T0192031

Lecture Notes in Computer Science   11237

Commenced Publication in 1973
Founding and Former Series Editors:
Gerhard Goos, Juris Hartmanis, and Jan van Leeuwen

More information about this series at http://www.springer.com/series/7408

Christian Colombo · Martin Leucker (Eds.)

Runtime Verification

18th International Conference, RV 2018
Limassol, Cyprus, November 10–13, 2018
Proceedings

 Springer

Editors
Christian Colombo
University of Malta
Msida, Malta

Martin Leucker
University of Lübeck
Lübeck, Germany

ISSN 0302-9743 ISSN 1611-3349 (electronic)
Lecture Notes in Computer Science
ISBN 978-3-030-03768-0 ISBN 978-3-030-03769-7 (eBook)
https://doi.org/10.1007/978-3-030-03769-7

Library of Congress Control Number: 2018960437

LNCS Sublibrary: SL2 – Programming and Software Engineering

Preface

This volume contains the proceedings of the 18th International Conference on Runtime Verification (RV 2018), which was held during November 10–13, 2018, at the Royal Apollonia Beach Hotel, Limassol, Cyprus. The RV series consists of annual meetings that gather together scientists from both academia and industry interested in investigating novel lightweight formal methods to monitor, analyze, and guide the runtime behavior of software and hardware systems. Runtime verification techniques are crucial for system correctness, reliability, and robustness; they provide an additional level of rigor and effectiveness compared with conventional testing, and are generally more practical than exhaustive formal verification. Runtime verification can be used prior to deployment, for testing, verification, and debugging purposes, and after deployment for ensuring reliability, safety, and security and for providing fault containment and recovery as well as online system repair.

RV started in 2001 as an annual workshop and turned into a conference in 2010. The workshops were organized as satellite events to an established forum, including CAV and ETAPS. The proceedings of RV from 2001 to 2005 were published in the *Electronic Notes in Theoretical Computer Science*. Since 2006, the RV proceedings have been published in Springer's *Lecture Notes in Computer Science*. The previous five RV conferences took place in Istanbul, Turkey (2012); Rennes, France (2013); Toronto, Canada (2014); Vienna, Austria (2015); Madrid, Spain (2016); and Seattle, USA (2017).

There were 49 submissions, 38 as regular contributions, six as short contributions and five as tool papers. Each submission was reviewed by at least three Program Committee members. The committee decided to accept 21 papers, 15 regular papers, three short papers, and three tool papers.

The evaluation and selection process involved thorough discussions among the members of the Program Committee and external reviewers through the EasyChair conference manager, before reaching a consensus on the final decisions. To complement the contributed papers, we included in the program three invited speakers covering both industry and academia:

- Rajeev Alur, University of Pennsylvania, USA
- Jim Kapinski, Toyota Motor North America (TMNA)
- Fritz Vaandrager, Radboud University, The Netherlands

Additionally, the proceedings also contain three invited contributions.

The conference included six tutorials that took place on the first day. The following tutorials were selected to cover a breadth of topics relevant to RV:

- Cesar Sanchez presented a tutorial on "Online and Offline Stream Runtime Verification of Synchronous Systems"
- Shaun Azzopardi, Joshua Ellul, and Gordon Pace presented a tutorial on "Monitoring Smart Contracts: ContractLarva and Open Challenges Beyond"

- Ylies Falcone presented a tutorial on "Can We Monitor Multi-threaded Java Programs?"
- Lukas Convent, Sebastian Hungerecker, Torben Scheffel, Malte Schmitz, Daniel Thoma, and Alexander Weiss presented a tutorial on "Hardware-Based Runtime Verification with Embedded Tracing Units and Stream Processing"
- Doron Peled and Klaus Havelund, presented a tutorial on "Runtime Verification – From Propositional to First-Order Temporal Logic"
- Ezio Bartocci presented a tutorial on "Monitoring, Learning and Control of Cyber-Physical Systems with STL"

We would like to thank the authors of all submitted papers, the members of the Steering Committee, the Program Committee, and the external reviewers for their exhaustive task of reviewing and evaluating all submitted papers. We highly appreciate the EasyChair system for the management of submissions.

We acknowledge the great support from our sponsors. Toyota InfoTech and Runtime Verification Inc. acted as gold sponsors and Denso as bronze sponsor.

September 2018   Martin Leucker
                                                                    Christian Colombo

Organization

Program Committee

Wolfgang Ahrendt	Chalmers University of Technology, Sweden
Ezio Bartocci	Vienna University of Technology, Austria
Andreas Bauer	KUKA
Eric Bodden	Paderborn University and Fraunhofer IEM, Germany
Borzoo Bonakdarpour	Iowa State University, USA
Christian Colombo	University of Malta, Malta
Ylies Falcone	University Grenoble Alpes, Inria, France
Lu Feng	University of Virginia, USA
Adrian Francalanza	University of Malta, Malta
Jean Goubault-Larrecq	LSV, ENS Paris-Saclay, CNRS, Université Paris-Saclay, France
Radu Grosu	Stony Brook University, USA
Kim Guldstrand Larsen	Aalborg University, Denmark
Sylvain Hallé	Université du Québec à Chicoutimi, Canada
Klaus Havelund	Jet Propulsion Laboratory, USA
Marieke Huisman	University of Twente, The Netherlands
Limin Jia	Carnegie Mellon University, USA
Felix Klaedtke	NEC Labs Europe
Shuvendu Lahiri	Microsoft
Insup Lee	University of Pennsylvania, USA
Axel Legay	IRISA/Inria, Rennes, France
Martin Leucker	University of Lübeck, Germany
David Lo	Singapore Management University, Singapore
Leonardo Mariani	University of Milano Bicocca, Italy
Ayoub Nouri	Verimag
Gordon Pace	University of Malta, Malta
Doron Peled	Bar-Ilan University, Israel
Ka I Pun	University of Oslo, Norway
Jorge A. Pérez	University of Groningen, The Netherlands
Giles Reger	The University of Manchester, UK
Grigore Rosu	University of Illinois at Urbana-Champaign, USA
Cesar Sanchez	IMDEA Software Institute, Spain
Gerardo Schneider	Chalmers — University of Gothenburg, Sweden
Nastaran Shafiei	University of York, UK
Rahul Sharma	Microsoft
Shinichi Shiraishi	Panasonic
Julien Signoles	CEA LIST
Scott Smolka	Stony Brook University, USA

Oleg Sokolsky	University of Pennsylvania, USA
Bernhard Steffen	University of Dortmund, Germany
Scott Stoller	Stony Brook University, USA
Volker Stolz	Høgskulen på Vestlandet, Norway
Neil Walkinshaw	The University of Sheffield, UK
Chao Wang	University of Southern California, USA
Eugen Zalinescu	Technical University of Munich, Germany

Additional Reviewers

Ahishakiye, Faustin
Attard, Duncan
Biondi, Fabrizio
Chen, Shuo
Dan, Li
El-Hokayem, Antoine
Enea, Constantin
Finkbeiner, Bernd
Fulton, Nathan
Given-Wilson, Thomas
Han, Minbiao
Herda, Mihai
Jakšić, Svetlana
Jiang, Zhihao
Kaur, Ramneet
Kuester, Jan-Christoph
Lange, Felix Dino

Lechner, Mathias
Ma, Meiyi
Mahyar, Hamidreza
Mallozzi, Piergiuseppe
Mediouni, Braham Lotfi
Mohan, Gautam
Park, Sangdon
Poulsen, Danny Bøgsted
Ratasich, Denise
Signoles, Julien
Stoller, Scott
Tan, Joshua
Vorobyov, Kostyantyn
Wang, Rui
Woo, Maverick
Zhang, Teng

Contents

Short Papers

Tool Papers

Invited Papers

Runtime Verification - 17 Years Later

Klaus Havelund[1](✉) and Grigore Roşu[2]

[1] Jet Propulsion Laboratory, California Institute of Technology, Pasadena, USA
klaus.havelund@jpl.nasa.gov
[2] University of Illinois at Urbana-Champaign, Urbana, USA

Abstract. Runtime verification is the discipline of analyzing program executions using rigorous methods. The discipline covers such topics as specification-based monitoring, where single executions are checked against formal specifications; predictive runtime analysis, where properties about a system are predicted/inferred from single (good) executions; specification mining from execution traces; visualization of execution traces; and to be fully general: computation of any interesting information from execution traces. Finally, runtime verification also includes fault protection, where monitors actively protect a running system against errors. The paper is written as a response to the 'Test of Time Award' attributed to the authors for their 2001 paper [45]. The present paper provides a brief overview of what lead to that paper, what has happened since, and some perspectives on the future of the field.

1 Introduction

Runtime verification (RV) [10,26,39,55] has emerged as a field of computer science within the last couple of decades. RV is concerned with the rigorous monitoring and analysis of software and hardware system executions. The field, or parts of it, can be encountered under several other names, including, e.g., runtime checking, monitoring, dynamic analysis, and runtime analysis. Since only single executions are analyzed, RV scales well compared to more comprehensive formal methods, but of course at the cost of coverage. Nonetheless, RV can be useful due to the rigorous methods involved. Conferences and workshops are now focusing specifically on this subject, including the Runtime Verification conference, which was initiated by the authors in 2001 as a workshop and became a conference in 2010, and runtime verification is now also often listed as a subject of interest in other conference calls for papers.

The paper is written as a response to the 'Test of Time Award' attributed to the authors for the 2001 paper [45] (*Monitoring Java Programs with Java PathExplorer*), presented 17 years ago (at the time of writing) at the first Runtime Verification workshop (RV'01) in Paris, July 23, 2001.

K. Havelund—The research performed by this author was carried out at Jet Propulsion Laboratory, California Institute of Technology, under a contract with the National Aeronautics and Space Administration.

© Springer Nature Switzerland AG 2018
C. Colombo and M. Leucker (Eds.): RV 2018, LNCS 11237, pp. 3–17, 2018.
https://doi.org/10.1007/978-3-030-03769-7_1

This paper reports on our own RV work, with some references to related work that specifically inspired us, and discusses the lessons learned and our perspective on the future of this field. Note that we do not try to identify all literature that inspired us. That task would be impossible. Previous publications of ours [26,42,44] have provided more technical tutorial-like presentations of the field. This paper rather offers information about the motivations for our work and philosophical considerations. As such this paper is closer in spirit to the longer paper [43]. It should be mentioned that most of the works over time have been done in collaboration with other people and inspired/initiated/driven by other people. We have just been lucky to be in the midst of all this work.

The paper is organized according to the time line of events, first leading up to [45], then the work described in that paper, the work that followed, and finally some thoughts on the future of this field.

2   In the Beginning

The initial interest of the first author in formal methods stems from his involvement in the design of the RAISE specification language RSL [30], during the period 1984–1991, and even with earlier work in the early 1980's on developing a parser and type checker for its predecessor VDM [14,15,28]. These are so-called wide-spectrum specification languages permitting formal specification at a high level, and "programming" at a low level, all within the same language, supported by a formal refinement relation between the different levels. These languages were impressively ahead of their time if one looks at these from a programming language perspective. For example, VDM^{++} has many similarities with today's SCALA programming language.

However, these languages were fundamentally still specification languages, and not programming languages, in spite of the fact that these languages have a lot in common with modern high-level programming languages, such as e.g. ML. The thought therefore was: why not benefit from the evolution of modern high-level programming languages and focus on verification of such? This was the first step: focus on programs rather than models. This lead to the work [34] of the first author on attempting to develop a specification language for an actual programming language, namely CONCURRENT ML (CML), an extension of Milner's ML with concurrency.

Later work with the very impressive PVS theorem prover [35] helped realize that theorem proving is hard after all, and that some form of more automated reasoning on programs would be useful as a less perfect alternative. Hence, thus far the realization was that *automated* verification of *programs* was a desirable objective. Note that at the time the main focus in the formal methods community was on models, not programs.

The next big move was the development of the JAVA PATHFINDER (JPF), a JAVA model checker, first as a translator from JAVA to the PROMELA modeling language of the SPIN model checker [41] (often referred to as JPF1), and later as a byte code model checker [50] (occasionally referred to as JPF2). The goal of this work was to explore how far model checking could be taken wrt. real code verification, either using JAVA as just a better modeling language, or, in the extreme case, for model checking real programs. A sub-objective was to explore the space between testing and full model checking.

JPF1 suffered from the problem of translating a complex language such as JAVA to the much simpler language PROMELA, resulting in a sensation that this approach worked for some programs but not for all programs. It was hard to go the last 20%. JPF2 solved part of this problem, but still suffered from the obvious problem of state space explosion. In addition, the model checker itself was a homemade JVM on top of the real JVM, and hence slow.

At this time we came across two inspiring invited talks at the SPIN 2000 workshop, which we organized. The first was a presentation by Harrow from Compaq on the VISUALTHREADS tool [33]. The purpose of this tool was to support Compaq's customers in avoiding multithreading errors. Specifically two algorithms appeared interesting: predictive data race and deadlock detection. These algorithms can detect the *potential* for a data race or deadlock by analyzing a run that does not necessarily encounter the error. The second invited talk was presented by Drusinsky, on the TEMPORAL ROVER [25] for monitoring temporal logic properties. We implemented the data race algorithm, also known as the Eraser algorithm [61], and a modification of the deadlock detection algorithm in JPF2. The idea was to first execute the program to check for data races and deadlocks using the two very scalable algorithms, and then only if error potentials were found between identified threads, to launch the model checker focusing specifically on those threads.

The two authors of [45] met at NASA Ames in 2000, when the second author started his first job right out of school, and this way, without knowing it, a fruitful, life-time collaboration and friendship with the first author. Inspired by recent joint work with his PhD adviser, Joseph Goguen, the second author was readily convinced that otherwise heavy-weight specification-based analysis techniques can very well apply to execution traces instead of whole systems, and thus achieve scalability by analyzing only what happens at runtime, as it happens. This, paired with provably correct recovery, gives the same level of assurance as formal verification of the whole system, but in a manner that allows us to divide-and-conquer the task. So the second author was "all in", ready to use his fresh algebraic specification and formal verification knowledge to rigorously analyze execution traces.

At this point, the previously mentioned observations about scalability of the traditional verification approaches, the experiments with data race and deadlock detection mentioned above, and some other less technical issues, led to our research focusing just on observing program executions. A constraint was that it should not be based on test case generation, since so many people were studying this already. We wanted to follow the path less explored. This is where the JAVA PATHEXPLORER project began, inspired by other work, but not too much other work.

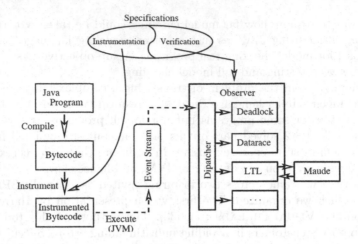

Fig. 1. The JPaX architecture.

3   Java PathExplorer

Our first pure runtime verification system was JAVA PATHEXPLORER (JPAX), described in the award winning paper [45], as well as in other papers [46–49,60]. The system is briefly described below.

3.1   Architecture

JPAX was a general framework for analyzing execution traces. It supported three kinds of algorithms: propositional temporal logic conformance checking, data race detection, and deadlock detection, as discussed earlier. Figure 1 shows JPAX's architecture. A Java program is instrumented (at byte code level) to issue events to the monitoring side, which is customizable, allowing the addition of new monitors. The temporal logic monitoring module was originally based on a propositional future time linear temporal logic, but was later extended to also cover past time.

An interesting aspect of the system was the use of the MAUDE [21] rewriting system for implementing monitoring logics as deep DSLs. One could in very few lines implement, e.g., linear temporal logic (LTL), with syntax and its monitoring algorithm, and have MAUDE function as the monitoring engine as well. There was a grander vision present at the time: to use a powerful Turing complete language, such as MAUDE, for monitoring, and not be restricted to just, e.g., LTL. However, that vision did not evolve beyond the thought stage, and had to wait some additional years, as discussed in Sect. 4. Below we briefly discuss some of the algorithms developed during the JPAX project.

Future Time LTL. The future time LTL monitoring used MAUDE to rewrite formulas. Consider, e.g., the LTL formula $p \mathcal{U} q$, meaning q eventually becomes true and until then p is true. The implementation of JPAX was based on classical equational laws for temporal operators, such as:

$$p \, \mathcal{U} \, q = q \wedge \bigcirc(p \, \mathcal{U} \, q) \qquad \text{and} \qquad \Box p = p \wedge \bigcirc(\Box p) \qquad (1)$$

Consider the sample formula $\Box(green \rightarrow \bigcirc(\neg red \, \mathcal{U} \, yellow))$. Upon encountering a $green$ in a trace, the formula will be rewritten into the following formula, which must be true in the next state: $(\neg red \, \mathcal{U} \, yellow) \wedge \Box(green \rightarrow (\neg red \, \mathcal{U} \, yellow))$. In MAUDE this was realized by a few simple rewrite rules, including the following two for the until operator (E is an event and T is a trace, the first rule handles the case of a trace consisting of only one event):

eq E $|$= X U Y = E $|$= Y.
eq E,T $|$= X U Y = E,T $|$= Y **or** E,T $|$= X **and** T $|$= X U Y.

3.2 Past Time LTL

Later, an efficient dynamic programming algorithm for monitoring *past time* linear temporal logic was developed [48], inspired by an initial encoding in MAUDE described in [45]. Consider the following past time formula: $red \rightarrow \blacklozenge green$ (whenever red is observed, in the past there has been a $green$). The algorithm for checking past time formulas like this uses two arrays, now and pre, recording the status of each sub-formula now and previously. Index 0 refers to the formula itself with positions ordered by the sub-formula relation. Then for this property, for each observed event the arrays are updated as follows.

```
bool pre [0..3],  now [0..3];

fun processEvent(e) {             // Sub−formula:
    now[3] := (event = red)       // red
    now[2] := (event = green)     // green
    now[1] := now[2] || pre [1]   // PREV green
    now[0] := !now[3] || now[1]   // red −> PREV green
    if !now[0] then output(" property violated ");
    pre := now;
}
```

This dynamic programming algorithm was generalized and optimized in [49,59] and later found way into three other systems for monitoring parametric temporal formulas, namely MOP [57], MonPoly [11], and DejaVu [40].

3.3 Data Races and Deadlocks

When used for bug finding, the effectiveness of runtime verification depends on the choice of test suite. For concurrent systems this is critical, due to the many possible non-deterministic execution paths. *Predictive runtime verification* approaches this problem by replacing a target property P with a stronger property Q such that there is a high probability that the program satisfies P iff a random trace of the program will satisfy Q. As already mentioned, one such algorithm was the Eraser algorithm [61], for detecting *potentials* for data races (where two threads can access a shared variable simultaneously). It is often referred to as the *lock set* algorithm as each variable is associated with a set of locks protecting it. The *lock graph* algorithm [33], would detect "dining philosopher"-like deadlock potentials by building a simple lock graph where a cycle indicates a deadlock potential. In [13] we augmented the original lock graph algorithm to reduce false positives in the presence of so-called guard locks (locks that prevent cyclic deadlocks). That paper was later followed by [12], which suggested a code instrumentation method (inserting wait statements) for confirming found deadlock potentials. Other forms of data races than those detected by Eraser are possible. In [3] a dynamic algorithm for detecting so-called high-level data races (races involving collections of variables) is described.

3.4   Code Instrumentation

JPAX code instrumentation was performed with Compaq's JTREK [22], a Java byte code instrumentation tool. Operating at the byte code level offers expressive power, but makes writing code instrumentation instructions inconvenient. An attempt was later made to develop an easier to use code instrumentation tool named JSPY [31] on top of JTREK. In this tool code instrumentation could be expressed as a set of high-level rules, formulated in JAVA (an internal JAVA DSL), each consisting of a predicate and an action.

3.5   Trace Visualization

Execution trace visualization is a subject that in our opinion has promising potential, although our own involvement in this direction is limited to [4]. The advantage of visualization is that it can provide a free-of-charge abstract view of the trace, from which a user potentially may be able to conclude properties about the program, or at least the execution, without having to explicitly formulate these properties. We can distinguish between two forms of trace visualization as outlined in [4]: *still visualization*, where all events are visualized in one view, and *animated visualization*. In [4], an extension of UML sequence diagrams with symbols is described for representing still visualizations of the execution of concurrent programs.

4   The Aftermath

The period after JPAX followed two tracks, which can be summarized as: experiments with aspect-oriented programming for program instrumentation, and so-called parametric monitoring of events carrying data.

4.1   Aspect-Oriented Programming

Whilst initial runtime verification frameworks targeted Java, the RMOR (Requirement Monitoring and Recovery) framework [36] targeted the monitoring of C programs against state machines using a homegrown aspect-oriented framework to perform program instrumentation. RMOR was implemented in OCAML using CIL (C Intermediate Language), a C program analysis and transformation system, itself written in OCAML. Later it was attempted to "go all aspect-oriented", meaning that aspects no longer were thought of as just the plumbing for performing code instrumentation, but instead that monitors *are* aspects. Some of our experiments went in the direction of what today is called *state-full aspects* [1,65]. Here one takes a starting point in an aspect-oriented language framework (such as e.g. ASPECTJ) and extends it with so-called *tracecuts*, denoting predicates on the execution trace. An advice can be associated with a tracecut, and executes when the tracecut is matched by the execution. We proposed this line of work already in [27]. Other later work included [16,51,62,63]. The main observation in these works was that aspect-oriented programming can be extended vertically (allowing more pointcuts) and horizontally (allowing temporal advice, essentially monitoring temporal constraints).

4.2   Runtime Verification with Data

JPAX had a number of limitations. The perhaps most important was the propositional nature of the temporal logics. One could not, for example, monitor parametric events carrying data, such as *openFile("data.txt")*, where *openFile* is an event name and *"data.txt"* is data. It is perhaps of interest to note, that at the time we were not (and are still not) aware of any system that at the time was able to monitor such parametric events in a temporal logic.

4.3   The Beginning of Data

These considerations lead to two different systems: EAGLE [6] and MOP [19]. EAGLE was a small and general logic having similarities with a linear time μ-calculus, supporting monitoring events with data, and allowing user-defined temporal operators. The later HAWK system [23] was an attempt to tie EAGLE to the monitoring of JAVA programs with automated code instrumentation using aspect-oriented programming, specifically ASPECTJ [53].

The same JPAX limitations that motivated the development of EAGLE also stimulated the apparition of monitoring-oriented programming (MOP) [18–20]. MOP proposed that runtime monitoring be supported and encouraged as a fundamental principle of software development, where monitors are automatically synthesized from formal specifications and integrated at appropriate places in the program. Violations and/or validations of specifications can trigger user-defined code at any points in the program, in particular recovery code, outputting/sending messages, or raising exceptions. MOP has made three important early contributions. First, it proposed specification formalism independence, allowing users to insert their favorite or domain-specific requirements specification formalisms via *logic plugin* modules. Second, it proposed automated code instrumentation as a means to weave the monitoring checking code within the application; the first version in 2003 used Perl for instrumentation [19], while the subsequent versions starting with 2004 [18] used ASPECTJ [53]. Finally, it proposed a formalism-independent semantics and implementation for parametric specifications. Conceptually, execution traces are sliced according to each observed instance of the parameters, and each slice is checked by its own monitor instance in a manner that is independent of the employed specification formalism. The practical challenge is how to deal with the potentially huge number of monitor instances. JAVAMOP proposed several optimizations, presented in [58] together with the mathematical foundations of parametric monitoring.

The EAGLE system mentioned earlier was considered quite an elegant system, but its implementation was complicated. The subsequent rule-based lower level RULER system [9] was meant as an "assembler" into which other temporal specification languages could be compiled for efficient trace checking. However, it assumed a life of its own as a specification language. RULER was given a finite-trace semantics with four verdicts. The verdicts STILL_TRUE and STILL_FALSE are given if the rule system would accept/reject the trace if it were to end at the current event, whilst the verdicts TRUE and FALSE were reserved for traces where every extension would be accepted/rejected. RULER allowed for very complex rule systems that could be *chained* together such that one rule system produced outputs for another rule system to consume as input events. Rule systems could be combined sequentially, in parallel, and conditionally.

A project solidly rooted in an actual space mission was the development of the LOGSCOPE temporal logic for log analysis [7]. The purpose of the project was to assist the team testing the flight software for JPL's Mars rover Curiosity, which successfully landed on Mars on August 6, 2012. The software produces rich log information. Traditionally, these logs are analyzed with complex PYTHON scripts. The LOGSCOPE logic was developed to support notations comprehensible to test engineers, including a very simple and convenient data parameterized temporal logic, which was translated to a form of data parameterized automata, which themselves could be used for specification of more complex properties that the temporal logic could not express. LOGSCOPE was furthermore implemented in PYTHON, allowing PYTHON code fragments to be included in specifications, all in order to integrate with the existing Python scripting culture at JPL.

4.4   Internal DSLs

Earlier we mentioned a grander vision to use a powerful Turing complete language for monitoring. The fundamental problem with a logic is that it likely may be insufficient for practical purposes if not designed extremely optimally. Engineers are, e.g., often observed using PYTHON for monitoring tasks. Of course in lack of a better notation, but also because it provides expressive power to perform arbitrary computations, e.g. on observed data. This observation led to several experiments with so-called internal DSLs, where one extends a programming language with monitoring features. This allows the user to use the features of the programming language when the features of the monitoring logic do not suffice. TRACECONTRACT [8,37] is such an internal SCALA DSL (effectively an API) for monitoring, based on a mixture of temporal logic and state machines. It is developed using SCALA's features for defining internal DSLs. TRACECONTRACT, although a research tool, was later used for analysis of command sequences sent to NASA's LADEE (Lunar Atmosphere and Dust Environment Explorer) spacecraft throughout its mission.

Another example of an internal Scala DSL is LOGFIRE [38]. LOGFIRE is a rule-based system similar to RULER, but based on a modification of the Rete algorithm [24,29], used in several rule-based systems. LOGFIRE was part of an investigation of the Rete algorithm's applicability for runtime verification. LOG-FIRE has become part of the software that daily processes telemetry data from JPL's Mars Curiosity rover. LOGFIRE's ability to generate facts can be used for Complex Event Processing (CEP) [56], where higher-level events (abstractions) are generated from lower-level events. CEP can be used for further analysis and/or human comprehension, e.g. through visualization. Another CEP system is NFER [52], which in part was influenced by our work on rule-based systems, and LOGFIRE in particular. The result of applying an NFER specification to an event stream is a set of time bounded intervals. The specification consists of rules of the form: name :− body (a rule name followed by a rule body). The semantics is similar to that of PROLOG (hence the :− symbol): when the body is true an interval is generated with that name. A difference from PROLOG is that rule bodies contain temporal constraints based on operators from Allen Temporal Logic [2]. NFER was created due to a need for comprehending large telemetry streams from Mars rovers. Abstracting these to higher level intervals, compared to the low level raw event stream, should ease human comprehension.

4.5   First-Order Beyond Slicing

RULER, as a layer of syntactic sugar on top of the rule formalism, offered a sub-formalism resembling a data parameterized automaton language. Likewise, LOGSCOPE, inspired by RULER, offered a data parameterized automaton notation (in addition to the temporal logic). Quantified event automata (QEA) [5] was an attempt to design a pure data parameterized automaton monitoring system logic, using the efficient trace slicing approach previously introduced in the JAVAMOP tool [57], but dealing with some of the limitations with respect to expressiveness. A QEA specification consists of a list of first-order quantifications (universal and existential) and an automaton. They can be compared to extended state machines (allowing arbitrary guards and actions on transitions operating on local state, but are more succinct due to the fact that automata are "spawned" according to parameters (there is a local state for each combination of parameters).

A different approach to optimizing monitoring of parametric data is implemented in the DEJAVU tool [40], which uses BDDs [17] to efficiently represent data observed in the trace. Logic-wise, the system supports a standard past time temporal logic with quantification. The logic in itself is not the innovation, rather it is the use of BDDs to represent the sets of values observed in the trace for the quantified variables. The representation of sets of assignments as BDDs allows a very simple algorithm that naturally extends the dynamic programming monitoring algorithm for propositional past time temporal logic shown on page 5 and presented in [47], using two vectors *now* and *pre*. However, while in [47] the vectors contain Boolean values, here the values are BDDs.

5   Discussion

Numerous runtime verification logics have been developed over time. They include various forms of temporal logics, state machines, regular expressions, context free grammars, rule systems, variations of the μ-calculus, process algebras, stream processing, timed versions of these, and even statistical versions, where data can be computed as part of monitoring. It is clear that parametric/first-order versions of these logics are needed. Some efforts have been made to combine two or more of these logics, such as, e.g., combining temporal logic and regular expressions. An interesting trend is logics which not just produce a Boolean value, but rather a data value of any type. This leads to systems computing arbitrary data values from traces. It is, however, nearly impossible at this point to estimate which of these approaches would potentially get infused in industrial settings.

Whether to develop a DSL as external or internal is a non-trivial decision. An external DSL is usually cleaner and more directly tuned towards the immediate needs of the user. In addition, they are easier to process and therefore optimize for efficiency. However, the richer the DSL becomes (moving towards Turing-completeness) the harder the implementation effort becomes. An internal DSL can be very fast to implement and augment with new (even user-defined) operators, and can provide an expressiveness that would require a major effort to support in an external DSL. One also gains the advantage of IDEs for the host language. A hypothesis is that monitoring logics used in practice will need to support very expressive expression languages to process data, such as strings and numbers that are part of the observed events. Temporal logic could become part of a programming language assertion language. This could be seen as part of a design-by contract approach also supporting pre/post conditions and class invariants.

An important topic may be inferring specifications from execution traces. Our own limited work in this area includes [54,64]. Related to specification mining is execution trace visualization (the visualization can be considered a learned model). The advantage of visualization is that it can provide a free-of-charge abstract view of the trace, from which a user potentially may be able to conclude properties about the program, or at least the execution, without having to explicitly formulate these properties.

Full verification is of course preferred over partial verification performed by a monitor. The combination of static and dynamic verification can provide the best of both worlds: prove as much as is feasible statically and verify the remaining proof obligations during runtime. To properly achieve this goal, we need formal specifications not only for the properties to verify, but also for the programming language itself. Moreover, we need provably correct monitor generation techniques, so we can put all the specification and proof artifacts together and assemble a proof of correctness for the entire system. Interestingly, once a specification of the programming language itself is available, then one can go even one step further and monitor the execution of the program even against the language specification. This may seem redundant at first, but it actually makes full sense for some languages with complex semantics, like C. For example, tools like VALGRIND or UBSAN detect undefined behaviors in C/C++ programs, which are essentially deviations from the intended language semantics. The RV-MATCH tool [32] is an attempt to push runtime verification in this direction.

In fault-protection strategies, the goal is to recover the system once it has failed. The general problem of how to recover from a bad program state is interesting and quite challenging. The ultimate solution to this problem can be found in planning and scheduling systems, where a planner creates a plan (straight-line program) to execute for a limited time period, an executive executes the plan, and a monitor monitors the execution. Upon failure detected by the monitor, a new plan (program) is generated online.

References

1. Allan, C., et al.: Adding trace matching with free variables to AspectJ. SIGPLAN Not. **40**, 345–364 (2005)
2. Allen, J.F.: Maintaining knowledge about temporal intervals. Commun. ACM **26**(11), 832–843 (1983)
3. Artho, C., Havelund, K., Biere, A.: High-level data races. Softw. Test. Verif. Reliab. **13**(4), 207–227 (2004)
4. Artho, C., Havelund, K., Honiden, S.: Visualization of concurrent program executions. In: 31st Annual International Computer Software and Applications Conference (COMPSAC 2007), vol. 2, pp. 541–546, July 2007
5. Barringer, H., Falcone, Y., Havelund, K., Reger, G., Rydeheard, D.: Quantified event automata: towards expressive and efficient runtime monitors. In: Giannakopoulou, D., Méry, D. (eds.) FM 2012. LNCS, vol. 7436, pp. 68–84. Springer, Heidelberg (2012). https://doi.org/10.1007/978-3-642-32759-9_9
6. Barringer, H., Goldberg, A., Havelund, K., Sen, K.: Rule-based runtime verification. In: Steffen, B., Levi, G. (eds.) VMCAI 2004. LNCS, vol. 2937, pp. 44–57. Springer, Heidelberg (2004). https://doi.org/10.1007/978-3-540-24622-0_5
7. Barringer, H., Groce, A., Havelund, K., Smith, M.: Formal analysis of log files. J. Aerosp. Comput. Inf. Commun. **7**(11), 365–390 (2010)
8. Barringer, H., Havelund, K.: TraceContract: a Scala DSL for trace analysis. In: Butler, M., Schulte, W. (eds.) FM 2011. LNCS, vol. 6664, pp. 57–72. Springer, Heidelberg (2011). https://doi.org/10.1007/978-3-642-21437-0_7
9. Barringer, H., Rydeheard, D.E., Havelund, K.: Rule systems for run-time monitoring: from Eagle to RuleR. J. Log. Comput. **20**(3), 675–706 (2010)

10. Bartocci, E., Falcone, Y., Francalanza, A., Reger, G.: Introduction to runtime verification. In: Bartocci, E., Falcone, Y. (eds.) Lectures on Runtime Verification. LNCS, vol. 10457, pp. 1–33. Springer, Cham (2018). https://doi.org/10.1007/978-3-319-75632-5_1

11. Basin, D., Klaedtke, F., Müller, S., Pfitzmann, B.: Runtime monitoring of metric first-order temporal properties. In: Proceedings of the 28th IARCS Annual Conference on Foundations of Software Technology and Theoretical Computer Science, volume 2 of Leibniz International Proceedings in Informatics (LIPIcs), pp. 49–60. Schloss Dagstuhl - Leibniz Center for Informatics (2008)

12. Bensalem, S., Fernandez, J.-C., Havelund, K., Mounier, L.: Confirmation of deadlock potentials detected by runtime analysis. In: Parallel and Distributed Systems: Testing and Debugging (PADTAD 2006), Portland, Maine, USA, July 2006

13. Bensalem, S., Havelund, K.: Dynamic deadlock analysis of multi-threaded programs. In: Ur, S., Bin, E., Wolfsthal, Y. (eds.) HVC 2005. LNCS, vol. 3875, pp. 208–223. Springer, Heidelberg (2006). https://doi.org/10.1007/11678779_15

14. Bjørner, D., Jones, C.B. (eds.): The Vienna Development Method: The Meta-Language. LNCS, vol. 61. Springer, Heidelberg (1978). https://doi.org/10.1007/3-540-08766-4

15. Bjørner, D., Jones, C.B.: Formal Specification and Software Development. Prentice Hall International (1982). ISBN 0-13-880733-7

16. Bodden, E., Havelund, K.: Aspect-oriented race detection in Java. IEEE Trans. Softw. Eng. **36**(4), 509–527 (2010)

17. Bryant, R.E.: Symbolic Boolean manipulation with ordered binary-decision diagrams. ACM Comput. Surv. (CSUR) **24**(3), 293–318 (1992)

18. Chen, F., D'Amorim, M., Roşu, G.: A formal monitoring-based framework for software development and analysis. In: Davies, J., Schulte, W., Barnett, M. (eds.) ICFEM 2004. LNCS, vol. 3308, pp. 357–372. Springer, Heidelberg (2004). https://doi.org/10.1007/978-3-540-30482-1_31

19. Chen, F., Roşu, G.: Towards monitoring-oriented programming: A paradigm combining specification and implementation. In: Proceedings of the 3rd International Workshop on Runtime Verification (RV 2003), volume 89(2) of Electronic Notes Theoretical Computer Science, pp. 108–127. Elsevier Science Inc. (2003)

20. Chen, F., Roşu, G.: MOP: an efficient and generic runtime verification framework. In: Object-Oriented Programming, Systems, Languages and Applications (OOPSLA 2007), pp. 569–588. ACM, ACM SIGPLAN Notices (2007)

21. Clavel, M., et al.: Maude: specification and programming in rewriting logic. Theor. Comput. Sci. **285**(2), 187–243 (2002)

22. Cohen, S.: JTrek. (2001)

23. d'Amorim, M., Havelund, K.: Event-based runtime verification of Java programs. ACM SIGSOFT Softw. Eng. Notes **30**(4), 1–7 (2005)

24. Doorenbos, R.B.: Production Matching for Large Learning Systems. Ph. D. thesis, Carnegie Mellon University, Pittsburgh, PA (1995)

25. Drusinsky, D.: The temporal rover and the ATG rover. In: Havelund, K., Penix, J., Visser, W. (eds.) SPIN 2000. LNCS, vol. 1885, pp. 323–330. Springer, Heidelberg (2000). https://doi.org/10.1007/10722468_19

26. Falcone, Y., Havelund, K., Reger, G.: A tutorial on runtime verification. In: Broy, M., Peled, D., Kalus, G., (eds.) Engineering Dependable Software Systems, volume 34 of NATO Science for Peace and Security Series - D: Information and Communication Security, pp. 141–175. IOS Press (2013)

27. Filman, R., Havelund, K.: Source-code instrumentation and quantification of events. In: Foundations of Aspect-Oriented Languages (FOAL 2002), Enschede, The Netherlands, April 2002
28. Fitzgerald, J., Larsen, P.G., Mukherjee, P., Plat, N., Verhoef, M.: Validated Designs for Object-oriented Systems. Springer, TELOS, Santa Clara (2005)
29. Forgy, C.: Rete: a fast algorithm for the many pattern/many object pattern match problem. Artif. Intell. **19**, 17–37 (1982)
30. George, C., et al.: The RAISE Specification Language. The BCS Practitioner Series. Prentice-Hall, Hemel Hampstead (1992)
31. Goldberg, A., Havelund, K.: Instrumentation of Java bytecode for runtime analysis. In: Fifth ECOOP Workshop on Formal Techniques for Java-like Programs (FTfJP 2003), Darmstadt, Germany, July 2003
32. Guth, D., Hathhorn, C., Saxena, M., Roşu, G.: RV-Match: practical semantics-based program analysis. In: Chaudhuri, S., Farzan, A. (eds.) CAV 2016, Part I. LNCS, vol. 9779, pp. 447–453. Springer, Cham (2016). https://doi.org/10.1007/978-3-319-41528-4_24
33. Harrow, J.J.: Runtime checking of multithreaded applications with visual threads. In: Havelund, K., Penix, J., Visser, W. (eds.) SPIN 2000. LNCS, vol. 1885, pp. 331–342. Springer, Heidelberg (2000). https://doi.org/10.1007/10722468_20
34. Havelund, K.: The Fork Calculus - Towards a Logic for Concurrent ML. Ph. D. thesis. DIKU, Department of Computer Science, University of Copenhagen, Denmark (1994)
35. Havelund, K.: Mechanical verification of a garbage collector. In: Rolim, J., et al. (eds.) IPPS 1999. LNCS, vol. 1586, pp. 1258–1283. Springer, Heidelberg (1999). https://doi.org/10.1007/BFb0098007
36. Havelund, K.: Runtime verification of C programs. In: Suzuki, K., Higashino, T., Ulrich, A., Hasegawa, T. (eds.) FATES/TestCom -2008. LNCS, vol. 5047, pp. 7–22. Springer, Heidelberg (2008). https://doi.org/10.1007/978-3-540-68524-1_3
37. Havelund, K.: Data automata in Scala. In: Proceedings of the 8th International Symposium on Theoretical Aspects of Software Engineering (TASE 2014). IEEE Computer Society (2014)
38. Havelund, K.: Rule-based runtime verification revisited. Int. J. Softw. Tools Technol. Trans. **17**(2), 143–170 (2015)
39. Havelund, K., Goldberg, A.: Verify your runs. In: Meyer, B., Woodcock, J. (eds.) VSTTE 2005. LNCS, vol. 4171, pp. 374–383. Springer, Heidelberg (2008). https://doi.org/10.1007/978-3-540-69149-5_40
40. Havelund, K., Peled, D.A., Ulus, D.: First order temporal logic monitoring with BDDs. In: Formal Methods in Computer Aided Design (FMCAD), pp. 116–123. IEEE (2017)
41. Havelund, K., Pressburger, T.: Model checking Java programs using Java PathFinder. Int. J. Softw. Tools Technol. Transf. **2**(4), 366–381 (2000)
42. Havelund, K., Reger, G.: Runtime verification logics - a language design perspective. In: Aceto, L., Bacci, G., Bacci, G., Ingólfsdóttir, A., Legay, A., Mardare, R. (eds.) Models, Algorithms, Logics and Tools. LNCS, vol. 10460, pp. 310–338. Springer, Cham (2017). https://doi.org/10.1007/978-3-319-63121-9_16
43. Havelund, K., Reger, G., Roşu, G.: Runtime verification - past experiences and future projections. volume 10000 of LNCS. Springer (2018)
44. Havelund, K., Reger, G., Thoma, D., Zălinescu, E.: Monitoring events that carry data. In: Bartocci, E., Falcone, Y. (eds.) Lectures on Runtime Verification. LNCS, vol. 10457, pp. 61–102. Springer, Cham (2018). https://doi.org/10.1007/978-3-319-75632-5_3

45. Havelund, K., Roşu, G.: Monitoring Java programs with Java PathExplorer. In: Proceedings of the 1st International Workshop on Runtime Verification (RV 2001), vol. 55(2) of Electronic Notes Theoretical Computer Science. Elsevier, Paris, France, 23 July 2001. Won the RV 2018 Test of Time Award

46. Havelund, K., Roşu, G.: Monitoring programs using rewriting. In: Proceedings of the 16th IEEE International Conference on Automated Software Engineering (ASE 2001), pp. 135–143 (2001)

47. Havelund, K., Roşu, G.: Synthesizing monitors for safety properties. In: Katoen, J.-P., Stevens, P. (eds.) TACAS 2002. LNCS, vol. 2280, pp. 342–356. Springer, Heidelberg (2002). https://doi.org/10.1007/3-540-46002-0_24

48. Havelund, K., Roşu, G.: An overview of the runtime verification tool Java PathExplorer. Form. Methods Syst. Des. **24**(2), 189–215 (2004)

49. Havelund, K., Roşu, G.: Efficient monitoring of safety properties. Int. J. Softw. Tools Technol. Transf. **6**(2), 158–173 (2004)

50. Havelund, K., Visser, W.: Program model checking as a new trend. STTT **4**(1), 8–20 (2002)

51. Havelund, K., Wyk, E.V.: Aspect-oriented monitoring of C programs. In: The Sixth IARP-IEEE/RAS-EURON Joint Workshop on Technical Challenges for Dependable Robots in Human Environments, Pasadena, CA, May 17–18 2008

52. Kauffman, S., Havelund, K., Joshi, R.: nfer – a notation and system for inferring event stream abstractions. In: Falcone, Y., Sánchez, C. (eds.) RV 2016. LNCS, vol. 10012, pp. 235–250. Springer, Cham (2016). https://doi.org/10.1007/978-3-319-46982-9_15

53. Kiczales, G., Hilsdale, E., Hugunin, J., Kersten, M., Palm, J., Griswold, W.G.: An overview of AspectJ. In: Knudsen, J.L. (ed.) ECOOP 2001. LNCS, vol. 2072, pp. 327–354. Springer, Heidelberg (2001). https://doi.org/10.1007/3-540-45337-7_18

54. Lee, C., Chen, F., Roşu, G.: Mining parametric specifications. In: Proceedings of the 33rd International Conference on Software Engineering, ICSE 2011, Waikiki, Honolulu, HI, USA, May 21–28 2011, pp. 591–600 (2011)

55. Leucker, M., Schallhart, C.: A brief account of runtime verification. J. Log. Algebr. Program. **78**(5), 293–303 (2008)

56. Luckham, D. (ed.): The Power of Events: An Introduction to Complex Event Processing in Distributed Enterprise Systems. Addison-Wesley, Boston (2002)

57. Meredith, P., Jin, D., Griffith, D., Chen, F., Roşu, G.: An overview of the MOP runtime verification framework. J. Softw. Tools Technol. Transf. **14**, 249–289 (2011)

58. Roşu, G., Chen, F.: Semantics and algorithms for parametric monitoring. Log. Methods Comput. Sci. **8**(1), 1–39 (2012)

59. Roşu, G., Chen, F., Ball, T.: Synthesizing monitors for safety properties: this time with calls and returns. In: Leucker, M. (ed.) RV 2008. LNCS, vol. 5289, pp. 51–68. Springer, Heidelberg (2008). https://doi.org/10.1007/978-3-540-89247-2_4

60. Roşu, G., Havelund, K.: Rewriting-based techniques for runtime verification. Autom. Softw. Eng. **12**(2), 151–197 (2005)

61. Savage, S., Burrows, M., Nelson, G., Sobalvarro, P., Anderson, T.: Eraser: a dynamic data race detector for multithreaded programs. ACM Trans. Comput. Syst. **15**(4), 391–411 (1997)

62. Seyster, J., et al.: InterAspect: aspect-oriented instrumentation with GCC. Form. Methods Syst. Des. **41**(3), 295–320 (2012)

63. Smith, D.R., Havelund, K.: Toward automated enforcement of error-handling policies. Technical Report number: TR-KT-0508, Kestrel Technology LLC, August 2005

64. Stoller, S.D., et al.: Runtime verification with state estimation. In: Khurshid, S., Sen, K. (eds.) RV 2011. LNCS, vol. 7186, pp. 193–207. Springer, Heidelberg (2012). https://doi.org/10.1007/978-3-642-29860-8_15
65. Walker, R., Viggers, K.: Implementing protocols via declarative event patterns. In: Taylor, R., Dwyer, M., (eds.) ACM Sigsoft 12th International Symposium on Foundations of Software Engineering (FSE-12), pp. 159–169. ACM Press (2004)

COST Action IC1402 Runtime Verification Beyond Monitoring

Christian Colombo[1]($\boxtimes$), Yliès Falcone[2], Martin Leucker[3], Giles Reger[4],
Cesar Sanchez[5], Gerardo Schneider[6], and Volker Stolz[7]

[1] University of Malta, Msida, Malta
christian.colombo@um.edu.mt
[2] Univ. Grenoble Alpes, CNRS, Inria, Grenoble INP, LIG, 38000 Grenoble, France
[3] Universtität zu Lübeck, Lübeck, Germany
[4] University of Manchester, Manchester, UK
[5] IMDEA Software Institute, Madrid, Spain
[6] University of Gothenburg, Gothenburg, Sweden
[7] Western Norway University of Applied Sciences, Bergen, Norway

Abstract. In this paper we report on COST Action IC1402 which studies Runtime Verification approaches beyond Monitoring. COST Actions are funded by the European Union and are an efficient networking instrument for researchers, engineers and scholars to cooperate and coordinate research activities. This COST action IC1402 lasted over the past four years, involved researchers from 27 different European countries and Australia and allowed to have many different working group meetings, workshops and individual visits.

1 Introduction

Runtime verification (RV) is a computing analysis paradigm based on observing a system at runtime to check its expected behavior. RV has emerged in recent years as a practical application of formal verification, and a less ad-hoc approach to conventional testing by building monitors from formal specifications. For tutorials and overviews of the field of Runtime Verification, we refer to [11,15,22,28].

There is a great potential applicability of RV beyond software reliability, if one allows monitors to interact back with the observed system, and generalizes to new domains beyond computers programs (like hardware, devices, cloud computing and even human-centric systems). Given the European leadership in computer-based industries, novel applications of RV to these areas can have an enormous impact in terms of the new class of designs enabled and their reliability and cost effectiveness.

COST Actions are a flexible, fast, effective and efficient networking instrument for researchers, engineers and scholars to cooperate and coordinate nationally funded research activities. COST Actions allow European researchers to jointly develop their own ideas in any science and technology field.

C. Colombo and M. Leucker (Eds.): RV 2018, LNCS 11237, pp. 18–26, 2018.
https://doi.org/10.1007/978-3-030-03769-7_2

This COST Action lasted from beginning of 2015 till the end of 2018. This paper describes its structure as well as the main results achieved in this action. Latest updates on this COST action can be found at https://www.cost-arvi.eu.

2 Working Groups

In this section, we briefly report on the activities carried by each of the working groups. Working groups served to structure and coordinate the work within the action.

2.1 Working Group 1: Core Runtime Verification

Working Group 1 (WG1) aimed at clarifying the dimensions of RV, its theory, algorithms and methods. These are the activities in which most of the work on RV has focused in the early stages of the discipline, with scattered results based on methods from other areas, notably formal methods and programming languages, and guided by application goals. Many outcomes from the other working groups posed new sets of problems and challenges for the core RV community. Specific activities of WG1 included research actions centered around establishing a common framework for RV, and challenges for new research and technology based on the other working groups. These activities led to several achievements, which are exposed in several publications and the report of WG1. We briefly summarize the achievements below:

- A *tutorial book* providing a collection of 7 lectures on introductory and advanced topics on RV [5].
- A *taxonomy of RV* aspects that "paves the road" to allow a classification and comparison of theoretical results, problems and techniques. The taxonomy has been published in [16].
- The identification of the *challenges and opportunities of instrumentation*, where the system under scrutiny is modified or harnessed to allow the monitoring process. The challenges are exposed in the report of this working group and in the introductory book chapter [7].
- A study of the *interplay* between RV and static analysis, between RV and model checking, and between RV and testing. All these activities usually serve to increase or assess system's reliability, but their interplay can potentially increase their applicability. The interplay study is exposed in the report of WG1.
- A study of potential applications of RV beyond system observation. This includes reflection to act upon the system, typically to control and prevent errors, or to replay allowing an error to be reproduced or even fixed. Potential applications beyond system observation are exposed in the report of this working group and in a chapter of the tutorial book dedicated to financial applications [14], and a chapter dedicated to runtime failure prevention and reaction [17]. We have also published a paper on the combination of reinforcement learning and RV monitors [29].

- To pose the *challenges in monitoring quantitative and statistical data*, beyond
property violation. The challenges are exposed in the report of WG1 and in
some chapters of the tutorial book, notably those on monitoring with data [25]
and monitoring cyber-physical systems [2].

Additionally, WG1 has organized several events and coordinated publications to
promote Runtime Verification as a field of research and favor the dissemination
of the core aspects of the field. These events include *two tracks* on RV at IsoLA
2016 [30] and 2018 focused on industrial aspects [3,4], *two special issues* in
Formal Methods in System Design [9,20], two successful *international schools*
on RV attracting around 40 students each [12,13] with one organized alongside
the 16th International Conference on Runtime Verification [19] and one as an
independent event, *competitions* on Software for Runtime Verification [1,18,32]
as well as an extensive report on the first edition [6].

2.2   Working Group 2: Standardization, Benchmarks, Tool Interoperability

This group aimed to clarify the landscape of formalisms and tools proposed and
built for RV, to design common input formats and to establish a large class of
benchmarks and challenges. We briefly summarise the main achievements of the
working group:

- *Classification of Tools.* The taxonomy mentioned above (in working group
1) was developed alongside a classification of Runtime Verification tools and
further refined with respect to this classification [16].
- *Exploration of Language Landscape.* The working group has encouraged a
number of activities exploring the links between specification languages for
Runtime Verification [24,35,36]. This has been both theoretically (defining
translations between languages) and pragmatically (discussing topics such as
usability).
- *Competitions.* Between 2014 and 2016 three competitions were carried out
comparing Runtime Verification tools for monitoring C programs, Java programs, and log files. These competitions compared 14 tools using over 100
different benchmarks. Full accounts of the competitions have been published
[1,6,18,32] and an ongoing account of these and future competitions can be
found at https://www.rv-competition.org/.
- *Trace Formats.* A number of trace formats were introduced and refined in the
above competitions including CSV, JSON, and XML formats. These have
been the subject of further exploration and discussion [26,33].
- *Encouraging a Conversation.* One of the most important jobs of this working
group was to get the different tool developers to talk to each other. We organised two events outside the Action to encourage this. Firstly, the RV-CuBES
workshop [31,34] was held alongside the 17th International Conference on
Runtime Verification [27]. This contained 11 short tool papers and 5 position
papers discussing how RV tools should be evaluated [10,37,39], describing

challenges of using RV tools in industry [21], and encouraging the community to use open standards [26]. Secondly, a Dagstuhl seminar [23] considered various issues around behavioural specification languages, inviting researchers from outside the RV community to join the discussion.

The activities of the working group are ongoing. The above taxonomy and classification continues to be refined and extended. The landscape of Runtime Verification languages is still not fully understood and more work is being carried out in this area. The competition continues, with a challenge focusing on benchmarks coinciding with the 18th International Conference on Runtime Verification and the end of this Action.

2.3 Working Group 3: Challenging Computational Domains

The main goal of this group has been to studied novel and important (but challenging) computational domains for RV and monitoring, that result from the study of other application areas other than programming languages. The concrete objectives of this Working Group was to identify concrete challenges for RV and monitoring in the following application domains:

Distributed Systems: where the timing of observations may vary widely in a non-synchronized manner.
Hybrid and Embedded Systems: where continuous and discrete behaviour coexist and the resources of the monitor are constrained.
Hardware: where the timing must be precise and the monitor must operate non disruptively.
Security & Privacy: where a suitable combination between static and dynamic analysis is needed.
Reliable Transactional Systems: where data consistency and strong guarantees of concurrent execution must be provided at network scale.
Contracts & Policies: where the connection between the legal world and the technical is paramount.
Unreliable Domains and Approximated Domains: where either the systems is not reliable, or aggregation or sampling is necessary due to large amounts of data.

The study of these areas has involved expertise from more than one domain, and has been possible by attacking them cooperatively. The first concrete outputs of this Working Group is a series of documents that give a roadmap for the application of RV techniques to the areas listed above, identifying connections with established work in the respective sub-areas of computer science, and challenges and opportunities. A summary of the content of these works where consolidated into a paper (60 pages, 336 references) and will appear in journal survey publication, currently under submission [38]. Second, a concrete case study has been defined, aiming at a RV solution for multicore systems using dedicated monitoring hardware based on FPGAs to show the feasibility and general applicability of RV techniques (ongoing work).

2.4   Working Group 4: Application Areas (Outside "Pure" Software Reliability)

This group have studied the potential applications of RV to important application areas beyond software and hardware reliability, including medical devices and legal contracts. This task required the direct interaction with experts from the respective communities. For example, for the safe interoperability of medical devices, it was important to enrich the interface COST specifications with temporal properties about the intended interaction of two devices and to synthesize monitoring code for runtime. If monitoring identifies unwanted behavior, the systems might go into some fail-safe mode. Another interesting application area that has been explored was how to monitor legal e-contracts (e.g., computer-mediated transactions). Some efforts have recently been done to formalize legal contracts using formal languages, where skeletons of runtime monitors could be extracted from the formal semantics. Other applications included robotics and hybrid systems, monitoring for business models and systems security. Concrete output of this Working Group consisted on documents describing challenges and potential applications of RV to these application areas. Moreover, a concrete case study in the medical domain has been performed identifying the safety enhancements of medical devices by using RV techniques.

Main application areas studied by the working group:

- Medical devices
- Legal contracts
- Financial transactions
- Security and privacy
- Electrical energy storage

This Working Group have organized few workshops with invited experts from application domains:

- ARVI Workshop on Financial Transaction Systems (organized by Christian Colombo).[1]
- Workshop on Medical Cyber Physical Systems (co-organised by Ezio Bartocci and Martin Leucker).[2]
- ARVI Workshop on the Analysis of Legal Contracts (co-organized by Christian Colombo, Gordon Pace and Gerardo Schneider).[3]
- ARVI Workshop on Privacy & Security (co-organized by Leonardo Mariani and Gerardo Schneider).[4]

---

[1] https://www.cost-arvi.eu/?page_id=166.
[2] http://mlab-upenn.github.io/medcps_workshop/.
[3] https://www.cost-arvi.eu/?page_id=862.
[4] https://www.cost-arvi.eu/?page_id=1431.

3   Short-Term Scientific Missions (STSMs)

The COST actions also provided financial support for so-called short-term scientific missions. The idea is to support individual mobility, strengthening existing networks and fostering collaboration. The visits should contribute to the scientific objectives of the COST Action that means concentrate on topics investigated in one of the four working groups while at the same time, allow to learn new techniques, gain access to specific data, instruments, methods not available in their own organizations.

The applications for an STSM were carefully reviewed by the STSM committee, which consisted of Tarmo Uustalu (Reykjavik University, Iceland), César Sénchez (IMDEA Software, Spain) and Martin Steffen (University of Olso, Norway).

Within this COST action, a total of 23 STSMs were carried out while another 2 are currently planned. Overall, the STSMs strengthened our joint interaction and resulted in many high-quality scientific contributions.

4   IC1402 in Numbers

Grant period:	17.12.2014 – 16.12.2018
Participating COST countries:	27
COST international Non-European partner countries:	1 (Australia)
Participating scientists:	Over 90
STSMs completed:	23 (+2 expected)
Including for young scientists:	9
Including female scientists:	7
Meetings:	13 completed
Workshops:	5
Training schools:	2
ITC conference grants	1 (Serbia)
Publications:	Over 40
Book published:	Lectures on RV: Introductory and Advanced Topics, Springer 2017

References

1. Bartocci, E., Bonakdarpour, B., Falcone, Y.: First international competition on software for runtime verification. In: Bonakdarpour, B., Smolka, S.A. (eds.) RV 2014. LNCS, vol. 8734, pp. 1–9. Springer, Cham (2014). https://doi.org/10.1007/978-3-319-11164-3_1
2. Bartocci, E., Deshmukh, J., Donzé, A., Fainekos, G.E, Maler, O., Ničković, D., Sankaranarayanan, S.: Specification-based monitoring of cyber-physical systems: a survey on theory, tools and applications. In: Bartocci and Falcone [5], pp. 135–175
3. Bartocci, E., Falcone, Y.: RV-TheToP: runtime verification from theory to the industry practice (track introduction). In: Margaria T., Steffen B. (eds.) Leveraging Applications of Formal Methods, Verification and Validation: Discussion, Dissemination, Applications - 8th International Symposium, ISoLA 2018, Limassol, Cyprus, 30 October–13 November 2018 Proceedings, Part II. Lecture Notes in Computer Science (2018, to appear)
4. Bartocci, E., Falcone, Y.: Runtime verification and enforcement, the (industrial) application perspective (track introduction). In: Margaria and Steffen [30], pp. 333–338. https://doi.org/10.1007/978-3-319-47169-3_24
5. Bartocci, E., Falcone, Y. (eds.): Lectures on Runtime Verification - Introductory and Advanced Topics. LNCS, vol. 10457. Springer, Cham (2018). https://doi.org/10.1007/978-3-319-75632-5
6. Bartocci, E., et al.: First international competition on runtime verification: rules, benchmarks, tools, and final results of CRV 2014. Int. J. Softw. Tools Technol. Transf. (2017)
7. Bartocci, E., Falcone, Y., Francalanza, A., Reger, G.: Introduction to runtime verification. In: Bartocci and Falcone [5], pp. 1–33
8. Bartocci, E., Majumdar, R. (eds.): RV 2015. LNCS, vol. 9333. Springer, Cham (2015). https://doi.org/10.1007/978-3-319-23820-3
9. Bartocci, E., Majumdar, R.: Introduction to the special issue on runtime verification. Formal Methods Syst. Des. **51**(1), 1–4 (2017). https://doi.org/10.1007/s10703-017-0287-6
10. Bianculli, D., Krstic, S.: On the risk of tool over-tuning in run-time verification competitions (position paper). In: Reger and Havelund [34], pp. 37–40. https://easychair.org/publications/paper/N6cC
11. Colin, S., Mariani, L.: 18: Run-Time Verification. In: Broy, M., Jonsson, B., Katoen, J.-P., Leucker, M., Pretschner, A. (eds.) Model-Based Testing of Reactive Systems. LNCS, vol. 3472, pp. 525–555. Springer, Heidelberg (2005). https://doi.org/10.1007/11498490_24
12. Colombo, C., Falcone, Y.: First international summer school on runtime verification - as part of the ArVi COST action 1402. In: Falcone and Sánchez [19], pp. 17–20
13. Colombo, C., Falcone, Y.: Second school on runtime verification. In: Colombo, C., Leucker, M. (eds.) Runtime Verification - 18th International Conference, RV 2018, Limassol, Cyprus, 11–13 November, 2018, Proceedings. Lecture Notes in Computer Science, vol. 11237, pp. 27–32. Springer, Cham (2018)
14. Colombo, C., Pace, G.J.: Industrial experiences with runtime verification of financial transaction systems: lessons learnt and standing challenges. In: Bartocci and Falcone [5], pp. 211–232
15. Falcone, Y., Havelund, K., Reger, G.: A tutorial on runtime verification. In: Broy, M., Peled, D.A., Kalus, G. (eds.) Engineering Dependable Software Systems, NATO Science for Peace and Security Series, D: Information and Communication

Security, vol. 34, pp. 141–175. IOS Press (2013). https://doi.org/10.3233/978-1-61499-207-3-141
16. Falcone, Y., Kristc, S., Reger, G., Traytel, D.: A taxonomy for classifying runtime verification tools. In: Colombo, C., Leucker, M. (eds.) Proceedings of the 18th International Conference on Runtime Verification, Lecture Notes in Computer Science, vol. 11237, pp. 241–262. Springer, Cham (2018)
17. Falcone, Y., Mariani, L., Rollet, A., Saha, S.: Runtime failure prevention and reaction. In: Bartocci and Falcone [5], pp. 103–134
18. Falcone, Y., Nickovic, D., Reger, G., Thoma, D.: Second international competition on runtime verification CRV 2015. In: Bartocci and Majumdar [8], pp. 405–422. https://doi.org/10.1007/978-3-319-23820-3
19. Falcone, Y., Sánchez, C. (eds.): RV 2016. LNCS, vol. 10012. Springer, Cham (2016). https://doi.org/10.1007/978-3-319-46982-9
20. Falcone, Y., Sánchez, C.: Introduction to the special issue on runtime verification. Formal Methods Syst. Des. **53**(1), 1–5 (2018). https://doi.org/10.1007/s10703-018-0320-4
21. Hallé, S., Khoury, R., Gaboury, S.: A few things we heard about RV tools (position paper). In: Reger and Havelund [34], pp. 89–95. https://easychair.org/publications/paper/q246
22. Havelund, K., Goldberg, A.: Verify your runs. In: Meyer, B., Woodcock, J. (eds.) VSTTE 2005. LNCS, vol. 4171, pp. 374–383. Springer, Heidelberg (2008). https://doi.org/10.1007/978-3-540-69149-5_40
23. Havelund, K., Leucker, M., Reger, G., Stolz, V.: A shared challenge in behavioural specification (Dagstuhl seminar 17462). Dagstuhl Rep. **7**(11), 59–85 (2017). https://doi.org/10.4230/DagRep.7.11.59
24. Havelund, K., Reger, G.: Runtime verification logics a language design perspective. In: Aceto, L., Bacci, G., Bacci, G., Ingólfsdóttir, A., Legay, A., Mardare, R. (eds.) Models, Algorithms, Logics and Tools. LNCS, vol. 10460, pp. 310–338. Springer, Cham (2017). https://doi.org/10.1007/978-3-319-63121-9_16
25. Havelund, K., Reger, G., Thoma, D., Zalinescu, E.: Monitoring events that carry data. In: Bartocci and Falcone [5], pp. 61–102
26. Jakšić, S., Leucker, M., Li, D., Stolz, V.: COEMS - open traces from the industry. In: Reger and Havelund [34], pp. 96–105. https://easychair.org/publications/paper/QljX
27. Lahiri, S., Reger, G. (eds.): RV 2017. LNCS, vol. 10548. Springer, Cham (2017). https://doi.org/10.1007/978-3-319-67531-2
28. Leucker, M., Schallhart, C.: A brief account of runtime verification. J. Logic Algebraic Program. **78**(5), 293–303 (2008). https://doi.org/10.1016/j.jlap.2008.08.004
29. Mallozzi, P., Pardo, R., Duplessis, V., Pelliccione, P., Schneider, G.: MoVEMo: a structured approach for engineering reward functions. In: Second IEEE International Conference on Robotic Computing (IRC 2018), pp. 250–257. IEEE Computer Society (2018). https://doi.org/10.1109/IRC.2018.00053
30. Margaria, T., Steffen, B. (eds.): ISoLA 2016. LNCS, vol. 9953. Springer, Cham (2016). https://doi.org/10.1007/978-3-319-47169-3
31. Reger, G.: A report of RV-CuBES 2017. In: Reger and Havelund [34], pp. 1–9. https://easychair.org/publications/paper/MVXk
32. Reger, G., Hallé, S., Falcone, Y.: Third international competition on runtime verification - CRV 2016. In: Falcone and Sánchez [19], pp. 21–37
33. Reger, G., Havelund, K.: What is a trace? A runtime verification perspective. In: Margaria and Steffen [30], pp. 339–355. https://doi.org/10.1007/978-3-319-47169-3_25

34. Reger, G., Havelund, K. (eds.): RV-CuBES 2017. In: An International Workshop on Competitions, Usability, Benchmarks, Evaluation, and Standardisation for Runtime Verification Tools, Kalpa Publications in Computing, vol. 3. EasyChair (2017)

35. Reger, G., Rydeheard, D.: From parametric trace slicing to rule systems. In: Colombo, C., Leucker, M. (eds.) Proceedings of the 18th International Conference on Runtime Verification, Lecture Notes in Computer Science, vol. 11237, pp. 334–352. Springer, Cham (2018)

36. Reger, G., Rydeheard, D.E.: From first-order temporal logic to parametric trace slicing. In: Bartocci and Majumdar [8], pp. 216–232 https://doi.org/10.1007/978-3-319-23820-3_14

37. Rozier, K.Y.: On the evaluation and comparison of runtime verification tools for hardware and cyber-physical systems. In: Reger and Havelund [34], pp. 123–137. https://easychair.org/publications/paper/877G

38. Sánchez, C., et al.: A Survey of Challenges for Runtime Verification from Advanced Application Domains (beyond software) (2018, under submission)

39. Signoles, J.: Online runtime verification competitions: how to possibly deal with their issues (position paper). In: Reger and Havelund [34], pp. 157–163. https://easychair.org/publications/paper/m1vV

Second School on Runtime Verification, as Part of the ArVi COST Action 1402
Overview and Reflections

Yliès Falcone[(✉)]

Univ. Grenoble Alpes, CNRS, Inria, Grenoble INP, LIG, 38000 Grenoble, France
ylies.falcone@univ-grenoble-alpes.fr

Abstract. This paper briefly reports on the second international school on Runtime Verification, co-organized and sponsored by Inria and COST Action IC1402 ArVi. The school was held March 19–21 2018, in Praz sur Arly (near Grenoble) in the French Alps. Most of the lectures dealt with introductory and advanced topics on Runtime Verification from the first tutorial book on Runtime Verification [2]. Additional lectures were given on cutting-edge research topics. We report the context and objectives of the school, overview its program, and propose outlooks for the future editions of the school.

1 Context and Objectives

Runtime Verification (RV) is the umbrella term to refer to the study of languages, (lightweight) techniques, and tools related to the verification of the executions of software and hardware systems against behavioral properties (see [4,5,7,10,11,14] for tutorials and overviews). Runtime Verification is a very effective technique to ensure that a system is correct, reliable, and robust. Compared to other verification techniques, RV is more practical than exhaustive verification techniques (e.g., model-checking, static analysis), at the price of losing completeness. Compared to conventional testing, RV is more powerful and versatile.

As a field of research, RV is endowed with a yearly conference[1], which exists since 2000. The field is getting more mature and diverse and the community is building documentation and lecture material to help students and practitioners entering the field. The international school on Runtime Verification constitutes one key element to facilitate the adoption of RV. This edition of the school shared the same objectives as the first edition [6] (which was held in Madrid as part of RV 2016 [9]):

- to present the foundations of the techniques;
- to expose participants to cutting-edge advances in the field;
- to provide a balance on theoretical and practical aspects of Runtime Verification;
- to adopt a hands-on approach and expose participants with the basics of building an RV tool.

---

[1] runtime-verification.org.

C. Colombo and M. Leucker (Eds.): RV 2018, LNCS 11237, pp. 27–32, 2018.
https://doi.org/10.1007/978-3-030-03769-7_3

2   Presentation

The second edition of the school on Runtime Verification was sponsored by COST Action IC1402 ArVi[2], Inria[3], and Persyval-Lab[4].

Table 1. Program overview - Day 1 - Monday 19th March

Time slot	Topic	Lecturer
08:00 10:00	*An Introduction to Runtime Verification and Monitorability* slides (https://www.cost-arvi.eu/wp-content/uploads/2018/04/2nd-School-on-RV-Francalenza.pdf) video (https://youtu.be/NDwiHfMXPMs)	A. Francalanza
10:30 12:00	*Monitoring Cyber-Physical Systems* slides (https://www.cost-arvi.eu/wp-content/uploads/2018/04/2nd-School-on-RV-Donze.pdf) video (https://youtu.be/GFVUpabVLQA)	A. Donze
13:00 14:30	*The Java Modeling Language a Basis for Static and Dynamic Verification* slides (https://www.cost-arvi.eu/wp-content/uploads/2018/04/2nd-School-on-RV-Ahrendt.pdf) video (https://youtu.be/9ItK0jxJ0oQ)	W. Ahrendt
14:30 15:30	*Foundations on Runtime Verification* video (https://youtu.be/wafR7Oe4Uk0)	M. Leucker
16:00 16:45	*Monitoring Data Minimization* slides (https://www.cost-arvi.eu/wp-content/uploads/2018/04/2nd-School-on-RV-Schneider.pdf) video (https://youtu.be/6JOGJLESTmw)	G. Schneider
16:45 17:30	*Runtime Assertion-Based Verification for Hardware and Embedded Systems* slides (https://www.cost-arvi.eu/wp-content/uploads/2018/04/2nd-School-on-RV-Pierre.pdf) video (https://youtu.be/L-H4qUkMDM)	L. Pierre

The school was organised over three days with a series of lectures from international experts (see Tables 1, 2 and 3). Lectures at the school ranged from the fundamentals of runtime verification to more practical aspects, but also covered cutting-edge research. All lectures were fully recorded. In Tables 1, 2 and 3, below each lecture title, one can find 3 clickable links to the slides and videos.

In the remainder, we report on some of the lessons learned from the organization of the school and make suggestions to future organizers of the school.

---

[2] www.cost-arvi.eu.

[3] www.inria.fr.

[4] persyval-lab.org.

Table 2. Program overview - Day 2 - Tuesday 20th March

Time slot	Topic	Lecturer
08:00 10:00	*Combined static and dynamic analyses in Frama-C: An Overview* slides (https://www.cost-arvi.eu/wp-content/uploads/2018/04/2nd-School-on-RV-Kosmatov.pdf) video (https://youtu.be/iC4i25jBaYg)	N. Kosmatov
10:30 12:00	*A Hands-On Introduction to Building a Runtime Verification Tool* slides (https://www.cost-arvi.eu/wp-content/uploads/2018/04/2nd-School-on-RV-Colombo1.zip) video (https://youtu.be/Vyz6kte4PVk)	C. Colombo
14:00 17:00	Social event: Outing to Mont Blanc	

Table 3. Program overview - Day 3 - Wednesday 21st March

Time slot	Topic	Lecturer
08:00 10:00	*Discovering Concurrency Errors* slides (https://www.cost-arvi.eu/wp-content/uploads/2018/04/2nd-School-on-RV-Lourenco.pdf) video (https://youtu.be/XqKpoOaomGQ)	J. Loureno
10:30 12:00	*Stream Runtime Verification* slides (www.cost-arvi.eu/wp-content/uploads/2018/04/2nd-School-on-RV-Sanchez.gz) video (https://youtu.be/pmLag5rcQIs)	C. Sanchez
13:00 14:30	*Industrial Experiences with Runtime Verification of Financial Transaction Systems: Lessons Learnt and Standing Challenges* slides (https://www.cost-arvi.eu/wp-content/uploads/2018/04/2nd-School-on-RV-Colombo2.pdf) video (https://youtu.be/Un5pJVqjUK0)	C. Colombo

3   Reflections

We summarize the most frequent comments obtained from the participants. The balance between practice and theory was really appreciated by the participants (with application-oriented lectures very welcome). However, we note that some participants (legitimately) found the practice sessions too short and that monitoring for concurrency errors was under-represented (only 2 h). Participants appreciated the format of the sessions: lectures last between one and two hours and focused on a topic. However, some participants with experience in RV would have preferred to opt for slightly more technical lectures with a greater focus on state of the art approaches, especially during the last sessions (as was actually the case with the first edition of the school). The participants appreciated the opportunities to discuss with experts and lecturers (thanks to the long breaks and social events); these opportunities allowed new connections to participants. Some participants suggested organizing additional group discussions in the form of panels dedicated to cutting-edge topics lead by the lecturers.

4 Outlooks

Given the great success of the last two editions, we hope that the school will proceed in the future. We make recommendations for future editions of the school. These recommendations are based on the experience gained from the organization of the two editions and the feedback received from the participants.

- First, we recommend that future editions of the school last longer: 3 to 4 full days would be the appropriate duration to dedicate one day to basics, one day to advanced topics, one day to cutting-edge research and recent results, and one day dedicated to tool construction (which is of importance for such a pragmatic technique as RV).
- Regarding practice sessions, we believe that sessions such as the ones organized during the first edition of the school would be more effective by allowing students to really address implementation issues. To save time, setup and configurations of the tools involved should be provided to the participants ahead of time. Using technologies such as virtual machines and containers is to be considered.
- Moreover, we would like to see a lecture dedicated to tool evaluation, detailing the methodology to compare a tool and assess its relevance.
- Furthermore, we would suggest future organizers to prepare overview slides providing participants with a big picture of the presented techniques. This shall help connect methods, techniques, and tools, and better see the complementarities. Similar to this is the concern of participants in seeing when to use RV compared to other techniques. Providing concrete example situations (upfront during the first lecture) where non-RV techniques fail and where RV techniques are complementary would clarify the position of RV in the big picture of verification techniques.
- To put the approaches in a better perspective, it would be nice to compare different approaches addressing the same problem. After an exposition of the approaches, a common interactive session could serve see the limits of each approach and study possible cross-fertilization between them.
- Finally, we would like to organize a small competition between the tools constructed by the students, in the same spirit as the competitions on Runtime Verification, usually held during the conference [1,3,8,12,13].

Acknowledgment. The organizer would like to warmly thank all the researchers for their lectures and all the participants to the winter school for their feedback.

The school lectures were based upon work from COST Action ARVI IC1402, supported by COST (European Cooperation in Science and Technology) and from the material in the tutorial book on introductory and advanced topics on Runtime Verification [2].

The organizer is grateful to several institutes who sponsored the school: the COST association, Inria, PERSYVAL-lab, and the Laboratoire d'Informatique de Grenoble.

The organizer is also much in debt with several fellows who largely contributed to making the school a successful event: Sophie Azzaro, Imma Presseguer, and Carmen Contamin for helping with logistic organization, and Djamel Hadji and Gilles Gardès for recording the lectures and handling all the audiovisual matters during the school.

References

1. Bartocci, E., Bonakdarpour, B., Falcone, Y.: First international competition on software for runtime verification. In: Bonakdarpour, B., Smolka, S.A. (eds.) RV 2014. LNCS, vol. 8734, pp. 1–9. Springer, Cham (2014). https://doi.org/10.1007/978-3-319-11164-3_1
2. Bartocci, E., Falcone, Y. (eds.): Lectures on Runtime Verification - Introductory and Advanced Topics. LNCS, vol. 10457. Springer, Cham (2018). https://doi.org/10.1007/978-3-319-75632-5
3. Bartocci, E., et al.: First international competition on runtime verification: rules, benchmarks, tools, and final results of CRV 2014. Int. J. Softw. Tools Technol. Transfer (2017)
4. Bartocci, E., Falcone, Y., Francalanza, A., Reger, G.: Introduction to runtime verification. In: Bartocci, E., Falcone, Y. (eds.) Lectures on Runtime Verification. LNCS, vol. 10457, pp. 1–33. Springer, Cham (2018). https://doi.org/10.1007/978-3-319-75632-5_1
5. Colin, S., Mariani, L.: Run-time verification. In: Broy, M., Jonsson, B., Katoen, J.-P., Leucker, M., Pretschner, A. (eds.) Model-Based Testing of Reactive Systems, Advanced Lectures [The volume is the outcome of a research seminar that was held in Schloss Dagstuhl in January 2004]. LNCS, vol. 3472, pp. 525–555. Springer, Heidelberg (2004). https://doi.org/10.1007/11498490_24
6. Colombo, C., Falcone, Y.: First international summer school on runtime verification. In: Falcone, Y., Sánchez, C. (eds.) RV 2016. LNCS, vol. 10012, pp. 17–20. Springer, Cham (2016). https://doi.org/10.1007/978-3-319-46982-9_2
7. Falcone, Y., Havelund, K., Reger, G.: A tutorial on runtime verification. In: Broy, M., Peled, D.A., Kalus, G. (eds.) Engineering Dependable Software Systems, NATO Science for Peace and Security Series, D: Information and Communication Security, vol. 34, pp. 141–175. IOS Press (2013)
8. Falcone, Y., Ničković, D., Reger, G., Thoma, D.: Second international competition on runtime verification. In: Bartocci, E., Majumdar, R. (eds.) RV 2015. LNCS, vol. 9333, pp. 405–422. Springer, Cham (2015). https://doi.org/10.1007/978-3-319-23820-3_27
9. Falcone, Y., Sánchez, C. (eds.): RV 2016. LNCS, vol. 10012. Springer, Cham (2016). https://doi.org/10.1007/978-3-319-46982-9
10. Havelund, K., Goldberg, A.: Verify your runs. In: Meyer, B., Woodcock, J. (eds.) VSTTE 2005. LNCS, vol. 4171, pp. 374–383. Springer, Heidelberg (2008). https://doi.org/10.1007/978-3-540-69149-5_40
11. Leucker, M., Schallhart, C.: A brief account of runtime verification. J. Logic Algebraic Program. **78**(5), 293–303 (2008)

12. Reger, G.: A report of RV-cubes 2017. In: Reger G., Havelund K. (eds.) RV-CuBES 2017. An International Workshop on Competitions, Usability, Benchmarks, Evaluation, and Standardisation for Runtime Verification Tools, 15 September 2017, Seattle, WA, USA. Kalpa Publications in Computing, vol. 3, pp. 1–9. EasyChair (2017)
13. Reger, G., Hallé, S., Falcone, Y.: Third international competition on runtime verification - CRV 2016. In: Falcone and Sánchez [9], pp. 21–37
14. Sokolsky, O., Havelund, K., Lee, I.: Introduction to the special section on runtime verification. STTT **14**(3), 243–247 (2012)

Tutorial Papers

Monitoring, Learning and Control
of Cyber-Physical Systems with STL
(Tutorial)

Ezio Bartocci[(✉)]

Technische Universität Wien, Vienna, Austria
ezio.bartocci@tuwien.ac.at

Abstract. Signal Temporal Logic (STL) is a popular specification language to reason about continuous-time trajectories of dynamical systems. STL was originally employed to specify and to monitor requirements over the temporal evolution of physical quantities and discrete states characterizing the behavior of cyber-physical systems (CPS). More recently, this formalism plays a key role in several approaches for the automatic design of safe systems and controllers satisfying an STL specification. However, requirements for CPS may include behavioral properties about the physical plant that are not always fully known a-priori and indeed cannot be completely manually specified. This has opened a new research direction on efficient methods for automatically mining and learning STL properties from measured data. In this tutorial we provide an overview of the state-of-the-art approaches available for monitoring, learning and control of CPS behaviors with STL focusing on some recent applications.

1 Introduction

Cyber-Physical Systems (CPS) [40, 46, 47] are defined as a networked computational embedded systems monitoring and controlling engineering, physical and biological systems. Their behavior is characterized by the evolution of physical quantities interleaved with the occurrence of discrete state transitions of the computational components.

Hybrid systems [29] are a suitable mathematical framework to model, at design time, the dynamics of CPS exhibiting both discrete and continuous behaviors. A hybrid automaton (HA) extends the logical, discrete-state representation of finite automata with continuous dynamics expressed as a set of differential equations in each state (or mode). Proving that a HA is safe (set of *bad states* is not reachable from an initial set of states) requires to solve the reachability analysis problem [2, 13, 22, 24–26, 37, 38, 50] that is in general undecidable [30].

A complementary approach, close to testing, is to monitor systematically the CPS behavior [8] under different initial conditions either at simulation-time [3, 17] or at runtime [32, 33, 52]. This approach consists in observing the evolution of the discrete and continuous variables characterizing the CPS dynamics and deciding whether the observed behavior is good or bad. These traces of values

© Springer Nature Switzerland AG 2018
C. Colombo and M. Leucker (Eds.): RV 2018, LNCS 11237, pp. 35–42, 2018.
https://doi.org/10.1007/978-3-030-03769-7_4

can be observed during the CPS simulation or execution through the instrumentation of the system under test (SUT) (more details concerning instrumentation techniques can be found in [9]). In this tutorial we provide an overview of the state-of-the-art approaches for specification-based monitoring of CPS behaviors using Signal Temporal Logic (STL) [41] and its recent applications to control synthesis and mining of requirements from data.

2 Tutorial Description

The tutorial is organized into three parts described in the following sections.

2.1 Part 1 - Monitoring Cyber-Physical Systems Using STL

STL [41] is a powerful formalism suitable to specify in a concise way complex temporal properties for CPS. STL enables to reason about real-time properties of components exhibiting both discrete and continuous dynamics. The classical Boolean semantics of STL decides whether a signal is correct or not with respect to a given specification. However, this answer may be not informative enough to reason about the CPS behavior. For example, let us consider an STL formula ϕ asserting that the value of a real-valued signal must be always less than a certain threshold. A signal with an initial value less than the threshold and approaching it, but never crossing it, satisfies ϕ in the same way as a real-valued signal with the same initial value that remains always constant. However, the application of a very small perturbation (the same) to both signals can make the first signal violating the specification while the second signal still satisfying the requirement. In general, the continuous dynamics of CPS are expected to satisfy the specification with a certain tolerance with respect to the value of certain parameters, thresholds, initial conditions and external inputs.

Different authors [20, 23] have proposed to address this issue by defining a *quantitative* semantics for STL. This semantics replaces the binary satisfaction relation with a quantitative *robustness degree* function, while not changing the original syntax of STL. The robustness degree function returns a real value that indicates how far is a signal from satisfying or violating a specification. The positive and negative sign of the robustness value indicates whether the formula is respectively satisfied or violated.

The notion of robustness was exploited in several tools [3, 17] for falsification-based analysis [16] and parameter synthesis [7, 19] of CPS models. One one hand, trying to minimize the robustness [3] can be suitable to search counterexamples in the input space violating the specification. On the other hand, maximizing the robustness [17] can be used to tune the parameters of the system to be more resilient. These optimisation problems can be solved using several heuristics (i.e., genetic algorithms [42], particle swarm optimization [5, 27], gradient ascent/descent [56], statistical emulations [7]) that systematically guide the search either in the parameter space or in the input space.

There has been a great effort to develop *offline* [3,17,18,44] and *online* monitoring algorithms [14,15,32,33] for both the Boolean and robust semantics of STL. These approaches are discussed thoughtfully in a recent survey [8].

2.2 Part 2 - Controller Specification and Synthesis

STL has also become a powerful formalism for control engineers to specify and automatically synthesize correct-by-construction controllers that can satisfy very complex time-dependent constraints [10]. This approach has been successfully employed in several application domains, ranging from biological networks to multi-agent robotics [3,49,54].

A typical approach to address this problem, presented first by Karaman et al. in [35], is to formulate a temporal logic control problems as Mixed Integer Linear or Quadratic Programs problems (MILP/MIQP) controlling the system directly in continuous space without the need of a discrete state-space abstraction as in automata-based solutions [36,48]. This approach has been followed later by many other researchers [21,28,48,51]. However, solving a MILP problem has an exponential complexity with respect to the number of its integer variables. Hence, this approach becomes unfeasible for very large and complex STL specifications with nested terms.

An alternative approach is to compute a smooth abstraction for the traditional STL quantitative semantics defined in [20]. The idea is to replace min/max operations with continuous differentiable functions such as exponential functions approximating min/max operators. In particular, Pant et al. in [45] have recently demonstrated that control problems can be solved using smooth optimization algorithms such as gradient descent in a much more computationally efficient way than MILP. Furthermore, this approach can be used to control any plant with smooth nonlinear dynamics while MILP/MIQP require the system dynamics to be linear or quadratic.

2.3 Part 3 - Learning STL Requirements from Data

CPS requirements may include behavioral properties about the physical plant that are not always fully known a-priori and indeed cannot be completely manually specified. Furthermore, classical machine learning methods typically produce very powerful black-box (statistical) models. However, these models are hard to interpret by humans, because they do not provide a comprehensible explanation of the phenomenon they capture. In contrast, temporal logics such as STL provide a precise and non-ambiguous formal specification of the behavioral requirements of interest and that can be easily interpreted by humans.

For this reason, learning STL requirements from observed traces is an emerging field of research supporting both the analysis and the control of CPS [1,4,6, 11,12,31,34,39,42,43,55,57]. Most of the literature focuses on learning the optimal parameters for given a specific template formula [4,6,31,34,42,43,55,57] in order to satisfy a particular training data set.

Learning both the structure and the parameters of a formula from data is a even more challenging [6,11,12,39]. This task is usually addressed in two steps: (i) learning the structure of the formula and (ii) synthesizing its parameters. For example, the approach described in [39] learns, by exploring a directed acyclic graph, a parametric template of the STL formula. The parameters of the formula (i.e., temporal intervals or the thresholds of the basic propositions) are then derived by applying standard *Support Vector Machine* (SVM) techniques over the training data.

The approach in [11] proposes instead a *decision tree*-based approach for learning the STL formula, while the optimality of the parameters is evaluated using heuristic impurity measures.

In our recent works [6,12,42] we have also tackled the problem of learning both the structure and the parameters of a temporal logic specification from data. In [6] the structure of the formula is learned using a heuristic algorithm, while [12,42] use a genetic algorithm. In both cases, the parameter synthesis is performed using the *Gaussian Process Upper Confidence Bound* (GP-UCB) [53] algorithm that statistically emulate the satisfaction probability of a formula for a given set of parameters.

Acknowledgements. The author acknowledges the partial support of the ICT COST Action IC1402 Runtime Verification beyond Monitoring (ARVI).

References

1. Ackermann, C., Cleaveland, R., Huang, S., Ray, A., Shelton, C., Latronico, E.: Automatic requirement extraction from test cases. In: Barringer, H., Falcone, Y., Finkbeiner, B., Havelund, K., Lee, I., Pace, G., Roşu, G., Sokolsky, O., Tillmann, N. (eds.) RV 2010. LNCS, vol. 6418, pp. 1–15. Springer, Heidelberg (2010). https://doi.org/10.1007/978-3-642-16612-9_1
2. Althoff, M.: Reachability analysis of nonlinear systems using conservative polynomialization and non-convex sets. In: Proceedings of HSCC 2013: The 16th International Conference on Hybrid Systems: Computation and Control, pp. 173–182. ACM (2013)
3. Annpureddy, Y., Liu, C., Fainekos, G., Sankaranarayanan, S.: S-TALiRo: a tool for temporal logic falsification for hybrid systems. In: Abdulla, P.A., Leino, K.R.M. (eds.) TACAS 2011. LNCS, vol. 6605, pp. 254–257. Springer, Heidelberg (2011). https://doi.org/10.1007/978-3-642-19835-9_21
4. Asarin, E., Donzé, A., Maler, O., Nickovic, D.: Parametric identification of temporal properties. In: Khurshid, S., Sen, K. (eds.) RV 2011. LNCS, vol. 7186, pp. 147–160. Springer, Heidelberg (2012). https://doi.org/10.1007/978-3-642-29860-8_12
5. Aydin-Gol, E., Bartocci, E., Belta, C.: A formal methods approach to pattern synthesis in reaction diffusion systems. In: Proceedings of CDC 2014: The 53rd IEEE Conference on Decision and Control, pp. 108–113. IEEE (2014)
6. Bartocci, E., Bortolussi, L., Sanguinetti, G.: Data-driven statistical learning of temporal logic properties. In: Legay, A., Bozga, M. (eds.) FORMATS 2014. LNCS, vol. 8711, pp. 23–37. Springer, Cham (2014). https://doi.org/10.1007/978-3-319-10512-3_3

7. Bartocci, E., Bortolussi, L., Nenzi, L., Sanguinetti, G.: System design of stochastic models using robustness of temporal properties. Theor. Comput. Sci. **587**, 3–25 (2015)
8. Bartocci, E., Deshmukh, J., Donzé, A., Fainekos, G., Maler, O., Ničković, D., Sankaranarayanan, S.: Specification-based monitoring of cyber-physical systems: a survey on theory, tools and applications. In: Bartocci, E., Falcone, Y. (eds.) Lectures on Runtime Verification - Introductory and Advanced Topics. LNCS, vol. 10457, pp. 135–175. Springer, Cham (2018). https://doi.org/10.1007/978-3-319-75632-5_5
9. Bartocci, E., Falcone, Y., Francalanza, A., Reger, G.: Introduction to runtime verification. In: Bartocci, E., Falcone, Y. (eds.) Lectures on Runtime Verification - Introductory and Advanced Topics. LNCS, vol. 10457, pp. 1–33. Springer, Cham (2018). https://doi.org/10.1007/978-3-319-75632-5_1
10. Belta, C., Yordanov, B., Aydin Gol, E.: Formal Methods for Discrete-Time Dynamical Systems. SSDC, vol. 89. Springer, Cham (2017). https://doi.org/10.1007/978-3-319-50763-7
11. Bombara, G., Vasile, C.I., Penedo, F., Yasuoka, H., Belta, C.: A decision tree approach to data classification using signal temporal logic. In: Proceedings of HSCC 2016: The 19th International Conference on Hybrid Systems: Computation and Control, pp. 1–10. ACM (2016)
12. Bufo, S., Bartocci, E., Sanguinetti, G., Borelli, M., Lucangelo, U., Bortolussi, L.: Temporal logic based monitoring of assisted ventilation in intensive care patients. In: Margaria, T., Steffen, B. (eds.) ISoLA 2014. LNCS, vol. 8803, pp. 391–403. Springer, Heidelberg (2014). https://doi.org/10.1007/978-3-662-45231-8_30
13. Chen, X., Ábrahám, E., Sankaranarayanan, S.: Flow*: an analyzer for non-linear hybrid systems. In: Sharygina, N., Veith, H. (eds.) CAV 2013. LNCS, vol. 8044, pp. 258–263. Springer, Heidelberg (2013). https://doi.org/10.1007/978-3-642-39799-8_18
14. Deshmukh, J.V., Donzé, A., Ghosh, S., Jin, X., Garvit, J., Seshia, S.A.: Robust online monitoring of signal temporal logic. Form. Methods Syst. Des. **51**, 5–30 (2017)
15. Dokhanchi, A., Hoxha, B., Fainekos, G.: On-line monitoring for temporal logic robustness. In: Bonakdarpour, B., Smolka, S.A. (eds.) RV 2014. LNCS, vol. 8734, pp. 231–246. Springer, Cham (2014). https://doi.org/10.1007/978-3-319-11164-3_19
16. Dokhanchi, A., Zutshi, A., Sriniva, R.T., Sankaranarayanan, S., Fainekos, G.: Requirements driven falsification with coverage metrics. In: Proceedings of EMSOFT: The 12th International Conference on Embedded Software, pp. 31–40. IEEE (2015)
17. Donzé, A.: Breach, A toolbox for verification and parameter synthesis of hybrid systems. In: Touili, T., Cook, B., Jackson, P. (eds.) CAV 2010. LNCS, vol. 6174, pp. 167–170. Springer, Heidelberg (2010). https://doi.org/10.1007/978-3-642-14295-6_17
18. Donzé, A., Ferrère, T., Maler, O.: Efficient robust monitoring for STL. In: Sharygina, N., Veith, H. (eds.) CAV 2013. LNCS, vol. 8044, pp. 264–279. Springer, Heidelberg (2013). https://doi.org/10.1007/978-3-642-39799-8_19
19. Donzé, A., Krogh, B., Rajhans, A.: Parameter synthesis for hybrid systems with an application to simulink models. In: Majumdar, R., Tabuada, P. (eds.) HSCC 2009. LNCS, vol. 5469, pp. 165–179. Springer, Heidelberg (2009). https://doi.org/10.1007/978-3-642-00602-9_12

20. Donzé, A., Maler, O.: Robust satisfaction of temporal logic over real-valued signals. In: Chatterjee, K., Henzinger, T.A. (eds.) FORMATS 2010. LNCS, vol. 6246, pp. 92–106. Springer, Heidelberg (2010). https://doi.org/10.1007/978-3-642-15297-9_9

21. Donzé, A., Raman, V.: BluSTL: Controller synthesis from signal temporal logic specifications. In: Proceedings of 1st and 2nd International Workshop on Applied veRification for Continuous and Hybrid Systems. EPiC Series in Computing, vol. 34, pp. 160–168. EasyChair (2015)

22. Duggirala, P.S., Mitra, S., Viswanathan, M., Potok, M.: C2E2: A verification tool for stateflow models. In: Baier, C., Tinelli, C. (eds.) TACAS 2015. LNCS, vol. 9035, pp. 68–82. Springer, Heidelberg (2015). https://doi.org/10.1007/978-3-662-46681-0_5

23. Fainekos, G.E., Pappas, G.J.: Robustness of temporal logic specifications for continuous-time signals. Theor. Comput. Sci. **410**(42), 4262–4291 (2009)

24. Fan, C., Meng, Y., Maier, J., Bartocci, E., Mitra, S., Schmid, U.: Verifying nonlinear analog and mixed-signal circuits with inputs. In: Proceedings of ADHS 2018 - IFAC Conference on Analysis and Design of Hybrid Systems, vol. 51(16), pp. 241–246 (2018)

25. Fränzle, M., Herde, C.: Hysat: an efficient proof engine for bounded model checking of hybrid systems. Form. Methods Syst. Des. **30**(3), 179–198 (2007)

26. Frehse, G., Le Guernic, C., Donzé, A., Cotton, S., Ray, R., Lebeltel, O., Ripado, R., Girard, A., Dang, T., Maler, O.: SpaceEx: scalable verification of hybrid systems. In: Gopalakrishnan, G., Qadeer, S. (eds.) CAV 2011. LNCS, vol. 6806, pp. 379–395. Springer, Heidelberg (2011). https://doi.org/10.1007/978-3-642-22110-1_30

27. Haghighi, I., Jones, A., Kong, Z., Bartocci, E., Grosu, R., Belta, C.: Spatel: A novel spatial-temporal logic and its applications to networked systems. In: Proceedings of HSCC 2015: The 18th International Conference on Hybrid Systems: Computation and Control, pp. 189–198. ACM (2015)

28. Haghighi, I., Sadraddini, S., Belta, C.: Robotic swarm control from spatio-temporal specifications. In: Proceedings of CDC 2016: The 55th IEEE Conference on Decision and Control, pp. 5708–5713. IEEE (2016)

29. Henzinger, T.A.: The theory of hybrid automata. In: Proceedings of IEEE Symposium on Logic in Computer Science, pp. 278–292 (1996)

30. Henzinger, T.A., Kopke, P.W., Puri, A., Varaiya, P.: What's decidable about hybrid automata ? J. Comput. Syst. Sci. **57**(1), 94–124 (1998)

31. Hoxha, B., Dokhanchi, A., Fainekos, G.E.: Mining parametric temporal logic properties in model-based design for cyber-physical systems. STTT **20**(1), 79–93 (2018)

32. Jaksic, S., Bartocci, E., Grosu, R., Kloibhofer, R., Nguyen, T., Ničković, D.: From signal temporal logic to FPGA monitors. In: Proceedings of MEMOCODE 2015: The 13th ACM/IEEE International Conference on Formal Methods and Models for Codesign, pp. 218–227. IEEE (2015)

33. Jakšić, S., Bartocci, E., Grosu, R., Ničković, D.: Quantitative monitoring of STL with edit distance. In: Falcone, Y., Sánchez, C. (eds.) RV 2016. LNCS, vol. 10012, pp. 201–218. Springer, Cham (2016). https://doi.org/10.1007/978-3-319-46982-9_13

34. Jin, X., Donzé, A., Deshmukh, J.V., Seshia, S.A.: Mining requirements from closed-loop control models. IEEE Trans. CAD Integr. Circuits Syst. **34**(11), 1704–1717 (2015)

35. Karaman, S., Sanfelice, R.G., Frazzoli, E.: Optimal control of mixed logical dynamical systems with linear temporal logic specifications. In: Proceedings of CDC 2008: The 47th IEEE Conference on Decision and Control, pp. 2117–2122. IEEE (2008)

36. Kim, E.S., Sadraddini, S., Belta, C., Arcak, M., Seshia, S.A.: Dynamic contracts for distributed temporal logic control of traffic networks. In: IEEE 56th Annual Conference on Decision and Control (CDC) 2017, pp. 3640–3645. IEEE (2017)
37. Kong, H., Bartocci, E., Henzinger, T.A.: Reachable set over-approximation for non-linear systems using piecewise barrier tubes. In: Chockler, H., Weissenbacher, G. (eds.) CAV 2018. LNCS, vol. 10981, pp. 449–467. Springer, Cham (2018). https://doi.org/10.1007/978-3-319-96145-3_24
38. Kong, S., Gao, S., Chen, W., Clarke, E.: dReach: δ-reachability analysis for hybrid systems. In: Baier, C., Tinelli, C. (eds.) TACAS 2015. LNCS, vol. 9035, pp. 200–205. Springer, Heidelberg (2015). https://doi.org/10.1007/978-3-662-46681-0_15
39. Kong, Z., Jones, A., Belta, C.: Temporal logics for learning and detection of anomalous behavior. IEEE Trans. Autom. Control. 62(3), 1210–1222 (2017)
40. Lee, E.A., Seshia, S.A.: An introductory textbook on cyber-physical systems. In: Proceedings of the 2010 Workshop on Embedded Systems Education, WESE 2010, pp. 1:1–1:6. ACM, New York (2010)
41. Maler, O., Nickovic, D.: Monitoring temporal properties of continuous signals. In: Lakhnech, Y., Yovine, S. (eds.) FORMATS/FTRTFT -2004. LNCS, vol. 3253, pp. 152–166. Springer, Heidelberg (2004). https://doi.org/10.1007/978-3-540-30206-3_12
42. Nenzi, L., Silvetti, S., Bartocci, E., Bortolussi, L.: A robust genetic algorithm for learning temporal specifications from data. In: McIver, A., Horvath, A. (eds.) QEST 2018. LNCS, vol. 11024, pp. 323–338. Springer, Cham (2018). https://doi.org/10.1007/978-3-319-99154-2_20
43. Nguyen, L., Kapinski, J., Jin, X., Deshmukh, J., Butts, K., Johnson, T.: Abnormal data classification using time-frequency temporal logic. In: Proceedings of HSCC 2017: The 20th ACM International Conference on Hybrid Systems: Computation and Control, pp. 237–242. ACM (2017)
44. Ničković, D., Lebeltel, O., Maler, O., Ferrère, T., Ulus, D.: AMT 2.0: qualitative and quantitative trace analysis with extended signal temporal logic. In: Beyer, D., Huisman, M. (eds.) TACAS 2018. LNCS, vol. 10806, pp. 303–319. Springer, Cham (2018). https://doi.org/10.1007/978-3-319-89963-3_18
45. Pant, Y.V., Abbas, H., Mangharam, R.: Smooth operator: control using the smooth robustness of temporal logic. In: Proceedings of CCTA 2017: The IEEE Conference on Control Technology and Applications, pp. 1235–1240. IEEE (2017)
46. Rajkumar, R.: A cyber-physical future. In: Proceedings of the IEEE 100 (Special Centennial Issue), pp. 1309–1312 (2012)
47. Rajkumar, R.R., Lee, I., Sha, L., Stankovic, J.: Cyber-physical systems: the next computing revolution. In: Proceedings of DAC 2010: The 47th Design Automation Conference, pp. 731–736. ACM, New York (2010)
48. Raman, V., Donzé, A., Maasoumy, M., Murray, R.M., Sangiovanni-Vincentelli, A.L., Seshia, S.A.: Model predictive control with signal temporal logic specifications. In: Proceedings of CDC 2014: The 53rd IEEE Conference on Decision and Control, pp. 81–87. IEEE (2014)
49. Raman, V., Donzé, A., Sadigh, D., Murray, R.M., Seshia, S.A.: Reactive synthesis from signal temporal logic specifications. In: Proceedings of the 18th International Conference on Hybrid Systems: Computation and Control, pp. 239–248. ACM (2015)
50. Ray, R., Gurung, A., Das, B., Bartocci, E., Bogomolov, S., Grosu, R.: XSpeed: accelerating reachability analysis on multi-core processors. In: Piterman, N. (ed.) HVC 2015. LNCS, vol. 9434, pp. 3–18. Springer, Cham (2015). https://doi.org/10.1007/978-3-319-26287-1_1

51. Sadraddini, S., Belta, C.: Model predictive control of urban traffic networks with temporal logic constraints. In: Proceedings of ACC 2016: The 2016 American Control Conference, p. 881. IEEE (2016)
52. Selyunin, K., Jaksic, S., Nguyen, T., Reidl, C., Hafner, U., Bartocci, E., Nickovic, D., Grosu, R.: Runtime monitoring with recovery of the SENT communication protocol. In: Majumdar, R., Kunčak, V. (eds.) CAV 2017. LNCS, vol. 10426, pp. 336–355. Springer, Cham (2017). https://doi.org/10.1007/978-3-319-63387-9_17
53. Srinivas, N., Krause, A., Kakade, S.M., Seeger, M.W.: Information-theoretic regret bounds for gaussian process optimization in the bandit setting. IEEE Trans. Inf. Theory **58**(5), 3250–3265 (2012)
54. Wongpiromsarn, T., Topcu, U., Murray, R.M.: Receding horizon temporal logic planning. IEEE Trans. Automat. Contr. **57**(11), 2817–2830 (2012)
55. Xu, Z., Julius, A.A.: Census signal temporal logic inference for multiagent group behavior analysis. IEEE Trans. Autom. Sci. Eng. **15**(1), 264–277 (2018)
56. Yaghoubi, S., Fainekos, G.: Hybrid approximate gradient and stochastic descent for falsification of nonlinear systems. In: Proceedings of ACC 2017: The 2017 American Control Conference, pp. 529–534. IEEE (2017)
57. Zhou, J., Ramanathan, R., Wong, W.-F., Thiagarajan, P.S.: Automated property synthesis of ODEs based bio-pathways models. In: Feret, J., Koeppl, H. (eds.) CMSB 2017. LNCS, vol. 10545, pp. 265–282. Springer, Cham (2017). https://doi.org/10.1007/978-3-319-67471-1_16

Hardware-Based Runtime Verification
with Embedded Tracing Units
and Stream Processing

Lukas Convent[1]([✉]), Sebastian Hungerecker[1]([✉]), Torben Scheffel[1]([✉]),
Malte Schmitz[1]([✉]), Daniel Thoma[1]([✉]), and Alexander Weiss[2]([✉])

[1] Institute for Software Engineering and Programming Languages,
University of Lübeck, Lübeck, Germany
{convent,hungerecker,scheffel,schmitz,thoma}@isp.uni-luebeck.de
[2] Accemic Technologies GmbH, Kiefersfelden, Germany
aweiss@accemic.com

Abstract. In this tutorial, we present a comprehensive approach to non-intrusive monitoring of multi-core processors. Modern multi-core processors come with trace-ports that provide a highly compressed trace of the instructions executed by the processor. We describe how these compressed traces can be used to reconstruct the actual control flow trace executed by the program running on the processor and to carry out analyses on the control flow trace in real time using FPGAs. We further give an introduction to the temporal stream-based specification language TeSSLa and show how it can be used to specify typical constraints of a cyber-physical system from the railway domain. Finally, we describe how light-weight, hardware-supported instrumentation can be used to enrich the control-flow trace with data values from the application.

1 Introduction

Software for embedded, hybrid and cyber-physical systems often operates under tight time and resource constraints. Therefore, testing, debugging and monitoring is particularly challenging in this setting. Strong limitations on timing and resource consumption prohibit usual approaches for the acquisition and analysis of execution information. First, comprehensive logging output during development built into the software (e.g. via instrumentation) decreases the performance significantly. Second, breakpoint-based debugging features of the processor are slow due to the potentially high number of interruptions. Both methods are highly intrusive as they modify the software temporarily for the analysis or interrupt the execution. This is especially problematic for concurrent programs running on multi-core processors or real-time applications. Errors due to race conditions or inappropriate timing may be introduced or hidden.

This work is supported in part by the European COST Action ARVI, the BMBF project ARAMiS II with funding ID 01 IS 16025, and the European Horizon 2020 project COEMS under number 732016.

C. Colombo and M. Leucker (Eds.): RV 2018, LNCS 11237, pp. 43–63, 2018.
https://doi.org/10.1007/978-3-030-03769-7_5

To allow for a non-intrusive observation of the program trace, many modern microprocessors feature an *embedded trace unit (ETU)* [3,11,13]. An ETU delivers runtime information to a debug port of the processor in a highly compressed format. State-of-the-art debugging solutions, such as ARM DSTREAM [4], allow the user to record this information for offline reconstruction and analysis.

The essential disadvantage of this technology is, however, that traces can be recorded for at most a few seconds because high-performance memory with very fast write access is required to store the delivered information. For example, the ARM DSTREAM solution offers a trace buffer of 4 GB for a recording speed of 10 Gbit/s or more which means that the buffer can only hold data of less than four seconds. While the majority of errors can be found immediately within a short program trace, some of them may only be observable on long-running executions or under specific, rarely occurring (logical or physical) conditions. It is therefore desirable for the developer and maintainer to be able to monitor the program execution for an arbitrary amount of time during development and testing and even in the field after deployment.

This paper is based on [9] which presented an earlier version of the monitoring techniques discussed in this paper. This tutorial gives a more extensive introduction into our monitoring approach and comprises the recent improvements made to the monitoring hardware, tools and specification language.

Related Work. For a general introduction into the field of runtime verification especially in comparison with static verification techniques such as model checking see [16,17].

Non-intrusive observation of program executions is a long-standing issue [21] and several approaches have been suggested. We rely on dedicated tracing interfaces as they are provided by many modern processors. Such interfaces have already been suggested in [26]. Another line of research focuses on the modification of processors [18] or complete systems on chips [25]. These approaches allow access to a wider range of information but require access to the processor or system hardware design and modifications have to be possible. In [6] a processor is monitored by synchronizing a second, emulated processor via a dedicated synchronisation interface. In [20] it is described that even side-channels can be used to monitor certain events on a processor.

There are also several approaches to execute monitors on FPGAs for various applications: synthesis for STL for observation of embedded systems is described in [14,15,24] and synthesis for past time LTL for observation of hardware buses is described in [22]. While these approaches directly synthesize FPGA designs from monitor specifications, we use processing units that are synthesized once and can be reconfigured quickly. Approaches also allowing for reconfiguration are described in [19] for past-time LTL and in [23] for past-time MTL.

The basic idea of stream-based runtime verification and stream transformations specified via recursive equations has been introduced with the language LOLA [8,10]. LOLA however is synchronous in the following sense: Events arrive in discrete steps and for every step, all input streams provide an event and all output streams produce an event, which means that it is not suitable for handling events with arbitrary real-time timestamps arriving at variable frequencies.

Outline. The rest of this paper is organized as follows: Sect. 2 gives an overview of the general workflow and mechanism of hardware-based runtime monitoring as discussed in this paper. Section 3 describes how the program flow can be reconstructed online and how events are generated and fed into the monitoring engine. Section 4 describes how to specify monitors in the stream processing language TeSSLa. Section 5 introduces a simple cyber-physical system that is used as an example throughout the rest of the paper. Section 6 demonstrates how to check timing constraints and Sect. 7 shows how to check event ordering constraints using hardware-based runtime monitoring. Section 8 describes how the tracing of data values works and demonstrates how to check data-values. Finally, Sect. 9 describes the practical hardware setup in order to do hardware-based runtime monitoring.

2   Interactive Hardware Monitoring Workflow

To overcome the limitations of current technology we developed a novel runtime verification methodology for evaluating long-term program executions which is suitable for development, debugging, testing, and in-field monitoring. Based on the runtime information provided by the ETU, we perform a real-time reconstruction of the program trace. The latter is evaluated with respect to a specification formulated by the user in the stream-based specification language TeSSLa [7]. To deliver sufficient performance for online analysis, both the reconstruction and monitoring system are implemented using FPGA hardware.

FPGAs have become a very popular technology to implement digital systems. They contain thousands of programmable logic elements which can be configured to realize different boolean functions. These functions can be connected to each other in an arbitrary way by means of configurable routing elements. Additional features like flip-flops, digital signal processing blocks and blocks of RAM add more flexibility and performance to the implemented circuit. Designing digital circuits with FPGAs typically starts from hardware description languages like VHDL or System Verilog. Synthesis software is responsible for mapping such designs to the elements available in an FPGA and then these elements must be positioned and routed on the FPGA fabric. Even for moderately large designs, this process can take hours. In case the design should run at high clock speed, this time is dramatically increased. Additionally, a designer must be familiar with the FPGA elements and must have thorough experience in FPGA design to be able to create fast designs.

Our monitoring system therefore does not rely on synthesizing a specific FPGA-design for each property specification that has to be evaluated. Instead, it builds on a set of event processing units implemented on the FPGA. These units can be configured quickly via memory to evaluate arbitrary specifications.

We provide a tool chain for mapping TeSSLa specifications to these units automatically within seconds. This allows the user to focus on writing the correctness properties instead of working with the complex FPGA synthesis tool chain. Formulating hypotheses, adapting property specification and checking them on the target system can be iterated quickly without time-intensive synthesis.

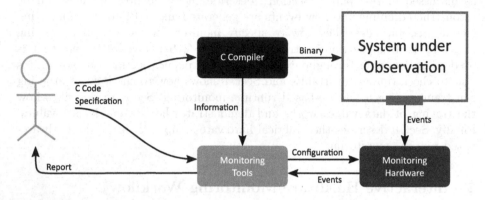

Fig. 1. General overview of the workflow cycle.

Figure 1 provides an overview of the proposed workflow based on our approach to rapidly adjustable embedded trace online monitoring. The user, e.g. the developer, tester, or maintainer, specifies the correct behaviour of the program under test based on program events such as function calls or variable accesses. The program is compiled and the binary is uploaded to the processor as usual. The property compiler automatically generates a corresponding configuration for the monitoring and trace reconstruction units that is then uploaded to the platform. When running the program on the processor, the monitoring platform reports the computed output stream to the user who can then use the information to adjust the program or the property.

Technically, all such events are represented in the reconstructed trace as so-called *watchpoints*, so the trace reconstruction provides a watchpoints stream to the monitoring platform. The reconstruction can already filter the full trace for those watchpoints (i.e., events) that are relevant for the property.

In this tutorial, we demonstrate how our approach can be applied to an example system from the railway domain. We first give an introduction to the specification language TeSSLa and show how it can be used to specify typical properties in such a setting. We then explain how our hardware implementation can be used to monitor these properties non-intrusively.

3 Monitoring Program Flow Trace

Figure 2 shows an overview of the program flow trace monitoring setup: The cores of the multi-core processor are communicating with periphery, such as the memory, through the system bus. Every core is observed by its own tracer. The core is not affected at all by this kind of tracing. The trace data is sent through the trace buffer and concentrator to the trace port without affecting the core. This tracing is separated from the system bus and does not interfere with it. The trace port of the processor is connected to the monitoring hardware, i.e. the FPGA on which the program flow reconstruction, the interpretation and the actual monitoring are located.

The user of this system provides the C code of the system under observation and the specification for the monitoring. The specification contains information about the events of interest and the actual monitor expressed in terms of these events. The C compiler compiles the C source code, so that the resulting binary can be executed on the processor. The C compiler provides debug information which can be used to determine the instruction pointer addresses of the events of interest in the program, the so called *tracepoints*. The trace reconstruction is configured with the observation configuration which contains the tracepoints. The TeSSLa compiler compiles the monitor specification to the monitor configuration which is used to configure the actual trace monitoring.

The final monitoring output coming from the dedicated monitoring hardware undergoes some post-processing on a regular PC using metadata provided by the frontend such as the names and types of the output events. The final monitoring report is a sequence of events that can be either stored or processed further.

We explain the concept of the trace reconstruction with the ARM CoreSight [3] trace technology as a widely available example of an ETU, which is included in every current ARM processor (Cortex M, R and A). In particular, we use the Program Flow Trace (PFT) [2] to acquire trace data of the operations executed by the ARM processors.

As stated in the PFT manual [2] the "PFT identifies certain instructions in the program, and certain events as waypoints. A waypoint is a point where instruction execution by the processor might involve a change in the program flow." With PFT we only observe as waypoints conditional and unconditional direct branches as well as all indirect branches and all other events, e.g. interrupts and other exceptions, that affect the program counter other than incrementing it. In order to save bandwidth on the trace bus, the Program Flow Trace Protocol (PFTP) does not report the current program counter address for every cycle. Especially for direct branches, the target address is not provided but only the information on whether a (conditional) jump was executed or not. The full program counter address is sent irregularly for synchronization (I-Sync message). In case of an indirect branch those address bits that have changed since the last indirect branch or the last I-Sync message are output.

In typical state-of-the-art applications the trace is recorded and the actual program flow is reconstructed from the trace offline. This approach does not work well for the purpose of runtime verification because we want to

1. react to detected failures as early as possible and
2. watch the system under test for a long time.

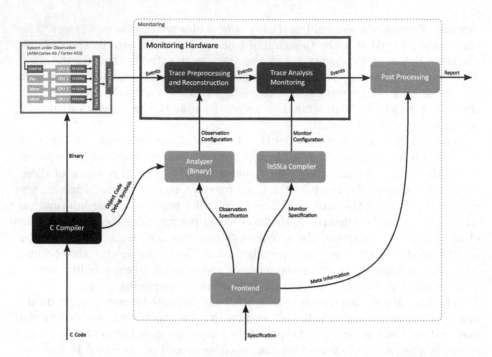

Fig. 2. Overview of the program flow trace monitoring setup. Operations of the cores are traced by the ETU, the trace is then reconstructed, filtered and monitored on the FPGA.

Currently, even with high technical effort, you can only record rather short sequences of trace data. For many real-world applications this might be not enough to spot errors, especially as you cannot start the recording based on complex events as you do not have the trace without reconstructing it from the waypoints.

Hence, we use an online (real time) program-flow-reconstruction method implemented on FPGA hardware [27,28]: From a static analysis of the binary running on the CPU we know all the jump targets of conditional direct jumps and can store those in a lookup table in the memory of the FPGA. Due to the high parallelism of the FPGA, we can split the trace data stream and reconstruct the program flow using the lookup table. The trace data stream can be split at the synchronization points that contain the full program counter address. A FIFO buffer stores the trace data stream until we reach the next synchronization point. For further processing we then immediately filter the reconstructed trace by comparing the reconstructed addresses to the tracepoints that correspond to the input events used in the TeSSLa specification. This comparison is realized by adding an additional tracepoint flag to the lookup table. After putting the slices back together in the right order we end up with a stream of tracepoints. Every tracepoint contains an ID and a timestamp. The timestamp is either assigned by the ARM processor if cycle accurate tracing is enabled or during the reconstruction on the FPGA otherwise. Cycle accurate tracing is only available for certain processor architectures, because it requires high bandwidth on the trace port in order to attach timing information to every message.

Note that PFT traces logical addresses used in the CPU before the memory management unit (MMU) translates them to physical addresses, which are used to address concrete cells in the memory. The MMU is part of the cores and translates logical addresses to physical addresses. Because logical addresses are used in the program binary and by the CPU, we do not need to handle physical addresses.

In a typical multithreaded application, we have multiple threads running on different cores and multiple threads running on the same core using any kind of scheduling. While we can distinguish instructions traced from the different CPUs, we have to consider the actual thread ID in order to distinguish different threads running on the same core. This information is provided by a so-called context ID message [3], sent every time when the operating system changes the context ID register of the CPU. The logical addresses for different threads might be exactly the same, because the MMU is reconfigured in the context switch to point to another physical memory region. If we see a context switch to another thread, we have to change the lookup table for the program flow reconstruction information.

4   Monitoring Properties with Stream Processing

The specification language TeSSLa has been designed as a general purpose stream-based specification language, but with the prerequisites in mind that come with the setting of hardware-based monitoring of embedded systems. That is, technical prerequisites stemming from the processor architectures and the evaluation on FPGAs and prerequisites from the targeted use cases and targeted user groups relevant for the field of embedded systems. The TeSSLa compiler and interpreter are available online[1].

4.1   Technical Prerequisites

The most important technical prerequisite arises from the fact that due to the large amounts of trace data generated by multi-core CPUs, monitoring has to be performed in hardware. More specifically the monitoring specification has to be executed by a specialized engine implemented on an FPGA. This imposes several limitations that have to be addressed by the language design.

On an FPGA only a very limited amount of memory is available. Therefore the specification language should make it easy to specify monitors that are guaranteed to require only a small amount of memory. If memory is required to monitor a certain property, the user should have precise control of when and how memory is used.

---

[1] https://www.tessla.io.

The complexity of logic on an FPGA is limited. While a CPU can process programs of practically unlimited size, on an FPGA all logic has to be represented in hardware. Hence the basic operations of the specification language have to be simple. Also, the number of operations required to express the properties of interest should be relatively low.

Some properties and analyses are too complex to be evaluated on an FPGA but the amount of observation data is too high to evaluate them completely in software. They have to be split up in simpler parts suitable for evaluation on an FPGA and more complex parts that can be evaluated on an reduced amount of data. TeSSLa has been designed to be suitable for the restricted hardware setting but at the same time be flexible enough to not limit the user in the software setting.

It has to be easy to specify properties involving time in TeSSLa, because timing is a crucial aspect of embedded and cyber-physical systems.

Another important aspect is that of data. For many properties it is not enough to only specify the order and timing relation between certain events. It is also important to analyse and aggregate the associated data values.

4.2   Design Goals

TeSSLa's design goals described in this section are based on the prerequisites discussed in the previous section. On one hand, TeSSLa is a specification language rather than a programming language, to allow for simple system descriptions. TeSSLa should provide a different and perhaps more abstract perspective on the system under observation than its actual implementation. Specifying correctness properties in the same programming language that was also used to implement the system might lead to a repetition of the same mistakes in the implementation and the specification. On the other hand, TeSSLa should feel natural to programmers and should not be too abstract or require previous knowledge in mathematical logic. TeSSLa is a stream processing language, which can be used to describe monitoring algorithms, and not a mathematical logic describing valid runs of the systems. Aside from making TeSSLa easier to use for the practical software engineer this also allows to use TeSSLa for event filtering and quantitative and statistical analysis as well as live debugging sessions.

Time is a first-class citizen in TeSSLa, making the specification of timed properties as simple as possible. This does not change the expressiveness of TeSSLa specifications but makes it more natural to reason about time constraints. In cyber-physical systems events are often caused by external inputs of the physical system and hence not following regular clock ticks, but are appearing with variable frequency. In order to simplify specifications over such event streams, every event in TeSSLa always carries a time stamp and a data value.

TeSSLa has a very small set of basic operators which have a simple semantics. Such a small operator set simplifies the implementation of software and hardware interpreters and the corresponding compilers. TeSSLa transforms streams by deriving new streams from existing streams in a declarative functional way: One can define new streams by applying operators to the existing streams but all streams are immutable. To gain the full expressiveness with such a small set of basic operators together with immutable streams we use recursive equation systems, which allow to express arbitrary computations over streams as combinations of the basic operators.

To allow adjustments of TeSSLa for different application domains and make it easier to use for practical software engineers without extending the set of basic operators we use a macro system. With TeSSLa's macro system we can build different libraries which support abstractions, code reuse and extension to allow the specification of more complex analyses. These libraries can use the domain knowledge and terms of the application knowledge without the need of adjusting the TeSSLa compiler and interpreter infrastructure.

TeSSLa's basic operators are designed to be implementable with limited memory, independent of the number of observed events. This allows for building TeSSLa evaluation engines in hardware without addressable memory. For every TeSSLa operator one only needs to store a fixed amount of data values, usually only one data value. TeSSLa allows to add additional data types to the language to adapt the language easily to different settings. Such data types can also be complex data types such as maps or sets, which then explicitly introduce infinite memory. To make the use of memory explicit via data types makes it very easy to identify the TeSSLa fragment that can be executed on hardware.

4.3   Basic Concepts

This section provides an overview on the monitoring specification language TeSSLa (Temporal Stream-based Specification Language).

Its basic modelling primitives are timed event streams, i.e. sequences of events carrying a time stamp and some arbitrary data value. These streams are well suited to model the (timed) behaviour of all kinds of systems with one or multiple time sources.

Properties and analyses are then described by stream transformations. These transformations are expressed via recursive equations over a set of basic operators. We cover here the operators directly available on the hardware. See [7] for a complete, formal definition of TeSSLa's semantics.

The most central operator is signal lift which allows to lift operations on arbitrary data types to streams. For example, the addition on integer numbers can be lifted to streams of integers. This operator follows the intuition of piecewise constant signals, i.e. a stream of events is interpreted as a piecewise constant signal where events indicate changes in the signal value. Addition of two integer streams therefore results in a stream of events indicating the changes of the sum of two corresponding signals. Further examples are the negation of booleans that can be lifted to a stream of booleans and the ternary if-then-else function that can be lifted to a stream of booleans and two streams of identical type.

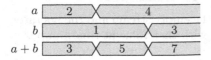
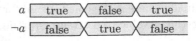

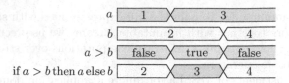

Note that the signal lift is implicitly applied when you use the built-in operators on integer numbers or booleans on streams of the corresponding types.

In order to define properties over sequences of events the operator last has been defined. It allows to refer to the values of events on one stream that occurred strictly before the events on another stream.

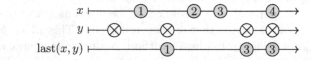

The time operator can be used to access the timestamp of events. It produces streams of events where the events carry their timestamps as data value. Hence all the computations available to data values can be applied to timestamps, too.

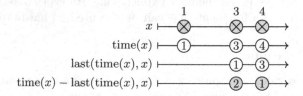

Furthermore, the language contains two operators to process streams in an event-oriented fashion, filter and merge. Filter allows to filter the events of one stream based on a second boolean stream interpreted as piecewise constant signal. Merge combines two streams into one, giving preference to the first stream when both streams contain identical timestamps.

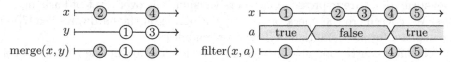

Using the last operator in recursive equations, aggregation operations like the sum over all values of a stream can be expressed. The merge operation allows to initialize recursive equations with an initial event from an other stream, e.g. $s := \text{merge}(\text{last}(s, x) + x, 0)$.

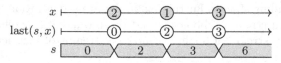

Finally, there is the constant nil for the empty stream and the operator const converting a value to a stream starting with that value at timestamp 0.

These operators are enough to express arbitrary stream transformations. The recursion is limited to recursive expressions involving last. This guarantees that the specifications are directly executable and thereby efficiently monitorable. It also allows the user to think of such specifications as programs which can be more convenient for programmers than the mathematical view of recursive equations.

All of these operators can be implemented using finite memory, i.e. a small amount of memory independent of the amount of data that has to be monitored.

The specification language facilitates abstract specifications and extensibility through a macro system. Here, macros are functions that can be evaluated at compile time. Therefore specifications can be structured in a functional fashion without requiring memory for a call stack at runtime. These macros can also be used to provide a library of common specification patterns.

Another extension point is that of data types. The language is defined agnostically with respect to any time or data domain. Depending on the application domain and the restrictions of the execution domain, different data structures can be used to represent time and data. For hardware monitoring this will typically be restricted to different atomic data types such as integer and floating point numbers. For software monitoring this might also comprise more complex data structures like lists, trees and maps.

5   Example Scenario

In this paper we use a highly simplified engine controller of a train as an example system that we want to analyse and monitor using the hardware monitoring technique presented in this paper. One of the most important aspects of (autonomous) train driving is adhering to the speed limits and the railway signals. Hence we only consider the process of braking a train in front of a stop signal. Since the braking distance for trains is rather long, there are additional distant signals positioned in front of the actual stop signal which indicate caution if the train has to stop at an stop signal further down the track. To make sure that the train really stops in front of the stop signal an automatic speed supervision system checks if the train never exceeds the allowed maximal speed.

To keep our example scenario simple, we consider the speed limits of the *intermittent automatic train running control* system (in German *Punktförmige Zugbeeinflussung, PZB*): We consider passenger trains with a maximal allowed speed of 165 km/h. If the train passes a distant signal indicating caution, it has to reduce its speed to 85 km/h in 23 s. The actual stop signal is located 1000 m after the distant signal. 250 m in front of the stop signal the train must have a speed below 65 km/h which must be reduced to 45 km/h over the next 153 m.

The intermittent automatic train running control system detects special inductors mounted on the tracks which indicate distant and stop signals as well as the point 250 m in front of the stop system. The maximal allowed speed is shown in red in Fig. 4. The speed of an allowed execution of the system is shown in blue in the same diagram.

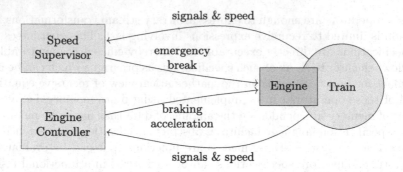

Fig. 3. Example scenario consisting of the train with its engine, the discrete speed supervisor and the engine controller.

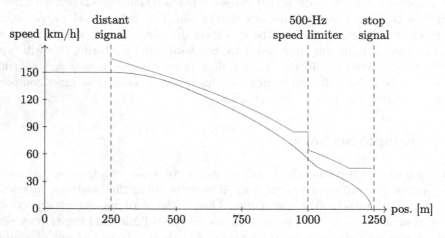

Fig. 4. Diagram showing the speed of the train (in blue) in relation to the train's position. The red curve shows the allowed speed of the train. (Color figure online)

The simulated system as depicted in Fig. 3 consists of three major components:

- The engine controller gets information about the current speed of the train and the signals and the 500 Hz inductor the train passed by. It controls the engine by setting the brake acceleration.
- The speed supervisor gets the same information about the train and computes the currently allowed speed. It compares this with the actual speed and performs an emergency brake if the current speed exceeds the currently allowed speed.
- The train is simulated using a highly simplified model with the initial speed and the acceleration set by the controller.

6   Measuring Timing Constraints

Timing is important for cyber-physical systems. Timing constraints encompass the runtime of tasks, functions or chains of dependant tasks, as well as response times and idle times. Checking such timing constraints or measuring the worst-case or average time consumed is an important task of hardware monitoring.

In this first example we want to measure the runtime of one execution of the speed supervisor. The supervisor is implemented in a function `supervisor`, hence we want to measure the runtime of this function. Therefore we have to specify that we are interested in the events of entering and leaving this function:

```
def call := function_call("supervisor")
def return := function_return("supervisor")
```

Using the `runtime` macro of the standard library we can now produce an event stream which has an event every time the functions returns. The data value of this event is the runtime of the function that did just return.

```
def supervisorRuntime := runtime(call, return)
```

The function `runtime` is defined in the standard library as follows:

```
def runtime(call: Events[Unit], return: Events[Unit]) :=
  at(return, time(return) - time(call))
```

```
def at[A,B](trigger: Events[A], values: Events[B]) :=
  filter(values, time(trigger) == time(values))
```

`Events[T]` is the type representing streams of elements of type T. The function at filters the `values` stream down to the events happening exactly when an event on the `trigger` stream happens. The runtime can then be defined as the difference of the timestamps of the last `return` and the last `call` event evaluated only at the `return` events.

Apart from measuring and checking timing constraints one can also use TeSSLa to aggregate statistical data. In this case lets compute the maximal runtime of the speed supervisor using the function max of the standard library:

```
def maxSupervisorRuntime := max(supervisorRuntime)
```

This maximum aggregation function is defined in the standard library by first defining the maximum of two integer values:

```
def maximum(a: Int, b: Int) := if a > b then a else b
```

This can now be aggregated in a similar recursive definition as the sum explained above:

```
def max(x: Events[Int]) := {
  def result := merge(maximum(last(result, x), x), 0)
  result
}
```

This pattern of aggregating functions can be generalized using TeSSLa's higher order functions. A fold function which takes a function and recursively folds it over an input stream is defined in TeSSLa as follows:

```
def fold[T,R](f: (Events[R], Events[T]) => Events[R],
    stream: Events[T], init: R) := {
  def result: Events[R] :=
    merge(f(last(result, stream), stream), init)
  result
}
```

Now we can define the aggregating max function simply by folding the maximum over the input stream x:

```
def max(x: Events[Int]) := fold(maximum, x, 0)
```

Especially these last examples show one of the strengths of the integrated hardware monitoring, where the online monitors are part of the system: We do not need to store the trace to analyse it. Hence we compute statistical data like the maximal runtime over very long executions of even multiple days or weeks since only the important events are stored and not the complete trace.

7   Checking Event Ordering Constraints

Another important class of properties of cyber-physical systems are event ordering constraints: Here we are not interested in the exact timing of the events, but in their order or presence. So for example one can check if certain events are always preceded or followed by other events.

As an example we again consider the speed supervisor which calls several local helper functions in order to compute the currently maximal allowed speed. The function getAllowedSpeed returns the currently allowed speed. Depending on the last seen signal or magnet it either calls computeAllowedSpeedDistant or computeAllowedSpeedMagnet. So first we want to assure that every call to getAllowedSpeed leads to a call of at least one of these two helper functions. To do so we have to declare these function calls as in the previous examples:

```
def call := function_call("getAllowedSpeed")
def return := function_return("getAllowedSpeed")
def computeDistant :=
  function_call("computeAllowedSpeedDistant")
def computeMagnet :=
  function_call("computeAllowedSpeedMagnet")
```

Using these three event streams we can now check every time the function getAllowedSpeed returns if one of the two other functions was called after the function getAllowedSpeed was entered. Such ordering constraints are expressed in TeSSLa as a comparison of the timestamps of the events:

```
def computation := on(return,
  time(computeDistant) > time(call) ||
  time(computeMagnet) > time(call))
```

As another example we can analyse a complete execution of the braking sequence: Once the function `computeAllowedSpeedMagnet` was called for the first time we must be past the 500 Hz inductor and hence the function `computeAllowedSpeedDistant` must not be called any more. The following TeSSLa specification checks whether all events on the stream `computeMagnet` are happening after all events on the `computeDistant` stream:

```
def magnetAfterDistant :=
  time(computeMagnet) > time(computeDistant)
```

By combining timing and event ordering constraints one can express arbitrary complex constellations. As an example we consider the burst pattern known from automotive modelling languages such as the AUTOSAR Timing Extension [5] and the EAST-ADL2 timing extension TADL2 [12]. Such a pattern checks if events happen in bursts. The pattern is parametrized in the maximum number of events allowed in the burst, the maximal length of the burst and the minimum time without any event after the burst. In TeSSLa such a pattern can be implemented as macro and used as follows:

```
def p := bursts(x, burstLength = 2s,
                   waitingPeriod = 1s,
                   burstAmount = 3)
```

The following event pattern satisfies this burst pattern:

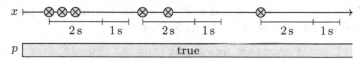

To violate the burst pattern you can either have too many events during one burst, or an event during the waiting period after the burst:

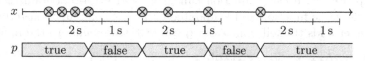

Such complex event patterns can be used to spot variations in event patterns of complex systems without a detailed knowledge of the dependencies of the individual events. For example in our scenario we can take the combination of all the function calls described above. If the supervisor is called roughly every second, this should adhere the following specification:

```
def e := merge3(call, computeDistant, computeMagnet)
def b := bursts(e, burstLength = 100ms,
                   waitingPeriod = 500ms,
                   burstAmount = 3)
```

With this specification you can spot abnormal behaviour, e.g. too many function calls during the computation. Such an abnormal behaviour is not necessarily a bug, but automatic detection of interesting parts of traces can be very helpful to speed up the debugging process, especially for partially unknown systems.

8   Monitoring Data Values

The previous examples were limited to the program flow trace, but in some situations one needs the actual values of variables or arguments to check the correct behaviour of the system under test. For example if we want to check that the allowed speed computed by the supervisor is equal to 85 km/h 23 s after the distant signal we need this computed value.

The *Instrumentation Trace Macrocell (ITM)* is part of the ARM CoreSight, see Chapter 12 of the CoreSight Technical Reference Manual [1], and allows programs to explicitly write small portions of data to the trace port. While the program flow trace can be monitored completely non-intrusively as described in the previous sections, one has to instrument the C code in order to use the ITM data trace. Figure 5 shows how the tooling and the workflow is adjusted in order to integrate such ITM trace messages into the system:

To make the usage of the ITM data trace comfortable, the instrumentation of the C code happens automatically. Therefore the C code and the given specification are analysed with regard to what data is used in the specification. The instrumenter than adds corresponding statements writing this information to the trace port.

Coming back to the example of verifying the computed allowed speed we need to know the last seen signal and the computed allowed speed. We can define TeSSLa signals of both values as follows:

```
def signal := function_argument("getAllowedSpeed", 1)
def allowed_speed := function_result("getAllowedSpeed")
```

signal now contains the value of the first argument of getAllowedSpeed and is updated with every function call. allowed_speed contains the return value of the same function and is updated every time the function returns. The instrumenter adds the following debug_output statements to the function:

```
double getAllowedSpeed(int signal, ...) {
  debug_output(1, (int64_t) signal);
  double result = ...
  tessla_debug(2, (int64_t) (result * 1000));
  return result;
}
```

The ITM tracing provides several data value slots, so in order to distinguish the two data values we are interested in we map them to the ITM slots 1 and 2. The TeSSLa specification is rewritten in terms of the current value and slot as follows:

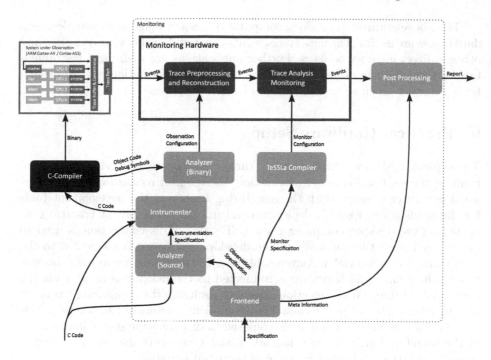

Fig. 5. Overview of the ITM trace setup.

```
in debug_slot: Events[Int]
in debug_value: Events[Int]
def signal := filter(debug_value, debug_slot == 1)
def allowed_speed := filter(debug_value, debug_slot == 2)
```

Now we can express the actual property: First we filter all changes of the signal stream for those where the value becomes DISTANT_SIGNAL_CAUTION. Then we check if the allowed speed is below 85 km/h if it was computed more than 23 s after we have seen the distant signal. We have to apply some unit conversions as the speed is internally represented in m/s.

```
def caution := filter(changes(signal),
                      signal == DISTANT_SIGNAL_CAUTION)
def valid :=
  if time(allowed_speed) - time(caution) > 23s
  then allowed_speed * 36 <= 85 * 1000
  else true
```

In the above specification we used the macro changes which returns only those events which have a different value than the previous one. Such a macro is defined in TeSSLa's standard library as follows:

```
def changes[A](signal: Events[A]) :=
  filter(signal, signal != last(signal, signal))
```

The above example of checking computation results is just one example where data traces are useful. The data trace can also be useful to check array indices and other indirect memory accesses. Further applications are additional instrumentations to enrich the program flow trace with extra information, e.g. additional timing data or clock values for synchronization purposes.

9   Practical Hardware Setup

The typical hardware setup comprises three components: a development board running the application under observation, the monitoring hardware and a personal computer running both the monitoring tools and the development tools for the application. Figure 6 depicts this setup. The development board is connected to the desktop computer via a USB cable. This connection is used to upload and start the application. The development board is connected to the monitoring hardware via an Aurora cable transmitting the compressed processor trace. The monitoring hardware is connected to the desktop computer via the second USB cable. This connection is used to configure the monitoring hardware and to receive the output events. The monitoring hardware has several LEDs that indicate its status and can also be used to display some status information of the monitor. Furthermore it has additional USB ports that are not used in normal operation and are only required to install updates.

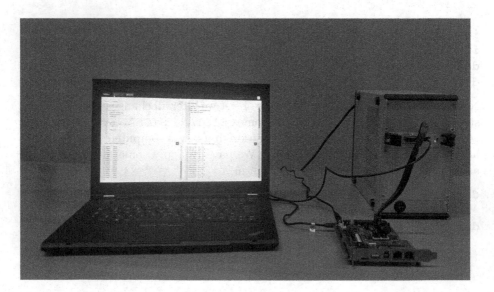

Fig. 6. The hardware setup comprising from left to right a personal computer, a development board and the monitoring hardware.

10   Conclusion

In this paper we demonstrated hardware-based runtime verification using the embedded tracing units of processors. While we discussed the technique in this paper using the example of the ARM CoreSight technology, other processor vendors recently developed similar tracing units: Intel's Processor Tracing IntelPT [13] supports program flow and data traces and for PowerPC the NEXUS tracing technology is already established. Combining the trace reconstruction discussed in this paper with stream-based online monitoring allows for long term monitoring of systems under observation without the need to store the processor traces. This technology can be seen as a milestone in the non-intrusive online-tracing of processors since all established solutions either need to modify the program and hence the timing of the system quite drastically or they can only analyse rather short executions, because they have to store the highly compressed processor trace in order to reconstruct it offline.

Online monitoring of processor traces can reduce costs for certification and development efforts as well as debugging costs. The ability to do long term analyses of systems in the field without the need to modify the source code, allows companies on the one hand to demonstrate the correct behaviour of their systems. On the other hand they can use this technology to identify root causes of bugs that occurred in productive systems faster. Currently bugs detected in productive systems often have to be reproduced in the lab to extract proper traces from the system which are needed to perform the root cause analysis. Using runtime verification of processor trace data can provide additional information already during the normal execution of the productive system and hence provide valuable information on errors faster and more accurate.

References

1. CoreSight Components: Technical Reference Manual. ARM DDI 0314H, July 2009. Issue H
2. ARM Limited, ARM IHI 0035B: CoreSight Program Flow Trace: PFTv1.0 and PFTv1.1 - Architecture Specification, March 2011. Issue B
3. ARM Limited, ARM IHI 0029B: CoreSightTM Architecture Specification v2.0 (2013). Issue D
4. ARM Limited: ARM DS-5 ARM DSTREAM User Guide Version 5.27 (2017)
5. AUTOSAR: Specification of Timing Extensions. Technical report, AUTOSAR (2017)
6. Backasch, R., Hochberger, C., Weiss, A., Leucker, M., Lasslop, R.: Runtime verification for multicore SoC with high-quality trace data. ACM Trans. Design Autom. Electr. Syst. **18**(2), 18:1–18:26 (2013)
7. Convent, L., Hungerecker, S., Leucker, M., Scheffel, T., Schmitz, M., Thoma, D.: TeSSLa: temporal stream-based specification language. In: Proceedings of the Formal Methods: Foundations and Applications - 21st Brazilian Symposium, SBMF 2018, Recife, Brazil, 26–30 November 2018. Lecture Notes in Computer Science. Springer (2018)

8. D'Angelo, B., et al.: LOLA: runtime monitoring of synchronous systems. In: TIME, pp. 166–174. IEEE (2005)
9. Decker, N., et al.: Rapidly adjustable non-intrusive online monitoring for multi-core systems. In: Cavalheiro, S., Fiadeiro, J. (eds.) SBMF 2017. LNCS, vol. 10623, pp. 179–196. Springer, Cham (2017). https://doi.org/10.1007/978-3-319-70848-5_12
10. Faymonville, P., Finkbeiner, B., Schirmer, S., Torfah, H.: A stream-based specification language for network monitoring. In: Falcone, Y., Sánchez, C. (eds.) RV 2016. LNCS, vol. 10012, pp. 152–168. Springer, Cham (2016). https://doi.org/10.1007/978-3-319-46982-9_10
11. Freescale Semiconductor, Inc.: P4080 Advanced QorIQ Debug and Performance Monitoring Reference Manual, Rev. F (2012)
12. Goknil, A., DeAntoni, J., Peraldi-Frati, M., Mallet, F.: Tool support for the analysis of TADL2 timing constraints using timesquare. In: 2013 18th International Conference on Engineering of Complex Computer Systems, Singapore, 17–19 July 2013, pp. 145–154. IEEE Computer Society (2013)
13. Intel Corporation: Intel (R) 64 and IA-32 Architectures Software Developer's Manual (2016)
14. Jaksic, S., Bartocci, E., Grosu, R., Kloibhofer, R., Nguyen, T., Nickovic, D.: From signal temporal logic to FPGA monitors. In: MEMOCODE, pp. 218–227 (2015)
15. Jakšić, S., Bartocci, E., Grosu, R., Ničković, D.: Quantitative monitoring of STL with edit distance. In: Falcone, Y., Sánchez, C. (eds.) RV 2016. LNCS, vol. 10012, pp. 201–218. Springer, Cham (2016). https://doi.org/10.1007/978-3-319-46982-9_13
16. Leucker, M.: Teaching runtime verification. In: Khurshid, S., Sen, K. (eds.) RV 2011. LNCS, vol. 7186, pp. 34–48. Springer, Heidelberg (2012). https://doi.org/10.1007/978-3-642-29860-8_4
17. Leucker, M., Schallhart, C.: A brief account of runtime verification. J. Logic Algebr. Progr. **78**(5), 293–303 (2009)
18. Lu, H., Forin, A.: Automatic processor customization for zero-overhead online software verification. IEEE Trans. VLSI Syst. **16**(10), 1346–1357 (2008)
19. Moosbrugger, P., Rozier, K.Y., Schumann, J.: R2U2: monitoring and diagnosis of security threats for unmanned aerial systems. Form. Methods Syst. Des. **51**(1), 31–61 (2017)
20. Moreno, C., Fischmeister, S.: Non-intrusive runtime monitoring through power consumption: a signals and system analysis approach to reconstruct the trace. In: Falcone, Y., Sánchez, C. (eds.) RV 2016. LNCS, vol. 10012, pp. 268–284. Springer, Cham (2016). https://doi.org/10.1007/978-3-319-46982-9_17
21. Nutt, G.J.: Tutorial: computer system monitors. SIGMETRICS Perform. Eval. Rev. **5**(1), 41–51 (1976)
22. Pellizzoni, R., Meredith, P.O., Caccamo, M., Rosu, G.: Hardware runtime monitoring for dependable cots-based real-time embedded systems. In: Proceedings of the 29th IEEE Real-Time Systems Symposium, RTSS 2008, Barcelona, Spain, 30 November–3 December 2008, pp. 481–491. IEEE Computer Society (2008)
23. Reinbacher, T., Függer, M., Brauer, J.: Runtime verification of embedded real-time systems. Form. Methods Syst. Des. **44**(3), 203–239 (2014)
24. Selyunin, K., et al.: Runtime monitoring with recovery of the SENT communication protocol. In: Majumdar, R., Kunčak, V. (eds.) CAV 2017. LNCS, vol. 10426, pp. 336–355. Springer, Cham (2017). https://doi.org/10.1007/978-3-319-63387-9_17
25. Shobaki, M.E., Lindh, L.: A hardware and software monitor for high-level system-on-chip verification. In: ISQED, pp. 56–61. IEEE Computer Society (2001)

26. Tsai, J.J.P., Fang, K., Chen, H., Bi, Y.: A noninterference monitoring and replay mechanism for real-time software testing and debugging. IEEE Trans. Softw. Eng. **16**(8), 897–916 (1990)
27. Weiss, A., Lange, A.: Trace-Data Processing and Profiling Device, US 9286186 B2, 15 March 2016
28. Weiss, A., Lange, A.: Trace-Data Processing and Profiling Device, EP 2873983 A1, 20 May 2015

Can We Monitor All Multithreaded Programs?

Antoine El-Hokayem and Yliès Falcone(✉)

Univ. Grenoble Alpes, CNRS, Inria, Grenoble INP, LIG, 38000 Grenoble, France
{antoine.el-hokayem,ylies.falcone}@univ-grenoble-alpes.fr

Abstract. Runtime Verification (RV) is a lightweight formal method which consists in verifying that an execution of a program is correct wrt a specification. The specification formalizes with properties the expected correct behavior of the system. Programs are instrumented to extract necessary information from the execution and feed it to monitors tasked with checking the properties. From the perspective of a monitor, the system is a black box; the trace is the *only* system information provided. Parallel programs generally introduce an added level of complexity on the program execution due to concurrency. A concurrent execution of a parallel program is best represented as a partial order. A large number of RV approaches generate monitors using formalisms that rely on total order, while more recent approaches utilize formalisms that consider multiple traces.

In this tutorial, we review some of the main RV approaches and tools that handle multithreaded Java programs. We discuss their assumptions, limitations, expressiveness, and suitability when tackling parallel programs such as producer-consumer and readers-writers. By analyzing the interplay between specification formalisms and concurrent executions of programs, we identify *four* questions RV practitioners may ask themselves to classify and determine the situations in which it is sound to use the existing tools and approaches.

1 Introduction

Analyzing and verifying programs typically relies on an abstraction of the program execution. One such abstraction, a *trace*, focuses on parts of the executed program. Traces typically contain operations and events that a program executes. They are versatile: they serve to analyze, verify and characterize the behavior of a program. A single trace records information of a program execution. Information serves to profile the run of a program [1] so as to optimize its performance. Alternatively, a trace abstracts a single program execution, to verify behavioral properties expressed using formal specifications. A collection of traces model the program behavior as it allows to reason about possible executions or states. As such, multiple traces serve to check for concurrency properties [48] such as absence of data races [42,57] and deadlock freedom [39].

© Springer Nature Switzerland AG 2018
C. Colombo and M. Leucker (Eds.): RV 2018, LNCS 11237, pp. 64–89, 2018.
https://doi.org/10.1007/978-3-030-03769-7_6

Thread 0 (Producer)	Thread 1 (Consumer)
① sq.produce(0);	② sq.consume(); //0
③ sq.produce(1);	④ sq.consume(); //1

Fig. 1. Operations for a single producer and a single consumer thread operating on a shared queue (sq). Shaded circles specify a given number associated with the statement.

Runtime Verification (RV) [9,31,46] is a lightweight formal method which consists in verifying that an execution of a program is correct wrt a specification. The specification formalizes with properties the expected correct behavior of the system. Programs are instrumented to extract necessary information from the execution and feed it to monitors. This information is typically referred to as the *trace* [56]. Monitors are synthesized from behavioral properties, they check if the trace complies with the properties. From the monitor perspective, the system is a black box; the trace is the *sole* system information provided. Therefore, for any RV technique, providing traces with correct and sufficient information is necessary for sound and expressive monitoring[1].

Listing 1.1: A shared queue for *producer-consumer*.

```
1  public class SynchQueue {
2    private LinkedList<Integer> q = new LinkedList<Integer >();
3    public void     produce(Integer v)    { q.add(v); }
4    public Integer consume()              { return q.poll(); }
5  }
```

Parallel programs introduce an added level of complexity because of concurrency. The introduction of concurrency can result in the collected trace not being representative of the actual *concurrent execution* of a parallel program. A concurrent execution is best modeled as a partial order over *actions* executed by the program. The actions can represent function calls, or even instructions executed at runtime. The order typically relates actions based on time, it states that some actions happened before other actions. Actions that are incomparable are typically said to be *concurrent*. This model is compatible with various formalisms that define the behavior of concurrent programs such as weak memory consistency models [2,3,49], Mazurkiewicz traces [36,50], parallel series [47], Message Sequence Charts graphs [51], and Petri Nets [53]. We introduce a textbook example of a multithreaded program, *producer-consumer* in Example 1.

Example 1 (Producer-consumer). We consider the classical *producer-consumer* example where a thread pushes items to a shared queue (generating a **produce** event), and another thread consumes items (one at a time) from the queue for processing (generating a **consume** event). We specify that consumers must not remove an item unless the queue contains one, and all items placed on the queue must be eventually consumed. Figure 1 illustrates the statements executed by two

---

[1] By soundness, we refer to the general principle of monitors detecting specification violation or compliance only when the actual system produces behavior that respectively violates or complies with the specification.

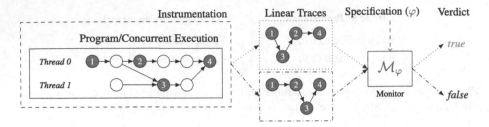

Fig. 2. RV flow and the impact of linearizing traces. Before runtime, RV is applied to a program with a concurrent execution (dashed): a monitor $\mathcal{M}_\varphi$ is synthesized from a property φ, and the program is instrumented to retrieve its relevant events. At runtime, we observe two possible linear traces that could lead to verdicts (*true* or *false*) when processed by the same monitor.

different threads: thread 0, and thread 1, representing respectively a producer and a consumer. Each statement is given a number for clarity. Both the producer and consumer use a shared queue shown in Listing 1.1. Statements in different threads can execute concurrently. We illustrate some correct and incorrect executions. Two correct executions have the following orders: ❶❷❸❹ and ❶❸❷❹; they comply with the specification. The execution with the order: ❷❶❸❹ is incorrect, as a `consume` attempts to retrieve an element from an empty queue. The execution with only the statements: ❶❸❷ is incorrect, as there remains an element to be consumed. The execution with the order: ❷❸❶❹ violates both conditions in the specification, since two `consume` events happen when the queue is empty, and after the executions there are two elements left to be consumed.

Monitoring Multithreaded Programs. RV has initially focused on utilizing totally ordered traces, as it uses formalisms inspired from Linear Temporal Logic (LTL) or finite-state machines as specifications [13,46,52,54], until recently with the introduction of stream-based RV [25,38,45], decentralized monitoring [11], and RV of hyperproperties [18]. Most of the top[2] existing tools for the online monitoring of Java programs rely on totally ordered traces and provide multithreaded monitoring support using one or more of the *three* modes. The first mode allows *per-thread* monitoring. The *per-thread* mode specifies that monitors are only associated with a given thread, and receive all events of the given thread. Monitors are unable to check properties that involve events across threads. This boils down to doing classical RV of single-threaded programs, assuming each thread is an independent program. When examining each thread or process while excluding others, one ignores the inter-thread dependencies, and it is therefore insufficient. For example, it is impossible to monitor *producer-consumer* illustrated in Example 1, as events happen on separate threads. In that setting, a specification cannot express behavior involving events across threads. The second

---

[2] Based on the first three editions of the Competition on Runtime Verification [6,8, 32,55].

mode allows for *global* monitoring. It spawns global monitors, and ensures that events are fed to the monitor *atomically*, by utilizing locks. As such, a program execution is *linearized* so that it can be processed by the monitors. Locks force events to be totally ordered across the entire execution, which oversimplifies and ignores concurrency, as illustrated in Example 2.

Example 2 (Linearization). Figure 2 illustrates the typical RV flow for some property φ with a monitor $\mathcal{M}_\varphi$, where during the execution, an instrumented parallel program feeds a trace to a monitor. Filled circles represent the events relevant to the RV specification, and are numbered simply to distinguish them. We notice that, in the case of a concurrent execution, the trace could differ based on the linearization strategy which influences the observation order. In the first trace, event 3 precedes event 2, while in the second trace, we have the opposite. This could potentially impact the verdict of the monitor if the specification relies on the order between events 2 and 3. We recall *producer-consumer* from Example 1: if the program is not properly synchronized, linearizing the concurrent events could lead two different traces: ❶❷❸❹, and ❷❶❸❹. The first trace complies with the specification while the second violates it.

The third mode allows monitors to receive events concurrently. This is typically done by providing a flag *unsynchronized*. In this mode, practitioners should handle the concurrency on their own, and in some cases specify their own monitoring logic. Writing additional concurrency logic, and managing concurrency has *three* disadvantages. First, by writing the monitors manually, we defeat the purpose of automatically generating monitors from a given formalism. Second, the manual monitors created may miss key information needed for managing concurrency. This extra information may require to implement additional instrumentation outside the tool. Third, the process is complicated due to concurrency, and is error-prone. We elaborate on the complications in Sect. 4. As such, we first ask if monitors are to be generated from a formalism.

Q0. *Is the developer using the tool to automatically generate monitor logic?*

For the scope of this tutorial, we focus on the formalisms from which monitors could be synthesized. As such, we consider the answer to **Q0** is *yes*.

Overview. In this tutorial, we explore RV tools that explicitly handle multithreaded programs. We illustrate the problem of monitoring a parallel program using existing techniques. In doing so, we overview the related approaches, some of the existing tools, and their shortcomings. We discuss their assumptions, advantages, limitations, and suitability when tackling two textbook parallel programs: producer-consumer and readers-writers. In particular, we use manually written monitors using AspectJ [43,58], Java-MOP [16,17,52], and RVPredict [42] to explore the challenges to monitoring multithreaded programs.

Overall, the challenges of monitoring multithreaded programs stem from the following facts:

- events in a concurrent program follow a partial order;
- most formalisms used by RV do not account for partial orders, but specify behavior over sequences of events (i.e., events are totally ordered); and
- an instrumented program must capture the order of events as it happens during the execution to pass it to monitors.

Moreover, we explore the situations where:

- a linear trace does not represent the underlying program execution;
- a linear trace hides some implicit assumptions which affect RV; and
- it is insufficient to use a linear trace for monitoring multithreaded programs.

By analyzing the interplay between specification formalisms and concurrent executions of programs, we propose *four* questions RV practitioners may ask themselves to classify and determine the situations in which it is reliable to use the existing tools and approaches as well as the situations where we believe more work is needed.

An online version of the tutorial [30] is provided with the programs, tools, and an interactive guide to reproduce and experiment with the examples provided in the tutorial. The examples included in the online tutorial are marked in the rest of the paper with the dagger sign (†).

2   Exploring Tools and Their Supported Formal Specifications

Runtime Verification approaches typically automatically synthesize monitors by relying on a formal specification of the expected behavior. A specification formalism allows to express properties that partition the system behaviors into correct and incorrect ones. As such, for a multithreaded program, we must first check the available properties that we can verify. We first classify the various approaches by considering the specification formalism alone.

2.1   Approaches Relying on Total-Order Formalisms

The first pool consists of tools and approaches where the specification language itself relies on a total order of events, as the input to monitors consists of words. We consider the tools commonly used for RV using those found in the RV competitions [8,32,55].

Java-MOP. Java-MOP [16,17,52] follows the design principle that specifications and programs should be developed together. Java-MOP provides *logic plugins* to express the specifications in several formalisms. Logic plugins include: finite-state machines, extended regular expressions, context-free grammars, past-time linear temporal logic, and string rewriting systems.

Tracematches. Tracematches [4,13] is another approach that uses regular expressions over user-specified events as specifications. Tracematches defines points in the execution where events occur, and specifies the actions to execute upon matching. Tracematches considers the semantics of such matching on large programs or multiple program runs, while binding the context associated with each event to the sequence. For example, it considers when a pattern matches multiple times, or matches multiple points in the program.

MarQ. MarQ [54] is designed for monitoring properties expressed as Quantified Event Automata (QEA) [5]. MarQ focuses on performing highly optimized monitoring, by providing full control of monitors lifecycles and garbage collection. Furthermore, it introduces quantification and distinguishes quantified from free variables in a specification, this allows finer control over the monitoring procedure by managing the replication of monitoring (slicing). MarQ relies on the developer to instrument the program with AspectJ to send the events to the QEA.

LARVA. LARVA [22] uses dynamic automata with timers and events [21]. LARVA focuses on monitoring real-time systems where timing is of importance. LARVA specifications feature timeouts and stopwatches. LARVA is also capable of verifying large programs by storing events in a database and allowing the monitors to "catch up" with the system as it executes [20].

Remark 1 (Unsynchronized monitors). While we focus on formalisms capable of automatically generating monitors, we note that it is still possible to write unsynchronized monitors manually. We explain in Sect. 4 the difficulties that make the process error-prone. Java-MOP provides the *unsynchronized* flag to specify that no additional locks should be added, thus allowing monitors to receive events concurrently. *Logic plugins* would no longer be used to automatically synthesize monitors. MarQ by default is not thread safe [54]. The developer must pre-process the events before passing them to the QEA monitor.

2.2   Approaches Focusing on Detecting Concurrency Errors

The second pool of tools is concerned with specific behavior for concurrent programs. We consider absence of data races and deadlock freedom. Tools used that can verify specific properties related to concurrency errors include RVPredict [42] and Java PathExplorer (JPaX) [39]. Further discussion on concurrency errors and additional tools are discussed in [48].

RVPredict. RVPredict relies on Predictive Trace Analysis (PTA) [42,57]. PTA approaches model the program execution as a set of traces corresponding to the different orderings of a trace. As such, they encode the trace minimally, then restrict the set of valid permutations based on the model that is allowed. The approach in [42] describes a general sound and complete model to detect data races in multithreaded programs and implement it in RVPredict. Traces are ordered permutations containing both control flow operations and memory accesses, and are constrained by axioms tailored to data race and sequential consistency. While [42] can, in theory, model behavioral properties, RVPredict monitors only data races, but does so very efficiently.

JPaX. Similar to RVPredict, Java PathExplorer (JPaX) [39] is a Java tool designed for multithreaded programs. JPaX uses bytecode-level instrumentation to detect both race conditions and deadlocks in a multithreaded program execution. To do so, JPaX tracks information on locks and variables accessed by various threads during an execution. JPaX supports standard formalisms such as LTL and finite-state machines. However, it separates those from the two mentioned concurrency properties, and defaults to providing an event stream to the monitors similar to automata-based approaches.

2.3 Approaches Utilizing Multiple Traces

The third pool consists of approaches specifying behavior that spans multiple traces.

Stream-based Techniques. Stream-based techniques include LOLA [25], BeepBeep [38], and more recently, the Temporal Stream-Based Specification Language [23,26,45]. Stream-based specifications rely on named streams to provide events. These streams are then aggregated using various functions that modify the timing, filter events, and output new events.

Decentralized Monitoring. Decentralized monitoring considers the system as a set of components sharing a logical timestamp. It uses monitoring algorithms and communication strategies to monitor one specification over components by avoiding synchronization and with the aim of minimizing the communication costs. Algorithms manage a decentralized trace associating each event with a component and a timestamp; essentially managing for each component a totally ordered trace. DecentMon [10,19] is a tool capable of simulating the behavior of decentralized monitoring algorithms.

Decentralized Specifications. Decentralized specifications [28] generalize decentralized monitoring by defining a set of monitors, additional atomic propositions that represent references to monitors, and attaches each monitor to a component. A monitor reference is evaluated as if it was an oracle. THEMIS [29] is a tool capable of monitoring decentralized specifications.

Hyperproperties. *Hyperproperties* [18] are specified over sets of traces. Typically, hyperproperties make use of variables that are quantified over multiple traces. RV approaches have been implemented to verify hyperproperties using rewriting [14], and using model checking and automata [34]. RVHyper [33] is a tool capable of verifying hyperproperties on sets of traces.

2.4 Outcome: A First Classification

Since concurrent executions exhibit a partial order between events, formalisms that rely on total order require that the partial order be coerced into a total order. Our first consideration for monitoring concurrent programs relies solely on the specification formalism.

Q1. *Are the models of the specification formalism based on a total order?*

If the answer to **Q1** is *yes*, then we are concerned with the first pool of tools.

We elaborate on further considerations for total order approaches in Sect. 3. Otherwise, we verify whether or not we are checking very specific properties on partial orders, such as data race or deadlock freedom.

Q2. *Are we only concerned with the absence of data races or deadlock freedom?*

If the answer to **Q2** is *yes*, then we are concerned with the second pool of tools, keeping in mind that they are unable to handle arbitrary specifications. Otherwise, we are concerned with the third pool, we elaborate on the potential of using these approaches in Sect. 5.2.

3 Linear Specifications for Concurrent Programs

In this section, we are concerned with RV approaches that rely on total-order formalisms (e.g., automata, LTL, regular expressions). We refer to specifications that use total-order formalisms to describe the behavior of the system as *linear specifications*. We explore the assumptions and outcomes of checking properties specifying total-order behavior.

3.1 Per-Thread Monitoring

Overview. A simple approach to monitor multithreaded programs is to consider each thread in the program execution independent. That is, the monitoring technique assumes that each thread is a separate serial program to monitor. A monitor is assigned to each thread and receives only events pertaining to that thread. This is called *per-thread* monitoring. Java-MOP and Tracematches support flag *perthread* [4,35] to monitor a property on each thread independently. It is also possible to use MarQ by quantifying over the threads, to monitor each thread independently for a given property.

Example 3 (Per-thread iterator[†]). We use for example the classical property described in [16] "An iterator's method hasNext() must always be called at least once before a call to method next()". Monitoring *per-thread* proves useful, when we are concerned about the usage of iterators in a given thread, and not across threads. Using Java-MOP, we can monitor a simple program that has two threads processing a shared list of integers concurrently. Each thread creates an iterator on the shared list, the first finds the minimum, while the second finds the maximum. In this case, it is sufficient to check that the iterator usage is correct for each thread independently.

Limitations. Since *per-thread* monitoring performs RV on a single thread, and all events in a given thread are totally ordered, it follows that monitoring is sound in such situations. However, in most cases, we may be interested in monitoring events across threads. This is the case with *producer-consumer* detailed in Example 1. To monitor the program we need to keep track of produces and consumes. By considering threads separately, one is not able at all to monitor the correct behavior, as producer and consumer are separate threads. Monitoring *per-thread* is not useful in this setting. Therefore, it becomes important to distinguish between properties for which events are shared across threads.

Q3. *Does there exist a model of the specification where events are generated by more than a single thread?*

We addressed in this section the tools and limitations when the answer to **Q3** is *no*. When the answer to **Q3** is *yes*, a developer has to consider *global* monitoring, explained in Sect. 3.2.

3.2 Global Monitoring

Overview. Whenever the specification formalism relies on events across threads, the existing approaches that use a total-order formalism typically define global monitors. This is the default mode for Java-MOP, MarQ, and for Tracematches this is called *"global tracematch"*. This is the only mode for LARVA. Furthermore, these tools typically include synchronization guards on such monitors. For example, LARVA synchronizes events passed to the monitors, such that a monitor cannot receive two events concurrently, while MarQ requires the developer to specify synchronization when needed, and Java-MOP offers an *unsynchronized* flag, to disable locking on monitors.

We discussed the implications of using *unsynchronized* in Sect. 1.

Example 4 (Monitoring producer-consumer[†]). We monitor *producer-consumer* (Example 1) using Java-MOP, LARVA, and MarQ[3]. The property can be expressed as a context-free grammar (CFG) using the rule: S -> S produce S consume | epsilon. We specify the property for each tool[4] and associate events produce and consume with adding and removing elements from a shared queue, respectively. We first verify this example using *per-thread* monitoring using Java-MOP, and notice quickly that the property is violated, as the first monitor is only capable of seeing produces, and the second only consumes. Using global monitoring, we monitor a large number of executions (10,000) of two variants of the program, and show the result in Table 1. For each execution, the producer generates a total of 8 produce events, which are then processed using up to 2 consumers. The first variant is a correctly synchronized *producer-consumer*, where locks ensure the atomic execution of each event. The second variant is a non-synchronized *producer-consumer*, and allows the two events to be fed to the

---

[3] On Java openjdk 1.8.0_172, using Java-MOP version 4.2, MarQ version 1.1 commit 9c2ecb4 (April 7, 2016), and LARVA commit 07539a7 (Apr 16, 2018).

[4] Equivalent monitors and specifications for each tools can be found in Appendix A.

Table 1. Monitoring 10,000 executions of 2 variants of *producer-consumer* using global monitors. Reference (REF) indicates the original program. Column **V** indicates the variant of the program. Column **Advice** indicates intercepting *after* (A) and *before* (B) the function call, respectively. Columns **True** and **False** indicate the number of executions (#) and the percentage over the total number of executions (%) for which the tool reported these verdicts.

V	Consumers	Tool	Advice	True		False		Timeout	
				#	%	#	%	#	%
1	1–2	REF	-					0	(0%)
		JMOP	A	10,000	(100%)	0	(0%)	0	(0%)
			B	10,000	(100%)	0	(0%)	0	(0%)
		MarQ	A	10,000	(100%)	0	(0%)	0	(0%)
			B	10,000	(100%)	0	(0%)	0	(0%)
		LARVA	A	10,000	(100%)	0	(0%)	0	(0%)
			B	10,000	(100%)	0	(0%)	0	(0%)
2	1	REF			-			631	(6.3%)
		JMOP	A	4,043	(40.43%)	5,957	(59.57%)	0	(0%)
			B	7,175	(71.75%)	6	(0.06%)	2,819	(28.19%)
		MarQ	A	4,404	(44.04%)	5,583	(55.83%)	13	(0.13%)
			B	9,973	(99.73%)	16	(0.16%)	11	(0.11%)
		LARVA	A	4,755	(47.55%)	5,245	(52.45%)	0	(0%)
			B	9,988	(99.88%)	2	(0.02%)	10	(0.10%)
2	2	REF			-			4,785	(47.85%)
		JMOP	A	128	(1.28%)	9,220	(92.20%)	652	(6.52%)
			B	1,260	(12.60%)	7,617	(76.17%)	1,123	(11.23%)
		MarQ	A	33	(0.33%)	9,957	(99.57%)	10	(0.10%)
			B	432	(4.32%)	9,530	(95.30%)	38	(0.38%)
		LARVA	A	250	(2.50%)	9,488	(94.88%)	262	(2.62%)
			B	5,823	(58.23%)	4,131	(41.31%)	46	(0.46%)

monitors concurrently. In both cases, the monitor is synchronized to ensure that the monitor processes each event atomically. Additional locks are included by Java-MOP and LARVA, we introduce a lock for MarQ, as it is not thread-safe. This is consistent as to check the CFG (or the automaton for LARVA and MarQ), we require a totally ordered word, as such traces are eventually linearized.

In the first variant, the monitor outputs verdict *true* for all executions. This is consistent with the expected behavior as the program is correctly synchronized, as such it behaves as if it were totally ordered. However, with no proper synchronization, produce and consume happen concurrently, we obtain one of two possible traces:

$$tr_1 = \text{produce} \cdot \text{consume} \quad \text{and} \quad tr_2 = \text{consume} \cdot \text{produce}.$$

While tr_1 seems correct and tr_2 incorrect, produce and consume happen concurrently. After doing 10,000 executions of the second variant, monitoring is unreliable: we observe verdict *true* for some executions, while for others, we observe verdict *false*. Even for the same tool, and the same number of consumers, we notice that the reported verdicts vary depending on whether or not we choose to intercept before or after the function call to create the event. For example, even when using a single consumer with Java-MOP, we see that the verdict rate for verdict *false* goes down from 60% when intercepting before the function call, to almost 0% when intercepting after the function call. We note that selecting to intercept before or after a method call can depend on the specification. For consistency reasons, we chose to intercept both events in the same way. Either choice produces inconsistent verdicts when concurrency is present, due to context switches.

In the second variant, the consumer must check that the queue has an element, and then poll it to recover it. Since it is badly synchronized, it is possible to deadlock as the check and the poll are not atomic. In this case, the program cannot terminate. To distinguish deadlocked executions, we terminate the execution after 1 second, and consider it a timeout, since a non-deadlocked execution takes less than 10 milliseconds to execute. It is important to note that when the specification detects a violation the execution is stopped, this could potentially lower the rate of timeouts. The rate of timeout of the original program (REF) is given as reference. We notice that the tools interfere with the concurrency behavior of the program in two ways. First, the locking introduced by the global monitoring can actually force a schedule on the program. We observe that when a single consumer is used and locks are used before the function call. In this case, the rate of getting verdict *true* is higher than when introduced after the call (72% for Java-MOP, 99.7% for MarQ, and 99.8% for LARVA). When the locks are applied naively, they can indeed correct the behavior of the program, as they force a schedule on the actions `produce` and `consume`. This, of course, is coincidental, when 2 consumers are used, we stop observing this behavior. Second, we observe that changing the interception from before to after the function call modifies the rate of timeout. For example, when using 1 consumer, the reference rate is 6% (REF). When using Java-MOP (B), the rate goes up to 28%, while for LARVA (B) it goes down to 0.1%. It is possible to compare the rate of timeout of Java-MOP (B) and LARVA (B) since the monitor is not forcing the process to exit early, as the rate of reaching verdict *false* is low for both ($<$ 0.1%). We elaborate more on the effect of instrumentation on concurrency in Sect. 4.

To understand the inconsistency in the verdicts, we look at the execution fragments of each variant in Fig. 3. In the first variant, the program utilizes locks to ensure the queue is accessed atomically. This allows the execution to be a total order. For the second variant, we see that while we can establish order between either `produce`, or `consume`, we cannot establish an order between events. During the execution, multiple total orders are possible, and thus different verdicts are possible.

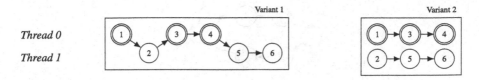

Fig. 3. Concurrent execution fragments of *producer-consumer* variants. Double circle: produce, normal: consume. Events are numbered to distinguish them.

Limitations. It is now possible to distinguish further situations where it is reliable to use global monitors. We notice that to evaluate a total order formalism, we require a trace which events are totally ordered. When dealing with a partial order, tools typically use locks and ensure that the partial order will be coerced into a total order. We see that the monitoring of the second variant failed since the program was not properly synchronized. One could assume that it is necessary to first check that the program is properly synchronized, and perhaps deadlock-free as well. To do so, one could use RVPredict or JPaX to verify the absence of data race (as shown in Example 5). Upon verifying that the program is synchronized, one could then run global monitors.

Listing 1.2: RVPredict (partial) output for *producer-consumer* variant 2.

```
 1 ────────Instrumented execution to record the trace────────
 2 [RV-Predict] Log directory: /tmp/rv-predict2523508450121758452
 3 [RV-Predict] Finished retransforming preloaded classes.
 4 main Complete in 28
 5 Data race on field java.util.LinkedList.$state:
 6     Read in thread 14
 7     > at SynchQueue.consume(SynchQueue.java:24)
 8       at Consumer.run(Consumer.java:14)
 9   Thread 14 created by thread 1
10       at java.util.concurrent.ThreadPoolExecutor.addWorker(Unknown Source)
11
12   Write in thread 13
13     > at SynchQueue.produce(SynchQueue.java:18)
14       at Producer.run(Producer.java:19)
15   Thread 13 created by thread 1
16       at java.util.concurrent.ThreadPoolExecutor.addWorker(Unknown Source)
```

Example 5 (Detecting data race[†]). Let us consider the second variant of *producer-consumer* as described in Example 4. Listing 1.2 displays the (partial) output of executing RVPredict on the program. Particularly, we focus on one data race report (out of 4). We notice that in this case, lines 7 and 13 indicate that the data race occurs during those function calls. Yet, these are the calls we used to specify the **produce** and **consume** events. In this case, we can see that the data race occurs at the level of the events we specified. Upon running RVPredict on the first variant, it reports no data races, as it is properly synchronized.

While checking the absence of data race is useful for the case of *producer-consumer*, it is not enough to consider a properly synchronized program to be safe when using global monitors. This is due to the possible existence of concurrent regions independently from data race. We illustrate the case of concurrent regions in Example 6.

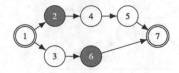

Fig. 4. Concurrent execution fragment of *1-Writer 2-Readers*. Double circle: `write`, normal: `read`. Events are numbered to distinguish them. Events 2 and 6 are an example of concurrent events as there is no order between them.

Example 6 (1-Writer 2-Readers[†]). Figure 4 illustrates a concurrent execution fragment of *1-Writer 2-Readers*, where a thread can write to a shared variable, and two other threads can read from the variable. The threads can read concurrently, but no thread can write or read while a write is occurring. In this execution, the first reader performs 3 reads (events 2, 4, and 5), while the second reader performs 2 reads (events 3 and 6). We notice that indeed, no reads happen concurrently. In this case, we see that the program is correctly synchronized (it is data-race free and deadlock-free). However, we can still end up with different total orders, as there still exists concurrent regions. By looking at the concurrent execution, we notice that we can still have events on which we can establish a total order[5].

On the one hand, a specification relying on the order of events found in concurrent regions (i.e., *"the first reader must always read before the second"*) can still result in inconsistent monitoring, similarly to *producer-consumer*. On the other hand, a specification relying on events that can always be totally ordered (i.e., *"there must be at least one read between writes"*) will not result in inconsistent monitoring. We notice that to distinguish these two cases, we rely (i) on the order of the execution (concurrent regions), and (ii) the events in the specification. Two events that cannot be ordered are therefore called *concurrent events*. For example, the events 2 and 6 are concurrent, as there is no order relation between them. Instrumenting the program to capture *concurrent events* may also be problematic as we will explain in Sect. 4.

3.3   Outcome: Refining the Classification

We are now able to formulate the last consideration for totally ordered formalisms.

Q4. *Is the satisfaction of the specification sensitive to the order of concurrent events?*

If the answer to **Q4** is *no*, then it is possible to linearize the trace to match the total order expressed in the specification. Otherwise, monitoring becomes *unreliable* as the concurrency can cause non-determinism, or even make it so the captured trace is not a representation of the execution as we explain in Sect. 4.

---

[5] This is similar to the notion of *linearizability* [40].

Remark 2 (Expressiveness). We noticed that utilizing linear specifications for monitoring multithreaded programs works well when the execution of the program can be reduced to a total order. On the one hand, we see *per-thread* monitoring (Sect. 3.1) restricting events to the same thread. On the other hand, we see *global* monitoring restricting the behavior to only those that can be linearized. As such, in these cases, the interplay between trace and specification constrains the expressiveness of the monitoring to either the thread itself, or the segments in the execution that can be linearized.

4   Instrumentation: Advice Atomicity

Generally, trace collection is done after instrumentation of the program using AspectJ, or other techniques (such as bytecode instrumentation). As mentioned in Sect. 1, it is still possible to specify *unsynchronized* monitors and handle concurrency without the tool support. We note that using AspectJ for instrumentation is found in Java-MOP, Tracematches, MarQ, and LARVA [8]. In this section, we show that instrumentation may lead to unreliable traces in concurrent regions.

4.1   Extracting Traces

Extracting a trace from a program execution often requires executing additional code at runtime. For example, to capture a method call, one could insert a print statement before or after the method call. This extra running code is referred to as *advice* by AspectJ. When an action is executed, *the code responsible for gathering the trace will not, in general, execute atomically with the action.* For multithreaded programs, the execution order may be incorrectly captured due to context switches between threads. To illustrate the issues caused by context switches, we have two threads with a race condition on a call to function f and g respectively, we match the call and execute the advice right after the call. We show this by adding a call to the advice code mon(), right after the function call. We see in Fig. 5 that in the execution the call to function f precedes the call to function g, however, due to context switches, the advice associated with g (mon(g)) executes before that associated with function f (mon(f)). In this case the order perceived by the monitors is g · f while the order of the execution is f · g. In this scenario, the generated trace is not representative of the execution, and thus the check performed by the monitor is unreliable.

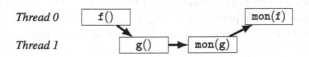

Fig. 5. Advice execution (mon) with context-switches leading to incorrect trace capture.

1	g	f_trace
2	f	g_trace
3	f	f_trace
4	g	g_trace
5	f	f_trace
6	g	g_trace
7	f	f_trace
8	g	g_trace
9	f	f_trace
10	g	f_trace
11	f	g_trace
12	f	f_trace
13	g	g_trace
14	g	g_trace

Tool	Advice	Sync	Identical	Different
AspectJ	A	✓	4,912	5,088
	B		9,170	830
Java-MOP	A	✓	1,737	8,263
	B		9,749	251
LARVA	A	✓	8,545	1,455
	B		9,992	8
Java-MOP	A	✗	2,026	7,974
	B		9,517	483

(a) Comparison between the system trace (left) and the trace collected by the monitor (right).

(b) Comparing traces collected with AspectJ, LARVA, and Java-MOP across 10,000 executions. The column **Advice** indicates respectively intercepting *after* (A) and *before* (B) the function call.

Fig. 6. Comparison of collected traces using instrumentation and the system trace.

Example 7 (Advice Atomicity[†]). For this example, we create two threads such that each calls a unique function (f and g, respectively) an equal number of times. Each function consists of a single print statement (to stdout) indicating the function name. We create a simple monitor that prints (to stderr) the same function name while appending "_trace". Then, we verify that the traces are identical, that is the prints from within the functions follow the same order as those in the monitor. Figure 6a shows a fragment of a trace that is different. We see at lines (1–2) that the trace of the monitor starts with f · g while the in the program execution the order is f · g. Figure 6b shows the difference between the captured trace by the monitor and the trace of the system, using monitors created manually with AspectJ, and automatically with Java-MOP and LARVA. The monitor created manually with AspectJ is also representative of MarQ as MarQ relies on the user writing the event matching in AspectJ, then calling the QEA monitor. Column **Sync** distinguishes the case when using *unsynchronized* in Java-MOP. We notice that the traces differ from the actual program execution for AspectJ, Java-MOP and LARVA. Traces appear to differ more when intercepting after the function call. In AspectJ, the rate of identical traces drops from 91% (B) to 49% (A). This drop is also visible for LARVA and Java-MOP. This is not surprising as Java-MOP and LARVA use AspectJ for instrumentation while introducing some variation as each tool has some additional computation performed on matching. The rate change could be associated with either the specific program or the virtual machine in this case, as the added computation from the monitors and AspectJ could affect the schedule. More importantly, we notice that even when the monitors are synchronized, the captured trace is not guaranteed to be identical to that of the execution.

This problem can only be solved if atomicity for the granularity level can be guaranteed. In general, source-level instrumentation of method calls with AspectJ, or even bytecode instrumentation at the INVOKE level will still not be atomic. Adding a lock not only increases overhead, but can also introduce deadlocks if the method invocation is external to the code being instrumented (e.g., calls to libraries). However, by adding locks one can modify the behavior of the program as illustrated in Example 7, as such one needs to minimize the area to which the lock is applied.

4.2 Discussion

In certain conditions, capturing traces can still be done in the case of concurrent events. First, a developer must have full knowledge of the program (i.e., it must be seen as a *white box*), this allows the developer to manually instrument the locks to ensure atomic capture, avoiding deadlocks and managing external function calls carefully. Second, we require that the instrumented areas tolerate the interference, and therefore must prove that the interference does not impact significantly the behavior of the program, by modifying the schedule. In this case, one could see that global monitoring (Sect. 3.2) reports correct verdicts *for the single execution.*

Remark 3 (Monitor placement). An additional important aspect for tools pertains to whether the monitors are inlined in the program or execute separately. For multithreaded programs, instrumentation can place monitors so that they execute in the thread that triggers the event, or in a separate thread, or even process. These constitute important implementation details that could limit or interfere with the program differently. However, for the scope of this paper, we focus on issues that are relevant for event orders and concurrency.

5   Reasoning About Concurrency

Section 3 shows that approaches relying on total order formalisms are only capable of reliably monitoring a multithreaded program when the execution boils down to a total order. Therefore, it is important to reason about concurrency when designing monitoring tools, while still allowing behavioral properties. We present GPredict [41] in Sect. 5.1, a concurrency analysis tool that can be used for specifying behavior over concurrent regions. We discuss in Sect. 5.2 the potential of multitrace approaches, first introduced in Sect. 2.3. In Sect. 5.3, we present certain approaches from outside RV that may prove interesting and provide additional insight.

5.1   Generic Predictive Concurrency Analysis

Concurrent Behavior as Logical Constraints Solving. The more general theory behind RVPredict (Sect. 2.2) develops a sound and maximal causal model

80   A. El-Hokayem and Y. Falcone

to analyze concurrency in a multithreaded program [42]. In this model, the correct behavior of a program is modeled as a set of logical constraints, thus restricting the possible traces to consider. The theory supports any logical constraints to determine correctness, it is possible to encode a specification on multithreaded programs as a set of logical constraints. However, allowing for arbitrary specifications to be encoded while supports in the model, is not supported in the provided tool (RVPredict).

GPredict. Using the same sound and maximal model for predictive trace analysis [42] discussed in Sect. 2.2, GPredict [41] extends the specification formalism past data-races to behavior. Specifications are able to include behavioral, user-specified events, and are extended with thread identifiers, atomic regions, and concurrency. Events are defined similarly to Java-MOP using AspectJ for instrumentation. Atomic regions are special events that denote either the start or end of an atomic region. Each atomic region is given an ID. The specification formalism uses regular expressions extended with the concurrency operator "||" which allows events to happen in parallel.

Example 8 (Specifying concurrency). Listing 1.3 shows a specification for GPredict written for a multithreaded program, we re-use the example from [41]. The program consists of a method (m) of an object which reads and writes to a variable (s). Lines 2 and 5 specify the events that denote respectively reaching the start and end of method (m). Line 3 and 4 specify respectively the **read** and **write** events. Lines 7 and 8 illustrate respectively specifications for atomic regions and concurrency. The events in the specification can be parametrized by the thread identifier, and a region delimiter. To specify an atomic regions, an event can indicate whether it is the start or end of a region using the characters > and < respectively. The delimiter is followed by a region identifier, which is used to distinguish regions in the specification. In this case, we see that the **begin** and **end** events emitted by thread t1 delimit an atomic regions in which a read by thread t1 must be followed by a write by thread t2, which is followed by a write by thread t1. The specification is violated if any of the events happen in a different order or concurrently. To specify concurrent events, one must utilize "||" as shown on Line 8. In this case, the specification says that a read in thread t1 can happen in parallel with a write in thread t2.

Listing 1.3: GPredict specification depicting atomic regions.

```
1  AtomicityViolation (Object o){
2     event begin  before(Object o)  : execution(m());
3     event read   before(Object o)  : get(* s) && target(o);
4     event write  before(Object o)  : set(* s) && target(o);
5     event end    after(Object o)   : execution(m());
6
7     pattern: begin(t1, <r1) read(t1) write(t2) write(t1) end(t1,>r1)
8  //pattern: read(t1) || write(t2)
9  }
```

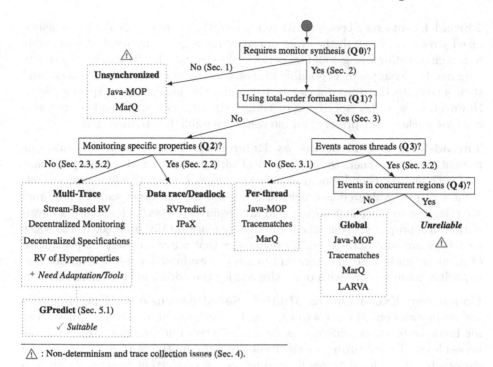

Fig. 7. RV approaches and considerations for monitoring multithreaded programs.

Limitations. While GPredict presents a general approach to reason about behavioral properties in concurrent executions, and hence constitutes a solution to monitoring when concurrency is present, it still requires additional improvements for higher expressiveness and usability. Notably, GPredict requires specifying thread identifiers explicitly in the specification. This requires specifications with multiple threads to become extremely verbose, and cannot handle a dynamic number of threads. For example, in the case of *readers-writers*, adding extra readers or writers requires rewriting the specification and combining events to specify each new thread. The approach behinds GPredict can also be extended to become more expressive, e.g. to support counting events to account for fairness in a concurrent setting.

5.2 Multi-trace Specifications: Possible Candidates?

RV approaches and tools that utilize multiple traces include approaches that rely on streams, decentralized specifications, and hyperproperties (as described in Sect. 2.3).

Thread Events as Streams. Stream-based RV techniques deal with synchronized streams in general, the order of the events is generally total. It is possible to imagine that ordering could be performed by certain functions that aggregate streams. For example, it is possible to create a stream per event per thread, and then aggregate them appropriately to handle the partial order specifications. However, as is, either specifying or adding streams to multithreaded programs remains unclear, but presents an interesting possible future direction.

Thread-level Specifications as References. Decentralized specifications present various manners to implicitly deal with threads, but do not in particular deal with multithreaded programs. Since monitors are merely references, and references can be evaluated as oracles at any point during the execution. Monitors are triggered to start monitoring, and are required to eventually return an evaluation of a property. Even when specifications are totally ordered, in the sense that they are automata-based, the semantics that allow for eventual evaluation of monitors make it so monitors on threads can evaluate local specifications and explicitly communicate with other threads for the additional information.

Concurrent Executions as Multiple Serial Executions. Hyperproperties are properties defined on a set of traces. Generally used for security, they allow for instance to check different executions of the same program from multiple access levels. By executing a concurrent program multiple times, we can obtain various totally ordered traces depending on the concurrent regions. As such, a possible future direction could explore how to express concurrency specifications as hyperproperties, and the feasibility of verifying a large set of totally ordered traces.

5.3   Inspiration from Outside RV

Detecting Concurrency Errors. Other approaches similar to RVPredict (Sect. 2.2) perform automatic verification and fence inference under relaxed memory models [12,44]. This ensures the correct execution of concurrent programs, but relies on static analysis and does not collect a runtime trace. Fence inference can be seen as determining concurrency segments in a program of interest with respect to the memory operations.

Relying on Heuristics. Determining exact concurrency regions is costly during execution or may interfere with the execution. An interesting direction is to utilize heuristics to determine concurrent regions. BARRACUDA [27] detects synchronization errors on GPUs by instrumenting CUDA applications and performing binary-level analysis. BARRACUDA avoids large overhead as it uses heuristics to approximate the synchronization in linear traces.

Testing Schedules. PARROT [24] is a *testing* framework that explores the interleavings of possible threads to test concurrent programs. PARROT analyzes the possible schedules of threads, and forces the application to explore them, thus exposing concurrency issues. The motivation behind PARROT is the realization that certain schedules occur in low probability under very specific circumstances.

6 Conclusions

We overviewed RV approaches that support multithreaded programs. By considering the various specifications formalisms, we are able to classify the tools by looking at whether or not they rely on total-order formalisms. We investigated the limitations of linear traces in the case of RV tools relying on formalisms that use total order, and noted the situations where linear traces lead to inconsistent verdicts. After presenting tools capable of checking specific properties, we mentioned various recent RV techniques using properties over multiple traces, and discussed their potential for monitoring multithreaded programs. Figure 7 summarizes the decisions a developer must consider when choosing RV tools for multithreaded monitoring, and the limitations of the existing approaches. We caution users of tools that using a formalism in which events are specified as a total order is not reliable when monitoring concurrent events (as we cannot reliably answer **Q4**). It is possible to monitor multithreaded programs that exhibit concurrency using GPredict (Sect. 5.1). However, issues with writing specifications easily and expressively need to be handled. Furthermore, RV techniques capable of specifying properties over multiple traces prove to be interesting candidates to extend to monitor multithreaded programs.

Acknowledgment. This article is based upon work from COST Action ARVI IC1402, supported by COST (European Cooperation in Science and Technology).

A   Monitors

We present the specifications used for monitoring *producer-consumer* using Java-MOP (Listing 1.4), LARVA (Listing 1.5), and MarQ (Listing 1.6). The detailed findings and description is found in Sect. 3.2. The monitors were designed for *global monitoring*, to ensure the trace is fed to the corresponding formalism as a total order. As such, for MarQ locking was needed.

Listing 1.4: Java-MOP specification and monitor for *producer-consumer*.

```
1  ProdCons() {
2    event produce before() :
3      call(* Queue.add(*))
4      && cflow(execution(* SynchQueue.produce(*)))
5      { }
6    event consume before() :
7      call(* Queue.poll())
8      && cflow(execution(* SynchQueue.consume()))
9      { }
10   cfg : S -> S produce S consume | epsilon
11   @fail {
12     System.out.println("Failed!");
13     System.exit(1);
14   }
15 }
```

Listing 1.5: LARVA specification and monitor for *producer-consumer*.

```
1  IMPORTS { import java.util.*; }
2  GLOBAL{
3    VARIABLES     { int cnt = 0;}
4    EVENTS{
5      produce() = { Queue.add()  }
6      consume() = { Queue.poll() }
7    }
8    PROPERTY prodcons {
9      STATES{
10       BAD { bad {
11         System.err.println("Failed!");
12         System.exit(1);
13       }}
14       NORMAL      { ok }
15       STARTING    { starting }
16     }
17
18     TRANSITIONS{
19       starting -> bad  [consume]
20       starting -> ok   [produce\          \cnt++;]
21       ok  -> ok        [consume\ cnt > 1  \cnt--;]
22       ok  -> starting  [consume\ cnt == 1 \cnt--;]
23       ok  -> ok        [produce\          \cnt++;]
24       ok  -> bad       [consume\ cnt == 0 \        ]
25       bad -> bad       [produce]
26       bad -> bad       [consume]
27     }
28   }
29 }
```

Listing 1.6: MarQ specification and monitor for *producer-consumer.*

```
1  public aspect MarQProdCon {
2    //Events
3    private final int PRODUCE = 1;
4    private final int CONSUME = 2;
5    //Produce Counter
6    private int counter = 0;
7    //Monitor + Lock
8    Monitor monitor;
9    private Object LOCK = new Object();
10
11   before() : //Handle Event: Produce
12     call(* Queue.add(*))
13     && cflow(execution(* SynchQueue.produce(*)))
14   {
15     synchronized(LOCK){
16       check(monitor.step(PRODUCE, counter));
17       counter++;
18     }
19   }
20   before() : //Handle Event: Consume
21     call(* Queue.poll())
22     && cflow(execution(* SynchQueue.consume()))
23   {
24     synchronized(LOCK){
25       check(monitor.step(CONSUME, counter));
26       counter--;
27     }
28   }
29   private void check(Verdict verdict){
30     if(verdict==Verdict.FAILURE){
31       System.err.println("Failed!");
32       System.exit(1);
33     }
34   }
35   //Create QEA Specification
36   public void init(){
37     QEABuilder b = new QEABuilder("ProdCon");
38     int ticket = 1;
39     b.addTransition(1, PRODUCE, new int[] {ticket},
40       Assignment.increment(ticket),      1);
41     b.addTransition(1, CONSUME, new int[] {ticket},
42       Guard.varIsGreaterThanVal(ticket, 0),
43       Assignment.decrement(ticket),      1);
44     b.addTransition(1, CONSUME, new int[] {ticket},
45       Guard.varIsEqualToIntVal(ticket, 0), 2);
46     b.addFinalStates(1);
47     monitor = MonitorFactory.create(b.make());
48   }
49   public MarQProdCon(){ init(); }
50 }
```

References

1. Adhianto, L., et al.: HPCTOOLKIT: tools for performance analysis of optimized parallel programs. Concurr. Comput. Pract. Exp. **22**(6), 685–701 (2010)
2. Adve, S.V., Gharachorloo, K.: Shared memory consistency models: a tutorial. Computer **29**(12), 66–76 (1996)
3. Ahamad, M., Neiger, G., Burns, J.E., Kohli, P., Hutto, P.W.: Causal memory: definitions, implementation, and programming. Distrib. Comput. **9**(1), 37–49 (1995)
4. Allan, C., et al.: Adding trace matching with free variables to AspectJ. In: Proceedings of the 20th Annual ACM SIGPLAN Conference on Object-oriented Programming, Systems, Languages, and Applications. pp. 345–364. OOPSLA 2005. ACM (2005)

5. Barringer, H., Falcone, Y., Havelund, K., Reger, G., Rydeheard, D.: Quantified event automata: towards expressive and efficient runtime monitors. In: Giannakopoulou, D., Méry, D. (eds.) FM 2012. LNCS, vol. 7436, pp. 68–84. Springer, Heidelberg (2012). https://doi.org/10.1007/978-3-642-32759-9_9
6. Bartocci, E., Bonakdarpour, B., Falcone, Y.: First international competition on software for runtime verification. In: Bonakdarpour, B., Smolka, S.A. (eds.) RV 2014. LNCS, vol. 8734, pp. 1–9. Springer, Cham (2014). https://doi.org/10.1007/978-3-319-11164-3_1
7. Bartocci, E., Falcone, Y. (eds.): Lectures on Runtime Verification. LNCS, vol. 10457. Springer, Cham (2018). https://doi.org/10.1007/978-3-319-75632-5
8. Bartocci, E., et al.: First international competition on runtime verification: rules, benchmarks, tools, and final results of CRV 2014. Int. J. Softw. Tools Technol. Transf. April 2017
9. Bartocci, E., Falcone, Y., Francalanza, A., Reger, G.: Introduction to runtime verification. In: Bartocci, E., Falcone, Y. (eds.) Lectures on Runtime Verification. LNCS, vol. 10457, pp. 1–33. Springer, Cham (2018). https://doi.org/10.1007/978-3-319-75632-5_1
10. Bauer, A., Falcone, Y.: Decentralised LTL monitoring. Form. Methods Syst. Des. **48**(1–2), 46–93 (2016)
11. Bauer, A., Falcone, Y.: Decentralised LTL monitoring. In: Giannakopoulou, D., Méry, D. (eds.) FM 2012. LNCS, vol. 7436, pp. 85–100. Springer, Heidelberg (2012). https://doi.org/10.1007/978-3-642-32759-9_10
12. Bender, J., Lesani, M., Palsberg, J.: Declarative fence insertion. In: Proceedings of the 2015 ACM SIGPLAN International Conference on Object-Oriented Programming, Systems, Languages, and Applications, pp. 367–385. OOPSLA 2015. ACM (2015)
13. Bodden, E., Hendren, L., Lam, P., Lhoták, O., Naeem, N.A.: Collaborative runtime verification with tracematches. J. Log. Comput. **20**(3), 707–723 (2010)
14. Brett, N., Siddique, U., Bonakdarpour, B.: Rewriting-based runtime verification for alternation-free HyperLTL. In: Legay, A., Margaria, T. (eds.) Tools and Algorithms for the Construction and Analysis of Systems, pp. 77–93. Springer, Berlin Heidelberg, Berlin, Heidelberg (2017)
15. Bultan, T., Sen, K. (eds.): Proceedings of the 26th ACM SIGSOFT International Symposium on Software Testing and Analysis, Santa Barbara, July 10–14, 2017. ACM (2017)
16. Chen, F., Roşu, G.: Java-MOP: a monitoring oriented programming environment for Java. In: Halbwachs, N., Zuck, L.D. (eds.) TACAS 2005. LNCS, vol. 3440, pp. 546–550. Springer, Heidelberg (2005). https://doi.org/10.1007/978-3-540-31980-1_36
17. Chen, F., Roşu, G.: Mop: an efficient and generic runtime verification framework. In: Proceedings of the 22nd Annual ACM SIGPLAN Conference on Object-oriented Programming Systems and Applications, pp. 569–588. OOPSLA 2007. ACM (2007)
18. Clarkson, M.R., Schneider, F.B.: Hyperproperties. J. Comput. Secur. **18**(6), 1157–1210 (2010)
19. Colombo, C., Falcone, Y.: Organising LTL monitors over distributed systems with a global clock. Form. Methods Syst. Des. **49**(1–2), 109–158 (2016)
20. Colombo, C., Pace, G.J., Abela, P.: Compensation-aware runtime monitoring. In: Barringer, H., Falcone, Y., Finkbeiner, B., Havelund, K., Lee, I., Pace, G., Roşu, G., Sokolsky, O., Tillmann, N. (eds.) RV 2010. LNCS, vol. 6418, pp. 214–228. Springer, Heidelberg (2010). https://doi.org/10.1007/978-3-642-16612-9_17

21. Colombo, C., Pace, G.J., Schneider, G.: Dynamic event-based runtime monitoring of real-time and contextual properties. In: Cofer, D., Fantechi, A. (eds.) FMICS 2008. LNCS, vol. 5596, pp. 135–149. Springer, Heidelberg (2009). https://doi.org/10.1007/978-3-642-03240-0_13

22. Colombo, C., Pace, G.J., Schneider, G.: LARVA – safer monitoring of real-time java programs (Tool Paper). In: Hung, D.V., Krishnan, P. (eds.) Seventh IEEE International Conference on Software Engineering and Formal Methods, SEFM 2009, Hanoi, 23–27 November 2009, pp. 33–37. IEEE Computer Society (2009). https://doi.org/10.1109/SEFM.2009.13

23. Convent, L., Hungerecker, S., Leucker, M., Scheffel, T., Schmitz, M., Thoma, D.: Tessla: Temporal stream-based specification language. CoRR abs/1808.10717 (2018)

24. Cui, H., et al.: Parrot: A practical runtime for deterministic, stable, and reliable threads. In: Proceedings of the Twenty-Fourth ACM Symposium on Operating Systems Principles, SOSP 2013, pp. 388–405, ACM (2013)

25. D'Angelo, B., et al.: LOLA: runtime monitoring of synchronous systems. In: 12th International Symposium on Temporal Representation and Reasoning (TIME 2005), pp. 166–174. IEEE Computer Society (2005)

26. Decker, N., et al.: Online analysis of debug trace data for embedded systems. In: 2018 Design, Automation & Test in Europe Conference & Exhibition, DATE 2018, pp. 851–856. IEEE (2018)

27. Eizenberg, A., Peng, Y., Pigli, T., Mansky, W., Devietti, J.: BARRACUDA: Binary-level analysis of runtime races in CUDA programs. In: Proceedings of the 38th ACM SIGPLAN Conference on Programming Language Design and Implementation, PLDI 2017, pp. 126–140. ACM (2017)

28. El-Hokayem, A., Falcone, Y.: Monitoring decentralized specifications. In: Bultan and Sen, Proceedings of the 26th ACM SIGSOFT International Symposium on Software Testing and Analysis, pp. 125–135. ACM (2017)

29. El-Hokayem, A., Falcone, Y.: THEMIS: a tool for decentralized monitoring algorithms. In: Bultan and Sen, Proceedings of the 26th ACM SIGSOFT International Symposium on Software Testing and Analysis, pp. 372-375. ACM (2017)

30. El-Hokayem, A., Falcone, Y.: RV for Multithreaded Programs Tutorial (2018). https://gitlab.inria.fr/monitoring/rv-multi

31. Falcone, Y., Havelund, K., Reger, G.: A tutorial on runtime verification. Eng. Dependable Softw. Syst. **34**, 141–175 (2013)

32. Falcone, Y., Ničković, D., Reger, G., Thoma, D.: Second International Competition on Runtime Verification. In: Bartocci, E., Majumdar, R. (eds.) RV 2015. LNCS, vol. 9333, pp. 405–422. Springer, Cham (2015). https://doi.org/10.1007/978-3-319-23820-3_27

33. Finkbeiner, B., Hahn, C., Stenger, M., Tentrup, L.: RVHyper: A runtime verification tool for temporal hyperproperties. In: Beyer, D., Huisman, M. (eds.) TACAS 2018. LNCS, vol. 10806, pp. 194–200. Springer, Cham (2018). https://doi.org/10.1007/978-3-319-89963-3_11

34. Finkbeiner, B., Rabe, M.N., Sánchez, C.: Algorithms for model checking Hyper-LTL and HyperCTL*. In: Kroening, D., Păsăreanu, C.S. (eds.) CAV 2015. LNCS, vol. 9206, pp. 30–48. Springer, Cham (2015). https://doi.org/10.1007/978-3-319-21690-4_3

35. Formal Systems Laboratory: JavaMOP4 Syntax (2018). http://fsl.cs.illinois.edu/index.php/JavaMOP4_Syntax

36. Gastin, P., Kuske, D.: Uniform satisfiability problem for local temporal logics over Mazurkiewicz traces. Inf. Comput. **208**(7), 797–816 (2010)

37. Giannakopoulou, D., Méry, D. (eds.): FM 2012. LNCS, vol. 7436. Springer, Heidelberg (2012). https://doi.org/10.1007/978-3-642-32759-9
38. Hallé, S., Khoury, R.: Event stream processing with BeepBeep 3. In: RV-CuBES 2017. An International Workshop on Competitions, Usability, Benchmarks, Evaluation, and Standardisation for Runtime Verification Tools. Kalpa Publications in Computing, vol. 3, pp. 81–88. EasyChair (2017)
39. Havelund, K., Roşu, G.: An overview of the runtime verification tool Java PathExplorer. Form. Methods Syst. Des. **24**(2), 189–215 (2004)
40. Herlihy, M., Wing, J.M.: Linearizability: a correctness condition for concurrent objects. ACM Trans. Program. Lang. Syst. **12**(3), 463–492 (1990)
41. Huang, J., Luo, Q., Rosu, G.: Gpredict: Generic predictive concurrency analysis. In: 37th IEEE/ACM International Conference on Software Engineering, ICSE 2015, vol. 1, pp. 847–857 (2015)
42. Huang, J., Meredith, P.O., Rosu, G.: Maximal sound predictive race detection with control flow abstraction. In: Proceedings of the 35th ACM SIGPLAN Conference on Programming Language Design and Implementation, PLDI 2014, pp. 337–348. ACM (2014)
43. Kiczales, G., Hilsdale, E., Hugunin, J., Kersten, M., Palm, J., Griswold, W.G.: An overview of AspectJ. In: Knudsen, J.L. (ed.) ECOOP 2001. LNCS, vol. 2072, pp. 327–354. Springer, Heidelberg (2001). https://doi.org/10.1007/3-540-45337-7_18
44. Kuperstein, M., Vechev, M., Yahav, E.: Partial-coherence abstractions for relaxed memory models. In: Proceedings of the 32nd ACM SIGPLAN Conference on Programming Language Design and Implementation, PLDI 2011, pp. 187–198. ACM (2011)
45. Leucker, M., Sánchez, C., Scheffel, T., Schmitz, M., Schramm, A.: TeSSLa: runtime verification of non-synchronized real-time streams. In: Haddad, H.M., Wainwright, R.L., Chbeir, R. (eds.) Proceedings of the 33rd Annual ACM Symposium on Applied Computing, SAC 2018, Pau, France, April 09–13, 2018, pp. 1925–1933. ACM (2018)
46. Leucker, M., Schallhart, C.: A brief account of runtime verification. J. Log. Algebraic Program. **78**(5), 293–303 (2009)
47. Lodaya, K., Weil, P.: Rationality in algebras with a series operation. Inf. Comput. **171**(2), 269–293 (2001)
48. Lourenço, J.M., Fiedor, J., Křena, B., Vojnar, T.: Discovering concurrency errors. In: Bartocci, E., Falcone, Y. (eds.) Lectures on Runtime Verification. LNCS, vol. 10457, pp. 34–60. Springer, Cham (2018). https://doi.org/10.1007/978-3-319-75632-5_2
49. Manson, J., Pugh, W., Adve, S.V.: The Java memory model. In: Proceedings of the 32nd ACM SIGPLAN-SIGACT Symposium on Principles of Programming Languages, POPL 2005, pp. 378–391. ACM (2005)
50. Mazurkiewicz, A.: Trace theory. In: Brauer, W., Reisig, W., Rozenberg, G. (eds.) ACPN 1986. LNCS, vol. 255, pp. 278–324. Springer, Heidelberg (1987). https://doi.org/10.1007/3-540-17906-2_30
51. Meenakshi, B., Ramanujam, R.: Reasoning about layered message passing systems. Comput. Lang. Syst. Struct. **30**(3–4), 171–206 (2004)
52. Meredith, P.O., Jin, D., Griffith, D., Chen, F., Rosu, G.: An overview of the MOP runtime verification framework. STTT **14**(3), 249–289 (2012)
53. Nielsen, M., Plotkin, G.D., Winskel, G.: Petri nets, event structures and domains, part I. Theor. Comput. Sci. **13**, 85–108 (1981)

54. Reger, G., Cruz, H.C., Rydeheard, D.: MARQ: Monitoring at runtime with QEA. In: Baier, C., Tinelli, C. (eds.) TACAS 2015. LNCS, vol. 9035, pp. 596–610. Springer, Heidelberg (2015). https://doi.org/10.1007/978-3-662-46681-0_55
55. Reger, G., Hallé, S., Falcone, Y.: Third international competition on runtime verification. In: Falcone, Y., Sánchez, C. (eds.) RV 2016. LNCS, vol. 10012, pp. 21–37. Springer, Cham (2016). https://doi.org/10.1007/978-3-319-46982-9_3
56. Reger, G., Havelund, K.: What is a trace? a runtime verification perspective. In: Margaria, T., Steffen, B. (eds.) ISoLA 2016. LNCS, vol. 9953, pp. 339–355. Springer, Cham (2016). https://doi.org/10.1007/978-3-319-47169-3_25
57. Said, M., Wang, C., Yang, Z., Sakallah, K.: Generating data race witnesses by an SMT-based analysis. In: Bobaru, M., Havelund, K., Holzmann, G.J., Joshi, R. (eds.) NFM 2011. LNCS, vol. 6617, pp. 313–327. Springer, Heidelberg (2011). https://doi.org/10.1007/978-3-642-20398-5_23
58. The Eclipse Foundation: The AspectJ project (2018). https://www.eclipse.org/aspectj/

Runtime Verification: From Propositional to First-Order Temporal Logic

Klaus Havelund[1] and Doron Peled[2(✉)]

[1] Jet Propulsion Laboratory, California Institute of Technology, Pasadena, USA
[2] Department of Computer Science, Bar Ilan University, Ramat Gan, Israel
doron.peled@gmail.com

Abstract. Runtime Verification is a branch of formal methods concerned with analysis of execution traces for the purpose of determining the state or general quality of the executing system. The field covers numerous approaches, one of which is specification-based runtime verification, where execution traces are checked against formal specifications. The paper presents syntax, semantics, and monitoring algorithms for respectively propositional and first-order temporal logics. In propositional logics the observed events in the execution trace are represented using atomic propositions, while first-order logic allows universal and existential quantification over data occurring as arguments in events. Monitoring of the first-order case is drastically more challenging than the propositional case, and we present a solution for this problem based on BDDs. We furthermore discuss monitorability of temporal properties by dividing them into different classes representing different degrees of monitorability.

1 Introduction

Runtime verification (RV) [2,13] allows monitoring (analysis) of executions of a system, directly, without the need for modeling the system. It has some commonality with other formal methods such as testing, model checking and formal verification, including the use of a specification formalisms[1]. However, it differs a lot in goals, the algorithms used, and the complexity and the coverage it suggests. Model checking performs a comprehensive search on a model of the system under test. Testing generates inputs to drive system executions, trying to provide a good coverage, yet keeping the complexity low, at the price of losing

The research performed by the first author was carried out at Jet Propulsion Laboratory, California Institute of Technology, under a contract with the National Aeronautics and Space Administration. The research performed by the second author was partially funded by Israeli Science Foundation grant 2239/15: "Runtime Measuring and Checking of Cyber Physical Systems".

[1] RV can be understood more broadly to mean: any processing of execution traces for the purpose of evaluating a system state or quality. Some approaches do not involve specifications but rather use pre-programmed algorithms as monitors.

© Springer Nature Switzerland AG 2018
C. Colombo and M. Leucker (Eds.): RV 2018, LNCS 11237, pp. 90–112, 2018.
https://doi.org/10.1007/978-3-030-03769-7_7

exhaustiveness. Formal verification attempts full proof of correctness based on deductive techniques. Runtime verification does not directly concern itself with coverage and the selection of execution paths, but rather focuses on analyzing a single execution trace (or a collection thereof). An execution trace is generated by the observed executing system, typically by instrumenting the system to generate events as important transitions take place. Instrumentation can be manual by inserting logging statements in the code, or it can be automated using instrumentation software, such as aspect-oriented programming frameworks.

Runtime verification can take place on-line, as the system executes, or off-line, by processing log files produced by the system. In the case of on-line processing, runtime verification obtains the information about the execution as it unfolds, oftentimes without seeing the complete sequence; yet it is required to provide a verdict as soon as possible. The critical complexity measure here is the *incremental complexity*, which is performed for each new event reported to the monitor. The calculation needs to be fast enough to keep in pace with the executing system.

Following in part [14,23], we present algorithms for the runtime verification of linear temporal logic properties, which is the most common specification formalism used for both runtime verification and model checking. We start with the propositional case, where an execution trace is checked against a future or past time propositional LTL formula. For an online algorithm, which observes the execution trace event by event, a verdict is not guaranteed in any finite time. Runtime monitorability identifies what kind of verdicts can be expected when monitoring an execution against a temporal property. Monitoring temporal properties is often restricted to safety properties. There are two main reasons for this restriction: the first is that the algorithm for checking safety is rather efficient, polynomial in the size of the property; the other reason is that for safety properties we are guaranteed to have a finite evidence for a negative verdict (albeit there is not always a bound on when such an evidence can be given).

After presenting the theory of monitoring propositional temporal logic we move on to the more demanding challenge of monitoring properties that depend on data reported to the monitor. This can be handled by a parametrized version of temporal logic (or using parametrized automata), but more generally it calls for using a first-order version of the temporal logic. We will concentrate on first-order safety properties. One of the challenges here is that the data may, in principle, be unbounded and we only learn about the actual values that are monitored as they appear in reported events. Another problem is that, unlike the propositional case, the amount of data that needs to be kept may keep growing during the execution. This calls for a clever representation that allows fast processing of many data elements. We present an algorithm based on BDDs, which is implemented in the tool DEJA VU [12].

The paper is organized as follows. Section 2 introduces propositional linear temporal logic, including future as well as past time operators, its syntax, semantics, and some pragmatics. Section 3 presents a general theory of monitorability of temporal properties, such as those formulated in LTL. Section 4 outlines algorithms for monitoring propositional LTL properties, first future time, and then past time. Section 5 introduces first-order past time LTL, its syntax, semantics, and some pragmatics. Section 6 outlines an algorithm for monitoring first-order past LTL properties. Finally, Sect. 7 concludes the paper.

2 Propositional LTL

The definition of linear temporal logic including future and past time operators is as follows [20]:

$$\varphi ::= true \mid p \mid (\varphi \wedge \varphi) \mid \neg\varphi \mid (\varphi\,\mathcal{U}\,\varphi) \mid \bigcirc \varphi \mid (\varphi \mathcal{S} \varphi) \mid \ominus \varphi$$

where p is a proposition from a finite set of propositions P, with $\mathcal{U}$ standing for *until*, $\bigcirc$ standing for *next-time*, $\mathcal{S}$ standing for *since*, and $\ominus$ standing for *previous-time*. One can also write $(\varphi \vee \psi)$ instead of $\neg(\neg\varphi \wedge \neg\psi)$, $(\varphi \rightarrow \psi)$ instead of $(\neg\varphi \vee \psi)$, $\Diamond\varphi$ (*eventually* φ) instead of $(true\,\mathcal{U}\,\varphi)$, $\Box\varphi$ (*always* φ) instead of $\neg\Diamond\neg\varphi$, $\mathbf{P}\,\varphi$ (*past* φ) instead of $(true\,\mathcal{S}\,\varphi)$ and $\mathbf{H}\,\varphi$ (*history* φ) instead of $\neg\mathbf{P}\,\neg\varphi$.

LTL formulas are interpreted over an infinite sequence of events $\xi = e_1.e_2.e_3 \ldots$, where $e_i \subseteq P$ for each $i > 0$. These are the propositions that *hold* in that event. LTL's semantics is defined as follows:

- $\xi, i \models true$.
- $\xi, i \models p$ iff $p \in e_i$.
- $\xi, i \models \neg\varphi$ iff not $\xi, i \models \varphi$.
- $\xi, i \models (\varphi \wedge \psi)$ iff $\xi, i \models \varphi$ and $\xi, i \models \psi$.
- $\xi, i \models \bigcirc\varphi$ iff $\xi, i+1 \models \varphi$.
- $\xi, i \models (\varphi\,\mathcal{U}\,\psi)$ iff for some $j \geq i$, $\xi, j \models \psi$, and for all $i \leq k < j$ it holds that $\xi, k \models \varphi$.
- $\xi, i \models \ominus\varphi$ iff $i > 1$ and $\xi, i-1 \models \varphi$.
- $\xi, i \models (\varphi\,\mathcal{S}\,\psi)$ iff $\xi, i \models \psi$ or the following hold[2]: $i > 1$, $\xi, i \models \varphi$ and $\xi, i-1 \models (\varphi\,\mathcal{S}\,\psi)$.

Then $\xi \models \varphi$ when $\xi, 1 \models \varphi$.

This definition of propositional temporal logic contains both future modalities ($\mathcal{U}$, $\Box$, $\Diamond$ and $\bigcirc$) and past modalities ($\mathcal{S}$, $\mathbf{H}$, $\mathbf{P}$ and $\ominus$). However, we do not always need to use all off them:

- Removing the past temporal operators does not affect the expressiveness of the logic [10]. On the other hand, there are examples of properties that are much more compact when expressed using both the past and the present operators.

---

[2] This definition is equivalent to the traditional definition $\xi, i \models (\varphi\,\mathcal{S}\,\psi)$ iff for some $0 < j \leq i$, $\xi, j \models \psi$, and for all $j < k \leq i$ it holds that $\xi, k \models \varphi$, but is more intuitive for the forthcoming presentation of the RV algorithm.

– Properties of the form $\Box\varphi$, where φ does *not* contain the future operators form an important class. There are several reasons for restricting runtime verification to such properties. These properties correspond to temporal *safety properties* [1,19]: failure can always be detected on a finite prefix [5]. Moreover, expressing safety properties in this form allows an efficient runtime verification algorithm that is only polynomial in the size of the specification [14][3].

3 Monitorability of Propositional Temporal Logic

Online runtime verification of LTL properties inspects finite prefixes of the execution. Assume an observed system S, and assume further that a finite execution of S up to a certain point is captured as an execution trace $\xi = e_1.e_2. \ldots .e_n$, which is a sequence of observed events, each of type $\mathbb{E}$. Each event e_i captures a snapshot of S's execution state. Then the RV problem can be formulated as constructing a program M with the type $M : \mathbb{E}^* \to D$, which when applied to the trace ξ, as in $M(\xi)$, returns some data value $d \in D$ in a domain D of interest. Typically M is generated from a formal specification, given as a temporal logic formula or a state machine. Because online RV observes at each time only a finite part of the execution, it can sometimes provide only a partial verdict on the satisfaction and violation of the inspected property [4,22]. This motivates providing three kinds of verdicts as possible values for the domain D:

failed when the current prefix cannot be extended in any way into an execution that satisfies the specification,
satisfied when any possible extension of the current prefix satisfies the specification, and
undecided when the current prefix can be extended to satisfy the specification but also extended to satisfy its negation.

For example, the property $\Box p$ (for some atomic proposition p), which asserts that p always happens, can be refuted by a runtime monitor if p does not hold in some observed event. At this point, no matter which way the execution is extended, the property will not hold, resulting in a *failed* verdict. However, no finite prefix of an execution can establish that $\Box p$ holds. In a similar way, the property $\Diamond p$ cannot be refuted, since p may appear at any time in the future; but once p happens, we know that the property is satisfied, independent on any continuation, and we can issue a *satisfied* verdict. For the property $(\Box p \vee \Diamond q)$ we may not have a verdict at any finite time, in the case where all the observed events satisfy both p and $\neg q$. On the other hand, we may never "lose hope" to have such a verdict, as a later event satisfying q will result in a positive verdict; at this point we can abandon the monitoring, since the property cannot be further violated. On the other hand, for the property $\Box\Diamond p$ we can never provide a verdict in finite

---

[3] There are examples of safety properties that are much more compact when expressed with the past temporal operators [21], and for symmetrical considerations also vice versa.

time: for whatever happens, p can still appear an infinite number of times, and we cannot guarantee or refute that this property holds when observing any finite prefix of an execution. The problem of monitorability of a temporal property was studied in [5,9,24], basically requiring that at any point of monitoring we still have a possibility to obtain a finite positive or negative verdict.

Safety and liveness temporal properties were defined informally on infinite execution sequences by Lamport [19] as *something bad cannot happen* and *something good will happen*. These informal definitions were later formalized by Alpern and Schneider [1]. Guarantee properties where used in an orthogonal characterization by Manna and Pnueli [20]. Guarantee properties are the dual of safety properties, that is, the negation of a safety property is a guarantee property and vice versa.

These classes of properties can be seen as characterizing finite monitorability of temporal properties: if a safety property is violated, there will be a finite prefix witnessing it; on the other hand, for a liveness property, one can never provide such a finite negative evidence. We suggest the following alternative definitions of classes of temporal properties.

AFR/safety Always Finitely Refutable: when the property does not hold on an infinite execution, a *failed* verdict can be identified after a finite prefix.

AFS/guarantee Always Finitely Satisfiable: when the property is satisfied on an infinite execution, a *satisfied* verdict can be identified after a finite prefix.

NFR/liveness Never Finitely Refutable: when the property does not hold on an infinite execution, refutation can never be identified after a finite prefix.

NFS/morbidity Never Finitely Satisfiable: When the property is satisfied on an infinite execution, satisfaction can never be identified after a finite prefix.

It is easy to see that the definitions of the classes AFR and safety in [1] are the same and so are those for AFS and guarantee. A liveness property φ is defined to satisfy that any finite prefix can be extended to an execution that satisfies φ. The definition of the class NFR only mentions prefixes of executions that do not satisfy φ; but for prefixes of executions that satisfy φ this trivially holds. The correspondence between NFS and morbidity is shown in a symmetric way.

The above four classes of properties, however, do not cover the entire set of possible temporal properties, independent of the actual formalism that is used to express them. The following two classes complete the classification.

SFR Sometimes Finitely Refutable: for some infinite executions that violate the property, refutation can be identified after a finite prefix; for other infinite executions violating the property, this is not the case.

SFS Sometimes Finitely Satisfiable: for some infinite executions that satisfy the property, satisfaction can be identified after a finite prefix; for other infinite executions satisfying the property, this is not the case.

Bauer, Leucker and Schallhart [5] define three categories of prefixes of elements from 2^P.

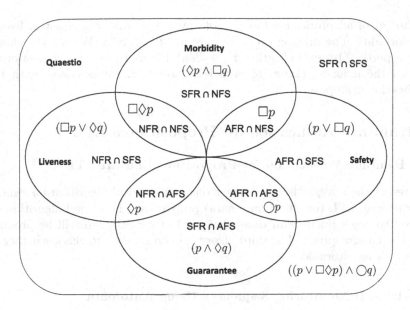

Fig. 1. Classification of properties: safety, guarantee, liveness, morbidity and quaestio.

- A *good* prefix is one where all its extensions (infinite sequences of elements from 2^P) satisfy the monitored property φ.
- A *bad* prefix is one where none of its infinite extensions satisfy φ.
- An *ugly* prefix cannot be extended into a good or a bad prefix.

When identifying a good or a bad finite prefix, we are done tracing the execution and can announce that the monitored property is satisfied or failed, respectively. After an ugly prefix, satisfaction or refutation of φ depends on the entire infinite execution, and cannot be determined in finite time. Note that a property has a good prefix if it is *not* a morbidity property, and a bad prefix if it is *not* a liveness property. *Monitorability* of a property φ is defined in [5] as the lack of ugly prefixes for the property φ. This definition is consistent with [24].

Any property that is in AFR (safety) or in AFS (guarantee) is monitorable [5, 9]. A property that is NFR ∩ NFS is non-monitorable. In fact no verdict is ever expected on any sequence that is monitored against such a property. This leaves the three classes SFR ∩ SFS, SFR ∩ NFS and NFR ∩ SFS, for which some properties are monitorable and others are not. This is demonstrated in the following table.

Class	Monitorable example	Non-monitorable example
SFR ∩ SFS	$((\Diamond r \lor \Box \Diamond p) \land \bigcirc q)$	$((p \lor \Box \Diamond p) \land \bigcirc q)$
SFR ∩ NFS	$(\Diamond p \land \Box q)$	$(\Box \Diamond p \land \bigcirc q)$
NFR ∩ SFS	$(\Box p \lor \Diamond q)$	$(\Box \Diamond p \lor \bigcirc q)$

The set of all properties *Prop* is not covered by safety, guarantee, liveness and morbidity. The missing properties are in SFR ∩ SFS. We call the class of such properties **Quaestio** (Latin for *question*). Figure 1 presents the relationship between the different classes of properties and their intersections, with LTL specification examples.

4   Runtime Verification for Propositional LTL

4.1   Runtime Verification for Propositional Future LTL

We present three algorithms. The first one is a classical algorithm for runtime verification of LTL (or Büchi automata) properties. The second algorithm can be used to check during run time what kind of verdicts can still be produced given the current prefix. The third algorithm can be used to check whether the property is monitorable.

Algorithm 1: Monitoring Sequences Using Automata

Kupferman and Vardi [17] provide an algorithm for detecting good and bad prefixes. For good prefixes, start by constructing a Büchi automaton $\mathcal{A}_{\neg\varphi}$ for $\neg\varphi$, e.g., using the translation in [11]. Note that this automaton is not necessarily deterministic [27]. States of $\mathcal{A}_{\neg\varphi}$, from which one cannot reach a cycle that contains an accepting state, are deleted. Checking for a positive verdict for φ, one keeps for each monitored prefix the set of states that $\mathcal{A}_{\neg\varphi}$ would be in after observing that input. One starts with the set of initial states of the automaton $\mathcal{A}_{\neg\varphi}$. Given the current set of successors S and an event $e \in 2^P$, the next set of successors S' is set to the successors of the states in S according to the transition relation Δ of $\mathcal{A}_{\neg\varphi}$. That is, $S' = \{s' | s \in S \wedge (s, e, s') \in \Delta\}$. Reaching the empty set of states, the monitored sequence is good, and the property must hold since the current prefix cannot be completed into an infinite execution satisfying $\neg\varphi$.

This is basically a *subset construction* for a deterministic automaton $\mathcal{B}_\varphi$, whose initial state is the set of initial states of $\mathcal{A}_{\neg\varphi}$, accepting state is the empty set, and transition relation as described above. The size of this automaton is $\mathcal{O}(2^{2^{|P|}})$, resulting in double exponential explosion from the size of the checked LTL property. But in fact, we do not need to construct the entire automaton $\mathcal{B}_\varphi$ in advance, and can avoid the double exponential explosion by calculating its current state on-the-fly, while performing runtime verification. Thus, the incremental processing per each event is exponential in the size of the checked LTL property. Unfortunately, a single exponential explosion is unavoidable [17].

Checking for a *failed* verdict for φ is done with a symmetric construction, translating φ into a Büchi automaton $\mathcal{A}_\varphi$ and then the deterministic automaton $\mathcal{B}_{\neg\varphi}$ (or calculating its states on-the-fly) using a subset construction as above. Note that $\mathcal{A}_{\neg\varphi}$ is used to construct $\mathcal{B}_\varphi$ and $\mathcal{A}_\varphi$ is used to construct $\mathcal{B}_{\neg\varphi}$. Runtime verification of φ uses both automata for the monitored input, reporting a *failed* verdict if $\mathcal{B}_{\neg\varphi}$ reaches an accepting state, a *satisfied* verdict if $\mathcal{B}_\varphi$ reaches an accepting state, and an *undecided* verdict otherwise. The algorithm guarantees to report a positive or negative verdict on the minimal good or bad prefix that is observed.

Algorithm 2: Checking Availability of Future Verdicts

We alter the above runtime verification algorithm to check whether positive or negative verdicts can still be obtained after the current monitored prefix at runtime. Applying DFS on $\mathcal{B}_\varphi$, we search for states from which one cannot reach the accepting state. We replace these states with a single state $\bot$ with a self loop, obtaining the automaton $\mathcal{C}_\varphi$. Reaching $\bot$, after monitoring a finite prefix σ with $\mathcal{C}_\varphi$ happens exactly when we will not have a good prefix anymore. This means that after σ, a *satisfied* verdict cannot be issued anymore for φ.

Similarly, we perform BFS on $\mathcal{B}_{\neg\varphi}$ to find all the states in which the accepting state is not reachable, then replace them by a single state $\top$ with a self loop, obtaining $\mathcal{C}_{\neg\varphi}$. Reaching $\top$ after monitoring a prefix means that we will not be able again to have a bad prefix, hence a *failed* verdict cannot be issued anymore for φ.

We can perform runtime verification while updating the state of both automata, $\mathcal{C}_\varphi$ and $\mathcal{C}_{\neg\varphi}$ on-the-fly, upon each input event. However, we need to be able to predict if, from the current state, an accepting state is not reachable. While this can be done in space exponential in φ, it makes an incremental calculation whose time complexity is doubly exponential in the size of φ, as is the algorithm for that by Pnueli and Zaks [24]. This is hardly a reasonable complexity for the incremental calculation performed between successive monitored events for an on-line algorithm. Hence, a pre-calculation of these two automata before the monitoring starts is preferable, leaving the incremental time complexity exponential in φ, as in Algorithm 1.

Algorithm 3: Checking Monitorability

A small variant on the construction of $\mathcal{C}_\varphi$ and $\mathcal{C}_{\neg\varphi}$ allows checking if a property is monitorable. The algorithm is simple: construct the product $\mathcal{C}_\varphi \times \mathcal{C}_{\neg\varphi}$ and check whether the state $(\bot, \top)$ is reachable. If so, the property is non-monitorable, since there is a prefix that will transfer the product automaton to this state and thus it is ugly. It is not sufficient to check separately that $\mathcal{C}_\varphi$ can reach $\top$ and that $\mathcal{C}_{\neg\varphi}$ can reach $\bot$. In the property $(\neg(p \wedge r) \wedge ((\neg p \, \mathcal{U} \, (r \wedge \Diamond q)) \vee (\neg r \, \mathcal{U} \, (p \wedge \Box q))))$: both $\bot$ and $\top$ can be reached, separately, depending on which of the predicates r or p happens first. But in either case, there is still a possibility for a good or a bad extension, hence it is a monitorable property.

If the automaton $\mathcal{C}_\varphi \times \mathcal{C}_{\neg\varphi}$ consists of only a single state $(\bot, \top)$, then there is no information whatsoever that we can obtain from monitoring the property.

The above algorithm is simple enough to construct, however its complexity is doubly exponential in the size of the given LTL property. This may not be a problem, as the algorithm is performed off-line and the LTL specifications are often quite short.

We show that checking monitorability is in EXPSPACE-complete. The upper bound is achieved by a binary search version of this algorithm[4]. For the lower bound we show a reduction from checking if a property is (not) a liveness property, a problem known to be in EXPSPACE-complete [18,25].

- We first neutralize bad prefixes. Now, when ψ is satisfiable, then $\Diamond\psi$ is monitorable (specifically, any prefix can be completed into a *good* prefix) iff ψ has a good prefix.
- Checking satisfiability of a property ψ is in PSPACE-complete [26][5].
- ψ has a good prefix iff ψ is not a morbidity property, i.e., if $\varphi = \neg\psi$ is not a liveness property.
- Now, φ is *not* a liveness property iff either φ is not satisfiable or $\Diamond\neg\varphi$ is monitorable.

4.2 Runtime Verification for Propositional Past LTL

Algorithm

The algorithm for past LTL, first presented in [14], is based on the observation that the semantics of the past time formulas $\ominus\varphi$ and $(\varphi\,\mathcal{S}\,\psi)$ in the current step i is defined in terms of the semantics in the previous step $i-1$ of a subformula, here recalled from Sect. 2:

- $\xi,i \models \ominus\varphi$ iff $i > 1$ and $\xi, i-1 \models \varphi$.
- $\xi,i \models (\varphi\,\mathcal{S}\,\psi)$ iff $\xi,i \models \psi$ or the following hold: $i > 1$, $\xi,i \models \varphi$ and $\xi, i-1 \models (\varphi\,\mathcal{S}\,\psi)$.

One only needs to look one step, or event, backwards in order to compute the new truth value of a formula and its subformulas. The algorithm, shown below, operates on two vectors (arrays) of values indexed by subformulas: pre for the state before that event, and now for the current state (after the last seen event).

1. Initially, for each subformula φ, $\mathsf{now}(\varphi) := \textit{false}$.
2. Observe a new event (as a set of ground predicates) s as input.
3. Let $\mathsf{pre} := \mathsf{now}$.
4. Make the following updates for each subformula. If φ is a subformula of ψ then $\mathsf{now}(\varphi)$ is updated before $\mathsf{now}(\psi)$.
   - $\mathsf{now}(\textit{true}) := \textit{true}$.
   - $\mathsf{now}((\varphi \wedge \psi)) := \mathsf{now}(\varphi)$ *and* $\mathsf{now}(\psi)$.
   - $\mathsf{now}(\neg\varphi) := \textit{not }\mathsf{now}(\varphi)$.
   - $\mathsf{now}((\varphi\,\mathcal{S}\,\psi)) := \mathsf{now}(\psi)$ *or* $(\mathsf{now}(\varphi)$ *and* $\mathsf{pre}((\varphi\mathcal{S}\psi)))$.
   - $\mathsf{now}(\ominus\,\varphi) := \mathsf{pre}(\varphi)$.
5. Goto step 2.

---

[4] To show that a property is not monitorable, one needs to guess a state of $\mathcal{B}_\varphi \times \mathcal{B}_{\neg\varphi}$ and check that (1) it is reachable, and (2) one cannot reach from it an empty component, both for $\mathcal{B}_\varphi$ and for $\mathcal{B}_{\neg\varphi}$. (There is no need to construct $\mathcal{C}_\varphi$ or $\mathcal{C}_{\neg\varphi}$.)

[5] Proving that liveness was PSPACE-hard was shown in [3].

An Example

As an example[6], consider the formula $close \land \ominus open$, and suppose we evaluate it against the trace $open.close$ at step $i = 2$ (after seeing the $close$ event). The algorithm performs the following assignments, resulting in the formula becoming true (assuming that $\mathsf{pre}(open)$ is true):

$$\mathsf{now}(open) := false$$
$$\mathsf{now}(close) := true$$
$$\mathsf{now}(\ominus open) := \mathsf{pre}(open)$$
$$\mathsf{now}(close \land \ominus open) := \mathsf{now}(close) \land \mathsf{now}(\ominus open)$$

The above suggested algorithm *interprets* a formula on a trace. As an alternative we can *synthesize* a program that is specialized for monitoring the property as in [14]. Figure 2 (left) shows a generated monitor program for the property. Two Boolean valued arrays pre for the previous state and now are declared and operated on. The indices $0 \ldots 3$ correspond to the enumeration of the subformulas shown in the Abstract Syntax Tree (AST) in Fig. 2 (right). For each observed event, the function evaluate() computes the now array from highest to lowest index, and returns true (property is satisfied in this position of the trace) iff now(0) is *true*.

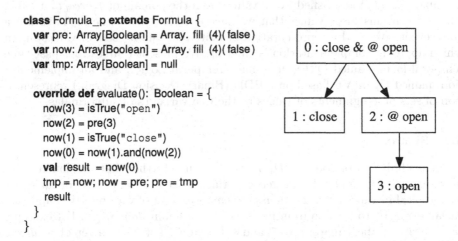

Fig. 2. Monitor (left) and AST (right) for propositional property.

---

[6] All examples of safety properties henceforth will omit the implied $\Box$ operator.

5   First-Order Past LTL

First-order past LTL allows universal and existential quantification over data occurring as parameters in events. Such events are referred to as *predicates* (or *parametric events*). Consider a predicate $open(f)$, indicating that a file f is being opened, and a predicate $close(f)$ indicating that f is being closed. We can formulate that a file cannot be closed unless it was opened before with the following first-order past LTL formula:

$$\forall f\,(close(f) \longrightarrow \mathbf{P}\,open(f)) \tag{1}$$

Here $\mathbf{P}$ is the "sometimes in the past" temporal operator. This property must be checked for every monitored event. Already in this very simple example we see that we need to store *all* the names of files that were previously opened so we can compare to the files that are being closed. A more refined specification would be the following, requiring that a file can be closed only if it was opened before, and has not been closed since. Here, we use the temporal operators $\ominus$ ("at previous step") and $\mathcal{S}$ ("since"):

$$\forall f\,(close(f) \longrightarrow \ominus(\neg close(f)\,\mathcal{S}\,open(f))) \tag{2}$$

One problem we need to solve is the unboundedness caused by negation. For example, assume that we have only observed so far one *close* event $close(\text{"ab"})$. The subformula $close(f)$ is therefore satisfied for the value $f = \text{"ab"}$. The subformula $\neg close(f)$ is satisfied by all values from the domain of f *except* for "ab". This set contains those values that we have not seen yet in the input within a *close* event. We need a representation of finite and infinite sets of values, upon which applying complementation is efficient. We present a first-order past time temporal logic, named QTL (Quantified Temporal Logic), and an implementation, named DEJA VU based on a BDD (Binary Decision Diagram) representation of sets of assignments of values to the free variables of subformulas.

5.1   Syntax

Assume a finite set of domains $D_1, D_2, \ldots$. Assume further that the domains are infinite, e.g., they can be the integers or strings[7]. Let V be a finite set of *variables*, with typical instances x, y, z. An *assignment* over a set of variables W maps each variable $x \in W$ to a value from its associated domain $domain(x)$. For example $[x \rightarrow 5, y \rightarrow \text{"abc"}]$ maps x to 5 and y to "abc". Let T be a set of *predicate names* with typical instances p, q, r. Each predicate name p is associated with some domain $domain(p)$. A predicate is constructed from a predicate name, and a variable or a constant of the same type. Thus, if the predicate name p and the variable x are associated with the domain of strings, we have predicates like $p(\text{"gaga"})$, $p(\text{"baba"})$ and $p(x)$. Predicates over constants are called *ground predicates*. An *event* is a finite set of ground predicates. For example, if $T = $

---

[7] For dealing with finite domains see [12].

$\{p, q, r\}$, then $\{p(\text{"xyzzy"}), q(3)\}$ is a possible event. An *execution* $\sigma = s_1 s_2 \ldots$ is a finite sequence of events.

For runtime verification, a property φ is interpreted on prefixes of a monitored sequence. We check whether φ holds for every such prefix, hence, conceptually, check whether $\Box\varphi$ holds, where $\Box$ is the "always in the future" linear temporal logic operator. The formulas of the core logic QTL are defined by the following grammar. For simplicity of the presentation, we define here the logic with unary predicates, but this is not due to any principle limitation, and, in fact, our implementation supports predicates with multiple arguments.

$$\varphi:: = true \mid p(a) \mid p(x) \mid (\varphi \wedge \varphi) \mid \neg\varphi \mid (\varphi \, \mathcal{S} \, \varphi) \mid \ominus\varphi \mid \exists x \, \varphi$$

The formula $p(a)$, where a is a constant in $domain(p)$, means that the ground predicate $p(a)$ occurs in the most recent event. The formula $p(x)$, for a variable $x \in V$, holds with a binding of x to the value a if a ground predicate $p(a)$ appears in the most recent event. The formula $(\varphi_1 \, \mathcal{S} \, \varphi_2)$ means that φ_2 held in the past (possibly now) and since then φ_1 has been true. The property $\ominus \varphi$ means that φ was true in the previous event. We can also define the following additional operators: $false = \neg true$, $(\varphi \vee \psi) = \neg(\neg\varphi \wedge \neg\psi)$, $(\varphi \longrightarrow \psi) = (\neg\varphi \vee \psi)$, $\mathbf{P} \, \varphi = (true \, \mathcal{S} \, \varphi)$ *(previously φ)*, $\mathbf{H} \, \varphi = \neg\mathbf{P} \, \neg\varphi$ *(historically φ, or φ always in the past)*, and $\forall x \, \varphi = \neg\exists x \neg\varphi$. The operator $[\varphi, \psi)$, borrowed from [16], has the same meaning as $(\neg\psi \, \mathcal{S} \, \varphi)$, but reads more naturally as an interval.

5.2   Semantics

Predicate Semantics

Let $free(\varphi)$ be the set of free (i.e., unquantified) variables of a subformula φ. Then $(\gamma, \sigma, i) \models \varphi$, where γ is an assignment over $free(\varphi)$, and $i \geq 1$, if φ holds for the prefix $s_1 s_2 \ldots s_i$ of the execution σ with the assignment γ. We denote by $\gamma|_{free(\varphi)}$ the restriction (projection) of an assignment γ to the free variables appearing in φ and by ϵ the empty assignment. The semantics of QTL can be defined as follows.

- $(\epsilon, \sigma, i) \models true$.
- $(\epsilon, \sigma, i) \models p(a)$ if $p(a) \in \sigma[i]$.
- $([x \mapsto a], \sigma, i) \models p(x)$ if $p(a) \in \sigma[i]$.
- $(\gamma, \sigma, i) \models (\varphi \wedge \psi)$ if $(\gamma|_{free(\varphi)}, \sigma, i) \models \varphi$ and $(\gamma|_{free(\psi)}, \sigma, i) \models \psi$.
- $(\gamma, \sigma, i) \models \neg\varphi$ if not $(\gamma, \sigma, i) \models \varphi$.
- $(\gamma, \sigma, i) \models (\varphi \mathcal{S} \psi)$ if $(\gamma|_{free(\psi)}, \sigma, i) \models \psi$ or the following hold: $i > 1$, $(\gamma|_{free(\varphi)}, \sigma, i) \models \varphi$, and $(\gamma, \sigma, i-1) \models (\varphi \mathcal{S} \psi)$.
- $(\gamma, \sigma, i) \models \ominus\varphi$ if $i > 1$ and $(\gamma, \sigma, i-1) \models \varphi$.
- $(\gamma, \sigma, i) \models \exists x \, \varphi$ if there exists $a \in domain(x)$ such that[8] $(\gamma[x \mapsto a], \sigma, i) \models \varphi$.

---

[8] $\gamma[x \mapsto a]$ is the overriding of γ with the binding $[x \mapsto a]$.

Set Semantics

It helps to present the BDD-based algorithm by first redefining the semantics of the logic in terms of sets of assignments satisfying a formula. Let $I[\varphi, \sigma, i]$ be the semantic function, defined below, that returns a set of assignments such that $\gamma \in I[\varphi, \sigma, i]$ iff $(\gamma, \sigma, i) \models \varphi$. The empty set of assignments $\emptyset$ behaves as the Boolean constant 0 and the singleton set that contains an assignment over an empty set of variables $\{\epsilon\}$ behaves as the Boolean constant 1. We define the union and intersection operators on sets of assignments, even if they are defined over non identical sets of variables. In this case, the assignments are extended over the union of the variables. Thus intersection between two sets of assignments A_1 and A_2 is defined like a database "join" operator; i.e., it consists of the assignments whose projection on the *common* variables agrees with an assignment in A_1 and with an assignment in A_2. Union is defined as the dual operator of intersection. Let A be a set of assignments over the set of variables W; we denote by $hide(A, x)$ (for "hiding" the variable x) the set of assignments obtained from A after removing from each assignment the mapping from x to a value. In particular, if A is a set of assignments over only the variable x, then $hide(A, x)$ is $\{\epsilon\}$ when A is nonempty, and $\emptyset$ otherwise. $A_{free(\varphi)}$ is the set of all possible assignments of values to the variables that appear free in φ. We add a 0 position for each sequence σ (which starts with s_1), where I returns the empty set for each formula. The assignment-set semantics of QTL is shown in the following. For all occurrences of i, it is assumed that $i > 0$.

- $I[\varphi, \sigma, 0] = \emptyset$.
- $I[true, \sigma, i] = \{\epsilon\}$.
- $I[p(a), \sigma, i] = $ if $p(a) \in \sigma[i]$ then $\{\epsilon\}$ else $\emptyset$.
- $I[p(x), \sigma, i] = \{[x \mapsto a] | p(a) \in \sigma[i]\}$.
- $I[(\varphi \wedge \psi), \sigma, i] = I[\varphi, \sigma, i] \bigcap I[\psi, \sigma, i]$.
- $I[\neg\varphi, \sigma, i] = A_{free(\varphi)} \setminus I[\varphi, \sigma, i]$.
- $I[(\varphi \, \mathcal{S} \, \psi), \sigma, i] = I[\psi, \sigma, i] \bigcup (I[\varphi, \sigma, i] \bigcap I[(\varphi \mathcal{S} \psi), \sigma, i - 1])$.
- $I[\ominus\varphi, \sigma, i] = I[\varphi, \sigma, i - 1]$.
- $I[\exists x \, \varphi, \sigma, i] = hide(I[\varphi, \sigma, i], x)$.

As before, the interpretation for the rest of the operators can be obtained from the above using the connections between the operators.

6   Runtime Verification for First-Order Past LTL

We describe an algorithm for monitoring QTL properties, first presented in [12] and implemented in the tool DEJA VU. To give a brief overview of the contents of this section, instead of storing the data values occurring in events, we enumerate these data values as soon as we see them and use Boolean encodings of this enumeration. We use BDDs to represent sets of such enumerations. For example, if the runtime verifier sees the input events *open*("a"), *open*("b"), *open*("c"), it will encode them as 000, 001 and 010 (say, we use 3 bits b_0, b_1 and b_2 to represent each enumeration, with b_2 being the most significant bit). A BDD that represents the set of values { "a", "c" } would be equivalent to a Boolean function $(\neg b_0 \wedge \neg b_2)$ that returns 1 for 000 and 010 (the value of b_1 can be arbitrary). This approach has the following benefits:

- It is highly compact. With k bits used for representing enumerations, the BDD can grow to $2^{\mathcal{O}(k)}$ nodes [6]; but BDDs usually compact the representation very well [8]. In fact, we often do not pay much in overhead for keeping surplus bits. Thus, we can start with an overestimated number of bits k such that it is unlikely to see more than 2^k different values for the domain they represent. We can also incrementally extend the BDD with additional bits when needed at runtime.
- Complementation (negation) is efficient, by just switching between the 0 and 1 leaves of the BDD. Moreover, even though at any point we may have not seen the entire set of values that will show up during the execution, we can safely (and efficiently) perform complementation: values that have not appeared yet in the execution are being accounted for and their enumerations are reserved already in the BDD before these values appear.
- Our representation of sets of assignments as BDDs allows a very simple algorithm that naturally extends the dynamic programming monitoring algorithm for propositional past time temporal logic shown in [14] and summarized in Sect. 4.2.

6.1 BDDs

We represent a set of assignments as an Ordered Binary Decision Diagram (OBDD, although we write simply BDD) [7]. A BDD is a compact representation for a Boolean valued function of type $\mathbb{B}^k \rightarrow \mathbb{B}$ for some $k > 0$ (where $\mathbb{B}$ is the Boolean domain $\{0, 1\}$), as a directed acyclic graph (DAG). A BDD is essentially a compact representation of a Boolean tree, where compaction glues together isomorphic subtrees. Each non-leaf node is labeled with one of the Boolean variables $b_0, \ldots, b_{k-1}$. A non-leaf node b_i is the source of two arrows leading to other nodes. A dotted-line arrow represents that b_i has the Boolean value 0, while a thick-line arrow represents that it has the value 1. The nodes in the DAG have the same order along all paths from the root. However, some of the nodes may be absent along some paths, when the result of the Boolean function does not depend on the value of the corresponding Boolean variable. Each path leads to a leaf node that is marked by either a 0 or a 1, representing the Boolean value returned by the function for the Boolean values on the path. Figure 3 contains five BDDs (a)-(e), over three Boolean variables b_0, b_1, and b_2 (referred to by their subscripts 0, 1, and 2), as explained below.

6.2 Mapping Data to BDDs

Assume that we see $p(\text{"ab"})$, $p(\text{"de"})$, $p(\text{"af"})$ and $q(\text{"fg"})$ in subsequent states in a trace, where p and q are predicates over the domain of strings. When a value associated with a variable appears for the first time in the current event (in a ground predicate), we add it to the set of values of that domain that were seen. We assign to each new value an *enumeration*, represented as a binary number, and use a hash table to point from the value to its enumeration.

Consistent with the DEJA VU implementation, the least significant bit in an enumeration is denoted in Fig. 3 (and in the rest of this paper) by BDD variable 0, and the most significant bit by BDD variable $n-1$, where n is the number of bits. Using e.g. a three-bit enumeration $b_2 b_1 b_0$, the first encountered value "ab" can be represented as the bit string 000, "de" as 001, "af" as 010 and "fg" as 011. A BDD for a subset of these values returns a 1 for each bit string representing an enumeration of a value in the set, and 0 otherwise. E.g. a BDD representing the set {"de", "af"} (2nd and 3rd values) returns 1 for 001 and 010. This is the Boolean function $\neg b_2 \wedge (b_1 \leftrightarrow \neg b_0)$. Figure 3 shows the BDDs for each of these values as well as the BDD for the set containing the values "de" and "af".

When representing a set of assignments for e.g. two variables x and y with k bits each, we will have Boolean variables $x_0, \ldots, x_{k-1}, y_0, \ldots, y_{k-1}$. A BDD will return a 1 for each bit string representing the concatenation of enumerations that correspond to the represented assignments, and 0 otherwise. For example, to represent the assignments $[x \mapsto$ "de", $y \mapsto$ "af"], where "de" is enumerated as 001 and "af" with 010, the BDD will return a 1 for 001010.

6.3   The BDD-based Algorithm

Given some ground predicate $p(a)$ observed in the execution matching with $p(x)$ in the monitored property, let **lookup**(x, a) be the enumeration of a. If this is a's first occurrence, then it will be assigned a new enumeration. Otherwise, **lookup** returns the enumeration that a received before. We can use a counter, for each variable x, counting the number of different values appearing so far for x. When a new value appears, this counter is incremented, and the value is converted to a Boolean representation. Enumerations that were not yet used represent the values not seen yet. In the next section we introduce data reclaiming, which allows reusing enumerations for values that no longer affect the checked property. This involves a more complicated enumeration mechanism.

The function **build**(x, A) returns a BDD that represents the set of assignments where x is mapped to (the enumeration of) v for $v \in A$. This BDD is independent of the values assigned to any variable other than x, i.e., they can have any value. For example, assume that we use three Boolean variables (bits) x_0, x_1 and x_2 for representing enumerations over x (with x_0 being the least significant bit), and assume that $A = \{a, b\}$, **lookup**$(x, a) = 011$, and **lookup**$(x, b) = 001$. Then **build**(x, A) is a BDD representation of the Boolean function $x_0 \wedge \neg x_2$.

Intersection and union of sets of assignments are translated simply to conjunction and disjunction of their BDD representation, respectively, and complementation becomes BDD negation. We will denote the Boolean BDD operators as **and**, **or** and **not**. To implement the existential (universal, respectively) operators, we use the BDD existential (universal, respectively) operators over the

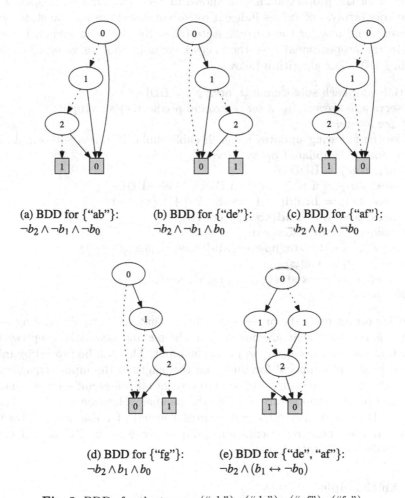

(a) BDD for {"ab"}:
$\neg b_2 \wedge \neg b_1 \wedge \neg b_0$

(b) BDD for {"de"}:
$\neg b_2 \wedge \neg b_1 \wedge b_0$

(c) BDD for {"af"}:
$\neg b_2 \wedge b_1 \wedge \neg b_0$

(d) BDD for {"fg"}:
$\neg b_2 \wedge b_1 \wedge b_0$

(e) BDD for {"de", "af"}:
$\neg b_2 \wedge (b_1 \leftrightarrow \neg b_0)$

Fig. 3. BDDs for the trace: $p("ab").p("de").p("af").q("fg")$.

Boolean variables that represent (the enumerations of) the values of x. Thus, if B_φ is the BDD representing the assignments satisfying φ in the current state of the monitor, then $\mathbf{exists}(\langle x_0, \ldots, x_{k-1} \rangle, B_\varphi)$ is the BDD that represents the assignments satisfying $\exists x\, \varphi$ in the current state. Finally, $\mathrm{BDD}(\bot)$ and $\mathrm{BDD}(\top)$ are the BDDs that return always 0 or 1, respectively.

The dynamic programming algorithm, shown below, works similarly to the algorithm for the propositional case shown in Sect. 4.2. That is, it operates on two vectors (arrays) of values indexed by subformulas: pre for the state before that event, and now for the current state (after the last seen event). However, while in the propositional case the vectors contain Boolean values, here they contain BDDs. The algorithm follows.

1. Initially, for each subformula φ, $\mathrm{now}(\varphi) := \mathrm{BDD}(\bot)$.
2. Observe a new event (as a set of ground predicates) s as input.
3. Let pre := now.
4. Make the following updates for each subformula. If φ is a subformula of ψ then $\mathrm{now}(\varphi)$ is updated before $\mathrm{now}(\psi)$.
   - $\mathrm{now}(true) := \mathrm{BDD}(\top)$.
   - $\mathrm{now}(p(a)) := $ if $p(a) \in s$ then $\mathrm{BDD}(\top)$ else $\mathrm{BDD}(\bot)$.
   - $\mathrm{now}(p(x)) := \mathbf{build}(x, A)$ where $A = \{a | p(a) \in s\}$.
   - $\mathrm{now}((\varphi \wedge \psi)) := \mathbf{and}(\mathrm{now}(\varphi), \mathrm{now}(\psi))$.
   - $\mathrm{now}(\neg\varphi) := \mathbf{not}(\mathrm{now}(\varphi))$.
   - $\mathrm{now}((\varphi \,\mathcal{S}\, \psi)) := \mathbf{or}(\mathrm{now}(\psi), \mathbf{and}(\mathrm{now}(\varphi), \mathrm{pre}((\varphi \mathcal{S} \psi))))$.
   - $\mathrm{now}(\ominus\, \varphi) := \mathrm{pre}(\varphi)$.
   - $\mathrm{now}(\exists x\, \varphi) := \mathbf{exists}(\langle x_0, \ldots, x_{k-1} \rangle, \mathrm{now}(\varphi))$.
5. Goto step 2.

An important property of the algorithm is that, at any point during monitoring, enumerations that are not used in the pre and now BDDs represent all values that have *not* been seen so far in the input. This can be proved by induction on the size of temporal formulas and the length of the input sequence. We specifically identify one enumeration to represent all values not seen yet, namely the largest possible enumeration, given the number of bits we use, $11 \ldots 11$. We let $(11 \ldots 11)$ denote the BDD that returns 1 exactly for this value. This trick allows us to use a finite representation and quantify existentially and universally over *all* values in infinite domains.

6.4   An Example

DEJA VU is implemented in SCALA. DEJA VU takes as input a specification file containing one or more properties, and synthesizes a self-contained SCALA program (a text file) - the monitor, as already illustrated for the propositional case in Sect. 4.2. This program (which first must be compiled) takes as input the trace file and analyzes it. The tool uses the JavaBDD library for BDD manipulations [15]. We shall illustrate the monitor generation using an example. Consider the following property stating that if a file f is closed, it must have been opened in the past with some access mode m (e.g. 'read' or 'write' mode):

$$\forall f\,(close(f) \longrightarrow \exists m\ \mathbf{P}\ open(f,m))$$

The property-specific part[9] of the synthesized monitor, shown in Fig. 4 (left), relies on the enumeration of the subformulas shown in Fig. 4 (right). As in the propositional case, two arrays are declared, indexed by subformula indexes: pre for the previous state and now for the current state, although here storing BDDs instead of Boolean values. For each observed event, the function evaluate() computes the now array from highest to lowest index, and returns true (property is satisfied in this position of the trace) iff now(0) is not BDD($\perp$). At composite subformula nodes, BDD operators are applied. For example for subformula 4, the new value is now(5).or(pre(4)), which is the interpretation of the formula $\mathbf{P}$ open(f, m) corresponding to the law: $\mathbf{P}\,\varphi = (\varphi \vee \ominus \mathbf{P}\,\varphi)$. As can be seen, for each new event, the evaluation of a formula results in the computation of a BDD for each subformula.

```
class Formula_p extends Formula {
  var pre: Array[BDD] = Array. fill (6)(False)
  var now: Array[BDD] = Array. fill (6)(False)
  var tmp: Array[BDD] = null
  val var_f :: var_m :: Nil =
    declareVariables("f", "m")

  override def evaluate(): Boolean = {
    now(5) = build("open")(V("f"),V("m"))
    now(4) = now(5).or(pre(4))
    now(3) = now(4).exist(var_m)
    now(2) = build("close")(V("f"))
    now(1) = now(2).not().or(now(3))
    now(0) = now(1).forAll (var_f)
    val result = !now(0).isZero
    tmp = now; now = pre; pre = tmp
    result
  }
}
```

Fig. 4. Monitor (left) and AST (right) for the property.

We shall briefly evaluate the example formula on a trace. Assume that each variable f and m is represented by three BDD bits. Consider the input trace, consisting of three events[10]:

$$open(\text{input,read}).\,open(\text{output,write}).\,close(\text{out})$$

----

[9] An additional 600+ lines of property independent boilerplate code is generated.

[10] Traces accepted by the tool are concretely in CSV format. For example the first event is a single line of the form: `open,input,read`.

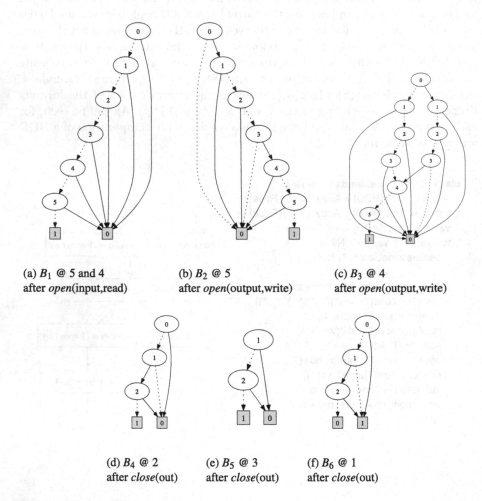

(a) B_1 @ 5 and 4
after *open*(input,read)

(b) B_2 @ 5
after *open*(output,write)

(c) B_3 @ 4
after *open*(output,write)

(d) B_4 @ 2
after *close*(out)

(e) B_5 @ 3
after *close*(out)

(f) B_6 @ 1
after *close*(out)

Fig. 5. Selected BDDs, named $B_1, \dots, B_6$, computed after each event at various sub-formula nodes, indicated by BDD B_i @ *node* (see Fig. 4), during processing of the trace: *open*(input,read).*open*(output,write).*close*(out).

When the monitor evaluates subformula 5 on the first event *open*(input, read), it will create a bit string composed of a bit string for each parameter f and m. As previously explained, bit strings for each variable are allocated in increasing order: 000, 001, 010,..., hence the first bit string representing the assignment [f ↦ input, m ↦ read] becomes 000000 where the three rightmost bits represent the assignment of input to f, and the three leftmost bits represent the assignment of read to m. Figure 5a shows the corresponding BDD B_1. Recall that most significant bits are implemented lower in the BDD, and that for each bit (node) in the BDD, the dotted arrow corresponds to this bit being 0 and the full drawn arrow corresponds to this bit being 1. In this BDD all bits have to be zero in order to be accepted by the function represented by the BDD. We will not show how all the tree nodes evaluate, except observe that node 5 assumes the same BDD value as node 4 (all the seen values in the past), and conclude that since no *close*(...) event has been observed, the top-level formula (node 0) is true at this position in the trace.

Upon the second *open*(output,write) event, new values (output,write) are observed as argument to the *open* event. Hence a new bit string for each variable f and m is allocated, in both cases 001 (the next unused bit string for each variable). The new combined bit string for the assignments satisfying subformula 5 then becomes 001001, forming a BDD representing the assignment [f ↦ output, m ↦ write], and appearing in Fig. 5b as B_2. The computation of the BDD for node 4 is computed by now(4) = now(5).or(pre(4)), which results in the BDD B_3, representing the set of the two so far observed assignments ($B_3 = \mathbf{or}(B_1, B_2)$).

Upon the third *close*(out) event, a new value out for f is observed, and allocated the bit pattern 010, represented by the BDD B_4 for subformula 2. At this point node 4 still evaluates to the BDD B_3 (unchanged from the previous step), and the existential quantification over m in node 3 results in the BDD B_5, where the bits 3, 4 and 5 for m have been removed, and the BDD compacted. Node 1 is computed as $\mathbf{or}(\mathbf{not}(B_4), B_5)$, which results in the BDD B_6. This BDD represents all bit patterns for f that are **not** 010, corresponding to the value: out. So for all such values the formula is true. This means, however, that the top-level formula in node 0 is not true (violated by bit pattern 010), and hence the formula is violated on the third event.

6.5   Dynamic Data Reclamation

Consider Property 1 on page 10 that asserts that each file that is closed was opened before. If we do not remember for this property *all* the files that were opened, then we will not be able to check when a file is closed whether it was opened before. Consider now the more refined Property 2 on page 10, requiring that a file can be closed only if it was opened before, and has not been closed. Observe here that if a file was opened and subsequently closed, then if it is closed again before opening, the property would be invalidated just as in the case where it was not opened at all. This means that we can "forget" that a file was opened when it is closed without affecting our ability to monitor the formula. This allows reusing enumerations of data values, when this does not affect the decision whether the property holds or not.

Let A be a set of assignments over some variables that include x. Denote by $A[x = a]$ the set of assignments from A in which the value of x is a. We say that the values a and b are *analogous* for variable x in A, if $hide(A[x = a], x) = hide(A[x = b], x)$. This means that a and b, as values of the variable x, are related to all other values in A in the same way. A value can be reclaimed if it is analogous to the values not seen yet in all the assignments represented in $pre(\psi)$, for each subformula ψ.

We shall now identify enumerations that can be reclaimed, and remove the values in the hash table that map to them, such that the enumerations can later be reused to represent new values. The search for reclaimable enumerations in a particular step during monitoring is performed on the pre BDDs. Recall that the enumeration $11 \ldots 11$ represents all the values that were *not* seen so far. Thus, we can check whether a value a for x is analogous to the values not seen so far for x by performing the checks on the pre BDDs between the enumeration of a and the enumeration $11 \ldots 11$. In fact, we do not have to perform the checks enumeration by enumeration, but use a BDD expression that constructs a BDD representing (returning 1 for) all enumerations that can be reclaimed for a variable x.

Assume that a subformula ψ has three free variables, x, y and z, each with k bits, i.e., $x_0, \ldots, x_{k-1}, y_0, \ldots, y_{k-1}$ and $z_0, \ldots, z_{k-1}$. The following expression returns a BDD representing the enumerations for values of x in assignments represented by $pre(\psi)$ that are related to enumerations of y and z in the same way as $11 \ldots 11$.

$$I_{\psi,x} = \forall y_0 \ldots \forall y_{k-1} \forall z_0 \ldots \forall z_{k-1} (pre(\psi)[x_0 \setminus 1, \ldots x_{k-1} \setminus 1] \leftrightarrow pre(\psi))$$

We now conjoin the above formula over each subformula that has a temporal operator at the outermost level, and subtract from this conjunction the $11 \ldots 11$ enumeration. This becomes the BDD *avail* of available enumerations. Any enumeration that is in *avail* can be reclaimed, and later reused as the enumeration of a new value. The selection of a "free" enumeration from *avail* can be performed by a SAT solver that picks any enumeration that satisfies it, followed by removing that enumeration from *avail* to indicate that it is no longer available. Note that if a value later reappears after its enumeration was reclaimed, it is likely to be assigned a different enumeration.

7   Conclusion

We presented a collection of runtime verification algorithms for linear temporal logics. First we introduced propositional temporal logic, including future as well as past time operators. We presented a theory of monitorability of temporal properties, introducing classes that reflect different degrees of monitorability. The notion of monitorability identifies the kinds of verdicts that one can obtain from observing finite prefixes of an execution. We then presented monitoring algorithms for the future time case as automata, and for the past time case as an instance of dynamic programming. We also provided algorithms for checking what kind of verdict (positive or negative) we can expect after monitoring a certain prefix against a given property, and whether a property is monitorable or not. We then introduced first-order past time linear temporal logic, and a monitoring algorithm for it. While the propositional version is independent of the length of the prefix seen so far, the first-order version may need to represent an amount of values that can grow linearly with the number of data values observed so far. The challenge is to provide a compact representation that will grow slowly and can be updated quickly with each incremental calculation that is performed per each new monitored event. We used a BDD representation of sets of assignments for the variables that appear in the monitored property.

References

1. Alpern, B., Schneider, F.B.: Recognizing safety and liveness. Distrib. Comput. **2**(3), 117–126 (1987)
2. Bartocci, E., Falcone, Y., Francalanza, A., Reger, G.: Introduction to runtime verification. In: Bartocci, E., Falcone, Y. (eds.) Lectures on Runtime Verification. LNCS, vol. 10457, pp. 1–33. Springer, Cham (2018). https://doi.org/10.1007/978-3-319-75632-5_1
3. Basin, D.A., Jiménez, C.C., Klaedtke, F., Zalinescu, E.: Deciding safety and liveness in TPTL. Inf. Process. Lett. **114**(12), 680–688 (2014)
4. Bauer, A., Leucker, M., Schallhart, C.: The good, the bad, and the ugly, but how ugly is ugly? In: Sokolsky, O., Taşıran, S. (eds.) RV 2007. LNCS, vol. 4839, pp. 126–138. Springer, Heidelberg (2007). https://doi.org/10.1007/978-3-540-77395-5_11
5. Bauer, A., Leucker, M., Schallhart, C.: Runtime verification for LTL and TLTL. ACM Trans. Softw. Eng. Method. **20**(4), 14:1–14:64 (2011)
6. Bryant, R.E.: On the complexity of VLSI implementations and graph representations of Boolean functions with application to integer multiplication. IEEE Trans. Comput. **40**(2), 205–213 (1991)
7. Bryant, R.E.: Symbolic Boolean manipulation with ordered binary-decision diagrams. ACM Comput. Surv. **24**(3), 293–318 (1992)
8. Burch, J.R., Clarke, E.M., McMillan, K.L., Dill, D.L., Hwang, L.J.: Symbolic model checking: 10^{20} states and beyond. In: LICS 1990, pp. 428–439 (1990)
9. Falcone, Y., Fernandez, J.-C., Mounier, L.: What can you verify and enforce at runtime? STTT **14**(3), 349–382 (2012)
10. Gabbay, D., Pnueli, A., Shelah, S., Stavi, J.: On the temporal analysis of fairness. In: POPL 1980, pp. 163–173. ACM (1980)
11. Gerth, R., Peled, D.A., Vardi, M.Y., Wolper, P.: Simple on-the-fly automatic verification of linear temporal logic. In: PSTV 1995, pp. 3–18 (1995)
12. Havelund, K., Peled, D., Ulus, D.: First-order temporal logic monitoring with BDDs. In: FMCAD 2017, pp. 116–123. IEEE (2017)
13. Havelund, K., Reger, G., Thoma, D., Zălinescu, E.: Monitoring events that carry data. In: Bartocci, E., Falcone, Y. (eds.) Lectures on Runtime Verification. LNCS, vol. 10457, pp. 61–102. Springer, Cham (2018). https://doi.org/10.1007/978-3-319-75632-5_3

14. Havelund, K., Roşu, G.: Synthesizing monitors for safety properties. In: Katoen, J.-P., Stevens, P. (eds.) TACAS 2002. LNCS, vol. 2280, pp. 342–356. Springer, Heidelberg (2002). https://doi.org/10.1007/3-540-46002-0_24
15. JavaBDD. http://javabdd.sourceforge.net
16. Kim, M., Kannan, S., Lee, I., Sokolsky, O.: Java-MaC: a run-time assurance tool for Java. In: RV 2001. Elsevier (2001). ENTCS **55**(2), 218–235
17. Kupferman, O., Vardi, M.Y.: Model checking of safety properties. Formal Methods Syst. Des. **19**(3), 291–314 (2001)
18. Kupferman, O., Vardi, G.: On relative and probabilistic finite counterability. Formal Methods Syst. Des. **52**(2), 117–146 (2018)
19. Lamport, L.: Proving the correctness of multiprocess programs. IEEE Trans. Softw. Eng. **3**(2), 125–143 (1977)
20. Manna, Z., Pnueli, A.: Completing the temporal picture. Theor. Comput. Sci. **83**, 91–130 (1991)
21. Markey, N.: Temporal logic with past is exponentially more succinct, concurrency column. Bull. EATCS **79**, 122–128 (2003)
22. Meredith, P.O., Jin, D., Griffith, D., Chen, F., Rosu, G.: An overview of the MOP runtime verification framework. STTT **14**(3), 249–289 (2012). Springer
23. Peled, D., Havelund, K.: Refining the safety-liveness classification of temporal properties according to monitorability. LNCS (2018, submitted)
24. Pnueli, A., Zaks, A.: PSL model checking and run-time verification via testers. In: Misra, Jayadev, Nipkow, Tobias, Sekerinski, Emil (eds.) FM 2006. LNCS, vol. 4085, pp. 573–586. Springer, Heidelberg (2006). https://doi.org/10.1007/11813040_38
25. Sistla, A.P.: Safety, liveness and fairness in temporal logic. Formal Aspects Comput. **6**(5), 495–512 (1994)
26. Sistla, A.P., Clarke, E.M.: The complexity of propositional linear temporal logics. In: STOC 1982, pp. 159–168 (1982). J. ACM (JACM), **32**(3), 733–749, July 1985. JACM Homepage archive
27. Thomas, W.: Automata on infinite objects. In: Handbook of Theoretical Computer Science, Volume B: Formal Models and Semantics, pp. 133–192 (1990)

Monitoring Smart Contracts: ContractLarva and Open Challenges Beyond

Shaun Azzopardi[1], Joshua Ellul[1,2], and Gordon J. Pace[1,2(✉)]

[1] Department of Computer Science, University of Malta, Msida, Malta
gordon.pace@um.edu.mt
[2] Centre for Distributed Ledger Technologies, University of Malta, Msida, Malta

Abstract. Smart contracts present new challenges for runtime verification techniques, due to features such as immutability of the code and the notion of gas that must be paid for the execution of code. In this paper we present the runtime verification tool CONTRACTLARVA and outline its use in instrumenting monitors in smart contracts written in Solidity, for the Ethereum blockchain-based distributed computing platform. We discuss the challenges faced in doing so, and how some of these can be addressed, using the ERC-20 token standard to illustrate the techniques. We conclude by proposing a list of open challenges in smart contract and blockchain monitoring.

1   Introduction

Although the general principles of runtime monitoring and verification are well established [5,15,24], applying these techniques and building tool support for new architectures frequently brings to the fore challenges in dealing with certain aspects of the architecture. Over the past few years, the domain of blockchain and distributed ledger technologies has increased in importance and pervasion, and with it came an arguably new software paradigm or architecture, that of smart contracts. Borrowing much from a multitude of existing technologies, including distributed computing and transaction-based systems, brings forth a new set of challenges for runtime monitoring and verification. In this paper, we expose our runtime verification tool CONTRACTLARVA for monitoring smart contracts, and discuss the open challenges in adapting dynamic verification for this domain.

The key novel idea behind distributed ledger technologies (DLTs), is how to achieve an implementation of a distributed and decentralised ledger, typically guaranteeing properties such as transaction immutability[1] i.e. achieving a form of ledger synchronisation without the need for central points of trust. Blockchain was one of the first algorithmic solutions proposed to achieve these

---

[1] In this context, one typically finds the use of the term *immutability* for immutability of transactions or data written in the past, whilst still allowing for appending new entries (in a controlled manner) to the ledger.

C. Colombo and M. Leucker (Eds.): RV 2018, LNCS 11237, pp. 113–137, 2018.
https://doi.org/10.1007/978-3-030-03769-7_8

goals, with the underlying ledger being used to enable keeping track of transactions in Bitcoin [26], the first instance of a cryptocurrency. Since then, various extensions and variants were proposed, with one major idea being that of *smart contracts*, allowing not only the immutable storage of transactions, but also that of logic which may perform such transactions. Smart contracts thus enable the enforcement of complex exchanges (possibly consisting of multiple transactions) between parties in an indisputable and immutable manner.

Smart contracts in themselves are not a new concept. They were originally proposed by Nick Szabo in 1996 [30] as *"contracts [. . .] robust against naïve vandalism and against sophisticated, incentive compatible breach."* Szabo's view was that while legal contracts typically specify ideal behaviour — the way things should be — e.g. *"The seller is obliged to deliver the ordered items on time,"* nothing stops the parties involved from behaving outside these bounds[2], a smart contract would *enforce* the behaviour, effectively ensuring that it is not violated in the first place. As most eminently highlighted by Lessig, *"code is law"* [23] — what code allows the parties to do or stops them from doing, effectively acts as theoretically inviolable legislation. The smart contract thus would typically chooses a path of action which ensures compliance with the agreement the parties have in mind. However, nothing stops the party entrusted with executing the code from modifying it or its behaviour, hence there remains the requirement of 4a regulatory structure to safeguard that such modifications do not occur — in practice, simply moving the need for a legal contract one step away.

Blockchain, however, provided a means of doing away with the need for such centralised trust in or legal agreement with the party executing the code, and the first realisation of this notion was the Ethereum blockchain [32], which supported smart contracts in the form of executable code running on a decentralised virtual machine, the Ethereum Virtual Machine (EVM), on the blockchain.

For instance, consider the natural language (legal) contract regulating a procurement process between a buyer and a seller, as shown in Fig. 1. Clause 8 states that: *"Upon placing an order, the buyer is obliged to ensure that there is enough money in escrow to cover payment of all pending orders."* This may be achieved in different ways. For example, this may be achieved by receiving payment upon the creation of every new order. However, since (according to clause 3) the buyer will already have put in escrow payment for the minimum number of items to be ordered, one may choose to use these funds as long as there are enough to cover the newly placed order, still satisfying clause 3. The legal contract does not enforce either of these behaviours, but rather insists that the overall effect is that of ensuring funds are available in escrow. In contrast, a (deterministic) executable enforcement of the contract would have to choose one of the behaviours to be executed.

The question as to whether specifications should be executable or not has a long history in computer science (see [17] vs. [20]). Executable specifications require a description of *how* to achieve a desired state as opposed to simply

---

[2] In practice, what stops these parties from doing so is the threat to be sued for breach of contract, which happens outside the realm of the contract itself.

1. *This contract is between ⟨buyer-name⟩, henceforth referred to as 'the buyer' and ⟨seller-name⟩, henceforth referred to as 'the seller'. The contract will hold until either party requests its termination.*
2. *The buyer is obliged to order at least ⟨minimum-items⟩, but no more than ⟨maximum-items⟩ items for a fixed price ⟨price⟩ before the termination of this contract.*
3. *Notwithstanding clause 1, no request for termination will be accepted before ⟨contract-end-date⟩. Furthermore, the seller may not terminate the contract as long as there are pending orders.*
4. *Upon enactment of this contract, the buyer is obliged to place the cost of the minimum number of items to be ordered in escrow.*
5. *Upon accepting this contract, the seller is obliged to place the amount of ⟨performance-guarantee⟩ in escrow.*
6. *Upon termination of the contract, the seller is guaranteed to have received payment covering the cost of the minimum number of items to be ordered unless less than this amount is delivered, in which case the cost of the undelivered items is not guaranteed.*
7. *The buyer has the right to place an order for an amount of items and a specified time-frame as long as (i) the running number of items ordered does not exceed the maximum stipulated in clause 2; and (ii) the time-frame must be of at least 24 hours, but may not extend beyond the contract end date specified in clause 2.*
8. *Upon placing an order, the buyer is obliged to ensure that there is enough money in escrow to cover payment of all pending orders.*
9. *Upon delivery, the seller receives payment of the order.*
10. *Upon termination of the contract, any undelivered orders are automatically cancelled, and the seller loses the right to receive payment for these orders.*
11. *Upon termination of the contract, if either any orders were undelivered or more than 25% of the orders were delivered late, the buyer has the right to receive the performance guarantee placed in escrow according to clause 5. Otherwise, it is released back to the seller.*

Fig. 1. A legal contract regulating a procurement process.

describing *what* that state should look like in a declarative specification — and the 'how' is often more complex than the 'what'[3], and leaves more room for error.

The possibility of error is a major issue. Smart contracts, being executable artifacts, do exactly what they say they do, but that might not be what the contract should have done. As smart contracts grow in size and complexity, this issue becomes more worrying, and there have been well-known instances of such smart contracts that allow for misbehaviour, for instance, on Ethereum [4]. Ideally, the correctness of smart contracts is verified statically at compile time, but using automated static analysis techniques to prove business-logic level properties of smart contracts has had limited success, with most work focussing on classes of non-functional bugs. This leaves great scope for runtime verification to provide guarantees over smart contracts.

In this paper, we present CONTRACTLARVA[4], a tool for the runtime verification of smart contracts written in Solidity, a smart contract programming language originally proposed for the use on Ethereum, but now also used on other blockchain systems. We summarise the salient features of Solidity in Sect. 2, and discuss the design of CONTRACTLARVA in Sect. 3. Given the immutable nature of smart contracts, bugs can be a major issue since simply updating the code

---

[3] NP-complete problems are a classical case of this — although there is no known deterministic polynomial algorithm which can find a solution to instances of any one of these problems, a known solution to an NP-complete problem instance can be verified in polynomial time on a deterministic machine.

[4] Available from https://github.com/gordonpace/contractLarva.

may not be an option. We discuss how this can be addressed using dynamic verification in Sect. 4. There are many other open challenges in smart contract monitoring, some of which are discussed in Sect. 5, while in Sect. 6 we discuss existing work in verification of smart contracts. Finally, we conclude in Sect. 7.

2   Smart Contracts and Solidity

Blockchains provide a decentralised means of a shared ledger which is tamper-proof and verifiable. Smart contracts built on a blockchain (like Ethereum) allow for decentralised execution of code, which could implement agreements between different parties, similarly in a tamperproof and verifiable manner. Solidity is the most popular language used to write Ethereum smart contracts. Solidity gets compiled down to EVM bytecode — a 256-bit stack-based instruction set which the Ethereum virtual machine will execute. At the bytecode execution level, the EVM can be seen as a 'one world computer' — a single shared abstract computer that can execute smart contract code. Once a smart contract is compiled to EVM bytecode, the contract may be uploaded and enacted on the blockchain having it reside at a particular address, thus allowing external entities to trigger its behaviour through function calls — therefore a smart contract's publicly executable functions represents the contract's Application Programming Interface (API). Functions are atomic i.e. they execute from beginning to end without interruption, and the EVM is single threaded which implies that only one function, or rather one instruction from all smart contracts is executed at a time, even though the EVM is distributed amongst all nodes. This implies that a long running function, or more so a function that never terminates, would slow down or stop all other smart contracts on the platform from executing. To prevent this, Ethereum requires an amount of *gas* to be sent by the initiator to be used to pay for the execution of code. If the gas runs out, then execution stops and all state changed since execution initiation is reverted. This mechanism ensures that infinite loops will eventually stop since the finite amount of gas associated with the execution will eventually run out. Although EVM bytecode is Turing complete, this limitation creates disincentives for creating sophisticated and resource-intensive smart contracts.

Using Solidity, the procurement legal contract from Fig. 1 can be transformed into a smart contract — the associated interface is shown in Listing 1. The contract allows the seller and buyer to invoke behaviour (such as placing an order, terminating the contract and specifying that a delivery was made).

We will now highlight Solidity's salient features required to appreciate this work. Solidity allows standard enumerated types (e.g. line 2 in Listing 1), and key-value associative arrays or mappings (e.g. line 4 defines a mapping from a 16-bit unsigned integer to an `Order` structure used to map from the order number to information, and line 7 of Listing 2 shows how the values can be accessed).

Functions can be defined as (i) `private`: can only be accessed by the smart contract itself; (ii) `internal`: the contract itself and any contract extending it can access the function; (iii) `external`: can be accessed from an external call;

Listing 1. The interface of a smart contract regulating procurement in Solidity.

```
 1   contract ProcurementContract {
 2     enum ContractStatus {Open, Closed}
 3     ContractStatus public status;
 4     mapping (uint16 => Order) public orders;
 5     ...
 6
 7     function ProcurementContract(
 8       uint _endDate, uint _price,
 9       uint _minimumItems, uint _maximumItems
10     ) public { ... }
11
12     function acceptProcurementContract() public { ... }
13
14     function placeOrder(
15       uint16 _orderNumber, uint _itemsOrdered,
16       uint _timeOfDelivery
17     ) public { ... }
18
19     function deliveryMade(
20       uint16 _orderNumber
21     ) public byBuyer { ... }
22
23     function terminateContract() public { ... }
24   }
```

and (iv) `public`: can be called from anywhere. These access modifiers only define from where a function can be called but not who can call such functions — a `public` function could be called from anyone. As part of a contract it is important to define which parties can initiate different contract functions.

Function *modifiers* provide a convenient reusable method to define ways of modifying the behaviour of functions in a uniform manner, such as this validation logic. Line 1 in Listing 2 defines a `byBuyer` modifier which checks whether the function invoker, retrieved using `msg.sender`, is indeed the `buyer` (the buyer's address would have had to be specified somewhere else in the contract), with the underscore indicating the execution of the original code of the function being affected by this modifier. Solidity provides such language construct validation guards including `require` which allows for testing of conditions in which case if the condition does not hold, execution will halt and all state changes will be reverted (this can also be done with the `revert()` instruction). It is worth noting that `revert` bubbles up normal function calls i.e. when a function call results in a revert, the calling function also fails and reverts. The only way to stop such revert cascades is to explicitly invoke the called function of another contract using the low-level `addr.call(...)` EVM opcode which calls the function given as parameter of the contract residing at the given address, but which returns a

Listing 2. Part of the implementation of the procurement smart contract.

```
1    modifier byBuyer {
2      require(msg.sender==buyer);
3      _;
4    }
5
6    function deliveryMade(uint16 _orderNumber) public
         byBuyer {
7      Order memory order = orders[_orderNumber];
8      // Ensure that the order exists and has
9      // not yet been delivered
10     require(
11       order.exists && order.status != OrderStatus.
           Delivered
12     );
13     // Order state update
14     order.status = OrderStatus.Delivered;
15     // Contract state update
16     if (order.deliveryTimeDue < now) {
17       lateOrdersCount++;
18     } else {
19       inTimeOrdersCount++;
20     }
21     // Sign delivery with the courier service
22     courierContract.call(
23       bytes4(keccak256("sign(uint256)")), buyer
24     );
25     // Pay the seller
26     seller.transfer(order.cost);
27
28     emit DeliveryMade(_orderNumber);
29   }
30
31   event DeliveryMade(uint16 _orderNumber);
```

boolean value stating whether the call failed or not. Line 19 triggers a signature on a separate contract with the courier, but avoiding the delivery to fail if the signature does not go through for whatever reason. If the call is to be made to a function from another contract, but within the state space of the current one (i.e. having access to the data and functions of the calling contract), a similar opcode `addr.delegatecall(...)` can be used.

The `byBuyer` modifier is used in line 6 to ensure that function `deliveryMade` can only be called by the buyer. Note how the underscore at line 3 specifies that the associated function logic (in this case `deliveryMade()`) should be performed after executing line 2.

Each smart contract inherently is also an Ethereum account, allowing it to hold Ether (Ethereum's cryptocurrency) as well as transfer it to other accounts. Incoming transfers are done with function calls which are tagged as `payable`, which enable the caller to send funds when triggering the function. Outgoing transfers can be done using the `addr.transfer(amount)` function, which sends the specified amount of cryptocurrency to the given address. For example, line 21 in Listing 2 performs a transfer of the amount of `order.cost` from the smart contract's internal account to the `seller` account. Finally, Solidity smart contracts can emit events that may be listened to (asynchronously) by applications off the chain. For example, a mobile application can listen to the event defined on line 26, and triggered on line 23 — thus notifying the seller that the buyer has acknowledged receipt and has affected payment.

3   Runtime Verification of Solidity Smart Contracts

CONTRACTLARVA is a runtime verification tool for contracts written in Solidity. It works at the Solidity source level of the smart contract and since once deployed, the code of a smart contract is immutable, it is meant to be applied before deployment. As shown in Fig. 2, extra code is instrumented into the smart contract based on a given specification, to add runtime checks ensuring that any violation of the specification is detected and may thus be reacted upon.

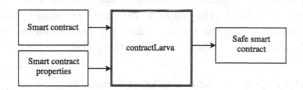

Fig. 2. Workflow using CONTRACTLARVA

The tool takes (i) a smart contract written in Solidity; and (ii) a specification written using an automaton-based formalism based on that used in the Larva runtime verification tool for Java [13], and produces a new smart contract which is functionally identical to the original as long as the specification is not violated, but has additional code to (i) track the behaviour of the smart contract with respect to the specification; and (ii) deal with violations as given in the specification.

3.1   Runtime Points-of-Interest in Smart Contracts

In any dynamic analysis technique with temporal specifications that express what should happen and in which order, one key element is the identification of which points during the execution of a smart contract can be captured by the analysis and thus analysed at runtime. These points-of-interest, or events[5] typically require balancing between what is required to specify the correctness of the system, with what can be efficiently extracted. Given that CONTRACTLARVA works at the source level, it makes sense to annotate points in the control flow of the smart contract in order to generate events when reached. Also of interest are updates to the global state (variable) which may happen at different control points e.g. the status of the procurement contract (whether it is proposed, active or terminated) is set in different functions, even though one may want to ensure that a terminated contract is never reactivated, thus requiring reasoning about runtime points when the status variable is updated. For this reason, CONTRACT-LARVA also allows the capture of data-flow points-of-interest. These are the two types of events which can be used in CONTRACTLARVA:

1. *Control-flow triggers* which trigger when a function is called or control exits that function: (a) `before:function`, triggers whenever `function` is called and before any of the function's code is executed; and (b) `after:function`, triggers the moment `function` terminates successfully (i.e. not reverted). In both cases, the value of the parameters can be accessed by being specified in the event e.g. `before:deliveryMade(_orderId)`, but may be left out if they are not used.
2. *Data-flow triggers*, trigger when an assignment on a global variable occurs (even if the value of the variable does not change) — `var@(condition)` triggers whenever variable `var` is assigned to (just after the assignment is performed), with the `condition` holding. The condition in variable assignment triggers can refer to the value of variable `var` before assignment using `LARVA_previous_var` e.g. to trigger when the procurement contract status goes from `Closed` to `Open`, one would use the event:

```
status@(
  LARVA_previous_status==ContractStatus.Closed &&
  status==ContractStatus.Open
)
```

It is worth remarking that all events trigger if they happen during an execution which succeeds (that is, not reverted). For instance, the control flow event `before:deliveryMade` would not be triggered when `deliveryMade` is called with an order number which does not exist and thus result in a revert due to a `require` statement. Similarly, if `deliveryMade` is called with insufficient gas to execute successfully, the event would not trigger.

3.2 Specifying Properties

In order to characterise correct and incorrect behaviour, CONTRACTLARVA uses automaton-based specifications in the form of dynamic event automata (DEAs)

---

[5] The choice of the term *event*, frequently used in runtime verification, is unfortunately overloaded with the notion of events in Solidity. In the rest of the paper, we use the term to refer to runtime points-of-interest.

— finite state automata with symbolic state, based on *dynamic automata with timers and events* (DATEs) used for specifications in Larva [13] but lacking timers and quantification, and *quantified event automata* (QEAs) as used in MarQ [29], but lacking quantification.

A DEA consists of a deterministic automaton, listening to contract event triggers. A number of the states are annotated as bad states which, when reached, denote that a violation has occurred, and other annotated as accepting states denoting that when reached, the trace has been accepted and monitoring is no longer required. DEAs thus categorise traces into three sets: rejected traces, accepted ones and others which cannot yet be given a verdict. The automata used are, however, symbolic automata — in that they may use and manipulate monitoring variables. Transitions are annotated by a triple: $e \mid c \mapsto a$, where (i) e is the event which will trigger the transition, (ii) c is a condition over the state of the smart contract and the symbolic monitoring state determining whether the transition is to be taken, and finally (iii) a is an executable action (code) which may have a side-effect on the monitoring state, and which will be executed if the transition is taken. Both condition and action can be left out if the condition is true or no action is to be taken respectively.

For instance, consider clause 6 of the legal contract which states that *"Upon termination of the contract, the seller is guaranteed to have received payment covering the cost of the minimum number of items to be ordered unless less than this amount is delivered, in which case the cost of the undelivered items is not guaranteed."* Figure 3(a) shows how this clause may be implemented. The DEA keeps track of (i) the number of items delivered (in a monitoring variable `delivered`); and (ii) the amount of money transferred to the seller (in the variable `payment`). If the contract is closed and the seller has not yet been sufficiently paid (for the minimum number of items to be ordered less any undelivered items), the DEA goes to a bad state marked with a cross. On the other hand, if during the lifetime of the contract, the seller has already received payment for the minimum number of items to be ordered, the DEA goes to an accepting state (marked with a checkmark) indicating that the property can no longer be violated. Note that any events happening not matching any outgoing transition of the current state leave the DEA in the same state.

However, runtime verification can be used to go beyond ensuring that the smart contract really enforces the legal contract. For instance, although not part of the legal contract, one may expect that the implementation ensures that once the procurement contract is terminated, it cannot be reactivated, a specification of which written using a DEA is shown in Fig. 3(b).

Formally, DEAs are defined as follows:

Definition 1. *A dynamic event automaton (DEA) defined over a set of monitorable events or points-of-interest Σ and system states Ω, is a tuple $\mathcal{M} = \langle Q, \Theta, q_0, \theta_0, B, A, t \rangle$, where (i) Q is a finite set of explicit monitoring states of the DEA; (ii) Θ is a (possibly infinite) set of symbolic monitoring states of $\mathcal{M}$; (iii) $q_0 \in Q$ and $\theta_0 \in \Theta$ are the initial explicit and symbolic state of $\mathcal{M}$; (iv) $B \subseteq Q$ and $A \subseteq Q$ are respectively the* bad *and* accepting *states of the*

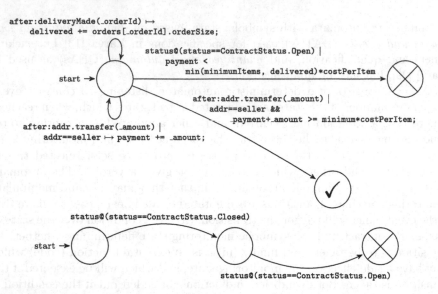

Fig. 3. (a) DEA encoding clause 6 of the procurement contract; and (b) Once terminated, the contract cannot be reactivated.

automaton; and (v) $t \subseteq Q \times \Sigma \times (\Theta \times \Omega \to Bool) \times (\Theta \to \Theta) \times Q$ *is the transition relation of* $\mathcal{M}$.

We will write $(q, \theta) \xrightarrow{e, \varphi}$ *to mean that* $\forall (q, e, c, a, q') \in t \cdot \neg c(\theta, \omega)$.

Informally, $(q, e, c, a, q') \in t$ denotes that if (i) the DEA is in state q; (ii) event e occurs; and (iii) condition c holds, then action a will be executed, updating the monitoring state from θ to $a(\theta)$, and the DEA moves to state q'. Formally the operational semantics are defined as follows:

Definition 2. *The configuration of a smart contract is a pair in* $Q \times \Theta$. *The operational semantics of a DEA* $\mathcal{M}$ *is given by the labelled transition relation over configurations such that* $(q, \theta) \xrightarrow{e, \omega} (q', \theta')$ *holds if and only if, upon receiving event* $e \in \Sigma$ *when the smart contract is in state* $\omega \in \Omega$, *the monitor evolves from explicit state* q *and symbolic state* θ *to* q' *and* θ':

$$\frac{(q, e, c, a, q') \in t \qquad c(\theta, \omega)}{(q, \theta) \xrightarrow{e, \omega} (q', a(\theta))} \ q \notin A \cup B$$

$$\frac{(q, \theta) \xrightarrow{e, \varphi}}{(q, \theta) \xrightarrow{e, \omega} (q, \theta)} \qquad \frac{q \in A \cup B}{(q, \theta) \xrightarrow{e, \omega} (q, \theta)}$$

The relation is extended over lists of observations, and we write $(q, \theta) \xRightarrow{w} (q', \theta')$ *(where* $w \in (\Sigma \times \Omega)^*$*) to denote the smallest relation such that: (i)*

$\forall q \in Q,\ \theta \in \Theta \cdot (q,\theta) \overset{\varepsilon}{\Rightarrow} (q,\theta);$ and (ii) for all $q, q' \in Q,\ \theta, \theta' \in \Theta,\ e \in \Sigma,$ $\omega \in \Omega,\ (q,\theta) \xRightarrow{(e,\omega):w} (q',\theta')$ if and only if for some $q_m \in Q$ and $\theta_m \in \Theta,$ $(q,\theta) \xrightarrow{e,\omega} (q_m, \theta_m)$ and $(q_m, \theta_m) \overset{w}{\Rightarrow} (q', \theta').$

The set of bad (respectively accepting) traces of a DEA $\mathcal{M}$, written $\mathcal{B}(\mathcal{M})$ (respectively $\mathcal{A}(\mathcal{M})$) is the set of traces which lead to a bad (respectively accepting) state: $\mathcal{B}(\mathcal{M}) \overset{df}{=} \{w \mid (q_0, \theta_0) \overset{w}{\Rightarrow} (q_b, \theta) \wedge q_b \in B\}$ and $\mathcal{A}(\mathcal{M}) \overset{df}{=} \{w \mid (q_0, \theta_0) \overset{w}{\Rightarrow} (q_a, \theta) \wedge q_a \in A\}.$

3.3 Reparation Strategies

One of the major challenges with smart contracts is what to do when a violation is detected. Runtime verification on traditional systems typically results in a bug report being filed, and code fixes to be released if the bug is deemed serious enough. In case of the state of the system being compromised due to the issue, the offending actions may be rolled back or manual intervention takes place to ensure correct future performance. In smart contracts reparation to deal with failure which already took place is typically not possible. The (by default) immutable nature of smart contracts means that bug fixes are not necessarily possible and transactions written to the blockchain cannot be easily undone. Immutability comes with caveats (we address this in Sect. 4) but modification of smart contracts and past transactions goes against the very selling point of using public blockchains: decentralised immutability of smart contracts and transactions.

We typically use dynamic analysis out of necessity when static analysis cannot handle the verification process completely. However in this case dynamic analysis comes with an advantage: logic to perform actions which override smart contract logic or past transactions can be guaranteed to trigger only when a violation occurs, thus ensuring immutability as long as the code is working as expected. However, the reparation logic itself is typically smart contract- and property-specific. For instance, while a transaction which wrongly disables an order may be fixed by reenabling it, a bug which locks the seller's performance guarantee in the contract (with no means to retrieve the funds) is more complex to address — with one possible reparatory strategy being that of requiring the buyer (or the developer of the contract) to place an amount of funds in the smart contract as a form of insurance, returning them when the contract terminates successfully but passed on to the seller if the performance guarantee becomes locked.

Flexibility of reparation techniques is thus crucial, possibly even more crucial than other domains. CONTRACTLARVA allows for custom actions (which may access the system state) which are triggered the moment the DEA moves to a bad or accepting state.

For instance, consider the property ensuring that the procurement contract is not reactivated after being closed. One possible reparation is that of closing it down immediately, which would be handled by the following CONTRACTLARVA script:

```
1     violation {
2        contractStatus = ContractStatus.Closed;
3     }
```

This would effectively close the contract immediately to make up for its reactivation. However, the reactivation may happen as part of a more complex transaction (e.g. a function call which, apart from opening the procurement contract, will also make other changes) which one may wish to abort altogether. Using Solidity's notion of reverted computations whose effects are effectively never written on the blockchain, one can build a form of runtime enforcement by effectively suppressing the call which led to the violation in the first place:

```
1     violation {
2        revert();
3     }
```

On the other hand, more complex reparation strategies may require additional code implementing them, as in the case of the minimum order constraint of clause 6 of the legal contract. For instance, the implementation of an insurance-based reparation strategy may work as follows: (i) the party providing insurance must start off by paying a stake before the contract is enabled; (ii) if the specification is violated, the insured party is given that stake; while (iii) if the specification reaches an accepting state, the insurer party gets to take their stake back.

In order to implement this behaviour, the specification would add the following auxiliary code to the original smart contract:

```
1     function payInsurance() payable {
2        require (insuranceStatus == UNPAID);
3        require (msg.value == getInsuranceValue());
4        require (msg.sender == getInsurer());
5
6        insuranceStatus = PAID;
7        LARVA_EnableContract();
8     }
9     function getInsuranceValue() { ... }
10    function getInsurer() { ... }
```

By default, CONTRACTLARVA starts off with the original smart contract disabled (i.e. functions automatically revert), and it is up to the monitoring logic to enable it. In this case, the function payInsurance() has to be called and the insurance paid by the insurer before the original contract is enabled — LARVA_EnableContract() and LARVA_DisableContract() are functions provided by CONTRACTLARVA to enable and disable the original smart contract. Specification satisfaction (in which case we simply return the stake to the insurer) and violation (in which case the stake is paid to the insured party and the original smart contract is disabled) would then be specified as follows:

```
1    satisfaction {
2        getInsurer().transfer(getInsuranceValue());
3    }
4    violation {
5        LARVA_DisableContract();
6        getInsured().transfer(getInsuranceValue());
7    }
```

For more sophisticated ways of dealing with reparation, including compensations, the reader is referred to [9].

3.4   Instrumentation

Monitor instrumentation into smart contracts can be done in different ways. For instance, instrumentation may be performed at the virtual machine level or at the source code level. It may be achieved by inlining verification code in the smart contract, or by adding only event generation to the original contract, and separate the monitoring and verification code — in the latter case, one may then choose to perform the verification on a separate smart contract or even off-chain. We discuss some of these options in Sect. 5, and focus on the approach taken by CONTRACTLARVA here.

CONTRACTLARVA instruments specifications directly into the smart contract at the Solidity source code level, promoting the idea that the new smart contract with instrumented verification code still being accessible at a high level of abstraction. The tool takes a smart contract written in Solidity and a specification, and creates a new smart contract with additional code to handle monitoring and verification.

In order to handle data-flow events, the tool adds setter functions, and replaces all assignments to the monitored variables to use the setter instead[6]. Using these setter functions, instrumenting for data-flow events effectively becomes equivalent to intercepting control-flow events on the setter function.

To instrument control-flow events, we add a modifier for each transition. For a particular event e, we define the set of transitions triggered by it to be $t \upharpoonright e = \{(q, e', c, a, q') \in t \mid e' = e\}$, with which the DEA operational semantics can be encoded. For instance, if $t \upharpoonright$ `before:f(x)` consists of two transitions $(q_1, \texttt{before:f(x)}, c_1, a_1, q_1')$ and $(q_2, \texttt{before:f(x)}, c_2, a_2, q_2')$ we define and use a Solidity modifier to carry out these transitions before `f` is called:

---

[6] The only case which is not covered by this approach is if the contract performs external delegate calls (which may result in the callee changing the state of the caller). However, this can be syntactically checked at instrumentation time.

```
1   modifier LARVA_before_f(uint x) {
2     if ((LARVA_STATE == q₁) && c₁) {
3         LARVA_STATE = q₁';
4         a₁;
5     } else {
6         if ((LARVA_STATE == q₂) && c₂) {
7         LARVA_STATE = q₂';
8         a₂;
9       }
10    }
11    _;
12  }
13
14  function f(uint _value) public LARVA_before_f(_value)
        { ... }
```

It is worth noting that the overheads induced when a function is called are linear in the number of transitions in the DEA which trigger on events related to that function. In practice, however, one finds that these overheads can be reasonable especially in the context of the critical nature of many smart contracts.

3.5 Runtime Overheads

Although, compared to other verification techniques, runtime verification is typically not that computationally expensive, it performs this computation at runtime, which can affect a program's performance. These runtime overheads can be avoided by performing verification asynchronously, however here we consider synchronous runtime verification since we require monitors to *ensure* that the smart contract conforms to the legal contract.

Unlike traditional systems, where one looks at different dimensions of monitoring overheads: time, memory, communication, etc., in the case of smart contracts on Ethereum, the metric for measuring overheads can be clearly quantified in terms of gas units. The main challenge is that gas is directly paid for in cryptocurrency, meaning that overheads have a direct economic impact[7].

When evaluating instrumented smart contracts we then can first measure the gas cost instrumentation adds to deployment of the smart contract (this additional gas cost reflects the instrumentation logic added), and secondly evaluate function calls to the smart contract to measure increased execution costs. We use this approach to evaluate an application of CONTRACTLARVA in the next section.

---

[7] Although in traditional systems, overheads in space, time and communication are still paid for financially (more memory, more CPU power or more bandwidth), the cost is indirect and the perception is that is a matter of *efficiency*, and not *cost management*..

4 Safe Mutability of Smart Contracts

An important aspect of smart contracts in Ethereum is that they are immutable (once deployed the smart contract's code cannot be changed). This ensures that no one can change the behaviour of the smart contract, protecting users from malicious changes. On the other hand immutability does not ensure this completely, given that smart contracts can call other smart contracts — any change in the target address of such calls changes the control-flow behaviour of the calling smart contract. Previous work shows that at least two out of five smart contracts are not control-flow immutable [16], and thus users cannot be completely sure that the behaviour will not be changed to their detriment and without notice.

4.1 Mutable Smart Contracts

Not allowing such external calls in contracts is not an option, since it is essential to support code reuse and to combine services. Moreover, since smart contracts are programs, they will have bugs, which must be repaired, thus some level of mutability allowing at least bug correction to occur is essential. Here we discuss an approach we proposed in [9] that allows safe mutability of a smart contract through the monitoring of a *behavioural contract*.

Listing 3. ERC-20 token interface standard [31].

```
1   interface ERC20 {
2      function totalSupply() public constant returns (uint);
3
4      function balanceOf(address tokenOwner) public constant
5         returns (uint balance);
6
7      function allowance(address tokenOwner, address spender
         )
8         public constant
9         returns (uint remaining);
10
11     function transfer(address to, uint tokens) public
12        returns (bool success);
13
14     function approve(address spender, uint tokens) public
15        returns (bool success);
16
17     function transferFrom(address from, address to, uint
         tokens)
18        public
19        returns (bool success);
20  }
```

As a case study we consider the ERC-20[8] token standard [31]. This standard, which is adhered to by over 100,000 smart contracts[9], is used by smart contracts which implement tokens — virtual assets which may be owned and transferred. Such tokens implement the Ethereum interface shown in Listing 3. Other, less widely used token standards exist, but they all carry out similar functionality and are thus amenable to roughly the same specification we use here.

An implementation of this standard may allow for possible updates to occur by introducing a *proxy* or *hub-spoke* pattern — a design pattern consisting of a hub (or proxy) contract that serves as the entry-point, which delegates the business logic to another contract. This common pattern allows one to deal with versioning in Ethereum (by allowing the implementation to be dynamically changed simply by updating the address to where the current version of the implementation resides), but does not provide any security to the user, since it allows the owner to change the behaviour unilaterally (e.g. the owner can change the implementation to one that steals commissions from token transfers). To provide the user with more guarantees, we propose the use of behavioural contracts that specify the behaviour the user can expect out when using this smart contract (i.e. the hub), which moreover we monitor for at runtime to revert any illicit behaviour.

As our hub or proxy, we create a smart contract that respects the interface in Listing 3, but which contains no logic except that it passes function calls to the implementation residing in another smart contract which contains the current version of the business logic:

```
1    ERC20 implementation;
2
3    function totalSupply() constant returns (uint){
4        return implementation.totalSupply();
5    }
```

In order to update versions, one can add simple logic to the hub or proxy that allows the owner to update the implementation to one residing at a new address:

```
1    address owner;
2
3    function updateImplementation(address
         newImplementation) public {
4        require(msg.sender == owner);
5        implementation = ERC20(newImplementation);
6    }
```

---

[8] ERC stands for *Ethereum Request for Comment,* with 20 being the number that was assigned to the request.

[9] As reported by Etherscan (see www.etherscan.io/tokens) in July 2018. The number of active, and trustworthy token implementations is, however, much lower than this figure.

The ERC-20 standard also comes with behavioural constraints, described informally in [31]. We can specify these using DEAs (see Figs. 4, 5 and 6). For specification legibility, we will use the condition denoted by an asterisk (*) to denote an *else* branch for the relevant event i.e. $e \mid * \mapsto a$ will trigger if and only if event e is detected, but no other outgoing transition from the current state is triggered.

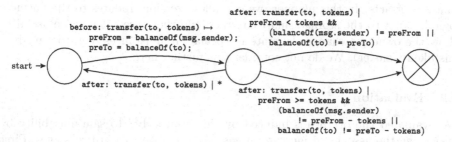

Fig. 4. Calling `transfer` (i) moves the amount requested if there are enough funds; but (ii) has no effect otherwise.

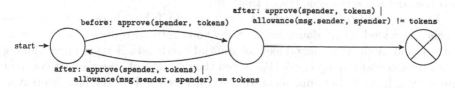

Fig. 5. Calling `approve` changes the allowance to the specified amount.

In order to ensure that updates to the implementation do not result in spurious, buggy or, even worse, malicious code, we instrument runtime checks to ensure that the effect of the ERC-20 functions on the state of the smart contract are as expected e.g. upon a call to the `transfer` function the balance of the sender and the recipient of the token value is stored, and this is used to check that the exact amount of tokens is transferred appropriately from the sender to the recipient (if the sender has enough tokens).

Thus, by instrumenting the entry-point (or hub) smart contract with this behavioural contract we ensure detection when smart contract mutability results in unexpected or wrong behaviour. If any non-conformant behaviour is detected, a bad state is reached and the transaction is reverted, thus protecting the user from malicious behaviour.

We give some examples of allowed and disallowed traces, using natural numbers as addresses, i.e. `0.transfer(1, 10)` denotes the address 0 calling the transfer function that sends ten tokens to address 1. Consider that `balanceOf(1) == 0` holds then the trace `0.transfer(1, 100);1.transfer(2, 101);` fails, due to Fig. 4, while `0.transfer(1, 100);1.transfer(2, 100);`

succeeds. For Fig. 6, `0.approve(1, 100);1.transferFrom(0, 1, 50);` is successful, but extending it with `1.transferFrom(0, 1, 51);` fails, given that after spending fifty tokens user 1 is only allowed to spend a further fifty tokens.

Note this still has some limitations, namely in terms of securing state, e.g. the owner can still update the implementation that behaviourally respects our contracts but that changes the token values assigned to certain users. To handle this, we can separate the business logic from storage, keeping them in different smart contracts. In this manner, we can allow version updates to the business logic but not to the storage smart contract. In other cases, it may be useful to allow the owner to change the state in special circumstances (e.g. to remedy a mistaken transfer). We do not consider this further here.

4.2   Evaluation

We evaluated the overheads induced by this approach[10] to safe mutability by measuring the associated increase in gas. We measure this in two stages. First we compare the overheads associated with adding versioning (and logic in the spoke to only allow the hub to use the spoke) against the simple case of just using the implementation directly. Secondly we compare the overheads associated with adding monitoring of the behavioural contracts on top of the versioning hub. We also consider some example traces that are

The magnitude of these overheads are shown in Table 1, along with the total overheads added when doing both. Note how both introducing a hub-spoke pattern and monitoring introduces substantial overheads. Setting up versioning increases gas costs by up to 65.11%, given the creation of a new smart contract and adding logic to the implementation to only be used by the hub. Moreover,

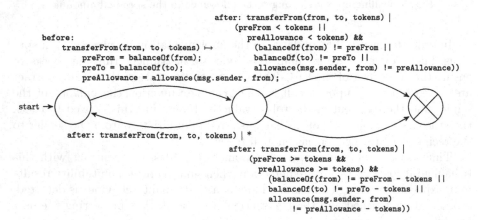

Fig. 6. Calling the `transferFrom` (i) moves the amount requested and reduces the allowance if there are enough funds and the caller has enough of an allowance; but (ii) has no effect otherwise.

---

[10] The case study can be found at: https://github.com/shaunazzopardi/safely-mutable-ERC-20-interface.

Table 1. Overheads associated with adding a behavioural interface to an ERC20 token.

Transactions	Overheads when adding Only versioning		Overheads when adding Behavioural contracts		Total	
	Gas units	Percentage	Gas units	Percentage	Gas units	Percentage
Setting up	1711984	65.11%	973794	37.03%	2685778	102.14%
totalSupply	4186	18.24%	734	3.2%	4920	21.44%
balanceOf	4494	18.71%	734	3.06%	5228	21.77%
allowance	4678	18.00%	756	2.91%	5434	20.91%
transferFrom	5324	5.78%	93320	101.34%	98644	107.12%
transfer	35362	71.47%	76152	153.92%	111514	225.39%
approve	5668	8.39%	43462	64.31%	49130	72.70%

there is a substantial increased cost to using the transfer function given it implicitly depends on the msg.sender which with versioning must be passed on directly from the hub (otherwise upon a call from the hub the implementation will see the hub's address for msg.sender, not the actual transaction initiator's address). When adding monitoring, calling transfer, transferFrom, and approve experience a significant increase in gas costs, which is to be expected given each call to these functions checks at least two monitor transitions. However, it is worth noting that the overhead induced is constant no matter how complex the token logic is. For the sake of this analysis, we used a trivial token implementation, but typically, tokens include more complex (i.e. more expensive) logic, thus reducing the percentage overhead for each call.

Furthermore, the major selling point of smart contracts has been that of guaranteed performance without the need for centralised trust (e.g. in a server), and yet there have been all too many cases of bugs in smart contracts which result in behaviour which resulted in losses of the equivalent of millions of dollars. Immutability (i.e. non-updatable code) results in bugs and exploits also being immutably present — the guaranteed performance is on the implemented behaviour, though possibly not the originally intended one. Unbridled version updates by the contract owner or developer, result in reintroducing the party who can update the code as a central point of trust, thus questioning the need for a smart contract in the first place. The need for controlled code updates is thus a real one, and the cost can be justified due to the immense potential losses. However, it is still a major question as to how these overheads can be significantly reduced.

5 Open Challenges

In this section we outline a number of research challenges and directions which are still to be addressed for smart contract monitoring.

5.1 Dealing with Failure

In many domains, failure to perform a subtask is handled within the normal execution of the systems, either through return values denoting failure or through exceptions. In either case, the side effects of the computation, both those leading to the failure and its handling can be monitored. In contrast, on Ethereum and Solidity, one can trigger failure through the use of `revert` which rolls back the prefix computation before the failure as though it never happened (apart from the fact that there was a reverted call). Although there has been some related work with runtime monitoring of rollback and compensation computation [10,11], in the context of smart contracts the notion of reverted execution goes beyond simply that of a computation which did not go through. With the view that smart contracts are effectively self-enforced contracts, a legal right such as *'The seller has the right to request an extension of the delivery deadline of an order'* goes beyond having a function `requestDeadlineExtension()`, since if every call to the function by the seller is reverted, the right is not really being respected.

The only way to handle reverted computation on the chain (on Ethereum) is by making the function calls from *another* contract, which allow capturing a `revert` within the logic of the (calling) smart contract, and we have already started experimenting with a variant of CONTRACTLARVA which handles an additional event modality `failure` such that the event `failure:f` triggers when function `f` is called but fails due to an explicit `revert` (or instances of the command hidden in syntactic sugar such as in `require`) [9]. If the cause for the failure is lack of gas, however, monitor execution cannot be carried out, which thus leaves the option of violating rights through excessive gas use.

Factoring in gas usage in monitoring for failures is a major challenge. Whether it is through the use of worst-case gas consumption analysis to statically reject monitored functions which may have a gas leak, or whether to leave sufficient gas to deal with monitoring upon a failure, static analysis could support these forms of violations. Some static analysis techniques to deal with potential gas attacks have already started being investigated [18]. Other options may use dynamic analysis to monitor gas usage for this form of denial-of-right attack.

5.2 Dealing with Monitoring Overheads

Over the past few years, much work has been done applying static analysis to make runtime verification cheaper, including [1,7,8,14]. In the domain of smart contracts, we believe that many of these approaches will perform better, and can be specialised to yield more optimisations. Although smart contract platforms such as Ethereum provide Turing-complete programming capabilities, in practice, few smart contracts use general recursion or loops other than using fixed patterns e.g. iteration through an array. This means that many static analysis techniques, such as abstraction or symbolic execution can yield much more precise results and hence are more effective in reducing runtime verification overheads.

In CONTRACTLARVA, we perform all monitoring and verification online and on-chain. Other alternative approaches could include pushing parts of the verification computation off-chain. For instance, for cases where the verification algorithms can be particularly expensive, one may simply log the relevant events (or even use the information written on the blockchain to extract it), and let the parties involved in the smart contract to perform verification, allowing progress only if they agree on the outcome of the verification e.g. using an external oracle, or via a voting mechanism or by all parties having to submit a hashed state of the verifying algorithm. The challenge in designing such an approach is to ensure that a smart contract is not stalled when things are detrimental to some party. Similarly, one may allow for asynchronous monitoring to avoid bottlenecks and enforce synchronisation only when critical situations are reached [12].

Another aspect is that on-chain stateful monitoring is simply impossible on DLTs which have stateless smart contracts, such as Ardor[11]. However, in the case of Ardor, only the relevant parties to a transaction execute the smart contract, and one may consider adding verification modules to clients in order to verify transactions before they are written to the blockchain.

5.3   Beyond Monitoring of Simple Smart Contracts

There are various other open challenges in the field. Our approach focusses on the behaviour of a single smart contract, even though they execute in a context. One may have properties across multiple interacting smart contracts e.g. the procurement smart contract may directly invoke and use a contract with a courier service to deliver the goods. If all the contracts are instrumented with monitoring code, the challenges are similar to those encountered in the monitoring of distributed systems e.g. where there should be a central monitoring orchestrator, or whether monitoring should be split and choreographed across contracts. If a contract cannot be instrumented with monitoring code, techniques such as assume-guarantee reasoning may need to be adopted to allow for compositional monitoring without being able to monitor within each component.

Although we have focussed on the monitoring of smart contracts, one may look at incorporating monitoring at the level of the DLT itself, beyond the effects of transactions, to include behaviour of miners and the data on the ledger itself. For instance, on Ethereum the order in which transactions are applied and recorded on a new block depends on the miners, which gives rise to a number of vulnerabilities due to a set of miners acting as *malicious schedulers*. Dynamic analysis of miner activity could be investigated to identify such behaviour.

6   Related Work

In this paper we have considered a runtime monitoring approach to the verification of smart contracts, however proving smart contracts safe before deployment

---

[11] See https://www.ardorplatform.org/.

is preferable, when possible. Although in their infancy, such approaches to formal verification in Ethereum exist. For instance, the approach proposed in [2] uses deductive analysis to verify business-logic properties of smart contracts at the Solidity level. In contrast, ZEUS [22] uses an abstraction of Solidity code that is translated to LLVM bitcode, allowing for conservative verification of safety properties expressed in a quantifier-free first order logic. This approach however does not soundly abstract all Solidity instructions, given lack of clear counterparts in LLVM, in fact reverting a program state is handled just as a program exit. Moreover external function calls are handled non-deterministically given that the target smart contract of such calls may change at runtime. The same behaviour for external calls is taken by other tools, e.g. [19]. In [19] the sound static analysis tool EtherTrust is used to show that an external call cannot call again the smart contract and reach another external call (then possibly causing an infinite loop that exhausts all gas). Given the external smart contract is not available, this depends on having appropriate logic preventing this in the smart contract. This is a good use case for runtime monitoring tools such as CONTRACTLARVA, that can be used to add this safety logic around external calls.

Other work, e.g. [3,21,28], translates EVM bytecode into established languages that amenable to theorem provers, however working at this low-level of bytecode abstracts away some valuable information (e.g. loops). Theorem provers also largely require interaction for full proofs, whereas we are interested in automated verification. Symbolic execution engines also exist for EVM bytecode, that allow for analysis of a smart contract in the context of the rest of the blockchain, e.g. [25,27]. [6] is an example of an approach capable of working at the level of Solidity code, where it translates this to F* code, making it amenable to the languages typechecking.

All this work has been recent and is not yet mature. Runtime verification, on the other hand, is simpler to implement, and gives precise results, unlike the tools we described whose precision varies. On these tools maturing runtime verification still has value, where it can be used as the tool of last resort — where other techniques only succeed in proving part of a property safe, runtime verification can be employed to prove the rest of the property, as in [1].

7   Conclusions

We have considered smart contracts and motivated the need for their verification, while illustrating the CONTRACTLARVA approach to monitoring Ethereum smart contracts by instrumenting smart contracts with event triggering and monitoring logic. Interestingly, this context allows the blocking of violating behaviour at the level of the smart contracting language, while CONTRACTLARVA further allows the specification of further flexible reparation strategies in case of violation. We have applied this approach to limit the mutability of a smart contract's behaviour once it is deployed to the blockchain, allowing updates to its logic while ensuring the behaviour is bounded by an immutable behavioural contract monitor. This allows more dependable services to be provided from the blockchain, and limiting the negative effect of bugs before they are corrected.

There are many open challenges left in smart contract verification. Particularly outstanding is the question of how to handle failure of a transaction. Considering an implementation of a legal contract, a failure of a transaction can have legal implications and verification methods can be used to detect such failures, assign blame, and enforce reparations. The role of off-chain analysis is also discussed, as are avenues for marrying this with on-chain enforcement. Monitoring also presents some challenges given it adds the need for more gas, possibly causing the failure of a transaction due to insufficient gas.

References

1. Ahrendt, W., Chimento, J.M., Pace, G.J., Schneider, G.: Verifying data- and control-oriented properties combining static and runtime verification: theory and tools. Form. Methods Syst. Des. **51**(1), 200–265 (2017)
2. Ahrendt, W., Pace, G.J., Schneider, G.: Smart contracts –a killer application for deductive source code verification. In: Festschrift on the Occasion of Arnd Poetzsch-Heffter's 60th Birthday (ARND 2018) (2018)
3. Amani, S., Bégel, M., Bortin, M., Staples, M.: Towards verifying Ethereum smart contract bytecode in Isabelle/Hol. In: Proceedings of the 7th ACM SIGPLAN International Conference on Certified Programs and Proofs, CPP 2018, pp. 66–77, New York, NY, USA. ACM (2018)
4. Atzei, N., Bartoletti, M., Cimoli, T.: A survey of attacks on ethereum smart contracts (SoK). In: Maffei, M., Ryan, M. (eds.) POST 2017. LNCS, vol. 10204, pp. 164–186. Springer, Heidelberg (2017). https://doi.org/10.1007/978-3-662-54455-6_8
5. Bartocci, E., Falcone, Y., Francalanza, A., Reger, G.: Introduction to runtime verification. In: Bartocci, E., Falcone, Y. (eds.) Lectures on Runtime Verification. LNCS, vol. 10457, pp. 1–33. Springer, Cham (2018). https://doi.org/10.1007/978-3-319-75632-5_1
6. Bhargavan, K., et al.: Formal verification of smart contracts. In: The 11th Workshop on Programming Languages and Analysis for Security (PLAS 2016) (2016)
7. Bodden, E., Hendren, L., Lhoták, O.: A staged static program analysis to improve the performance of runtime monitoring. In: Ernst, E. (ed.) ECOOP 2007. LNCS, vol. 4609, pp. 525–549. Springer, Heidelberg (2007). https://doi.org/10.1007/978-3-540-73589-2_25
8. Bodden, E., Lam, P., Hendren, L.: Clara: a framework for partially evaluating finite-state runtime monitors ahead of time. In: Barringer, H., Falcone, Y., Finkbeiner, B., Havelund, K., Lee, I., Pace, G., Roşu, G., Sokolsky, O., Tillmann, N. (eds.) RV 2010. LNCS, vol. 6418, pp. 183–197. Springer, Heidelberg (2010). https://doi.org/10.1007/978-3-642-16612-9_15
9. Colombo, C., Ellul, J., Pace, G.J.: Contracts over smart contracts: recovering from violations dynamically. In: Proceedings of the 8th International Symposium, ISoLA 2018. LNCS Vol. 11247, Limassol, Cyprus, 5-9 November 2018. Springer, (2018)
10. Colombo, C., Pace, G.J.: Monitor-oriented compensation programming through compensating automata. In: ECEASST, vol. 58 (2013)
11. Colombo, C., Pace, G.J.: Comprehensive monitor-oriented compensation programming. In: FESCA, vol. 147, pp. 47–61. EPTCS (2014)

12. Colombo, C., Pace, G.J., Abela, P.: Compensation-aware runtime monitoring. In: Barringer, H., Falcone, Y., Finkbeiner, B., Havelund, K., Lee, I., Pace, G., Roşu, G., Sokolsky, O., Tillmann, N. (eds.) RV 2010. LNCS, vol. 6418, pp. 214–228. Springer, Heidelberg (2010). https://doi.org/10.1007/978-3-642-16612-9_17
13. Colombo, C., Pace, G.J., Schneider, G.: Safe runtime verification of real-time properties. In: 7th International Conference Formal Modeling and Analysis of Timed Systems, FORMATS 2009, pp. 103–117 (2009)
14. de Boer, F.S., de Gouw, S., Johnsen, E.B., Kohn, A., Wong, P.Y.H.: Run-time assertion checking of data- and protocol-oriented properties of Java programs: an industrial case study. In: Chiba, S., Tanter, É., Bodden, E., Maoz, S., Kienzle, J. (eds.) Transactions on Aspect-Oriented Software Development XI. LNCS, vol. 8400, pp. 1–26. Springer, Heidelberg (2014). https://doi.org/10.1007/978-3-642-55099-7_1
15. Falcone, Y., Havelund, K., Reger, G.: A tutorial on runtime verification. In: Broy, M., Peled, D.A., Kalus, G. (eds.) Engineering Dependable Software Systems, vol. 34. NATO Science for Peace and Security Series, D: Information and Communication Security, pp. 141–175. IOS Press (2013)
16. Fröwis, M., Böhme, R.: In code we trust? In: Garcia-Alfaro, J., Navarro-Arribas, G., Hartenstein, H., Herrera-Joancomartí, J. (eds.) Data Privacy Management. Cryptocurrencies and Blockchain Technology, pp. 357–372. Springer, Cham (2017)
17. Fuchs, N.E.: Specifications are (preferably) executable. Softw. Eng. J. **7**(5), 323–334 (1992)
18. Grech, N., Kong, M., Jurisevic, A., Lexi, B., Scholz, B., Smaragdakis, Y.: Madmax: surviving out-of-gas conditions in Ethereum smart contracts. In: PACMPL, (OOPSLA) (2018)
19. Grishchenko, I., Maffei, M., Schneidewind, C.: Foundations and tools for the static analysis of ethereum smart contracts. In: Chockler, H., Weissenbacher, G. (eds.) Computer Aided Verification, pp. 51–78. Springer, Cham (2018)
20. Hayes, I., Jones, C.B.: Specifications are not (necessarily) executable. Softw. Eng. J. **4**(6), 330–338 (1989)
21. Hirai, Y.: Defining the ethereum virtual machine for interactive theorem provers. In: Brenner, M., Rohloff, K., Bonneau, J., Miller, A., Ryan, P.Y., Teague, V., Bracciali, A., Sala, M., Pintore, F., Jakobsson, M. (eds.) Financial Cryptography and Data Security, pp. 520–535. Springer, Cham (2017)
22. Kalra, S., Goel, S., Dhawan, M., Sharma, S.: ZEUS: analyzing safety of smart contracts. In: 25th Annual Network and Distributed System Security Symposium, NDSS 2018, San Diego, California, USA, 18–21 February 2018
23. Lessig, L.: Code 2.0. CreateSpace, 2nd edn. Paramount (2009)
24. Leucker, M., Schallhart, C.: A brief account of runtime verification. J. Log. Algebr. Program. **78**(5), 293–303 (2009)
25. Luu, L., Chu, D.-H., Olickel, H., Saxena, P., Hobor, A.: Making smart contracts smarter. In: Proceedings of the 2016 ACM SIGSAC Conference on Computer and Communications Security, CCS 2016, pp. 254–269, New York, NY, USA. ACM (2016)
26. Nakamoto, S.: Bitcoin: a peer-to-peer electronic cash system (2008). https://bitcoin.org/bitcoin.pdf
27. Nikolic, I., Kolluri, A., Sergey, I., Saxena, P., Hobor, A.: Finding the greedy, prodigal, and suicidal contracts at scale. CoRR, abs/1802.06038 (2018)

28. Park, D., Zhang, Y., Saxena, M., Daian, P., Roşu, G.: A formal verification tool for Ethereum VM Bytecode. In: Proceedings of the 26th ACM Joint European Software Engineering Conference and Symposium on the Foundations of Software Engineering (ESEC/FSE 2018). ACM, November 2018

29. Reger, G.: An overview of MARQ. In: Falcone, Y., Sánchez, C. (eds.) RV 2016. LNCS, vol. 10012, pp. 498–503. Springer, Cham (2016). https://doi.org/10.1007/978-3-319-46982-9_34

30. Szabo, N.: Smart contracts: building blocks for digital markets. Extropy, vol. 16 (1996)

31. Vogelsteller, F.: ERC-20 Token Standard (2005). https://github.com/ethereum/EIPs/blob/master/EIPS/eip-20.md

32. Wood, G.: Ethereum: a secure decentralised generalised transaction ledger. Ethereum Proj. Yellow Pap. **151**, 1–32 (2014)

Online and Offline Stream Runtime Verification of Synchronous Systems

César Sánchez[✉]

IMDEA Software Institute, Madrid, Spain
cesar.sanchez@imdea.org

Abstract. We revisit Stream Runtime Verification for synchronous systems. Stream Runtime Verification (SRV) is a declarative formalism to express monitors using streams, which aims to be a simple and expressive specification language. The goal of SRV is to allow engineers to describe both correctness/failure assertions and interesting statistical measures for system profiling and coverage analysis. The monitors generated are useful for testing, under actual deployment, and to analyze logs.

The main observation that enables SRV is that the steps in the algorithms to monitor temporal logics (which generate Boolean verdicts) can be generalized to compute statistics of the trace if a different data domain is used. Hence, the fundamental idea of SRV is to separate the temporal dependencies in the monitoring algorithm from the concrete operations to be performed at each step.

In this paper we revisit the pioneer SRV specification language LOLA and present in detail the online and offline monitoring algorithms. The algorithm for online monitoring LOLA specifications uses a partial evaluation strategy, by incrementally constructing output streams from input streams, maintaining a storage of partially evaluated expressions. We identify syntactically a class of specifications for which the online algorithm is trace length independent, that is, the memory requirement does not depend on the length of the input streams. Then, we extend the principles of the online algorithm to create an efficient offline monitoring algorithm for large traces, which consist on scheduling trace length independent passes on a dumped log.

Keywords: Runtime verification · Formal verification
Formal methods · Stream runtime verification synchronous systems
Dynamic analysis · Monitoring

1 Introduction

Runtime Verification (RV) is an applied formal method for software reliability that analyzes the system by processing one trace at a time. In RV a specification is transformed automatically into a monitor, and algorithms are presented

This research has been partially supported by: the EU H2020 project Elastest (num. 731535), by the Spanish MINECO Project "RISCO (TIN2015-71819-P)" and by the EU ICT COST Action IC1402 ARVI (*Runtime Verification beyond Monitoring*).

C. Colombo and M. Leucker (Eds.): RV 2018, LNCS 11237, pp. 138–163, 2018.
https://doi.org/10.1007/978-3-030-03769-7_9

to evaluate monitors against traces of observations from the system. There are two kinds of monitoring algorithms in RV depending on when the trace is generated and processed. In online monitoring the monitor checks the trace while the system runs, while in offline monitoring a finite collection of previously generated traces are analyzed. Online monitoring is used to detect violations of the specification when the system is in operation, while offline monitoring is used in post-mortem analysis and for testing large systems before deployment.

Static verification techniques like model checking intend to show that every (infinite) run of a system satisfies a given specification, while runtime verification is concerned only with a single (finite) trace. Thus, RV sacrifices completeness to provide an applicable formal extension of testing. See [21,24] for modern surveys on runtime verification and the recent book [4].

The first specification languages studied for runtime verification were based on temporal logics, typically LTL [6,13,22], regular expressions [28], timed regular expressions [1], rules [3], or rewriting [27]. In this paper we revisit the Stream Runtime Verification specification formalism, in particular the LOLA specification language for synchronous systems [12]. The LOLA language can express properties involving both the past and the future and their arbitrary combination. In SRV, specifications declare explicitly the dependencies between input streams of values—that represent the observations from the system—and output streams of values—that represent monitoring outputs, like error reports and diagnosis information. The fundamental idea of SRV is to cleanly separate the temporal reasoning from the individual operations to be performed at each step. The temporal aspects are handled in a small number of constructs to express the offsets between observations and their uses. For the data, SRV uses off-the-self domains with interpreted functions so function symbols can be used as constructors to create expressions, and their interpretation is used for evaluation during the monitoring process. The domains used for SRV are not restricted to Booleans and allow richer domains like Integers, Reals (for computing quantitative verdicts) and even queues, stacks, etc. These domains do not involve any reasoning about time. The resulting expressiveness of SRV surpasses that of temporal logics and many other existing formalisms including finite-state automata. The restriction of SRV to the domain of Booleans is studied in [10], including the expressivity, the comparison with logics and automata and the complexity of the decision problems.

The online monitoring problem of past specifications can be solved efficiently using constant space and linear time in the trace size. For future properties, on the other hand, the space requirement depends on the length of the trace for rich types (even though for LTL, that is for the verdict domain of the Booleans, one can use automata techniques to reduce the necessary space to exponential in the size of the specification). Consequently, online monitoring of future temporal formulas quickly becomes intractable in practical applications with long traces. On the other hand, the offline monitoring problem for LTL-like logics is known to be easy for purely past or purely future properties. We detail in the paper a syntactic characterization of *efficiently monitorable* specifications (introduced in [12]), for which the space requirement of the online monitoring algorithm is independent of the size of the trace, and linear in the specification size. This property was later popularized as *trace length independence* [5] and is a very desirable property as it allows online monitors to scale to arbitrarily large traces. In practice, most properties of interest in online monitoring can be expressed as efficiently monitorable properties. For the offline monitoring problem, we show an efficient monitoring strategy in the presence of arbitrary past and future combinations by scheduling trace length independent passes. We describe here the algorithm and results using the LOLA specification language. An execution of the monitor extracted from a LOLA specification computes data values at each position by evaluating the expressions over streams of input, incrementally computing the output streams.

Two typical specifications are properties that specify correct behavior, and statistical measures that allow profiling the system that produces the input streams. One important limitation of runtime verification is that liveness properties can never be violated on a finite trace. Hence, most of these properties have been typically considered as non-monitorable (for violation) as every finite prefix can be extended to a satisfying trace, at least if the system is considered as a black box and can potentially generate any suffix. An appealing solution that SRV supports is to compute quantitative measures from the observed trace. For example, apart from "there are only finitely many retransmissions of each package," which is vacuously true over finite traces, SRV allows to specify "what is the average number of retransmissions." Following this trend, runtime monitors can be used not only for bug-finding, but also for profiling, coverage, vacuity and numerous other analyses. An early approach for combining proving properties with data collection, which inspired SRV, appeared in [16].

In the present paper we present a simplified semantics of LOLA [12] together with a detailed presentation of the monitoring algorithms as well as the necessary definitions and proofs. In the rest of the paper we use SRV and LOLA interchangeably.

Related Work. The expressions that declare the dependencies between input streams and output streams in SRV are functional, which resemble synchronous languages—which are also functional reactive stream computation languages—like LUSTRE [20], ESTEREL [9] and SIGNAL [17], with additional features that are relevant to monitoring. The main difference is that synchronous languages are designed to express behaviors and therefore assume the causality assumption and forbid future references, while in SRV future references are allowed to describe dependencies on future observations. This requires additional expressiveness in the language and the evaluation strategies to represent that the monitor cannot decide a verdict without observing future values. These additional verdicts were also introduced for this purpose in LTL-based logics, like LTL_3 and LTL_4 [6–8], to encode that the monitor is indecisive.

An efficient method for the online evaluation of *past* LTL properties is presented in [22], which exploits that past LTL can be recursively defined using only values in the previous state of the computation. The *efficiently monitorable* fragment of SRV specifications generalize this idea, and apply it uniformly to both verification and data collection. One of the early systems that most closely resembles LOLA is Eagle [3], which allows the description of monitors using greatest and least fixed points of recursive definitions. LOLA differs from Eagle in the descriptive nature of the language, and in that LOLA is not restricted to checking logical formulas, but can also express numerical queries.

The initial application domain of LOLA was the testing of synchronous hardware by generating traces of circuits and evaluating monitors against these traces. Temporal testers [26] were later proposed as a monitoring technique for LTL based on Boolean streams. Copilot [25] is a domain-specific language that, similar to LOLA, declares dependencies between streams in a Haskell-based style, to generate C monitors that operate in constant time and space (the fragment of specifications that Copilot can describe is efficiently monitorable). See also [18].

The simple version of LOLA presented here does not allow to quantify over objects and instantiate monitors to follow the actual objects observed, like in Quantified Event Automata [2]. Lola2.0 [14] is an extension of Lola that allows to express parametrized streams and dynamically generates monitors that instantiate these streams for the observed data items. The intended application of Lola2.0 is network monitoring.

Stream runtime verification has a also been extended recently to asynchronous and real-time systems. RTLola [15] extends SRV from the synchronous domain to timed streams. In RTLola streams are computed at predefined periodic instants of time, collecting aggregations between these predefined instants using a library of building blocks. TeSSLa [11] also offers a small collection of primitives for expressing stream dependencies (see also [23]) but allows to compute timed-streams at arbitrary real-time instants. The intended application of TeSSLa is hardware based monitoring. Striver [19] offers a Lola-like language with time offsets, that allows to express explicit instants of time in the expressions between streams. Striver is aimed at testing and monitoring of cloud based systems.

The rest of the paper is structured as follows. Section 2 revisits the syntax and semantics of SRV. Section 3 presents the online monitoring of SRV specifications, including the notion of efficient monitorability. Section 4 presents the algorithm for offline monitoring, and finally Sect. 5 concludes.

2   Overview of Stream Runtime Verification

In this section we describe SRV using the LOLA specification language. The monitoring algorithms will be presented in Sects. 3 and 4.

2.1   Specification Language: Syntax

We use many-sorted first order interpreted theories to describe data domains. A theory is given by a finite collection T of types and a finite collection F of function symbols. Since our theories are interpreted every type T is associated with a domain D of values and every symbol f is associated with a computable function that, given elements of the domains of the arguments compute a value of the domain of the resulting type. We use sort and type interchangeably in this paper.

For example, the theory *Boolean* uses the type *Bool* associated with the Boolean domain with two values $\{\top, \bot\}$, and has constant symbols *true* and *false*, and binary function symbols $\wedge$, and $\vee$, unary function symbol $\neg$, etc. all with their usual interpretations. A more sophisticated theory is *Naturals*, the theory of the Natural numbers, that uses two types *Nat* and *Bool*. The type *Nat* is associated with the domain $\{0, 1, \ldots\}$ of the Natural numbers, and has constant symbols $0, 1, 2, \ldots$ and binary symbols $+$, $*$, etc. of type $Nat \times Nat \rightarrow Nat$. Other function symbols in this theory are predicates $<, \leq, \ldots$ of type $Nat \times Nat \rightarrow Bool$. All our theories include equality and also, for every type T, a ternary predicate if $\cdot$ then $\cdot$ else $\cdot$ of type $Bool \times T \rightarrow T$. For simplicity we restrict the rest of the paper to types *Nat* and *Bool*.

Definition 1 (Stream Expression). *Given a finite set Z of stream variable (each with a given type) the set of stream expressions is defined as follows:*

- *Variable: If s is a stream variable of type T, then s is a stream expression of type T;*
- *Function Application: Let $f : T_1 \times T_2 \times \cdots \times T_k \mapsto T$ be a k-ary function symbol. If for $1 \leq i \leq k$, e_i is an expression of type T_i, then $f(e_1, \ldots, e_k)$ is a stream expression of type T.*
- *Offset: If v is a stream variable of type T, c is a constant of type T, and k is an integer value, then $v[k, c]$ is a stream expression of type T.*

We use $Expr(Z)$ for the set of stream expressions using stream variables Z.

Constants c (that is, 0-ary function symbols) and stream variables v are called *atomic stream expressions*. Stream variables are used to represent streams. Informally, the offset term $v[k, c]$ refers to the value of v offset k positions from the current position, where a negative offset refers to a past position in the stream and a positive offset refers to a future position in the stream. The constant c is the *default* value of type T assigned to positions from which the offset is past the end or before the beginning of the stream. For example $v[-1, true]$ refers to the previous position of stream v, with the value *true* when v does not have a previous position (that is when $v[-1, true]$ is evaluated at the beginning of the trace).

A LOLA specification describes a relation between input streams and output streams. A *stream* σ of type T and length N is a *finite* sequence of values from the domain of T; $\sigma(i)$, $i \geq 0$ denotes the value of the stream at time step i.

Definition 2 (Lola specification). *A LOLA specification $\varphi : \langle I, O, E \rangle$ consists of:*

- *a finite set I of typed* independent *stream variables;*
- *a collection O of typed* dependent *stream variables; and*
- *a collections E of defining expressions, with one expression $E_y \in Expr(I \cup O)$ for each output variable $y \in O$, where y and E_y must have the same type.*

We write $y := E_y$ to denote that the stream y is defined by its defining expression E_y, which can use every stream variable in $I \cup O$ (including y itself) as atomic terms. Sometimes, LOLA specifications include a collection of *triggers* defined by expressions of type *Bool* over the stream variables, with the intended meaning of informing the user when the corresponding expressions become true, but we do not use triggers in the presentation in this paper.

Independent variables refer to input streams and dependent variables refer to output streams. It is often convenient to partition the dependent variables into output variables and intermediate variables to distinguish streams that are of interest to the user from those that are used only to facilitate the description of other streams. However, for the semantics and the algorithm this distinction is not important, and hence we will ignore this classification in the rest of the paper.

Example 1. Let x_1 and x_2 be stream variables of type Boolean and x_3 be a stream variable of type integer. The following is an example of a LOLA specification with $I = \{x_1, x_2, x_3\}$ as independent variables, $O = \{y_1, \ldots, y_{10}\}$ as dependent variables and the following defining equations:

$$y_1 := \textbf{true}$$
$$y_2 := x_3$$
$$y_3 := x_1 \vee (x_3 \leq 1)$$
$$y_4 := ((x_3)^2 + 7) \bmod 15$$
$$y_5 := \textbf{if } y_3 \textbf{ then } y_4 \textbf{ else } y_4 + 1$$

$$y_6 := \textbf{if } x_1 \textbf{ then } x_3 \leq y_4 \textbf{ else } \neg y_3$$
$$y_7 := x_1[+1, false]$$
$$y_8 := x_1[-1, true]$$
$$y_9 := y_9[-1, 0] + (x_3 \bmod 2)$$
$$y_{10} := x_2 \vee (x_1 \wedge y_{10}[1, true])$$

Stream variable y_1 denotes a stream whose value is *true* at all positions, while y_2 denotes a stream whose values are the same at all positions as those in x_3. The values of the streams corresponding to $y_3, \ldots, y_6$ are obtained by evaluating their defining expressions place-wise at each position. The stream corresponding to y_7 is obtained by taking at each position i the value of the stream corresponding to x_1 at position $i + 1$, except at the last position, which assumes the default value *false*. Similarly for the stream for y_8, whose values are equal to the values of the stream for x_1 shifted by one position, except that the value at the first position is the default value *true*. The stream specified by y_9 counts the number of odd entries in the stream assigned to x_3 by accumulating $(x_3 \bmod 2)$. Finally, y_{10} denotes the stream that gives at each position the value of the temporal formula $x_1 \mathcal{U} x_2$ with the stipulation that unresolved eventualities be regarded as satisfied at the end of the trace.   □

To present formal results, it is sometimes convenient to work with a simpler class of specifications.

Definition 3 (Flat). *A specification is flat if each defining expression E_y is one of the following*

- *A constant c*
- *A stream variable v*
- *A constructor over stream variables* $f(v_1, \ldots, v_n)$
- *An offset expression* $v[k, c]$.

Definition 4 (Normalized). *A specification is normalized if it only contains offsets* 1 *or* −1.

Any LOLA specification can be converted into a flat specification by introducing extra stream variables as place-holders for complex sub-expressions. Similarly, any LOLA specification can be converted into a normalized specification by introducing additional stream variables defined to carry value $n-1$ for offsets of $n > 1$ (and $n + 1$ for offsets of $n < -1$). This transformation also preserves flatness so every LOLA specification can be converted into a normalized flat specification.

Example 2. Consider the LOLA specification with $I = \{x_1, \ldots, x_5\}$, $O = \{y\}$ and
$$y := x_1[1, 0] + \text{if } x_2[-1, \textit{true}] \text{ then } x_3 \text{ else } x_4 + x_5.$$
The normalized specification uses $O = \{y, y_1, \ldots, y_4\}$ with equations:

$$y := y_1 + y_2 \qquad \begin{aligned} y_1 &:= x_1[1, 0] \\ y_2 &:= \text{if } y_3 \text{ then } x_3 \text{ else } y_4 \end{aligned} \qquad \begin{aligned} y_3 &:= x_2[-1, \textit{true}] \\ y_4 &:= x_4 + x_5 \end{aligned}$$

□

2.2 Specification Language: Semantics

In order to define the semantics of SRV specifications we first define how to evaluate expressions. Consider a map σ_I that assigns one stream σ_x of type T and length N for each input stream variable x of type T, and a map $\sigma_O : \{\ldots, \sigma_y, \ldots\}$ that contains one stream σ_y of length N for each defined stream variable y (again of the same type as y). We call (σ_I, σ_O) an interpretation of φ, and use σ as the map that assigns the corresponding stream as σ_I or σ_O (depending on whether the stream variable is an input variable or an output variable).

Definition 5 (Valuation). *Given an interpretation* (σ_I, σ_O) *a valuation is a map* $[\![\cdot]\!]$ *that assigns to each expression a stream of length N of the type of the expression as follows:*

$$\begin{aligned} [\![c]\!](j) &= c \\ [\![v]\!](j) &= \sigma_v(j) \\ [\![f(e_1, \ldots, e_k)]\!](j) &= f([\![e_1]\!](j), \ldots, [\![e_k]\!](j)) \\ [\![\text{if } e_1 \text{ then } e_2 \text{ else } e_3]\!](j) &= \text{if } [\![e_1]\!](j) \text{ then } [\![e_2]\!](j) \text{ else } [\![e_3]\!](j) \\ [\![v[k, c]]\!](j) &= \begin{cases} [\![v]\!](j + k) & \text{if } 0 \le j + k < N \\ c & \text{otherwise} \end{cases} \end{aligned}$$

We now can define when an interpretation (σ_I, σ_O) of φ is an *evaluation model*, which gives denotational semantics to LOLA specifications.

Definition 6 (Evaluation Model). *An interpretation (σ_I, σ_O) of φ is an evaluation model of φ whenever*

$$\llbracket y \rrbracket = \llbracket E_y \rrbracket \quad \text{for every } y \in O$$

In this case we write $(\sigma_I, \sigma_O) \models \varphi$.

For a given set of input streams, a LOLA specification may have zero, one, or multiple evaluation models.

Example 3. Consider the LOLA specifications (all with $I = \{x\}$ and $O = \{y\}$) where x has type *Nat* and y has type *Bool*.

$$\varphi_1 : y := (x \leq 10)$$
$$\varphi_2 : y := y \wedge (x \leq 10)$$
$$\varphi_3 : y := \neg y$$

For any given input stream σ_x, φ_1 has exactly one evaluation model (σ_x, σ_y), where $\sigma_y(i) = true$ if and only if $\sigma_x(i) \leq 10$, for $1 \leq i \leq N$. The specification φ_2, however, may give rise to multiple evaluation models for a given input stream. For example, for input stream $\sigma_x : \langle 0, 15, 7, 18 \rangle$, both $\sigma_y : \langle false, false, false, false \rangle$ and $\sigma_y : \langle false, true, false, true \rangle$ make (σ_x, σ_y) an evaluation model of φ_2. The specification φ_3, on the other hand, has no evaluation models, because there is no solution to the equations $\sigma_y(i) = \neg \sigma_y(i)$. $\qquad \square$

2.3 Well-Definedness and Well-Formedness

SRV specifications are meant to define monitors, which intuitively correspond to queries of observations of the system under analysis (input streams) for which we want to compute a unique answer (the output streams). Therefore, the intention of a specification is to define a function from input streams to output streams, and this requires that there is a unique evaluation model for each instance of the input streams. The following definition captures this intuition.

Definition 7 (Well-defined). *A LOLA specification φ is well-defined if for any set of appropriately typed input streams σ_I of the same length $N > 0$, there exists a unique valuation σ_O of the defined streams such that $(\sigma_I, \sigma_O) \models \varphi$.*

A well-defined LOLA specification maps a set of input streams to a unique set of output streams. Unfortunately well-definedness is a semantic condition that is hard to check in general (even undecidable for rich types). Therefore, we define a more restrictive (syntactic) condition called *well-formedness*, that can be easily checked on every specification φ and implies well-definedness. We first add an auxiliary definition.

Definition 8 (Dependency Graph). *Let φ be a LOLA specification. The dependency graph for φ is the weighted directed multi-graph $D = \langle V, E \rangle$, with vertex set $V = I \cup O$. The set E contains an edge $y \xrightarrow{0} v$ if v is occurs in E_y and an edge $y \xrightarrow{k} v$ if $v[k, d]$ occurs in E_y.*

An edge $y \xrightarrow{k} v$ encode that y at a particular position potentially depends on the value of v, offset by k positions. Note that there can be multiple edges between x and y with different weights on each edge. Also note that vertices that correspond to input variables do not have outgoing edges.

A *walk* of a graph is a sequence $v_1 \xrightarrow{k_1} v_2 \xrightarrow{k_2} v_3 \cdots v_n \xrightarrow{k_n} v_{n+1}$ of vertices and edges. A walk is *closed* if $v_1 = v_{n+1}$. The weight of a walk is the sum of the weights of its edges. A simple walk is a walk in which no vertex is repeated. A *cycle* is a simple closed walk.

Definition 9 (Well-Formed Specifications). *A* LOLA *specification φ is well-formed if its dependency graph has no closed walk with weight zero.*

Example 4. Consider the LOLA specification with $I : \{x_1, x_2\}$ and $O : \{y_1, y_2\}$ and the following defining equations:

$$y_1 := y_2[1,0] + \text{if } (y_2[-1,7] \leq x_1[1,0]) \text{ then } (y_2[-1,0]) \text{ else } y_2$$
$$y_2 := (y_1 + x_2[-2,1]).$$

Its normalized specification is

$$\begin{array}{lll} y_1 := y_5 + y_9 & y_2 := y_1 + y_4 & y_3 := x_1[1,0] \\ y_4 := x_2[-2,1] & y_5 := y_2[1,0] & y_6 := y_2[-1,0] \\ y_7 := y_2[-1,7] & y_8 := y_7 \leq y_3 & y_9 := \text{if } y_8 \text{ then } y_6 \text{ else } y_2 \end{array}$$

The dependency graph of the normalized specifications is:

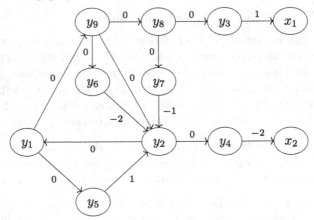

This specification has a zero-weight closed walk, namely $y_1 \xrightarrow{0} y_9 \xrightarrow{0} y_2 \xrightarrow{0} y_1$, and hence the specification is not well-formed.   □

To prove that well-formedness implies well-definedness, we first define the notion of an evaluation graph which captures the dependencies for a given input length N.

Definition 10 (Evaluation Graph). *Given a specification φ and a length N, the evaluation graph is the directed graph $G_N : \langle V, E \rangle$ where V contains one vertex v^j for each position j of each stream variable v and*

- there is an edge $y^j \to v^j$ if E_y contains v as an atom, and
- there is an edge $y^j \to v^{j+k}$ if E_y contains $v[k, c]$ and $0 \leq j + k < N$.

The vertices v^j are called *position variables* as they encode the value of stream variable v at position j. We will prove later that a specification is guaranteed to be well-defined if no evaluation graph for any length contains a cycle, because in this case the value of each position variable can be uniquely determined. The following lemma relates this acyclicity notion with the absence of zero-weight cycles in the dependency graph.

Lemma 1. *Let φ be a specification with dependency graph D, let N be a trace length and G_N the explicit dependency graph. If G_N has a cycle then D has a zero-weight closed walk.*

Proof. Assume G_N has a cycle

$$y_1^{j_1} \to y_2^{j_2} \to \cdots \to y_k^{j_k} \to y_1^{j_1}$$

The corresponding closed walk in D is

$$y_1 \xrightarrow{j_2 - j_1} y_2 \to \cdots \to y_k \xrightarrow{j_1 - j_k} y_1$$

with weight $\sum_{i=1}^{k} (j_{i \oplus 1} - j_i) = 0$. $\qquad\square$

Note that the closed walk induced in D needs not be a cycle since some of the intermediate nodes may be repeated, if they correspond to the same y_k for different position j.

Lemma 2. *Let φ be a specification and N a length. If G_N has no cycles, then for every tuple σ_I of input streams of length N, there is a unique evaluation model.*

Proof. Assume G_N has no cycles, so G_N is a DAG. Then we can define a topological order $>$ on G_N by taking the transitive closure of $\to$. We prove by induction on this order that the value of each vertex is uniquely determined, either because this value is obtained directly from an input stream or constant value in the specification, or because the value can be computed from values computed before according to $>$.

For the base case, the value of a vertex v^j without outgoing edges does not depend on other streams. The only possible value is either the value of an input stream (if v is an input stream variable) at position j, or a value obtained from an equation with no variables or offsets as atoms. In all these cases the value is uniquely determined.

For the inductive case, the value of v^j can be computed uniquely from the values of its adjacent vertices in G_N. Indeed, by Definition 10, if the value of v^j depends on the value of v^k then there exists an edge $v^j \to v^k$ in G_N and thus $v^j > v^k$ and, by the inductive hypothesis, the value of v^k is uniquely determined. Then, since every atom in $[\![E_v]\!](j)$ is uniquely determined, the value of $[\![E_v]\!](j)$ is uniquely determined. Since this value has been computed only from inputs, this is the only possible value for $\sigma_v(j)$ to form an evaluation model. $\qquad\square$

Consider now a well-formed specification φ. Then, by Lemma 1, no evaluation graph has cycles, and thus by Lemma 2 for every set of input streams, there exists a unique solution for the output streams, and hence there is exactly one evaluation model.

Theorem 1. *Every well-formed* LOLA *specification is well-defined.*

Note that the converse of Theorem 1 does not hold. First, the absence of cycles in G_N does not imply the absence of a zero-weight closed walk in D. For example, the evaluation graph for the specification

$$y_1 := y_2[-k, c]$$
$$y_2 := y_1[k, c]$$

for $N < k$ has no cycles (since it has no edges), but it is easy to see that D has a zero-weight closed walk. Second, a cycle in G_N does not necessarily imply that φ is not well-defined. For example, the evaluation graph of the specification

$$y := (z \ \vee \ \neg z) \ \wedge \ x$$
$$z := y$$

has a cycle for all N, but for every input stream, φ has exactly one evaluation model, namely $\sigma_y = \sigma_z = \sigma_x$, and thus, by definition, the specification is well-defined.

2.4   Checking Well-Formedness

A LOLA specification φ is well-formed if its dependency graph D has no closed walks, so checking well-formedness is reduced to construct D and check for closed walks. In turn, this can be reduced to checking for cycles as follows.

Let a gez-cycle be a cycle in which the sum of the weight of the edges is greater than or equal to zero, and let a gz-cycle be a cycle in which the sum of the weight of the edges is strictly greater than zero. Similarly, a lez-cycle is a cycle where the sum is less than or equal zero and a lz-cycle is one where the sum is less than zero. The reduction is based on the observation that a graph has a zero-weight closed walk if and only if it has a maximally strongly component (MSCC) with both a gez-cycle and a lez-cycle.

Lemma 3. *A weighted and directed multigraph D has a zero-weight closed walk if and only if it has a vertex v that lies on both a gez-cycle and a lez-cycle.*

Proof. ($\Rightarrow$) Assume v is part of gez-cycle C_1 and lez-cycle C_2, with weights $w_1 \geq 0$ and $w_2 \leq 0$, respectively. The closed walk consisting of traversing w_1 times C_2 and then traversing $|w_2|$ times C_1 has weight $w_1 w_2 + |w_2| w_1 = 0$, as desired.

($\Leftarrow$) Assume D has a zero-weight closed walk. If D has a zero-weight cycle C we are done, as C is both a gez-cycle and a lez-cycle and any vertex in C has the desired property.

For the other case, assume D has no zero-weight cycles. It is easy to show by induction in the length of W that every closed walk can be decomposed into cycles that share one vertex. If one of these cycles is a lez-cycle or a gez-cycle the result follows. Now, not all the cycles can be strictly positive, because then the total weight of W would not be zero. Consequently there must a positive cycle and a negative cycle, and therefore there must be two consecutive cycles C_1 and C_2 that share one node and C_1 is positive and C_2 is negative.   □

Theorem 2. *A directed weighted multigraph D has no zero-weight closed walk if and only if every MSCC has only gz-cycles or only lz-cycles.*

Proof. ($\Rightarrow$) Consider an arbitrary MSCC with only gz-cycles (the case for only lz-cycles is analogous). By the proof of Lemma 3, a closed walk is the multiset union of one or more cycles with weight the sum of the weights of the cycles. Hence the weight of any closed walk within the MSCC must be strictly greater than zero. Since any closed walk must stay within an MSCC, the weight of any closed walk must be strictly greater than zero.

($\Leftarrow$) Assume D has no zero-weight closed walk. Then, by Lemma 3, D has no vertex that lies on both a gez-cycle and a lez-cycle. Suppose D has an MSCC with a gz-cycle C_1 and a lz-cycle C_2. Consider an arbitrary vertex v_1 on C_1 and v_2 on C_2. If $v_1 = v_2 = v$, v lies on both a gez-cycle and a lez-cycle, a contradiction. If $v_1 \neq v_2$, since v_1 and v_2 are in the same MSCC, there exists a cycle C_3 that contains both v_1 and v_2. C_3 is either a zero-weight cycle, a gz-cycle or a lz-cycle. In all three cases either v_1 or v_2 or both lie on both a gez-cycle and a lez-cycle, a contradiction.   □

Thus to check well-formedness of a SRV specification φ it is sufficient to check that each MSCC in G has only gz-cycles or only lz-cycles. This can be checked efficiently, even for large dependency graphs.

3 Online Monitoring

We distinguish two situations for monitoring—*online* and *offline* monitoring. In online monitoring, the traces from the system under observation are received as the system run, and the monitor works in tandem with the system. This leads to the following restriction for online monitoring: the traces are available a few points at a time starting at the initial instant on-wards, and need to be processed to make way for more incoming data. In particular, random access to the traces is not available. The length of the trace is assumed to be unknown upfront and very large.

In offline monitoring, on the other hand, we assume that the system has run to completion and the trace of data has been dumped to a storage device. Offline monitoring is covered in Sect. 4.

3.1   Monitoring Algorithm

We start by exhibiting a general monitoring algorithm for arbitrary LOLA specifications, and then study its efficiency. Let φ be a LOLA specification with independent stream variables I, dependent stream variables O and defining expressions E. Let j be the current position, at which the latest data is available from all input streams. The monitoring algorithm maintains two sets of equations as storage:

- *Resolved* equations R of the form (v^k, c) for a given position variable v^k (with $k \in \{1, \ldots, j\}$) and concrete value c.
- *Unresolved* equations U of the form (y^k, e) for position variable y^k expression e (for e different from a constant).

An equation (v^k, c) stored in R denotes that stream variable v at position k in the trace has been determined to have value c. This happens in two cases: input streams whose reading has been performed, and dependent stream variables whose value has been computed. Equations in U relate position variables y^k— where y is a dependent stream variable—with a (possibly partially simplified) expression over position variables whose values have not yet been determined. Note that if (y^k, e) is in U then e must necessarily contain at least one position variable, because otherwise e is a ground expression and the interpreted functions from the domain can transform e into a value.

The monitoring algorithm is shown in Algorithm 1. After initializing the U and R stores to empty and j to 0, the monitoring algorithm executes repeatedly the main loop (lines 5 to 11). This main loop first reads values for all inputs at the current position and adds these values to R (line 6). Then, it instantiates the defining equations for all outputs and adds these to U (line 7). Finally, it propagates new known values (v^k, c) in R by substituting all occurrences of v^k in unresolved equations by c and then simplifies resulting equations (procedure PROPAGATE). This procedure simply uses all the information in R to substitute occurrences of known values in unresolved equations. In some cases, these equations become resolved (the term becomes a value) and the corresponding pair is moved to R (lines 23 and 24). Then, the procedure PRUNE is used to eliminate unnecessary information from R as described below. Finally, procedure FINALIZE is invoked at the end of the trace. This procedure is used to determine whether a given offset expression that remains in an unresolved equation falls beyond the end of the trace, which is converted into its default value. This procedure also performs a final call to PROPAGATE, which is guaranteed (see below) to resolve all position variables, and therefore U becomes empty.

Procedure INST, shown in Algorithm 2, instantiates the defining equation for v into the corresponding equation for v^j at given position j by propagating the value into the atomic stream variable references and offsets atoms, which become instance variables. Note that the default value c is recorded in line 57 in case the computed position $k + j$ falls beyond the end of the trace N, which is not known at the point of the instantiation. Whether $k + j$ is inside the trace will be determined after k steps or resolved by FINALIZE.

Algorithm 1. Monitoring algorithm

1: **procedure** MONITOR
2:     $U \leftarrow \emptyset$
3:     $R \leftarrow \emptyset$
4:     $j \leftarrow 0$
5:     **while** not finished **do**
6:         $R \leftarrow R \cup \{(y^j, \sigma_y(j)) \mid \text{for every } y \in I\}$ ▷ Add new inputs to R
7:         $U \leftarrow U \cup \{(x^j, \text{INST}(e_x, j)) \mid \text{for every } x \in O\}$ ▷ Add output instances to U
8:         PROPAGATE()
9:         PRUNE(j)
10:        $j \leftarrow j + 1$
11:    **end while**
12:    $N \leftarrow j + 1$
13:    FINALIZE(N)
14: **end procedure**

15: **procedure** PROPAGATE
16:    **repeat**
17:        $change \leftarrow false$
18:        **for all** $(v^k, e) \in U$ **do**   ▷ Try to resolve every v^k in U
19:            $e' \leftarrow simplify(subst(e, R))$
20:            $U.replace(v^k, e')$ ▷ update v^k
21:            **if** e' is value **then**
22:                $change \leftarrow true$ ▷ v^k is resolved
23:                $R \leftarrow R + \{(v^k, e')\}$ ▷ add v^k to R
24:                $U \leftarrow U - \{(v^k, e)\}$ ▷ remove v^k from U
25:            **end if**
26:        **end for**
27:    **until** $\neg change$
28: **end procedure**

29: **procedure** PRUNE(j)
30:    **for all** $(v^k, c) \in R$ **do**
31:        **if** $\nabla v + k \leq j$ **then**   ▷ Prune R
32:            $R \leftarrow R - \{(v^k, c)\}$
33:        **end if**
34:    **end for**
35: **end procedure**

36: **procedure** FINALIZE(N)
37:    **for all** $(v^k, e) \in U$ **do**
38:        **for all** u_c^l subterm of e with $l \geq N$ **do**
39:            $e \leftarrow e[u_c^l \leftarrow c]$
40:        **end for**
41:        $U.replace(v^k, e)$
42:    **end for**
43:    PROPAGATE()
44: **end procedure**

Algorithm 2. Instantiate a defining expression for position j

---
45: **procedure** INST($expr, j$)
46:     **switch** $expr$ **do**
47:         **case** c
48:             **return** c
49:         **case** $f(e_1, \ldots, e_n)$
50:             **return** $f(\text{INST}(e_1, j), \ldots, \text{INST}(e_n, j))$
51:         **case** v
52:             **return** v^j
53:         **case** $v[k, c]$
54:             **if** $k + j < 0$ **then**
55:                 **return** c
56:             **else**
57:                 **return** v_c^{k+j}
58:             **end if**
59: **end procedure**

We show now how the resolved storage R can be pruned by removing information that is no longer necessary. The back reference distance of a stream variable represents the maximum time steps that its value needs to be remembered.

Definition 11 (Back Reference Distance). *Given a specification φ with dependency graph D the* back reference distance ∇v *of a vertex v is*

$$\nabla v = max(0, \left\{ k \mid s \xrightarrow{-k} v \in E \right\})$$

Example 5. We illustrate the use of back reference distances for pruning R (lines 31 and 32) revisiting Example 4. The back reference distances are $\nabla y_1 = \nabla y_{10} = \nabla y_{11} = \nabla y_{12} = \nabla y_{13} = \nabla y_{14} = \nabla y_{15} = \nabla y_{16} = \nabla x_1 = 0$ and $\nabla y_2 = \nabla x_2 = 2$. Consequently, all equations (v^j, c) are removed from R in the same time step that they are entered in R, except for y_2^j and x_2^j, which must remain in R for two time steps until instant $j + 2$.   □

Example 6. Consider the following specification

$$y := q \lor (p \land z)$$
$$z := y[1, false]$$

which computes $p\,\mathcal{U}\,q$. For input streams $\sigma_p : \langle false, false, true, false \rangle$ and $\sigma_q : \langle true, false, false, false \rangle$ the equations in stores R and U at the completion of step (3) of the algorithm at each position are:

j	0	1	2	3
R	$p^0 = false$ $q^0 = true$ $y^0 = true$	$p^1 = false$ $q^1 = false$ $y^1 = false$ $z^0 = false$	$p^2 = true$ $q^2 = false$	$p^3 = false$ $q^3 = false$ $z^3 = false$ $y^3 = false$ $z^2 = false$ $y^2 = false$ $z^1 = false$
U	$z^0 = y^1$	$z^1 = y^2$	$y^2 = z^2$ $z^2 = y^3$ $z^1 = y^2$	$\emptyset$

Since the back reference distance of all stream variables is 0, all equations can be removed from R at each position.   □

Theorem 3 (Correctness). *Let φ be a specification and σ_I be input streams of length N. If φ is well-formed, then Algorithm 1 computes the unique evaluation model of φ for σ_I. That is, at the end of the trace the unique value has been computed for each y^k, and U is empty.*

Proof. Assume φ is well-formed. By Definition 9 the dependency graph D has no zero-weight closed walks and hence by Lemma 1, the evaluation graph G_N has no cycles, and we can define a topological order $<$ in G_N.

As in the proof of Lemma 1, every vertex of G_N can be mapped to the corresponding value of the unique evaluation model. We prove by induction on G_N that at the end of the trace each of these values has been computed and that each value has been available in R at some point $j < N$ during the computation.

For the base case, leaf vertices v^j correspond to either input stream variables or values from equations of the form $x = c$ or $x = y[k, c]$ such that $j + k < 0$. In both cases the value is uniquely obtained and the corresponding equation is added to R.

For the inductive case, the value for vertex v^j is uniquely computed from the values for vertices w^k such that $v^j \rightarrow w^k$, and hence $w^k < v^j$ and by the inductive hypothesis, the value for w^k is uniquely computed or obtained and is at some point available in R. It remains to be shown that these values are available in R for substitution. We distinguish three cases:

1. $j = k$. In this case (v^j, e) and (w^k, e') are added to U (or R) at position j (either in line 6 or in line 7). If (w^k, e') is added to R, the value of w^k in e is substituted in e' in line 19. If (w^k, e') is added to U, by the inductive hypothesis, it is available at some later point in the computation. Then it must be moved to R in line 23, and hence in the same step it is substituted in e.
2. $j < k$. In this case (w^k, e') is added to U (or R) after (v^j, e) is added to U. Again, by the inductive hypothesis, (w^k, c) will be resolved and become available in R at some position $l < N$ and thus at that same position is substituted in e if (v^j, e) is still in U.

3. $j > k$. In this case E_v contains $w[i, c]$ and thus $k = j + i$ (i.e. $i < 0$). Now, (w^k, c) is added to R or U before (v^j, e) is added to U. Again, by the inductive hypothesis, w^k will be resolved at some position $l \leq N$, which must be after k. By the definition of k, (w^k, c) will be in R at least until $k + \nabla w$ which is guaranteed to be at j or after and hence be available when v^j is added to U.

This finishes the proof. $\square$

3.2   Efficiently Monitorable Specifications

In the general case the algorithm MONITOR described above is linear in both time and space in the length of the trace and the size of the specification. In these bounds, we assume that the value of a type can be stored in a single register of the type, and that a single function is computed in a single step.

  In online monitoring, since the traces are assumed to be large, it is generally assumed that a specification can be monitored efficiently only if the memory requirements are independent of the trace length.

Example 7. Consider the following specification with $I = \{x\}$ and $O = \{y, last, w, z\}$:

$$
\begin{aligned}
y &:= false \\
last &:= y[1, true] \\
w &:= z[1, 0] \\
z &:= \textbf{if } last \textbf{ then } x \textbf{ else } w
\end{aligned}
$$

For the input stream σ_x $\langle 37, 31, 79, 17, 14 \rangle$ the unique evaluation model is

σ_x	37	31	79	17	14
σ_y	false	false	false	false	false
σ_{last}	false	false	false	false	true
σ_w	14	14	14	14	0
σ_z	14	14	14	14	14

In general, for any input stream σ_x, output stream σ_z has all its values equal to the last value of σ_x. However, for all j, equations

$$(w^j, z_0^{j+1}) \quad \text{and} \quad (z^j, \textbf{if } last^j \textbf{ then } x^j \textbf{ else } w^j)$$

remain unresolved until the end of the trace, and thus the memory requirements of Algorithm 1 for this specification are linear in the length of the trace. $\square$

  The worst-case memory usage of a LOLA specification for a given trace length can be derived from the evaluation graph with the aid of the following definitions.

Definition 12 (Fan and Latency). *The fan of a vertex v^j of an evaluation graph G_N is the set of vertices reachable v^j:*

$$fan(v^j) \overset{def}{=} \{w^k \mid v^j \rightarrow^* w^k\}$$

The latency of a position variable v^j is the difference between j and the position of the furthest vertex in $fan(v^j)$:

$$lat(v^j) \overset{def}{=} max \left(0, \{ k \mid w^{j+k} \in fan(v^j) \} \right).$$

The fan of v^j is an over-approximation of the set of vertices on which the value of v^j depends. The latency is an upper-bound on the number of trace steps it takes before a value at a given position is guaranteed to be resolved.

Theorem 4. *If a vertex v^j has latency k, then the corresponding equation (v^j, e) will be fully resolved by* MONITOR *at or before step $j + k$.*

Proof. Since the specification is well-formed the evaluation graph is acyclic. We show the results by induction on a topological order $<$ of the evaluation graph. Note that if $v^j \to w^i$ then $lat(v^j) \geq lat(w^i)$ directly by the definition of latency. Then, at position $j+k$ it is guaranteed that w^i is resolved. Since all atoms in the expression e of equation (v^j, e) are resolved at $j+k$ or before, the corresponding values are substituted in e (line 19) at step $j+k$ or before, so e is simplified into a value at $j+k$ or before. $\qquad\square$

Example 8. Consider again the specification of Example 7. The latency of z^2 is $N-2$, so equations for z^2 may reside in U for $N-2$ steps, so this specification cannot be monitored online in a trace-length independent manner. $\qquad\square$

Definition 13 (Efficiently Monitorable). *A* LOLA *specification is efficiently monitorable if the worst case memory usage of* MONITOR *is independent of the length of the trace.*

Some specifications that are not efficiently monitorable may be rewritten into equivalent efficiently monitorable form, as illustrated by the following example.

Example 9. Consider the specification "*Every request must be eventually followed by a grant before the trace ends*", expressed as φ_1 as follows:

$$reqgrant \ \ := \textbf{if } request \textbf{ then } evgrant \textbf{ else } true$$
$$evgrant \ \ := grant \lor nextgrant$$
$$nextgrant := evgrant[1, false]$$

This specification encodes the temporal assertion $\square(request \to \lozenge grant)$. Essentially, $evgrant$ captures $\lozenge grant$ and $reqgrant$ corresponds to $\square(request \to \lozenge grant)$ (see [12] and [10] for a description of translation from LTL to Boolean SRV). An alternative specification φ_2 of the same property is

$$waitgrant := \neg grant \land (request \lor nextgrant)$$
$$nextgrant := waitgrant[-1, false]$$
$$ended \ \ \ := false[1, true]$$

It is easy to see that, for the same input, $ended \land waitgrant$ is true at the end of the trace (for φ_2) if and only if $\neg nextgrant$ is true at the beginning of the trace for φ_1. Hence, both specifications can report a violation at the end of the trace if a request was not granted. The second specification, however, is efficiently monitorable, while the first one is not. $\qquad\square$

Similar to the notion of well-definedness, checking whether a specification is efficiently monitorable is a semantic condition and cannot be checked easily in general. Therefore we define a syntactic condition based on the dependency graph of a specification that guarantees that a specification is efficiently monitorable.

Definition 14 (Future Bounded). *A well-formed specification φ is future bounded if its dependency graph D has no positive-weight cycles.*

We show that every future bounded specification is efficiently monitorable by showing that in the absence of positive-weight cycles every vertex in the dependency graph can be mapped to a non-negative integer that provides an upper-bound on the number of trace steps required to resolve the equation for the corresponding instance variable.

Definition 15 (Look-ahead Distance). *Given a future bounded specification with dependency graph D, the look-ahead distance Δv of a vertex v is the maximum weight of a walk starting from v (or zero if the maximum weight is negative).*

Note that the look-ahead distance is well defined only in the absence of positive-weight cycles. The look-ahead distance of a vertex can be computed easily using shortest path traversals on the dependency graph D.

Example 10. Consider the specification

$$y_1 := y_4 \wedge y_5 \qquad\qquad y_4 := p[1, \textit{false}] \qquad\qquad y_7 := q[2, 0]$$
$$y_2 := \textbf{if } y_6 \textbf{ then } y_7 \textbf{ else } y_8 \qquad y_5 := y_3[-7, \textit{false}] \qquad y_8 := q[-1, 2]$$
$$y_3 := y_9 \leq 5 \qquad\qquad y_6 := y_1[2, \textit{true}] \qquad\qquad y_9 := y_2[4, \textit{true}]$$

The dependency graph D of this specification is:

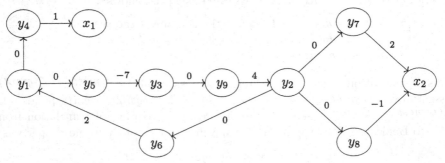

Consequently, the values of the look-ahead distance are:

$$\Delta y_1 = 1 \qquad \Delta y_4 = 1 \qquad \Delta y_7 = 2$$
$$\Delta y_2 = 3 \qquad \Delta y_5 = 0 \qquad \Delta y_8 = 0$$
$$\Delta y_3 = 7 \qquad \Delta y_6 = 3 \qquad \Delta y_9 = 7$$

which are easily computer from D.   □

The look-ahead distance provides an upper-bound on the number of equations that may simultaneously be in U.

Lemma 4. *For every vertex v^j in an evaluation graph G_N of a future bounded specification $lat(v^j) \leq \Delta c$.*

Proof. Consider a vertex v^j in an evaluation graph, with latency $lat(v, j) = d$. Then, there exists a sequence of vertices

$$v^j \rightarrow y_1^{j_1} \rightarrow \cdots \rightarrow y_n^{j_n}$$

with $j_n - j = d$. The walk in the dependency graph of the corresponding vertices

$$v \xrightarrow{j_1 - j} y_1 \xrightarrow{j_2 - j_1} \cdots \xrightarrow{j_n - j_{n-1}} y_n$$

has total weight

$$\sum_{i=1}^{n} j_{i+1} - j_i = j_n - j_i = d$$

and hence $lat(v^j) \leq \Delta v$. □

Theorem 5 (Memory Requirements). *Let φ be a future bounded specification. Algorithm 1 requires to store in U and R, at any point in time, a number of equations linear in the size of φ.*

Proof. From the description of the algorithm and Lemma 4 it follows that the maximum number of equations in U is less than or equal to

$$\sum_{y \in O} \Delta y + |O|$$

where the second term reflects that all equations for the dependent variables are first stored in U in line 7 and after simplification moved to R in line 23.

Moreover, the maximum number of equations stored in R is bounded by ∇v and the number of stream variables v. □

Example 11. Consider again the specification of Example 10. The back reference distance is 0 for all variables except for x_2 and y_3, which are $\nabla x_2 = 1, \nabla y_3 = 7$. Hence, at the end of every main loop, R only contains one instance of x_2 and seven instances of y_3. Additionally, the look-ahead distance of a stream variable v bounds linearly the number of instances of v in U. □

Corollary 1. *Every future-bounded specification is efficiently monitorable.*

Note that the converse does not hold. In practice, it is usually possible to rewrite an online monitoring specification with a positive cycle into one without positive cycles, as illustrated in Example 9.

4   Offline Monitoring

In offline monitoring we assume that all trace data is available on tape, and therefore we can afford more flexibility in accessing the data. In this section we show that every well-formed SRV specification can be monitored efficiently offline, in contrast to online monitoring where we required that the dependency graph not have any positive-weight cycles. The reason why we can efficiently monitor in an offline manner all specifications is that we can perform both forward and backward passes over the trace. We will show that every well-formed specification can be decomposed into sub-specifications such that each sub-specification needs to be checked only once and can be done so efficiently by either traversing the trace in a forward or in a backward direction. In this manner, all values of the output streams of a sub-specification can written to tape and are accessible for subsequent traversals.

We first define the notions of *reverse efficiently monitorable* and its corresponding syntactic condition, *past bounded*, as the duals of efficiently monitorable and future bounded. A reverse monitoring algorithm REVMONITOR can be easily obtained by initializing j to N (line 4) decreasing j (line 10), pruning j on the dual of the back-reference distance in line 31 and performing substitutions when the offset becomes negative (so FINALIZE is not necessary for reverse monitoring). This is essentially the same algorithm as MONITOR but performing the index transformation $j' = N - (j + 1)$.

Definition 16 (Reverse Efficiently Monitorable). *A* LOLA *specification is reverse efficiently monitorable if its worst-case memory requirement when applying* REVMONITOR *is independent of the length of the trace.*

Definition 17 (Past Bounded). *A well-formed* LOLA *specification is past bounded if its dependency graph has no negative-weight cycles.*

Lemma 5. *Every past-bounded specification is reverse efficiently monitorable.*

Proof. The dual of the argument for Corollary 1.   □

We construct now an offline algorithm that can check a well-formed LOLA specification in a sequence of forward and reverse passes over the tapes, such that the number of passes is linear in the size of the specification and each pass is trace-length independent.

Let φ be a well-formed specification with dependency graph D. From the definition of well-formedness it follows that D has no zero-weight cycles, so each MSCC consists of only negative-weight or only positive-weight cycles. Let $G_M : \langle \{V_p, V_n\}, E_M \rangle$ be the graph induced by the MSCCs of D defined as follows. For each positive-weight MSCC in D there is a vertex in V_p and for each negative-weight MSCC in D there is a vertex in V_n. For each edge between two MSCCs there is an edge in E_M connecting the corresponding vertices. Clearly, G_M is a DAG.

Now we assign each MSCC a stage that will determine the order of computing the output for each MSCC following the topological order of G_M. Positive

MSCCs will be assigned even numbers and negative MSCCs will be assigned odd numbers. Every MSCC will be assigned the lowest stage possible that is higher than that of all its descendants with opposite polarity. In other words, the stage of an MSCC v is at least the number of alternations in a path in G_M from v.

Formally, let the opposite descendants be defined as follows:

$$op(v) = \{v' \mid (v, v') \in E_M^* \text{ and } (v \in V_p \text{ and } v' \in V_n, \text{ or } v \in V_n \text{ and } v' \in V_p)\}$$

Then,

$$stage(v) = \begin{cases} 0 & \text{if } op(v) \text{ is empty and } v \in V_n \\ 1 & \text{if } op(v) \text{ is empty and } v \in V_p \\ 1 + max\{stage(v') \mid v' \in op(v)\} & \text{otherwise} \end{cases}$$

which can be computed following a topological order on G_M. Each vertex v in G_M can be viewed as representing a sub-specification φ_v whose defining equations refer only to stream variables in sub-specifications with equal or lower stage processing order. Based on this processing order we construct the following algorithm.

Algorithm 3. Offline Trace Processing

1: **procedure** OFFLINEMON
2:     **for** $i = 0$ to $max(stage(v))$ with increment 2 **do**
3:         **for all** v with $stage(v) = i$ **do**
4:             MONITOR(φ_v)   ▷ Forward pass
5:         **end for**
6:         **for all** v with $stage(v) = i + 1$ **do**
7:             REVMONITOR(φ_v)   ▷ Backward pass
8:         **end for**
9:     **end for**
10: **end procedure**

Theorem 6. *Given a well-formed specification, a trace can be monitored in time linear in the size of the specification and the length of the trace, with memory requirements linear in the size of the specification and independent of the length of the trace.*

Proof. Follows directly from Lemmas 1 and 5 and Algorithm 3.   □

Example 12. Figure 1 shows the dependency graph of a LOLA specification and its decomposition into MSCCs, along with its induced graph G_M annotated with the processing order of the vertices. MSCCs G_1 and G_4 are positive, while G_2 and G_5 are negative. G_3 is a single node MSCC with no edges, which can be chosen to be either positive or negative. The passes are: G_5 is first monitored forward because it is efficiently monitorable. Then, G_4 is monitored backwards. After that, G_3 and G_2 are monitored forward. Finally, G_1 is monitored backwards.

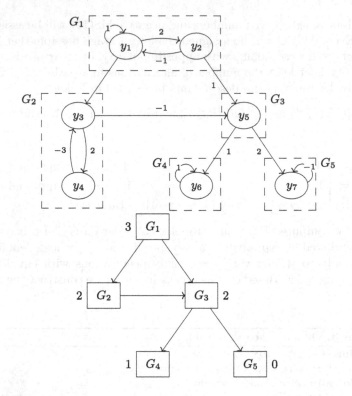

Fig. 1. A dependency graph G and its MSCC induced graph G_M.

5   Conclusions

We have revisited Stream Runtime Verification, a formalism for runtime verification based on expressing the functional relation between input streams and output streams, and we have presented in detail evaluation strategies for online and offline monitoring.

SRV allows both runtime verification of temporal specifications and collection of statistical measures that estimate coverage and specify complex temporal patterns. The LOLA specification language is sufficiently expressive to specify properties of interest to applications like large scale testing, and engineers find the language easy to use. Even specifications with more than 200 variables could be constructed and understood relatively easily by engineers. Even though the language allows ill-defined specifications, SRV provides a syntactic condition that is easy to check and that guarantees well-definedness, using the notion of a dependency graph. Dependency graphs are also used to check whether a specification is efficiently monitorable online, that is, in space independent of the trace length. In practical applications most specifications of interest are in fact efficiently monitorable or can be rewritten into an efficiently monitorable fashion. We revisited the online algorithm for LOLA specifications, and presented an algorithm for offline monitoring whose memory requirements are independent of the trace length for any well-formed specification.

The design of the LOLA specification language was governed by ease of use by engineers. In runtime verification, unlike in static verification, one is free to choose Turing-complete specification languages. As a result researchers have explored the entire spectrum from temporal logics to programming languages. The advantage of a programming language in comparison with a temporal logic is that a declarative programming language is more familiar to engineers and large specifications are easier to write and understand. The disadvantage is that the semantics is usually tied to the evaluation strategy (typically in an informal implicit manner) and the complexity is hard to determine, while the semantics of a logic is independent of the evaluation strategy and upper bounds for its complexity are known. In practice, the choice is motivated by the intended use. Stream Runtime Verification is usually employed to facilitate the task of writing large specifications for engineers, so the natural choice was a programming-language. SRV retains, however, most of the advantages of a logic: the semantics is independent of the evaluation strategy and the efficiently monitorable specifications provide a clear bound on complexity. See [10] where we study decision procedures and complexities of decision problems for Boolean Stream Runtime Verification. For example, comparing LOLA with specification languages at the other end of the spectrum, such as Eagle [3], LOLA usually allows simpler specifications, as illustrated in Fig. 2.

Eagle encoding of the operator $\Box_p F$ with intended meaning that F holds with at least probability p over a given sequence [3]:

$$\underline{\min}\ A(\textit{Form } F, \textit{float } p, \textit{int } f, \textit{int } t) =$$

$$\left(\bigcirc Empty() \wedge \left(\begin{matrix} (F\ \wedge (1 - \frac{f}{t}) \geq p) \\ \vee \\ (\neg F \wedge (1 - \frac{f+1}{t}) \geq p) \end{matrix} \right) \right) \vee$$

$$\left(\neg Empty() \wedge \left(\begin{matrix} (F\ \rightarrow \bigcirc A(F, p, f, t+1)) \\ \wedge \\ (\neg F \rightarrow \bigcirc A(F, p, f+1, t+1)) \end{matrix} \right) \right)$$

Corresponding LOLA specification:

$$countF = F[1, 0] + \mathtt{ite}(F, 1, 0)$$
$$total\ \ = total[1, 0] + 1$$
$$BoxFp = (F/total) \geq p$$

Fig. 2. Comparison between the LOLA and Eagle specification language

References

1. Asarin, E., Caspi, P., Maler, O.: Timed regular expressions. J. ACM **49**(2), 172–206 (2002)
2. Barringer, H., Falcone, Y., Havelund, K., Reger, G., Rydeheard, D.: Quantified event automata: towards expressive and efficient runtime monitors. In: Giannakopoulou, D., Méry, D. (eds.) FM 2012. LNCS, vol. 7436, pp. 68–84. Springer, Heidelberg (2012). https://doi.org/10.1007/978-3-642-32759-9_9
3. Barringer, H., Goldberg, A., Havelund, K., Sen, K.: Rule-based runtime verification. In: Steffen, B., Levi, G. (eds.) VMCAI 2004. LNCS, vol. 2937, pp. 44–57. Springer, Heidelberg (2004). https://doi.org/10.1007/978-3-540-24622-0_5
4. Bartocci, E., Falcone, Y. (eds.): Lectures on Runtime Verification. LNCS, vol. 10457. Springer, Cham (2018). https://doi.org/10.1007/978-3-319-75632-5
5. Bauer, A., Küster, J.-C., Vegliach, G.: From propositional to first-order monitoring. In: Legay, A., Bensalem, S. (eds.) RV 2013. LNCS, vol. 8174, pp. 59–75. Springer, Heidelberg (2013). https://doi.org/10.1007/978-3-642-40787-1_4
6. Bauer, A., Leucker, M., Schallhart, C.: Runtime verification for LTL and TLTL. ACM T. Softw. Eng. Meth. **20**(4), 14 (2011)
7. Bauer, A., Leucker, M., Schallhart, C.: Monitoring of real-time properties. In: Arun-Kumar, S., Garg, N. (eds.) FSTTCS 2006. LNCS, vol. 4337, pp. 260–272. Springer, Heidelberg (2006). https://doi.org/10.1007/11944836_25
8. Bauer, A., Leucker, M., Schallhart, C.: The good, the bad, and the ugly, but how ugly is ugly? In: Sokolsky, O., Taşıran, S. (eds.) RV 2007. LNCS, vol. 4839, pp. 126–138. Springer, Heidelberg (2007). https://doi.org/10.1007/978-3-540-77395-5_11
9. Berry, G.: The foundations of Esterel. In: Plotkin, G., Stirling, C., Tofte, M. (eds.) Proof, Language, and Interaction: Essays in Honour of Robin Milner, pp. 425–454. MIT Press, Cambridge (2000)
10. Bozzelli, L., Sánchez, C.: Foundations of Boolean stream runtime verification. In: Bonakdarpour, B., Smolka, S.A. (eds.) RV 2014. LNCS, vol. 8734, pp. 64–79. Springer, Cham (2014). https://doi.org/10.1007/978-3-319-11164-3_6
11. Convent, L., Hungerecker, S., Leucker, M., Scheffel, T., Schmitz, M., Thoma, D.: TeSSLa: temporal stream-based specification language. In: Proceedings of the 21st Brazilian Symposium on Formal Methods (SBMF 2018). LNCS. Springer (2018)
12. D'Angelo, et al.: LOLA: runtime monitoring of synchronous systems. In: Proceedings of TIME 2005, pp. 166–174. IEEE CS Press (2005)
13. Eisner, C., Fisman, D., Havlicek, J., Lustig, Y., McIsaac, A., Van Campenhout, D.: Reasoning with temporal logic on truncated paths. In: Hunt, W.A., Somenzi, F. (eds.) CAV 2003. LNCS, vol. 2725, pp. 27–39. Springer, Heidelberg (2003). https://doi.org/10.1007/978-3-540-45069-6_3
14. Faymonville, P., Finkbeiner, B., Schirmer, S., Torfah, H.: A stream-based specification language for network monitoring. In: Falcone, Y., Sánchez, C. (eds.) RV 2016. LNCS, vol. 10012, pp. 152–168. Springer, Cham (2016). https://doi.org/10.1007/978-3-319-46982-9_10
15. Faymonville, P., Finkbeiner, B., Schwenger, M., Torfah, H.: Real-time stream-based monitoring. CoRR, abs/1711.03829 (2017)
16. Finkbeiner, B., Sankaranarayanan, S., Sipma, H.B.: Collecting statistics over runtime executions. ENTCS **70**(4), 36–54 (2002)
17. Gautier, T., Le Guernic, P., Besnard, L.: SIGNAL: a declarative language for synchronous programming of real-time systems. In: Kahn, G. (ed.) FPCA 1987.

LNCS, vol. 274, pp. 257–277. Springer, Heidelberg (1987). https://doi.org/10.1007/3-540-18317-5_15

18. Goodloe, A.E., Pike, L.: Monitoring distributed real-time systems: a survey and future directions. Technical report, NASA Langley Research Center (2010)
19. Gorostiaga, F., Sánchez, C.: Striver: stream runtime verification for real-time event-streams. In: Colombo, C., Leucker, M. (eds.) RV 2018. LNCS, vol. 11237, pp. 282–298. Springer, Cham (2018)
20. Halbwachs, N., Caspi, P., Raymond, P., Pilaud, D.: The synchronous data-flow programming language LUSTRE. Proc. IEEE **79**(9), 1305–1320 (1991)
21. Havelund, K., Goldberg, A.: Verify your runs. In: Meyer, B., Woodcock, J. (eds.) VSTTE 2005. LNCS, vol. 4171, pp. 374–383. Springer, Heidelberg (2008). https://doi.org/10.1007/978-3-540-69149-5_40
22. Havelund, K., Roşu, G.: Synthesizing monitors for safety properties. In: Katoen, J.-P., Stevens, P. (eds.) TACAS 2002. LNCS, vol. 2280, pp. 342–356. Springer, Heidelberg (2002). https://doi.org/10.1007/3-540-46002-0_24
23. Leucker, M., Sánchez, C., Scheffel, T., Schmitz, M., Schramm, A.: TeSSLa: runtime verification of non-synchronized real-time streams. In: Proceedings of the 33rd Symposium on Applied Computing (SAC 2018). ACM (2018)
24. Leucker, M., Schallhart, C.: A brief account of runtime verification. J. Logic Algebr. Progr. **78**(5), 293–303 (2009)
25. Pike, L., Goodloe, A., Morisset, R., Niller, S.: Copilot: a hard real-time runtime monitor. In: Barringer, H., et al. (eds.) RV 2010. LNCS, vol. 6418, pp. 345–359. Springer, Heidelberg (2010). https://doi.org/10.1007/978-3-642-16612-9_26
26. Pnueli, A., Zaks, A.: PSL model checking and run-time verification via testers. In: Misra, J., Nipkow, T., Sekerinski, E. (eds.) FM 2006. LNCS, vol. 4085, pp. 573–586. Springer, Heidelberg (2006). https://doi.org/10.1007/11813040_38
27. Roşu, G., Havelund, K.: Rewriting-based techniques for runtime verification. Autom. Softw. Eng. **12**(2), 151–197 (2005)
28. Sen, K., Roşu, G.: Generating optimal monitors for extended regular expressions. ENTCS **89**(2), 226–245 (2003)

Regular Papers

METIS: Resource and Context-Aware Monitoring of Finite State Properties

Garvita Allabadi[1]([✉]), Aritra Dhar[2], Ambreen Bashir[1], and Rahul Purandare[1]

[1] IIIT-Delhi, New Delhi, India
{garvita12133,ambreen1233,purandare}@iiitd.ac.in
[2] ETH Zurich, Zurich, Switzerland
aritra.dhar@inf.ethz.ch

Abstract. Runtime monitoring of finite state properties may incur large and unpredictable overheads in terms of memory and execution time, which makes its deployment in a production environment challenging. In this work, we present a monitoring approach that investigates the trade-offs between memory overheads of monitoring, execution times of monitoring operations, and error reporting. Our approach is motivated by two key observations. First, there is a prominent behavioral redundancy among monitors. Second, the events on the same or related objects are often temporally segregated. We have implemented our approach in a prototype tool, METIS. Its evaluation indicates that it can reduce the memory footprint effectively and provide compact worst-case execution time bounds to monitoring operations with little to no compromise in error reporting.

1 Introduction

Modern software applications are complex and functionally diverse. They come in forms ranging from large web-based systems to applications that run on small hand-held mobile devices. Irrespective of their forms, they pose challenges for tools that analyze them for correctness. Even though useful, static analysis often produces numerous false positives that are hard to analyze [21]. Hence, researchers have invested time and effort to develop runtime monitoring tools [1,3,9,25].

In spite of their effectiveness, monitoring tools have been found to incur considerable memory and execution overheads making their deployment challenging in a production environment [24]. This may happen particularly when the properties of interest are associated with objects that are generated in large numbers [20]. Monitoring overheads can be an even bigger concern considering that in practice, programmers would like to track several properties simultaneously [18,24].

Monitoring overheads are difficult to estimate since they depend on program and property interactions, which in turn, depend on executed program paths. When properties are associated with multiple objects [8,20,24], monitoring operations may take arbitrarily long even for similar events owing to the fact that

© Springer Nature Switzerland AG 2018
C. Colombo and M. Leucker (Eds.): RV 2018, LNCS 11237, pp. 167–186, 2018.
https://doi.org/10.1007/978-3-030-03769-7_10

variable number of monitors may get associated with them at different times and each one of the monitors needs to be tracked after the occurrence of these events. This number can grow rapidly. Up to 1548 monitors associated with a single event have been reported [24].

Large and unpredictable overheads pose severe challenges to monitoring since they adversely impact the system performance. Even web-based and cloud-based systems have practical constraints on their resources since the applications they run are often CPU- and memory-intensive, and their performance is expected to be high and predictable. Hence, to employ monitoring in a production environment, we need novel techniques that consume fewer resources and provide performance guarantees.

Researchers have proposed several approaches in the past to control overheads, such as turning off monitoring if it exceeds the time budget [3,5,27]. However, these approaches do not deal with properties that are related to multiple objects. Other approaches either do not deal with finite state properties or do not perform inline monitoring. Finite state property monitoring allows us to check programs for properties with multiple objects, whereas inline monitoring allows us to keep detection latency within limits and provides opportunities to avoid failure by performing evasive actions [15].

In this work, we propose a novel inline monitoring technique that investigates the trade-offs between program resources, namely, memory and execution time, and error reporting. Our approach is motivated by a key observation that there is a large behavioral redundancy among monitors that results in the majority of them undergoing similar life cycle. Even when some monitors report errors they may report the same error. This is wasteful from the monitoring perspective because it consumes resources and programmers are interested in catching only distinct errors. Our technique limits the number of monitors based on the program's execution context[1] and puts a hard limit on the number of monitors associated with an event. As a result, it consumes much less memory and provides tight worst-case bounds on event monitoring times. Another key observation is that events on the same or related objects often occur together. Therefore, recent events are likely to be associated with newly created objects. We develop monitor allocation heuristics based on these observations to maintain the soundness of the system.

This paper makes two contributions. First, we present a novel approach in Sect. 4 that is memory-efficient and time-deterministic. Second, we present a study using a prototype implementation tool, METIS in Sect. 6 and evaluate it first on challenging DACAPO benchmarks in Sect. 7, and then on two resource-constrained web applications in Sect. 7.7. The results indicate that the technique has a potential to detect all distinct violations that an unoptimized approach could detect using much fewer resources.

---

[1] The execution context of an error report is the path of the call graph from the root function to the current function where that error report was triggered.

2 Background and Motivation

2.1 Finite State Properties

This work considers properties that are either typestate or typestate-like that may involve multiple objects and can be modeled using a finite state automaton (FSA) [28]. Figure 1a depicts an FSA which models the `UnsafeIterator` property. This property codifies that a `Collection` must not be updated while being iterated over. The symbols *create*, *update*, and *next* correspond to creating an `Iterator` from a `Collection`, modifying the `Collection`, and iterating over the `Collection`, respectively. The symbol *next* observed following *update* pushes the FSA to the *error* state. Similarly, Fig. 1b encodes the `HasNext` property, which states that *hasNext* must always be invoked prior to invoking *next* to ensure that an element exists before it is operated upon. Figure 1c illustrates the property `HashSet`, which checks that an object added to a hashset can be safely accessed from the set only before it is removed from the set and only if its hashcode is not changed in the meantime.

2.2 Monitoring System

Figure 2a depicts a general monitoring scheme that takes as input an instrumented program and a property to be monitored. The instrumentation corresponds to the extra code added to program statements, which are relevant to the property. This extra code generates events that are tracked by the monitoring system. An event is parameterized by objects and has a symbol associated with it. This information is analyzed first by the monitor creation module to see if

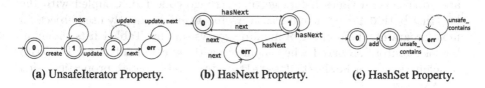

(a) UnsafeIterator Property.   (b) HasNext Propterty.   (c) HashSet Property.

Fig. 1. FSA for finite state properties.

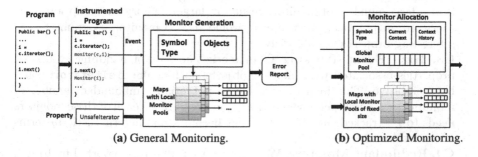

(a) General Monitoring.   (b) Optimized Monitoring.

Fig. 2. Schematics of monitoring systems.

Table 1. Original benchmark memory consumption in MB, number of monitors and events generated, and memory consumption in MB while monitoring the programs for various properties.

	Orig. Mem.	HasNext			UnsafeIterator			HashSet		
		#mon	#event	memory	#mon	#event	memory	#mon	#event	memory
Avrora	51	0.9 M	2.5 M	160	0.9 M	1.4 M	419	106	11 K	61
Bloat	94	1.9 M	144 M	1433	1.9 M	82 M	1158	66 K	171 K	1505
Pmd	157	1.9 M	49 M	1288	1.9 M	26 M	1120	6.8 M	6.8 M	1356

a monitor needs to be created. A monitor contains a property FSA, references to the related objects, and its current state. A newly created monitor is added to the pools associated with the related objects and then tracked for all related future events. The tracking involves performing a state transition according to the symbol and the current state. In case a monitor moves to the error state, the error is reported. For example, for property UnsafeIterator, a monitoring system instantiates a *monitor* corresponding to every pair of Collection and Iterator after observing a *creation* event, which corresponds to an invocation to the Iterator() method on the Collection interface. It then pushes the monitor from state 0 to state 1. As long as the Iterator is used, the monitor remains in state 1. If the Collection is updated, the monitor moves to state 2. Any subsequent use of the Iterator pushes the monitor to the error state which is then reported as the error.

CHALLENGES. Monitoring of finite state properties can be challenging due to:

C1. High Monitor Count: In practice, a Collection object may get iterated over several times before getting garbage collected. Coupled with the fact that both Collection and Iterator objects are frequently used objects in most programs, the number of monitors grows rapidly. Table 1 lists the number of monitors observed when monitoring three commonly used DACAPO benchmarks [6] for HasNext, UnsafeIterator, and HashSet properties using JAVAMOP v2.3.

C2. High Memory Usage: Table 1 also lists the memory consumption of the benchmarks with and without monitoring using JAVAMOP v2.3. We observe that a large number of monitors results in large memory consumption. Furthermore, in practice, programmers would like to monitor programs for *all* interesting properties collectively.

C3. High Event Tracking Overhead: The cost of handling events for properties associated with multiple objects, such as UnsafeIterator, could be prohibitive. This high cost is due to potentially unbounded number of monitors that might get associated with an event. Since each of these monitors needs to be tracked, handling an event becomes non-deterministic in terms of execution time.

C4. Redundant Monitors: We observed that all errors reported by bloat, pmd, and avrora for property HasNext can be grouped into exactly one unique class of errors each for the benchmarks based on their execution context, i.e., sequence of method calls. This observation indicates that several monitors catch the same redundant errors, which clearly is not intelligent reporting to the developer. Ideally, the monitors should report only distinct errors, i.e., one for each benchmark in this case.

3   Terminology and Definitions

Finite state properties can be modeled using a Deterministic Finite Automaton represented by a tuple $(Q, \Sigma, q_0, \delta, F, err)$, where Q is the set of states, Σ is the set of symbols, $q_0 \in Q$ is the start state, $\delta : Q \times \Sigma \to Q$ is the state transition function, $F \subset Q$ is the set of accept states, and err is the designated error state. Typically, $F \bigcup err = Q$ and $F \bigcap err = \emptyset$.

Let ϕ be a program property to be monitored, and let O be the set of objects associated with ϕ. An event η in the program under execution is represented by a pair (β, σ), where $\beta \in 2^O$ is a set of objects associated with the event and $\sigma \in \Sigma$.

We define a monitor $m \in M$ parameterized by a set of objects α, where $\alpha \in 2^O$, and $cur \in Q$ is the current state of the monitor. We assume the presence of $\Sigma_c \subseteq \Sigma$ which are symbols associated with monitor creation events. We define a mapping $\psi : 2^O \nrightarrow 2^M$ that after receiving an event $\eta = (\beta, \sigma)$ returns a set of monitors θ corresponding to β, where $\beta \subseteq \alpha$. Note that α uniquely identifies a monitor, and β has exactly one monitor associated when $\beta = \alpha$. However, there may be more than one monitors associated with β when $\beta \subset \alpha$. The current state of every monitor that belongs to θ is updated according to the symbol associated with the event. Formally, $\forall m \in \theta : m.cur \leftarrow \delta(m.cur, \sigma)$. We report the error when $m.cur = err$.

A traditional approach uses ψ for locating monitors, whereas our approach generates ψ' such that the approach ignores an event $\eta = (\beta, \sigma)$ if $\psi'(\beta)$ is undefined. Moreover, it returns $\theta_b \subseteq \theta$ to limit the number of monitors to be updated for an event to b.

Classes of Errors. Even with the reduced number of monitors, our approach still tries to detect all distinct errors. Let P be the set of error reports generated by an unoptimized monitoring system for a given program run. Let Π be the set of program execution contexts under which P was generated. Let $\pi \in \Pi$ be the context under which the report $\rho \in P$ was generated. We partition the set P into classes $c_1, \ldots, c_n$ as follows – $\rho_i \in c_k$ and $\rho_j \in c_k$ if and only if ρ_i and ρ_j were created under the context π_k. In other words, all error reports that fall under one class are created under the same program execution context and hence we treat them equivalent. The aim of our approach is to generate *distinct* error reports, that is ideally one report for every class of errors.

4   Monitoring Approach

Figure 2b shows the main elements of our approach. The key difference with the general scheme depicted in Fig. 2a is the monitor allocation module which keeps information about the current execution context, the observed execution contexts, and the global monitor pool in addition to the symbol types. The module maintains the observed contexts as a forest in which a newly observed context adds a node with one or more branches corresponding to method calls in exactly one of the trees. A leaf node represents a context and the module keeps its observed frequency.

Context-Based Sampling: We use context-based sampling of objects to control the number of monitors. The motivation comes from our observation that monitors created under similar program execution contexts tend to go through a similar life cycle and show a redundant behavior. Our approach works by (i) identifying the monitor creation sites which are specified as creation events in the monitoring specification, and then by (ii) obtaining the current execution context, and finally by (iii) making a decision about the allocation of the monitor based on the number of times this context was seen in the past. More often the system has seen the context, less likely it is to allocate a monitor. An execution context that we consider in this work is the limited length suffix of the method calling sequence. We describe its implementation in Sect. 6.

Fixed-Size Global Pool of Monitors: The global monitor pool is implemented as a circular array of fixed size that preserves the chronological ordering. In case the allocation module chooses to allocate a monitor, it picks the next available monitor from this pool. The monitor being allocated could be already in use in which case it is first deallocated, reset, and then reallocated to the current set of objects. The heuristic that we use to reclaim a monitor is based on our observations that events related to the same objects are often temporally segregated, and recent events are more likely to be generated by newly created objects. We exploit this observation by making the oldest active monitor available for reallocation.

Fixed-Size Local Pool of Monitors for Indexed Objects: In the case of a property related to multiple objects, an object can get associated with numerous monitors in its life-time depending on its interaction with other objects. As a result, an event related to the object results in updating the states of arbitrarily large number of monitors making handling such events *nondeterministic* in terms of their execution times. For this work, we consider a monitoring behavior as time-deterministic if we can compute and limit the worst-case execution time for monitoring every event. Binding the number of monitors associated with an object allows us to limit the execution time for any monitoring operation associated with that object. Our approach implements this constraint by restricting the size of local pools. In case this pool is full, we return the oldest monitor from it to the global pool to make space for the new monitor.

Algorithm 1 . Resource- and Context-Aware Monitoring. Input: $\phi = (Q,\Sigma,\delta,q_0,F,\text{err})$, $\eta = (\beta,\sigma)$ where η is an event and $\beta \in 2^O$ be the set of associated objects and $\sigma \in \Sigma$.

1: **let** $\Sigma_c \subseteq \Sigma$ be the set of creation symbols.
2: **let** A be the global array of monitors.
3: **let** $\psi': 2^O \rightarrowtail 2^M$ be the map that returns the monitors associated with a set of objects.
4: **let** $\tau: M \rightarrowtail 2^O$ be the map that returns the objects associated with a monitor.
5: **let** $\pi \in \Pi$ be a finite sequence of methods.
6: **let** ζ hold observed execution contexts.
7: **if** $\sigma \in \Sigma_c$ **then**
8:     $\pi \leftarrow getExecutionContextInfo()$
9:     **if** isPresent(π, ζ) = TRUE **then**
10:        $k \leftarrow$ threshold(π, ζ)
11:    **else**
12:        $k \leftarrow 1$
13:    $updateExecutionContext(\pi, \zeta)$
14:    **if** Random$() \leq k$ **then**
15:        $m \leftarrow A.\text{nextMonitor}()$
16:        **for all** $\alpha \subseteq \tau(m)$ **do**
17:            $\psi'(\alpha) \leftarrow \psi'(\alpha)/\{m\}$
18:        reset(m)
19:        **for all** $\alpha \subseteq \beta$ **do**
20:            **if** $\psi'(\alpha).\text{size}() = max\_mon$ **then**
21:                $m' \leftarrow \psi'(\alpha).\text{first}()$;
22:                **for all** $\alpha' \subseteq \tau(m')$ **do**
23:                    $\psi'(\alpha') \leftarrow \psi'(\alpha') / \{m'\}$
24:            $\psi'(\alpha) \leftarrow \psi'(\alpha) \cup \{m\}$
25: **for all** $m \in \psi'(\beta)$ **do**
26:    $m.\text{cur} \leftarrow \delta(m.\text{cur},\sigma)$
27:    **if** $m.\text{cur} =$ err **then**
28:        report **error**

All the parameters mentioned above including the monitor pool sizes and the method call sequence length are configurable depending on the available resources.

5 Monitoring Algorithm

Algorithm 1 depicts the steps that implement our monitoring scheme. It takes a property ϕ and an event η as input. Lines 7–24 describe the operations that are performed when a creation event is encountered and a new monitor may need to be allocated. Line 8 reads the program execution context. If the execution context is already seen which is checked at line 9, then a *threshold* value between 0 and 1 is generated based on the frequency of the observed context. If the context is unseen, the threshold is assigned the highest value which is 1 to ensure that a monitor will be allocated to observe this unseen context. In either case line 13 updates the execution context history.

Lines 14–24 describe the steps when the threshold value is found to be large enough to justify allocation of a monitor which is checked at line 14. As a result, a new monitor from the global circular array is allocated at line 15. Lines 16–17 reclaim the monitor in case it was previously assigned. This step ensures that all previous bindings are removed. The monitor is then reset at line 18 and is made ready for the assignment.

Lines 19–24 describe the steps to insert new monitor in all relevant pools. The condition at line 20 checks that all local monitor pools are still within the size limit. In case the limit is getting exceeded for any pool, the oldest monitor in the pool is identified at line 21 and then reclaimed by removing it from related lists of all maps as shown in lines 22–23. The new monitor is then inserted in the list at line 24.

Finally, as shown in lines 25–28, the relevant monitors are retrieved and their states are updated. In case any of the states is the *error* state, then the error is reported.

Correctness: We argue about the correctness of our algorithm by arguing about its *soundness* and *completeness* with respect to the unoptimized version. Runtime monitoring is inherently unsound since errors may not be reported if the paths that encounter them are not exercised [30]. However, monitoring is expected to be sound with respect to the observed traces and complete so that it produces no false positives.

The unoptimized approach creates a monitor for every creation event, whereas the optimized approach either allocates one from the pool or skips the allocation completely. If a monitor is reused, it is reset first before its realloca-tion. For non-creation events, the optimized approach either skips monitoring if no monitor was earlier allocated or tracks them in a way similar to the unopti-mized approach. In other words, if a monitor picked by the optimized approach for tracking reaches the error state, then the system guarantees that the monitor was tracked from the beginning similar to the unoptimized approach. Therefore, optimized approach cannot produce any false positives, since the unoptimized approach cannot. As a result, the optimized approach retains the completeness. The degree of soundness, however, depends on whether the optimized approach skipped events that would have otherwise led to an error.

Memory and Time Efficiency: The algorithm preallocates monitors from a pool of constant size, and then if required, monitors are reused. This reduces the number of required monitors drastically. In fact, as mentioned in the study in Sect. 7, for some configurations the system ended up consuming even less moni-tors than the size of the global monitor pool due to limited program execution contexts that were observed during runtime. The number of dynamic instances of execution contexts can often be much less than the static instances which are computed more conservatively. The reduced number of monitors allow us to skip monitoring actions. The fact that other events are generally much higher in number than creation events also helps. Even though maintaining and checking execution contexts and reallocating monitors add to the overhead, the efficient memory management scheme helps maintain the system's efficiency. In addition, it reduces the system's dependence on the garbage collector saving the execution time and reducing the unpredictability introduced by the garbage collector.

Execution Time-Determinism: The fact that the algorithm has fairly tight worst-case execution time bounds can be explained by analysing the bounds on the steps involved in handling monitoring events which can be divided into two categories.

Handling Creation Events: This event may result in a monitor allocation. Accessing the execution context on line 8 is a constant time operation. Method `isPresent` on line 9 may traverse the height of the context tree in the worst case, which still makes it constant time since the tree has a limited height equal to the length of the execution context. Similar argument applies to updating the context on line 13. The loop on lines 16–17 iterates 2^n times where n is $\mid \tau(m) \mid$ and $\tau(m)$ is the number of associated objects typically ranging from 1 to 3. Hence, this operation takes $O(1)$ time. By the same arguments loops on lines 22–23 and 19–24 iterate $2^{|\tau(m)|}$ and 2^β times and take $O(1)$ time. Hence, the running time of the outer loop on lines 19–24 is constant. Therefore the overall time taken by a creation event is constant.

Handling Other Events: Since the size of the local monitor pools is limited to a small constant, say k, the loop on lines 25–28 executes at most k times. Hence, the handling of other events takes a constant time.

Therefore, the running time of the algorithm is a constant and for a program execution that generates n events, the time taken to handle these events is $\Theta(n)$. In comparison, in the worst case, the unoptimized algorithm may create $O(n)$ monitors, assign all of them to a set of objects, and then receive $O(n)$ events of similar kind on the same set of objects requiring all of the created monitors to be tracked for every event. Therefore, the worst-case complexity of the unoptimized algorithm is $O(n^2)$.

5.1 Soundness, Memory, Efficiency, and Time-Determinism: Tradeoffs

There is a direct relation between soundness and the number of monitors allocated, which in turn, corresponds to the memory allocated for monitoring. We stretch the inherent unsoundness of any monitoring system a little further to achieve substantial benefits in terms of memory savings using heuristics that help limit the unsoundness. Similar tradeoffs exist between soundness and efficiency, and soundness and time-determinism where we pick one at a potential loss of the other. However, as indicated by the study in Sects. 7 and 7.7, our approach can save considerable amount of memory, maintain its efficiency, and can also make monitoring time-deterministic without compromising much with its error reporting. As a result, our technique should enable developers to employ monitoring in environments where traditional techniques might not be feasible.

6   METIS Implementation

METIS, the prototype of our approach (as described in Sect. 4) is implemented in JAVA. We use SOOT [26] for program instrumentation, and leverage the ajc v1.8.0 compiler to weave aspects. Some salient features of METIS are described below.

Lightweight Execution Context and Static Analysis Optimization: While the Java method `getStackTrace()` fetches the current stack trace, it introduces significant performance penalties. To mitigate this overhead, we instrument program methods with a static `Integer` field and populate it with a unique 16-bit identifier. We maintain method calling sequence by using a circular array containing these identifiers. In our implementation, the sequence is of length 3. The circular array is implemented as a 64 bit `Long` integer. The array is of the format $id_1|id_2|id_3$, where id_i is the id corresponding to method f_i and is a 16 bit integer. Note that the method call sequence is populated by bit-wise $<<$ and | operations, which makes any query operation over the stack-trace lightweight. To further reduce the execution time, we employ static analysis to identify and instrument the methods which are within the distance equal to the length of the context from the method calls that may lead to the error state.

Aspects and Monitors Allocation: METIS takes as input the regular expression based mop files from JAVAMOP v2.3. It then generates the aspect file for the specified property. We modify these aspects by adding logic corresponding to the monitor allocation.

Context Matching: A `HashMap` is added to the aspect that maps a context (`long`) to a `ArrayList` of monitors associated with it. Each monitor is associated with a unique context value. Whenever a new monitor creation pointcut is encountered, the context matching module checks the number of the monitor associated with that context and probabilistically decides whether to allocate more monitors or not.

7   Evaluation

7.1   Artefacts

The evaluation of our approach is divided into two parts: In the first part we perform our experiments on DACAPO benchmarks which have also been used in the related work [7,9,24]. We considered three benchmarks from DACAPO benchmark suite [6,11], namely `bloat`, `pmd` and `avrora`. We ignored other benchmarks in the suite as they do not contain sufficient monitor events. We consider `HasNext`, `UnsafeIterator` and `HashSet` as the finite state properties of interest since they have been reported to generate considerable monitors and overheads in the prior work [20,24]. In the second part, we present two case studies on two popular real world applications. The first is a marketplace and e-commerce platform called `Mayocat Shop` [19] and the second is a Java graph library called

JGraphT [16]. Both are open source applications written in Java. We define new customized typestate properties for these platforms and perform our experiments on them. The case study is covered in detail in Sect. 7.7.

7.2 Experimental Setup

We performed the experiments on a laptop provisioned with 2.3 GHz processor, 16 GB RAM and running 64-bit Windows 10. We use JVM v8 with 8 GB heap. For evaluation, we use DACAPO benchmarks versions $2006 - 10 - MR2$ and 9.12 [6,11]. We host the application in Sect. 7.7 on the Apache Tomcat Server v8.0.46. For calculating the execution times, we ran the experiments 5 times and reported the mean values.

7.3 Evaluation Criteria

We list the key research questions about the effectiveness of our approach that we address in this section below.

RQ1: Does it consume less memory?
RQ2: Does it incur higher execution time overhead than the unoptimized approach?
RQ3: Does it bound the worst case execution time for all monitoring operations?
RQ4: Does it effectively catch errors?

7.4 Resource Consumption

In this section, we answer questions **RQ1** and **RQ2** to understand the resource consumption of our approach. We execute the three DACAPO benchmarks and measure the total execution time and memory consumption. Tables 2 and 3 list the results. We compare the performance against the aspects generated by JAVA-MOP, which is denoted as *Unoptimized* in the table. *Optimized*$(\mathcal{L}(a) = 1\,K)$ denotes the optimized monitors with 1K limit on the size of monitor pool. We observe that for all cases the benchmarks with the optimized monitors execute faster than the unoptimized ones. This indicates that our optimizations decrease the time overhead. There is upto 55% reduction in execution times compared to the unoptimized approach.

Table 2. Runtime (ms.) of DACAPO benchmarks, $\mathcal{L}(A)$ denotes size of monitor pool.

	HasNext			UnsafeIterator			HashSet		
	Avrora	Bloat	Pmd	Avrora	Bloat	Pmd	Avrora	Bloat	Pmd
Without monitoring	7221	3221	3746	7221	3221	3746	7221	3221	3746
Unoptimized	44766	27126	15085	48456	25355	13506	44754	13695	15785
Optimized $(\mathcal{L}(A) = 1\,K)$	39864	16053	8240	39302	17772	7941	40177	12350	8178
Optimized $(\mathcal{L}(A) = 10\,K)$	42107	16424	10250	43008	18396	8581	44098	12700	9390

Table 3. Peak Memory consumption (in GB).

	HasNext			UnsafeIterator			HashSet		
	Avrora	Bloat	Pmd	Avrora	Bloat	Pmd	Avrora	Bloat	Pmd
Without monitoring	0.05	0.09	0.15	0.05	0.09	0.15	0.05	0.09	0.15
Unoptimized	0.157	1.4	1.2	0.41	1.15	1.11	0.06	1.5	1.35
Optimized $(\mathcal{L}(A) = 1\,\mathrm{K})$	0.067	0.12	0.268	0.067	0.26	0.247	0.06	0.10	0.422
Optimized $(\mathcal{L}(A) = 10\,\mathrm{K})$	0.079	0.12	0.36	0.079	0.27	0.526	0.06	0.12	0.423

Table 4. Comparison of event execution times (nano second) of UnsafeIterator property.

Create									
	Bloat			Pmd			Avrora		
	Max	Mean	Std Dev	Max	Mean	Std Dev	Max	Mean	Std Dev
Unoptimized	26 M	1.2 K	38.21 K	84M	996.95	101.87 K	74M	2.12 K	106.68 K
Optimized $(\mathcal{L}(A) = 10\,\mathrm{K})$	625 K	5.14 K	9.64 K	395 K	4.25 K	7.94 K	998 K	13.75 K	17.80 K
Update									
Unoptimized	418 K	265.22	1.66 K	807 K	76.06	294.09	33 M	26.38 K	687.12 K
Optimized $(\mathcal{L}(A) = 10\,\mathrm{K})$	40 K	127.28	294.09	67 K	38.21	218.02	90 K	319.74	427.85 K

Table 3 represents the memory consumption for the benchmarks. Unsurprisingly, the memory consumption of the optimized approach is always substantially less (by up to 77% compared to the unoptimized approach) than the unoptimized approach, and is only marginally higher than the consumption of the uninstrumented benchmarks. The very low memory overhead is because our approach spawns considerably less number of monitors (see Table 5) which should allow developers to employ monitoring even in severely resource-constrained environments.

7.5   Bounded Execution Time

We now address **RQ3**, i.e., bound on worst case execution time. We consider the UnsafeIterator property for this analysis, since it is a multi-object property which can take highly variable execution time for update events due to variable number of monitors associated with these events. We also consider create events since they involve monitor allocations, object bindings, map entries and lookups. The unoptimized approach performs extra memory allocations whereas the optimized approach performs extra context tree lookups and context matching. This makes the comparison with respect to their abilities to provide tighter bounds interesting. Table 4 compares the maximum and mean execution times along with the standard deviations. We observe that even though mean execution

Table 5. Errors reported and monitors generated for different properties. Errors denote the #errors reported along with the #unique contexts where errors are encountered and #unique contexts created in parantheses. $\mathcal{N}(A)$ and $\mathcal{T}(A)$ denote #monitor allocated and #monitor targeted respectively. - denotes no error event observed.

HasNext						
	Bloat		Pmd		Avrora	
	Errors	$\mathcal{N}(A)$	Errors	$\mathcal{N}(A)$	Errors	$\mathcal{N}(A)$
Unoptimized	44 (1/3)	1.9 M	400 (1/3)	1.94 M	79 K (1/9)	898 K
Optimized ($\mathcal{L}(A) = 1$ K)	3 (1/3)	1 K	254 (1/3)	1 K	446 (1/9)	1 K
Optimized ($\mathcal{L}(A) = 10$ K)	3 (1/3)	10 K	398 (1/3)	10 K	735 (1/9)	8.2 K
Randomized ($\mathcal{T}(A) = 1$ K)	0 (0/1)	1.2 K	0 (0/1)	1.1 K	85 (1/2)	1 K
Randomized ($\mathcal{T}(A) = 10$ K)	0 (0/1)	10 K	68 (1/1)	10 K	962 (1/2)	9.9 K
UnsafeIterator						
Unoptimized	-	1.96 M	-	1.94 M	-	898 K
Optimized ($\mathcal{L}(A) = 10$ K)	-	10 K	-	10 K	-	8.4 K
HashSet						
Unoptimized	-	66.8 K	-	6.8 M	-	106
Optimized($\mathcal{L}(A) = 10$ K)	-	10 K	-	10 K	-	103

times for `create` events are higher for optimized monitors, the maximum execution times as well as standard deviation values are much lower. These values including the standard deviation are much lower for `update` events in the case of optimized monitors. This indicates that the optimized approach can effectively bound the execution time even for the events that are the hardest to monitor.

7.6 Effectiveness of the Approach

We test the effectiveness of our approach by determining if it missed out on errors due to the fewer monitors generated (**RQ4**). We measure the number of reported errors and the number of monitors allocated under following scenarios : **(a)** *Unoptimized*: aspects generated by JavaMop, **(b)** *Optimized*($\mathcal{L}(a) = 1\,K$) optimized aspect with 1 K bound on global monitor pool, and **(c)** *Optimized*($\mathcal{L}(a) = 10\,K$) optimized aspect with 10 K monitor bound on global monitor pool. We then present two additional scenarios **(d)** *Randomized*($\mathcal{T}(a) = 1\,K$) and **(e)** *Randomized*($\mathcal{T}(a) = 10\,K$) in which we perform monitoring by probabilistically generating monitors[2] which in terms of numbers are close to **(b)** and **(c)**, respectively. We compare the effectiveness of our approach with the randomized approach when the monitors generated in two scenarios are similar.

Table 5 lists the results of our study. We observe that across all the benchmarks and properties, our approach enables significant reduction of allocated monitors, which results in lesser memory consumption (refer Sect. 7.4). Note

---

[2] The probability of generating the monitor decreases multiplicatively with the number of monitors that are already in the pool.

that even though our approach reports lesser number of errors, a closer inspection of the context trace reveals that all the errors reported by the unoptimized approach are generated from just one unique context which is captured by our approach with only 1 K monitors. Moreover, our approach investigates all distinct contexts which are 3 each for `bloat` and `pmd`, and 9 for `avrora`. Thus, **the optimized monitors do not miss any distinct error report; they rather exclude duplicate errors.** In comparison with our approach, the randomized approach misses errors for `bloat` and `pmd` when the generated monitors are 1 K and misses errors for `bloat` even when the number of generated monitors is increased to 10 K. Moreover, it fails to investigate several contexts which could have potentially led to errors. These results indicate that our approach can effectively catch errors.

7.7   Case Studies

Mayocat Shop. In the first case study, we analyze the performance of our technique when deployed in an eCommerce environment that can support large number of concurrent users. Typically, these applications are resource-constrained and their performance is determined by various factors such as bandwidth, CPU, memory, and I/O capacity. These applications have tight bounds on these resources and cannot tolerate high and unpredictable overheads. Most businesses use eCommerce solutions to market their services and products to a larger audience base. Consequently there are numerous providers which provide these online businesses a platform for managing their website, sales and operations. `Mayocat Shop` [19] is one such open source marketplace and eCommerce platform. It is developed in Java and uses other technologies such as ElasticSearch, PostgreSQL, Jersey, and Jetty. The basic features include management of product, inventory, shipping, order, and internationalization.

To determine customized properties for our monitoring system we studied the Cart, Billing and Shipping modules in the application. We define two properties: `ShipOps` and `CartOps` based on the functionality of these modules. The `ShipOps` property states that the shipping/delivery address associated with that order should not be changed once the order has been shipped. While the `CartOps` property states that for a particular item in the cart, it can only be updated or removed after it has been added to the cart. We then implemented the unoptimized and optimized aspects for these properties. These properties are based on different operations performed on the following entities: Customer, Order, Cart and Address. For our experiments we vary the number of users in the application from 100 to 10 K and report the number of monitors created, errors caught, program execution times, and the memory consumption for both approaches in Table 7. We also report the event monitoring execution times in Table 6.

JGraphT. For the second case study we used an open source graph library called JGraphT [16] which provides mathematical graph-theory objects and algorithms. This library contains Java implementation for a variety of graphs like

Table 6. Comparison of event execution times (nano second) of ShipOps property.

	Create			Shipped		
	Max	Mean	Std Dev	Max	Mean	Std Dev
Unopt (100)	280 K	15.14 K	15.66 K	19 K	4.06 K	1.68 K
Opt	116 K	12.32 K	11.62 K	10 K	1.97 K	1.37 K
Unopt (1 K)	726 K	9.94 K	18.79 K	55 K	1.88 K	1.77 K
Opt	406 K	7.96 K	12.33 K	46 K	793.38	1.64 K
Unopt (10 K)	2M	2.44 K	18.83 K	701 K	479.84	4.57 K
Opt	838 K	2.28 K	8.10 K	397 K	205.47	2.34 K

Table 7. #monitors generated, #errors reported, peak memory consumption (MB) and runtimes (ms) along with percentage overheads in parantheses. Errors denote #errors reported along with #unique contexts where errors are encountered and #unique contexts created in parantheses.

		Unopt	Opt	Unopt	Opt	Unopt	Opt
ShipOps	Monitors	100	54	1K	112	10K	224
	Errors	61 (3/5)	30 (3/5)	711 (3/4)	82 (3/4)	7K (2/5)	154 (2/5)
	Memory	3.8 (52)	3.8 (52)	5.1 (104)	3.8 (52)	17.7 (133)	12.7 (67)
	Runtime	48 (500)	40 (400)	90 (275)	72 (200)	212 (179)	180 (137)
CartOps	Monitors	100	60	1 K	108	10 K	201
	Errors	445(4/5)	241 (4/5)	4741 (4/4)	563 (4/4)	47K (4/5)	1K (4/5)
	Memory	3.8 (52)	3.8 (52)	3.8 (52)	3.8 (52)	10.2 (34)	8.8 (16)
	Runtime	44 (450)	36 (350)	78 (225)	72 (200)	172 (126)	164 (116)

directed and undirected graphs, weighted and unweighted graphs, simple-graphs, multigraphs, pseudographs, cycles etc. It also has an extensive test suite which we use for our analysis.

We studied the jgrapht-core module to determine customized properties for our monitoring system. We define two properties: JSCO and HSCO based on the functionality of the JohnsonSimpleCycles, HawickJamesSimpleCycles and DirectedGraph classes. The JSCO property states that for a DefaultDirected-Graph in a JohnsonSimpleCycles, an edge can only be removed after it has been added to the graph. While the HSCO property states that for a SimpleDirect-edGraph in a HawickJamesSimpleCycle should not be updated (add or remove edge) once the countSimpleCycles function has been called. We then implemented the unoptimized and optimized aspects for these properties. For our experiments we modified the existing test suite in the application to vary the number of instances of each of these cycles and graphs. The instances range from 100 to 10 K. We report the number of monitors created, errors caught, program execution times, and the memory consumption for both approaches in Table 9. We also report the event monitoring execution times in Table 8.

Table 8. Comparison of event execution times (nano second) of HSCO property.

	Create			CountCycles		
	Max	Mean	Std Dev	Max	Mean	Std Dev
Unopt (100)	124K	37.3 K	19.83 K	112 K	1.49 K	2.30 K
Opt	96 K	36.22 K	16.21 K	89 K	1.15 K	1.81 K
Unopt (1 K)	666 K	24.34 K	41.81 K	2M	531.92	14.34 K
Opt	165 K	13.89 K	15.89 K	282 K	222.17	2.08 K
Unopt (10 K)	2M	7.56 K	38.04 K	3M	179.51	5.03 K
Opt	838 K	2.28 K	8.10 K	195 K	67.73	609.67

Table 9. #monitors generated, #errors reported, peak memory consumption (MB) and runtimes (ms) along with percentage overheads in parantheses. Errors denote #errors reported along with #unique contexts where errors are encountered and #unique contexts created.

		Unopt	Opt	Unopt	Opt	Unopt	Opt
JSCO	Monitors	100	52	1 K	109	10 K	208
	Errors	20 K (2/2)	10 K (2/2)	197 K (3/3)	19 K (3/3)	1M (2/2)	23 K (2/2)
	Memory	3.8 (52)	3.8 (52)	3.8 (52)	3.8 (52)	8.8 (25)	7.6 (10)
	Runtime	78 (420)	70 (360)	125 (400)	110 (340)	324 (210)	240 (130)
HSCO	Monitors	100	53	1 K	110	10 K	212
	Errors	99(1/1)	52 (1/1)	991 (2/2)	108 (2/2)	9 K (1/1)	207 (1/1)
	Memory	3.8 (52)	3.8 (52)	7.6 (200)	3.8 (52)	18.6 (160)	11.4 (63)
	Runtime	90 (500)	66 (340)	129 (410)	96 (284)	387 (270)	252 (140)

Discussion. Our observations for both the case studies are fourfold. First, we observe that there is a significant reduction in the number of monitors in the case of the optimized approach as the number of creation events increase. Consequently, the peak memory consumed also decreases in the same proportion (upto 50% reduction in memory compared to the unoptimized approach). Second, we see that although the number of errors caught in the optimized approach is lesser, **the unique errors caught by both the approaches are same**. Third, the execution times of programs with optimized monitoring are less than the ones with unoptimized monitoring (upto 40% reduction compared to the unoptimized approach). Finally, the mean and standard deviation values of execution times of monitoring operations of optimized monitors are lower than the corresponding values of unoptimized monitors. Hence, overall the optimized approach does significantly better than the unoptimized approach in terms of memory and execution times without compromising with the error detection. This indicates that our approach is a promising step toward deploying runtime monitoring of realistic applications with resource constraints in a production environment.

8   Threats to Validity

We used JAVAMOP 2.3 as a baseline tool for our prototype implementation.
However, the results of the study may change if we use a different tool or a
more recent version of JAVAMOP. Using an older version of JAVAMOP had an
advantage of being easier to understand, which allowed us to ensure that our
optimizations do not interfere with JAVAMOP's optimizations. Our goal is not
to compare the performance with JAVAMOP, but to show that our technique is
complementary to JAVAMOP optimizations and can be used to extend JAVAMOP
or similar tools to further improve their effectiveness.

The choices of hardware and software platforms, in particular the server
settings, may influence the results. In the future, we plan to repeat the study on
a variety of platforms to understand their impact on the results.

9   Related Work

In this section, we briefly discuss some of the notable monitor optimization
works.

Approaches for Real-Time Systems. Real-time systems demand time-
deterministic monitoring. The challenge is in scheduling monitoring activities
such that they do not interfere with the software operation and do not violate
the nonfunctional properties. Some approaches depend on event sampling and
optimized time-triggering [2,22,29]. Other approaches include predictable monitoring that provide bounds on detection latency [17,31,32]. These approaches are
effective, However, they do not target finite state properties. and are unsuitable
for inline monitoring. Another approach by Colombo et al. [10] tries to decrease
the runtime overheads by performing the monitoring operations by carrying
out the monitoring operations on a remote site. This has shortcomings such as
increased communication between the server and remote site. Our approach, in
contrast, performs inline monitoring without the need for any communication
channel.

Sampling-Based Approaches. Researchers have presented approaches that
are based on sampling object space [3], time [5,27], and properties [13]. The
approach presented by Arnold et al. [3] is the closest to our approach in its spirit.
They develop Quality Virtual Machine (QVM) that tracks safety properties, Java
assertions and heap properties for violations. It also has an overhead manager
to enforce a user specified overhead budget. Even though effective for general-
purpose applications, QVM is not designed for timing requirements. It is not
easily portable and it tracks only single-object properties. None of these reuses
monitors to control overheads.

Aspect-Based and Similar Monitoring Approaches. A number of finite
state runtime monitoring tools including MarQ [25], JAVAMOP[20], and Tracematches [1] have been developed to detect violations of typestate properties.
In spite of this efficiency, for certain program and property combinations, all

of these tools incur heavy overheads. These scenarios act as the motivation to our research. Various approaches [4,18,20,24] have been proposed to control the memory and to avoid unnecessary monitoring. However, monitoring still remains challenging for some properties.

Hybrid Approaches. Several hybrid approaches have been proposed that combine static program analysis with monitoring to reduce overheads [7,8,14,23]. The static component of the analysis filters program points that need no monitoring. These approaches are effective, and have been found to control overheads in many cases but not all. Moreover, they have not been effective in controlling the space requirements. None of these approaches provide bounds on the execution times of monitoring operations.

Data Structure Based Optimization Approaches. Different data structures have been used to keep track of the different states of the monitors associated with runtime monitoring. The time taken to search, read and write to these data structures determines the performance of a monitoring system. JAVAMOP[20], and MarQ [25] use data structures based on lookup tables, implemented as hash maps, to store this mapping of objects to their individual state. Decker et al. [12] use union-find data structures to store the state of program objects. Although these techniques optimize the inherent runtime overhead, they can quickly become infeasible in production environments as the number of tracked objects increase.

10   Conclusion and Future Work

We presented a novel inline finite state monitoring technique that explores the trade-offs between efficiency and determinism, and reported violations. It samples objects for monitoring in order to reduce the memory overhead based on program execution contexts. At the same time, it strives to catch all distinct errors that an unoptimized approach would catch. The approach provides worst-case execution time bounds for all monitoring operations. General monitoring approaches do not take into consideration the limited availability of resources. These approaches can degrade software performance. We hope that our approach would help employ inline monitoring in production environments even for resource-constrained systems.

Acknowledgements. We thank Dr. Mohan Dhawan (IBM Research) and the anonymous reviewers for their valuable suggestions. This work was partly supported by Infosys Center for Artificial Intelligence.

References

1. Allan, C., et al.: Adding trace matching with free variables to AspectJ. In: Proceedings of the 20th Annual ACM SIGPLAN Conference on Object-Oriented Programming, Systems, Languages, and Applications, OOPSLA 2005, pp. 345–364 (2005)
2. Arafa, P., Kashif, H., Fischmeister, S.: DIME: time-aware dynamic binary instrumentation using rate-based resource allocation. In: Proceedings of the Eleventh ACM International Conference on Embedded Software, EMSOFT 2013, pp. 1–10 (2013)
3. Arnold, M., Vechev, M., Yahav, E.:. QVM: an efficient runtime for detecting defects in deployed systems. In: Proceedings of the 23rd ACM SIGPLAN Conference on Object-Oriented Programming Systems Languages and Applications, OOPSLA 2008, pp. 143–162 (2008)
4. Avgustinov, P., Tibble, J., de Moor, O.: Making trace monitors feasible. In: Proceedings of the 22nd Annual ACM SIGPLAN Conference on Object-Oriented Programming Systems and Applications, OOPSLA 2007, pp. 589–608 (2007)
5. Bartocci, E., et al.: Adaptive runtime verification. In: Qadeer, S., Tasiran, S. (eds.) RV 2012. LNCS, vol. 7687, pp. 168–182. Springer, Heidelberg (2013). https://doi.org/10.1007/978-3-642-35632-2_18
6. Blackburn, S.M., et al.: The DaCapo benchmarks: java benchmarking development and analysis. In: OOPSLA, OOPSLA 2006, pp. 169–190. ACM, New York (2006)
7. Bodden, E.: Efficient hybrid typestate analysis by determining continuation-equivalent states. In: Proceedings of the 32nd ACM/IEEE International Conference on Software Engineering, vol. 1, ICSE 2010, pp. 5–14 (2010)
8. Bodden, E., Lam, P., Hendren, L.: Finding programming errors earlier by evaluating runtime monitors ahead-of-time. In: Proceedings of the 16th ACM SIGSOFT International Symposium on Foundations of Software Engineering, SIGSOFT 2008/FSE-16, pp. 36–47 (2008)
9. Chen, F., Roşu, G.: Java-mop: a monitoring oriented programming environment for java. In: 11th International Conference, TACAS 2005, Held as Part of the Joint European Conferences on Theory and Practice of Software, ETAPS 2005, Edinburgh, UK, 4–8 April, pp. 546–550 (2005)
10. Eleftherakis, G., Hinchey, M., Holcombe, M. (eds.): SEFM 2012. LNCS, vol. 7504. Springer, Heidelberg (2012). https://doi.org/10.1007/978-3-642-33826-7
11. http://www.dacapobench.org/
12. Decker, N., Harder, J., Scheffel, T., Schmitz, M., Thoma, D.: Runtime monitoring with union-find structures. In: Chechik, M., Raskin, J.-F. (eds.) TACAS 2016. LNCS, vol. 9636, pp. 868–884. Springer, Heidelberg (2016). https://doi.org/10.1007/978-3-662-49674-9_54
13. Dwyer, M.B., Diep, M., Elbaum, S.: Reducing the cost of path property monitoring through sampling. In: Proceedings of the 23rd IEEE/ACM International Conference on Automated Software Engineering, pp. 228–237 (2008)
14. Dwyer, M.B., Purandare, R.: Residual dynamic typestate analysis exploiting static analysis: results to reformulate and reduce the cost of dynamic analysis. In: Proceedings of the Twenty-Second IEEE/ACM International Conference on Automated software Engineering, ASE 2007, pp. 124–133 (2007)
15. Dwyer, M.B., Purandare, R., Person, S.: Runtime verification in context: can optimizing error detection improve fault diagnosis? In: Barringer, H., et al. (eds.) RV 2010. LNCS, vol. 6418, pp. 36–50. Springer, Heidelberg (2010). https://doi.org/10.1007/978-3-642-16612-9_4

16. http://www.jgrapht.org/
17. Kochanthara, S., Nelissen, G., Pereira, D., Purandare, R.: REVERT: runtime verification for real-time systems. In: IEEE Real-Time Systems Symposium RTSS 2016, p. 365 (2016)
18. Luo, Q., Zhang, Y., Lee, C., Jin, D., Meredith, P.O.N., Şerbănuţă, T.F., Roşu, G.: RV-Monitor: efficient parametric runtime verification with simultaneous properties. In: Bonakdarpour, B., Smolka, S.A. (eds.) RV 2014. LNCS, vol. 8734, pp. 285–300. Springer, Cham (2014). https://doi.org/10.1007/978-3-319-11164-3_24
19. https://github.com/jvelo/mayocat-shop
20. Meredith, P., Jin, D., Chen, F., Roşu, G.: Efficient monitoring of parametric context-free patterns. Autom. Softw. Eng. ASE, 148–157 (2008)
21. Naeem, N.A., Lhotak, O.: Typestate-like analysis of multiple interacting objects. In: Proceedings of the 23rd ACM SIGPLAN Conference on Object-Oriented Programming Systems Languages and Applications, OOPSLA 2008, pp. 347–366 (2008)
22. Navabpour, S., Bonakdarpour, B., Fischmeister, S.: Path-aware time-triggered runtime verification. In: Qadeer, S., Tasiran, S. (eds.) RV 2012. LNCS, vol. 7687, pp. 199–213. Springer, Heidelberg (2013). https://doi.org/10.1007/978-3-642-35632-2_21
23. Purandare, R., Dwyer, M.B., Elbaum, S.: Monitor optimization via stutter-equivalent loop transformation. In: Proceedings of the ACM International Conference on Object Oriented Programming Systems Languages and Applications, OOPSLA 2010, pp. 270–285 (2010)
24. Purandare, R., Dwyer, M.B., Elbaum, S.: Optimizing monitoring of finite state properties through monitor compaction. In: Proceedings of the 2013 International Symposium on Software Testing and Analysis, ISSTA 2013, pp. 280–290 (2013)
25. Reger, G., Cruz, H.C., Rydeheard, D.: MARQ: monitoring at runtime with QEA. In: Baier, C., Tinelli, C. (eds.) TACAS 2015. LNCS, vol. 9035, pp. 596–610. Springer, Heidelberg (2015). https://doi.org/10.1007/978-3-662-46681-0_55
26. http://sable.github.io/soot/
27. Stoller, S.D., et al.: Runtime verification with state estimation. In: Khurshid, S., Sen, K. (eds.) RV 2011. LNCS, vol. 7186, pp. 193–207. Springer, Heidelberg (2012). https://doi.org/10.1007/978-3-642-29860-8_15
28. Strom, R.E., Yemini, S.: Typestate: a programming language concept for enhancing software reliability. IEEE Trans. Softw. Eng. 12(1), 157–171 (1986)
29. Wu, C.W.W., Kumar, D., Bonakdarpour, B., Fischmeister, S.: Reducing monitoring overhead by integrating event- and time-triggered techniques. In: Legay, A., Bensalem, S. (eds.) RV 2013. LNCS, vol. 8174, pp. 304–321. Springer, Heidelberg (2013). https://doi.org/10.1007/978-3-642-40787-1_18
30. Xie, Y., Naik, M., Hackett, B., Aiken, A.: Soundness and its role in bug detection systems. In: Proceedings of the Workshop on the Evaluation of Software Defect Detection Tools (BUGS 2005), pp. 22–37 (2005)
31. Zhu, H., Dwyer, M.B., Goddard, S.: Predictable runtime monitoring. In: 21st Euromicro Conference on Real-Time Systems, ECRTS, pp. 173–183 (2009)
32. Zhu, H., Goddard, S., Dwyer, M.B.: Selecting server parameters for predictable runtime monitoring. In: 16th IEEE Real-Time and Embedded Technology and Applications Symposium, RTAS, pp. 227–236 (2010)

Predictive Run-Time Verification of Discrete-Time Reachability Properties in Black-Box Systems Using Trace-Level Abstraction and Statistical Learning

Reza Babaee$^{(\boxtimes)}$, Arie Gurfinkel, and Sebastian Fischmeister

Electrical and Computer Engineering, University of Waterloo, Waterloo, Canada
{rbabaeec,arie.gurfinkel,sebastian.fischmeister}@uwaterloo.ca

Abstract. Run-time Verification (RV) has become a crucial aspect of monitoring black-box systems. Recently, we introduced $\mathcal{P}revent$, a predictive RV framework, in which the monitor is able to predict the future extensions of an execution, using a model inferred from the random sample executions of the system. The monitor maintains a table of the states of the prediction model, with the probability of the extensions from each state that satisfy a safety property.

The size of the prediction model directly influences the monitor's memory usage and computational performance, due to the filtering techniques used for run-time state estimation, that depends on the size of the model. Hence, achieving a small prediction model is key in predictive RV.

In this paper, we use symmetry reduction to apply abstraction, that, in the absence of a model in black-box systems, is performed on the observation space. The symmetry relation is inferred based on k-gapped pair model, that lumps symbols with similar empirical probability to reach a set of target labels on a set of samples. The obtained equivalence classes on the observation space are used to abstract traces that are used in training the prediction model.

We demonstrate the soundness of the abstraction, in the case that the generating abstract model is a deterministic Discrete-Time Markov Chain (DTMC). We use Hidden Markov Models (HMMs) to handle the abstraction-induced non-determinism by learning the distribution of a hidden state variable. We implemented our approach in our tool, $\mathcal{P}revent$, to empirically evaluate our approach on the Herman's randomised self-stabilising algorithm. Our results show that the inferred abstraction significantly reduces the size of the model and the training time, without a meaningful impact on the prediction accuracy, with better results from the HMM models.

1 Introduction

Run-time Verification (RV) [28] has become a crucial element in monitoring and analysing safety aspects of black-box stochastic systems [29,39], where there is almost surely a non-zero probability of failure. In RV, a monitor checks the current execution, that is a finite prefix of an infinite path, against a given property,

© Springer Nature Switzerland AG 2018
C. Colombo and M. Leucker (Eds.): RV 2018, LNCS 11237, pp. 187–204, 2018.
https://doi.org/10.1007/978-3-030-03769-7_11

typically expressed in Linear Temporal Logic (LTL) [36], that represents a set of acceptable infinite paths. If any infinite extension of a prefix belongs (does not belong) to the set of infinite paths that satisfy the property, the monitor accepts (resp. rejects) the prefix. However, if the monitor is not able to reach a verdict with the given prefix because it can be extended to satisfy or violate the property, the monitor outputs *unknown* [5].

We introduced the predictive RV framework [3], where the monitor finitely extends the prefix based on a *prediction model* that is trained on the set of *independent and identically distributed (iid)* sample traces. This gives the monitor the ability to detect a monitorable [14] property's satisfaction/violation before its occurrence. In this paper, we propose inferring trace-level abstraction to reduce the size of the prediction model. Our focus is on the discrete-time reachability properties, specified as *target labels* on the observation space Σ. The maximum length of the extensions is specified as the *prediction horizon* (Fig. 1).

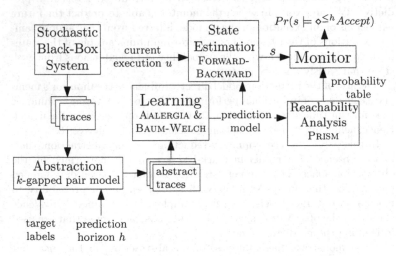

Fig. 1. Overview of predictive RV with abstraction.

Abstraction. The key idea in our abstraction is to decrease the size of the observation space by extracting symbols that have similar *transient probability* [24] to reach the target labels. Therefore, our approach can be seen as a form of symmetry reduction [23] on the observation space that is implemented at the trace-level [33]. We use *k-gapped pair model* [13] to detect the symbols that have similar empirical probability to reach the target symbols within k steps. The symbols that have probability *zero* are considered irrelevant in the prediction. The *symmetrical* symbols are then lumped into equivalence partition over the observation space to convert the traces of the training set into *abstract* traces.

Learning. If there is no non-determinism in the generating model of the abstract traces, given that the property is a bounded reachability LTL formula, any learning technique to infer the deterministic model, such as AALERGIA [30], suffices to provide the prediction model that in the limit is as accurate as the actual model. However, the trace-level abstraction may induce non-determinism in the trained model [33]. We use Hidden Markov Model [37] (HMM) to infer the induced non-determinism by the abstraction, and compare the results with the deterministic as well as the actual model [30]. We train an HMM using BAUM-WELCH algorithm [37], that is an approximation to find the parameters of the HMM that maximizes the likelihood of the training data.

Reachability Analysis and Monitor Construction. The monitor in our framework is the result of a bounded reachability analysis on the prediction model. We use PRISM [34] to perform the probabilistic bounded reachability analysis on the prediction model. The monitor is implemented as a lookup table, where each entry is a combination of three elements: an integer variable t, a state of the prediction model, and the probability that from that state the system reaches the states with the target labels, within t steps. The value of t is constrained by the prediction horizon that is expected from the prediction model.

State Estimation. Given that the original DTMC is deterministic, the system state can be determined by the observed path u. However, if the prediction model is non-deterministic, the state of the system needs to be estimated [40] based on the prefix u. Any *filtering techniques* [38] can be exploited to estimate the state at run-time. If the size of the model is large, approximate techniques such as the VITERBI algorithm [3,43] can be applied too. Since the purpose of the current paper is to reduce the size of the prediction model, and also for evaluation purposes, we apply a direct approach and compute the posterior probability distribution of the states in the prediction model after observing u, using FORWARD-BACKWARD algorithm [37].

The output of the monitor is the probability that from the estimated state s the system reaches the target labels within at most h steps. This probability is retrieved from the probability table after estimating the current state. Respectively, the size of the prediction model dictates both the size and the computational overload of the monitor.

In summary, our paper makes the following contributions:

- define trace-level abstraction as a symmetry relation in the observation space, and infer it using k-gapped pair model
- resolve non-determinism induced by the abstraction using hidden state variable
- demonstrate the validity of our approach on a distributed randomized algorithm, by showing the significant reduction in the prediction models with minimum impact on the prediction accuracy.

The rest of the paper is organized as follows: in Sect. 2 we introduce our running example, followed by preliminaries in Sect. 3, and a brief description of the prediction procedure in Sect. 4. In Sect. 5 we explain the trace-level abstraction using symmetry relation on the observation space and our algorithm to infer the symmetry. Learning deterministic models, and some theoretical guarantee, as well as learning non-deterministic models are described in Sect. 6. We conclude the paper by discussing the results of our case study in Sect. 7.

2 Running Example

We use the die example [34] as the running example throughout the paper. This example demonstrates the simulation of throwing a fair 6-sided die with flipping a fair coin [22]. Let C be the output of the flipped coin ($C \in \{ii, hh, tt\}$), where hh, tt display *head* and *tail*, resp., and ii is a special symbol to indicate the initial state of the coin. Also, let D be the output of the simulated die ($D \in \{0, \ldots, 6\}$), where $1, \ldots, 6$ is the simulated output of the die, and 0 shows that the coin needs to be flipped again, and the output of the die is not determined yet. The coin needs to be flipped at least three times to simulate observing a number on the die. We define $\Sigma_{die} : C \times D$ as the observation space, that denotes the output of the coin and the die in the process.

Suppose checking the reachability property *eventually the outcome of the die is either "1" or "6"*, at run-time, which translates to the LTL property $\varphi : \Diamond D = 6\ or\ D = 1$, based on the symbols in the defined observation space. Any (infinite) execution paths with the prefix $u : (ii, 0)(tt, 0)(hh, 0)(hh, 6)$ satisfies φ. However, the result on the prefix $u' : (ii, 0)(tt, 0)(hh, 0)(tt, 0)$ is *unknown* [6], as it can be extended to an infinite path that satisfies φ (e.g., $(ii, 0)(tt, 0)(hh, 0)\ (tt, 0)(hh, 0)(hh, 6)^\omega$), or an infinite path that violates φ (e.g., $(ii, 0)(tt, 0)(hh, 0)(tt, 0)(tt, 0)(tt, 5)^\omega$).

To deal with the inconclusive results due to unknown extensions [5], we provide the monitor with a *prediction model* to extend the prefix and generate the results based on the probability of the extensions that satisfy the given property. In the die example, the model in Fig. 2 is created from 1000 *iid* samples, with which the monitor is able to compute the probability of all the extensions that satisfy φ (the shaded states). We

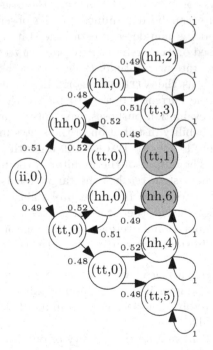

Fig. 2. The learned model of the die example from 1000 samples used as the prediction model.

limit the length of the extensions to some boundary, which we call the *prediction horizon*.

3   Preliminaries

In this section, we briefly introduce definitions and notations. A probability distribution over a finite set S is a function $P : S \rightarrow [0,1]$ such that $\sum_{s \in S} P(s) = 1$. We use $X_{1:n}$ to denote a sequence $x_1, x_2, \ldots, x_n$ of values of a random variable X, and use u and w to, respectively, denote a finite and an infinite path.

Discrete-Time Markov Chains (DTMC).

Definition 1 (DTMC). *A Discrete-Time Markov Chain (DTMC) is a tuple* $\mathcal{M} : (S, \Sigma, \pi, \mathbf{P}, L)$, *where S is a non-empty finite set of states, Σ is a non-empty finite alphabet, $\pi : S \rightarrow [0,1]$ is the initial probability distribution over S, $\mathbf{P} : S \times S \rightarrow [0,1]$ is the transition probability, such that for any $s \in S$, $P(s, \cdot)$ is a probability distribution, and $L : S \rightarrow \Sigma$ is the labeling function.*

Let $\mathcal{M}$ be a DTMC. The sequence $\sigma_0 \sigma_1 \ldots$ is an execution path on $\mathcal{M}$ iff $\mathbf{P}(s_i, s_{i+1}) > 0$, where $L(s_i) = \sigma_i, i \geq 0$. An execution path can be finite or infinite. The probability measure on the execution paths is defined using cylinder sets [24]. We deal with finite paths in the remaining of the paper. We denote by $Path_k(\sigma)$ the set of all finite execution paths of length k that start with σ. In the following, we define the finite extension of a path.

Definition 2 (Finite Extensions of a Path). *Let $\sigma_0 \sigma_1 \cdots \sigma_n$ be a finite execution path on a DTMC. The set of finite extensions of u is denoted by Ext_u and defined as follows:*

$$Ext_u = \{ u \in Path_k(\sigma_n) | k \geq 0 \}$$

We denote by $Ext_u^{\leq h}$, if $k \leq h$ in Definition 2.

Definition 3 (Deterministic State). *State $s \in S$ of a DTMC is called deterministic iff for all $\sigma \in \Sigma$, there exists at most one $s' \in S$ such that $\mathbf{P}(s, s') > 0$ and $L(s') = \sigma$.*

Definition 4 (Deterministic DTMC [30]). *A DTMC is deterministic iff:*

– *There exists $s_{init} \in S$ such that $\pi(s_{init}) = 1$.*
– *For all $s \in S$, s is deterministic.*

Hypothesis Testing. Let X be some random variable with *unknown* mean μ and variance σ^2. Let $x_1, \ldots, x_n$ be *iid* random samples of X, with mean $\bar{X}$ and variance v^2. A two-sided null hypothesis test enables us to check $H_0 : |\mu - \bar{X}| = 0$. According to the central theorem [15], as the number of samples grows $|\mu - \bar{X}|$ follows a student's t-distribution [15]. Therefore using confidence α and the t-distribution we are able to accept H_0, if $\frac{|\bar{X} - \mu|}{\frac{\sqrt{v}}{n}} \leq t_{n-1,\alpha}$.

4   Prediction as Quantitative Bounded Reachability Analysis

Let $\mathcal{M}$ be a DTMC, $\mathcal{G} \subseteq \Sigma$ be the set of *target* labels of some goal states in $\mathcal{M}$, and $\mathcal{L}(\mathcal{G})$ be the set of finite execution paths on $\mathcal{M}$ that end with $\sigma \in \mathcal{G}$. The monitor's purpose is to estimate the probability of all the extensions of length at most h that satisfy $\Diamond\mathcal{G}$. In a discrete-time setting, the variable h is a positive integer, which we call the *prediction horizon*. Computing the probability of the satisfying extensions is achieved by performing a bounded reachability analysis on the prediction model.

Let $u \notin \mathcal{L}(\mathcal{G})$ be the execution on $\mathcal{M}$ observed so far, and Ext_u be the set of finite extensions of u. The output of the monitor is the probability measure of the set of the paths of length at most h that satisfy $\Diamond\mathcal{G}$, i.e.,

$$Pr(\mathcal{C}), \text{ where } \mathcal{C} = \{v \in Ext_u^{\leq h} | uv \in \mathcal{L}(\mathcal{G})\}) \tag{1}$$

Suppose also that s is the state corresponding to the last label in u, which is obtained by some state estimation technique [3,21,40]. As u expands, the new state is consequently estimated at run-time.

The probability (1) can be obtained by recursively computing the *transient probability* in $\mathcal{M}$ [24]: starting from s the probability of being at state s' after h steps, such that $L(s') \in \mathcal{G}$. We can effectively turn computing the transient probability into checking the following quantitative PCTL property [17,24]:

$$\mathrm{P}_{=?}[s \models \Diamond^{\leq h}\mathcal{G}] \tag{2}$$

Due to multiplications of large and typically sparse matrices, the calculation of (2) is not practical during run-time [24]. As a result, we use PRISM [34] to execute the quantitative reachability analysis [4] on all the states of $\mathcal{M}$ off-line, and store the values in a look-up table. The size of the table is $O(|\mathcal{M}|)$ [3], where $|\mathcal{M}|$ is the size of the prediction model. Subsequently, reducing the size of the model results in a smaller look-up table, in addition to the performance improvement due to a faster state estimation.

In our example, $\mathcal{G}_\varphi = \{(tt, 1), (hh, 1), (hh, 6), (tt, 6)\}$. Using the model in Fig. 2, the monitor is able to retrieve the value of $\mathrm{P}_{=?}(s_{u'} \models \Diamond^{\leq h}\mathcal{G}_\varphi)$, where $s_{u'}$ is the state of the model after generating u'. For instance, $\mathrm{P}_{=?}(s_{u'} \models \Diamond^{\leq 20}\mathcal{G}_\varphi) = 0.34$, which translates to the probability of all the extensions of length at most 20, that terminate with the labels where the outcome of the die is 6 or 1.

5   Trace-Level Abstraction by Inferring Symmetry in the Observation Space

We use a finite partitioning of the observation space, Σ, to achieve the trace-level abstraction in the form of a *projection*. The abstract traces are then used to train the prediction models, which ideally have smaller sizes than the model trained from the concrete traces, but are good enough approximates.

The simplest abstraction is to divide the observation space into two partitions, the atomic propositions that appear in the target labels and the non-target labels [33], i.e., $\mathcal{G}$, and $\Sigma - \mathcal{G}$, which we denote by $\Sigma_{\bar{\mathcal{G}}}$. The projection $R_{\mathcal{G}} : \Sigma \to \{gg, nn\}$ simply maps a symbol of a path to the symbol gg, if it is a target label, i.e., $R(\sigma) = gg$ iff $\sigma \in \mathcal{G}$, and to the symbol nn otherwise. Consider $\mathcal{G}_{\varphi}$ and the traces u and u'. The projection of u and u', using the projection relation $R_{\mathcal{G}_{\varphi}}$, are respectively, $\tilde{u} : (nn)(nn)(nn)(gg)$ and $\tilde{u}' : (nn)(nn)(nn)(nn)$.

The projection $R_{\mathcal{G}}$ may collapse the non-target symbols, that have a non-zero probability to reach a target label within some bounded steps, with symbols that never reach the target labels, i.e., have probability zero. For instance, compare the symbols $(hh, 0)$ and $(hh, 4)$. The former appears immediately before the target label $(hh, 6)$ often in a simulated path; whereas the latter has no appearance before any of the target labels (see Fig. 2). Both are replaced with nn in $R_{\mathcal{G}}$, thus the predictive information from $(hh, 0)$ and $(hh, 4)$ are combined.

The key insight in our abstraction method is to not only detect the symbols with no significant correlation with the target labels, but also recognize the ones that have similar empirical probability to reach the target labels within a fixed number of steps, and collapse them together. As a result, we leverage the notion of *symmetry* [23] on the observation space to recognize the symbols with similar prediction power and lump them into the same partition. We define the symmetry relation with respect to reaching the target labels. More specifically, we say two symbols are symmetrical *iff* the probability measure of a fixed length path, that starts from either symbols and ends with some target labels, is equal.

Let $\mathcal{M}$ be a deterministic DTMC. Let $P_k : \Sigma_{\bar{\mathcal{G}}} \to \Sigma_{\bar{\mathcal{G}}}$ be the permutations on the non-target labels, such that $Pr(Path_k^{\mathcal{G}}(P_k(\sigma))) = Pr(Path_k^{\mathcal{G}}(\sigma))$ for all $\sigma \in \Sigma_{\bar{\mathcal{G}}}$, and some fixed integer $k > 0$, where $Path_k^{\mathcal{G}}(.) = Path_k(.) \cap \mathcal{L}(\mathcal{G})$. A group of permutations defined by P_k on $\Sigma_{\bar{\mathcal{G}}}$ provides an equivalence relation (so-called the *orbits*) on $\Sigma_{\bar{\mathcal{G}}}$ that with $\mathcal{G}$ defines the equivalence classes over the observation space. We denote by Σ_k the abstract alphabet set that contains a unique representative symbol for each partition, and by $R_k : \Sigma \to \Sigma_k$ the corresponding projection that maps each symbol to its rep. in the abstract alphabet.

Let $\mathcal{M}_k$ be the quotient of $\mathcal{M}$, where Σ is replaced with Σ_k, and $L_k : S \to \Sigma_k$ such that $L_k(s) = R_k(L(s))$. Given that $\mathcal{M}_k$ is deterministic, we can show that $\mathcal{M}_k$ is bisimilar to $\mathcal{M}$. Therefore bounded predictions from any state in both models are equal (see Theorem 1). In the case that $\mathcal{M}_k$ is non-deterministic, we employ a hidden state variable to infer the non-determinism imposed by abstraction (see Sect. 6.2).

In the remainder, we use k-gapped pair model (Sect. 5.1) combined with hypothesis testing (Sect. 5.2) to infer R_k, and consequently, Σ_k.

5.1 k-gapped Pair Model

The k-gapped pair model [13] has been successfully applied in mining biological sequences [20], and in context-dependent text prediction [11]. We use the k-gapped pair model to extract the predictive symbols with respect to the target labels in the training set.

1 COMPUTEPREDICTIONSUPPORT$(S, \sigma, \mathcal{G}, k)$

   inputs : The *iid* sample set $S = [u_1 \dots u_m]$, $\sigma \in \Sigma$, the set of target
             labels $\mathcal{G}$, and an integer $k \geq 0$

   output: $[F_{u_1} \dots F_{u_m}]$

2 **begin**

3   **foreach** $u_i \in S$ **do**

4        $n \leftarrow length(u_i)$

5        $F_{u_i} \leftarrow \frac{1}{n-k-1} \sum\limits_{j=1}^{n-k-1} \mathbb{1}_{(\sigma_j = \sigma \text{ and } \sigma_{j+k+1} \in \mathcal{G})}$

6   **end**

7 **end**

Algorithm 1: Computing the k-prediction support of σ over the sample set.

A k-gapped pair model is a triplet (σ, σ', k), where $\sigma, \sigma' \in \Sigma$, and $k \geq 0$ is an integer that indicates the number of steps (gaps) between σ and σ'. If $k = 0$ the k-gapped pair is equivalent to a *bigram* [31].

The *k-gapped occurrence frequency* of the symbols σ and σ', is the frequency that σ appeared within exactly k steps before σ' over the sample path. Assuming that $\sigma' \in \mathcal{G}$, we use the sum of k-gapped occurrence frequency of a given symbol over all the target labels in the sample set, and define it as the k-*prediction support*. Algorithm 1 shows computing k-prediction support of symbol σ. Symbols σ_j and σ_{j+k+1} are the jth and $(j + k + 1)^{th}$ symbols of the sample path u_i in each iteration of the loop in line **3**, and $\mathbb{1}_{(\sigma_i = \sigma \text{ and } \sigma_{i+k+1} = \sigma')}$ in line **5** is the indicator function that returns 1 if $\sigma_i = \sigma$ and $\sigma_{i+k+1} = \sigma'$; and 0 otherwise. The output of Algorithm 1 is the vector $[F_{u_1} \dots F_{u_m}]$, the k-prediction support values of each sample path for symbol σ.

The k-prediction support of σ is essentially the empirical estimation of $Pr(Path_k^{\mathcal{G}}(\sigma))$. Under the assumption that $F_{u_1}, \dots, F_{u_m}$ is *covariance-stationary* [16], i.e., the mean is time-invariant and the autocovarinace function depends only on the distance k, both of which hold if the samples are *iid*, and the underlying generating model is a deterministic DTMC, we are able to use hypothesis testing to extract R_k.

5.2 Using Hypothesis Testing to Extract Symbols with Equivalent Prediction Support

Algorithm 2 demonstrates the procedure of extracting the abstract alphabet set, based on the symmetry between the k-prediction support of the symbols. The algorithm receives the sample set, the alphabet set, the set of target labels, and k, as inputs, and infer R_k, by generating the partitions $V_1, \dots, V_t$.

The algorithm iterates over the symbols not considered in any equivalence classes, that are stored in $\mathcal{R}$ (the loop in lines **5–17**). In each iteration, the symbol with the maximum k-prediction support score is found in $\mathcal{R}$ and stored in σ_{max} with its score in F_{max} (line **6**). The score 0 indicates that there is no

1 EXTRACTABSTRACTALPHABET(Sample set $S, \Sigma, \mathcal{G}, k$)

  output: Partition $[\mathcal{G} \cup V_1 \cup \cdots \cup V_t \cup \mathcal{R}]$ over Σ
2 **begin**
3      $t \leftarrow 1$
4      $\mathcal{R} \leftarrow \Sigma - \mathcal{G}$
5   **while** $\mathcal{R} \neq \emptyset$ **do**
6          $[\sigma_{max} \; F_{max}] \leftarrow \max_{\sigma \in R} \sum_{i=1}^{m} F_{u_i}$
7   **if** $F_{max} = 0$ **then break**
8
9          $V_t \leftarrow \{\sigma_{max}\}$
10   **for** $\sigma \in \mathcal{R} - \{\sigma_{max}\}$ **do**
11              $F_\sigma \leftarrow$ COMPUTEPREDICTIONSUPPORT$(S, \sigma, \mathcal{G}, k)$
12   **if** HYPOTHESISTESTING$(F_{max} - F_\sigma)$ **then**
13                  $V_t \leftarrow V_t \cup \{\sigma'\}$
14   **end**
15   **end**
16          $\mathcal{R} \leftarrow \mathcal{R} - V_t$
17          $t \leftarrow t + 1$
18   **end**
19 **end**

Algorithm 2: Extracting the equivalence classes on the alphabet set.

path of length k to any target labels from the symbols in $\mathcal{R}$ and we can end the procedure (line **7**); otherwise, the symbols with statistically similar k-prediction support score to σ_{max} are extracted from $\mathcal{R}$, and inserted in V_t (for loop in **9–13**). The statistical testing is conducted via the function HYPOTHESISTESTING, which performs a two-sided hypothesis t-test to check $H_0 : F_{max} - F_\sigma = 0$. Depending on the number of samples, a proper confidence is chosen to test H_0.

Algorithm 2 terminates, if there is no more symbol to classify, i.e., $\mathcal{R} = \emptyset$, or if all the remaining symbols in $\mathcal{R}$ have no k-prediction support. We dedicate a representative symbol for each extracted partition, including $\mathcal{G}$ and $\mathcal{R}$ if it is not empty, and define R_k accordingly.

At worst, a total number of $O(|\Sigma|^2)$ comparisons is required to extract the abstract alphabet set. Given that the size of the actual model is at least as large as $|\Sigma|$, storing the entire vector of k-prediction support score for all symbols is impractical for large models. In fact, to make the usage of memory independent of the size of the alphabet, the computation of F in Algorithm 1 is performed on-the-fly, which only depends on the size of sample data. Compared to inferring the abstract alphabet from a model that is trained from the concrete traces, our approach is more memory-efficient.

Table 1 demonstrates the k-prediction support of the symbols $(tt, 0)$ and $(hh, 0)$, for $k = 0, 1, 2$, over 1000 samples. The equivalence classes obtained by Algorithm 2 for $k = 2$, where $R_2(\sigma_g) = gg, \sigma_g \in \mathcal{G}_\varphi, R_2(\sigma_v) = v1, \sigma_v \in V_1 = \{(ii, 0), (hh, 0), (tt, 0)\}, R_2(\sigma_n) = nn, \sigma_n \in \mathcal{R} = \Sigma_{die} - \mathcal{G}_\varphi - V_1$. Notice that according to the original model in Fig. 2 the probability of reaching any of the labels in $\mathcal{G}_{\varphi}$ from $(ii, 0), (hh, 0), (tt, 0)$ in 3 steps (within 2 gaps) is equal.

6 Learning

6.1 Learning Deterministic DTMC

Amongst *probably almost correct* (PAC) techniques to train deterministic DTMCs [42], state-merging algorithms [9], are known to be effective. We use AALERGIA [1, 30], that generates a *frequency prefix tree acceptor* (FPTA) from the training data, and then applies data-dependent compatibility criterion, parameterized by α, to merge the states of the FPTA, and finally transforms it into a DTMC by normalizing the frequencies. The learned model converges to the generating deterministic DTMC, $\mathcal{M}$, in the limit for any $\alpha > 1$ [33]. Figure 3 depicts the learned model from the abstract traces, based on the extracted symbols in Table 1.

In the following, we demonstrate the correctness of the predictions made by the deterministic DTMC trained from the abstract traces.

Theorem 1. *Let* $\mathcal{M}_k : (S, \Sigma_k, \pi, \mathbf{P}, L_k)$ *be the representation of* $\mathcal{M}$*, where the states are relabelled based on the symbols in* Σ_k*. Suppose* $\mathcal{G} \subseteq \Sigma$ *is the set of target symbols, and* $'gg'$ *is their representative symbol in* Σ_k*. Also let* $\mathcal{M}^{\#} : (\tilde{S}, \Sigma_k, \tilde{\pi}, \tilde{\mathbf{P}}, \tilde{L})$ *be the learned model from the samples of* $\mathcal{M}_k$*, using any PAC learning algorithm. Then, under the assumptions of the convergence of the learning algorithm,*

$$\Pr(\tilde{s} \models \Diamond^{\leq h}(gg)) = Pr(s \models \Diamond^{\leq h}\mathcal{G}), \forall \tilde{s} \in \tilde{S}, s \in S. \tag{3}$$

Table 1. The k-prediction support of all the symbols except the target labels, $(hh, 6)$ and $(tt, 1)$, for $k = 0, 1, 2$, obtained from 1000 sample paths of the die example (scale $\times 10^{-3}$).

	$k = 0$	$k = 1$	$k = 2$
$(ii, 0)$	0	0	22.01
$(hh, 0)$	9.26	20.05	23.20
$(tt, 0)$	10.21	21.05	23.22
$(hh, 2)$	0	0	0
$(tt, 3)$	0	0	0
$(hh, 4)$	0	0	0
$(tt, 5)$	0	0	0

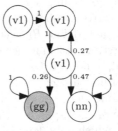

Fig. 3. The learned deterministic DTMC from the abstract traces using the alphabet $\{gg, v1, nn\}$ using 2-prediction support.

Proof. Notice that since prediction in our setting is a *bounded* LTL property, (3) is valid for the initial state, regardless of whether $\mathcal{M}_k$ is deterministic or not (see Theorem 1 in [33]). If $\mathcal{M}_k$ is a deterministic DTMC, the states of the trained model $\mathcal{M}^\#$, almost surely bisimulates the states of $\mathcal{M}_k$ in the limit (see Theorem 1 in [30]). As a result, under the assumptions of the convergence of the learning algorithm, (3) is followed.   □

6.2   Learning Non-deterministic DTMC Using HMM

A Hidden Markov Model (HMM) specifies the distribution of a sequence as the joint distribution of two random variables: the hidden state variable, and the observation variable. More particularly, an HMM is the joint distribution over $X_{1:n}$, the sequence of the state variable, and $Y_{1:n}$, the sequence of observations (both with identical lengths). The joint distribution is such that $Pr(y_i \mid X_{1:i}, Y_{1:i}) = Pr(y_i \mid x_i)$ for $i \in [1, n]$, i.e., the current observation is conditioned only on the current state, and $Pr(x_i \mid X_{1:i-1}, Y_{1:i-1}) = Pr(x_i \mid x_{i-1})$ for $i \in [1, n]$ i.e., the current state is only conditioned on the previous hidden state. We use π to denote the initial probability distribution over the state space, i.e., $Pr(x_1) = \pi(x_1)$. As a result, an HMM can be defined with three distributions:

Definition 5 (HMM). *A finite discrete Hidden Markov Model (HMM) is a tuple $\mathcal{H} : (S, \Sigma, \pi, T, O)$, where S is the non-empty finite set of states, Σ is the non-empty finite set of observations, $\pi : S \to [0, 1]$ is the initial probability distribution over S, $T : S \times S \to [0, 1]$ is the transition probability, and $O : S \times \Sigma \to [0, 1]$ is the observation probability. We use $\Theta_{\mathcal{H}}$ to denote π, T, and O.*

In our setting, observations are the symbols of the abstract alphabet, Σ_k, and hidden states are the states of the generating model, i.e., the deterministic DTMC. The random hidden state variable creates an extra degree of freedom which allows to distinguish states that emit the same symbol but have different joint probability distributions.

Notice that the PAC learning of an HMM is a hard problem under cryptographic assumptions [10, 41] because the probability distribution over the state sequence X is unknown, therefore, the likelihood function does not have a closed form [41]. Subsequently, approximate algorithms, such as Expectation-Maximization (EM) [8], are employed. Training an HMM using EM is known as the BAUM-WELCH algorithm [37] (BWA), which calculates the parameters of the HMM by finding the maximum likelihood of the sample data. BWA requires the number of hidden states in a finite state HMM as an input, or *hyper-parameter*. The hyper-parameters are typically chosen based on some criterion that prevents overfitting (e.g., Bayesian Information Criterion (BIC) [12]).

To run the reachability analysis on the HMM, $\mathcal{H} : (S, \Sigma, \pi, T, O)$, we adopt the direct method in [45] to create an equivalent DTMC, $\mathcal{M}_H : (S \times \Sigma, \Sigma, \pi(s, .), \mathbf{P}, L(., \sigma))$, where $\mathbf{P}((s, \sigma), (s', \sigma')) = T(s, s') \times O(s', \sigma')$.

Figure 4 displays the non-deterministic DTMC and the trained HMM over the abstract traces obtained by R_2 from Table 1. The DTMC in Fig. 4a is similar to the DTMC in Fig. 2, except that the states are relabeled using R_2 (see Sect. 5.2). Relabeling the model creates non-determinism as the sequence $(v1, v1, v1)$ corresponds to several state sequences in the model. The HMM in Fig. 4b is obtained by training HMM that has 4 hidden states. Each hidden state corresponds to the set of states in the DTMC in Fig. 4a with the same labels. There are two hidden states associated with $(v1)$ to distinguish between the states of the model in Fig. 4a that reach the target states (labelled (gg)) with different joint probabilities.

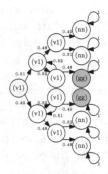

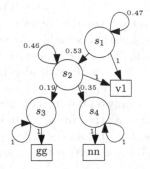

(a) The abstract DTMC obtained by relabeling the states of the DTMC in Fig. 2 using R_2.

(b) The learned HMM from the abstract traces created by R_2 with 4 hidden states.

Fig. 4. Training non-deterministic DTMC using HMM.

7   Case Study: Randomised Self-Stabilising Algorithm

We use Herman's self-stabilising algorithm [18] to experiment our approach in $\mathcal{P}revent$.[1] The algorithm provides a protocol for N identical processes (N is odd) in a token ring network, with unidirectional synchronous communication. Starting from an arbitrary configuration, the network will eventually converge to a defined *stable* state within a finite number of steps. The token is infinitely circulated in the ring amongst the processes in a fair manner. The stable state is defined as such that there is exactly one process that has the token. The process i has a local Boolean variable x_i. If $x_i = x_{i-1}$ there is a token with process i, in which case process i randomly chooses to set x_i to the next value or leave it unchanged (i.e., equal to x_{i-1}).

The observation space for a ring with N processes has 2^N symbols, each representing the values of the local variable in each process. The observation space maps one-to-one to the state space of the corresponding DTMC. We are interested in monitoring the property $\varphi_{stable} : \Diamond^{\leq h}\text{``}stable\text{''}$ which translates into the target symbols in which only one process has the same label as its

---

[1] Available at https://bitbucket.org/rbabaeecar/prevent/.

left neighbour, i.e., there exists only one i such that $x_i = x_{i-1}$. The monitoring procedure throughout our experiments is performed off-line; however, in principle the on-line monitoring procedure would be the same, except that the execution path keeps expanding as the system continues running.

We collected 1000 *iid* samples from the DTMC using PRISM simulation tool [34]. The length of the samples is constrained by a maximum, and is distributed uniformly. We first run Algorithm 2 to extract the predictive symbols for the target symbols specified by φ_{stable}. We replaced the symbols of the sampled traces based on the found partitioning, and performed the training algorithms to learn a deterministic DTMC as well as an HMM. The number of states in the HMM is chosen so that it is comparable to the size of the learned DTMC.

Prediction Evaluation: Using the values obtained from the actual models, we use Mean-Square Prediction Error (MSPE) [15] to measure the performance of the predictions by each model. The evaluation is conducted on a separate *iid* sample from the training samples, where the following is computed for each instance i that the prediction is made (i.e., a target label is not still observed):

$$\varepsilon_i^2 = (Pr(s \models \Diamond^{\leq h}\mathcal{G}) - Pr(\hat{s} \models \Diamond^{\leq h}\mathcal{G}))^2 \qquad (4)$$

where s is the state in the actual DTMC, and $\hat{s}$ is the state in the prediction model, estimated using FORWARD-BACKWARD algorithm [37]. The FORWARD-BACKWARD algorithm computes the posterior probability of the state space given the observation u, i.e., $Pr(X_n = s \mid u, \Theta)$, where n is the length of u. We define MSPE as the average of (4), i.e., $\frac{1}{t}\sum_{i=1}^{t}\varepsilon_i^2$ where t indicates the number of points on the sample where a prediction is made.

Table 2. The prediction results of different models on 100 random samples.

N	Orig. Alph.	Learned DTMC *conc.*		Abst. Alph.	Learned DTMC *abst.*			Learned HMM		
		Size	Training time (s)		Size	Training time (s)	MSPE $e-02$	Size	Training time (s)	MSPE $e-02$
5	32	18	1047.12	5	5	16.12	27.57	4(7)	9.95	0.70
7	128	1319	19605.47	3	3	866.27	32.28	3(5)	61.13	1.39
9	512	7914	135004.38	2	2	275.54	79.36	3(4)	47.16	1.79
11	2048	O/M	–	2	2	2696.73	87.52	2(3)	2496.20	1.35

Table 2 summarizes our results of three different prediction models compared to the prediction results obtained from the original model for $N \in \{5, 7, 9, 11\}$, $k = 0$ (a bigram model), and prediction horizon equal to one step. The size of the original model is identical to the size of the alphabet, as there is exactly one state corresponding to the valuation of the local variables in each process. We used AALERGIA [1] to train DTMC from both the concrete and abstract traces, and Matlab HMM toolbox to train the HMMs. The training was performed on an Ubuntu 17.10 machine with 24 GB RAM. Training a DTMC from concrete traces was aborted for $N = 11$ due to lack of memory, as the length of the FPTAs grows exponentially with the size of the alphabet. The trained DTMCs from abstract traces have significantly smaller size in direct relation to the size of the inferred abstract alphabet, and consequently a shorter training time. This result is consistent with the fact that the actual model is highly symmetrical with respect to the stable states, i.e., the probability of reaching the stable states from the states within an equivalence class in one step is equal.

The sizes of the trained HMMs are determined by the BIC score, and the size of their equivalent DTMCs are shown in parentheses. As we can see an HMM with comparable size is substantially more accurate in making predictions than a DTMC. The state estimation also benefits from the small size of the HMM with virtually no computational overhead. Since the prediction horizon is formulated as an upper-bound, the probability of an accepting extension increases as the prediction horizon increases, which in turn results in a lower MSPE. However, as depicted in Fig. 5a trained HMM has lower error-rate even for shorter range of predictions, e.g., for $h = 5$, the MSPE of the HMM is $0.03e{-}02$ as opposed to $0.85e{-}2$ for the DTMC.

Figure 5b demonstrates the prediction results of the DTMC trained from concrete traces, and the traces abstracted by k-prediction support, using $k = 0, 5, 10$. The prediction results are from the initial state, and as we can see, the models learned from abstract traces almost follow the values of the actual model. The best result belongs to $k = 10$, which echos the maximum expected time to reach a stable state, i.e., that the path to the target symbols from the initial state is of length at most about 9.

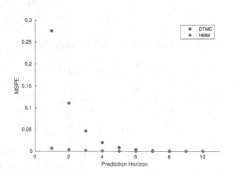

(a) MSPE of the trained DTMC and HMM on abstract traces with $k = 0$, $N = 5$ (prediction horizon [1,10]).

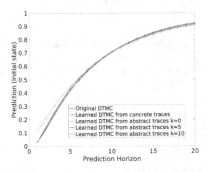

(b) The prediction results from the initial state of different prediction models compared to the original model for $N = 9$.

Fig. 5. The experiment results for abstract models in the Herman algorithm.

8 Related Work

To the best of our knowledge our approach is novel in terms of applying learning and abstraction to predictive RV, and using HMM to handle non-determinism at the trace level. Xian Zhang *et al.* [46] introduce a predictive LTL semantics definition, that is applied on white-box systems (i.e., using the control flow graphs), to find the extensions that evaluate an LTL formula to *true* or *false*. Martin Leucker [27] follows the same idea and extends the semantics and the monitor construction for when an over-approximation of the program is given. Our approach works on black-box systems and finds the probability of the extensions that satisfy a reachability property based on the sample executions of the system that form a probabilistic model. Furthermore, we define the abstraction by inferring a projection function over the observation space using the sample executions.

Sistla *et al.* [39] propose an *internal* monitoring approach (i.e., the property is specified over the hidden states) using specification automata and HMMs with infinite states. Learning an infinite-state HMM is a harder problem than the finite HMMs, but does not require inferring the size of the model [7].

Nouri *et al.* [33] use abstraction and learning to expedite statistical model checking [25]. Their approach is the probabilistic variant of *black box checking* [35] in which the inferred model, in the form of definite finite automata (DFA), is checked against some properties. In our case, we use abstraction to obtain a smaller prediction model for predictive RV. In [33] the atomic propositions in the property are used for abstracting the traces. We perform a statistical analysis on the traces to obtain partitions that leave the prediction probability intact. We also use HMM to handle the potential non-determinism introduced by the abstraction.

Aichernig and Tappler [2] employ black box checking in the context of reachability analysis of stochastic systems with controllable inputs. They use Markov Decision Process (MDP), an extension of a Markov chain with non-deterministic choices, as a model that is trained from random samples. They use the inferred MDP to obtain an *adversary* with which they collect new samples and incrementally train new MDPs. LAR [44] is a combination of probabilistic model learning and counterexample guided abstraction refinement (CEGAR) [19]. These approaches are orthogonal to our technique and it is straightforward to extend the training to other models such as MDP, and apply probabilistic CEGAR to obtain a model that guarantees checking affirmative properties.

9 Conclusion

We propose inferring a projection relation from a random set of samples to abstract traces that are used in building prediction models to monitor a discrete-time reachability property. Our inference technique is based on finding a symmetrical relation between the symbols of the alphabet, using k-gapped pair model, and lumping them into same equivalence classes. We use the abstract traces to train deterministic DTMC as well as HMM to handle the possible non-determinism induced by abstraction. We show that the prediction results remain intact with the model trained from abstract traces, under the condition that the generating DTMC of the abstract traces is deterministic and under the constraints of the learning algorithm. We evaluated our approach on a distributed randomized algorithm, and demonstrated that in general the trained HMM from the abstract traces is more accurate than the trained DTMCs.

Our approach is most effective on the systems with large observation space, and where the model benefits from symmetry in the probability of reaching some states. The statistical analysis of the traces proposed in this paper to reduce the observation space requires enough number of executions with the target labels to reliably detect similar symbols. If the target labels indicate some rare events (e.g., *error* with very low probability), techniques such as [26] are required to simulate enough traces with target labels. The trained model from such simulated sample traces need to be adjusted.

Lastly, an implementation of $\mathcal{P}revent$ with the application of on-line learning methods (such as state merging or splitting techniques [32]) is necessary to apply the framework to the real-world scenarios.

References

1. Aalergia: http://mi.cs.aau.dk/code/aalergia/. Accessed 15 Mar 2018
2. Aichernig, B.K., Tappler, M.: Probabilistic black-box reachability checking. In: Lahiri, S., Reger, G. (eds.) RV 2017. LNCS, vol. 10548, pp. 50–67. Springer, Cham (2017). https://doi.org/10.1007/978-3-319-67531-2_4
3. Babaee, R., Gurfinkel, A., Fischmeister, S.: $\mathcal{P}revent$: A Predictive Run-Time Verification Framework Using Statistical Learning. In: Johnsen, E.B., Schaefer, I. (eds.) SEFM 2018. LNCS, vol. 10886, pp. 205–220. Springer, Cham (2018). https://doi.org/10.1007/978-3-319-92970-5_13
4. Baier, C., Katoen, J.: Principles of Model Checking. MIT Press, Cambridge (2008)
5. Bauer, A., Leucker, M., Schallhart, C.: The good, the bad, and the ugly, but how ugly is ugly? In: 7th International Workshop RV, pp. 126–138 (2007)
6. Bauer, A., Leucker, M., Schallhart, C.: Comparing LTL semantics for runtime verification. J. Log. Comput. **20**(3), 651–674 (2010)
7. Beal, M.J., Ghahramani, Z., Rasmussen, C.E.: The infinite hidden Markov model. In: Proceedings of the 14th International Conference on Neural Information Processing Systems: Natural and Synthetic, NIPS 2001, pp. 577–584. MIT Press, Cambridge (2001)
8. Bilmes, J.A.: A gentle tutorial of the EM algorithm and its applications to parameter estimation for Gaussian mixture and hidden Markov models. Technical report TR-97-021, International Computer Science Institute, Berkeley, CA (1997)
9. Carrasco, R.C., Oncina, J.: Learning stochastic regular grammars by means of a state merging method. In: Carrasco, R.C., Oncina, J. (eds.) ICGI 1994. LNCS, vol. 862, pp. 139–152. Springer, Heidelberg (1994). https://doi.org/10.1007/3-540-58473-0_144
10. Castro, J., Gavaldà, R.: Learning probability distributions generated by finite-state machines. In: Heinz, J., Sempere, J.M. (eds.) Topics in Grammatical Inference, pp. 113–142. Springer, Heidelberg (2016). https://doi.org/10.1007/978-3-662-48395-4_5

11. Chan, S.W.K., Franklin, J.: A text-based decision support system for financial sequence prediction. Decis. Support Syst. **52**(1), 189–198 (2011)
12. Claeskens, G., Hjort, N.L.: Model Selection and Model Averaging. Series in Statistical and Probabilistic Mathematics. Cambridge University Press, Cambridge (2008)
13. Dong, G., Pei, J.: Sequence data mining. In: Advances in Database Systems, vol. 33, Kluwer (2007)
14. Falcone, Y., Fernandez, J.-C., Mounier, L.: Runtime verification of safety-progress properties. In: Bensalem, S., Peled, D.A. (eds.) RV 2009. LNCS, vol. 5779, pp. 40–59. Springer, Heidelberg (2009). https://doi.org/10.1007/978-3-642-04694-0_4
15. Geisser, S.: Predictive Inference, Chapman & Hall/CRC Monographs on Statistics & Applied Probability. Taylor & Francis, UK (1993)
16. Hamilton, J.D.: Time Series Analysis. Princeton University Press, Princeton (1994)
17. Hansson, H., Jonsson, B.: A logic for reasoning about time and reliability. Formal Asp. Comput. **6**(5), 512–535 (1994)
18. Herman, T.: Probabilistic self-stabilization. Inf. Process. Lett. **35**(2), 63–67 (1990)
19. Hermanns, H., Wachter, B., Zhang, L.: Probabilistic CEGAR. In: Gupta, A., Malik, S. (eds.) CAV 2008. LNCS, vol. 5123, pp. 162–175. Springer, Heidelberg (2008). https://doi.org/10.1007/978-3-540-70545-1_16
20. Huang, S., Liu, R., Chen, C., Chao, Y., Chen, S.: Prediction of outer membrane proteins by support vector machines using combinations of gapped amino acid pair compositions. In: Fifth IEEE International Symposium on Bioinformatic and Bioengineering (BIBE 2005), 19–21 October 2005, Minneapolis, MN, USA, pp. 113–120. IEEE Computer Society (2005)
21. Kalajdzic, K., Bartocci, E., Smolka, S.A., Stoller, S.D., Grosu, R.: Runtime verification with particle filtering. In: Legay, A., Bensalem, S. (eds.) RV 2013. LNCS, vol. 8174, pp. 149–166. Springer, Heidelberg (2013). https://doi.org/10.1007/978-3-642-40787-1_9
22. Knuth, D.: The complexity of nonuniform random number generation. In: Algorithm and Complexity, New Directions and Results, pp. 357–428 (1976)
23. Kwiatkowska, M., Norman, G., Parker, D.: Symmetry reduction for probabilistic model checking. In: Ball, T., Jones, R.B. (eds.) CAV 2006. LNCS, vol. 4144, pp. 234–248. Springer, Heidelberg (2006). https://doi.org/10.1007/11817963_23
24. Kwiatkowska, M., Norman, G., Parker, D.: Stochastic model checking. In: Bernardo, M., Hillston, J. (eds.) SFM 2007. LNCS, vol. 4486, pp. 220–270. Springer, Heidelberg (2007). https://doi.org/10.1007/978-3-540-72522-0_6
25. Legay, A., Delahaye, B., Bensalem, S.: Statistical model checking: an overview. In: Barringer, H. (ed.) RV 2010. LNCS, vol. 6418, pp. 122–135. Springer, Heidelberg (2010). https://doi.org/10.1007/978-3-642-16612-9_11
26. Legay, A., Sedwards, S., Traonouez, L.-M.: Rare events for statistical model checking an overview. In: Larsen, K.G., Potapov, I., Srba, J. (eds.) RP 2016. LNCS, vol. 9899, pp. 23–35. Springer, Cham (2016). https://doi.org/10.1007/978-3-319-45994-3_2
27. Leucker, M.: Sliding between model checking and runtime verification. In: Qadeer, S., Tasiran, S. (eds.) RV 2012. LNCS, vol. 7687, pp. 82–87. Springer, Heidelberg (2013). https://doi.org/10.1007/978-3-642-35632-2_10
28. Leucker, M., Schallhart, C.: A brief account of runtime verification. J. Log. Algebr. Program. **78**(5), 293–303 (2009)
29. Maler, O.: Some thoughts on runtime verification. In: Falcone, Y., Sánchez, C. (eds.) RV 2016. LNCS, vol. 10012, pp. 3–14. Springer, Cham (2016). https://doi.org/10.1007/978-3-319-46982-9_1

30. Mao, H., Chen, Y., Jaeger, M., Nielsen, T.D., Larsen, K.G., Nielsen, B.: Learning probabilistic automata for model checking. In: Eighth International Conference on Quantitative Evaluation of Systems, QEST 2011, Aachen, Germany, 5–8 September, pp. 111–120 (2011)
31. Mikolov, T., Chen, K., Corrado, G., Dean, J.: Efficient estimation of word representations in vector space. CoRR, abs/1301.3781 (2013)
32. Mukherjee, K., Ray, A.: State splitting and merging in probabilistic finite state automata for signal representation and analysis. Sign. Process. **104**, 105–119 (2014)
33. Nouri, A., Raman, B., Bozga, M., Legay, A., Bensalem, S.: Faster statistical model checking by means of abstraction and learning. In: Bonakdarpour, B., Smolka, S.A. (eds.) RV 2014. LNCS, vol. 8734, pp. 340–355. Springer, Cham (2014). https://doi.org/10.1007/978-3-319-11164-3_28
34. Parker, D., Norman, G., Kwiatkowska, M.: Prism model checker. http://www.prismmodelchecker.org/. Accessed 14 Aug 2017
35. Peled, D.A., Vardi, M.Y., Yannakakis, M.: Black box checking. J. Automata, Lang. Comb. **7**(2), 225–246 (2002)
36. Pnueli, A.: The temporal logic of programs. In: 18th Annual Symposium on Foundations of Computer Science, pp. 46–57 (1977)
37. Rabiner, L.R.: A tutorial on hidden Markov models and selected applications in speech recognition. Proc. IEEE **77**(2), 257–286 (1989)
38. Roweis, S.T., Ghahramani, Z.: A unifying review of linear Gaussian models. Neural Comput. **11**(2), 305–345 (1999)
39. Sistla, A.P., Žefran, M., Feng, Y.: Monitorability of stochastic dynamical systems. In: Gopalakrishnan, G., Qadeer, S. (eds.) CAV 2011. LNCS, vol. 6806, pp. 720–736. Springer, Heidelberg (2011). https://doi.org/10.1007/978-3-642-22110-1_58
40. Stoller, S.D., Bartocci, E., Seyster, J., Grosu, R., Havelund, K., Smolka, S.A., Zadok, E.: Runtime verification with state estimation. In: Khurshid, S., Sen, K. (eds.) RV 2011. LNCS, vol. 7186, pp. 193–207. Springer, Heidelberg (2012). https://doi.org/10.1007/978-3-642-29860-8_15
41. Terwijn, S.A.: On the learnability of hidden Markov models. In: Adriaans, P., Fernau, H., van Zaanen, M. (eds.) ICGI 2002. LNCS (LNAI), vol. 2484, pp. 261–268. Springer, Heidelberg (2002). https://doi.org/10.1007/3-540-45790-9_21
42. Verwer, S., Eyraud, R., de la Higuera, C.: PAUTOMAC: a probabilistic automata and hidden Markov models learning competition. Mach. Learn. **96**(1–2), 129–154 (2014)
43. Viterbi, A.J.: Error bounds for convolutional codes and an asymptotically optimum decoding algorithm. IEEE Trans. Inform. Theor. **13**(2), 260–269 (1967)
44. Wang, J., Sun, J., Qin, S.: Verifying complex systems probabilistically through learning, abstraction and refinement. CoRR, abs/1610.06371 (2016)
45. Zhang, L., Hermanns, H., Jansen, D.N.: Logic and model checking for hidden Markov models. In: Wang, F. (ed.) FORTE 2005. LNCS, vol. 3731, pp. 98–112. Springer, Heidelberg (2005). https://doi.org/10.1007/11562436_9
46. Zhang, X., Leucker, M., Dong, W.: Runtime verification with predictive semantics. In: Goodloe, A.E., Person, S. (eds.) NFM 2012. LNCS, vol. 7226, pp. 418–432. Springer, Heidelberg (2012). https://doi.org/10.1007/978-3-642-28891-3_37

Efficient Timed Diagnosis Using Automata with Timed Domains

Patricia Bouyer[1], Samy Jaziri[1], and Nicolas Markey[2(✉)]

[1] LSV – CNRS & ENS Paris-Saclay, Univ. Paris-Saclay, Cachan, France
[2] IRISA – Univ. Rennes & CNRS & INRIA, Rennes, France
nmarkey@irisa.fr

Abstract. We consider the problems of efficiently diagnosing and predicting what did (or will) happen in a partially-observable one-clock
timed automaton. We introduce *timed sets* as a formalism to keep track
of the evolution of the reachable configurations over time, and use our
previous work on automata over timed domains to build a candidate
diagnoser for our timed automaton. We report on our implementation of
this approach compared to the approach of [Tripakis, *Fault diagnosis for
timed automata*, 2002].

1 Introduction

Formal Methods in Verification. Because of the wide range of applications of
computer systems, and of their increasing complexity, the use of formal methods
for checking their correct behaviours has become essential [10,16]. Numerous
approaches have been introduced and extensively studied over the last 40 years,
and mature tools now exist and are used in practice. Most of these approaches
rely on building mathematical models, such as automata and extensions thereof,
in order to represent and reason about the behaviours of those systems; various algorithmic techniques are then applied in order to ensure correctness of
those behaviours, such as *model checking* [11,12], *deductive verification* [13,17]
or *testing* [25].

Fault Diagnosis. The techniques listed above mainly focus on assessing correctness of the set of all behaviours of the system, in an offline manner. This is usually
very costly in terms of computation, and sometimes too strong a requirement.
Runtime verification instead aims at checking properties of a running system [19].
Fault diagnosis is a prominent problem in runtime verification: it consists in
(deciding the existence and) building a diagnoser, whose role is to monitor real
executions of a (partially-observable) system, and decide *online* whether some
property holds (e.g., whether some unobservable fault has occurred) [24,26].
A diagnoser can usually be built (for finite-state models) by determinizing a
model of the system, using the powerset construction; it will keep track of all

Work supported by ERC project EQualIS.

possible states that can be reached after each (observable) step of the system, thereby computing whether a fault may or must have occurred. The related problem of *prediction*, a.k.a. prognosis, (that e.g. no fault may occur in the next five steps) [15], is also of particular interest in runtime verification, and can be solved using similar techniques.

Verifying Real-Time Systems. Real-time constraints often play an important role for modelling and specifying correctness of computer systems. Discrete models, such as finite-state automata, are not adequate to model such real-time constraints; timed automata [1], developed at the end of the 1980's, provide a convenient framework for both representing and efficiently reasoning about computer systems subject to real-time constraints. Efficient offline verification techniques for timed automata have been developed and implemented [2,3]. Diagnosis of timed automata however has received less attention; this problem is made difficult by the fact that timed automata can in general not be determinized [14,27]. This has been circumvented by either restricting to classes of determinizable timed automata [6], or by keeping track of all possible configurations of the automaton after a (finite) execution [26]. The latter approach is computationally very expensive, as one step consists in maintaining the set of all configurations that can be reached by following (arbitrarily long) sequences of unobservable transitions; this limits the applicability of the approach.

Our Contribution. In this paper, we (try to) make the approach of [26] more efficiently applicable (over the class of one-clock timed automata). Our improvements are based on two ingredients: first, we use *automata over timed domains* [7] as a model for representing the diagnoser. Automata over timed domains can be seen as an extension of timed automata with a (much) richer notion of time and clocks; these automata enjoy determinizability. The second ingredient is the notion of *timed sets*: timed sets are pairs (E, I) where E is any subset of $\mathbb{R}$, and I is an interval with upper bound $+\infty$; such a timed set represents a set of clock valuations evolving over time: the timed set $(E; I)$ after a delay d represents the set $(E + d) \cap I$. As we prove, timed sets can be used to finitely represent the evolution of the set of all reachable configurations after a finite execution.

In the end, our algorithm can compute a finite representation of the reachable configurations after a given execution, as well as all the configurations that can be reached from there after any delay. This can be used to very quickly update the set of current possible configurations (which would be expensive with the approach of [26]). Besides diagnosis, this can also be used to efficiently predict the occurrence of faults occurring after some delay (which is not possible in [26]). We implemented our technique in a prototype tool: as we report at the end of the paper, our approach requires heavy precomputation, but can then efficiently handle delay transitions.

Related Works. Model-based diagnosis has been extensively studied in the community of discrete-event systems [23,24,28]. This framework gave birth to a number of ramifications (e.g. active diagnosis [22], fault prediction [15], opacity [18]), and was applied in many different settings besides discrete-event systems (e.g. Petri nets, distributed systems [4], stochastic systems [5,20], discrete-time systems [9], hybrid systems [21]).

Much fewer papers have focused on continuous-time diagnosis: Tripakis proposed an algorithm for deciding diagnosability [26]. Cassez developed a uniform approach for diagnosability of discrete and continuous time systems, as a reduction to Büchi-automata emptiness [8]. A construction of a diagnoser for timed systems is proposed in [26]: the classical approach of determinizing using the powerset construction does not extend to timed automata, because timed automata cannot in general be determinized [14,27]. Tripakis proposed the construction of a diagnoser as an online algorithm that keeps track of the possible states and zones the system can be in after each event (or after a sufficiently-long delay), which requires heavy computation at each step and is hardly usable in practice. Bouyer, Chevalier and D'Souza studied a restricted setting, only looking for diagnosers under the form of deterministic timed automata with limited resources [6].

2 Definitions

2.1 Intervals

In this paper, we heavily use intervals, and especially unbounded ones. For $r \in \mathbb{R}$, we define

$$\mathord{\uparrow} r = [r; +\infty) \qquad \mathord{\uparrow} r = (r; +\infty) \qquad \mathord{\downarrow} r = (-\infty; r) \qquad \mathord{\downarrow} r = (-\infty; r].$$

We let $\widehat{\mathbb{R}}_{\geq 0} = \{\mathord{\uparrow} r, \mathord{\uparrow} r \mid r \in \mathbb{R}_{\geq 0}\}$ for the set of upward-closed intervals of $\mathbb{R}_{\geq 0}$; in the sequel, elements of $\widehat{\mathbb{R}}_{\geq 0}$ are denoted with $\hat{r}$. Similarly, we let $\widecheck{\mathbb{R}}_{\geq 0} = \{\mathord{\downarrow} r, \mathord{\downarrow} r \mid r \in \mathbb{R}_{\geq 0}\}$, and use notation $\underaccent{\sim}{r}$ for intervals in $\widecheck{\mathbb{R}}_{\geq 0}$. The elements of $\widehat{\mathbb{R}}_{\geq 0}$ can be (totally) ordered using inclusion: we write $\hat{r} \prec \hat{r}'$ whenever $\hat{r}' \subset \hat{r}$ (so that $r < r'$ entails $\mathord{\uparrow} r \prec \mathord{\uparrow} r'$).

2.2 Timed Automata

Let Σ be a finite alphabet.

Definition 1. *A one-clock timed automaton over Σ is a tuple $\mathcal{A} = (S, \{s_0\}, T, F)$, where S is a finite set of states, $s_0 \in S$ is the initial state, $T \subseteq S \times \widehat{\mathbb{R}}_{\geq 0} \times \mathbb{R}_{\geq 0} \times (\Sigma \uplus \{\epsilon\}) \times \{0, id\} \times S$ is the set of transitions, and $F \subseteq S$ is a set of final states. A configuration of $\mathcal{A}$ is a pair $(s, v) \in S \times \mathbb{R}_{\geq 0}$. There is a transition from (s, v) to (s', v') if*

- *either $s' = s$ and $v' \geq v$. In that case, we write $(s, v) \xrightarrow{d} (s', v')$, with $d = v' - v$, for such delay transitions (notice that we have no invariants);*

– *or there is a transition* $e = (s, \widehat{l}, \underline{u}, a, r, s')$ *s.t.* $v \in \widehat{l} \cap \underline{u}$ *and* $v' = v$ *if* $r = id$, *and* $v' = 0$ *otherwise. For those* action transitions, *we write* $(s, v) \to_e (s', v')$. *We assume that for each transition* $e = (s, \widehat{l}, \underline{u}, a, r, s')$, *it holds* $\widehat{l} \cap \underline{u} \neq \emptyset$.

Fix a one-clock timed automaton $\mathcal{A}$; we write T_{id} for the set of *non-resetting* transitions, i.e., having id as their fifth component, and T_0 for the complement set of *resetting* transitions.

For a transition $e = (s, \widehat{l}, \underline{u}, a, r, s')$, we write $\widehat{e}$ and $\underline{e}$ for $\widehat{l}$ and $\underline{u}$, respectively. We write $\mathsf{src}(e) = s$ and $\mathsf{tgt}(e) = s'$, and $\mathsf{lab}(e) = a \in \Sigma$. We extend these definitions to sequences of transitions $w = (e_i)_{0 \le i < n}$ as $\mathsf{src}(w) = \mathsf{src}(e_0)$, $\mathsf{tgt}(w) = \mathsf{tgt}(e_{n-1})$, and $\mathsf{lab}(w) = (\mathsf{lab}(e_i))_{0 \le i < n}$.

Let w be a sequence $(e_{2i+1})_{0 \le 2i+1 < n}$ of transitions of T, and $d \in \mathbb{R}_{\ge 0}$. We write $(s, v) \xrightarrow{d}_w (s', v')$ if there exist finite sequences $(s_i, v_i)_{0 \le i \le n} \in (S \times \mathbb{R}_{\ge 0})^{n+1}$ and $(d_{2i})_{0 \le 2i < n} \in \mathbb{R}_{\ge 0}^{\lfloor n/2 \rfloor}$ such that $\sum_{0 \le 2i < n} d_{2i} = d$, and $(s_0, v_0) = (s, v)$ and $(s_n, v_n) = (s', v')$, and for all $0 \le j < n$, $(s_j, v_j) \xrightarrow{d_j} (s_{j+1}, v_{j+1})$ if j is even and $(s_j, v_j) \to_{e_j} (s_{j+1}, v_{j+1})$ if j is odd. We write $(s, v) \to (s', v')$ when $(s, v) \xrightarrow{d}_w (s', v')$ for some $w \in T^*$ and some $d \in \mathbb{R}_{\ge 0}$.

For any $\lambda \in \Sigma^*$ and any $d \in \mathbb{R}_{\ge 0}$, we write $(s, v) \xrightarrow{d}_\lambda (s', v')$ whenever there exists a sequence of transitions w such that $\lambda = \mathsf{lab}(w)$ and $(s, v) \xrightarrow{d}_w (s', v')$. Notice that[1] $(s, v) \xrightarrow{d}_\perp (s', v')$ (sometimes simply written $(s, v) \xrightarrow{d} (s', v')$) indicates a delay-transition (hence it must be $s = s'$). The untimed language $\mathcal{L}(\mathcal{A})$ of $\mathcal{A}$ is the set of words $\lambda \in \Sigma^*$ such that $(s_0, 0) \xrightarrow{d}_\lambda (s', v')$ for some $s' \in F$ and $d \in \mathbb{R}_{\ge 0}$.

We borrow some of the formalism of [7], in order to define a kind of *powerset construction* for timed automata. For a one-clock timed automaton $\mathcal{A} = (S, \{s_0\}, T, F)$ on Σ, we write $\mathrm{M} = (\mathcal{P}(\mathbb{R}_{\ge 0}))^S$ for the set of *markings*, mapping states of $\mathcal{A}$ to sets of valuations for the unique clock of $\mathcal{A}$. For a marking $m \in \mathrm{M}$, we write $\mathsf{supp}(m) = \{s \in S \mid m(s) \neq \emptyset\}$. For any $l \in \Sigma$, we define the function $\mathbf{O}_l \colon \mathrm{M} \to \mathrm{M}$ by letting, for any $m \in \mathrm{M}$ and any $s' \in S$,

$$\mathbf{O}_l(m) \colon s' \mapsto \{v' \in \mathbb{R}_{\ge 0} \mid \exists s \in S.\ \exists v \in m(s).\ (s, v) \to_l (s', v')\}.$$

Similarly, for any $d \in \mathbb{R}_{\ge 0}$, we let

$$\mathbf{O}_d(m) \colon s' \mapsto \{v' \in \mathbb{R}_{\ge 0} \mid \exists s \in S.\ \exists v \in m(s).\ (s, v) \xrightarrow{d} (s', v')\}.$$

Notice that $\mathbf{O}_d$ simply shifts all valuations by d.

Definition 2 ([7]). *The* powerset automaton *of a timed automaton* $\mathcal{A} = (S, \{s_0\}, T, F)$ *is a tuple* $\mathbf{D}\mathcal{A} = (\mathcal{P}(S), \{\{s_0\}\}, \mathbf{PT}, \mathbf{PF})$, *where* $\mathcal{P}(S)$ *is the set of states,* $\{s_0\}$ *is the initial state,* $\mathbf{PT} = \{(q, m, a, q') \in \mathcal{P}(S) \times \mathrm{M} \times \Sigma \times \mathcal{P}(S) \mid q = \mathsf{supp}(m),\ q' = \mathsf{supp}(\mathbf{O}_a(m))\}$ *is the set of transitions, and* $\mathbf{PF} = \{E \in \mathcal{P}(S) \mid E \cap F \neq \emptyset\}$ *is a set of final states.*

---

[1] In this paper, we write $\perp$ for the empty word (or empty sequences) over any alphabet.

Configurations of $\mathbf{D}\mathcal{A}$ are all pairs $(q, m) \in \mathcal{P}(S) \times \mathbb{M}$ for which $q = \text{supp}(m)$. There is a transition from a configuration (q, m) to a configuration (q', m') labelled with $l \in \Sigma \cup \mathbb{R}_{\geq 0}$ whenever $m' = \mathbf{O}_l(m)$. We extend this definition to sequences alternating delay- and action transitions, and write $(q, m) \xrightarrow{d}_w (q', m')$ when there is a path from (q, m) to (q', m') following the transitions of w in d time units. Similarly, we write $(q, m) \xrightarrow{d}_\sigma (q', m')$ if $(q, m) \xrightarrow{d}_w (q', m')$ and $\text{lab}(w) = \sigma$.

Following [7], the automaton $\mathbf{D}\mathcal{A}$ is deterministic, and it simulates $\mathcal{A}$ in the sense that given two marking m and m' and a word σ of Σ^*, we have $(\text{supp}(m), m) \xrightarrow{d}_\sigma (\text{supp}(m'), m')$ if, and only if, $m'(s') = \{v' \in \mathbb{R}_{\geq 0} \mid \exists s \in S. \ \exists v \in m(s). \ (s, v) \xrightarrow{d}_\sigma (s', v')\}$ for all $s' \in S$.

2.3 Timed Automata with Silent Transitions

The work reported in [7] only focuses on the case when there are no silent transitions. In that case, for any $d \in \mathbb{R}_{\geq 0}$, the operation $\mathbf{O}_d$ can be computed easily, since it amounts to adding d to each item of the marking (in other terms, for any marking m, any state $s \in S$, and any $v \in \mathbb{R}_{\geq 0}$ such that $v + d \in \mathbb{R}_{\geq 0}$, we have $v \in m(s)$ if, and only if, $v + d \in \mathbf{O}_d(m)(s)$). This leads to an efficient expression of a (deterministic) powerset automaton simulating $\mathcal{A}$.

However fault diagnosis should deal with timed automata with unobservable transitions (unobservable transitions then correspond to internal transitions). So we now assume that Σ contains a special *silent letter* ϵ, whose occurrence is not *visible*. This requires changing the definition of lab: we now let

$$\text{lab}(\bot) = \bot$$
$$\text{lab}(w \cdot e) = \text{lab}(w) \qquad\qquad\qquad \text{if } \text{lab}(e) = \epsilon$$
$$\text{lab}(w \cdot e) = \text{lab}(w) \cdot \text{lab}(e) \qquad\qquad \text{if } \text{lab}(e) \neq \epsilon$$

Notice that $\text{lab}(w) \in (\Sigma \setminus \{\epsilon\})^*$. We may write $\rightarrow_\epsilon$ in place of $\rightarrow_\bot$, to stick to classical notations and make it clear that it allows silent transitions.

In that case, $\mathbf{D}\mathcal{A}$ still is a (deterministic) powerset automaton that simulates $\mathcal{A}$, and hence is still a *diagnoser*, but the function $\mathbf{O}_d$ cannot be computed by just shifting valuations by d. In its raw form, the function $\mathbf{O}_d$ can be obtained by the computation of the set of reachable configurations in a delay d by following silent transitions. This is analogous to the method proposed by Tripakis [26], and turns out to be very costly. However, a diagnoser must be able to simulate all possible actions of the diagnosed automaton quickly enough, so that it can be used at runtime. In this paper, we introduce a new data structure called *timed sets*, which we use to represent markings in the timed powerset automaton; as we explain, using timed sets we can compute $\mathbf{O}_d$ more efficiently (at the expense of more precomputations).

3   (Regular) Timed Sets

3.1   Timed Sets

For a set E and a real d, we define the set $E + d = \{x + d \mid x \in E\}$. We introduce *timed sets* as a way to represent sets of clock valuations (and eventually markings), and their evolution over time.

Definition 3. *An* atomic timed set *is a pair* $(E; \widehat{r})$ *where* $E \subseteq \mathbb{R}$ *and* $\widehat{r} \in \widehat{\mathbb{R}}_{\geq 0}$. *With an atomic timed set* $F = (E; \widehat{r})$, *we associate a mapping* $F \colon \mathbb{R}_{\geq 0} \to 2^{\mathbb{R}}$ *defined as* $F(d) = (E + d) \cap \widehat{r}$.

We define the union of two timed sets F and F', denoted as $F \sqcup F'$, as their pointwise union: $(F \sqcup F')(d) = F(d) \cup F'(d)$.

Definition 4. *A* timed set *is a countable set* $F = \{F_i \mid i \in I\}$ *(intended to be a union, hence sometimes also denoted with* $\bigsqcup_{i \in I} F_i$*) of atomic timed sets. With such a timed set, we again associate a mapping* $F \colon \mathbb{R}_{\geq 0} \to 2^{\mathbb{R}_{\geq 0}}$ *defined as* $F(d) = \bigcup_{i \in I} F_i(d)$. *A timed set is* finite *when it is made of finitely many atomic timed sets. We write* $\mathcal{T}(\mathbb{R})$ *for the set of timed sets of* $\mathbb{R}$.

Given two timed sets F and F', we write $F \sqsubseteq F'$ whenever $F(d) \subseteq F'(d)$ for all $d \in \mathbb{R}_{\geq 0}$. This is a pre-order relation; it is not anti-symmetric as for instance $(\{1\}; {\uparrow}0) \sqsubseteq (\{1\}; {\uparrow}1)$ and $(\{1\}; {\uparrow}1) \sqsubseteq (\{1\}; {\uparrow}0)$. We write $F \equiv F'$ whenever $F \sqsubseteq F'$ and $F' \sqsubseteq F$.

Example 1. Figure 1 displays an example of an atomic timed set $F = (E; {\uparrow}1)$, with $E = [-3; -1] \cup [0; 2]$. The picture displays the sets $F(0) = [1; 2]$ and $F(3) = [1; 2] \cup [3; 5]$.   ◁

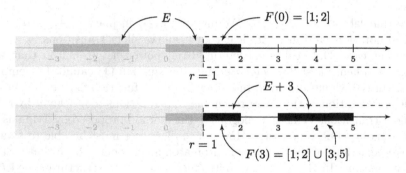

Fig. 1. Example of an atomic timed set $F = ([-3; -1] \cup [0; 2]; {\uparrow}1)$.

3.2 Regular Timed Sets

In order to effectively store and manipulate timed sets, we need to identify a class of timed sets that is expressive enough but whose timed sets have a finite representation.

Definition 5. *A regular union of intervals is a 4-tuple $E = (I, J, p, q)$ where I and J are finite unions of intervals of $\mathbb{R}$ with rational (or infinite) bounds, $p \in \mathbb{Q}_{\geq 0}$ is the period, and $q \in \mathbb{N}$ is the offset. It is required that $J \subseteq (-p; 0]$ and $I \subseteq \hat{\uparrow}(-q \cdot p)$.*

The regular union of intervals $E = (I, J, p, q)$ represents the set (which we still write E) $I \cup \bigcup_{k=q}^{+\infty} J - k \cdot p$.

Regular unions of intervals enjoy the following properties:

Proposition 6. *Let E and E' be regular unions of intervals, K be an interval, and $d \in \mathbb{Q}$. Then $E \cup E'$, $\overline{E}$, $E + d$ and $E - K$ are regular unions of intervals.*

Definition 7. *A regular timed set is a finite timed set $F = \{(E_i; \hat{r}_i) \mid i \in I\}$ such that for all $i \in I$, the set E_i is a regular union of intervals.*

4   Computing the Powerset Automaton

In this section, we fix a one-clock timed automaton $\mathcal{A} = (S, \{s_0\}, T, F)$ over alphabet Σ, assumed to contain a silent letter ϵ. We assume that some silent transitions are *faulty*, and we want to detect the occurrence of such faulty transitions based on the sequence of actions we can observe. Following [26], this can be reduced to a *state-estimation problem*, even if it means duplicating some states of the model in order to keep track of the occurrence of a faulty transition. In the end, we aim at computing (a finite representation of) the powerset automaton $\mathbf{D}\mathcal{A}$, which amounts to computing the transition functions $\mathbf{O}_l$ for any $l \in \Sigma$ and $\mathbf{O}_d$ for any $d \in \mathbb{R}_{\geq 0}$. Computing $\mathbf{O}_l(m)$ for $l \in \Sigma$ is not very involved: for each state $s \in S$ and each transition e labelled with l with source s and target s', it suffices to intersect $m(s)$ with the guard $\hat{e} \cap e$, and add the resulting interval (or the singleton $\{0\}$ if e is a resetting transition) in $\mathbf{O}_l(m)(s')$.

From now on, we only focus on computing $\mathbf{O}_d$, for $d \in \mathbb{R}_{\geq 0}$. For this, it is sufficient to only consider silent transitions of $\mathcal{A}$: we let $U = U_0 \uplus U_{id}$ be the subset of T containing all transitions labelled ϵ, partitioned into those transitions that reset clock x (in U_0), and those that do not (in U_{id}). We write $\mathcal{A}_\epsilon$ for the restriction of $\mathcal{A}$ to silent transitions, and only consider that automaton in the sequel. All transitions are silent in $\mathcal{A}_\epsilon$, but for convenience, we assume that transitions are labelled with their name in $\mathcal{A}$, so that the *untimed language* of $\mathcal{A}_\epsilon$ is the set of sequences of consecutive (silent) transitions firable from the initial configuration.

4.1   Linear Timed Markings and Their ϵ-Closure

We use markings to represent sets of configurations; in order to compute $\mathbf{O}_d$, we need to represent the evolution of markings over time. For this, we introduce *timed markings*. A timed marking is a mapping $M\colon S \to (\mathbb{R}_{\geq 0} \to 2^{\mathbb{R}_{\geq 0}})$. For any $s \in S$ and any $d \in \mathbb{R}_{\geq 0}$, $M(s)(d)$ is intended to represent all clock valuations that can be obtained in s after a delay of d time units. For any delay $d \in \mathbb{R}$, we may (abusively) write $M(d)$ for the marking represented by M after delay d (so that for any $s \in S$ and any $d \in \mathbb{R}_{\geq 0}$, both notations $M(d)(s)$ and $M(s)(d)$ represent the same subset of $\mathbb{R}$).

A special case of timed marking are those timed markings that can be defined using timed sets; timed markings of this kind will be called *linear timed markings* in the sequel. As we prove below, linear timed markings are expressive enough to represent how markings evolve over time in one-clock timed automata. Atomic (resp. finite, regular) timed markings are linear timed markings whose values are atomic (resp. finite, regular) timed sets (we may omit to mention linearity in these cases to alleviate notations). Union, inclusion and equivalence of (timed) markings are defined statewise.

With any marking m, we associate a linear timed marking, which we write $\overrightarrow{m}$ (or sometimes m if no ambiguity arises), defined as $\overrightarrow{m}(s)(d) = \{v+d \mid v \in m(s)\}$. This timed marking is linear since it can be defined e.g. as $\overrightarrow{m}(s) = (m(s); \uparrow\!0)$. This timed marking can be used to represent all clock valuations that can be reached from marking m after any delay $d \in \mathbb{R}_{\geq 0}$.

Given a marking m, a delay d and a sequence $w \in U^*$ of silent transitions of $\mathcal{A}_\epsilon$, we define the marking $m \oplus_w d$ as follows:

$$m \oplus_w d\colon s' \mapsto \{v \in \mathbb{R}_{\geq 0} \mid \exists s \in S.\ \exists v \in m(s).\ (s,v) \xrightarrow{d}_w (s',v')\}$$

(remember that w here represents a sequence of silent transitions). This corresponds to all configurations reachable along w from a configuration in m with a delay of exactly d time units. By definition of the transition relation $\to_w$, for $m \oplus_w d$ to be non-empty, w must be a sequence of consecutive transitions. With this definition, for any sequence w of silent transitions and any marking m, we can define a timed marking $m^w\colon d \mapsto m \oplus_w d$. In particular, for the empty sequence $\perp$, the timed marking $m^\perp$ is equivalent to the timed marking $\overrightarrow{m}$ (hence it is linear).

For any $d \in \mathbb{R}_{\geq 0}$, we define $m \oplus_\epsilon d$ as $(m \oplus_\epsilon d)(s) = \bigcup_{w \in U^*} (m \oplus_w d)(s)$. The marking $m \oplus_\epsilon d$ represents the set of configurations that can be reached after a delay d through sequences of silent transitions. This gives rise to a timed marking, which we write m^ϵ. By definition of $\mathbf{O}_d$, we have $\mathbf{O}_d(m) = m^\epsilon(d)$ for any marking m and any delay d.

The definition is extended to timed markings as follows: for a timed marking M and a delay d, we let

$$M \oplus_w d\colon s' \mapsto \{v' \in \mathbb{R}_{\geq 0} \mid \exists s \in S.\ \exists d_0 \leq d.\ \exists v \in M(d_0)(s).\ (s,v) \xrightarrow{d-d_0}_w (s',v')\},$$

Again, this gives rise to a timed marking $M^w \colon d \mapsto M \oplus_w d$. Observe that for any *linear* timed marking, we have $M^\perp \equiv M$. Notice also that for any marking m, it holds $(\overrightarrow{m})^w \equiv m^w$. We let $M \oplus_\epsilon d$ be the union of all $M \oplus_w d$ when w ranges over U^*, and M^ϵ be the associated timed marking.

Definition 8. *Let M be a timed marking. A timed marking N is an ϵ-closure of M if $N \equiv M^\epsilon$. The timed marking M is said ϵ-closed if it is an ϵ-closure of itself.*

Our aim in this section is to compute (a finite representation of) an ϵ-closure of any given initial marking (defined using regular unions of intervals).

Example 2. Consider the (silent) timed automaton of Fig. 2. The initial configuration can be represented by the timed marking M with $M(s_0) = ([0;0]; \mathop{\uparrow} 0)$ and $M(s_1) = (\emptyset; \mathop{\uparrow} 0)$, corresponding to the single configuration $\{(s_0, x = 0)\}$. This timed marking is not closed under delay- and silent-transitions, as for instance configuration $(s_1, x = 0)$ is reachable; however, this configuration cannot be reached after any delay: it is only reachable after delay 0, or after a delay larger than or equal to 2 time units. In the end, an ϵ-*closed* timed marking for this automaton is $M^\epsilon(s_0) = M(s_0)$, and $M^\epsilon(s_1) = ((-\infty; -2] \cup [0;0]; \mathop{\uparrow} 0)$.   ◁

Fig. 2. A silent timed automaton

4.2   Computing ϵ-Closures

Let E and F be two subsets of $\mathbb{R}$. We define their *gauge* as the set $E \bowtie F = (E - F) \cap \mathbb{R}_{\leq 0}$. Equivalently, $E \bowtie F = \{d \in \mathbb{R}_{\leq 0} \mid F + d \cap E \neq \emptyset\}$.

Lemma 9. – *If $E \leq F$ (in particular, if $E \subseteq \mathbb{R}_{\leq 0}$ and $F \subseteq \mathbb{R}_{\geq 0}$), then $E \bowtie F = E - F$.*
 – *if $E > F$, then $E \bowtie F = \emptyset$.*
 – *If E and F are two intervals, then $E \bowtie F$ is an interval.*
 – *IF E is a regular union of intervals and J is an interval, then $E \bowtie F$ is a regular union of intervals.*
 – *If $F' \subseteq \mathbb{R}_{\geq 0}$, then $(E \bowtie F) \bowtie F' = (E \bowtie F) - F'$.*

We now define a mapping $\epsilon\colon \mathcal{T}(\mathbb{R}) \times U^* \to \mathcal{T}(\mathbb{R})$, intended to represent the timed set that is reached by performing sequences of silent transitions from some given timed set. We first consider atomic timed sets, and the application of a single silent transition. The definition is based on the type of the transition:

$$\epsilon((E,\widehat{r}), (s,\widehat{e},\underline{e},\epsilon,\mathsf{op},s')) = \begin{cases} (\emptyset; \uparrow 0) & \text{if } \widehat{r} \cap \underline{e} = \emptyset \\ (E \cap \underline{e}; \widehat{p}) & \text{if } \widehat{r} \cap \underline{e} \neq \emptyset \text{ and } \mathsf{op} = id \\ (E \bowtie (\widehat{p} \cap \underline{e}); \uparrow 0) & \text{if } \widehat{r} \cap \underline{e} \neq \emptyset \text{ and } \mathsf{op} = 0 \end{cases}$$

where $\widehat{p} = \widehat{r} \cap \widehat{e}$. We extend ϵ to sequences of transitions inductively by letting $\epsilon((E;\widehat{r}), \perp) = (E;\widehat{r})$ and, for $w \in U^+$,

$$\epsilon((E;\widehat{r}), w \cdot e) = \begin{cases} \epsilon(\epsilon((E;\widehat{r}), w), e) & \text{if } \mathsf{tgt}(w) = \mathsf{src}(e) \\ (\emptyset; \uparrow 0) & \text{otherwise.} \end{cases}$$

Finally, we extend this definition to unions of atomic timed sets by letting $\epsilon(F_1 \sqcup F_2, w) = \epsilon(F_1, w) \sqcup \epsilon(F_2, w)$. We now prove that this indeed corresponds to applying silent- and delay-transitions from a given timed set.

Lemma 10. *Let F be a timed set and $w \in U^*$. Then for any $d \in \mathbb{R}_{\geq 0}$ and any $v \in \mathbb{R}_{\geq 0}$,*

$$v \in (\epsilon(F,w))(d) \;\Leftrightarrow\; \exists d_0 \in [0;d].\ \exists v' \in F(d_0).\ (\mathsf{src}(w),v') \xrightarrow{d-d_0}_w (\mathsf{tgt}(w),v).$$

Proof. We carry the proof for the case where F is an atomic timed set. The extension to unions of atomic timed sets is straightforward. The proof for atomic timed sets is in two parts: we begin with proving the result for a single transition (the case where $w = \perp$ is easy), and then proceed by induction to prove the full result.

We begin with the case where w is a single transition $e = (s,\widehat{e},\underline{e},\epsilon,\mathsf{op},s')$. In case F is empty, then also $\epsilon(F,e)$ is empty, and the result holds. We now assume that F is not empty, and consider three cases:

- if $\widehat{r} \cap \underline{e} = \emptyset$, then $\epsilon(F,e) = (\emptyset; \uparrow 0)$. On the other hand, for any d_0 and any $v' \in F(d_0)$, it holds $v' \in \widehat{r}$, so that $v' \notin \underline{e}$, and the transition cannot be taken from that valuation. Hence both sides of the equivalence evaluate to false, and the equivalence holds.
- now assume that $\widehat{r} \cap \underline{e} \neq \emptyset$, and consider the case where e does not reset the clock. Then $v \in (\epsilon(F,w))(d)$ means that $v \in (E+d) \cap (\underline{e}+d) \cap \widehat{p}$. If such a v exists, then $\widehat{p} \cap \underline{e} \cap [v-d;v]$ is non-empty: indeed, this is trivial if either $v \in \underline{e}$, or $v - d \in \widehat{p}$, or $d = 0$; otherwise, we have $\underline{e} \subseteq {\downarrow}v$ and $\widehat{p} \subseteq {\uparrow}v - d$, so that $\widehat{p} \cap \underline{e} \subseteq (v-d;v)$. Moreover, $\widehat{p} \cap \underline{e} \neq \emptyset$ since $\widehat{r} \cap \underline{e} \neq \emptyset$ and $\widehat{e} \cap \underline{e} \neq \emptyset$. Then for any v' in that set $\widehat{p} \cap \underline{e} \cap [v-d;v]$, letting $d_0 = v' - (v-d)$, we have $v' \in E+d_0$. In the end, $v' \in F(d_0)$, and $v' \in \widehat{e} \cap \underline{e}$, so that $(\mathsf{src}(e),v') \xrightarrow{d-d_0}_e (\mathsf{tgt}(e),v)$. Conversely, if $d_0 \in [0;d]$ and $v' \in F(d_0)$ exist such that $(\mathsf{src}(w),v') \xrightarrow{d-d_0}_w (\mathsf{tgt}(w),v)$, then $v' \in E+d_0 \cap \widehat{r}$, and for some $d_1 \leq d - d_0$, $v' + d_1 \in \widehat{e} \cap \underline{e}$.

Then letting $v = v' + d - d_0$, we have $v \in E + d$ and $v \in \hat{r} + (d - d_0) \subseteq \hat{r}$ and $v \in \hat{e} + (d - d_0 - d_1) \subseteq \hat{e}$ and $v \in \underline{e} + (d - d_0 - d1) \subseteq \underline{e} + d$. This proves our result for this case.

- we finally consider the case where $\hat{r} \cap \underline{e} \neq \emptyset$ and e resets the clock. In this case, $v \in (\epsilon(F, w))(d)$ means that $v \in {\uparrow}0$ and $v - d \in E \bowtie (\hat{p} \cap \underline{e})$, which rewrites as $0 \leq v \leq d$ and $(E + d - v) \cap (\hat{p} \cap \underline{e}) \neq \emptyset$. Let $d_0 = d - v$. The property above entails that $0 \leq d_0 \leq d$, and that there exists some $v' \in (E + d_0) \cap (\hat{p} \cap \underline{e})$, so that $0 \leq d_0 \leq d$, $v' \in F(d_0)$ and $(\mathsf{src}(e), v') \xrightarrow{d - d_0}_e (\mathsf{tgt}(e), v)$. Conversely, if those conditions hold, then for some $0 \leq d_1 \leq d - d_0$, we have $v' + d_1 \in \hat{e} \cap \underline{e}$, and $v = d - (d_0 + d_1)$ (remember that e resets the clock). Then $v' + d_1 \in E + (d_0 + d_1) \cap \hat{r} \cap \hat{e} \cap \underline{e}$, so that $-(d_0 + d_1) \in E \bowtie (\hat{p} \cap \underline{e})$, and finally $v \in \epsilon(F, w)(d)$.

We now extend this result to sequences of transitions. The case where $w = \perp$ is straightforward. Now assume that the result holds for some word w, and consider a word $w \cdot e$. In case $\mathsf{tgt}(w) \neq \mathsf{src}(e)$, the result is trivial.

The case of single transitions has been handled just above. We thus consider the case of $w \cdot e$ with $w \in U^+$. First assume that $v' \in (\epsilon(F, w \cdot e))(d)$, and let $F' = \epsilon(F, w)$. Then $v' \in (\epsilon(F', e))(d)$, thus there exist $0 \leq d_0 \leq d$ and $v \in F'(d_0)$ s.t. $(\mathsf{src}(e), v) \xrightarrow{d - d_0}_e (\mathsf{tgt}(e), v')$. Since $v \in F'(d_0)$, there must exist $0 \leq d_1 \leq d_0$ and $v'' \in F(d_1)$ such that $(\mathsf{src}(w), v'') \xrightarrow{d_0 - d_1}_w (\mathsf{tgt}(w), v)$. We thus have found $0 \leq d_1 \leq d$ such that $(\mathsf{src}(w), v'') \xrightarrow{d - d_1}_{w \cdot e} (\mathsf{tgt}(e), v')$.

Conversely, if $(\mathsf{src}(w), v'') \xrightarrow{d - d_1}_{w \cdot e} (\mathsf{tgt}(e), v')$ for some $0 \leq d_1 \leq d$ and $v'' \in F(d_1)$, then we have $(\mathsf{src}(w), v'') \xrightarrow{d_0 - d_1}_w (\mathsf{tgt}(w), v) \xrightarrow{d - d_0}_e (\mathsf{tgt}(e), v')$ for some $d_0 \in [d_1; d]$ and some v. We prove that $v \in (\epsilon(F, w))(d_0)$: indeed, we have $d_1 \in [0; d_0]$, and $v'' \in F(d_1)$ such that $(\mathsf{src}(w), v'') \xrightarrow{d_0 - d_1}_w (\mathsf{tgt}(w), v)$, which by induction hypothesis entails $v \in (\epsilon(F, w))(d_0)$. Thus we have $d_0 \in [0; d]$ and $v \in F'(d_0)$, where $F' = \epsilon(F, w)$, such that $(\mathsf{tgt}(w), v) \xrightarrow{d - d_0}_e (\mathsf{tgt}(e), v')$, which means $v' \in \epsilon(F', e)(d)$, and concludes the proof.   □

Thanks to this semantic characterization of $\epsilon(F, w)$, we get:

Corollary 11. *For any sequence w of transitions, and any two equivalent timed sets F and F', the timed sets $\epsilon(F, w)$ and $\epsilon(F', w)$ are equivalent.*

Finally, we extend ϵ to linear timed markings in the expected way: given a linear timed marking M, and a sequence w of transitions, we let

$$\epsilon(M, w) \colon s \mapsto \epsilon(M(\mathsf{src}(w)), w) \quad \text{if } s = \mathsf{tgt}(w),$$
$$s \mapsto (\emptyset; {\uparrow}0) \quad \text{otherwise.}$$

Again, we have $\epsilon(M_1 \sqcup M_2, w) \equiv \epsilon(M_1, w) \sqcup \epsilon(M_2, w)$ for any $w \in U^*$. Then:

Lemma 12. $\epsilon(M, w) \equiv M^w$ *for all $w \in U^*$ and all linear timed marking M.*

Letting $\epsilon(M, \mathcal{L}) = \bigsqcup_{w \in \mathcal{L}} \epsilon(M, w)$ for any subset $\mathcal{L}$ of U^*, and $\epsilon(M) = \epsilon(M, U^*)$, we immediately get:

Theorem 13. *For any linear timed marking M, it holds $\epsilon(M) \equiv M^\epsilon$.*

It follows that the closure of any marking can be represented as a linear timed marking. However, this linear timed marking is currently defined as an infinite union over all sequences of consecutive silent transitions. We make the computation more effective in the next section.

4.3   Finite Representation of the Closure

In this section, we prove that we can effectively compute a finite representation of the closure of any regular timed marking. More precisely, we show how to compute such a closure as a regular timed marking.

Finiteness. Indeed, let M be (a finite representation of) a regular timed marking: then M can be written as the finite union of atomic regular timed markings $M_{(s,E,\widehat{r})}$, defined as $M_{(s,E,\widehat{r})}(s) = (E;\widehat{r})$ and $M_{(s,E,\widehat{r})}(s') = (\emptyset; \mathord{\uparrow}0)$ for all $s' \neq s$. In the end, any regular timed marking M can be written as the finite union $\bigsqcup_{i \in I} M_i$ of atomic regular timed markings. Thus we have $\epsilon(M) \equiv \bigsqcup_{i \in I} \epsilon(M_i)$, and it suffices to compute ϵ for atomic regular timed markings $M_{(s,E,\widehat{r})}$. We prove that those closures can be represented as regular timed markings.

We write $\epsilon_1((E;\widehat{r}), w)$ and $\epsilon_2((E;\widehat{r}), w)$ for the first and second components of $\epsilon((E;\widehat{r}), w)$. Notice that $\epsilon_2((E;\widehat{r}), w)$ does not depend on E (so that we may denote it with $\epsilon_2(\widehat{r}, w)$ in the sequel). In particular,

- $\epsilon_2((E;\widehat{r}), w) = \mathord{\uparrow}0$ if $w \in U^* \times U_0$ is a sequence of consecutive transitions ending with a resetting transition;
- $\epsilon_2((E;\widehat{r}), w) = \widehat{r} \cap \bigcap_{i<k} \widehat{e}_i$ if $w = e_1 \ldots e_k \in U_{id}{}^*$ is a sequence of consecutive non-resetting transitions.

Letting $\mathbb{J}_{\widehat{r}} = \{\mathord{\uparrow}0, \widehat{r}\} \cup \{\widehat{e} \mid e \in U_{id}\}$, it follows that $\epsilon_2((E;\widehat{r}), w) \in \mathbb{J}_{\widehat{r}}$ for any $(E;\widehat{r})$ and any w. Thus $\epsilon(M)$ can be written as a finite union of atomic timed markings.

Regularity. To prove regularity, we first introduce some more formalism:

- we let $\widehat{G_{id}} = \{\widehat{e} \mid e \in U_{id}\}$ and $\underline{G_{id}} = \{\underline{e} \mid e \in U_{id}\}$. We thus have $\mathbb{J}_{\widehat{r}} = \{\mathord{\uparrow}0, \widehat{r}\} \cup \widehat{G_{id}}$;
- for $\widehat{r} \in \widehat{\mathbb{R}}_{\geq 0}$ and $e \in U$, we write $\Phi(\widehat{r}, e)$ for the interval $\widehat{r} \cap \widehat{e} \cap \underline{e}$;
- we define a mapping $\mathcal{J}_{\widehat{r}} \colon U^* \to \mathbb{N}^{\mathbb{J}_{\widehat{r}} \times U_0}$ that counts the number of occurrences of certain timing constraints at resetting transitions along a path: precisely, it is defined inductively as follows (where $\uplus$ represents addition of an element to a multiset):

$$
\begin{aligned}
\mathcal{J}_{\widehat{r}}(\bot) &= \{0\}^{\mathbb{J}_{\widehat{r}} \times U_0} & \\
\mathcal{J}_{\widehat{r}}(w \cdot e) &= \mathcal{J}_{\widehat{r}}(w) \uplus \{(\epsilon_2(\widehat{r}, w), e)\} & \text{if } e \in U_0 \\
\mathcal{J}_{\widehat{r}}(w \cdot e) &= \mathcal{J}_{\widehat{r}}(w) & \text{if } e \in U_{id}.
\end{aligned}
$$

By induction on w, we prove:

Lemma 14. *Let $(E; \widehat{r})$ be a timed set with $E \subseteq \mathbb{R}_{\leq 0}$, and $w \in U^*$. Then*

$$\epsilon_1((E; \widehat{r}), w) = E - \sum_{J = (\widehat{g}, e) \in \mathbb{J}_{\widehat{r}}} \mathcal{J}_{\widehat{r}}(w)(J) \times \Phi(\widehat{g}, e) \subseteq \mathbb{R}_{\leq 0}.$$

Now, we fix an atomic regular timed marking $M_{(s, E, \widehat{r})}$. For any state s' of $\mathcal{A}_\epsilon$, we let $\mathcal{L}(s, s')$ be the set of all sequences of consecutive transitions from s to s' in $\mathcal{A}_\epsilon$. Then

$$(M_{(s, E, \widehat{r})})^\epsilon = \bigsqcup_{s' \in S} \epsilon(M_{(s, E, \widehat{r})}, \mathcal{L}(s, s')).$$

Hence we need to prove that $\epsilon_1(M_{(s, E, \widehat{r})}, \mathcal{L}(s, s'))$ is regular.

For any set $\mathcal{L}$ of sequences of consecutive transitions, and for any $\widehat{r}$ and $\widehat{r}'$ in $\widehat{\mathbb{R}}_{\geq 0}$, we let $\mathcal{L}_{\widehat{r}}^{\widehat{r}'} = \{w \in \mathcal{L} \mid \widehat{r}' = \epsilon_2(\widehat{r}, w)\}$. One easily observes that for any $\widehat{r} \in \widehat{\mathbb{R}}_{\geq 0}$ and any $\mathcal{L}$, it holds $\mathcal{L} = \bigcup_{\widehat{r}' \in \mathbb{J}_{\widehat{r}}} \mathcal{L}_{\widehat{r}}^{\widehat{r}'}$, so that

$$\epsilon_1(M_{(s, E, \widehat{r})}, \mathcal{L}(s, s')) = \bigcup_{\widehat{r}' \in \mathbb{J}_{\widehat{r}}} \epsilon_1(M_{(s, E, \widehat{r})}, [\mathcal{L}(s, s')]_{\widehat{r}}^{\widehat{r}'}).$$

The following property entails that this set is a regular union of intervals:

Lemma 15. *Let E be a regular union of intervals, $\widehat{r}$ and $\widehat{r}'$ be two elements of $\widehat{\mathbb{R}}_{\geq 0}$, and $\mathcal{L} \subseteq \mathcal{L}(\mathcal{A}_\epsilon)$ be a regular language. Then $\epsilon_1(M_{(s, E, \widehat{r})}, \mathcal{L}_{\widehat{r}}^{\widehat{r}'})$ is a regular union of intervals.*

5 Experimentations

In order to evaluate the possible improvement of our approach compared to the diagnoser proposed in [26], we implemented and compared the performances of both approaches. Sources can be downloaded at http://www.lsv.fr/~jaziri/DOTA.zip.

5.1 Comparison of the Approaches

In the approach of [26], the set of possible current configurations is stored as a marking. If an action l occurs after some delay d, the diagnoser computes the set of all possible configurations reached after delay d (possibly following silent transitions), and applies from the resulting markings the set of all available transitions labelled l. This amounts to computing the functions $\mathbf{O}_d$ and $\mathbf{O}_l$ at each observation. There is also a timeout, which makes the diagnoser update the marking (with $\mathbf{O}_d$) regularly if no action is observed. The computation of $\mathbf{O}_d$ is heavily used, and has to be performed very efficiently so that the diagnoser can be used at runtime.

In our approach, we use *timed markings* to store sets of possible configurations. Given a timed marking, when an action l is observed after some delay d, we can easily compute the set of configurations reachable after delay d, and have to apply $\mathbf{O}_l$ and recompute the ϵ-closure. Following [7], $\mathbf{O}_l$ can be performed as a series of set operations on intervals. The ϵ-closure can be performed as a series of subtractions between an interval and regular unions of intervals (see Lemma 14). Those regular unions can be precomputed; while this may require exponential time and space to compute and store, this makes the simulation of a delay transition very efficient.

5.2   Implementation

In our experimentations, in order to only evaluate the benefits of the precomputation and of the use of ϵ-closures in our approach compared to that of [26], we use the same data structure for both diagnosers. In particular, both diagnosers are implemented as automata over timed domains [7], where the timed domain is the set of timed markings. The only difference lies in the functions computing the action- and the delay transitions. As a consequence, both implementations benefit from the data structure we chose for representing timed intervals, which allows us to compute basic operations in linear time. Also, both structures use the same reachability graphs for either computing the sets of reachable configurations or the Parikh images.

Our implementation is written in Python3. One-clock timed automata and both diagnosers are instances of an abstract class of automata over timed markings; timed markings are implemented in a library TILib. Simulations of those automata are performed using an object called ATDRunner, which takes an automaton over timed markings and simulates its transitions according to the actions it observes on a given *input channel*. It may also write what it does on an *output channel*. A channel is basically a way of communicating with ATDRunners.

In order to diagnose a given one-clock timed automaton, stored in an object OTAutomata, we first generate a diagnoser object, either a DiagOTA or a TripakisDOTA, depending of which version we want to use. Then we launch two threads: one is an ATDRunner simulating the timed automaton, listening to some channel object Input, and writing every non-silent action it performs on some other channel object Comm. The other one is another ATDRunner simulating the diagnoser and listening to the Comm channel.

In a DiagOTA object, which corresponds to our approach, we have already precomputed the relevant timed intervals; action transitions are then made by operations over timed markings, and delay transitions are encoded by increasing a *padding information* on the timed markings, which is applied when performing the next action transition. In such a simulation, we can thus keep track of which states may have been reached, but also predict which states may be reached in the future and the exact time before we can reach them.

In a TripakisDOTA object, which corresponds to the approach of [26], action and delay transitions are simulated by computing all configurations reachable through that action or delay, also allowing arbitrarily many silent transitions. This does not allow for prediction.

5.3 Results

Figure 3 reports on the performances of both implementations on a small set of (randomly generated) examples. Those examples are distributed with our prototype. In Fig. 3, we give the important characteristics of each automaton (number of states and of silent transitions), the amount of precomputation time used by our approach, and the average time (over 400 random runs) used in the two approaches to simulate action- and delay transitions.

	Example2	Example3	Example4	Example6	Example8
#State/#Silent Trans	3/6	4/6	4/7	7/10	7/5
Precomputation Time	173.25s	0.38s	791.06s	11.01s	4.96s
Actions DiagOTA	0.014s	0.019s	0.029s	0.17s	0.15s
Actions TripakisDOTA	0.020s	0.078s	0.049s	0.26s	0.042
Ratio (actions)	0.73	0.25	0.59	0.64	3.71
Delays DiagOTA	0.000012s	0.0000011s	0.000011s	0.000011s	0.000012s
Delays TripakisDOTA	0.032s	0.057s	0.049s	0.30s	0.033s
Ratio (delays)	0.0004	0.0002	0.0002	0.00003	0.0004

Fig. 3. Bench for 5 examples over 400 runs with 10 to 20 actions

As could be expected, our approach outperforms the approach of [26] on delay transitions by several orders of magnitude in all cases. The performances of both approaches are comparable when simulating action transitions.

The precomputation phase of our approach is intrinsically very expensive. In our examples, it takes from less than a second to more than 13 min, and it remains to be understood which factors make this precomputation phase more or less difficult. We may also refine our implementation of the computation of Parikh images, which is heavily used in the precomputation phase.

6   Conclusion and Future Works

In this paper, we presented a novel approach to fault diagnosis for one-clock timed automata; it builds on a kind of powerset construction for automata over timed domains, using our new formalism of *timed sets* to represent the evolution of the set of reachable configurations of the automaton. Our prototype implementation shows the feasibility of our approach on small examples.

There remains space for improvements in many directions: first, our implementation can probably be made more efficient on the precomputation phase, and at least we need to better understand why some very small examples are so hard to handle.

A natural continuation of this work is an extension to n-clock timed automata. This is not immediate, as it requires a kind of *timed zone*, and an adaptation of our operator $\bowtie$. Another possible direction of research could target priced timed automata, with the aim of monitoring the cost of the execution in the worst case.

References

1. Alur, R., Dill, D.L.: A theory of timed automata. Theor. Comput. Sci. **126**(2), 183–235 (1994)
2. Behrmann, G., et al.: Uppaal 4.0. In: Proceedings of the 3rd International Conference on Quantitative Evaluation of Systems (QEST 2006), pp. 125–126. IEEE Computer Society Press, September 2006
3. Bengtsson, J., Yi, W.: Timed automata: semantics, algorithms and tools. In: Desel, J., Reisig, W., Rozenberg, G. (eds.) ACPN 2003. LNCS, vol. 3098, pp. 87–124. Springer, Heidelberg (2004). https://doi.org/10.1007/978-3-540-27755-2_3
4. Benveniste, A., Fabre, É., Haar, S., Jard, C.: Diagnosis of asynchronous discrete event systems: a net-unfolding approach. IEEE Trans. Autom. Control. **48**(5), 714–727 (2003)
5. Bertrand, N., Haddad, S., Lefaucheux, E.: Foundation of diagnosis and predictability in probabilistic systems. In: Raman, V., Suresh, S.P. (eds.) Proceedings of the 34th Conference on Foundations of Software Technology and Theoretical Computer Science (FSTTCS 2014). Leibniz International Proceedings in Informatics, vol. 29, pp. 417–429. Leibniz-Zentrum für Informatik, December 2014
6. Bouyer, P., Chevalier, F., D'Souza, D.: Fault diagnosis using timed automata. In: Sassone, V. (ed.) FoSSaCS 2005. LNCS, vol. 3441, pp. 219–233. Springer, Heidelberg (2005). https://doi.org/10.1007/978-3-540-31982-5_14
7. Bouyer, P., Jaziri, S., Markey, N.: On the determinization of timed systems. In: Abate, A., Geeraerts, G. (eds.) FORMATS 2017. LNCS, vol. 10419, pp. 25–41. Springer, Cham (2017). https://doi.org/10.1007/978-3-319-65765-3_2
8. Cassez, F.: A note on fault diagnosis algorithms. In: Proceedings of the 48th IEEE Conference on Decision and Control (CDC 2009), pp. 6941–6946. IEEE Computer Socirty Press, December 2009
9. Chen, Y.-L., Provan, G.: Modeling and diagnosis of timed discrete event systems - a factory automation example. In: Proceedings of the 1997 American Control Conference (ACC 1997), pp. 31–36. IEEE Computer Society Press, June 1997
10. Clarke, E.M., Allen Emerson, E., Sifakis, J.: Model checking: algorithmic verification and debugging. Commun. ACM **52**(11), 74–84 (2009)
11. Clarke, E.M., Grumberg, O., Peled, D.A.: Model Checking. MIT Press, Cambridge (2000)
12. Clarke, E.M., Henzinger, T.A., Veith, H., Bloem, R.: Handbook of Model Checking. Springer, Cham (2018). https://doi.org/10.1007/978-3-319-10575-8
13. Filliâtre, J.-C.: Deductive software verification. Int. J. Softw. Tools Technol. Transf. **13**(5), 397–403 (2011)
14. Finkel, O.: Undecidable problems about timed automata. In: Asarin, E., Bouyer, P. (eds.) FORMATS 2006. LNCS, vol. 4202, pp. 187–199. Springer, Heidelberg (2006). https://doi.org/10.1007/11867340_14

15. Genc, S., Lafortune, S.: Predictability of event occurrences in partially-observed discrete-event systems. Automatica **45**(2), 301–311 (2009)
16. Henzinger, T.A., Sifakis, J.: The embedded systems design challenge. In: Misra, J., Nipkow, T., Sekerinski, E. (eds.) FM 2006. LNCS, vol. 4085, pp. 1–15. Springer, Heidelberg (2006). https://doi.org/10.1007/11813040_1
17. Hoare, C.A.R.: An axiomatic basis for computer programming. Commun. ACM **12**(10), 576–580 (1969)
18. Lafortune, S., Lin, F., Hadjicostis, C.N.: On the history of diagnosability and opacity in discrete event systems. Annu. Rev. Control. **45**, 257–266 (2018)
19. Leucker, M., Schallart, C.: A brief account of runtime verification. J. Log. Algebr. Program. **78**(5), 293–303 (2009)
20. Lunze, J., Schröder, J.: State observation and diagnosis of discrete-event systems described by stochastic automata. Discret. Event Dyn. Syst. **11**(4), 319–369 (2001)
21. Narasimhan, S., Biswas, G.: Model-based diagnosis of hybrid systems. IEEE Trans. Syst., Man, Cybern. Part A Syst. Hum. **37**(3), 348–361 (2007)
22. Sampath, M., Lafortune, S., Teneketzis, D.: Active diagnosis of discrete-event systems. IEEE Trans. Autom. Control. **43**(7), 908–929 (1998)
23. Sampath, M., Sengupta, R., Lafortune, S., Sinnamohideen, K., Teneketzis, D.: Diagnosability of discrete-event systems. IEEE Trans. Autom. Control. **40**(9), 1555–1575 (1995)
24. Sampath, M., Sengupta, R., Lafortune, S., Sinnamohideen, K., Teneketzis, D.: Failure diagnosis using discrete-event models. IEEE Trans. Comput. **35**(1), 105–124 (1996)
25. Tretmans, J.: Conformance testing with labelled transition systems: Implementation relations and test generation. Comput. Netw. ISDN Syst. **29**(1), 49–79 (1996)
26. Tripakis, S.: Description and schedulability analysis of the software architecture of an automated vehicle control system. In: Sangiovanni-Vincentelli, A., Sifakis, J. (eds.) EMSOFT 2002. LNCS, vol. 2491, pp. 123–137. Springer, Heidelberg (2002). https://doi.org/10.1007/3-540-45828-X_10
27. Tripakis, S.: Folk theorems on the determinization and minimization of timed automata. Inf. Process. Lett. **99**(6), 222–226 (2006)
28. Zaytoon, J., Lafortune, S.: Overview of fault diagnosis methods for discrete event systems. Annu. Rev. Control. **37**(2), 308–320 (2013)

Bringing Runtime Verification Home

Antoine El-Hokayem and Yliès Falcone[(⊠)]

Univ. Grenoble Alpes, CNRS, Inria, Grenoble INP, LIG, 38000 Grenoble, France
{antoine.el-hokayem,ylies.falcone}@univ-grenoble-alpes.fr

Abstract. We use runtime verification (RV) to check various specifications in a smart apartment. The specifications can be broken down into
three types: behavioral correctness of the apartment sensors, detection
of specific user activities (known as activities of daily living), and composition of specifications of the previous types. The context of the smart
apartment provides us with a complex system with a large number of
components with two different hierarchies to group specifications and
sensors: geographically within the same room, floor or globally in the
apartment, and logically following the different types of specifications.
We leverage a recent approach to decentralized RV of decentralized specifications, where monitors have their own specifications and communicate
together to verify more general specifications. This allows us to re-use
specifications, and combine them to: (1) scale beyond existing centralized RV techniques, and (2) greatly reduce computation and communication costs.

Sensors and actuators are used to create "smart" environments which track
the data across sensors and human-machine interaction. One particular area of
interest consists of homes (or apartments) equipped with a myriad of sensors
and actuators, called *smart homes* [11]. Smart homes are capable of providing added services to users. These services rely on detecting the user behavior
and the context of such activities [7], typically detecting activities of daily living (ADL) [9,29] from sensor information. Detecting ADL allows to optimize
resource consumption (such as electricity [1]), improve the quality of life for the
elderly [27] and users suffering from mild impairment [30].

Relying on information from multiple sources and observing behavior is not
just constrained to activities. It is also used with techniques that verify the correct behavior of systems. *Runtime Verification* (RV) [3–5,20] is a lightweight
formal method which consists in verifying that a run of a system is correct wrt a
specification. The specification formalizes the behavior of the system typically in
logics (such as variants of Linear Temporal Logic, LTL) or finite-state machines.

This work is supported by the French national program "Programme Investissements
d'Avenir IRT Nanoelec" (ANR-10-AIRT-05). The authors thank the Amiqual4Home
(ANR-11-EQPX-0002) team, in particular S. Borkowski and J. Crowley for assisting
in the case study and J. Cumin, for providing the collected data. This article is based
upon work from COST Action ARVI IC1402, supported by the European Cooperation
in Science and Technology.

C. Colombo and M. Leucker (Eds.): RV 2018, LNCS 11237, pp. 222–240, 2018.
https://doi.org/10.1007/978-3-030-03769-7_13

Based on the provided specification, monitors are automatically synthesized to run alongside the system and verify whether or not the system execution complies with the specification. RV techniques have been used for instance in the context of automotive [10] and medical [26] systems. In both cases, RV is used to verify communication patterns between components and their adherence to the architecture and their formal specifications.

While RV can be used to check that the devices in a smart home are performing as expected, we believe it can be extended to monitor ADL, and complex behavior on the activities themselves. We identify three classes of specifications for applying RV to a smart home. The first class pertains to the system behavior. These specifications are used to check the correct behavior of the sensors, and detect faulty sensors. Ensuring that the system is behaving correctly is what is generally checked when performing RV. However, it is also possible to use RV to verify other specifications. The second class consists of specifications for detecting ADL, such as detecting when the user is cooking, showering or sleeping. The third class contains combinations of the other two. These specifications can be seen as meta-specifications for both system correctness and ADL, they can include specifications such as ensuring that the user does not sleep while cooking, or ensuring that certain activities are only done under certain conditions.

However, standard RV techniques are not directly suitable to monitor the three classes of specifications. This is mainly due to scalability issues arising from the large number of sensors, as typically RV techniques rely on a single large formula to describe all behavior. Synthesizing centralized monitors from certain large formulas considered in this paper is not possible using the current tools. Instead, we make use of RV with decentralized specifications [16], as it allows monitors to reference other monitors in a hierarchical fashion. The advantage of this is twofold. First, it provides an abstraction layer to relate specifications to each others. This allows specifications to be organized and changed without affecting other specifications, and even to be expressed with different specification languages. Second, it leverages the structure and layout of the devices to organize the hierarchies. On the one hand, we have a geographical hierarchy resulting from the spacial structure of the apartment from a given device, to a room, a floor, or the full apartment. On the other hand, we have a logical hierarchy defined by the interdependence between specifications, i.e. ADL specifications that use other ADL specifications, and specifications that combine sensor safety with ADL. For example, informally, consider checking two activities: sleeping and cooking, which can be expressed using formulae φ_s and φ_c respectively. A monitor that checks whether the user is sleeping and cooking requires to check $\varphi_s \wedge \varphi_c$ and as such will replicate the monitoring logic of another monitor that checks φ_s alone, instead of re-using the output of that monitor. The formula will be written twice, and changing the formula for detecting sleeping requires changing the formula for the monitor that checks both specifications.

Overall, we see our contributions as follows[1]:

- Applying decentralized RV to analyze traces of over 36,000 timestamps spanning 27 sensors in a real smart apartment (Sect. 1.1).
- Going beyond system properties, to specify ADL using RV, and more complex inter-dependent specifications defined on up to 27 atomic propositions (Sect. 1.2).
- Taking advantage of hierarchies, modularity and re-use of decentralized specifications (Sect. 2) to both be able to synthesize monitors and to reduce overhead when monitoring complex inter-dependent specifications (Sect. 3.1).
- Using RV to effectively monitor ADL and identifying some insights and limitations inherent to using formal LTL specifications to determine user behavior (Sect. 3.2).

1   Writing Specifications for the Apartment

1.1   Devices and Organization

We consider a single actual apartment, with multiple rooms, where activities are logged using sensors. Amiqual4Home is an experimental platform consisting of a smart apartment, a rapid prototyping platform, and tools for observing human activity.

Overview of Amiqual4Home. The Amiqual4Home apartment is equipped with 219 sensors and actuators spread across 2 floors [25]. Amiqual4Home uses the OpenHab 6 integration platform for all the sensors and actuators installed. Sensors communicate using KNX, MQQT or UPnP protocols sending measurements to OpenHab over the local network, so as to preserve privacy. The general layout of the apartment consists of 2 floors: the ground and first floor. On the ground floor (resp. first floor), we have the following rooms: `entrance`, `toilet`, `kitchen`, and `livingroom` (resp. `office`, `bedroom`, and `bathroom`). Between the two floors, there is a connecting `staircase`. This layout reveals a geographical hierarchy of components, where we can see the rooms at the leaves, grouped by floors then the whole apartment. While in effect all device data is fed to a central observation point, it is reasonable to consider the hierarchy in the apartment as a simpler model to consider hierarchies in general, as one is bound to encounter a hierarchy at a higher level (from houses, to neighborhoods, to smart cities, etc.). Furthermore, hierarchies appear when integrating different providers for devices in the same house.

---

[1] An artifact [15] that contains data, documentation, and software, is provided to replicate and extend on the work. An extended version of this paper is available in [18].

Reusing the Orange4Home Dataset. Amiqual4Home has been used to generate multiple datasets that record all sensor data, this includes an ADL recognition dataset [25] (ContextAct@A4H), and an energy consumption dataset [12] (Orange4Home). In this paper, we reuse the dataset from [12]. The case study involved a person living in the home and following (loosely) a schedule of activities spread out across the various rooms of the house, set out by the authors. This allows us to nicely reconstruct the schedule from the result of monitoring the sensors. Furthermore, the person living in the home provided manual annotations of the activities done, which helps us assess our specifications. We chose to use [12] over [25] as it involves only one person living in the house at a time which simplifies writing and validating specifications (Fig. 1).

Fig. 1. Schedule for Jan 31 2017

Monitoring Environment. In total, we formalize 22 specifications that make use of up to 27 sensors, and evaluate them over the course of a full day of activity in the apartment[2]. That is, we monitor the house (by replaying the trace) from 07:30 to 17:30 on a given day, by polling the sensors every 1 second, creating a trace of a total of 36,000 timestamps. Specifications are elaborated in Sect. 1.2 and expressed as decentralized specifications [16] (introduced in Sect. 2.2). Traces are replayed using the THEMIS tool [17] which supports decentralized specifications and provides a wide range of metrics. We elaborate on the trace replay in Sect. 2.4.

1.2 Specification Groups

We now specify specifications that describe different behaviors of components in the smart apartment. Specifications can be subdivided into 3 groups: system-behavior properties, user-behavior specifications, and meta-specifications on both system and user behavior. The specifications we considered are listed in Table 1.

System Behavior. The first group of specifications consists in ensuring that the system behaves as expected. That is, verifying that the sensors are working properly. These specifications are the subject of classical RV techniques [6,20] applied to systems. For the scope of this case study, we verify light switches as

---

[2] [19] is a more detailed version of this paper including all the specifications.

Table 1. Specifications considered in this paper. (*) indicates added ADL specifications. G indicates specification group: system (S), ADL (A), and meta-specifications (M). $|AP|^d$ (resp. ($|AP|^c$): atomic propositions needed in formula for decentralized (resp. centralized) specifications. d is the maximum depth of monitor dependencies.

G	Scope	Name	Description	$|AP|^d$	$|AP|^c$	d
S	Room	sc_light(i)	light switch turns on light ($i \in [0..3]$)	2	2	1
M	House	sc_ok	All light switches are ok	4	8	2
A	Toilet	toilet*	Toilet is being used	1	1	0
A	Bathroom	sink_usage	Sink is being used	1	2	1
A	Bathroom	shower_usage	Shower is being used	1	2	1
A	Bedroom	napping	Tenant is sleeping on the bed	1	1	1
A	Bedroom	dressing	Tenant is dressing, using the closet	2	3	1
A	Bedroom	reading	Tenant is reading	3	5	2
A	Office	office_tv	Tenant is watching TV	1	1	1
A	Office	computing	Tenant is using the computer	1	1	1
A	Kitchen	cooking	Tenant is cooking food	2	2	1
A	Kitchen	washing_dishes	Tenant is cleaning dishes	2	3	1
A	Kitchen	kactivity*	Using cupboards and fridge	4	9	1
A	Kitchen	preparing	Tenant is preparing to cook food	2	11	2
A	Living	livingroom_tv	Tenant is watching TV	2	2	1
A	Floor 0	eating	Tenant is eating on the table	2	2	1
M	Floor 0	actfloor(0)	Activity triggered on floor 0	6	16	3
M	Floor 1	actfloor(1)	Activity triggered on floor 1	7	11	3
M	House	acthouse	Activity triggered in house	2	27	4
M	House	notwopeople	No 2 simultaneous activities on dif. floors	2	27	4
M	House	restricttv	No watching TV for more than 10s	2	3	3
M	House	firehazard	No cooking while sleeping	2	3	2

system properties. We verify that for a given room i, whenever the switch is toggled, then the light must turn on until the switch is turned off. We verify the property at two scopes, for a given room, and the entire apartment. While this property appears simple to check, it does highlight issues with existing centralized techniques applied in a hierarchical way. We develop the property in Sect. 2.1, and show the issues in Sect. 2.2.

ADL. The second group of specifications is concerned with defining the behavior of the user inferred from sensors. The sensors available in the apartment provide us with a wealth of information to determine the user activities. The list of activities of interest is detailed in [24] and includes activities such as cooking and sleeping. By correctly identifying activities, it is possible to decide when to interact with the user in a smart setting [1], provide custom care such as nursing for the elderly [27], or help users who suffer from mild impairment [30]. Inferring activities done by the user is an interesting problem typically addressed through either data-based or knowledge-based methods [9]. The first method consists in learning activity models from preexisting large-scale datasets of users' behaviors by utilizing data mining and machine learning techniques. The built models

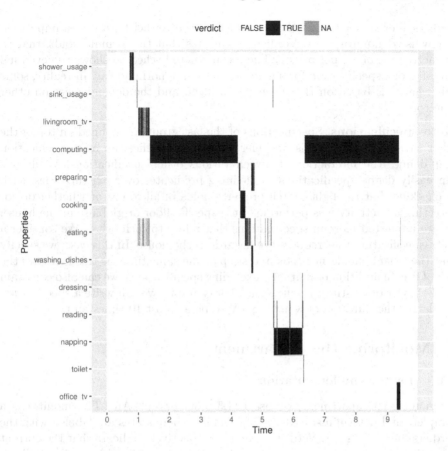

Fig. 2. Detected ADL for Tuesday, Jan 31 2017. Time is in hours starting from 7:30.

are probabilistic or statistical activity models such as Hidden Markov Model
(HMM) or Bayesian networks, followed by training and learning processes. Data-
driven approaches are capable of handling uncertainty, while often requiring large
annotated datasets for training and learning. The second method consists in
exploiting prior knowledge in the domain of interest to construct activity models directly using formal logical reasoning, formal models, and representation.
Knowledge-driven approaches are semantically clear, but are typically poor at
handling uncertainty and temporal information [9]. We elaborate on such limitations in Sect. 3.2. Writing specifications can be seen as a knowledge-based
approach to describe the behavior of sensors. As such, we believe that runtime
verification is useful to describe the activity as a specification on sensor output.
We formalize a specification for the following ADL activities described in [12] (see
Table 1). We re-use the traces to verify that our detected activities are indeed
in line with the schedule proposed. Figure 2 displays the reconstructed schedule after detecting ADL with runtime verification. Each specification is represented by a monitor that outputs (with some delay) for every timestamp (second)

verdicts $\top$ or $\bot$. To do this, the monitor finds the verdict for a timestamp t then respawns to monitor $t + 1$. Verdict $\top$ indicates that the formula holds, that is, the activity is being performed. The reconstructed schedule shows the eventual outcome of a specification for a given timestamp ignoring delay. In reality, some delay happens based on the specification itself, and the dependencies on other monitors.

Meta-specifications. Specifications of the last group are defined on top of the other specifications. That is, we refer to a meta-specification as a specification that defines the interactions between various other specifications. While one can easily define specifications by defining predicates over existing ones, such as checking that the light switch property holds in all rooms or whether or not detecting an activity was performed on a specific floor or globally in the house, we are interested more in specifications that relate to each other. We consider a meta-specification that reduces fire hazards in the house. In this case, we specify that the tenant should not cook and sleep at the same time, as this increases the risk of fire. In addition to mutually excluding specifications, we can also constrain the behavior of existing specifications. For example, we can write a specification regulating the duration of watching TV to be at most 10 timestamps.

2   Monitoring the Appartment

2.1   Monitor Implementation

To monitor the apartment, we use LTL3 monitors [6]. An LTL3 monitor is a complete and deterministic Moore automaton where states are labeled with the verdicts $\mathbb{B}_3 = \{\top, \bot, ?\}$. Verdicts $\top$ and $\bot$ respectively indicate that the current execution complies and does not comply with the specification, while verdict ? indicates that the verdict has not been determined yet. Verdicts $\top$ and $\bot$ are called final, as once the monitor outputs $\top$ or $\bot$ for a given trace, it cannot output a different verdict for any suffix of that trace. Using LTL3 monitors for representing our specificaitons allows us to take advantage of the multiple RV tools that convert different specification languages to LTL3 monitors. For our monitoring, we use the THEMIS tool which is able to use both ltl2mon [6] and LamaConv [22] to generate monitors.

Example 1 (Check light switch). Let us consider property sc_light(i) (sensor check light): "Whenever a light switch is triggered in a room i at some timestamp t, then the light must turn on at $t + 1$ until the switch is turned off again". Figure 3a shows the Moore automaton that represents the property. Starting from q_0 with verdict ?, the automaton verifies that the property is falsified (as it is a safety property). That is, upon reaching q_2 the verdict will be $\bot$ for all possible suffixes of a trace.

For the scope of this paper and for clarity, we use LTL extended with two (syntactic) operators, mostly to strengthen and relax time constraints. We consider the operator *eventually within t* ($\Diamond_{\leq t}$) which considers a disjunction of next

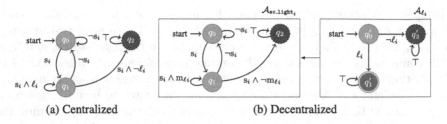

(a) Centralized   (b) Decentralized

Fig. 3. Monitor(s) for $\texttt{sc\_light}(i)$, for a given room i in the house. The verdicts associated with the states are $\bot$: dotted red, $\top$: double green, and ?: single yellow.

operators. It is defined as: $\Diamond_{\leq t} ap \stackrel{\text{def}}{=} ap \vee \mathrm{X}ap \vee \mathrm{XX}ap \vee ... \mathrm{X}^t ap$. Where ap is an atomic proposition. Intuitively, the eventually within states that ap holds within a given number of timestamps. Operator $\Diamond_{\leq t}$ allows us to relax the time constraints for a given atomic proposition. Similarly, we consider the operator *globally within* t ($\Box_{\leq t}$) which the dual of the previous operator. The operator $\Box_{\leq t}$ is a conjunction of next operators. $\Box_{\leq t} ap \stackrel{\text{def}}{=} ap \wedge \mathrm{X}ap \wedge \mathrm{XX}ap \wedge \mathrm{X}^t ap$.

Example 2 (Check light switch modalities). The property expressed in Example 1 can be expressed in LTL as: $\texttt{sc\_light}(i) \stackrel{\text{def}}{=} \Box(s_i \implies \mathrm{X}(\ell_i \mathrm{U} \neg s_i))$. The property can be modified with the extra operators relax or constrain the time on the light. The relaxed property $\texttt{sc\_light}'(i) \stackrel{\text{def}}{=} \Box(s_i \implies \Diamond_{\leq 3}(\ell_i \mathrm{U} \neg s_i))$ allows the right-hand side of the implication to hold within any of the next 3 timestamps instead of immediately after. The bounded property $\texttt{sc\_light}''(i) \stackrel{\text{def}}{=} \Box(s_i \implies \Box_{\leq 3}(\ell_i))$ states that the light is on starting from the timestamp the switch is turned on and the subsequent two (for a total of 3). An example of such a property is the restriction on watching TV for a specific duration (Table 1) where $\texttt{restricttv} \stackrel{\text{def}}{=} \Box(\texttt{tv} \implies \Diamond_{\leq 10} \neg \texttt{tv})$.

2.2 Decentralized Specifications

While simple specifications can be expressed with both LTL and automata, it quickly becomes a problem to scale the formulae or account for hierarchies (see Sect. 2.3). As such, we use decentralized specifications [16].

Informally, a decentralized specification considers the system as a set of components, defines a set of monitors, additional atomic propositions that represent references to monitors, and attaches each monitor to a component. A decentralized trace is a partial function that assigns to each component and timestamp an event. Each monitor is a Moore automaton as described in Sect. 2.1 where the transition label is restricted to only atomic propositions related to the component on which the monitor is attached, and references to other monitors. A monitor reference is evaluated as if it were an oracle. That is, to evaluate a monitor reference m_i at a timestamp t, the monitor referenced ($\mathcal{A}_i$) is executed starting from the initial state on the trace starting at t. The atomic proposition m_i at t takes the value of the final verdict reached by the monitor.

Example 3 (Decentralized light switch). Figure 3b shows the decentralized specification for the check light property from Example 1. We have two monitors $\mathcal{A}_{\mathtt{sc\_light}_i}$ and $\mathcal{A}_{\ell_i}$. They are respectively attached to the light switch, and light bulb components. In the former, the atomic propositions are either related to observations on the component ($\mathtt{s}_i$, switch on), or references to other monitors ($\mathtt{m}_{\ell_i}$). The light switch monitor first waits for the switch to be on to reach q_1. In q_1, at some timestamp t, it needs to evaluate reference $\mathtt{m}_{\ell_i}$ by running the trace starting from t on monitor $\mathcal{A}_{\ell_i}$.

The assumptions of decentralized specifications on the system are as follows: no monitors send messages that contain wrong information; no messages are lost, they are eventually delivered in their entirety but possibly out-of-order; all components share one logical discrete clock marked by round numbers indicating relevant transitions in the system specification. While security is a concern in the smart apartment setting, the first two assumptions are met in this case study as the apartment sensor network operates on the local network, and we expect monitors to be deployed by the sensor providers, and users of the apartment. The last assumption is also met in the smart setting, as all sensors share a global clock.

2.3   Advantages of Decentralized Specifications

Modularity and Re-use. Monitor references in decentralized specifications allow specifications writers to modularize behavior. Given that a monitor represents a specific behavior, this same monitor can be re-used to define more complex specifications at a higher level, without consideration for the details needed for this specification. This allows specification writers to reason at various levels about the system specification.

Let us consider the ADL specification `cooking` (resp. `sleeping`) which specifies whether the tenant is cooking (resp. sleeping) in the apartment. One can reason about the meta-specification `firehazard` using both `cooking` and `sleeping` specifications without considering the lower level sensors that determine these specifications, that is `firehazard` $\stackrel{\text{def}}{=}$ $\Box(\mathtt{sleeping} \implies \neg\mathtt{cooking})$. While we can define `cooking` as `cooking` $\stackrel{\text{def}}{=}$ `kitchen_presence`$\land\Diamond_{\leq 5}$(`kitchen_cooktop`$\lor$ `kitchen_oven`). Additionally, any specification that requires either `sleeping` or `cooking` can re-use the verdict outputted by their respective monitors. For example the specifications `actfloor(0)` and `actfloor(1)` require the verdicts from monitors associated with `cooking` and `sleeping`, respectively, since cooking happens on the ground floor while sleeping on the first floor. Furthermore, we can disjoin `actfloor(0)` and `actfloor(1)` to easily specify that an activity has happened in the house, `acthouse` $\stackrel{\text{def}}{=}$ `actfloor(0)` $\lor$ `actfloor(1)`. While specification `acthouse` can be seen as a quantified version of `actfloor(i)`, we can use modular specifications for behavior, for example we can verify the triggering of an alarm in the house within 5 timestamps of detecting a fire hazard, i.e. `checkalert` $\stackrel{\text{def}}{=}$ `firehazard` $\implies$ $\Diamond_{\leq 5}$(`firealert`).

In addition to providing a higher level of abstraction and reasoning about specifications, the modular structure of the specifications present three additional advantages. The first allows the sub-specifications to change without affecting the meta-specifications, that is if the sub-specification cooking is changed (possibly to account for different sensors), no changes need to be propagated to specifications firehazard, actfloor(0), acthouse, and checkalert. The second advantage is controlling duplication of computation and communication, as such sensors do not have to send their observations constantly to all monitors that verify the various specifications. The specification cooking requires knowledge from the kitchen presence sensor, the kitchen cooktop (being enabled) and the kitchen oven. Without any re-use these three sensors (presence, cooktop, and oven) need to send their information to monitors checking: firehazard, actfloor(0), acthouse, and checkalert. The third advantage is a consequence of modeling explicitly the dependencies between specifications. This allows the monitoring to take advantage of such dependencies and place the monitors that depend on each other closer depending on the hierarchy, either geographically (i.e., in the same room or floor) or logically (i.e., close to the monitors of the dependent sub-specifications). Furthermore, knowing the explicit dependencies between specifications allows the user to choose a placement for their monitors, adjusting the placement to the system architecture. In the case a placement is not possible, it is possible to create intermediate specifications that simply relay verdicts of other monitors, to transitively connect all components that are not connected.

Abstraction From Implementation. Decentralized specifications define modular specifications that can be composed together to form bigger and more complex specifications. One setback for learning-based techniques to detect ADL is their specificity to the environment. That is, the training set is specific to a house layout, user profile (i.e., elderly versus adults) [23].

By using references to monitors, we leave the implementation of the specification to be specific for the house or user profile. Using our existing example, cooking is implemented based on the available sensors in the house, which would change for different houses. However, meta-specifications such as firehazard can be defined independently from the implementation of both cooking and sleeping.

Furthermore, using monitor references, which are treated as oracles, opens the door to utilizing existing techniques in the literature for non-automata based monitors. That is, as a reference is expected to eventually evaluate to $\top$ or $\bot$, any implementation of a monitor that can return a final verdict for a given timestamp can be incorporated to form more complex specifications. For example, one can use the various machine learning techniques [7,23,29] to define monitors that detect specific ADLs, then reference them in order to define more complex specifications.

Scalability. Decentralized specifications allow for a higher level of scalability when writing specifications, and also when monitoring. By using decentralized specifications, we restrict a given monitor to atomic propositions local to the component on which it is attached, and references to other monitors (see Sect. 2.2). This greatly reduces the number of atomic propositions to consider when synthesizing the monitor and reduces its size, as the sub-specifications are offloaded to another monitor.

For example, let us consider writing specifications using LTL formulae. The classical algorithm that converts LTL to Moore automata is doubly exponential in the size of the formula including all permutations of atomic propositions (to form events) [6]. As such reducing both the size of the formula and the number of atomic propositions used in the formula helps significantly when synthesizing the monitors, allowing us to scale beyond the limits of existing tools. For a large formula, it becomes impossible to generate a central monitor using the existing synthesis techniques. Decentralized specifications provide a way to manage the large formula by subdividing it into subformulae. The decomposition ensures that the formula evaluates to the same verdict given the same observations, at the cost of added delay.

Example 4 (Synthesizing check light). Recall the system property $\texttt{sc\_light}(i)$ in Example 2 responsible for verifying that in a room i a light switch does indeed turn a light bulb on until it is turned off. We recall the LTL specification $\texttt{sc\_light}(i) \stackrel{\text{def}}{=} \Box(\texttt{s}_i \implies X(\ell_i \, U \, \neg \texttt{s}_i))$. To verify the property across n rooms of the house, we formulate a property $\texttt{sc\_ok} \stackrel{\text{def}}{=} \bigwedge_{i \in [0..n]} \texttt{sc\_light}(i)$. In the case of a decentralized specification the formula will reference each monitor in each room, leading to a conjunction of at n atomic propositions. However, in the case of a centralized specification, the specification needs to be written as: $\texttt{sc\_ok}^{\text{cent}} \stackrel{\text{def}}{=} \bigwedge_{i \in [0...n]} \Box(\texttt{s}_i \implies X(\ell_i \, U \, \neg \texttt{s}_i))$, which is significantly more complex as a formula consisting of $4n$ operators (to cover the sub-specification), along n conjunctions, and defined over each sensor and light bulb atomic propositions ($2n$). Given that monitor synthesis is doubly exponential, both $\texttt{ltl2mon}$ [6] and $\texttt{lamaconv}$ [22] require significant resources and time to generate the minimal Moore automaton (in our case we were unable to generate the monitor for $n = 3$ after an hour to timeout with both tools).

2.4 Trace Replay with THEMIS

To perform monitoring we use THEMIS [17]. THEMIS is designed to define and handle decentralized specifications. The trace from [12] is given as a database with a table for each sensor. We extract each table as a csv file for each sensor and treat them as observations, we then assign a logical component for multiple related sensors.

Each sensor is implemented as an input (**Periphery** in THEMIS) to a logical component. For example, for the shower water, we use both cold and hot water sensors but define only a single component ("shower water"), from an RV perspective, "hot" and "cold" are multiple observations passed to the "shower water" component. We implemented two peripheries to process sensor trace data: **SensorBool** and **SensorThresh**. The first periphery reads Boolean values from the csv file associated with timestamps, and associates them with an atomic proposition. The second periphery reads real (double) values, converts them Boolean values based on whether the number is below or above a certain threshold, and associates them with an atomic proposition.

Since the system has a global clock, to synchronize observations, our periphery implementations synchronize on a date at the start and an increment (in our case 1 second) and a default Boolean value for the observation. When polled, the periphery returns the default value if nothing is observed yet, or the last value observed otherwise.

Managing the trace length (36,000) is an issue for the monitoring techniques presented in [16] as they rely on eventual consistency and will wait on input for the length of the trace, which requires a lot of memory. We optimized the datastructure used to store observations (Memory) to add garbage collection and thus reduce memory usage.

3   Assessing the Monitoring of the Appartment

Monitoring the smart apartment requires leveraging the interdependencies between specifications to be able to scale, beyond monitoring system properties, to more complex meta-specifications (as detailed in Sect. 1.2). We assess using decentralized specifications to monitor the apartment by conducting two separate scenarios. The first scenario (Sect. 3.1) evaluates the advantages of using decentralized specifications presented in Sect. 2.3 (modularity, scalability, and re-use) by looking at the complexity of monitor synthesis, and communication and computation costs when adding more complex specifications that re-use sub-specifications. The second scenario (Sect. 3.2) evaluates the effectiveness of detecting ADL by looking at various detection measures such as precision and recall.

3.1   Monitoring Efficiency and Hierarchies

Monitor Synthesis. Table 1 displays the number of atomic propositions referenced by each specification for the decentralized ($|AP^d|$) and the centralized ($|AP^c|$) settings. Column d indicates the maximum depth of the dependencies directed acyclic graph, so as to assess how many levels of sub-specifications need to be computed. When $d = 0$, it indicates that the specification can be determined directly by the monitor placed on the component, while $d = 1$ indicates that the monitor has to pull at most 1 monitor (which typically relays the component observations). More generally, when $d = n$, it indicates that the specification depends on a monitor that has at most depth $n - 1$. The atomic propositions indicate either direct references to sensor observations (in the centralized setting) or references to either sensor observations and dependent monitors (in the decentralized setting). It is possible to notice that for certain specifications such as `toilet` which relies only on the water sensor in the toilet to be detected, there is no difference between using a centralized or decentralized specification, as it resolves to the observations. Reduction becomes more pronounced when specifications re-use other specifications. For example, specification acthouse $\overset{\text{def}}{=}$ actfloor(0) ∨ actfloor(1), when decentralized, uses only 2 references (for each of the sub-specification). However, when expanded, it references all 27 sensors used to detect activities. Additionally, specification notwopeople $\overset{\text{def}}{=}$ ¬(actfloor(0) ∧ actfloor(1)) does not re-use the sub-specifications and requires all sensors again. This greatly reduces the formula size and allows us to synthesize the monitors needed to check the formulae, as the synthesis algorithm is doubly exponential as mentioned in Sect. 2.3.

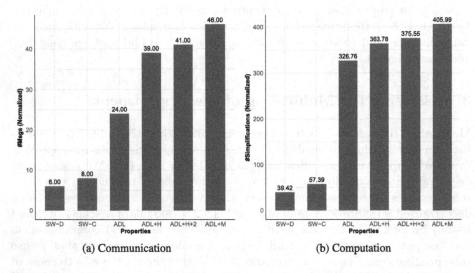

(a) Communication   (b) Computation

Fig. 4. Scalability of communication and computations in decentralized specifications.

Assessing Re-use and Scalability. Reducing the size of the atomic propositions needed for a specification not only affects monitor synthesis, but also performance, as atomic propositions represent the information needed (Sect. 2.3). To assess re-use and scalability, we perform two tasks and gather two measures pertaining to computation and communication, and present results in Fig. 4. The first task compares a centralized (SW-C) and a decentralized (SW-D) version of property sc_ok presented in Example 4 using only 2 rooms. The second task introduces large meta-specifications on top of the ADL specifications to check scalability. Firstly, we measure the communication and computation for monitoring ADL specifications (ADL). Secondly, we introduce specifications actfloor(0), actfloor(1) and acthouse (ADL+H) as they require information about all sensors for ADL. Thirdly, we add specification notwopeople (ADL+H+2), as it re-uses the same sub-specifications as specification acthouse. Lastly, we show all measures for all meta-specifications in Table 1 (ADL+M). We re-use two measures from [16]: the total number of simplifications the monitors are doing, and the total number of messages transferred. These measures are provided directly with THEMIS [17]. The total number of simplifications

(**#Simplifications**) abstracts the computation done by the monitors, as they attempt to simplify Boolean expressions that represent automaton states, which are the basic operations for maintaining the monitoring data structures in [16]. The total number of messages abstracts the communication (**#Msgs**), as our messages are of fixed length, they also represent the total data transferred. Both measures are normalized by the number of timestamps in the execution (36,000).

Results. Figure 4a shows the normalized number of messages sent by all monitors. For the first task, we notice that the number of messages is indeed lower in the decentralized setting, SW-D sends on average 2 messages per timestamp less than SW-C, which corresponds to the difference in the number of atomic propositions referenced (6 for SW-D and 8 for SW-C). For the second task, we notice that on the baseline for ADL, we observe 24 messages per timestamp, a smaller number than the sensors count (27). This is because some ADL like `toilet` are directly evaluated on the sensor without communicating, and other ADL like `preparing`, re-use other ADL specifications like `kactivity`. By introducing the 3 meta-specifications stating that an activity occurred on a floor or globally in a house, the number of messages per round only increases by 15. This also coincides with the number of atomic propositions for the specifications (6 for `actfloor(0)`, 7 for `actfloor(1)`, and 2 for `acthouse`) as those monitors depend in total on 15 other monitors to relay their verdicts. This costs much less than polling 16 sensors to determine `actfloor(0)`, 11 sensors to determine `actfloor(1)`, and 27 (a total of 54) to determine `acthouse`. To verify this, we notice that the addition of `notwopeople` (ADL+H+2) that needs information from all 27 sensors, only increases the total number of messages per timestamp by 2. The specification `notwopeople` reuses the verdicts of the two monitors associated with each `actfloor` specification. After adding all the meta-specifications (ADL+M), the total number of messages per timestamp is 46, which is less than the number needed to verify adding `actfloor`, and `acthouse` in a centralized setting (54). We notice a similar effect for computation (Fig. 4b).

3.2   ADL Detection Using RV

Measurements. Table 2a displays the effectiveness of using RV to monitor all ADL specifications on the trace of Tuesday, Jan 31 2017. To assess the effectiveness, we considered the provided self-annotated data from [12], where the user annotated the start and end of each activity. We measure precision, recall and F1 (the geometric mean of precision and recall). To measure precision, we consider a true positive when the verdict $\top$ of a monitor for a given timestamp fell indeed in the self-annotated interval for the activity. To measure recall, we measure the proportion of the intervals that have been determined $\top$ using RV. This approach is more fine-grained than the approach used in [25] where the precision and recall are computed for the start and end of intervals.

Results. The effectiveness of detection depends highly on the specification. Our approach performs well for the specifications `computing`, `cooking`, `office_tv`, as it exhibits high precision and high recall. The second group of specifications

Table 2. Precision, Recall, and F1 of monitoring Tuesday, Jan 31 2017.

(a) Monitoring all ADL specifications.

Specification	Precision	Recall	F1
computing	0.98	0.99	0.99
office_tv	1.00	0.80	0.89
cooking	0.88	0.88	0.88
shower_usage	1.00	0.50	0.67
washing_dishes	1.00	0.47	0.64
livingroom_tv	1.00	0.43	0.60
dressing	1.00	0.41	0.58
toilet*	1.00	0.18	0.30
sink_usage	1.00	0.13	0.23
eating	0.61	0.35	0.44
napping	0.43	0.95	0.60
preparing	0.23	0.77	0.35
reading	0.37	0.04	0.06

(b) Variations on the napping specification.

Formula	Precision	Recall	F1
$\Box_{\leq 25}(\texttt{weight})$	0.43	0.95	0.60
$\Box_{\leq 3}(\texttt{weight})$	0.43	0.99	0.60
$\Diamond_{\leq 3}(\texttt{weight})$	0.43	1.0	0.60
$\Box_{\leq 3}(\texttt{pres} \wedge \texttt{weight})$	0.34	0.14	0.20
$\Box_{\leq 3}(\neg \ell \wedge \texttt{weight})$	1.00	0.97	0.99

weight: bed pressure sensor
pres : bedroom presence sensor
ℓ : bedroom light sensor

contains specifications such as shower_usage, and livingroom_tv. It exhibits high precision but medium recall, that is, we were able to determine around 40 to 50% of all the timestamps where the specifications held according to the person annotating, without any false positives. The third group is similar to the second group but has very low recall (13–18%) and contains the specifications toilet and sink_usage. The fourth group, which includes the specifications napping and preparing, shows high recall but a high rate of false positives. And finally, specification reading is not properly detected, as it has a high rate of false positives and covers almost no annotated intervals.

Limitations of RV for Detecting ADL. The limitations of using RV to detect ADL are due to the modeling. As mentioned in Sect. 1.2, RV can be seen as a knowledge-based approach to activity detection, as such it suffers from similar weaknesses and limitations [9]. The activity is described as a rigid formal specification over the sensor data, and this has two consequences. Firstly, since RV relies purely on sensor data, activities which cannot be inferred from existing sensors will be poorly detected or not detected at all. This is the case for reading, as there are no sensors to indicate that the tenant is reading. We infer reading by checking that the light is on in the room and no other specified activity holds. Secondly, given that specifications are rigid, we expect the user to behave exactly as specified for the activity to be detected, any minor deviation results in the activity not being detected. To illustrate this point, the specification computing relies on the power consumption of the plug in the office. Had the tenant been charging his phone instead of computing, the recall would have suffered greatly. Another great example of this is the shower_usage specification, that is captured by inspecting the water usage of the shower. The time the tenant spends getting into the shower and out of the shower will not be considered, which greatly impacts recall. Table 2b shows how we can modify the specification napping to attempt to better capture the activity. In this case, using the additional light sensor to detect lights are off, helps us increase precision. The above issues are further compounded by the annotation being carried out by a person. The annotator can for example take a few seconds to annotate some events which could impact recall, especially for short intervals of activity. However, even with the inherent limitations of using knowledge-based approaches, our observed groups and results fall within the expected range, of knowledge-based approaches such as [25], and also have similar effectiveness as model-based SVM approaches such as [8].

4 Related Work

We present similar or useful techniques for detecting ADL activities in a smart apartment that use log analysis and complex event processing. Then, we present techniques from stream-based RV that can be extended for monitoring smart apartments.

ADL Detection Using Log Analysis. Detecting ADL can be performed using trace analysis tools. The approach in [25] defines parametric events using Model Checking Language (MCL) [28] based on the modal mu-calculus (inspired by temporal logic and regular expressions). Traces are read and transformed into actions, then actions are matched against the specifications to determine locations in the trace that match ADL. Five ADL (sleep, using toilets, cooking, showering, and washing dishes) are specified and checked in the same smart apartment as our work. While this technique is able to detect ADL activities, it amounts to checking traces offline, and a high level of post-processing is required to analyze the data.

ADL Detection Using Complex Event Processing. Reasoning at a much higher level of abstraction than sensor data, the approach in [21] attempts to detect ADL by analyzing the electrical consumption in the household. To do so, it employs techniques from Complex Event Processing (CEP), in which data is fed as streams and processed using various functions to finally output a stream of data. In this work, the ADL detection is split into two phases, one which detects peaks and plateaus of the various electrical devices, and the second phase uses those to indicate whether or not an appliance is being used. This illustrates a transformation from low-level data (sensor signal) to a high-level abstraction (an appliance is being used). The use of CEP for detecting ADL is promising, as it allows for similar scalability and abstraction. However, CEP's model of named streams makes it hard to analyze the specification formally, making little distinction between specification and implementation of the monitoring logic.

ADL Detection Using Runtime Verification. Similarly to CEP but focusing on Boolean verdicts, various stream-based RV techniques have been elaborated such as LOLA [13] which are used to verify correctness properties for synchronous systems such as the PCI bus protocol and a memory controller.

A more recent approach uses the Temporal Stream-Based Specification Language (TeSSLa) to verify embedded systems using FPGAs [14]. Stream-based RV is particularly fast and effective for verifying lengthy parametric traces. However, it is unclear how these approaches handle monitor synthesis for a large number of components and account for the hierarchy in the system.

Discussion. Stream-based systems such as stream-based RV and CEP are bottom-up. Data in streams is eventually aggregated into more complex information and relayed to a higher level. Decentralized specifications also support top-down approaches, which would increase the efficiency of monitoring large and hierarchical systems. To illustrate the point, consider the decentralized specification in Fig. 3b. In the automaton $\mathcal{A}_{sc\_light_i}$, the evaluation of the dependent monitor $\mathcal{A}_{\ell_i}$ only occurs when reaching q_1, so long as the automaton is in q_0, no interaction with the dependent monitor is necessary. This top-down feedback can be used to naturally optimize dependencies and increase efficiency. Because of the the oracle-based implementation of decentralized specifications, it is possible to integrate any monitoring reference that eventually returns a verdict. One could imagine integrating other stream-based monitors or even data-driven ADL detection approaches. The integration works both ways, as monitors can be considered a (blocking) stream of verdicts for the other techniques.

5   Conclusion

Monitoring a smart apartment presents RV with interesting new problems as it requires a scalable approach that is compositional, dynamic, and able to handle a multitude of devices. This is due to the hierarchical structure imposed by either limited communication capabilities of devices across geographical areas or the dependencies between various specifications. Attempting to solve such problems with centralized specifications is met with several obstacles at the level of monitor synthesis techniques (as we are presented with large formulae), and also at the level of monitoring as one needs to model interdependencies between formulae and re-use the sub-specifications used to build more complex specifications. We illustrate how decentralized specifications tackle such systems by explicitly modeling of interdependencies between specifications. Furthermore, we illustrate monitoring specifications that detect ADL in addition to system properties and even more specifications defined over both types of specifications.

References

1. Aimal, S., Parveez, K., Saba, A., Batool, S., Arshad, H., Javaid, N.: Energy optimization techniques for demand-side management in smart homes. In: Barolli, L., Woungang, I., Hussain, O.K. (eds.) INCoS 2017. LNDECT, vol. 8, pp. 515–524. Springer, Cham (2018). https://doi.org/10.1007/978-3-319-65636-6_46
2. Proceedings of the 26th ACM SIGSOFT International Symposium on Software Testing and Analysis, Santa Barbara, CA, USA, 10–14 July 2017. ACM (2017)

3. Bartocci, E., Falcone, Y. (eds.): Lectures on Runtime Verification. LNCS, vol. 10457. Springer, Cham (2018). https://doi.org/10.1007/978-3-319-75632-5

4. Bartocci, E., et al.: First international competition on runtime verification: rules, benchmarks, tools, and final results of CRV 2014. Int. J. Softw. Tools Technol. Transfer (2017)

5. Bartocci, E., Falcone, Y., Francalanza, A., Reger, G.: Introduction to runtime verification. In: Bartocci, E., Falcone, Y. (eds.) Lectures on Runtime Verification. LNCS, vol. 10457, pp. 1–33. Springer, Cham (2018). https://doi.org/10.1007/978-3-319-75632-5_1

6. Bauer, A., Leucker, M., Schallhart, C.: Runtime verification for LTL and TLTL. ACM Trans. Softw. Eng. Methodol. **20**(4), 14 (2011)

7. Brdiczka, O., Crowley, J.L., Reignier, P.: Learning situation models in a smart home. IEEE Trans. Syst. Man Cybern. Part B **39**(1), 56–63 (2009)

8. Chen, B., Fan, Z., Cao, F.: Activity recognition based on streaming sensor data for assisted living in smart homes. In: 2015 International Conference on Intelligent Environments, IE 2015, pp. 124–127. IEEE (2015)

9. Chen, L., Hoey, J., Nugent, C.D., Cook, D.J., Yu, Z.: Sensor-based activity recognition. IEEE Trans. Syst. Man Cybern. Part C **42**(6), 790–808 (2012)

10. Cotard, S., Faucou, S., Béchennec, J., Queudet, A., Trinquet, Y.: A data flow monitoring service based on runtime verification for AUTOSAR. In: 14th IEEE International Conference on High Performance Computing and Communication & 9th IEEE International Conference on Embedded Software and Systems, HPCC-ICESS 2012, pp. 1508–1515. IEEE Computer Society (2012)

11. Crowley, J.L., Coutaz, J.: An ecological view of smart home technologies. In: De Ruyter, B., Kameas, A., Chatzimisios, P., Mavrommati, I. (eds.) AmI 2015. LNCS, vol. 9425, pp. 1–16. Springer, Cham (2015). https://doi.org/10.1007/978-3-319-26005-1_1

12. Cumin, J., Lefebvre, G., Ramparany, F., Crowley, J.L.: A dataset of routine daily activities in an instrumented home. In: Ochoa, S.F., Singh, P., Bravo, J. (eds.) UCAmI 2017. LNCS, vol. 10586, pp. 413–425. Springer, Cham (2017). https://doi.org/10.1007/978-3-319-67585-5_43

13. D'Angelo, B., et al.: LOLA: runtime monitoring of synchronous systems. In: 12th International Symposium on Temporal Representation and Reasoning (TIME 2005), pp. 166–174. IEEE Computer Society (2005)

14. Decker, N., et al.: Online analysis of debug trace data for embedded systems. In: 2018 Design, Automation & Test in Europe Conference & Exhibition, DATE 2018, pp. 851–856. IEEE (2018)

15. El-Hokayem, A., Falcone, Y.: THEMIS Smart Home Artifact Repository. https://gitlab.inria.fr/monitoring/themis-rv18smarthome

16. El-Hokayem, A., Falcone, Y.: Monitoring decentralized specifications. In: El-Hokayem, A., Falcone, Y. (eds.) [2], pp. 125–135

17. El-Hokayem, A., Falcone, Y.: THEMIS: a tool for decentralized monitoring algorithms. In: El-Hokayem, A., Falcone, Y. (eds.) [2], pp. 372–375

18. El-Hokayem, A., Falcone, Y.: Bringing runtime verification home - a case study on the hierarchical monitoring of smart homes. CoRR abs/1808.05487 (2018). http://arxiv.org/abs/1808.05487

19. El-Hokayem, A., Falcone, Y.: Bringing Runtime Verification Home - A case study on the Hierarchical Monitoring of Smart Homes. CoRR abs/1808.05487 (2018)
20. Falcone, Y., Havelund, K., Reger, G.: A tutorial on runtime verification. In: Engineering Dependable Software Systems, NATO Science for Peace and Security Series, D: Information and Communication Security, vol. 34, pp. 141–175. IOS press (2013)
21. Hallé, S., Gaboury, S., Bouchard, B.: Activity recognition through complex event processing: First findings. In: Artificial Intelligence Applied to Assistive Technologies and Smart Environments, Papers from the 2016 AAAI Workshop, vol. WS-16-01. AAAI Press (2016)
22. Institute for Software Engineering and Programming Languages: LamaConv - Logics and Automata Converter Library. http://www.isp.uni-luebeck.de/lamaconv
23. van Kasteren, T.L.M., Englebienne, G., Kröse, B.J.A.: Transferring knowledge of activity recognition across sensor networks. In: Floréen, P., Krüger, A., Spasojevic, M. (eds.) Pervasive 2010. LNCS, vol. 6030, pp. 283–300. Springer, Heidelberg (2010). https://doi.org/10.1007/978-3-642-12654-3_17
24. Katz, S.: Assessing self-maintenance: activities of daily living, mobility, and instrumental activities of daily living. J. Am. Geriatr. Soc. 31(12), 721–727 (1983)
25. Lago, P., Lang, F., Roncancio, C., Jiménez-Guarín, C., Mateescu, R., Bonnefond, N.: The ContextAct@A4H real-life dataset of daily-living activities. In: Brézillon, P., Turner, R., Penco, C. (eds.) CONTEXT 2017. LNCS (LNAI), vol. 10257, pp. 175–188. Springer, Cham (2017). https://doi.org/10.1007/978-3-319-57837-8_14
26. Leucker, M., Schmitz, M., à Tellinghusen, D.: Runtime verification for interconnected medical devices. In: Margaria, T., Steffen, B. (eds.) ISoLA 2016. LNCS, vol. 9953, pp. 380–387. Springer, Cham (2016). https://doi.org/10.1007/978-3-319-47169-3_29
27. Majumder, S., Aghayi, E., Noferesti, M., Memarzadeh-Tehran, H., Mondal, T., Pang, Z., Deen, M.J.: Smart homes for elderly healthcare - recent advances and research challenges. Sensors 17(11), 2496 (2017)
28. Mateescu, R., Thivolle, D.: A model checking language for concurrent value-passing systems. In: Cuellar, J., Maibaum, T., Sere, K. (eds.) FM 2008. LNCS, vol. 5014, pp. 148–164. Springer, Heidelberg (2008). https://doi.org/10.1007/978-3-540-68237-0_12
29. Tapia, E.M., Intille, S.S., Larson, K.: Activity recognition in the home using simple and ubiquitous sensors. In: Ferscha, A., Mattern, F. (eds.) Pervasive 2004. LNCS, vol. 3001, pp. 158–175. Springer, Heidelberg (2004). https://doi.org/10.1007/978-3-540-24646-6_10
30. Thapliyal, H., Nath, R.K., Mohanty, S.P.: Smart home environment for mild cognitive impairment population: solutions to improve care and quality of life. IEEE Consum. Electron. Mag. 7(1), 68–76 (2018)

A Taxonomy for Classifying Runtime Verification Tools

Yliès Falcone[1](✉), Srđan Krstić[2](✉), Giles Reger[3](✉), and Dmitriy Traytel[2](✉)

[1] Univ. Grenoble Alpes, CNRS, Inria, Grenoble INP, LIG, 38000 Grenoble, France
`ylies.falcone@univ-grenoble-alpes.fr`
[2] Institute of Information Security, Department of Computer Science, ETH Zürich,
Zurich, Switzerland
`{srdan.krstic,traytel}@inf.ethz.ch`
[3] University of Manchester, Manchester, UK
`giles.reger@manchester.ac.uk`

Abstract. Over the last 15 years Runtime Verification (RV) has grown into a diverse and active field, which has stimulated the development of numerous theoretical frameworks and tools. Many of the tools are at first sight very different and challenging to compare. Yet, there are similarities. In this work, we classify RV tools within a high-level taxonomy of concepts. We first present this taxonomy and discuss the different dimensions. Then, we survey RV tools and classify them according to the taxonomy. This paper constitutes a snapshot of the current state of the art and enables a comparison of existing tools.

1 Introduction

Runtime Verification (RV) [7,28,29,38] (or runtime monitoring) is (broadly) the study of methods to analyze the dynamic behavior of computational systems. The most typical analysis is to check whether a given run of a system satisfies a given specification and it is this general setting (and its variants) that we consider in this paper. Whilst topics such as *specification mining* or *trace visualization* are generally considered to be within this broad field, we do not include them in our discussion.

This paper presents a taxonomy of RV frameworks and tools and uses this to classify 20 selected tools. This work is timely for a number of reasons. Firstly, after more than 15 years of maturing, the field has reached a point where such a general view is needed. The last significant attempt at a taxonomy was in 2004 [24] and had a distinctly different focus to our own. Secondly, a number

The authors warmly thank Martin Leucker for the early discussions on the taxonomy and mind map representation. This article is based upon work from COST Action ARVI IC1402, supported by COST (European Cooperation in Science and Technology). In particular, the taxonomy and classification benefited from discussions within working groups one and two of this action. We would also like to acknowledge input from participants of Dagstuhl seminar 17462 [34].

© Springer Nature Switzerland AG 2018
C. Colombo and M. Leucker (Eds.): RV 2018, LNCS 11237, pp. 241–262, 2018.
https://doi.org/10.1007/978-3-030-03769-7_14

of activities, such as the runtime verification competitions [4,6,30,48], the RV-CuBES workshop [46,49], two schools dedicated to RV [16], and a COST action [1] (including the development of a tutorial book on the topic [5]), have put the development of runtime verification tools into focus.

Terminology. The field of RV is broad and the used terminology is not yet unified. For the sake of clarity, let us fix the following terms:

- *Monitored system.* The system consisting of software, hardware, or a combination of the two, that is being monitored. Its behavior is usually abstracted as a *trace* object.
- *Trace.* A finite sequence of observations that represents (or in some cases approximates) the behavior of interest in the monitor system. The process of extracting/recording the trace is usually referred to as *instrumentation*.
- *Property.* A partition of traces. This may simply be a separation of traces into two sets or a more refined classification of traces.
- *Specification.* A concrete description of a property using a well-defined formalism.
- *Monitor.* A runtime object that is used to check properties. The monitor will receive observations from the trace (usually incrementally) and may optionally send information back to the monitored system, or to some other source.
- *RV framework.* A collection of a specification formalism, monitoring algorithm(s) (for generating and executing monitors), and (optional) instrumentation techniques that allows for runtime verification.
- *RV tool.* A concrete instantiation of an RV framework.

Contributions and Structure. This paper has two main contributions:

- *The Taxonomy.* We present a detailed taxonomy that defines seven major concepts used to classify runtime verification approaches (Sect. 2). Each of these seven concepts are refined and explained, with areas of possible further refinement identified.
- *The Classification.* We take 20 runtime verification tools and classify them in our taxonomy (Sect. 3). Tools were taken from the recent runtime verification competitions and RV-CuBES workshop and therefore represent a recent and relevant snapshot.

We then discuss what we have learned from these two activities (Sect. 4) before concluding with some comments on how we see this work developing in the future (Sect. 5).

2 A Taxonomy of Runtime Verification

This section describes a taxonomy of runtime verification approaches. Figure 1 provides a general overview of the taxonomy which identifies the seven major concepts (and is limited to the first two levels for readability reasons). This taxonomy provides a hierarchical organization of the major concepts used in the field.

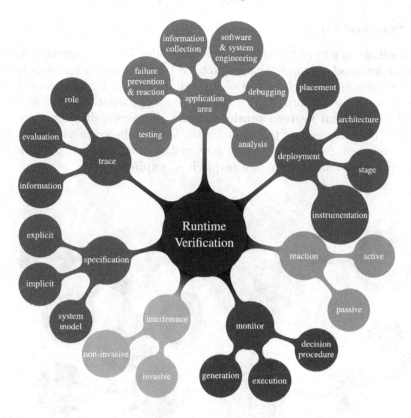

Fig. 1. Mindmap overviewing the taxonomy of Runtime Verification

Development Process. This taxonomy was developed in an iterative process alongside the classification presented in Sect. 3. The seven main conceptual areas were identified as an initial starting point and extended with established dichotomies (e.g., offline vs online). Sub-concepts were then added and refined based on the focused classification process and a wider survey of tools (involving over 50 tools, not described in this paper). We have attempted to ensure that the taxonomy remains as general and flexible as possible.

Relations Between Nodes. We do not capture concepts such as mutual exclusion or interdependence between nodes diagrammatically but aim to describe these in the text. In most cases the final level of the taxonomy captures some concrete instances of a particular (sub)concept and it is at this level where such relations are most important.

The remainder of this section focusses on each of the seven major concepts and expands the description along the corresponding branches.

2.1 Specification

The specification part of the taxonomy is depicted in Fig. 2. A specification indicates the intended system behavior (property), that is *what one wants to check* on the system behavior. It is one of the main inputs of a runtime verification framework designed before running the system. A specification exists within the context of a general **system model** i.e., the abstraction of the system being specified. The main part of this model is the form of observations (traces) made about the system (see Sect. 2.5) but may include other contextual information. A specification itself can be either **implicit** or **explicit**.

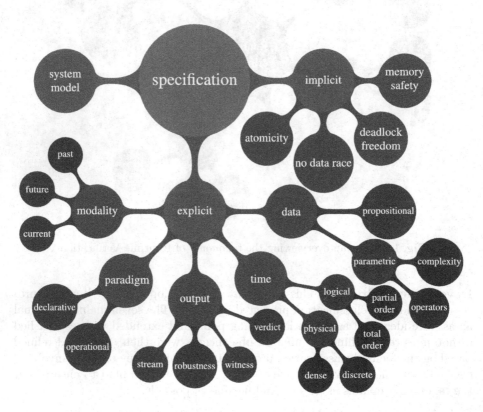

Fig. 2. Mindmap for the specification part of the taxonomy

Implicit Specifications. An **implicit** specification is used in a runtime verification framework when there is a general understanding of the particular desired behavior. Runtime verification tools do not require their users to explicitly formulate and enter implicit specifications. Implicit specifications generally aim at avoiding runtime errors (that would typically be not caught by a compiler). Such runtime errors can be critical. An example is memory safety, whose purpose is to ensure proper accesses to the system memory. Implicit specifications often also describe correct concurrent behavior such as the absence of deadlocks, the atomicity of operations, and the absence of data races. The final layer here is a non-exhaustive list of prominent examples.

Explicit Specifications. An explicit specification is one provided by the user of the runtime verification framework and formally expresses functional or non-functional requirements. It can complement the properties checked by the compiler of a language (e.g., errors that would not be caught by type checking). An explicit specification denotes a function from traces to some **output** domain and is written in a specification formalism belonging to some **paradigm** e.g., specifications may describe this function **operationally** (e.g., by a finite-state automaton) or **declarative** (e.g., by a temporal logic formula). The specification formalism can offer different features used to model the expected behavior according to the dimensions discussed below.

The specification formalism may support different **modalities**. Some formalisms may restrict assertions to the **current** observation whereas others may support constraints over **past** or **future** observations. In some cases, different modalities represent distinct expressiveness classes; in other cases it is merely a matter of usability.

A key dimension is how specifications or a specification formalism handle data in observations. The simple case is the **propositional** case where observations are assumed to be atomic and unstructured (e.g., simple names). Otherwise, we say that the approach is **parametric**: observations (events or states) are associated with a list of (possibly named) runtime values. The structure of these runtime values may have different **complexity** e.g. they may be simple primitive values or complex XML documents or runtime objects. The **operators** over these values supported by the specification language may also vary. For example, whether it is possible to compare values in different ways (e.g. more than equality) or whether quantification (e.g. first-order, freeze quantification, or pseudo-quantification via templates) over parameters is supported [34–36].

A specification can also express constraints over **time**. Constraints can refer either to **logical time** or **physical time**. In the case of logical time, constraints are placed on the relative ordering between events. Such an order can be **total** (e.g., when monitoring a monolithic single-threaded program) or **partial** (e.g., when monitoring a multi-threaded program or a distributed system). In the case of physical time, timing constraints are related to the actual physical time that elapses when running the system. The domain of this timing information can be **discrete** or **dense**. There is a special case where *time is treated as data*. Such approaches typically do not offer native support for expressing quantitative temporal relationships, but use the parametrization operators to refer to timestamps.

The last dimension of an explicit specification formalism is that of the **outputs** assigned to the input executions e.g., the range of the denoted function. In the standard case, the specification associates **verdicts** with an execution. Those verdicts indicate specification fulfillment or violation and may range over a domain extending the Boolean domain. A more refined output might include a **witness** for the verdict, e.g., a set of bindings of values to free variables in the specification that lead to violations. **Robustness** information extends classical verdicts by providing a quantitative assessment of the specification fulfillment or violation. Finally, in the most general case, specifications can describe output **streams**, which is any form of continuously produced information. This may be a stream of verdicts or witnesses, e.g., by evaluating the specification at each observation point, or more generally may be any data computed from the observations.

2.2   Monitor

The monitor part of the taxonomy is depicted in Fig. 3. A monitor is a main component of a runtime verification framework. By monitor, we refer to a component executed along the system for the purposes of the runtime verification process. A monitor implements a decision procedure which produces the expected output (either the related information for an implicit specification or the specification language output for an explicit specification).

The **decision procedure** of the monitor can be either **analytical** or **operational**. Analytical decision procedures query and scan records (e.g., from a

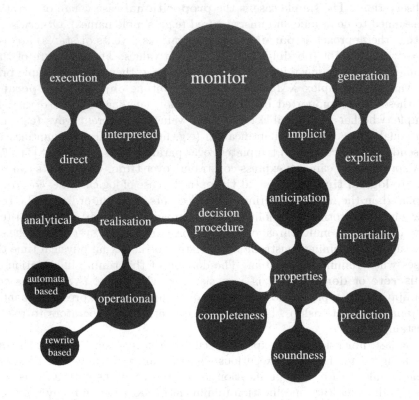

Fig. 3. Mindmap for the monitor part of the taxonomy

database) to determine whether some relations hold between the records and the current execution. Operational decision procedures are those based on automata or formula rewriting. In an **automata-based** monitor, the code relies on some form of automata-like formalism (either classical finite-state automata or richer forms). In a **rewrite-based** monitor, the decision procedure is based on a set of (possibly pre-defined) rewriting rules trigged by a new event. When designing monitors, it is desirable that its decision procedure guarantee several properties. Intuitively, a **sound** monitor never provides incorrect output, while a **complete** monitor always provide an output. The properties reflect how much confidence one can have in the output of monitor and how much confidence one can have that a monitor will produce an output, respectively. Soundness and completeness cannot be guaranteed in situations where, for instance, some form of sampling is used, not all necessary events can be observed by the monitor, or when the observation order does not correspond to the execution order. In such cases, the monitor can perform two kinds of **prediction**. Firstly, when the monitor produces its output as soon as possible, meaning that it uses a model of the monitored system to predict the possible futures of the trace and evaluate these possible futures before they actually happen. Secondly, when the monitor predicts potential errors in alternative concurrent executions (which are not actually observed by the monitor). A monitor is **impartial** when the produced outputs are not contradictory over time. Finally, a monitor can **anticipate** the output. This resembles prediction but the knowledge used by the monitor in this case comes from the monitored specification. Impartiality and anticipation are properties of the semantics of the specification language itself.

The decision procedure will act on an object (e.g. an automaton) which is itself often referred to as the monitor. This may be **generated explicitly** from the specification (e.g. an automaton synthesized from an LTL formula) or may exist **implicitly** (e.g. a rewrite system defined in an internal domain-specific language). Finally, a monitor must be **executed**. This might be **directly** if the monitor is given as code e.g., it is either already implemented as some extension of a programming language (i.e., an internal domain-specific language, or the synthesis step from generation directly produced executable code. Otherwise, the monitor is said to be **interpreted**. The key difference between the two approaches is whether each monitor is implemented by a different piece of code (direct) or there is a generic monitoring code that is parametrized by some monitor information (interpreted).

2.3   Deployment

The deployment part of the taxonomy is depicted in Fig. 4. By deployment, we refer to how the monitor is effectively implemented, organized, how it retrieves the information from the system, and when it does so.

The notion of **stage** describes *when* the monitor operates, with respect to the execution of the system. Runtime verification is said to apply **offline** when the monitor runs after the system finished executing and thus has access to the complete system execution (e.g., a log file). It is said to apply **online** when the

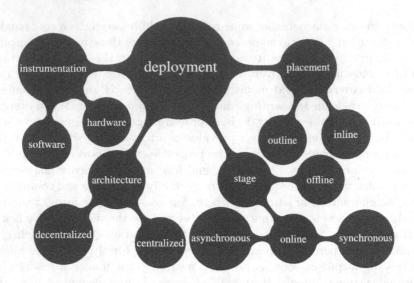

Fig. 4. Mindmap for the deployment part of the taxonomy

monitor runs while the system executes and thus observes the current execution and a part of its history. In the online case, the communication and connection between the monitor and the system can be **synchronous** or **asynchronous**, respectively depending on whether the initial program code stops executing when the monitor analyzes the retrieved information. It is possible for a monitor to be *partially* synchronous if it synchronises on some but not all observations.

The notion of **placement** describes where the monitor operates, with respect to the running system. Therefore, this concept only applies when the stage is online. Traditionally, the monitor is said to be **inline** (resp. **outline**) when it executes in the same (resp. in a different) address space as/than the running system. Pragmatically, the difference between inline and outline is a matter of **instrumentation**. An inline tool implicitly includes some form of instrumentation, used to inline the monitor in the monitored system. Conversely, outline tools typically provide an interface for receiving observations. This interface may exist within the same language and be called directly, or it may be completely separate with communication happening via other means (e.g., pipes). There is a (not uncommon) grey area between the two in the instance of tools that provide an outline interface but may also automatically generate instrumentation code. Instrumentation itself may be at the **hardware** or **software** level and there are further subdivisions within this that we do not cover here. Finally, the architecture of the monitor may be **centralized** (e.g., in one monolithic procedure) or **decentralized** (e.g., by utilising communicating monitors, which may be synchronous or asynchronous).

2.4 Reaction

The reaction part of the taxonomy is depicted in Fig. 5. By reaction, we refer to how the monitor affects the execution of the system; this can be passive or active.

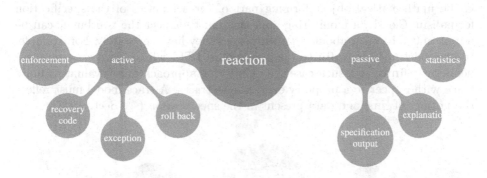

Fig. 5. Mindmap for the reaction part of the taxonomy

Reaction is said to be **passive** when the monitor does not influence or minimally influences the initial execution of the program. A passive monitor is typically an observer, only collecting information. This means that there are some sorts of guarantees that the analysis performed by monitor did not alter the execution and that the reported information is accurate. Such guarantees could be some form of behavioral equivalence (e.g., simulation, bisimulation, or weak bisimulation) between the initial system and the monitored system. In that case, the purpose of monitoring typically pertains to producing the **specification outputs** (e.g., verdicts or robustness information) or providing a form of **explanation** of a specification output (e.g., a witness trace containing the important events leading to a specific verdict) or **statistics** (for instance violated/satisfied specifications, number of times intermediate verdicts were output before a final verdict is reached).

Reaction is said to be **active** when the monitor affects the execution of the monitored system. An active monitor would typically affect the execution of the system when a violation is reported or detected to be irremediably happening. Various interventions are possible. A so-called **enforcement** monitor can try to prevent property violations from occurring by forcing the system to adhere to the specification. When a violation occurs, a monitor can execute **recovery code** to mitigate the effect of the fault and let the program either terminate or pursue the execution from a safer state. A monitor can also raise **exceptions** that were already present in the initial system. Finally, recovery mechanisms can be launched to **roll the system back** in a previous correct state.

2.5   Trace

The trace part of the taxonomy is depicted in Fig. 6. The notion of trace appears in two places in a runtime verification framework and this distinction is captured by the **role** concept. By **observed** trace we refer to the object extracted from the monitored system and examined by the monitor. Conversely the trace **model** is the mathematical object forming part of the semantics of the specification formalism. Clearly, a monitoring approach must connect the two but it can be important to be clear about what properties they have separately. For example, trace models may be **infinite** (as in standard LTL) whilst observed traces are necessarily **finite** – in such case the monitoring approach must evaluate a finite trace with respect to a property over infinite traces. A trace model must reflect the notions of time and data present in the specification (see Sect. 2.1).

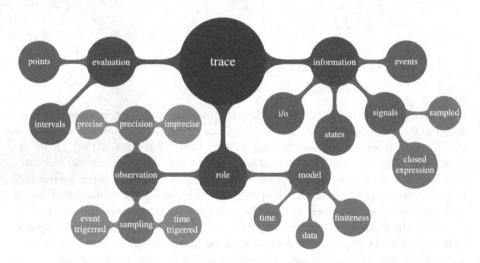

Fig. 6. Mindmap for the trace part of the taxonomy

The construction of the observed trace is also parameterized by a **sampling** decision and a **precision** decision. Sampling is said to be **event triggered** when the monitor gets information from the target system when an event of interest happens in the program. This can be the case when an event occurs in the system (in case the trace consists of a collection of events), when a relevant part of the program state changes, or when a new input is received or an output produced by the system. Sampling is said to be **time triggered** when there exists a more or less regular period at which information is collected on the program. The term sampling here reflects the fact that any trace will only collect a relevant subset of actual behaviours. If the trace contains *all* relevant traces then it is **precise**, otherwise it is **imprecise**. Reasons for imprecision might be imperfect trace collection methods, or purposefully for reasons of overhead.

Either form of trace object is an abstraction of the system execution and only contains some of the runtime information. The **information** retrieved from the program can take the form of isolated information. For instance, the trace can contain information on the internal **state** of the program or notifications that some **events** occurred in the program (or both). Not exclusive of the previous option, the monitor can also process the **input and output** information from a transformational program. Finally, the analyzed object can consist in time-continuous information in the form of a **signal**, which may be captured as a **closed-expression** or by discrete **sampling**.

The runtime information retrieved by the monitor represents an **evaluation** of the system state. This information can be related to an identified **point** (in time or at a program location) or an **interval**.

2.6   Interference

The **interference** part of the taxonomy (see Fig. 1) characterizes monitoring frameworks as **invasive** or **non-invasive**. In absolute, a non-invasive monitoring framework being impossible (observer effect), this duality corresponds more in reality to a spectrum. There are two sources of interference for a monitoring framework with a system. The interference with the system execution can be for instance related to the induced overhead (time and memory wise) or by a modification of scheduling. First, how much a runtime verification framework interferes with the initial system depends on the effect of the instrumentation applied to the system, which itself depends on the specification as instrumentation is purposed mainly to collect a trace. Thus, the quantity of information in the trace and the frequency at which this information is collected (depending on the sampling) affects the instrumentation. Moreover, interference also depends on the monitor deployment. Offline monitoring is considered to be less intrusive because the observation made on the system consists only in dumping events to a trace. Online monitoring is considered to be more intrusive to a degree depending on the coupling between the system and the monitor. Second, interference with the monitored system also occurs when actively steering the system.

2.7   Application Areas

We have included **application areas** as a top-level concept of the taxonomy (see Fig. 1) as it can have a large impact on other aspects of the runtime verification tools. There are numerous application areas of runtime verification. We have identified the following (certainly non-exhaustive) categories. First, runtime verification can be used for the purpose of **collecting information** on a system. This includes visualizing the execution (e.g., with traces, graphs, or diagrams) and evaluating the runtime performance (in a broad sense) over some metrics (execution time, memory consumption, communication, etc.) to collect statistics. Second, runtime verification can be used to perform an **analysis** of the system, usually to complement or in conjunction with static analysis techniques. This could focus on assessing concerns for a system in a large sense (e.g., requirements, properties, or goals) of **security and privacy**, **safety** and **progress/liveness** natures. Third, runtime verification can be used to augment software engineering techniques with a rigorous analysis of runtime information. Fourth, runtime verification can be used to complement techniques for finding defects and locating faults in systems such as **testing** and **debugging**. Finally, leveraging the previous techniques, runtime verification can be used to address the general problem of runtime **failure prevention and reaction**, by offering ways to detect faults, contain them, recover from them, and repair the system.

3   Classification

This section considers a snapshot of runtime verification tools with respect to the previously introduced taxonomy. As discussed later, this is the first major step in our effort to achieve a full classification of all existing runtime verification tools.

Tool Selection. For our initial classification we wanted a reasonably sized set that represented reasonably active, well documented, and recent tools. In particular, a recent source of information about the tool was of utmost importance. We therefore focussed on the entrants to the runtime verification competitions taking place between 2014 and 2016 [6,30,48] and the submissions to the RV-CuBES workshop [49], which took place in 2017. This led to a selection of 20 tools (14 from the competition and 6 from the workshop). Our selection method is biased as the competition focussed only on tools for Java, C, or offline monitoring. Therefore, we expect our initial classification to be biased towards this area of the taxonomy. The selection is also favoring tools that had the resources to participate in either the competition or workshop.

Participating Tools. The 20 participating tools are listed in Table 1 along with hyperlinks (where applicable), references, the name of their specification formalism and some additional remarks. The given references are those that were used to fill in the classification, along with any additional information provided in competition reports [6,30,48].

Classification. The classification is given in Table 3 with a legend found in Table 2. We leave a general discussion of the classification to the next section. The classification also exists as a living document found at https://goo.gl/Mmuhdd. This document welcomes comments from the community and will be updated as our work continues.

The classification non-uniformly instantiates levels for different parts of the taxonomy. We omit parts of the taxonomy that are too abstract to be properly instantiated for the participating tools (e.g., system model) or if the source material of all the tools does not contain enough information for classification. Moreover, the major concepts application area and interference are omitted since there is a large space of non-exclusive possibilities that each tool can instantiate in this part of the taxonomy.

Table 1. Details of the participating tools.

Tool	References	Specification formalism name + some remarks
Aerial	[8, 12, 13]	MDL
ARTiMon	[44]	ARTiMon (no quantification; only aggregation)
BeepBeep	[31, 32]	Stateful stream function API + DSLs for LTL-FO+, FSM
DANA	[27]	UML state machines
detectEr	[15]	μHML (only universal quantification)
E-ACSL	[23, 53]	ACSL/implicit
JavaMOP	[37, 40]	MOP with plugins (LTL, FMS, ERE, CFG, SRS, CaReT)
jUnitRV	[21, 22]	Temporal Data Logic
Larva	[17–19]	DATEs
LogFire	[33]	LogFire DSL
MarQ/QEA	[3, 45, 47]	QEA
MonPoly	[9–11]	MFOTL
Mufin	[20]	Projection Automata
R2U2	[42, 50, 51]	MTL + mission time LTL
RiTHM	[14, 43]	LTL_3
RTC	[41]	- (implicit)
RV-Monitor	[39]	MOP (see above)
STePr	-	Scala-internal DSL
TemPsy/OCLR-Check	[25, 26]	TemPsy
VALOUR	[2]	Valour Script/Rules

The classification also refines the taxonomy. For instance, software instrumentation is refined based on how it is implemented (using AspectJ or reflection). We also provide more detailed description of the decision procedure, whenever the tools' material provides such information. Besides the values specified in Table 2, the cells in Table 3 may contain values "all", or "none" indicating that the tool supports all, or none of the features defined by that part of the taxonomy. Value "na" states that this part of the taxonomy is not applicable to the tool, while "?" means that there is insufficient information about the tool to establish a definitive classification. We have devised the classification mostly without involvement of the tools' developers, based on the available materials. As future work, we will validate our understanding of the tools through targeted interviews whenever this will be possible. (Any corrections will appear in the online version of the classification.)

Threats to Validity. Whilst we argue that this classification represents a reasonable snapshot of current runtime verification tools, there are two possible threats to its validity. Firstly, the sample of tools is heavily focussed towards software-monitoring with explicit specifications. Although, within this focus the coverage of tools is broad. It is important to be clear about the *scope* of this work. Few tools supporting implicit specifications (e.g. MemorySanitizer [54] or ThreadSanitizer [52]) identify themselves as runtime verification tools and most existing work does not share much of the terminology with runtime verification e.g. it is not usual to abstract a system by a trace. Whilst such tools can be categorised in the taxonomy, their classification will remain coarse as such tools are not the focus of the taxonomy. In general, this suggests that some areas of the taxonomy may require a refinement in the future, but also that these refinements will be orthogonal to the work presented here. We discuss this further later.

Secondly, the classification does not cover all known tools (over 50). However, many tools not included in this classification are mostly of historic interest. Others have influenced the taxonomy without taking part in the classification (e.g. stream-based approaches). Nonetheless, it will be important to achieve maximal coverage in the future.

4 Discussion

This section makes some observations about the taxonomy and classification.

4.1 General Observations

The majority of tools handled explicit specifications based on totally ordered logical time. There was a mixture of propositional and parametric tools and different approaches to physical time. Almost all tools were event-based with event-triggered sampling.

Unsurprisingly, the monitor decision procedures were varied, with many not quite fitting the mould. The majority of tools were online – it is perhaps worth observing that RV-Monitor added an offline interface for the competition. Only one tool is purely offline. The distinction between operational and declarative specification languages results in two sets of tools of roughly the same size. Both approaches are useful and favored by different sub-communities of RV. A few tools support both kinds of specification languages.

Some parts of the taxonomy were relatively straightforward to complete, whereas others were more controversial. The most discussed part of the taxonomy was the monitor concept as the term "monitor" is highly overloaded in our field and many frameworks do not have an explicit notion of a monitor. In the end, we decided to split how a monitor is generated and how it is executed as there is not necessarily a close link between the two. Another area that was difficult to fix was the relation between trace model and observed trace. It would be wrong to conflate the two, however often these concepts overlap.

Table 2. Key for Table 3.

Column	Values
Specification	
implicit	ms = *memory safety*
data	p = *propositional*, s = *simple parametric*, c = *complex parametric*
output	s = *stream*, v = *verdict*, w = *witness*, r = *robustness*
logical time	tot = *total order*, par = *partial order*
physical time	$\mathbb{N}$ = *discrete*, $\mathbb{R}$ = *dense*, none = *no time*
modality	f = *future*, p = *past*, c = *current*
Monitor	
generation	e = *explicit*, i = *implicit*
execution	i = *interpreted*, d = *direct*
Deployment	
stage	on = *online*, off = *offline*
synchronisation	sync = *synchronous*, async = *asynchronous*
architecture	c = *centralised*, d = *decentralised*
placement	out = *outline*, in = *inline*
instrumentation	sw = *software*, swAJ = *software with AspectJ*, swR = *software with reflection*
Reaction	
active	e = *exception*, r = *recovery*
passive	so = *specification output*, e = *explanations*
Trace	
information	e = *events*, s = *states*
sampling	et = *event-triggered*, tt = *time-triggered*
evaluation	p = *points*, i = *intervals*
precision	p = *precise*, i = *imprecise*
model	f = *finite trace model*, i = *infinite trace model*
General	
	all = *all features supported*, none = *no features supported*
	na = *not applicable*, ? = *insufficient information*

4.2 Underpopulated Areas of the Taxonomy

The classification unveils areas that are not populated by any tools. We discuss the main ones here and what this might mean.

Decentralized Architecture. This appears to be an area that has not received much attention. This may be due to the inherent complexity of decentralization, or it may reflect a lack of need. They may also be interdependencies with the

Table 3. Classification of participating tools.

Column groups — Specification: implicit, data, output, logical, physical, modality, paradigm (data/output = explicit; logical/physical = time); Monitor: decision procedure; Deployment: generation, execution (= stage), synchronisation, architecture, placement, instrumentation; Reaction: active, passive; Trace: information, sampling, evaluation, precision, model.

Tool	implicit	data	output	logical	physical	modality	paradigm	decision procedure	generation	execution	synchronisation	architecture	placement	instrumentation	active	passive	information	sampling	evaluation	precision	model
Aerial	none	p	s	tot	$\mathbb{N}$	all	d	dynamic programming	i	i	on none	c	out	none	none	so	e	et	p	p	i
ARTiMon	none	s	s	tot	$\mathbb{N}\mathbb{R}$	all	d	?	i	i	on none	c	out	none	none	so	e	et	i	p	i
BeepBeep	none	c	s	tot	none	f	all	stream-processing	i	d	on all	c	out	sw	none	so	e	et	p	p	i
DANA	none	p	s	tot	$\mathbb{R}$	all	o	?	i	d	on sync	c	?	?	none	so	e	et	p	p	f
detectEr	none	s	v	par	none	f	d	dynamic programming	e	i	on all	c	in	sw	none	so	e	et	p	p	i
E-ACSL	ms	na	r	?	na	na	o	code rewriting with assertions	e	d	on sync	c	in	sw	e	e	s	na	na	na	na
JavaMOP	none	s	w	tot	none	all	d	trace slicing plugin-based	e	d	on sync	c	in	swAJ	r	e	e	et	p	p	f
jUnitRV	none	s	v	tot	none	f	d	automata-based (modulo theories e.g. SMT solver)	e	d	on sync	c	in	swR	?	?	e	et	p	p	f
Larva	none	s	v	tot	$\mathbb{N}$	f	o	automata-based	e	d	on all	c	all	sw	r	so	e	et	p	p	f
LogFire	none	s	w	tot	none	all	o	rewriting-based (RETE)	i	d	all sync	c	out	none	none	so	e	et	p	p	f
MarQ/QEA	none	s	v	tot	$\mathbb{N}$	f	o	automata-based	i	d	all sync	c	all	sw	none	so	e	et	p	p	f
MonPoly	none	s	s	tot	$\mathbb{N}$	all	d	first-order queries	i	i	on none	c	out	none	none	so	s	na	na	na	all
Mufin	none	s	v	tot	none	f	o	automata-based (union-find)	i	d	on sync	c	out	none	none	so	e	et	p	p	f
R2U2	none	p	s	tot	$\mathbb{N}$	all	d	automata-based	e	i	on async	c	out	none	none	so	e	et	p	p	i
RiTHM	none	p	s	tot	none	f	o	time-triggered runtime verification	e	d	on async	c	in	sw	none	so	s	all	p	p	i
RTC	ms	na	w	?	na	na	o	?	i	d	on sync	c	in	sw	r	?	?	et	p	p	na
RV-Monitor	none	s	w	tot	$\mathbb{N}$	all	all	(see JavaMOP)	i	d	all sync	c	all	sw	r	e	e	et	p	p	f
STePr	none	s	s	tot	$\mathbb{N}$	all	o	?	i	d	on ?	c	out	none	none	so	e	et	p	p	?
TemPsy/OCLR-Check	none	p	v	tot	$\mathbb{N}$	all	d	OCL constraint	i	i	off na	c	out	none	none	so	e	et	p	p	f
VALOUR	none	s	v	tot	$\mathbb{N}$	all	o	automata-based	i	d	on all	c	in	swAJ	none	all	e	all	p	p	f

monitoring setting (e.g. the language of interest) that make such an approach less desirable. Also the selection of the tools based on the competitions might have contributed to this topic being underrepresented: the competitions did not focus on the distributed setting.

Monitoring States. None of the tools in our classification monitor states of a program directly. This may be a result of the popularity of event-oriented specification languages. This is an interesting observation as it is commonly stated as a common dichotomy (observing events or states) but we do not see this in our classification. Although, arguably E-ACSL monitors states even though it has no formal notion of a trace. Furthermore, the distinction between state and event is not always clear; it is always possible to encode state in events and some inline tools allow specifications to directly query runtime state.

Richer Reactions. Most tools only provide passive reactions and the active reactions provided were relatively weak. It would be interesting to see more work in the areas of enforcement, recovery, and explanations for declarative specifications.

Applications. Many of the tools were not developed with a single application area in mind, making this part of the taxonomy irrelevant. However, in cases where an application exists it is significant. For example, R2U2 is designed to monitor unmanned aerial vehicles and this is heavily reflected in the tool's design. This is less an underpopulated area and more an area that only applies in certain cases.

4.3   Relation to Other Classifications

We briefly compare our taxonomy to the previous most complete taxonomy for runtime monitoring [24]. The context of this taxonomy is slightly different as their focus was software-fault monitoring. We have chosen to focus more on issues related to the monitoring of *explicit specifications* and include fewer operational issues. Delgado et al. identify four top-level concepts: *Specification*, *Monitor*, *Event-Handler*, and *Operational Issues*. Below we summarise the most significant differences in each area.

Specification. In the previous taxonomy the focus is more on the kind of property being captured (e.g. safety) and the abstraction at which the property is captured (e.g. whether it directly refers to implementation details). There is little discussion of issues such as the handling of data or modalities (although one concept is *language type* which may be algebra, automata, logic, or HL/VHL). They also consider which parts of a program are/can be instrumented as part of the specification.

Monitor. Again there is a focus on instrumentation, which is something that we do not consider in depth as we tend to draw a line between instrumentation and monitoring. They differentiate whether instrumentation is manual or automatic. They key observation here is that they view *placement* slightly differently, as they classify monitoring occurring using different resources (e.g. running in a different process) as *offline*. We refer to [7] for a discussion on the recent alternatives when considering instrumentation.

Event-Handler. This concept has the same meaning as our concept of *reaction* and their sub-concepts are subsumed by ours.

Operational Issues. This is a concept that we have not considered in our taxonomy. They focus on *source program type* i.e. the types of programs that it can work with (e.g. just Java), *dependencies* (e.g. on specific hardware), and *maturity* of the tool. This is something we could extend our taxonomy with but we found that many tools are actively developed and such data may quickly become outdated.

5 Conclusion

We have introduced a taxonomy for classifying runtime verification tools and used it to classify an initial set of 20 tools taken from recent competitions and workshops. We believe that this classification activity is important for a number of reasons. Firstly, the taxonomy fixes shared terminology and dimensions for discussing tools – it is important that the community has a shared language for what it does. Secondly, the classification exercise gives an overview of comparable tools, making it more straightforward to identify the tools against which new contributions should be compared. Additionally, the taxonomy can help shape evaluation and benchmark activities in general, in particular the design of competitions. Finally, we believe this kind of activity can identify interesting directions for future research, in particular in underpopulated areas of the taxonomy.

Our work is ongoing and our next step is to extend the classification. We have collected information about over 50 runtime verification tools and plan to extend the classification to these tools. This may constitute a challenge because many of the tools from this extended list do not provide sufficient information for classification.

References

1. IC1402 Runtime Verification beyond Monitoring (ARVI). https://www.cost-arvi.eu/
2. Azzopardi, S., Colombo, C., Ebejer, J.P., Mallia, E., Pace, G.: Runtime verification using VALOUR. In: Reger, G., Havelund, K. (eds.) RV-CuBES 2017. Kalpa Publications in Computing, vol. 3, pp. 10–18. EasyChair (2017)
3. Barringer, H., Falcone, Y., Havelund, K., Reger, G., Rydeheard, D.: Quantified event automata: towards expressive and efficient runtime monitors. In: Giannakopoulou, D., Méry, D. (eds.) FM 2012. LNCS, vol. 7436, pp. 68–84. Springer, Heidelberg (2012). https://doi.org/10.1007/978-3-642-32759-9_9

4. Bartocci, E., Bonakdarpour, B., Falcone, Y.: First international competition on software for runtime verification. In: Bonakdarpour, B., Smolka, S.A. (eds.) RV 2014. LNCS, vol. 8734, pp. 1–9. Springer, Cham (2014). https://doi.org/10.1007/978-3-319-11164-3_1

5. Bartocci, E., Falcone, Y. (eds.): Lectures on Runtime Verification. LNCS, vol. 10457. Springer, Cham (2018). https://doi.org/10.1007/978-3-319-75632-5

6. Bartocci, E., et al.: First international competition on runtime verification: rules, benchmarks, tools, and final results of CRV 2014. STTT, 1–40 (2017)

7. Bartocci, E., Falcone, Y., Francalanza, A., Reger, G.: Introduction to runtime verification. In: Bartocci, E., Falcone, Y. (eds.) Lectures on Runtime Verification. LNCS, vol. 10457, pp. 1–33. Springer, Cham (2018). https://doi.org/10.1007/978-3-319-75632-5_1

8. Basin, D.A., Bhatt, B.N., Traytel, D.: Almost event-rate independent monitoring of metric temporal logic. In: Legay, A., Margaria, T. (eds.) TACAS 2017. LNCS, vol. 10206, pp. 94–112. Springer, Heidelberg (2017). https://doi.org/10.1007/978-3-662-54580-5_6

9. Basin, D.A., Harvan, M., Klaedtke, F., Zălinescu, E.: MONPOLY: monitoring usage-control policies. In: Khurshid, S., Sen, K. (eds.) RV 2011. LNCS, vol. 7186, pp. 360–364. Springer, Heidelberg (2012). https://doi.org/10.1007/978-3-642-29860-8_27

10. Basin, D.A., Klaedtke, F., Müller, S., Zalinescu, E.: Monitoring metric first-order temporal properties. J. ACM **62**(2), 15:1–15:45 (2015)

11. Basin, D.A., Klaedtke, F., Zalinescu, E.: The MonPoly monitoring tool. In: Reger, G., Havelund, K. (eds.) RV-CuBES 2017. Kalpa Publications in Computing, vol. 3, pp. 19–28. EasyChair (2017)

12. Basin, D.A., Krstić, S., Traytel, D.: Almost event-rate independent monitoring of metric dynamic logic. In: Lahiri, S., Reger, G. (eds.) RV 2017. LNCS, vol. 10548, pp. 85–102. Springer, Cham (2017). https://doi.org/10.1007/978-3-319-67531-2_6

13. Basin, D.A., Krstić, S., Traytel, D.: AERIAL: almost event-rate independent algorithms for monitoring metric regular properties. In: Reger, G., Havelund, K. (eds.) RV-CuBES 2017. Kalpa Publications in Computing, vol. 3, pp. 29–36. EasyChair (2017)

14. Bonakdarpour, B., Navabpour, S., Fischmeister, S.: Time-triggered runtime verification. Form. Methods Syst. Des. **43**(1), 29–60 (2013)

15. Cassar, I., Francalanza, A., Attard, D.P., Aceto, L., Ingólfsdóttir, A.: A suite of monitoring tools for Erlang. In: Reger, G., Havelund, K. (eds.) RV-CuBES 2017. Kalpa Publications in Computing, vol. 3, pp. 41–47. EasyChair (2017)

16. Colombo, C., Falcone, Y.: First international summer school on runtime verification. In: Falcone, Y., Sánchez, C. (eds.) RV 2016. LNCS, vol. 10012, pp. 17–20. Springer, Cham (2016). https://doi.org/10.1007/978-3-319-46982-9_2

17. Colombo, C., Pace, G.J.: Runtime verification using LARVA. In: Reger, G., Havelund, K. (eds.) RV-CuBES 2017. Kalpa Publications in Computing, vol. 3, pp. 55–63. EasyChair (2017)

18. Colombo, C., Pace, G.J., Schneider, G.: Dynamic event-based runtime monitoring of real-time and contextual properties. In: Cofer, D., Fantechi, A. (eds.) FMICS 2008. LNCS, vol. 5596, pp. 135–149. Springer, Heidelberg (2009). https://doi.org/10.1007/978-3-642-03240-0_13

19. Colombo, C., Pace, G.J., Schneider, G.: LARVA — safer monitoring of real-time java programs (tool paper). In: Hung, D.V., Krishnan, P. (eds.) SEFM 2009, pp. 33–37. IEEE Computer Society (2009)

20. Decker, N., Harder, J., Scheffel, T., Schmitz, M., Thoma, D.: Runtime monitoring with union-find structures. In: Chechik, M., Raskin, J.-F. (eds.) TACAS 2016. LNCS, vol. 9636, pp. 868–884. Springer, Heidelberg (2016). https://doi.org/10.1007/978-3-662-49674-9_54

21. Decker, N., Leucker, M., Thoma, D.: jUnit^{RV}–adding runtime verification to jUnit. In: Brat, G., Rungta, N., Venet, A. (eds.) NFM 2013. LNCS, vol. 7871, pp. 459–464. Springer, Heidelberg (2013). https://doi.org/10.1007/978-3-642-38088-4_34

22. Decker, N., Leucker, M., Thoma, D.: Monitoring modulo theories. STTT **18**(2), 205–225 (2016)

23. Delahaye, M., Kosmatov, N., Signoles, J.: Common specification language for static and dynamic analysis of C programs. In: Shin, S.Y., Maldonado, J.C. (eds.) SAC 2013, pp. 1230–1235. ACM (2013)

24. Delgado, N., Gates, A.Q., Roach, S.: A taxonomy and catalog of runtime software-fault monitoring tools. IEEE Trans. Softw. Eng. **30**(12), 859–872 (2004)

25. Dou, W., Bianculli, D., Briand, L.: A model-driven approach to offline trace checking of temporal properties with OCL. Technical report SnT-TR-2014-5, Interdisciplinary Centre for Security, Reliability and Trust (2014). http://hdl.handle.net/10993/16112

26. Dou, W., Bianculli, D., Briand, L.: TemPsy-Check: a tool for model-driven trace checking of pattern-based temporal properties. In: Reger, G., Havelund, K. (eds.) RV-CuBES 2017. Kalpa Publications in Computing, vol. 3, pp. 64–70. EasyChair (2017)

27. Drabek, C., Weiss, G.: DANA - description and analysis of networked applications. In: Reger, G., Havelund, K. (eds.) RV-CuBES 2017. Kalpa Publications in Computing, vol. 3, pp. 71–80. EasyChair (2017)

28. Falcone, Y.: You should better enforce than verify. In: Barringer, H., et al. (eds.) RV 2010. LNCS, vol. 6418, pp. 89–105. Springer, Heidelberg (2010). https://doi.org/10.1007/978-3-642-16612-9_9

29. Falcone, Y., Havelund, K., Reger, G.: A tutorial on runtime verification. In: Broy, M., Peled, D.A., Kalus, G. (eds.) Engineering Dependable Software Systems, NATO SPS D: Information and Communication Security, vol. 34, pp. 141–175. IOS Press, Amsterdam (2013)

30. Falcone, Y., Ničković, D., Reger, G., Thoma, D.: Second international competition on runtime verification. In: Bartocci, E., Majumdar, R. (eds.) RV 2015. LNCS, vol. 9333, pp. 405–422. Springer, Cham (2015). https://doi.org/10.1007/978-3-319-23820-3_27

31. Hallé, S.: When RV meets CEP. In: Falcone, Y., Sánchez, C. (eds.) RV 2016. LNCS, vol. 10012, pp. 68–91. Springer, Cham (2016). https://doi.org/10.1007/978-3-319-46982-9_6

32. Hallé, S., Khoury, R.: Event stream processing with BeepBeep 3. In: Reger, G., Havelund, K. (eds.) RV-CuBES 2017. Kalpa Publications in Computing, vol. 3, pp. 81–88. EasyChair (2017)

33. Havelund, K.: Rule-based runtime verification revisited. STTT **17**(2), 143–170 (2015)

34. Havelund, K., Leucker, M., Reger, G., Stolz, V.: A shared challenge in behavioural specification (Dagstuhl seminar 17462). Dagstuhl Rep. **7**(11), 59–85 (2017)

35. Havelund, K., Reger, G.: Runtime verification logics a language design perspective. In: Aceto, L., Bacci, G., Bacci, G., Ingólfsdóttir, A., Legay, A., Mardare, R. (eds.) Models, Algorithms, Logics and Tools. LNCS, vol. 10460, pp. 310–338. Springer, Cham (2017). https://doi.org/10.1007/978-3-319-63121-9_16

36. Havelund, K., Reger, G., Thoma, D., Zălinescu, E.: Monitoring events that carry data. In: Bartocci, E., Falcone, Y. (eds.) Lectures on Runtime Verification. LNCS, vol. 10457, pp. 61–102. Springer, Cham (2018). https://doi.org/10.1007/978-3-319-75632-5_3

37. Jin, D., Meredith, P.O., Lee, C., Rosu, G.: JavaMOP: efficient parametric runtime monitoring framework. In: Glinz, M., Murphy, G.C., Pezzè, M. (eds.) ICSE 2012, pp. 1427–1430. IEEE Computer Society (2012)

38. Leucker, M., Schallhart, C.: A brief account of runtime verification. J. Log. Algebr. Program. **78**(5), 293–303 (2009)

39. Luo, Q., et al.: RV-Monitor: efficient parametric runtime verification with simultaneous properties. In: Bonakdarpour, B., Smolka, S.A. (eds.) RV 2014. LNCS, vol. 8734, pp. 285–300. Springer, Cham (2014). https://doi.org/10.1007/978-3-319-11164-3_24

40. Meredith, P.O., Jin, D., Griffith, D., Chen, F., Rosu, G.: An overview of the MOP runtime verification framework. STTT **14**(3), 249–289 (2012)

41. Milewicz, R., Vanka, R., Tuck, J., Quinlan, D., Pirkelbauer, P.: Lightweight runtime checking of C programs with RTC. Comput. Lang. Syst. Str. **45**, 191–203 (2016)

42. Moosbrugger, P., Rozier, K.Y., Schumann, J.: R2U2: monitoring and diagnosis of security threats for unmanned aerial systems. Form. Methods Syst. Des. **51**(1), 31–61 (2017)

43. Navabpour, S., et al.: RiTHM: a tool for enabling time-triggered runtime verification for C programs. In: Meyer, B., Baresi, L., Mezini, M. (eds.) ESEC/FSE 2013, pp. 603–606. ACM (2013)

44. Rapin, N.: ARTiMon monitoring tool, the time domains. In: Reger, G., Havelund, K. (eds.) RV-CuBES 2017. Kalpa Publications in Computing, vol. 3, pp. 106–122. EasyChair (2017)

45. Reger, G.: An overview of MARQ. In: Falcone, Y., Sánchez, C. (eds.) RV 2016. LNCS, vol. 10012, pp. 498–503. Springer, Cham (2016). https://doi.org/10.1007/978-3-319-46982-9_34

46. Reger, G.: A report of RV-CuBES 2017. In: Reger, G., Havelund, K. (eds.) RV-CuBES 2017. Kalpa Publications in Computing, vol. 3, pp. 1–9. EasyChair (2017)

47. Reger, G., Cruz, H.C., Rydeheard, D.: MARQ: monitoring at runtime with QEA. In: Baier, C., Tinelli, C. (eds.) TACAS 2015. LNCS, vol. 9035, pp. 596–610. Springer, Heidelberg (2015). https://doi.org/10.1007/978-3-662-46681-0_55

48. Reger, G., Hallé, S., Falcone, Y.: Third international competition on runtime verification. In: Falcone, Y., Sánchez, C. (eds.) RV 2016. LNCS, vol. 10012, pp. 21–37. Springer, Cham (2016). https://doi.org/10.1007/978-3-319-46982-9_3

49. Reger, G., Havelund, K. (eds.): RV-CuBES 2017. An International Workshop on Competitions, Usability, Benchmarks, Evaluation, and Standardisation for Runtime Verification Tools, Kalpa Publications in Computing, vol. 3. EasyChair (2017)

50. Reinbacher, T., Rozier, K.Y., Schumann, J.: Temporal-logic based runtime observer pairs for system health management of real-time systems. In: Ábrahám, E., Havelund, K. (eds.) TACAS 2014. LNCS, vol. 8413, pp. 357–372. Springer, Heidelberg (2014). https://doi.org/10.1007/978-3-642-54862-8_24

51. Schumann, J., Moosbrugger, P., Rozier, K.Y.: Runtime analysis with R2U2: a tool exhibition report. In: Falcone, Y., Sánchez, C. (eds.) RV 2016. LNCS, vol. 10012, pp. 504–509. Springer, Cham (2016). https://doi.org/10.1007/978-3-319-46982-9_35

52. Serebryany, K., Iskhodzhanov, T.: ThreadSanitizer: data race detection in practice. In: Proceedings of the Workshop on Binary Instrumentation and Applications, WBIA 2009, pp. 62–71. ACM, New York (2009). https://doi.org/10.1145/1791194.1791203, http://doi.acm.org/10.1145/1791194.1791203
53. Signoles, J., Kosmatov, N., Vorobyov, K.: E-ACSL, a runtime verification tool for safety and security of C programs (tool paper). In: Reger, G., Havelund, K. (eds.) RV-CuBES 2017. Kalpa Publications in Computing, vol. 3, pp. 164–173. EasyChair (2017)
54. Stepanov, E., Serebryany, K.: MemorySanitizer: fast detector of uninitialized memory use in C++. In: Proceedings of the 2015 IEEE/ACM International Symposium on Code Generation and Optimization (CGO), San Francisco, CA, USA, pp. 46–55 (2015)

Verifying and Validating Autonomous Systems: Towards an Integrated Approach

Angelo Ferrando[1], Louise A. Dennis[2], Davide Ancona[1], Michael Fisher[2], and Viviana Mascardi[1(✉)]

[1] Università di Genova, Genova, Italy
{angelo.ferrando,davide.ancona,viviana.mascardi}@dibris.unige.it
[2] Liverpool University, Liverpool, UK
{L.A.Dennis,MFisher}@liverpool.ac.uk

Abstract. When applying formal verification to a system that interacts with the real world we must use a *model* of the environment. This model represents an *abstraction* of the actual environment, but is necessarily incomplete and hence presents an issue for system verification. If the actual environment matches the model, then the verification is correct; however, if the environment falls outside the abstraction captured by the model, then we cannot guarantee that the system is well-behaved. A solution to this problem consists in exploiting the model of the environment for statically verifying the system's behaviour and, if the verification succeeds, using it also for validating the model against the real environment via runtime verification. The paper discusses this approach and demonstrates its feasibility by presenting its implementation on top of a framework integrating the Agent Java PathFinder model checker. Trace expressions are used to model the environment for both static formal verification and runtime verification.

Keywords: Runtime verification · Model checking
Autonomous systems · Trace expressions · MCAPL

1 Introduction

Static formal verification of autonomous systems that interact with the real world requires a model of the world to successfully accomplish the verification process. In [23] we recommended using the simplest environment model, in which any combination of the environmental predicates that correspond to possible perceptions of the autonomous system is possible. Consider an intelligent cruise control in an autonomous vehicle that can perceive the environmental predicates

Work supported by EPSRC as part of the Verifiable Autonomy research project [EP/L024845] and the FAIR-SPACE [EP/R026092], ORCA [EP/R026173], and RAIN [EP/R026084] Robotics and AI Hubs.

safe, meaning it is safe to accelerate, at_speed_limit, meaning that the vehicle reached its speed limit, driver_brakes and driver_accelerates, meaning that the driver is braking/accelerating. In order to formally verify the behaviour of the cruise control agent, we might randomly supply subsets of {safe, at_speed_limit, driver_brakes, driver_accelerates}: the generation of each subset causes branching in the state space exploration during verification so that, ultimately, all possible combinations are explored.

This model is an *unstructured abstraction* of the world, as it makes no specific assumptions about the world behaviour and deals only with the possible incoming perceptions that the system may react to. Unstructured abstractions obviously lead to significant state space explosion. The state space explosion problem can be addressed by making assumptions about the environment. For instance, we might assume that a car can not both brake and accelerate at the same time: subsets of environmental predicates containing both driver_brakes and driver_accelerates should not be supplied to the agent during the static verification stage, as they do not correspond to situations that we believe likely in the actual environment. This *structured abstraction* of the world is grounded on assumptions that help prune the possible perceptions and hence control state space explosion. Structured abstractions have advantages over unstructured ones, provided that the assumptions they rely on are correct. Let us suppose that the cruise control system crashes if the driver is accelerating and braking at the same time. If the subsets of environmental predicates generated to verify it never contain both driver_brakes and driver_accelerates, then the static formal verification succeeds but if one real driver, for whatever reason, operates both the acceleration and brake pedals at the same time, the real system crashes!

In this paper, which extends our AAMAS'18 extended abstract [31], we propose an approach for exploiting the advantages of structured abstractions, while mitigating their risks. Our proposal consists in modelling the structured abstraction in a formalism that can be used both for statically verifying the autonomous system's behaviour via model checking and for validating the model against the real environment by means of runtime verification (RV). If performed during a testing stage, RV of the actual environment against its structured abstraction allows the developer to identify situations not foreseen in the initial assumptions. He/she can revise them, generate a new structured abstraction, re-verify it via model checking, re-validate it via RV once again, reaching in the end a "safe" abstraction. If RV takes place after system deployment and assumption violations are detected, mechanisms for handing control to a human, a failsafe system, or for performing ad hoc reasoning about the current system safety should be invoked. To demonstrate the feasibility of the proposed approach, we implemented it on top of the MCAPL framework developed by Dennis, Fisher, et al. [21,24] (which provides a model-checker for rational agents) using trace expressions developed by Ancona, Ferrando, Mascardi, et al. [3,10,11] as the single formalism to generate both the environment model and the runtime monitor. We choose trace expressions instead of more widely used formalisms for model checking like Linear Temporal Logic (LTL [39]) because of their expressive power. In our previous work [10], we demonstrated that trace expressions are able to express and verify sets of traces that are context-free. When working in a RV scenario, trace expressions are more expressive than LTL. In this paper we keep the presentation as simple as possible and do not stress the potential of such expressive power. However, this power opens up interesting scenarios discussed in the conclusions.

2 Related Work

The growing popularity of model checking in industry is due to the possibility of transforming domain-specific input models familiar to the developers into "under the hood models" invisible to them and amenable to model checking using existing techniques [36]. The idea behind this work is similar: we use trace expressions as the front-end formalism suitable for modeling behaviour patterns in systems made up of autonomous entities [4,5,30] and we transform them into under the hood models suitable for both model checking and runtime verification (RV). The main difference is that trace expressions are not domain-specific, and although initially devised for modeling protocols in multiagent system (MASs), they have been successfully adopted for specifying different kinds of behavioural patterns, including interactions among objects in Java-like programs [7] and Internet of Things applications developed with Node.js [12]. This is both a strength and a weakness: a customised formalism for different domains would make it more usable by domain experts, at the cost of some loss in generality.

"Enabling sufficiently precise yet tractable verification" with models – be they explicit or under the hood – of the real environment is a main issue [46]. Developing "safe" structured abstractions of the environment (also named "environment models") for model checking that are sufficiently precise to enable effective reasoning yet not so over-restrictive that they mask faulty system behaviours has been understood as a significant challenge since the early 2000s [38]. The Bandera Environment Generator [46] is a toolset that automates the generation of environments to provide a restricted form of modular model checking of Java programs. Although the addressed problem is the same as ours, the approach is different. We do not automatically generate "safe by construction" trace expressions starting from observations of the environment. Rather, we manually design and implement a trace expression encoding our assumptions and validate it against the real environment to empirically show that it is "safe". Although our approach requires a more accurate design stage and more manual work, it can be applied to any system and environment; the automatic generation of the environment model is instead inherently domain-dependent, and the Bandera Environment Generator is in fact customized for model checking Java programs. The approach of Dhaussy et al. [27] is closer to ours; the state space explosion is mitigated with requirements relative to scenarios which are verified instead of the full environment. In that work the context – corresponding to our structured abstraction – is modelled with the domain-specific Context Description Language, CDL. The main difference is that CDL is less expressive than trace expressions (recursion and concatenation are not supported), and no methodology for checking the CDL specification against the real environment is discussed. In a similar way, in [25] Desai et al. present a framework to combine model checking and runtime verification for robotic applications. They represent the discrete model of their system using the P language [26], check the model and extract the assumptions deriving from such abstraction. Despite sharing the same purpose, our work is not committed to any specific case study and trace expressions are more expressive than STL specifications [35] used in [25]. Besides CDL, hybrid automata [2,32] are another widely adopted formalism for precise modelling of the real world. They do not solve the question of whether the model accurately captures the environment, and although RV of cyber-physical systems modelled with hybrid automata is a lively and promising research field [37,45], we are not aware of proposals where the same hybrid automaton model undergoes both a model checking and a RV process.

Investigation of model checking for MASs dates back to 1998 [13] and has continued to generate much follow up work, for instance the Model Checking Agent Programming Languages project which involves two authors of this paper (http://cgi.csc.liv.ac.uk/MCAPL/, [15,24]), and works by Lomuscio and Raimondi [34,41]. Approaches to MAS RV complement these and include the proposals spun off from the SOCS project where the SCIFF computational logic framework [1] is used to provide the semantics of social integrity constraints. To model MAS interaction, expectation-based semantics specifies the links between observed and expected events, providing a means to test run-time conformance of an actual conversation with respect to a given interaction protocol [47]. Similar work has been performed using commitments [18]. A more recent strand is related to the exploitation of trace expressions for MAS RV and monitoring, along with their ancestor formalism [6]. None of the contributions above tackles the problem of recognising assumption violations in structured abstractions via RV, for model checking autonomous systems immersed in a real environment. This makes our proposal original in the panorama of model checking both "in general" and, more specifically, for autonomous systems and MASs.

3   Background and Running Example

MCAPL: Model Checking BDI Agents. The belief-desire-intention (BDI) model, originally proposed by Bratman [16] as a philosophical theory of the practical reasoning, inspired both architectures [43] and programming languages [14,40,44] for agents. BDI languages are based on *rational agency* [42]. Beliefs represent the agent's (possibly incorrect) information about its environment, desires represent the agent's long-term goals, and intentions represent the goals that the agent is actively pursuing. The MCAPL framework [21,24] supports model checking of programs in BDI-style languages via the implementation of interpreters for those languages in Java. The framework implements *program model-checking* in which the *actual* program to be verified, not a model of it, is checked, and contains the Agent Java PathFinder (AJPF) model checker which customises the Java PathFinder (JPF) model checker for Java bytecodes (https://babelfish.arc.nasa.gov/trac/jpf). We use the "Engineering Autonomous Space Software" (EASS) variant of GWENDOLEN [20], a language developed for programming agent-based autonomous systems and verifying them in AJPF. EASS assumes an architecture in which the rational agents are partnered with an *abstraction engine* that discretises continuous information from sensors in an explicit fashion [19, 22]. We adopt the methodology from [23] setting out the formal verification of rational agent components in autonomous systems. This uses model checking to demonstrate that the rational agent always tries to act in line with requirements and never *deliberately* chooses options that lead to states the agent believes to be unsafe.

Running Example: Autonomous Cruise Control. The (slightly simplified) EASS code in Example 1 is for an agent implementing intelligent cruise control in an autonomous vehicle. It uses standard syntactic conventions from BDI agent languages: +!g indicates the addition of a goal, g; +b indicates the addition of a belief, b; and −b indicates the removal of a belief. Plans follow the pattern trigger : guard ← body;. The trigger is the addition of a goal or a belief (beliefs may be acquired thanks to the operation of perception or as a result of internal deliberation); the guard states conditions about the agent's beliefs which must be true before the plan can become active; and the body is a stack of *deeds* the agent performs in order to execute the plan. These deeds typically involve the addition or deletion of goals and beliefs, as well as *actions* (e.g. perf(accelerate), meaning "perform the action of accelerating") which indicate code delegated to non-rational parts of the system.

According to the operational semantics of GWENDOLEN [20], the agent moves through a *reasoning cycle* polling an external environment for perceptions; converting these into beliefs and creating intentions from new beliefs; selecting an intention for consideration; if the intention has no associated plan body, then the agent seeks a plan that matches the trigger event and places the body of this plan on the deed stack; the agent then processes the first deed, and places the intention at the end of the intention queue before again performing perception. As an intention may be suspended while it waits for some belief to become true, we use *b to indicate a deed that suspends processing of an intention until b is believed. Plan guards are evaluated using Prolog-style reasoning with *reasoning rules* of the form h :− body and literals drawn from agent's belief base. Negation is indicated with ~ and its semantics is negation by failure as in Prolog. All of this is part of the standard Gwendolen semantics.

Example 1 *(Cruise Control Agent). When the car has an initial goal to be at the speed limit, +! at_speed_limit, it can accelerate if it believes it to be safe, that there are no incoming instructions from the human driver, and it does not already believe it is accelerating or is at the speed limit — it does this by removing any belief that it is braking, adding a belief that it is accelerating, performing acceleration, then waiting until it no longer believes it is accelerating. If it does not believe it is safe, believes the driver is accelerating or braking, or believes it*

*is already accelerating, then it waits for the situation to change. If it believes it
is at the speed limit, it maintains its speed having achieved its goal (which will
be dropped automatically, having been achieved).*

*If new beliefs arrive from the environment that the car is at the speed limit, no
longer at the speed limit, no longer safe, or the driver has accelerated or braked,
then it reacts appropriately. Note that even if the driver is trying to accelerate,
the agent only does so if it is safe.*

```
:Reasoning Rules:                                                          1
can_accelerate :− safe, ~ driver_accelerates, ~ driver_brakes;             2
                                                                           3
:Initial Goals:                                                            4
at_speed_limit                                                             5
                                                                           6
:Plans:                                                                    7
+! at_speed_limit: {can_accelerate, ~accelerating, ~at_speed_lim}          8
    ← −braking, +accelerating, perf(accelerate), *~accelerating;           9
+! at_speed_limit: {~safe} ← *safe;                                        10
+! at_speed_limit: {driver_accelerates} ← *~driver_accelerates;            11
+! at_speed_limit: {driver_brakes} ← *~driver_brakes;                      12
+! at_speed_limit: {accelerating} ← *~accelerating;                        13
+at_speed_lim: {can_accelerate, at_speed_lim}                              14
    ← −accelerating, −braking, perf(maintain_speed);                       15
−at_speed_lim: {~at_speed_lim} ← +! at_speed_limit;                        16
−safe: {~driver_brakes, ~safe, ~braking} ← −accelerating, +braking,        17
    perf(brake);                                                           18
+driver_accelerates: {safe, ~driver_brakes, driver_accelerates, ~accelerating}  19
    ← +accelerating, −braking, perf(accelerate);                          20
+driver_brakes: {driver_brakes, ~braking} ← +braking, −accelerating,       21
    perf(brake);                                                           22
```

The cruise control agent has to be connected to either a physical vehicle or
a simulation. Similar EASS agents have been connected to both detailed simulations of ground vehicles and physical vehicles [22,33]. Here we will consider
embedding the agent within a multi-lane, multi-vehicle motorway (highway) simulation. The agent is connected to the simulator via a *thin Java environment*
that communicates using sockets. The environment reads simulated speeds of
the vehicles from the socket and publishes values for acceleration to the socket.
The information from sensors is then passed on to an *abstraction engine* that
converts it to discrete representations, shared with the rational agent as logical
predicates. The rational agent accesses these *shared beliefs* as perceptions. Previously, the model of the combined behaviour of simulator, thin Java environment,
and abstraction engine used for verification was unstructured: all the possible
combinations of the shared beliefs were explored. This is where our proposal for
modeling structured abstractions as trace expressions and validating them via
RV, as well as using them for model checking, comes into play.

Trace Expressions. Trace expressions are a specification formalism specifically
designed for RV and constrain the ways in which a stream of events may occur.
An *event trace* over a fixed universe of events $\mathcal{E}$ is a (possibly infinite) sequence
of events from $\mathcal{E}$. The *juxtaposition*, $e\,u$, denotes the trace where e is the first
event, and u is the rest of the trace. A trace expression (over $\mathcal{E}$) denotes a set of
event traces over $\mathcal{E}$. More generally, trace expressions are built on top of event

types (chosen from a set $\mathcal{ET}$), rather than single events; an event type denotes a subset of $\mathcal{E}$. A *trace expression*, τ, represents a set of possibly infinite event traces, and is defined on top of the following operators:

- ε, the set containing only the empty event trace.
- $\vartheta{:}\tau$ (*prefix*), denoting the set of all traces whose first event e matches the event type ϑ ($e \in \vartheta$), and the remaining part is a trace of τ.
- $\tau_1{\cdot}\tau_2$ (*concatenation*), denoting the set of all traces obtained by concatenating the traces of τ_1 with those of τ_2.
- $\tau_1{\wedge}\tau_2$ (*intersection*), the intersection of traces τ_1 and τ_2.
- $\tau_1{\vee}\tau_2$ (*union*), denoting the union of traces of τ_1 and τ_2.
- $\tau_1{|}\tau_2$ (*shuffle*), denoting the union of the sets obtained by shuffling each trace of τ_1 with each trace of τ_2 (see [17] for a more precise definition).
- $\vartheta{\gg}\tau$ (*filter*), denoting the set of all traces contained in τ, when "deprived" of all events that do not match ϑ.

Trace expressions can be easily represented as Prolog terms. To support recursion without introducing an explicit construct, trace expressions are regular (a.k.a. rational or cyclic) terms which can be represented by a finite set of syntactic equations, as happens in most modern Prolog implementations where unification supports cyclic terms. The semantics of trace expressions is specified by the transition relation $\delta \subseteq \mathcal{T} \times \mathcal{E} \times \mathcal{T}$, where $\mathcal{T}$ denotes the sets of trace expressions. As customary, we write $\tau_1 \overset{e}{\to} \tau_2$ to mean $(\tau_1, e, \tau_2) \in \delta$. If the trace expression τ_1 specifies the current valid state of the system, then an event e is valid *iff* there exists a transition $\tau_1 \overset{e}{\to} \tau_2$; in such a case, τ_2 specifies the next valid state of the system after event e. Otherwise, the event e is not valid in τ_1. The rules for the transition functions are presented in [10]. A Prolog implementation exists which allows a system's developer to use trace expressions for RV by automatically building a trace expression-driven monitor able to both observe events taking place in the environment, and execute the δ transition rules. If the observed event is allowed in the current state – which is represented by a trace expression itself – it is consumed and the δ transition function generates a new trace expression representing the updated current state. If, on observing an event, no δ transition can be performed, the event is not allowed in the current state. In this situation an error is "thrown" by the monitor. When a system terminates, if the trace expression representing the current state can halt (formally meaning that it contains the empty trace), the RV process ends successfully; otherwise an error is again "thrown" since the system should not stop here.

AJPF Static Formal Verification. The EASS implementation provides a Java class supporting the creation of abstract models. Unstructured abstractions can be created by overriding in a *subclass* its method **add_random_beliefs** which is called when the agent requests an action execution or sleeps. This method should generate a set of beliefs and add them to the environment's *percept base* which the agent then polls. It is assumed this implementation will randomly generate all possible sub-sets of the shared beliefs relevant to the agent. For static verification, therefore, we want to generate this subclass from our trace expression.

In normal operation, EASS abstraction engines communicate with the agent-based reasoning engine (the 'agent') by performing assert_belief and remove_belief actions. These actions are implemented by Java environments which also connect to sensors and simulators. There are four such actions: assert_belief(b) asserts a shared belief for all agents and remove_belief(b) removes shared belief b from all agents. assert_belief(a, b) and remove_belief(a, b) alter the available beliefs for a specific agent a. For reasons of space we do not describe these further. Our runtime monitor needs to observe these events. We are also interested in any action performed by an agent, so our runtime monitor must also observe calls to the executeAction method that all EASS environments implement.

4   Recognising Assumption Violations

In this section we discuss how trace expressions can be suitably adopted for specifying structured abstractions of the real world for use in AJPF. The idea is to generate *both* a suitable Java model for AJPF model checking *and* a runtime monitor from the same trace expression. The monitor can detect if the real (or simulated) environment violates the assumptions used during the static verification. Figure 1 gives an overview of this system. A trace expression τ is used to generate an abstract model in Java used to verify an agent in AJPF (the dotted box on the right of the Figure). Once this verification is successfully completed, the verified agent is used with an abstraction engine, a thin Java environment, and the real world or external simulator. This is shown in the dotted box on the left of the Figure. If, at any point, the monitor observes an inconsistent event, then the abstraction used during verification was incorrect. Depending on the development stage reached so far different measures will be possible, ranging from refining the trace expression and re-executing the verification-validation steps, to involving a human or a failsafe system in the loop.

Event Types for AJPF Environments. We have identified the assertion and removal of shared beliefs and the performance of actions as the "events of interest" in our Java environments. Our runtime monitor receives notification of all actions in the environment as events. It is possible to flexibly create a number of different event types (we remind that an event type is a set of events) on top of this structure: $bel(b)$ and $not\_bel(b)$ are singleton sets and model events involving shared beliefs. They are defined as $bel(b) = \{assert\_belief(b)\}$ and $not\_bel(b) = \{remove\_belief(b)\}$. We coalesce these as event set $\mathcal{E}_b$ and define event types $action(any\_action)$ where $e \in action(any\_action)$ iff $e \notin \mathcal{E}_b$; not_action where $e \in not\_action$ iff $e \in \mathcal{E}_b$; $action(A)$ where $e \in action(A)$ iff $e \notin \mathcal{E}_b$ and $e = A$. Clearly, $e \in \mathcal{E}_b$ and $e = A$ are mutually exclusive.

Representing Abstract Models in AJPF. Abstract models in AJPF can be represented as automata. The automaton states can be divided into two parts: *initial beliefs* and *actions*. Initial Beliefs represent all the shared beliefs that may be asserted before the system starts executing. After an action is performed, more shared beliefs may be asserted. In the unstructured abstractions used by

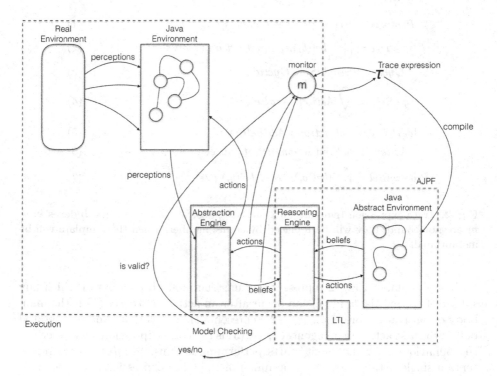

Fig. 1. General view.

the "standard" AJPF system the initial beliefs, and the beliefs after each action, were generated at random. Any structured abstraction will be one that places constraints upon the possible transitions in the automaton.

Representing Abstract Models as Trace Expressions. We represent an abstract model of the real world as a set of possibly cyclic trace expressions modelled in Prolog. The basic structure of the Prolog code is given in Fig. 2. We abuse regular expression syntax: as parentheses are used for grouping in trace expressions, we adopt [and] to represent groupings within a regular expression; similarly, since | is a trace expression operator, we use || to indicate alternatives within the regular expression. Here, $e?$ indicates zero or one occurrences of the element e. As we use Prolog, variables are represented by terms starting with an upper case letter (e.g., $Action_i$) and constants are represented by terms starting with a lower case letter (e.g., b_i, $action_i$). $\Big|_{i=1}^{n}$ indicates one or more trace expressions composed via the trace expression shuffle operator, $|$. Similarly, $\bigvee_{i=1}^{n}$ composes expressions using $\vee$ and $\bigwedge_{i=1}^{n}$ composes expressions using $\wedge$. Variables with the same name will be unified. Occurrences of Pre in (1) and (2) are intended to unify, and the variable names used in these positions in any instantiation of this template should be the same. Pre is needed to model (optional) constraints on the beliefs that can be observed before the first action takes place, and the trace expression cycle ($Cyclic$) starts.

$$Protocol = Pre \cdot (Cyclic\,[\wedge Constrs]?) \tag{1}$$

$$Pre = [\;\Big|_{i=1}^{n}\; bel(b_i){:}\epsilon]\;\|\;[not\_action : Pre\vee\epsilon] \tag{2}$$

$$Cyclic = SingleStep \cdot Cyclic \tag{3}$$

$$SingleStep = \bigvee_{i=1}^{m} Action_i \cdot AddBelEv \tag{4}$$

$$AddBelEv = not\_action : AddBelEv\vee\epsilon \tag{5}$$

$$Action_i = action(action_i){:}ProtocolBel \tag{6}$$

$$ProtocolBel = \Big|_{i=1}^{k}\;(bel(b_i){:}\epsilon\vee not\_bel(b_i){:}\epsilon\vee\epsilon) \tag{7}$$

Fig. 2. Trace expression template for generating abstract environments. Indexes k, n, m are not bound: they will be replaced by actual numbers when the template will be instantiated.

The template in Fig. 2 represents an unstructured abstraction in which any subset of the beliefs, b_i in (7) can occur after an action. *Protocol* (1) is the main body of our trace expression. *Pre* (2) represents all events that can be generated before the first action of an agent. *Cyclic* (3) is the trace expression that describes the behaviour once the agent starts performing actions. *SingleStep* (4) represents a single action step. It is the union of the trace expressions that describe the possible results of each action the agent may take followed by *AddBelEv* which describes additional belief events after the immediate results of the action – for instance if the agent sleeps and other agents are acting. *Action* (6) consists of an action event followed by *ProtocolBel* (7) which describes the possible belief events. Any given belief, b_i may appear in the shared belief base ($bel(b_i)$), disappear ($not\_bel(b_i)$) or its status may be unchanged (ϵ).

Figure 2 contains an optional variable *Constrs*. If present this provides *constraints* that structure the abstraction. The template for constraints is shown in Fig. 3. *Constrs* consists of an intersection of trace expressions of the form $FilterEventType_j \gg C_j^x$. It appears at the top level of the trace expression in an intersection ($\wedge$) with the repeating *Cyclic* step. This allows us to put constraints on belief events without considering at which action step they occur. In this way,

$$Constrs = \bigwedge_{j=1}^{o} FilterEventType_j \gg [C_j^1 \;\|\; C_j^2] \tag{8}$$

$$C_j^1 = (((B_{j,1}{:}\epsilon) \vee (NB_{j,2}{:}\epsilon)) \cdot C_j^1) \vee (NB_{j,1} : C_j^2) \tag{9}$$

$$C_j^2 = (((NB_{j,1}{:}\epsilon) \vee (NB_{j,2}{:}\epsilon)) \cdot C_j^2) \vee$$
$$(B_{j,1}{:}C_j^1) \vee (B_{j,2}{:}C_j^3) \tag{10}$$

$$C_j^3 = (((B_{j,2}{:}\epsilon) \vee (NB_{j,1}{:}\epsilon)) \cdot C_j^3) \vee (NB_{j,2} : C_j^2) \tag{11}$$

Fig. 3. Trace expressions for Constrs: $B_{j,i}$ must be the "opposite operation" of $NB_{j,i}$.

each time a constrained belief event is observed in a *SingleStep*, we can keep track of the fact. $B_{j,i}$ and $NB_{j,i}$ are event types, and they must meet the condition (not modeled in Fig. 3) that if $B_{j,i} = bel(b_{j,i})$ then $NB_{j,i} = not\_bel(b_{j,i})$ and vice versa. *FilterEventType$_j$* is an event type which denotes only the events involved in C_j^x. Its purpose is to filter out any events that are not constrained by C_j^x, and matches $bel(b_{j,1})$, $not\_bel(b_{j,1})$, $bel(b_{j,2})$ and $not\_bel(b_{j,2})$. It ensures that the trace expression can move to the next state without getting stuck.

Each constraint represents a pairwise relationship between two belief events. These are captured by the three trace expressions in (9), (10) and (11) which describe the evolving behaviour of the four belief events of interest where $B_{j,i}$ is either the assertion or removal of $b_{j,i}$ and $NB_{j,i}$ is its converse. The three equations capture the constraint that if $B_{j,1}$ has occurred then $B_{j,2}$ can not occur until after $NB_{j,1}$ has been observed and vice versa. The constraint either starts in the state described by C_j^1 or C_j^2 depending upon whether only one of the constrained belief events is possible in the initial state (C_j^1) or both are (C_j^2).

Abstract Model Generation. Once we have created a trace expression, we translate it into Java by implementing **add_random_beliefs**. We omit the involved low level details (e.g., constructing appropriate class and package names) but just focus on the core aspects[1]. Our trace expression is defined according to the template in Figs. 2 and 3. Many parts of these trace expressions are not directly translated into Java; the sub-expressions relevant to the generation of abstract models are *Pre* (2), *SingleStep* (4) and *Constrs* (8). Note that the MCAPL framework provides support for constructing logical predicates and adding them to the belief base.

If *Pre* specifies particular initial beliefs then the subclass adds these to the agent's belief base at the start. *SingleStep* contains a union of trace expressions of the form $Action = action(action\_name):ProtocolBel$. $ProtocolBel = |_{i=1}^k$ $(bel(b_i) \lor not\_bel(b_i) \lor \epsilon)$ defines the set of belief events that may occur. We define the set $\mathcal{B}(ProtocolBel)$ as $b_i \in \mathcal{B}(ProtocolBel)$ iff $(bel(b_i) \lor not\_bel(b_i) \lor \epsilon)$ is one of the interleaved trace expressions in *ProtocolBel*. For each $b_i \in \mathcal{B}(ProtocolBel)$ we define a predicate in the environment class and bind it to a Java field called b_i. *Constrs* constrains events by specifying mutual exclusion between some couples of them. For each *Action* trace expression we generate a corresponding *if statement* inside the **add_random_beliefs** method.

```
if(act.getFunctor().equals("action_name")) { translation(ProtocolBel,Constrs) }    1
```

We construct a set of mutually exclusive belief events, $\mathcal{M}_x(Constrs)$, from *Constrs* where $(B_{j,1}, B_{j,2}) \in \mathcal{M}_x(Constrs)$ iff *FilterEventType$_j$* $\gg$ *Constraint$_j$* is one of the conjuncts of *Constrs* and $C_j^1 = (((B_{j,1}:\epsilon) \lor (NB_{j,2}:\epsilon)) \cdot C_j^1) \lor (NB_{j,1} : C_j^2)$ and $C_j^3 = (((B_{j,2}:\epsilon) \lor (NB_{j,1}:\epsilon)) \cdot C_j^3) \lor (NB_{j,2} : C_j^2)$.

---

[1] Full source code can be found in the MCAPL distribution: mcapl.sourceforge.net. Code for the examples is also available from the University of Liverpool together with experimental data – DOI: https://doi.org/10.17638/datacat.liverpool.ac.uk/438.

The set of possible sets of belief events for our structured environment is:

$$\mathcal{PB}(ProtocolBel, Constrs) = \{S \mid (\forall b_i \in \mathcal{B}(ProtocolBel). \; bel(b_i) \in S \lor not\_bel(b_i) \in S)$$
$$\land(\forall(B_1, B_2) \in \mathcal{M}_x(Constrs). \; B_1 \in S \leftrightarrow B_2 \notin S)\} \quad (12)$$

Say that $\mathcal{PB}(ProtocolBel, Constrs)$ contains k sets of belief events, S_j, $0 \leq j < k$. We generate $translation(ProtocolBel, Constrs)$, as follows:

```
int assert_random_int = random_int_generator(k);                              1
```

where random_int_generator is a special method that generates random integers in a way that optimises the model checking in AJPF. For each S_j we generate

```
if (assert_random_int == j) { add_percepts(S_j) }                             1
```

Here $add\_percepts(S_j)$ adds b_i to the percept base for each $bel(b_i) \in S_j$. We do not need to handle the belief removal events, $not\_bel(b_i) \in S_j$, because AJPF automatically removes all percepts before calling add_random_beliefs.

5   Case Study and Experiments

Figures 4 and 5 show the trace expression modeling the cruise control agent from Example 1. *Pre* is reused for *AddBelEnv* since, in this case, they are the same trace expression. *SingleStep* contains only one branch which matches any action. *ProtocolBel* specifies that the possible belief events are the assertion and removal of *safe*, *at_speed_lim*, *driver_accelerates* and *driver_brakes*.

We have two constraints. Firstly we assume that the driver never brakes and accelerates at the same time. This establishes a mutual exclusion

$$Protocol = Pre \cdot (Cyclic \land Constrs) \qquad (13)$$
$$Pre = ((not\_action{:}Pre) \lor \epsilon) \qquad (14)$$
$$Cyclic = SingleStep \cdot Cyclic \qquad (15)$$
$$SingleStep = action(any\_action){:}(ProtocolBel \cdot Pre) \qquad (16)$$
$$Safe = ((bel(safe){:}\epsilon) \lor (not\_bel(safe){:}\epsilon) \lor \epsilon) \qquad (17)$$
$$AtSpeedLimit = ((bel(at\_speed\_lim){:}\epsilon) \lor$$
$$(not\_bel(at\_speed\_lim){:}\epsilon) \lor \epsilon) \qquad (18)$$
$$Accel = ((bel(driver\_accelerates){:}\epsilon) \lor$$
$$(not\_bel(driver\_accelerates){:}\epsilon) \lor \epsilon) \qquad (19)$$
$$Brakes = ((bel(driver\_brakes){:}\epsilon) \lor$$
$$(not\_bel(driver\_brakes){:}\epsilon) \lor \epsilon) \qquad (20)$$
$$ProtocolBel = (Safe \mid AtSpeedLimit \mid Accel \mid Brakes) \qquad (21)$$

Fig. 4. Trace expression for a Cruise Control Agent.

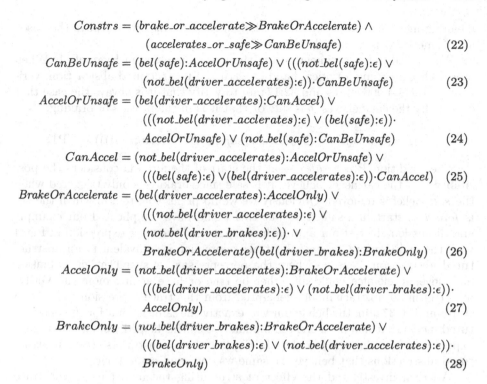

$$Constrs = (brake\_or\_accelerate \gg BrakeOrAccelerate) \wedge$$
$$(accelerates\_or\_safe \gg CanBeUnsafe) \tag{22}$$
$$CanBeUnsafe = (bel(safe){:}AccelOrUnsafe) \vee (((not\_bel(safe){:}\epsilon) \vee$$
$$(not\_bel(driver\_accelerates){:}\epsilon)){\cdot}CanBeUnsafe) \tag{23}$$
$$AccelOrUnsafe = (bel(driver\_accelerates){:}CanAccel) \vee$$
$$(((not\_bel(driver\_acclerates){:}\epsilon) \vee (bel(safe){:}\epsilon)){\cdot}$$
$$AccelOrUnsafe) \vee (not\_bel(safe){:}CanBeUnsafe) \tag{24}$$
$$CanAccel = (not\_bel(driver\_accelerates){:}AccelOrUnsafe) \vee$$
$$(((bel(safe){:}\epsilon) \vee (bel(driver\_accelerates){:}\epsilon)){\cdot}CanAccel) \tag{25}$$
$$BrakeOrAccelerate = (bel(driver\_accelerates){:}AccelOnly) \vee$$
$$(((not\_bel(driver\_accelerates){:}\epsilon) \vee$$
$$(not\_bel(driver\_brakes){:}\epsilon)){\cdot} \vee$$
$$BrakeOrAccelerate)(bel(driver\_brakes){:}BrakeOnly) \tag{26}$$
$$AccelOnly = (not\_bel(driver\_accelerates){:}BrakeOrAccelerate) \vee$$
$$(((bel(driver\_accelerates){:}\epsilon) \vee (not\_bel(driver\_brakes){:}\epsilon)){\cdot}$$
$$AccelOnly) \tag{27}$$
$$BrakeOnly = (not\_bel(driver\_brakes){:}BrakeOrAccelerate) \vee$$
$$(((bel(driver\_brakes){:}\epsilon) \vee (not\_bel(driver\_accelerates){:}\epsilon)){\cdot}$$
$$BrakeOnly) \tag{28}$$

Fig. 5. Trace expression for the Constraints on a Car where the driver only accelerates when it is safe to do so, and never uses both brake and acceleration pedal together.

between $bel(driver\_accelerates)$ and $bel(driver\_brakes)$. Initially either belief may appear. Secondly, we assume the driver only accelerates if it is safe to do so. This establishes a mutual exclusion between $bel(driver\_accelerates)$ and $not\_bel(safe)$. Initially we are in the state were we cannot observe $bel(driver\_accelerates)$. $brake\_or\_accelerate$ and $accelerates\_or\_safe$ are event types that match the relevant events for each constraint.

MCAPL Runtime Verification. Since the MCAPL framework is implemented in Java, its integration with the trace expressions runtime verification engine or "monitor" (namely, the Prolog engine that "executes" the δ transitions) was easy using the JPL interface, http://jpl7.org, between Java and Prolog. In order to verify a trace expression τ modelled in Prolog, we supply the runtime verification engine with Prolog representations of the events taking place in the environment. These are easily obtained from the abstraction engine and the Java environment that links to sensors and actuators. The Java environment reports instances of assert_shared_belief, remove_shared_belief and executeAction to the runtime verification engine which checks if the event is compliant with the current state of the modelled environment and reports any *violations* that occur during execution. AJPF's property specification language uses LTL extended with modalities for BDI concepts such as beliefs ($B(a,b)$ is interpreted as meaning agent a believes b). In this language $\Box$ means "it is always the case" and $\Diamond$ means "it is eventually the case".

We carried out experiments using the agent discussed in Example 1. When model checked using a typical hand-constructed unstructured abstraction, verification takes 4,906 states and 32:17 min to verify that it is always the case that eventually the car believes it is safe or that it is in the process of braking:

$$\Box(B(car, safe) \rightarrow \Box(\Diamond(B(car, safe) \vee B(car, braking)))) \quad (P1)$$

The condition $B(car, safe) \rightarrow$ at the start of the formula considers the possibility that the car never believes it is safe since braking is only triggered when the *safe* belief is removed. Obviously we would prefer a system in which the car is *forced* to start in a safe state but this would have complicated our example and discussion. To test our approach, we first used the trace expression in Fig. 4 with the omission of *Constrs*: this trace expression is equivalent to an unstructured abstraction, i.e., one where the percepts safe, at_speed_lim, driver_brakes, and driver_accelerates could all either be true or false at any moment. Verifying (P1) in an abstract model generated from this trace expression took 4,906 states and 30:37 min: the behaviour was exactly the same as that for the unstructured model that had been created manually, and this helped validate that trace expressions following the template in Fig. 2 without constraints create unstructured abstractions that behave the same way as hand crafted ones.

We then investigated the effect of structuring the model using the trace expression in Fig. 5, which adds constraints to that in Fig. 4. With this abstraction (P1) takes 8:22 min to prove using 1,677 states – this has more than halved the time and the state space.

To illustrate how we cope with the risk that a structured abstraction may not reflect reality, we consider a version of the cruise control agent with slight variations. It is widely considered important that an autonomous vehicle *should not* be able to override the actions of a driver. In our previous example the vehicle violates this rule – it would only let the driver accelerate if it was safe to do so, and it would brake *whenever* it detected unsafe conditions even if the driver was currently trying to accelerate. We adapted the program, removing these restrictions. This modified program could *not* be verified in the unstructured model because our property is *not* actually true in that model – if the driver continually accelerates in an unsafe situation then the car can *never* brake. However, it is true in the structured model which assumes that the driver never accelerates if the situation is unsafe. When we run this program in our simulator it is indeed possible to cause a crash by accelerating in unsafe conditions. This is where the runtime verification engine fits in. The engine logs an exception at the moment when the unsafe acceleration takes place. It generates the error message shown below and also shows the current state of the trace expression, which is the equivalent of (23) in Fig. 5.

```
*** DYNAMIC TYPE–CHECKING ERROR ***
Message event(abstraction_car0 , assert_shared(driver_accelerates))
cannot be accepted in the current state

S_8=(bel(safe):S_6)\/((not_bel(safe):epsilon)\/
      (not_bel(driver_accelerates):epsilon))*S_8])
```

This identifies the system as now being in an unverified state, as this acceleration has violated the trace expression. The example shows how we have addressed the development of a principled mechanism for creating structured abstractions in a way that allows us to provide at least some guarantee of the validity of our results.

6   Conclusions and Future Work

In this paper, we have shown how trace expressions can be used as a unifying formalism to generate both a structured abstraction for model checking and a runtime monitor, providing a route for guarantees of the behaviour of a system that has been verified against an abstract model of the real world. Their expressive power would pave the way to addressing challenging scenarios where:

1. the behaviour of the system is modeled with a trace expression τ without expressive power limitations (for example, an expression representing the set of all $a^n b^n$ traces, for any $n \in \mathbb{N}$; this set of traces cannot be modeled in LTL) to allow specifications of complex environments;
2. τ is over-approximated by a Java model as shown in [28];
3. the model checking stage is performed using the generated over-approximating Java model;
4. the runtime verification stage uses τ, with all its expressive power; empirical results show that in most cases verifying whether a trace belongs to the language defined by a trace expression is linear in the length of the trace: this means that – even when the highest modeling expressiveness of the formalism is exploited – performances of RV remain acceptable.

In the future, we aim to provide arguments (ideally proofs) that the behaviour of the abstract environments generated by the system genuinely expresses the behaviour specified by the trace expressions, also in case of noise and uncertainties in the formation of beliefs. We recently started working on partial observability of events [8], which is related to noise and uncertainty, and we plan to adapt and integrate the achieved results in the Verification and Validation framework presented in this paper. We also point out that discovering a violation does not necessarily mean that the system is in danger: for example, braking and accelerating at the same time – although tagged as a violation during the RV stage – might not cause the system to crash. Although discriminating between safety-critical violations and acceptable ones was out of the scope of this paper, it is a significant issues and deserves further exploration. We will also explore how to express a greater range of constraints in these models – for instance, the constraint that some belief can only occur after some action is taken (e.g., that a car can only reach the speed limit after an acceleration has been performed).

From the practical side, we are currently designing a user friendly language for specifying trace expressions, as the current formalism is not easy to read and write for a human, and we will extend RIVERtools [9,29] to support the simplified notation. We also plan to apply our approach to a real case study. The scenario we have in mind is a cyberphysical system which must demonstrate its dependability in order to be acceptable to society and be trusted by its users. As an example, in a remote patient monitoring system where the program integrates sensory input, formal guarantees should be provided that the system respects given medical guidelines (model checking stage), and a RV stage looking at sensors perceptions should monitor that those guidelines are continuously met.

References

1. Alberti, M., Gavanelli, M., Lamma, E., Mello, P., Torroni, P.: The SCIFF abductive proof-procedure. In: Proceedings of the 9th Congress of the Italian Association for Artificial Intelligence, AI*IA 2005, pp. 135–147 (2005)
2. Alur, R., Henzinger, T.A., Lafferriere, G., Pappas, G.J.: Discrete abstractions of hybrid systems. Proc. IEEE **88**(7), 971–984 (2000)
3. Ancona, D., Barbieri, M., Mascardi, V.: Constrained global types for dynamic checking of protocol conformance in multi-agent systems. In: Proceedings of the 28th Annual ACM Symposium on Applied Computing, SAC 2013, pp. 1377–1379 (2013)
4. Ancona, D., Briola, D., Ferrando, A., Mascardi, V.: Global protocols as first class entities for self-adaptive agents. In: Proceedings of the 2015 International Conference on Autonomous Agents and Multiagent Systems, AAMAS 2015, pp. 1019–1029 (2015)
5. Ancona, D., Briola, D., Ferrando, A., Mascardi, V.: Runtime verification of fail-uncontrolled and ambient intelligence systems: a uniform approach. Intelligenza Artificiale **9**(2), 131–148 (2015)
6. Ancona, D., Drossopoulou, S., Mascardi, V.: Automatic generation of self-monitoring MASs from multiparty global session types in Jason. In: Baldoni, M., Dennis, L., Mascardi, V., Vasconcelos, W. (eds.) DALT 2012. LNCS (LNAI), vol. 7784, pp. 76–95. Springer, Heidelberg (2013). https://doi.org/10.1007/978-3-642-37890-4_5
7. Ancona, D., Ferrando, A., Franceschini, L., Mascardi, V.: Parametric trace expressions for runtime verification of Java-like programs. In: Proceedings of the 19th Workshop on Formal Techniques for Java-like Programs, FTFJP 2017 (2017)
8. Ancona, D., Ferrando, A., Franceschini, L., Mascardi, V.: Coping with bad agent interaction protocols when monitoring partially observable multiagent systems. In: Demazeau, Y., An, B., Bajo, J., Fernández-Caballero, A. (eds.) PAAMS 2018. LNCS (LNAI), vol. 10978, pp. 59–71. Springer, Cham (2018). https://doi.org/10.1007/978-3-319-94580-4_5
9. Ancona, D., Ferrando, A., Franceschini, L., Mascardi, V.: Managing Bad AIPs with RIVERtools. In: Demazeau, Y., An, B., Bajo, J., Fernández-Caballero, A. (eds.) PAAMS 2018. LNCS (LNAI), vol. 10978, pp. 296–300. Springer, Cham (2018). https://doi.org/10.1007/978-3-319-94580-4_24

10. Ancona, D., Ferrando, A., Mascardi, V.: Comparing trace expressions and linear temporal logic for runtime verification. In: Theory and Practice of Formal Methods: Essays Dedicated to Frank de Boer on the Occasion of His 60th Birthday (2016)

11. Ancona, D., Ferrando, A., Mascardi, V.: Parametric runtime verification of multiagent systems. In: Proceedings of the 2017 International Conference on Autonomous Agents and Multiagent Systems, AAMAS 2017, pp. 1457–1459. ACM (2017)

12. Ancona, D., Franceschini, L., Delzanno, G., Leotta, M., Ribaudo, M., Ricca, F.: Towards runtime monitoring of Node.js and its application to the Internet of Things. In: Proceedings of the 1st workshop on Architectures, Languages and Paradigms for IoT, ALP4IoT@iFM. EPTCS, vol. 264, pp. 27–42 (2017)

13. Benerecetti, M., Giunchiglia, F., Serafini, L.: Model checking multiagent systems. J. Log. Comput. **8**(3), 401–423 (1998)

14. Bordini, R.H., Hübner, J.F., Wooldridge, M.: Programming Multi-agent Systems in AgentSpeak Using Jason. Wiley (2007)

15. Bordini, R.H., Fisher, M., Visser, W., Wooldridge, M.: Verifying multi-agent programs by model checking. Auton. Agents Multi-Agent Syst. **12**(2), 239–256 (2006)

16. Bratman, M.E.: Intention, Plans, and Practical Reason. Harvard University Press, Cambridge (1987)

17. Broda, S., Machiavelo, A., Moreira, N., Reis, R.: Automata for regular expressions with shuffle. Inf. Comput. **259**(2), 162–173 (2018)

18. Chesani, F., Mello, P., Montali, M., Torroni, P.: Commitment tracking via the reactive event calculus. In: Proceedings of the 21st International Joint Conference on Artifical Intelligence, IJCAI 2009, pp. 91–96 (2009)

19. Dennis, L.A., Fisher, M., Lincoln, N., Lisitsa, A., Veres, S.M.: Declarative abstractions for agent based hybrid control systems. In: Proceedings 8th International Workshop on Declarative Agent Languages and Technologies (DALT), pp. 96–111 (2010)

20. Dennis, L.A.: Gwendolen semantics: 2017. Technical report ULCS-17-001, University of Liverpool, Department of Computer Science (2017)

21. Dennis, L.A.: The MCAPL framework including the agent infrastructure layer and agent Java Pathfinder. J. Open Source Softw. **3**(24) (2018). https://doi.org/10.21105/joss.00617

22. Dennis, L.A., et al.: Agent-based autonomous systems and abstraction engines: theory meets practice. In: Alboul, L., Damian, D., Aitken, J.M.M. (eds.) TAROS 2016. LNCS (LNAI), vol. 9716, pp. 75–86. Springer, Cham (2016). https://doi.org/10.1007/978-3-319-40379-3_8

23. Dennis, L.A., Fisher, M., Lincoln, N.K., Lisitsa, A., Veres, S.M.: Practical verification of decision-making in agent-based autonomous systems. Autom. Softw. Eng., 1–55 (2014)

24. Dennis, L.A., Fisher, M., Webster, M.P., Bordini, R.H.: Model checking agent programming languages. Autom. Softw. Eng. **19**(1), 5–63 (2012)

25. Desai, A., Dreossi, T., Seshia, S.A.: Combining model checking and runtime verification for safe robotics. In: Lahiri, S., Reger, G. (eds.) RV 2017. LNCS, vol. 10548, pp. 172–189. Springer, Cham (2017). https://doi.org/10.1007/978-3-319-67531-2_11

26. Desai, A., Gupta, V., Jackson, E.K., Qadeer, S., Rajamani, S.K., Zufferey, D.: P: safe asynchronous event-driven programming. In: Proceedings of the ACM SIGPLAN Conference on Programming Language Design and Implementation 2013, PLDI 2013, pp. 321–332. ACM (2013)

27. Dhaussy, P., Roger, J., Boniol, F.: Reducing state explosion with context modeling for model-checking. In: Proceedings of the 13th IEEE International Symposium on High-Assurance Systems Engineering, HASE 2011, pp. 130–137 (2011)

28. Ferrando, A.: The early bird catches the worm: first verify, then monitor! (2016). presented at Vortex'16. Downloadable from http://trace2buchi.altervista.org/wp-content/uploads/2017/10/paper.pdf

29. Ferrando, A.: RIVERtools: an IDE for RuntIme VERification of MASs, and beyond. In: PRIMA Demo Track 2017. CEUR, Vol. 2056 (2017)

30. Ferrando, A., Ancona, D., Mascardi, V.: Monitoring patients with hypoglycemia using self-adaptive protocol-driven agents: a case study. In: Proceedings of Engineering Multi-Agent Systems - 4th International Workshop, EMAS, pp. 39–58 (2016)

31. Ferrando, A., Dennis, L.A., Ancona, D., Fisher, M., Mascardi, V.: Recognising assumption violations in autonomous systems verification. In: Proceedings of the 2018 International Conference on Autonomous Agents and Multiagent Systems, AAMAS 2018 (2018)

32. Henzinger, T.A.: The theory of hybrid automata. In: Proceedings of the 11th Annual IEEE Symposium on Logic in Computer Science (LICS), pp. 278–292 (1996)

33. Kamali, M., Dennis, L.A., McAree, O., Fisher, M., Veres, S.M.: Formal verification of autonomous vehicle platooning. Sci. Comput. Program. **148**, 88–106 (2017). Special issue on Automated Verification of Critical Systems (AVoCS 2015)

34. Lomuscio, A., Raimondi, F.: MCMAS: a model checker for multi-agent systems. In: Hermanns, H., Palsberg, J. (eds.) TACAS 2006. LNCS, vol. 3920, pp. 450–454. Springer, Heidelberg (2006). https://doi.org/10.1007/11691372_31

35. Maler, O., Nickovic, D.: Monitoring temporal properties of continuous signals. In: Lakhnech, Y., Yovine, S. (eds.) FORMATS/FTRTFT -2004. LNCS, vol. 3253, pp. 152–166. Springer, Heidelberg (2004). https://doi.org/10.1007/978-3-540-30206-3_12

36. van der Merwe, H., van der Merwe, B., Visser, W.: Verifying android applications using Java PathFinder. ACM SIGSOFT Softw. Eng. Notes **37**(6), 1–5 (2012)

37. Nguyen, L.V., Schilling, C., Bogomolov, S., Johnson, T.T.: Runtime verification for hybrid analysis tools. In: Bartocci, E., Majumdar, R. (eds.) RV 2015. LNCS, vol. 9333, pp. 281–286. Springer, Cham (2015). https://doi.org/10.1007/978-3-319-23820-3_19

38. Penix, J., Visser, W., Engstrom, E., Larson, A., Weininger, N.: Verification of time partitioning in the DEOS scheduler kernel. In: Proceedings of the 22nd International Conference on Software Engineering, pp. 488–497 (2000)

39. Pnueli, A.: The temporal logic of programs. In: Proceedings of the 18th Annual Symposium on Foundations of Computer Science, SFCS 1977, pp. 46–57. IEEE Computer Society, Washington, DC (1977)

40. Pokahr, A., Braubach, L., Lamersdorf, W.: Jadex: a BDI reasoning engine. In: Bordini, R.H., Dastani, M., Dix, J., El Fallah Seghrouchni, A. (eds.) Multi-Agent Programming: Languages, Platforms and Applications, Multiagent Systems, Artificial Societies, and Simulated Organizations, vol. 15, pp. 149–174. Springer, Boston (2005). https://doi.org/10.1007/0-387-26350-0_6

41. Raimondi, F., Lomuscio, A.: Automatic verification of multi-agent systems by model checking via ordered binary decision diagrams. J. Appl. Logic **5**(2), 235–251 (2007)

42. Rao, A.S., Georgeff, M.: BDI agents: from theory to practice. In: Proceedings of the 1st International Conference Multi-Agent Systems (ICMAS), San Francisco, USA, pp. 312–319, June 1995
43. Rao, A.S., Georgeff, M.P.: Modeling agents within a BDI-architecture. In: Proceedings of the 2nd International Conference on Principles of Knowledge Representation and Reasoning (KR&R), pp. 473–484 (1991)
44. Rao, A.: Agentspeak(L): BDI agents speak out in a logical computable language. In: Agents Breaking Away: Proceedings of the 7th European Workshop on Modelling Autonomous Agents in a Multi-Agent World (MAAMAW), pp. 42–55 (1996)
45. Sistla, A.P., Žefran, M., Feng, Y.: Runtime monitoring of stochastic cyber-physical systems with hybrid state. In: Khurshid, S., Sen, K. (eds.) RV 2011. LNCS, vol. 7186, pp. 276–293. Springer, Heidelberg (2012). https://doi.org/10.1007/978-3-642-29860-8_21
46. Tkachuk, O., Dwyer, M.B., Pasareanu, C.S.: Automated environment generation for software model checking. In: Proceedings of the 18th IEEE International Conference on Automated Software Engineering (ASE 2003), pp. 116–129 (2003)
47. Torroni, P., et al.: Modelling interactions via commitments and expectations. In: Handbook of Research on Multi-Agent Systems: Semantics and Dynamics of Organizational Models. IGI Global (2009)

Striver: Stream Runtime Verification for Real-Time Event-Streams

Felipe Gorostiaga[✉] and César Sánchez[✉]

IMDEA Software Institute, Madrid, Spain
{felipe.gorostiaga,cesar.sanchez}@imdea.org

Abstract. We study the problem of monitoring rich properties of real-time event streams, and propose a solution based on Stream Runtime Verification (SRV), where observations are described as output streams of data computed from input streams of data. SRV allows a clean separation between the temporal dependencies among incoming events, and the concrete operations that are performed during the monitoring.

SRV specification languages typically assume that all streams share a global synchronous clock and input events arrive in a synchronous manner. In this paper we generalize the time assumption to cover real-time event streams, but keep the essential explicit time dependencies present in synchronous SRV languages. We introduce Striver, which shares with SRV the simplicity, and the separation between the timing reasoning and the data domain. Striver is a general language that allows to express other real-time monitoring languages. We show in this paper translations from other formalisms for (piece-wise constant) signals and timed event streams. Finally, we report an empirical evaluation of an implementation of Striver.

1 Introduction

Runtime verification (RV) is a lightweight formal method that studies the problem of whether a single trace from the system under analysis satisfies a formal specification. From the point of view of coverage, static verification must consider all possible executions of the system while RV only considers the traces observed. In this manner, RV sacrifices completeness but offers a readily applicable formal method that can be combined with testing or debugging. See [16,20] for surveys on RV, and the recent book [2]. Early specification languages proposed in RV were based on temporal logics [7,12,17], regular expressions [25], timed regular expressions [3], rules [5], or rewriting [24].

Stream runtime verification (SRV), pioneered by Lola [11] defines monitors by declaring the dependencies between output streams (results) and input streams (observations). The main idea of SRV is that the same sequence of operations

---

This research has been partially supported by: the EU H2020 project Elastest (num. 731535), by the Spanish MINECO Project "RISCO (TIN2015-71819-P)" and by the EU ICT COST Action IC1402 ARVI (*Runtime Verification beyond Monitoring*).

C. Colombo and M. Leucker (Eds.): RV 2018, LNCS 11237, pp. 282–298, 2018.
https://doi.org/10.1007/978-3-030-03769-7_16

performed during the monitoring of a temporal logic formula can be followed to compute statistics of the input trace, if the data type and the operations are changed. The generalization of the outcome of the monitoring process to richer verdict values brings runtime verification closer to monitoring and data stream-processing. See [8,15,22] for further works on SRV. Temporal testers [23] were later proposed as a monitoring technique for LTL based on Boolean streams. SRV was initially conceived for monitoring synchronous systems, where all observations proceed in cycles. In this paper we present a specification formalism for timed asynchronous observations, where streams are sequences of timed events, not necessarily happening at the same time in all input streams, but where all time-stamps are totally ordered according to a global clock (following the timed asynchronous model of distributed systems [10]). The formalism that we propose in this paper targets the outline, non-intrusive monitoring (see [18] for definitions), where the model of time is that of timed asynchronous distributed systems. Our target application is the monitoring and testing of cloud systems and multi-core hardware monitoring, where this assumption is reasonable.

Related Work. The work [19] presents an asynchronous evaluation engine for a simple event stream language for timed events, based on a collection of language constructs that compute aggregations. This language does not allow explicit time references and offsets. Moreover, recursion is not permitted and all recursive computations are encapsulated implicitly in the language constructs. A successor work of [19] is TeSSLa [9] which allows recursion and offers a smaller collection of language constructs. Still, TeSSLa precludes explicit offset dependencies, and the target application domain is hardware based monitoring. We sketched that Striver subsumes TeSSLa. Another similar work is RTLola [14], which also aims to extend SRV from the synchronous domain to timed streams. However, in RTLola defined streams are computed at predefined periodic instants of time, collecting aggregations between these predefined instants using language constructs. In this manner, the output streams in RTLola are *isochronous*[1], while in Striver defined streams are computed at the specific real-time instants where they are required, resulting in a completely *asynchronous* SRV system (in the sense that streams can tick at arbitrary time points). Striver can be used as a low level language to compile TeSSLa, RTLola and similar specifications.

The rest of the paper is organized as follows. Section 2 describes the Striver specification language. Section 3 presents a trace-lenght independent online algorithm. Section 4 shows some extensions of Striver. Section 5 reports on an empirical evaluation and Sect. 6 concludes the paper.

2   The Striver Specification Language

In this section we introduce Striver, a specification language that allows defining efficiently monitorable specifications [11], those for which all streams can be

---

[1] We borrow this term from telecomunications and signal processing where an isochronous signal is one in which events happen at regular intervals.

resolved immediately. We show in Sect. 3 an online monitoring algorithm and prove that this algorithm is also trace length independent.

2.1 Preliminaries

The main idea behind SRV is to separate two concerns: the temporal dependencies and the data manipulated, for which we use data domains.

Data Domains. We use many-sorted first order logic to describe data domains. A simple theory, *Booleans*, has only one sort[2], *Bool*, two constants `true` and `false`, binary functions $\wedge$ and $\vee$, unary function $\neg$, etc. A more sophisticated signature is *Naturals* that consists of two sorts (*Nat* and *Bool*), with constant symbols 0, 1, 2... of sort *Nat*, binary symbols $+$, $*$, etc (of sort $Nat \times Nat \to Nat$) as well as predicates $<$, $\leq$, etc of sort $Nat \times Nat \to Bool$, with their usual interpretation. All theories have equality and are typically (e.g. *Naturals*, *Booleans*, *Queues*, *Stacks*, etc) equipped with a ternary symbol `if · then · else·`. In the case of *Naturals*, the `if · then · else·` symbol has sort $Bool \times Nat \times Nat \to Nat$.

Our theories are interpreted, so each sort S is associated with a domain D_S (a concrete set of values), and each function symbol `f` is interpreted as a total computable function f, with the given arity and that produces values of the domain of the result given elements of the arguments' domains. For simplicity, we omit the sort S from D_S.

We will use *stream variables* with an associated sort, but from the point of view of the theories, these stream variables are atoms. As usual, given a set of sorted atoms A and a theory, the set of terms is the smallest set containing A and closed under the use of function symbols in the theory as a constructors (respecting sorts).

We consider a special *time* domain $\mathbb{T}$, whose interpretation is a (possibly infinite, possibly dense) set with a total order and a minimal element 0, and a binary addition symbol $+$. Examples of time domains are $\mathbb{R}_0^+$, $\mathbb{Q}_0^+$ and $\mathbb{N}_0$ with their usual order. Given $t_a, t_b \in \mathbb{T}$ we use $[t_a, t_b] = \{t \in \mathbb{T} \mid t_a \leq t \leq t_b\}$, and also (t_a, t_b), $[t_a, t_b)$ and $(t_a, t_b]$ with the usual meaning. We say that a set of time points $S \subseteq \mathbb{T}$ does not contain bounded infinite subsets, whenever for every $t_a, t_b \in \mathbb{T}$, the set $S \cap [t_a, t_b]$ is finite, in which case we say that S is a non-Zeno set.

We extend every domain D into $D^\perp$ that includes two special fresh symbols $\perp_{notick}^D$ and $\perp_{outside}^D$. These new symbols allow capturing when a stream does not generate an event, and when the time offset falls off the beginning and the end of the trace.

Streams. Monitors observe sequences of events as inputs, where each event is time-stamped and contains a data value from its domain.

---

[2] We use sort and type interchangeably in the rest of the paper.

Definition 1 (Event stream). *An event stream of sort D is a partial function* $\eta : \mathbb{T} \rightharpoonup D$ *such that* $dom(\eta)$ *does not contain bounded infinite subsets, where* $dom(\eta)$ *is the subset of* $\mathbb{T}$ *where* η *is defined.*

The set $dom(\eta)$ is called the set of *event points* of η. An event stream η can be naturally represented as a *timed word*: $s_\eta = (t_0, \eta(t_0))(t_1, \eta(t_1)) \cdots \in (dom(\eta) \times D)^*$, or as an ω-timed word $s_\eta = (t_0, \eta(t_0))(t_1, \eta(t_1)) \cdots \in (dom(\eta) \times D)^\omega$ for infinite streams, such that:

(1) s_η is ordered by time $(t_i < t_{i+1})$; and
(2) for every $t_a, t_b \in \mathbb{T}$ the set $\{(t, d) \in s_\eta \mid t \in [t_a, t_b]\}$ is finite.

The set of all event streams over D is denoted by $\mathcal{E}_D$.

We introduce some notation for event streams. The functions $prev_<$ and $prev_\le$ with type $\mathcal{E}_D \times \mathbb{T} \to \mathbb{T}^\perp$ are defined as follows. Note that the functions can return a value in $\mathbb{T}^\perp$ because sup can return $\perp_{outside}^\mathbb{T}$ when the stream has no event in the interval provided.

$$prev_<(\sigma, t) \stackrel{\text{def}}{=} sup(dom(\sigma) \cap [0, t))$$
$$prev_\le(\sigma, t) \stackrel{\text{def}}{=} sup(dom(\sigma) \cap [0, t])$$

$$sup(S) \stackrel{\text{def}}{=} \begin{cases} max(S) & \text{if } S \neq \emptyset \\ \perp_{outside}^\mathbb{T} & \text{otherwise} \end{cases}$$

Essentially, given a stream σ and a time instant $t \in \mathbb{T}$, the expression $prev_<(\sigma, t)$ provides the nearest time instant in the past of t at which σ is defined. Similarly, $prev_\le(\sigma, t)$ returns t if $t \in dom(\sigma)$, otherwise it behaves as $prev_<$.

Synchronous SRV. In synchronous SRV, specifications are given by associating every output stream variable y with a defining equation that, once the input streams are known, associates y to an output stream. For example:

```
define bool always_p := p /\ always_p[-1,true]
define int   count_p := (count_p[-1,0]) + if p then 1 else 0
```

defines two output streams: `always_p`, which calculates whether Boolean input stream p was true at every point in the past (that is, $\Box p$) and `count_p`, which counts the number of times p was true in the past. Offset expressions like `count_p[-1,0]` allow referring to streams in a different position (in this case in the previous position) with a default value when there is no previous position (the beginning of the trace). In this paper we introduce a similar formalism for timed event streams. Our goal is to provide a simple language with few constructs including explicit references to the previous position at which some stream contains an event, contrary to other stream languages like TeSSLa [9] and RTLola [14] which preclude to reason about real-time instants. We say that Striver is an *explicit time* SRV formalism.

2.2 Syntax of Striver

A Striver specification describes the relation between input event-streams and output event-streams, where an input stream is a sequence of observations from the system under analysis.

> The key idea in Striver is to associate each defined stream variable with:
>
> - a *ticking expression* that captures when the stream may contain an event;
> - a *value expression* that defines the value contained in the event.

Note that in synchronous SRV, only a value expression is necessary because every stream has a value at every clock tick.

Formally, a Striver specification $\varphi : \langle I, O, V, T \rangle$ consists of input stream variables $I = \{x_1, \ldots, x_n\}$, output stream variables $O = \{y_1, \ldots, y_m\}$, a collection of ticking expressions $T = \{T_1, \ldots, T_m\}$ and a collection of value expressions $V = \{V_1, \ldots, V_m\}$. For output variable y, T_y captures when stream y ticks and V_y what the value is when y ticks. All input and output streams are associated with a sort. It is sometimes convenient to partition output streams into proper outputs and intermediate streams, that are introduced only to simplify specifications.

In practice, it is very useful that T_y defines an over-approximation of the set of instants at which y ticks, and then allow the value expression to evaluate to $\perp_{\text{notick}}^D$. The stream associated with y does not contain an event at t if V_y evaluates to $\perp_{\text{notick}}^D$ at t, even if t is in T_y. For example, if one wishes y to filter out events from a given stream x it is simple to define in T_y that y ticks whenever x does, and delegate to V_y to decide whether an event is relevant of should be filtered out.

Expressions. We fix a set of stream variables $Z = I \cup O$. Apart from ticking expressions and value expressions, offset expressions (used inside value expressions) allow defining temporal dependencies between ticking instants.

- *Ticking Expressions*:
$$\alpha := \{c\} \mid v.\texttt{ticks} \mid \alpha \cup \alpha \mid \texttt{delay } w$$

  where $c \in \mathbb{T}$ is a time constant, v is an arbitrary stream variable, and w is a stream variable of type $\mathbb{T}_\epsilon$, and $\cup$ is used for the union of sets of ticks. The type $\mathbb{T}_\epsilon$ is defined as $\mathbb{T}_\epsilon = \{t \mid t \geq \epsilon\}$ for a given $\epsilon > 0$. This restriction on the argument of delay guarantees that the ticking instants are non-zeno if all their inputs are non-zeno (see Sect. 3).
- *Offset Expressions*, which allow fetching previous events from streams:
$$\tau_x :: = x <\!\sim \tau' \mid x << \tau' \qquad \tau' :: = \texttt{t} \mid \tau_z \text{ for } z \in Z$$

  Offset expressions have sort $\mathbb{T}$. Here, $\texttt{t}$ represents the current value of the clock. The intended meaning of $x << \tau'$ is to refer to the previous instant strictly in the past of τ' where x ticks (or $\perp_{\text{outside}}^D$ if there is not such an instant). The expression $x <^\sim \tau'$ also considers the present as a candidate.

- *Value Expressions*, which give the value of a defined stream at a given ticking point candidate:

$$E::= d \mid x(\tau_x) \mid f(E_1, \ldots, E_k) \mid t \mid \tau_x \mid \text{outside}_D \mid \text{notick}_D$$

where d is a constant of type D, $x \in Z$ is a stream variable of type D and f is a function symbol of return type D. Note that in $x(\tau_x)$ the value of stream x is fetched at an offset expression indexed by x, which captures the ticking points of x and guarantees the existence of an event. Expressions t and τ_x build expressions of sort $\mathbb{T}$. The two additional constants outside_D and notick_D allow to reason about accessing the end of the streams, or not generating an event at ticking candidate instant.

We also use the following syntactic sugar:

$$x(^\sim e) \stackrel{\text{def}}{=} x(x<^\sim e) \qquad x(^\sim e, d) \stackrel{\text{def}}{=} \text{if } (x <^\sim e)\text{==outside then } d \text{ else } x(^\sim e)$$
$$x(<e) \stackrel{\text{def}}{=} x(x << e) \qquad x(<e, d) \stackrel{\text{def}}{=} \text{if } (x << e)\text{==outside then } d \text{ else } x(<e)$$

Essentially, $x(^\sim t)$ provides the value of x at the previous ticking instant of x (including the present) and $x(<t)$ is similar but not including the present. Also, $x(<t, d)$ is the analogous to $x[-1, d]$ in synchronous SRV allowing to fetch the value in the previous event in stream x, or d if there is not such previous event.

Example 1. Consider two input event streams: `sale` that represents sales of a certain product, and `arrival` which represents the arrivals to the store:

```
input int sale, int arrival
ticks stock := sale.ticks U arrival.ticks
define int stock := stock(<t,0) +
    (if isticking(arrival) then arrival(~t) else 0) -
    (if isticking(sale  ) then sale(~t  ) else 0)
```

where `isticking(sale)` is defined as `(sale<~t)==t`. Note that `stock` is defined to tick when either `sale` or `arrival` (or both) tick.   □

Example 2. To illustrate the use of `delay` consider the following specification:

```
ticks clock        := {0} U delay clock
define Time_eps clock := 1sec
```

The stream `clock` emits an event every second since time 0.   □

2.3   Semantics

As common in SRV, the semantics is defined denotationally first. This semantics establishes whether a given input and a given output satisfy the specification, which is defined in terms of *valuations*. Given a set of variables Z, a valuation σ is a map that associates every x in Z of sort D with an event stream from

$\mathcal{E}_D$. Given a valuation σ we define the result of evaluating an expression for σ. We define three evaluation maps $[\![.]\!]_\sigma$, $[\![.]\!]_\sigma$, $[\![.]\!]_\sigma$ depending on the type of the expression[3]:

- *Ticking Expressions.* The semantic map $[\![.]\!]_\sigma$ assigns a set of time instants to each ticking expression as follows:

$$[\![\{c\}]\!]_\sigma \overset{\text{def}}{=} \{c\}$$
$$[\![v.\texttt{ticks}]\!]_\sigma \overset{\text{def}}{=} dom(\sigma_v)$$
$$[\![a \cup b]\!]_\sigma \overset{\text{def}}{=} [\![a]\!]_\sigma \cup [\![b]\!]_\sigma$$
$$[\![\texttt{delay}(w)]\!]_\sigma \overset{\text{def}}{=} \{t' \mid \text{ there is a } t \in dom(\sigma_w) \text{ such that } t + \sigma_w(t) = t' \text{ and } dom(\sigma_w) \cap (t, t') = \emptyset \}$$

- *Offset Expressions.* For offset expressions $[\![.]\!]_\sigma$ provides, given a time instant t, another time instant:

$$[\![t]\!]_\sigma(t) \overset{\text{def}}{=} t$$

$$[\![x << e]\!]_\sigma(t) \overset{\text{def}}{=} \begin{cases} \perp^T_{\text{outside}} & \text{if } [\![e]\!]_\sigma(t) = \perp^T_{\text{outside}} \\ prev_<(\sigma_x, [\![e]\!]_\sigma(t)) & \text{otherwise} \end{cases}$$

$$[\![x <\sim e]\!]_\sigma(t) \overset{\text{def}}{=} \begin{cases} \perp^T_{\text{outside}} & \text{if } [\![e]\!]_\sigma(t) = \perp^T_{\text{outside}} \\ prev_\le(\sigma_x, [\![e]\!]_\sigma(t)) & \text{otherwise} \end{cases}$$

- *Value Expressions.* Finally, value expressions are evaluated into event streams of the appropriate type. For a given instant t:

$$[\![d]\!]_\sigma(t) \overset{\text{def}}{=} d$$

$$[\![x(e)]\!]_\sigma(t) \overset{\text{def}}{=} \begin{cases} \perp^D_{\text{outside}} & \text{if } [\![e]\!]_\sigma(t) = \perp^T_{\text{outside}} \\ v & \text{if } [\![e]\!]_\sigma(t) = t' \text{ and } \sigma_x(t') = v \end{cases}$$

$$[\![f(E_1, \ldots, E_k)]\!]_\sigma(t) \overset{\text{def}}{=} f([\![E_1]\!]_\sigma(t), \ldots, [\![E_k]\!]_\sigma(t))$$
$$[\![t]\!]_\sigma(t) \overset{\text{def}}{=} t$$
$$[\![\tau_x]\!]_\sigma(t) \overset{\text{def}}{=} [\![\tau_x]\!]_\sigma(t)$$
$$[\![\texttt{outside}_D]\!]_\sigma(t) \overset{\text{def}}{=} \perp^D_{\text{outside}}$$
$$[\![\texttt{notick}_D]\!]_\sigma(t) \overset{\text{def}}{=} \perp^D_{\text{notick}}$$

Note that $[\![x(e)]\!]_\sigma$ includes the possibility that (1) the expression cannot be evaluated because the time instant given by $[\![e]\!]_\sigma(t)$ is outside the boundaries of domain of the stream and (2) the expression is not defined because the stream does not tick at t. It is easy to see that the cases for $[\![x(e)]\!]_\sigma$ are exhaustive because $[\![e]\!]_\sigma(t)$ guarantees that $\sigma_x(t')$ is defined.

For example, consider the following stream $(1.0, 17), (2.5, 21), (3.5, 12)$ for variable `sale` from Example 1. Then

$$[\![\texttt{sale}(\sim t)]\!]_\sigma(3.1) = [\![\texttt{sale}(\texttt{sale}<\sim t)]\!]_\sigma(3.1) = [\![\texttt{sale}]\!]_\sigma(2.5) = 21$$

---

[3] we use colors to better distinguish between semantic maps.

Definition 2 (Evaluation Model). *Given a valuation σ of variables $I \cup O$ the evaluation of the equations for stream $y \in O$ is:*

$$[\![T_y, V_y]\!]_\sigma \overset{\text{def}}{=} \{(t,d) \mid t \in [\![T_y]\!]_\sigma \text{ and } d = [\![V_y]\!]_\sigma(t) \text{ and } d \neq \bot_{notick}^D\}$$

An evaluation model is a valuation σ such that for every $y \in O$: $\sigma_y = [\![T_y, V_y]\!]_\sigma$.

The goal of a Striver specification is to define a monitor, that intuitively should be a computable function from input streams into output streams. The following definition captures whether a specification indeed corresponds to such a function.

Definition 3 (Well-defined). *A specification φ is well-defined if for all σ_I, there is a unique σ_O, such that $\sigma_I \cup \sigma_O$ is an evaluation model of φ.*

As with synchronous SRV, specifications can be ill-defined. For example, the following specification (`define bool a:= not a`) admits no evaluation model, and (`define bool a:= a`) admits many evaluation models. Additionally, a specification is efficiently monitorable if the output at time t only depends on the input at time t, which enable the incremental computation of the output stream.

Definition 4 (Efficiently monitorable). *A well-defined specification φ is efficiently monitorable whenever for every two input σ_I and σ_I' with evaluation models σ_O and σ_O', and for every time t, if $\sigma_I|_t = \sigma_I'|_t$ then $\sigma_O|_t = \sigma_O'|_t$.*

2.4 Well-Formedness

The condition of well-definedness is a semantic condition, which is not easy to check for a given specification (undecidable for expressive enough domains). We present here a syntactic condition, called well-formedness, that is easy to check on input specifications and guarantees that specifications are well-defined. Most specifications encountered in practice are well-formed.

We first define a subset of the offset expressions, called the *Present* subset, as the smallest subset that contains t and such that if $e \in$ *Present* then $(x \mathrel{<^\sim} e) \in$ *Present*. We say that an output stream variable y directly depends on a stream variable x (and we write $x \to y$) if x appears in T_y or V_y. We say that y has a present direct dependency on x (and write $x \overset{0}{\to} y$) if $x \to y$ and either

- $x.ticks$ appears in T_y, or
- $(x \mathrel{<^\sim} e)$ appears in V_y and $e \in$ *Present*.

A direct dependency captures whether in order to compute a value of a stream variable y at position t, it is necessary to know the value of stream variable x up to t. If $x \to y$ but $x \overset{0}{\nrightarrow} y$ we say that y directly depends on x in the past (and we write $x \overset{-}{\to} y$).

Definition 5 (Dependency Graph). *The dependency graph of a specification φ is a graph (V, E) where $V = I \cup O$ and $E = V \times V \times \{\xrightarrow{0}, \xrightarrow{-}\}$.*

The dependency graph of Example 1 is:

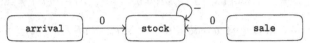

The following definition captures whether an output stream variable cannot depend on itself at the present moment.

Definition 6 (Well-Formed Specifications). *A specification φ is well-formed if every closed path in its dependency graph contains a past dependency edge $\xrightarrow{-}$.*

Closed paths in the dependency graph correspond to dependencies between a stream and itself in the specification φ. These closed paths do not create problems if the path corresponds to accessing the strict past of the stream. Note that if one removes $\xrightarrow{-}$ edges from the dependency graph of a well-formed specification, the resulting graph is necessarily a DAG. In other words $\xrightarrow{0}{}^{*}$ is irreflexive. The following lemma formally captures the information that is sufficient to determine the value of a given stream at a given time instant.

Lemma 1. *Let y be an output stream variable of a specification φ, σ, σ' be two evaluation models of φ, such that, for time instant t:*
  (i) For every variable x, $\sigma_x(t') = \sigma'_x(t')$ for every $t' < t$, and
  (ii) For every x, such that $x \xrightarrow{0}{}^{*} y$, $\sigma_x(t') = \sigma'_x(t')$ for every $t' \leq t$
Then $\sigma_y(t) = \sigma'_y(t)$.

The proof proceeds by structural induction on expressions, with the observation that only values in the past are necessary, as in conditions (i) and (ii). We are now ready to show that well-formed specifications cannot have two different evaluation models.

Theorem 1. *Every well-formed Striver specification is well-defined.*

The proof proceeds by showing that for well-formed specifications two evaluation models must be equal. This is shown by induction on the events in the traces to prove that the i-th event must be identical. Lemma 1 guarantees that induction can be applied.

3   Operational Semantics

The semantics of Striver specifications introduced in the previous section are denotational in the sense that these semantics associate for a given input stream valuation exactly one output stream valuation, but does not provide a procedure to compute the output streams, let alone do it incrementally. We provide in this section an operational semantics that computes the output incrementally. We fix a specification φ with dependency graph G and we let $G^=$ be its pruned dependency graph (obtained from G by removing $\xrightarrow{0}$ edges). We also fix $<$ to be an arbitrary total order between stream variables that is a reverse topological order of $G^=$.

We first present an online monitoring algorithm that stores the full history computed so far for every output stream variable. Later we will provide bounds on the portion of the history that needs to be remembered by the monitor, showing that only a bounded number of events needs to be recorded, and that this bound depends only on the size of the specification (number of streams) and not on the length of trace. This modified algorithm is a trace-length independent monitor for efficiently monitorable Striver specifications. The algorithm maintains the following state (H, t_q):

- **History**: H is a finite event stream one for each output stream variable. We use H_y for the event stream prefix for stream variable y.
- **Quiescence time**: t_q is the time up to which all output streams have been computed.

The monitor runs a main loop, calculating first the next relevant time t_q for the monitoring evaluation and then computing all outputs (if any) for time t_q. We show that no event exists in any stream in the interval between two consecutive quiescence time instants. We assume that at time t, the next event for every input stream is available to the monitor, even though knowing that there is no event up-to some t_q is sufficient.

The core observation follows from Lemma 1, which limits the information that is necessary to compute whether stream y at instant t contains an event (t, d). All this information is contained in H, so we write $[\![T_y]\!]_H$ and $[\![V_y]\!]_H$ to remark that only H is needed to compute $[\![T_y]\!]_\sigma$ and $[\![V_y]\!]_\sigma$.

The main algorithm, MONITOR, is shown in Algorithm 1. Lines 2 and 3 set the history and initial quiescence time. The main loop continues until no more events can be generated.

Line 5 computes the next quiescence time, by taking the minimum instant after the last quiescence time at which some output stream may tick. A stream y "votes" (see Algorithm 2) for the next possible instant at which its ticking equation T_y can possibly contain a value. Consequently, if no input stream votes for an earlier time it is guaranteed that no ticking equation will contain a value t lower than the lowest vote. Note that recursive calls at line 28 terminate because the graph $G^=$ is acyclic (recall that the specification is well-formed).

The algorithm follows a topological order over the $G^=$, so the information about the past required in Lemma 1 is contained in H. The following result shows that, assuming that σ_I is non-zeno, the output is also non-zeno. Hence, for every instant t, the algorithm eventually reaches $t_q > t$ in a finite number of executions of the main loop.

Lemma 2. MONITOR *generates non-zeno output for a given non-zeno input.*

Algorithm 1. MONITOR: Online Monitor

1: **procedure** MONITOR
2:     $H_s \leftarrow \langle \rangle$ for every s
3:     $t_q \leftarrow -\infty$
4:     **loop**   ▷ Step
5:         $t_q \leftarrow \min\limits_{s \in O}\{t \mid t = \text{VOTE}(H, T_s, t_q)\}$
6:         **if** $t_q = \infty$ **then break**
7:         **for** s in $G^=$ following $<$ **do**
8:             **if** $t_q \in [\![T_s]\!]_H$ **then**
9:                 $v \leftarrow [\![V_s]\!]_H(t_q)$
10:                **if** $v \neq \perp^D_{\text{notick}}$ **then**
11:                    $H_s \leftarrow H_s ++ (t_q, v)$ ▷ Updates history H
12:                    $emit(t_q, v, s)$
13:        **end for**
14:    **end loop**

Algorithm 2. VOTE: Compute the next ticking instant

15: **function** VOTE($H, expr, t$)
16:     **switch** $expr$ **do**
17:         **case** delay(s)
18:             **if** $(t' + v) > t$ (where $(t', v) = last(H_s)$) **then return** $t' + v$
19:             **else return** ∞
20:         **case** $\{c\}$
21:             **if** $c > t$ **then return** c
22:             **else return** ∞
23:         **case** $a \cup b$
24:             **return** $min(\text{VOTE}(H, a, t), \text{VOTE}(H, b, t))$
25:         **case** $y.ticks$ with $y \in O$
26:             **return** VOTE(H, T_y, t)
27:         **case** $s.ticks$ with $s \in I$
28:             **return** $succ_>(\sigma_s, t_q)$

The proof proceeds by contradiction assuming a t with non-zeno output, and the minimum output stream in $G^=$ that has a non-zeno output, and then showing that there must be a non-zeno output for $t - \epsilon$. This can be applied $\frac{t}{\epsilon}$ times to conclude that there is non-zeno output before 0 which is a contradiction.

We finally show that the output of MONITOR is an evaluation model. We use $H^i_s(\sigma_I)$ for the history of events H_s after the i-th execution of the loop body, and $H^*_s(\sigma_I)$ for the sequence of events generated after a continuous execution of the monitor. Note that $H^*_s(\sigma_I)$ can be a finite sequence of events (if the input is bounded and no repetition is introduced in the specification using delay) or an infinite sequence of events. In the first case, the vote is eventually ∞ and the monitoring algorithm halts.

Theorem 2. *Let σ_I be an input event stream, and let σ_O consist of $\sigma_x = H^*_x(\sigma_I)$ for every output stream x. Then (σ_I, σ_O) is an evaluation model of φ.*

The proof proceeds by induction on the number of rounds in the loop, showing that the output is an evaluation model up-to the quiescence time. Putting together Theorem 2, Lemmas 1 and 2 we obtain the following result.

Corollary 1. *Let φ be a well-formed specification, σ_I a non-zeno input stream and H^* the result of* MONITOR. *Then, H^* is the only evaluation model for input σ_I, and H^* is non-zeno.*

Trace Length Independent Monitoring. The algorithm MONITOR shown above computes incrementally the only possible evaluation model for a given input stream, but this algorithm stores the whole prefix H_y for every output stream variable y. We show now a modification of the algorithm that is trace length independent, based on flattening the specification. A specification is *flat* if every occurrence of an offset expression in every T_y is either $x(<^\sim \text{t})$ or $x(<< \text{t})$. In other words, there can be no nested term of the form $x(<^\sim (y<^\sim \text{t}))$ or $x(<^\sim (y<< \text{t}))$ or $x(<< (y<^\sim \text{t}))$ or $x(<< (y<< \text{t}))$. We first show that every specification can be transformed into a flat specification. The flattening applies incrementally the following steps to every nested term $x(E(y<< \text{t}))$, where E is an arbitrary offset term:

1. introduce a fresh stream s with equations $T_s = y.ticks$ and $V_s = x(E(\text{t}))$
2. replace every occurrence of $x(E(y << \text{t}))$ by $s(<\text{t})$.

Example 3. Consider the following specification of a continuous integration process in software engineering. The intended meaning is to report in `faulty` those commits to a repository that fail the unit tests.

```
input commit_id commits, unit push, bool tests
ticks faulty               := tests.ticks
define commit_id faulty := if tests(~t) then notick
                                else commits(<push<<t)
```

After applying the flattening process the specification becomes:

```
define commit_id faulty := if tests(~t) then notick else s(<t)
ticks              s := push.ticks
define  commit_id s := commits(<t)
```

Here, `s` stores the `commit_id` of the last commit at the point of a `push`, which is precisely the information to report at the time of a `faulty` commit.   □

Lemma 3. *Let φ be a specification. There is an equivalent flat specification φ' that is linear in the size of φ.*

Now, let φ' be the flat specification obtained from φ and let y be an output stream variable. Consider the cases for offset sub-expressions in the computation of $[\![V_y]\!]_H(t)$ in line 9 of MONITOR:

- $s<^\sim t$: the evaluation fetches the value H_s at time t (if s ticks at t) of at the previous ticking time (if s does not tick at t).

– $s \ll t$: the evaluation fetches the value H_s at the previous ticking time of s.

In either case, only the last two elements of H_s are needed. The similar argument can be made to compute T_y because only the last event of s is needed for $\mathtt{delay}(s)$. Hence, to evaluate MONITOR on flat specifications, the algorithm only needs to maintain the last two elements in the history for every output stream variable to compute the next value of every value and ticking equation.

Theorem 3. *Every flat specification φ can be monitored online with linear memory in the size of the specification and independently of the length of the trace. Moreover, every step can be computed in linear time on the size φ.*

4   Extensions and Comparison

We first sketch how to define the most complex operator[4] of TeSSLa: $x = delay\langle s_0, s_1 \rangle$, which creates an event stream x which will tick at an instant t if there is an event (t', v) in s_0 such that $t' + v = t$ and also $dom(s_1) \cap (t', t) = \emptyset$ TeSSLa does not handle explicit time and offsets but builds specifications from building blocks like *delay*. Given inputs s0 and s1 the Striver specification is:

```
ticks aux  := s0.ticks U s1.ticks
define Time_eps aux := if isticking(s1) then infty
    else if aux(<t,infty) = infty || aux(<t) + aux<<t <= t
        then s0(~t) else notick
ticks x := delay x_aux
define unit x := ()
```

We now present three extensions to the basic Striver introduced previously.

Accessing Successors. The first extension allows accessing future events, via the dual of the offset operators $x >^{\sim} e$ and $x \gg e$, and the syntactic sugar to access the successor value $x(e>)$, $x(e^{\sim})$, $x(e,d>)$ and $x(e,d^{\sim})$. As for Lola, well-formedness can be guaranteed as long as all strongly connected components in the dependency graph contain only $\xrightarrow{-}$ and $\xrightarrow{0}$ edges, or only $\xrightarrow{+}$ and $\xrightarrow{0}$ edges, and additionally, there is no cycle with only $\xrightarrow{0}$ edges. For example, this guarantees that there is no cyclic dependency, as every stream either depends on itself in the future or in the past (or none at all).

All Delays. This allows defining tick sets that consider all delays. The ticking expressions are extended with an operator $\mathtt{delayall}$ with the following semantics:

$$[\![\mathtt{delayall}(w)]\!]_\sigma \stackrel{\text{def}}{=} \{t' \mid \text{ there is a } t \in dom(\sigma_w) \text{ such that } t + \sigma_w(t) = t'\}$$

---

[4] Due to limitations a full comparison against TeSSLa and STL is not presented here.

This extension requires only to change VOTE to accommodate for a set of possible pending delays and not just a single delay. In general, this cannot be implemented in finite memory for arbitrary event rates and delays, but MONITOR works directly for the online monitoring this construct.

Windows. The last extension allows implementing computations over precise windows, like *"count the number of events in every window of one second"*. This cannot be described in TeSSLa [9], which is limited to finite memory monitors, or in RTLola [14] because this specification is not isochronous. Note that this property cannot be monitored by splitting the time in intervals of one second and counting the events in each of the intervals obtained (as in RTLola) as this approach misses the case of counting the events in part of one window and the remaining time in the adjacent window. The main idea of this extension is to enrich time expressions with a tag, in such a way that every tick carries an additional value (we called this extension *dependent time*). Then, `delay` and `delayall` are enriched with the ability to use tagged time streams, with the caveat that the U combinator must now indicate how to combine tags. Consider the following example with input `int s`:

```
ticks wcount :=  (const 1 s)  U delayall (const (-1,5) s)
define int wcount t aux := wcount(<t,0) + aux
```

The stream `wcount` must only be computed when a new event arrives in s (adding 1) or when an event leaves the window (subtracting 1), which is monitored with a constant number of operations per event, but requires storing a number of events that depends on the event rate.

The Signal Temporal Logic STL [1,21]—when interpreted over piecewise-constant signals—is subsumed by Striver. First note that event streams have a dual interpretation as piece-wise constant signals, where the signal only changes at the point where events are produced. The translation to Striver opens the door to a quantitative computation of STL by enriching the data types of expressions and verdicts. We show the operator $x \, \mathcal{U}_{[0,b]} \, y$:

```
ticks v := x U y U delayall -b x U delayall -b y
define bool v t := if  y(~t,false) then true else
    if !x(~t,false) then false else
    let t' := yT(t~) in
    if t'==outside || t' > t+b then false else t' <= xF(t~)
```

5   Empirical Evaluation

We report an empirical evaluation of a prototype sequential Striver implementation, written in the Go programming language[5]. We measure the memory usage and time per event for two collections of specifications. The first collection, from Example 1, computes the stocks of p independent products. These specifications contain a number of streams proportional to p, where each defining equation is

---
[5] Striver is available at http://github.com/imdea-software/striver.

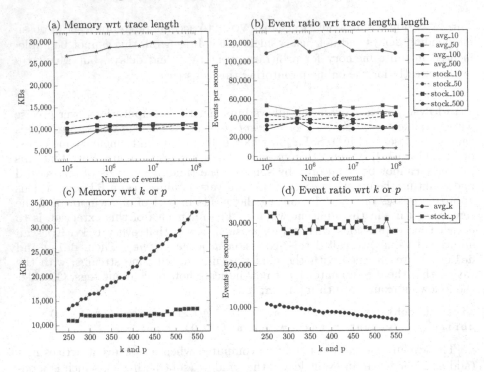

Fig. 1. Empirical evaluation

of constant size. The second collection computes the average of the last k sales of a fixed product, via streams that tick at the selling instants and compute the sum of the last k sales (see the appendix for the concrete specs). The resulting specifications has depth proportional to k. We instantiate k and p from 10 to 500 and run each resulting specification with a set of generated input traces. We run the experiments on a virtual machine on top of an Intel Xeon at 3 GHz with 32GB of RAM, and measure the average memory usage (using the OS) and the number of events processed per second.

In the first experiment, we run the synthesized monitors with traces of varying length (top two plots in Fig. 1). The results illustrate that the memory needed to monitor each specification is independent of the length of the trace (the curves are roughly constant). Also, the ratio of events processed is independent of the length of the trace. In the second experiment, we fix a trace of 1 million events and run the specifications with k and p ranging from 250 to 550. The results (lower diagrams) indicate that the memory needed to monitor stock_p is independent of the number of products while the memory needed to monitor each avg_k specification grows linearly with k. Recall that theoretically all specifications can be monitored with memory linearly on the size of the specification.

6 Conclusion and Future Work

We have introduced Striver, a specification language with explicit time and off-set reference for the stream runtime verification of timed event streams. We have presented a trace-length independent online monitoring algorithm for the efficiently monitorable fragment. Future work includes the extension of the language with parametrization, (like in QEA [4], MFOTL [6] and Lola2.0 [13]), to dynamically instantiate monitors for observed data items. We are also studying offline evaluation algorithms, and algorithms that tolerate deviations in the time-stamps and asynchronous arrival of events from the different input streams.

References

1. Bartocci, E., Deshmukh, J., Donzé, A., Fainekos, G., Maler, O., Ničković, D., Sankaranarayanan, S.: Specification-based monitoring of cyber-physical systems: a survey on theory, tools and applications. In: Bartocci, E., Falcone, Y. (eds.) Lectures on Runtime Verification. LNCS, vol. 10457, pp. 135–175. Springer, Cham (2018). https://doi.org/10.1007/978-3-319-75632-5_5
2. Bartocci, E., Falcone, Y. (eds.): Lectures on Runtime Verification - Introductory and Advanced Topics. LNCS, vol. 10457. Springer, Cham (2018). https://doi.org/10.1007/978-3-319-75632-5
3. Asarin, E., Caspi, P., Maler, O.: Timed regular expressions. J. ACM 49(2), 172–206 (2002)
4. Barringer, H., Falcone, Y., Havelund, K., Reger, G., Rydeheard, D.: Quantified event automata: towards expressive and efficient runtime monitors. In: Giannakopoulou, D., Méry, D. (eds.) FM 2012. LNCS, vol. 7436, pp. 68–84. Springer, Heidelberg (2012). https://doi.org/10.1007/978-3-642-32759-9_9
5. Barringer, H., Goldberg, A., Havelund, K., Sen, K.: Rule-Based runtime verification. In: Steffen, B., Levi, G. (eds.) VMCAI 2004. LNCS, vol. 2937, pp. 44–57. Springer, Heidelberg (2004). https://doi.org/10.1007/978-3-540-24622-0_5
6. Basin, D.A., Klaedtke, F., Müller, S., Zalinescu, E.: Monitoring metric first-order temporal properties. J. ACM 62(2) 2015
7. Bauer, A., Leucker, M., Schallhart, C.: Runtime verification for LTL and TLTL. ACM T. Softw. Eng. Meth. 20(4), 14 (2011)
8. Bozzelli, L., Sánchez, C.: Foundations of boolean stream runtime verification. In: Bonakdarpour, B., Smolka, S.A. (eds.) RV 2014. LNCS, vol. 8734, pp. 64–79. Springer, Cham (2014). https://doi.org/10.1007/978-3-319-11164-3_6
9. Convent, L., Hungerecker, S., Leucker, M., Scheffel, T., Schmitz, M., Thoma, D.: TeSSLa: temporal stream-based specification language. In: Proceedings of the 21st Brazilian Symposium on Formal Methods (SBMF 2018), LNCS. Springer (2018)
10. Cristian, F., Fetzer, C.: The timed asynchronous distributed system model. IEEE Trans. Parallel Distrib. Syst. 10(6), 642–657 (1999)
11. D'Angelo, B., et al.: LOLA: runtime monitoring of synchronous systems. In: Proceedings of TIME 2005, pp. 166–174. IEEE (2005)
12. Eisner, C., Fisman, D., Havlicek, J., Lustig, Y., McIsaac, A., Van Campenhout, D.: Reasoning with temporal logic on truncated paths. In: Hunt, W.A., Somenzi, F. (eds.) CAV 2003. LNCS, vol. 2725, pp. 27–39. Springer, Heidelberg (2003). https://doi.org/10.1007/978-3-540-45069-6_3

13. Faymonville, P., Finkbeiner, B., Schirmer, S., Torfah, H.: A stream-based specification language for network monitoring. In: Falcone, Y., Sánchez, C. (eds.) RV 2016. LNCS, vol. 10012, pp. 152–168. Springer, Cham (2016). https://doi.org/10.1007/978-3-319-46982-9_10

14. Faymonville, P., Finkbeiner, B., Schwenger, M., Torfah, H.: Real-time stream-based monitoring. CoRR, abs/1711.03829 (2017)

15. Goodloe, A.E., Pike, L.: Monitoring distributed real-time systems: A survey and future directions. Technical report, NASA Langley Research Center (2010)

16. Havelund, K., Goldberg, A.: Verify your runs. In: Meyer, B., Woodcock, J. (eds.) VSTTE 2005. LNCS, vol. 4171, pp. 374–383. Springer, Heidelberg (2008). https://doi.org/10.1007/978-3-540-69149-5_40

17. Havelund, K., Roşu, G.: Synthesizing monitors for safety properties. In: Katoen, J.-P., Stevens, P. (eds.) TACAS 2002. LNCS, vol. 2280, pp. 342–356. Springer, Heidelberg (2002). https://doi.org/10.1007/3-540-46002-0_24

18. Leucker, M.: Teaching runtime verification. In: Khurshid, S., Sen, K. (eds.) RV 2011. LNCS, vol. 7186, pp. 34–48. Springer, Heidelberg (2012). https://doi.org/10.1007/978-3-642-29860-8_4

19. Leucker, M., Sánchez, C., Scheffel, T., Schmitz, M., Schramm, A.: TeSSLa: runtime verification of non-synchronized real-time streams. In: Proceedings of the 33rd Symposium on Applied Computing (SAC 2018). ACM (2018)

20. Leucker, M., Schallhart, C.: A brief account of runtime verification. J. Logic Algebr. Progr. **78**(5), 293–303 (2009)

21. Maler, O., Nickovic, D.: Monitoring temporal properties of continuous signals. In: Lakhnech, Y., Yovine, S. (eds.) FORMATS/FTRTFT -2004. LNCS, vol. 3253, pp. 152–166. Springer, Heidelberg (2004). https://doi.org/10.1007/978-3-540-30206-3_12

22. Pike, L., Goodloe, A., Morisset, R., Niller, S.: Copilot: a hard real-time runtime monitor. In: Barringer, H., Falcone, Y., Finkbeiner, B., Havelund, K., Lee, I., Pace, G., Roşu, G., Sokolsky, O., Tillmann, N. (eds.) RV 2010. LNCS, vol. 6418, pp. 345–359. Springer, Heidelberg (2010). https://doi.org/10.1007/978-3-642-16612-9_26

23. Pnueli, A., Zaks, A.: PSL model checking and run-time verification via testers. In: Misra, J., Nipkow, T., Sekerinski, E. (eds.) FM 2006. LNCS, vol. 4085, pp. 573–586. Springer, Heidelberg (2006). https://doi.org/10.1007/11813040_38

24. Roşu, G., Havelund, K.: Rewriting-based techniques for runtime verification. Autom. Softw. Eng. **12**(2), 151–197 (2005)

25. Sen, K., Roşu, G.: Generating optimal monitors for extended regular expressions. ENTCS **89**(2), 226–245 (2003)

Efficient Monitoring of Real Driving Emissions

Maximilian A. Köhl$^{(\boxtimes)}$, Holger Hermanns, and Sebastian Biewer

Saarland University, Saarland Informatics Campus, Saarbrücken, Germany
{mkoehl,hermanns}@cs.uni-saarland.de
biewer@depend.uni-saarland.de

Abstract. The diesel emissions scandal has demonstrated that real-world behavior of systems can deviate excessively from the behavior shown under certification conditions. In response to the massive revelation of fraudulent behavior programmed inside diesel cars across Europe, the European Union has defined a procedure to test for *Real Driving Emissions* (RDE) [22]. This is gradually being put into force since September 2017 [23]. To avoid misinterpretation, the RDE regulation comes with an informal but relatively precise specification that spells out in how far a real trip, i.e., a trajectory driven with a car, constitutes an RDE test, or not. This paper presents a formalization of the RDE test procedure which is used to monitor for RDE violations at runtime and thereby fosters perspicuity. To this end, we extend the stream-based specification language LOLA [5, 10] with sliding aggregation windows. We evaluate the approach experimentally using data from real trips and further present a low-cost variant of the RDE test which can be conducted without expensive test equipment solely with on-board sensors.

Keywords: Automotive testing · Runtime monitoring
Specification languages · Software doping · Perspicious systems

1 Introduction

The recent diesel emissions scandal has put the problem of doped software [6] in the spotlight: proprietary embedded control software may decide to exploit functionality offered by a device against the best interest of the device owner or of society, in favor of interests of the manufacturer. Concretely, the controllers embedded in many diesel-powered cars are programmed in ways that induce substantial environmental pollution, in violation of many emission regulations around the world. This escapes detection through official test procedures because the behavior is programmed to surreptitiously change whenever the car is deemed to be in a test setting. This is easily possible, since, at least so far, emission test procedures were carried out in a precisely defined environment, and were

This research was supported in part by the Saarbrücken Graduate School of Computer Science and by ERC Advanced Grant 695614 (POWVER).

C. Colombo and M. Leucker (Eds.): RV 2018, LNCS 11237, pp. 299–315, 2018.
https://doi.org/10.1007/978-3-030-03769-7_17

following a precisely defined driving profile, with the car under test fixed on a chassis dynamometer. This precision is needed so as to ensure reproducibility of the tests and to enable comparisons of exhaust footprint and fuel consumption across different car models.

For about a decade, the binding standard to be used during type approval of a new car model has been the *New European Driving Cycle* (NEDC), which has recently been replaced by the *Worldwide harmonized Light vehicles Test Procedure* (WLTP) [23]. The latter is considered to be more realistic, but it still shares the problematic characteristics of the NEDC in that the WLTP driving profile is very much a singularity, and therefore easy to identify by control software doped by the manufacturer. To overcome this conceptual problem, the European Union has lately defined a new procedure to test for *Real Driving Emissions* (RDE). This comes with broad certification conditions for tests which are to be conducted under real-world conditions, on public roads and during working days. The RDE is gradually being put into force since September 2017. The RDE complements the WLTP—while the RDE is intended to measure emissions under real-world conditions the WLTP is intended to measure fuel consumption in a reproducible manner enabling comparability.

To avoid misinterpretation, the RDE regulation comes with an informal but relatively precise specification document [23] that spells out in how far a road trip, i.e., a trajectory driven with a car in-the-wild, constitutes an RDE test, or not. This specification contains constraints on the route, allowed altitude and speed, and on the dynamics of the driving profile, that make use of percentiles. The specification also accounts for dynamic conditions like the weather. Conducting an RDE test requires a PEMS, a *Portable Emissions Measurement System*. This is a device that measures the emissions at the tailpipe of a vehicle and is small and light enough to be carried inside or moved with the vehicle during the test drive. The unit price of a PEMS is in the order of \$250,000. Commercial software such as "AVL Concerto for PEMS" is used to effectuate the measurement, collect the relevant data, and to decide if the test performed is indeed an RDE or not [1]. As usual for proprietary software, the source code of AVL Concerto and similar programs is not available, so there is no direct check available to reassure the verdict of the program after a test drive.

This paper phrases the question of RDE compliance as a runtime monitoring problem. Its central contribution is a formalization of the RDE regulation. For this, we extend the stream-based specification language LOLA [5,10] with sliding aggregation windows enabling the efficient computation of percentiles and moving averaging windows as needed by the RDE regulation.

We exploit this formalization in a low-cost variant of the RDE test procedure for NO_x emissions which only uses on-board sensors instead of an expensive PEMS. The hardware cost of our system is in the order of \$100. With our openly available formalization[1] at its core, the system implements the blueprint of an independent emission control and compliance system which we use to empirically

---

[1] All details of the monitor, including the source code of the LOLA specification and RDE trip data, can be found at https://www.powver.org/real-driving-emissions/.

monitor real vehicles under real driving conditions. The empirical results we can report are very encouraging. We discuss the pros and cons of our solution. In addition, we show that our extension of LOLA can be compiled into plain LOLA, albeit at the price of losing succinctness.

The contributions of this paper are an extended version of the stream-based specification language LOLA with sliding aggregation windows, an elaborate study on the formalization of the RDE test procedure using this extended version of LOLA, and the presentation of experimental results which make use of a low-cost version of the RDE without expensive equipment.

Organization of the Paper. In Sect. 3 we briefly introduce LOLA [10] and the RDE regulation [23]. In Sect. 4 we extend LOLA with sliding aggregation windows. In Sect. 5 we present the RDE test procedure and its formalization displaying the capabilities of the freshly introduced sliding aggregation windows. In Sect. 6 we evaluate the RDE formalization and the thereof constructed monitor experimentally using data from real trips. Furthermore, we show how a runtime monitor can be used to continuously supervise cars in use.

2   Related Work

We implement our RDE monitor using an extended version of the stream-based specification language LOLA 2.0 [5,10]. LOLA can express complex temporal properties referring to the past and the future. It can be used for checking if single traces satisfy given properties and generating statistical measures. LOLA allows the computation of output streams, which are instances of *templates* specifying when and how streams are computed. *Triggers* are used to define boolean properties based on input and output streams. LOLA 2.0 supports instance aggregation functions (e.g. exists, forall, count, ...) for output streams enabling reasoning about all active instances of a certain stream template.

Recently, LOLA 2.0 has been extended to RTLOLA, which supports real-time properties [11] and is especially useful when data does not arrive with a fixed frequency. The RDE, however, is based on test parameters provided with a fixed sampling frequency. Statistical measurements for real-time data have been realized by using *sliding aggregation windows* over discrete real-time intervals, and due to the real-time semantics, arbitrary many sample points. Currently, no implementation of RTLOLA is available. In our work, we follow a similar approach by extending LOLA with sliding aggregation windows over a fixed number of data points. In LOLA 2.0, aggregation functions can only be used to aggregate data of several instances at the *current time*, whereas sliding aggregation windows aggregate data from an interval.

Temporal logic [15,16] has been extended for real-time systems in MITL [2]. Signal Temporal Logic (STL) [13,14] introduces real-valued signals to MITL. The logic can specify past or future behavior. However, unlike LOLA, it cannot relate values of the stream at different points in time. Further, it is not possible to generate the statistical measures required to validate an RDE test. Hence, it is not suitable for encoding the RDE regulation. An approach to extend STL for properties, that need a global view on the data, has already been proposed [8].

The semantics of temporal logics has been extended from boolean satisfaction of a formula to robustness values [7,9,17]. Positive numbers indicate that the property is satisfied, a negative value shows the opposite. Falsification techniques for reactive systems try to make such a value smaller to eventually make it negative and disprove the property [3].

Efficient algorithms for the incremental computation of sliding window aggregations have been extensively studied [12]. This work allows us to make use of these algorithms within LOLA using a standardized interface.

Currently, RDE tests are conducted using Portable Emissions Measurement Systems, e.g., [1]. The commercial software that is delivered with these systems includes ready-to-use RDE monitors.

3 Preliminaries

3.1 Real Driving Emissions

Although the RDE regulation specifies broad testing conditions, there are still some constraints which should guarantee that a trip is close to real-driving conditions making it neither too easy nor too hard for the vehicle to pass the test. For this, valid RDE drives take 90 to 120 min and traverse three phases: urban, rural, and motorway. The regulation defines minimum and maximum permissible ratios of each phase w.r.t. the whole test distance. Moreover, the regulation defines speed constraints, minimum distances, ambient conditions, and more. Table 1 shows some of those constraints which we will formalize in Sect. 5.

Table 1. Some constraints for the urban, rural and motorway phase of RDE tests

	Urban	Rural	Motorway
Ratio range [%]	[29, 44]	[23, 43]	[23, 43]
Speed range [km/h]	[0, 60]	]60, 90]	]90, 160]
Distance [km]	≥16	≥16	≥16
Additional constraints	Stop percentage between 6% and 30% of urban time; average velocity in range [15, 40] km/h		>100 km/h for at least 5 mins
Temperature [K]	Moderate: [273, 303]; extended: [266, 273[or]303, 308]		
Altitude [m]	Moderate: <700; extended:]700, 1300]		
Speed limit [km/h]	145 (]145,160] for at most 3% of motorway time)		

3.2   Lola 2.0: An Introduction

LOLA 2.0 [10] is a stream-based specification language based on its predecessor LOLA [5]. This paper uses LOLA 2.0, however, for readability reasons we draw this distinction explicitly only where it is relevant and otherwise refer to LOLA 2.0 simply as LOLA. This section aims to give a brief introduction to LOLA, for further details we refer to the original publications [5,10].

LOLA provides an evaluation model based on synchronous streams where output streams are computed based on input streams. To this end, a LOLA 2.0 specification comprises a declaration of N typed input stream variables t_i and M typed parameterized output stream variables s_j that get assigned stream expressions which specify how the respective output streams are computed from values of the input streams, output streams, and parameters.

Input stream variables are declared by

```
input  Ti  ti
```

where T_i is the type of input stream variable t_i.

Parameterized *output stream variables* are declared by *templates* of the form

```
output  Tj  sj⟨p1 : T1ʲ,...,pk : Tkʲ⟩  :  inv:  s_inv;  ext:  s_ext;  ter:  s_ter
     :=  e(t1,...,tN,s1,...,sM,p1,...,pk)
```

where T_j is the type of output stream variable s_j. Concrete streams $s_j(\alpha)$, i.e., *instances* of s_j, are identified by *parameter valuations* $\alpha \in T_1^j \times \ldots \times T_k^j$. Each instance has a local clock. Instances $s_j(\alpha)$ are invoked with local time 0 whenever a tuple α appears on the *invocation stream* s_{inv} for which there does not already exist an instance. The local time of an instance advances with an increment of 1 whenever **true** appears on the boolean *extension stream* s_{ext} which is required to have the same *parameter signature* $\vec{P} = \langle p_1 : T_1^j, \ldots, p_k : T_k^j \rangle$ as the template for s_j. Whenever the extension stream is **true**, a new value is computed by the *stream expression* e over stream variables and parameters which is then appended to the stream. Otherwise, the previous value remains valid and the local time does not advance. If **true** appears on the boolean *termination stream* s_{ter}, again with signature $\vec{P}$, the instance is terminated. Intuitively, the invocation of a new instance creates a new output stream that produces values with each tick of its local clock and which ends on termination of the instance. An instance is *alive* starting with its invocation until its termination. Input streams are alive from the beginning until termination of the monitor.

In addition to the input and output streams, there is a stream producing the constant empty tuple in every global step. If streams without parameters are defined, then this stream is used as the invocation stream which thus is omitted in the template. Additionally, if s_{ext} is omitted instances are extended with every global step and if s_{ter} is omitted instances are never terminated.

Stream expressions are defined inductively. Constants c and *parameter variables* p_i are *atomic stream expressions*. Let $e_1, \ldots, e_k$ be stream expressions of types $T_1, \ldots, T_k$. If f is a k-ary function of type $T_1 \times T_2 \times \ldots \times T_k \to T$, then

$f(e_1, \ldots, e_k)$ is a stream expression of type T. If b is a boolean stream expression and $T_1 = T_2$, then $ite(b, e_1, e_2)^2$ is a stream expression of type T_1. Let $k \in \mathbb{Z}$, d be a constant of type T_1, and s be an output stream variable. Then $s(\vec{p})[k, d]$ is a stream expression of type T_1 where $\vec{p}$ are *parameters* comprised of atomic stream expressions matching the signature of s. Further, for an *instance aggregation operator* O, $O(s)$ is an expression.

Semantically, constants, parameter variables, functions, and if-then-else constructs are defined as usual. The semantics of *offset expressions* $s(\vec{p})[k, d]$ are defined as follows: if the parameter tuple $\vec{p}$ evaluates to α, then $s(\vec{p})[k, d]$ is the value of the instance $s(\alpha)$ at local time $t + k$ where t is the local time of instance $s(\alpha)$ at the global time step that the expression is evaluated. If the instance $s(\alpha)$ is not alive at the global time the expression is evaluated or if the local time $t + k$ refers to a point before the invocation or after the termination, the value of the offset expression is the default value d. Instance aggregation operators compute properties about all instances of a template. For example, COUNT(S) returns the number of active instances of output stream template s.

Notice that input stream variables can be used wherever output stream variables are expected by copying the input to an output stream.

LOLA allows the declaration of triggers,

```
trigger φ
```

where φ is a boolean stream expression. The trigger is activated if φ becomes true. Triggers usually indicate the violation of a property.

4 Sliding Aggregation Windows

In the previous section, we briefly introduced the RDE regulation and the LOLA specification language in which we aim to formalize the regulation. The RDE regulation assesses the overall driving dynamics of a trip in terms of the 95% percentile of speed times positive acceleration. In this section, we extend LOLA 2.0 with *sliding aggregation windows* which enable the efficient computation and perspicuous specification of percentiles.

In [11] LOLA 2.0 has been extended with *real-time* sliding aggregation windows which allow for efficient aggregation over windows comprising an unbounded amount of values specified in terms of real-time intervals. Our extension of LOLA 2.0 complements this extension by allowing the computation of aggregated values over windows of fixed width in terms of values taken into account.

For an introductory example, see the definition of stream $\widetilde{va_{95}}$

```
output float ṽa₉₅ := percentile95(va[-n:0 | a_is_positive])
```

---

[2] *ite* is short for if-then-else.

which computes the 95% percentile of speed times positive acceleration over the last n samples. In general, an aggregation window comprises an *aggregation function* (`percentile95`) and a *window expression* which is composed of a parameterized stream variable (`va`), a *window specifier* (`-n:0`), and an optional condition (`a_is_positive`).

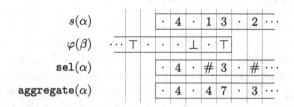

Fig. 1. Example of an unrolled aggregation window: $sum(s(\alpha)[-3:0 \mid \varphi(\beta)])$

Intuitively a sliding aggregation window aggregates over those values within the bounds of the window specifier for which the condition is satisfied by applying the aggregation function to the sequence of these values.

Formally, we extend the syntax of LOLA 2.0's stream expressions with sliding aggregation window expressions of the form

$$f\left(s(\vec{p_s})\,[i:j \mid \varphi(\vec{p_\varphi})]\right) \tag{1}$$

where $f : T^* \to T'$ is an aggregation function mapping possibly empty sequences of values of type T to a value of type T', $s(\vec{p_s})$ is a stream variable of type T with parameters $\vec{p_s}$, $i, j \in \mathbb{Z}$ with $j \geq i$ define the window boundaries, and $\varphi(\vec{p_\varphi})$ is a boolean stream variable with parameters $\vec{p_\varphi}$. We further require that the parameters $\vec{p_\varphi}$ only contain parameter variables also occurring in $\vec{p_s}$ or constants, which relates exactly one φ instance to each s instance. The type of the whole expression (1) is the target set T' of the aggregation function.

As we will show in the following, technically the introduction of sliding aggregation windows does not allow us to express any new properties, because aggregation windows can be rewritten to ordinary LOLA 2.0 syntax. Nevertheless, they have the advantage that they are much more succinct making them more intuitive and easier to write than their rewritten equivalents. Thereby they foster perspicuity of the specification—for which we strive.

4.1   Explicit Unrolling Semantics

We start with a naive rewriting rule for an explicit unrolling of the sliding aggregation window into the syntax of LOLA 2.0.

To unroll an aggregation window expression we define a new n-ary function f' where n is the window width, i.e., $n = j - i$, and manually hand over every value of the respective s instance to f' for each position in the window where the condition holds using an offset. To this end, we introduce a new unique value

to the type of s and define an auxiliary stream template `sel` whose instances run in tandem with the respective instances of s. Whenever a new value for an s instance becomes available, we extend the respective `sel` instance with this value if the condition holds, otherwise with #. See Fig. 1 for an example.

```
output T_s^# sel⟨P⃗⟩ : inv: s_inv; ext: s_ext; ter: s_ter :=
    ite(φ(p⃗_φ')[0,false], s(p⃗)[0,#], #)
```

The invocation, extension, and termination streams are the same as for the stream template s we aggregate over, i.e., the instances $s(\alpha)$ and $\mathtt{sel}(\alpha)$ for parameter valuation α are invoked, terminated, and extended together. $\vec{P}$ denotes the parameter signature of s and $\vec{p}$ passes those parameters on to s to select the corresponding instance of s. By requiring that $\vec{p}_\varphi$ contains only parameters also appearing in $\vec{p}_s$ or constants, we can reconstruct the parameters for φ using only the parameters passed to $\mathtt{sel}$. This reconstruction is denoted by $\vec{p}_\varphi'$.

The result are streams that only contain those values of the respective s instances for which the condition holds. Notice that, although we specify a default value for $s(\vec{p})$ in the consequence of the conditional, $s(\vec{p})$ will never be undefined. It remains to pass those values with explicit offsets to the function f'.

```
output T' aggregate⟨P⃗⟩ : inv: s_inv; ext: s_ext; ter: s_ter :=
    f'(sel(p⃗)[i+1,#], sel(p⃗)[i+2,#], ..., sel(p⃗)[j,#])
```

The function f' computes the value of the aggregation using f by constructing a sequence from its parameters in parameter order ignoring those that are #. Now, the aggregation window can be rewritten as follows

$$f(s(\vec{p_s})[i:j \mid \varphi(\vec{p_\varphi})]) \rightsquigarrow \mathtt{aggregate}(\vec{p_s})[0, f'(\#^n)]$$

where $f'(\#^n) = f(\epsilon)$ is the aggregation function's default value in case there is no s instance for the respective parameters—which implies, that there also is no instance of `aggregate` for the respective parameters.

4.2   Efficient Aggregation Windows

With explicit unrolling, we can rewrite sliding aggregation windows to the usual syntax of LOLA and hence use the LOLA monitoring algorithm as is. However, the standard monitoring algorithm of LOLA will recompute the aggregation functions from scratch for every window change, although many aggregation functions like summation or average allow for a much more efficient incremental updating strategy [11,12]. To this end, we present a more sophisticated rewrite rule which utilizes incremental updates and thereby allows us to compute aggregation functions much more efficiently. Table 2 provides an overview of selected aggregation functions as well as their space and update costs.

We follow [12] and define an abstract interface to aggregation algorithms that reuse intermediate results. For an aggregation function $f : T^* \to T'$ let D be an intermediate aggregation domain and $\epsilon \in D$ a unique initial value. We

Table 2. Aggregation function costs as a function of window size [12]

Functions	Space	Update cost
sum, avg, width	$\mathcal{O}(n)$	worst-case $\mathcal{O}(1)$
count, any, all	$\mathcal{O}(n)$	worst-case $\mathcal{O}(1)$
max, min	$\mathcal{O}(n)$	amortized $\mathcal{O}(1)$
median, percentile	$\mathcal{O}(n)$	worst-case $\mathcal{O}(\log n)$

define three operations on intermediate aggregation values, *insert* : $D \times T \to D$ adds a new value of type T to an intermediate aggregate, *evict* : $D \times T \to D$ evicts an old value from an intermediate aggregate, and *lower* : $D \to T'$ lowers an intermediate aggregate into an aggregated value of type T'. Insertions and evictions happen in FIFO order, which will be guaranteed by our translation. For each aggregation function, we choose an aggregation algorithm.

Computing aggregation windows over streams with the defined interface is then straightforward. For each window one constructs the `sel` stream template as given in Sect. 4.1. Instead of computing the value with `aggregate` from scratch for every change, one stores an intermediate aggregation, inserts new values $v \neq \#$ whenever they become available on the corresponding `sel` instance and evicts old values $v \neq \#$ when they shift out of the window. This algorithm can be directly implemented within LOLA 2.0 itself:

```
output D ins⟨P⃗⟩  : inv: s_inv; ext: s_ext; ter: s_ter  :=
  ite(sel[j,#] ≠ #, insert(agg[-1,ϵ], sel[j,#]), agg[-1,ϵ])
output D agg⟨P⃗⟩  : inv: s_inv; ext: s_ext; ter: s_ter  :=
  ite(sel[i,#] ≠ #, evict(ins[0,ϵ], sel[i,#]), ins[0,ϵ])
```

The stream template `agg` produces instances running in tandem with s instances and stores the intermediate results. First, the stream `ins` inserts new values appearing on the respective `sel` instance. Then, if a value is sliding out of the window, it is evicted by the `agg` stream. With this, rewriting aggregation windows is possible as follows:

$$f(s(\vec{p_s})[i : j \mid \varphi(\vec{p_\varphi})]) \rightsquigarrow lower(\mathbf{agg}(\vec{p_s})[0, \epsilon])$$

Rewriting the specification instead of extending the monitoring algorithm has the advantage that the core of LOLA 2.0 stays small and is, therefore, easier to implement and reduces the chance for bugs. Additionally, our extension can be used directly with existing implementations of and optimizations for LOLA 2.0. Using the standardized interface suggested in [12] we utilize existing research on sliding aggregation windows.

5   Formalizing Real Driving Emissions

We now have everything needed to formalize the RDE test procedure. The regulation is a contract imposing emission limits whenever a trip is a valid RDE

308   M. A. Köhl et al.

test. We split our formalization into two main parts where the first part decides whether a trip qualifies as a valid test and the other assesses whether the emission limits are violated.

We use a trigger that indicates an RDE violation

```
trigger is_valid_test & emission_limits_exceeded
```

when the trip is a valid test but the emissions are exceeded. It remains to define boolean streams indicating a valid test and exceeded emissions.

As we will see our extension of LOLA provides a very intuitive and natural way of formalizing the RDE test procedure. The specification is structured as follows: We first declare input streams for all test parameters, we then formalize the various preconditions of the regulation to determine the validity of a trip. Finally, we formalize the computation of the distance specific emissions and whether the respective emission limits are exceeded, or not. We describe selected and interesting parts of the formalization (see footnote 1) in this section.

5.1 Test Parameters

As the test parameters are provided as synchronous streams with a fixed sampling frequency f prescribed by the regulation, we can directly declare them as inputs to our monitor. To asses whether a trip meets basic requirements regarding its route and ambient conditions, we need the speed v of the vehicle, the altitude, and the ambient temperature. To calculate the emissions, we further need the concentration of the various regulated emission gasses and the *Exhaust Mass Flow* (EMF), i.e., the weight of the exhaust emitted per second. For this, we declare an input stream *gas*_ppm for each regulated emission gas and another input stream exhaust_mass_flow for the EMF. Given the gas concentration and the EMF we can compute the mass flow of the respective gas. Usually, all inputs come from the *On-Board Diagnostics II* (OBD-II) [19] interface and the PEMS which includes a GPS tracker. Given an appropriately equipped vehicle, the NO_x concentration can be obtained via OBD-II. Since the early 2000s all new U.S. and European cars are equipped with an OBD-II port [18]. However, an NO_x sensor is not mandatory yet.

5.2 Preconditions

The preconditions a trip shall satisfy to qualify as a valid test are divided into *trip requirements*, stipulating basic requirements regarding, for instance, the route and the velocity, *ambient conditions*, stating acceptable temperature and altitude ranges, *overall trip dynamics*, encompassing the driving behavior, and *dynamic conditions*, accounting for road grade, weather, and other dynamic factors. While the trip requirements and ambient conditions are relatively straightforward to specify, the overall trip dynamics and dynamic conditions are more of a challenge.

Trip Requirements. After declaring the input streams we formalize the trip requirements as specified in Section 6 of ANNEX IIIA of the RDE regulation. Compare Table 1 in Sect. 3 for an overview of the constraints and our full formalization for further details. To formalize the trip requirements, we first compute useful auxiliary streams e.g.

```
output bool   is_urban := v <= 60 // 6.3
output float u_avg_v   := avg(v[-N:0 | is_urban])
```

which we use to comprehensively assert the trip requirements. According to the regulation, values need to be binned according to the current speed in one of three bins, *urban*, *rural*, or *motorway*. The stream u_avg_v computes the average velocity in the urban speed bin using a sliding aggregation window. N is a constant denoting the maximal number of samples an RDE trip could have. An RDE trip must not last longer than 2 h which is $N = 7200f$ samples. Computing the average only over that sampling interval instead of the whole data allows us to specify a monitor considering only the temporally maximal suffix of a trip. A trip with more than N samples is not a valid RDE trip in any case.

We use the auxiliary streams to compute a boolean stream which is the conjunction of all trip requirements, for instance, for the average velocity of the urban segment: 15 <= u_avg_v <= 40.

Ambient Conditions. The RDE regulation specifies the ambient conditions in terms of temperature (in Kelvin), e.g., 273 <= temperature <= 303, and altitude ranges which can be directly translated to boolean formulae.

Overall Trip Dynamics. The overall trip dynamics asses the drivers driving behavior. They require that the driver neither drives too aggressive nor too restrained. To this end, they require to compute the 95% percentile of speed times acceleration for acceleration values at least 0.1 for each speed bin. We show this exemplary for the urban speed bin:

```
output float a   := (v[+1,0] - v[-1,0]) / (2 * 3.6)
output float va := (v * a / 3.6)
output bool u_a_ge_01 := a >= 0.1 & is_urban
output float u_va_pct :=
  percentile95(va[-N:0 | u_a_ge_01])
```

These values can be efficiently computed with an update cost of $\mathcal{O}(\log n)$ and storage cost of $\mathcal{O}(n)$. Although, in general specifications with future references are not efficiently monitorable [10] this does not hold here, as v is extended in every step and cannot delay the computation indefinitely. We again use these values as part of boolean equations as specified in the RDE regulation, e.g.

```
u_va_pct > (0.136*u_avg_v + 14.44)
```

which invalidates the trip if less than 95% of the va values are below the given threshold, i.e., if the driving was too aggressive.

Dynamic Conditions. The dynamic conditions encompass road grade, weather, and other factors that may influence the performance of the vehicle under test, but are out of control of the driver. They serve as built-in plausibility checks based on the reproducible CO_2 measurements of WLTP. To validate the dynamic conditions one considers variable width windows where a new window is instantiated with each sample point. Owed to the parameterized stream templates of LOLA 2.0 this can be expressed nicely by:

```
output bool win_completed(start: int) :
  inv: sample; ter: win_completed
  := total_co2_mass - win_start_co2(start) >= MCO2REF

output float win_v(start: int) :
  inv: sample; ter: win_completed := v

output float win_avg_v(start: int) :
  inv: sample; ter: win_completed
  := avg(win_v(start)[-N:0])
```

With each `sample` a new window is invoked. The values of these windows are extended in each step, and a window is completed in the step where the CO_2 emissions so far generated are at least a reference value determined by the WLTP test results. The RDE requires to compute the distance specific emissions for each window as well as the average speed. The earlier introduced sliding aggregation windows can be used to compute these values. Each window is then checked for normality by comparing the distance specific CO_2 emissions given the average speed to a reference curve. If at least 50% of windows are normal, the test is considered valid.

In the above, we are formalizing the computation of the values to demonstrate that we are indeed able to cover dynamic conditions faithfully with our formalization. However, our actual experiments do not include the checks regarding these conditions, which merely serve as plausibility check. The practical reason is that the needed WLTP values for our test vehicles were unavailable to us.

Calculating Emissions. As already stated above the emissions are calculated using the exhaust mass flow and the gas concentrations. The emissions are then accumulated and based on the distance of the trip the distance specific emissions are calculated which are compared to the respective threshold [21], e.g.:

```
output bool nox_exceeded :=
  ite(d > 0, sum(D_nox_mass[-N:0]) / d, 0) > 0.08
```

5.3   RDE Violation

Given the boolean formulae of the preconditions, we compute whether the trip is indeed valid. Given the boolean formulae indicating whether the various regulated emission gases exceed the thresholds, we compute whether the emissions are exceeded. This gives us the boolean streams needed for our trigger.

Monitoring for RDE violations allows us to asses whether a car is compliant or not. In addition, one can ask the question of how difficult is it to detect a running test as early as possible. Some of the preconditions, e.g., the total duration and the maximal velocity are monotonic and cannot be satisfied once violated. To build an RDE defeat device one needs to be able to tell whether the current trip prefix could still become a valid RDE trip or not.

6   Experimental Evaluation

We show that the formalization and the thereof constructed monitor are not only useful for certification purposes but can further be used by a layperson without expensive equipment to get an insight into exhaust emissions and whether her car does indeed adhere to the RDE regulation, or not.

Usually, the test parameters are obtained with a Portable Emissions Measurement System. We present two use cases for our monitor—one that requires a quite expensive PEMS and another that does not.

Case 1: Genuine RDE The first use case of the constructed RDE monitor is a genuine RDE test performed with a PEMS, for instance as part of an official certification process. The input streams for our monitor are directly generated by the PEMS and the control unit of the car.

Case 2: Low-Cost RDE The more interesting use case, however, is a *low-cost* RDE test without a PEMS. At best such a test can be conducted by a layperson without expensive equipment and expertise how to use it. The key challenge of a low-cost RDE is obtaining the test parameters.

A PEMS is a whole emission measurement laboratory in a box and therefore costs a significant amount of money. In addition, its setup procedure is rather complicated and usually requires an expert. Therefore, genuine RDE tests cannot be conducted by a layperson. As we will show, a low-cost variant of the RDE can be performed solely based on on-board sensors for a fraction of the cost with an easy to use monitor plugged into a standardized debug port.

The key challenge here is to obtain the test parameters—especially the concentrations of the regulated emission gasses. While the vehicle speed and altitude can be determined via GPS with an ordinary smartphone, measuring emissions requires specific sensors. Fortunately, many modern cars with a Selective Catalytic Reduction (SCR) system are already equipped with NO_x sensors measuring the NO_x concentration in the after-treatment exhaust stream, i.e., the stream of exhaust after it ran through the cleaning process as it leaves the tailpipe. Further, the CO_2 emissions can be approximated using data obtained from the engine control unit. Thanks to the standardized OBD-II interface [19] the required values can be obtained using a standard debug port.

We conducted a low-cost RDE with an Audi A7 3.0 TDI 200 kW which is known to contain a defeat device which chokes the injected amount of urea

312   M. A. Köhl et al.

shortly before it runs out of urea [24]. Urea is used as part of the SCR system to lower the NO_x emissions. We assume that the car indeed conforms with the EURO 6 emission limits in case the urea tank contains enough urea. If this were not the case, this would have been likely unrevealed by now based on the extensive testing that was necessary to detect the defeat device in the first place. In order to convince ourselves that the RDE specification and monitor we provide is correct, we first checked the input validation by correctly validating recorded data of genuine RDE tests. For trips that obviously are not RDE, the monitor complained as expected. In a second step, we drove a valid RDE with the Audi A7 mentioned above with full urea tank. We briefly discuss the test setup, main obstacles, and the result of this test in the rest of this section.

While our test vehicle provides the NO_x concentration in the exhaust stream, it does not directly provide the exhaust mass flow, which is needed to calculate the emissions. We thus approximate the exhaust mass flow as follows: [23] describes a procedure to compute the exhaust mass flow based on the mass air flow and the mass fuel flow, i.e., the rate of mass of air and fuel used in the combustion process. We approximate the fuel mass flow based on the rate of fuel consumption in liters and the fuel density, which is approximately 0.835 kg/l [20] for Diesel. In LOLA this is then calculated by:

```
output float exhaust_mass_flow :=   // in [kg/h]
    mass_air_flow + fuel_rate * 0.835
```

CO_2 emissions can be calculated based on the fuel rate and an oxidation factor specifying how much of the carbon is fully oxidized to CO_2. Cars do emit CO which is a regulated emission gas. Thus the oxidation factor has to be less than 1. For our tests, we assumed an oxidation factor of 0.99 [25].

Besides acquiring the test parameters, there is yet another challenge for a successful low-cost RDE conducted by a layperson—she needs to drive a valid RDE test trip. To assist with that, we augmented our specification with additional streams and triggers computing the urban, rural, and motorway distances which still need to be driven and other indicators, e.g., emitting a warning when the stop percentage comes close to the allowed boundaries.

With that assistance system in place, it was relatively easy to drive a valid test trip. See Fig. 2 for the speed profile of the trip. Our monitor computed a value of 68 mg/km NO_x which is within the EURO 6 emission limits of 80 mg/km [21] and almost matches the value of the data-sheet [4], which is 67 mg/km. For CO_2 the monitor computed 151 g/km which is a deviation of +9% from the value of the datasheet, but CO_2 is only used to check plausibility in any case. This shows that a low-cost RDE test conducted by a layperson using inexpensive equipment can provide very good results.

Knowing that the vehicle chokes the urea injected into the exhaust stream whenever it runs low on urea, we tried to repeat our experiment with a close to empty urea tank. Unfortunately, we were unable to drain the urea from the tank of the car which is prevented by the construction of the vehicle.

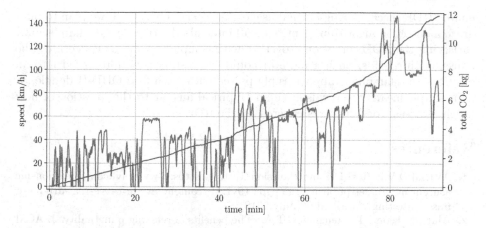

Fig. 2. Profile of a low-cost RDE with an Audi A7 3.0 TDI 200 kW

To conclude the experimental evaluation and given those results, we envisage that in the future cars are equipped with more sophisticated emission measurement systems such that a low-cost RDE eventually becomes possible not only for NO_x but also for other emission gasses.

7 Conclusion

We presented an extension of the stream-based specification language LOLA 2.0 with sliding aggregation windows and showcased its application with a formalization of the Real Driving Emissions (RDE) regulation. The constructed monitor has been successfully used as a basis for a low-cost, easy-to-use, and fully transparent tool, which can be plugged into the standardized OBD-II port with which every modern car is equipped. This enables laypersons to perform RDE tests for a fraction of the cost of a genuine RDE test. These measurements then rely on the on-board NO_x sensors. Research about their precision is still in progress. However, the tests we conducted suggest high precision measurements. Nevertheless, it should be mentioned that the sensors and their driver software are shipped with the car, so it is imaginable that the sensors are doped by the manufacturer, thereby invalidating the test results. We are indeed looking into the option to instead hook a separate sensor to the exhaust pipe.

The formalization of regulations is an essential step towards precise and succinct perspicuity enablers. The existing formalization already captures the heart of the RDE regulation. There are some corner cases and details for regions with peculiar geographic conditions that we did not implement yet, but we are planning to add. Our monitor is working *online*, i.e., the car's driving information is passed to the monitor in real-time. However, the decision whether the trip satisfies the RDE requirements, or not, does not consider possible continuations of the trip. Thus far, it does not detect that a current trip cannot be prolonged to a valid RDE drive anymore. We are working on this. Additionally, our goal is to enable RDE checks during normal usage of the car. To this end, we plan to integrate a detection algorithm identifying all intervals of a trip (longer than 90 min) satisfying the RDE conditions together with compliance checks concerning the emission thresholds. Such a monitor could, for instance, be integrated into an easy-to-use smartphone app, possibly paired with a wireless OBD-II dongle, or as a simple means to crowdsource an empirical answer to the question of how much of actual road traffic is covered by the RDE.

References

1. AVL M.O.V.E Real Driving Emission Testing. https://www.avl.com/emission-me asurement/-/asset_publisher/gYjUpY19vEA8/content/avl-m-o-v-e-real-driving-e mission-testing. Accessed 06 July 2018
2. Alur, R., Feder, T., Henzinger, T.A.: The benefits of relaxing punctuality. J. ACM **43**(1), 116–146 (1996)
3. Annpureddy, Y., Liu, C., Fainekos, G., Sankaranarayanan, S.: S-TaLiRo: a tool for temporal logic falsification for hybrid systems. In: Abdulla, P.A., Leino, K.R.M. (eds.) TACAS 2011. LNCS, vol. 6605, pp. 254–257. Springer, Heidelberg (2011). https://doi.org/10.1007/978-3-642-19835-9_21
4. Audi: Technische Daten - Audi A7–3.0 TDI 200 kW s-tronic quattro EU6W, March 2015
5. D'Angelo, et al.: LOLA: runtime monitoring of synchronous systems. In: 12th International Symposium on Temporal Representation and Reasoning (TIME 2005), pp. 166–174. IEEE Computer Society Press, June 2005
6. D'Argenio, P.R., Barthe, G., Biewer, S., Finkbeiner, B., Hermanns, H.: Is your software on dope? In: Yang, H. (ed.) ESOP 2017. LNCS, vol. 10201, pp. 83–110. Springer, Heidelberg (2017). https://doi.org/10.1007/978-3-662-54434-1_4
7. Donzé, A., Ferrère, T., Maler, O.: Efficient robust monitoring for STL. In: Sharygina, N., Veith, H. (eds.) CAV 2013. LNCS, vol. 8044, pp. 264–279. Springer, Heidelberg (2013). https://doi.org/10.1007/978-3-642-39799-8_19
8. Donzé, A., Maler, O., Bartocci, E., Nickovic, D., Grosu, R., Smolka, S.: On temporal logic and signal processing. In: Chakraborty, S., Mukund, M. (eds.) ATVA 2012. LNCS, pp. 92–106. Springer, Heidelberg (2012). https://doi.org/10.1007/978-3-642-33386-6_9
9. Fainekos, G.E., Pappas, G.J.: Robustness of temporal logic specifications for continuous-time signals. Theor. Comput. Sci. **410**(42), 4262–4291 (2009)
10. Faymonville, P., Finkbeiner, B., Schirmer, S., Torfah, H.: A stream-based specification language for network monitoring. In: Falcone, Y., Sánchez, C. (eds.) RV 2016. LNCS, vol. 10012, pp. 152–168. Springer, Cham (2016). https://doi.org/10.1007/978-3-319-46982-9_10
11. Faymonville, P., Finkbeiner, B., Schwenger, M., Torfah, H.: Real-time stream-based monitoring. CoRR abs/1711.03829 (2017). http://arxiv.org/abs/1711.03829
12. Hirzel, M., Schneider, S., Tangwongsan, K.: Sliding-window aggregation algorithms: tutorial. In: Proceedings of the 11th ACM International Conference on Distributed and Event-Based Systems, DEBS 2017, pp. 11–14. ACM, New York (2017)
13. Maler, O., Nickovic, D.: Monitoring temporal properties of continuous signals. In: Lakhnech, Y., Yovine, S. (eds.) FORMATS/FTRTFT -2004. LNCS, vol. 3253, pp. 152–166. Springer, Heidelberg (2004). https://doi.org/10.1007/978-3-540-30206-3_12

14. Maler, O., Nickovic, D., Pnueli, A.: Checking temporal properties of discrete, timed and continuous behaviors. In: Avron, A., Dershowitz, N., Rabinovich, A. (eds.) Pillars of Computer Science. LNCS, vol. 4800, pp. 475–505. Springer, Heidelberg (2008). https://doi.org/10.1007/978-3-540-78127-1_26
15. Pnueli, A.: The temporal logic of programs. In: 18th Annual Symposium on Foundations of Computer Science, Providence, Rhode Island, USA, 31 October–1 November 1977, pp. 46–57. IEEE Computer Society (1977), http://ieeexplore.ieee. org/xpl/mostRecentIssue.jsp?punumber=4567914
16. Pnueli, A.: The temporal semantics of concurrent programs. Theor. Comput. Sci. **13**, 45–60 (1981)
17. Rizk, A., Batt, G., Fages, F., Soliman, S.: On a continuous degree of satisfaction of temporal logic formulae with applications to systems biology. In: Heiner, M., Uhrmacher, A.M. (eds.) CMSB 2008. LNCS (LNAI), vol. 5307, pp. 251–268. Springer, Heidelberg (2008). https://doi.org/10.1007/978-3-540-88562-7_19
18. The European Parliament and the Council of the European Union: 98/69/EC, October 1998. http://data.europa.eu/eli/dir/1998/69/oj
19. The European Parliament and the Council of the European Union: Directive 98/69/EC of the European parliament and of the council. Official Journal of the European Communities (1998), http://eur-lex.europa.eu/LexUriServ/LexUriServ. do?uri=CELEX:31998L0069:EN:HTML
20. The European Parliament and the Council of the European Union: Directive 2005/55/EC, September 2005. http://data.europa.eu/eli/dir/2005/55/oj
21. The European Parliament and the Council of the European Union: Commission Regulation (EU) 2007/715, June 2007. http://data.europa.eu/eli/reg/2007/715/oj
22. The European Parliament and the Council of the European Union: Commission Regulation (EU) 2016/427, March 2016. http://data.europa.eu/eli/reg/2016/427/oj
23. The European Parliament and the Council of the European Union: Commission Regulation (EU) 2017/1151, June 2017. http://data.europa.eu/eli/reg/2017/1151/oj
24. Traufetter, G.: Audi manipulierte beliebtes Dienstwagenmodell - Produktion gestoppt, May 2018. http://www.spiegel.de/auto/aktuell/audi-manipulierte-beliebtes-dienstwagenmodell-a-1206722.html
25. U.S. Environmental Protection Agency: Emission Facts: Average Carbon Dioxide Emissions Resulting from Gasoline and Diesel Fuel, February 2005. https://nepis. epa.gov/Exe/ZyPURL.cgi?Dockey=P1001YTF.TXT

Property-Driven Runtime Resolution of Feature Interactions

Santhana Gopalan Raghavan[1], Kosuke Watanabe[2], Eunsuk Kang[3(✉)],
Chung-Wei Lin[4], Zhihao Jiang[5], and Shinichi Shiraishi[2]

[1] University of Southern California, Los Angeles, USA
santhanr@usc.edu
[2] Toyota InfoTechnology Center, Mountain View, USA
{kwatanabe,sshiraishi}@us.toyota-itc.com
[3] Carnegie Mellon University, Pittsburgh, USA
eskang@cmu.edu
[4] National Taiwan University, Taipei, Taiwan
cwlin@csie.ntu.edu.tw
[5] ShanghaiTech University, Shanghai, China
jiangzhh@shanghaitech.edu.cn

Abstract. The feature interaction problem occurs when two or more features interact and possibly conflict with each other in unexpected ways, resulting in undesirable system behaviors. Common approaches to resolving feature interactions are based on priorities, which are ineffective in scenarios where the set of features may evolve past the design phase, and where desirability of features may change dynamically depending on the state of the environment. This paper introduces a *property-driven* approach to feature-interaction resolution, where a desired system property is leveraged to determine which feature action should be enabled at a given context. Compared to existing approaches, our approach is capable of (1) providing resolutions even if the system evolves with new or modified features, and (2) handling complex resolution scenarios where the preference of one feature over the others may change dynamically. We demonstrate the effectiveness of our approach through a case study involving resolution of safety-critical features in an intelligent vehicle.

1 Introduction

The *feature interaction* problem occurs when two or more features interact and possibly conflict with each other in unexpected ways, resulting in undesirable system behaviors [3]. Feature interactions are becoming an important issue in emerging domains such as the Internet of Things and intelligent automotive systems, where the outcome of an unexpected interaction may pose significant safety or security risks [8,16,26]. For instance, a pair of independent safety features in a vehicle may attempt to send conflicting acceleration commands to the engine controller, possibly violating a safety requirement that would have been satisfied if each feature had existed in isolation.

© Springer Nature Switzerland AG 2018
C. Colombo and M. Leucker (Eds.): RV 2018, LNCS 11237, pp. 316–333, 2018.
https://doi.org/10.1007/978-3-030-03769-7_18

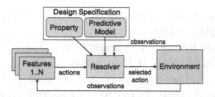

Fig. 1. Overview of the proposed resolution framework.

Most common approaches to resolving conflicts between features leverage some notion of *priorities* [4,5,13,24,28]. Typically, a total or partially-ordered ranking of features is determined at design time, and an arbitration procedure is applied at runtime to enable the actions of the highest ranking feature when a conflict occurs. However, a priority-based resolution strategy suffers from two major shortcomings. First, in certain domains, it may be difficult or impossible to predict the set of potential features that may be integrated into a system. Many modern vehicles, for example, are designed with a capability to download new applications or modify existing ones through over-the-air (OTA) updates, and the architecture of an in-vehicle software system is likely to evolve well beyond its deployment into the market.

Second, certain types of resolution decisions are *context-dependent*, in that the most desirable feature may depend on the state of the surrounding environment at a particular time. For instance, to reduce the risk of collision, a feature that results in increased acceleration may sometimes be preferable to one that attempts to reduce speed (e.g., in scenarios where a vehicle is being tailgated by another speeding vehicle within an unsafe distance). A static resolution strategy that always favors certain features over the others is insufficient to support this type of dynamic resolution, where contextual information plays a crucial role.

This paper introduces a novel *property-driven* approach to feature-interaction resolution that is designed to address these two shortcomings. The high-level overview of the proposed approach is shown in Fig. 1. Along with a set of feature actions, our resolver takes three different types of inputs: (1) a desired *property* to be fulfilled (e.g., "The distance to the preceding vehicle must be at least some minimum value"), (2) a *predictive model* that describes how the system and its environment evolve given a particular action (e.g., a model of changes in velocity over time given an acceleration), and (3) a set of *observations* that represent the current *context*, i.e., the state of the environment (e.g., velocities of the surrounding vehicles). The resolver then uses the model to evaluate potential consequences of each action and determine which of the conflicting features should be enabled to satisfy the property in the current context.

Instead of relying on a pre-determined priority list, our approach decouples resolution decisions from the presence of particular features and thus, is capable of providing resolutions even if the system evolves with new or modified features. In addition, since our approach does not rely on fixed resolution strategies, it is capable of handling complex resolution scenarios where the preference of one feature over the others may change dynamically depending on their satisfactions of the property in a given context.

In particular, we are interested in investigating the problem of feature interaction in *cyber-physical systems* (CPS), where the behavior of the system and the environment can be represented as an evolution of continuous variables (e.g., velocity or distance) over time. To express properties about these types of systems, we adopt Signal Temporal Logic (STL) as the underlying property specification language [15]. Sometimes, multiple actions may satisfy the desired property in a given context and thus, cannot be distinguished from each other. To resolve this issue, we leverage the notion of *robustness* of satisfaction [11] as a quantitative metric to measure how well the property is satisfied by a given action and distinguish competing features that both (dis-)satisfy the property.

We have built a prototype implementation of the proposed resolution framework as a part of an in-house simulation environment for designing and testing vehicle systems. To demonstrate the effectiveness of our approach, we applied this framework to a case study involving a set of safety features from the automotive domain. The outcome of this study shows that our approach can effectively resolve conflicts among features and ensure that the system performs the actions that are most satisfactory with respect to a given safety property.

This paper makes the following contributions:

- A novel, *property-driven* approach to feature-interaction resolution, which applies the notion of the *robustness* of property satisfaction to resolve conflicts among competing features (Sect. 4),
- A prototype implementation of the proposed approach (Sect. 5.1), and
- A case study demonstrating the effectiveness of the approach on a set of automotive safety features (Sect. 5.2).

The paper concludes with a discussion of the related work (Sect. 6), current limitations with the proposed framework and potential directions for further extending the property-driven approach (Sect. 7).

2 Motivating Example

Modern vehicles are equipped with a set of safety features called *advanced driver-assistance systems* (ADAS). One common ADAS feature is called *cruise control* (CC), which is intended to automatically maintain the speed of the *ego* vehicle (i.e., the vehicle being controlled) to the driver-set speed. To achieve its objective, CC sends an acceleration request to the engine controller, which, in turn, generates a corresponding actuator command to increase the engine torque until the vehicle reaches the desired acceleration.

Another ADAS feature, called speed limit control (SLC), is designed to automatically reduce the speed of the vehicle to a legal limit that is obtained from the surrounding environment (e.g., by detecting a speed limit sign or a GPS location). SLC operates by sending a sequence of requests to the brake controller until the vehicle reaches the desired speed limit.

One desirable safety property of the ego vehicle can be stated as:

P1: *The time to collision (TTC) between this vehicle and a nearby vehicle must always be above TTC_{min}.*

where TTC_{min} is some constant threshold determined by automotive engineers (enough time for a driver to react; e.g., 5 s). The actual time-to-collision at a given moment depends on the acceleration, velocity, and distance between a pair of vehicles, and computed using information from on-board sensors.

Conflict Scenario. Consider a scenario with three vehicles sharing a single lane, as shown in Fig. 2. For the purpose of this example, vehicle B is designated to be the system that we wish to control, and the leading and following vehicles (A and C) are considered to be part of the environment. Initially, vehicle A is moving at a constant speed of 60 km per hour (km/h), and B decides to catch up to A from its initial speed of 40 km/h by enabling CC.

Suppose that vehicle B approaches an area with a speed limit of 40 km/h, and the SLC feature begins sending brake requests in order to limit the vehicle acceleration. This results in one type of *feature conflict*: Two independent features (i.e., CC and SLC), each trying to achieve its own goal, attempt to manipulate the same system variable (i.e., acceleration) in an inconsistent manner.

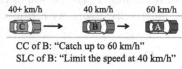

CC of B: "Catch up to 60 km/h"
SLC of B: "Limit the speed at 40 km/h"

Fig. 2. Sample driving scenario.

Existing Methods. One way to resolve this conflict is to assign to each feature a *priority rank* that indicates the level of criticality, and have the feature with the highest priority (e.g., SLC) be selected over those with lower ranks when a conflict arises (e.g., CC). An alternative approach is to design and assign a specific resolution strategy to each system variable that may be manipulated by multiple features. For instance, one possible strategy, given multiple features that attempt to manipulate the acceleration, may select the one that results in the lowest acceleration (e.g., SLC)—the reasoning being that the slower the vehicle speed is, the safer it is likely to be.

While the latter approach has the advantage that it is feature-agnostic, it may still lead to unsafe outcomes in scenarios that the specific resolution strategy is not designed to handle. For instance, suppose that the following vehicle C begins to rapidly accelerate and exceed the speed of vehicle B. As vehicle C approaches B within an unsafe distance (thus, reducing the TTC between the two vehicles), the safer action to take in this scenarios is arguably to increase, not decrease, the acceleration of vehicle B to avoid a possible collision.

Proposed Method. Our approach to resolution, in comparison, evaluates the feature actions *with respect to the property* and selects the one that is most likely to satisfy it. For instance, as vehicle C speeds towards B from the rear and the TTC approaches the safe threshold (TTC_{min}), our resolver determines that accelerating the vehicle is more likely to satisfy the above property (**P1**) and selects CC over SLC.

Suppose, however, that as vehicle B speeds up towards 60 km/h, the leading vehicle A begins to slow down, and the TTC between A and B begins approaching the safety threshold (thus increasing the chance of collision ahead). Under this circumstance, the resolver determines that the safer action (as determined by property **P1**) is to decelerate vehicle B, and chooses SLC over CC.

Challenges. Note that the desirability of a feature may change depending on the context; i.e., a feature action may satisfy a desired property in one scenario while failing to satisfy it in a different scenario. To make this type of *context-dependent* decision, the system must explicitly take into account the information about the current and future states of the environment. Furthermore, if none of the competing features satisfies the property (or if all of them do), the system must still be able to make a meaningful choice between them. In the following sections of the paper, we introduce how our resolution framework leverages (1) a model of the environment to evaluate the desirability of a feature within a given context, and (2) the notion of *robustness* of satisfaction to select the action that is *most satisfactory* with respect to the given property.

3   Background

We are interested in designing a resolution framework to ensure the safety of CPSs, which share two common characteristics: (1) timing is often an important part of system requirements (e.g., "the vehicle must come to a full stop within the next 3 s"), and (2) certain aspects of system states are best captured using continuous domains (e.g., velocity). To express properties about such a system, we adopt a formal specification logic called *signal temporal logic* (STL) [15].

Behavior as Signals. In this approach, the state of a system and its evolution over time is captured using the notion of a *signal*. A signal over domain D is a function $\mathbf{s} : T \rightarrow D$, where *time domain* T is a finite or infinite set of real numbers that represent a particular point in time ($T \subseteq \mathbb{R}_{\geq 0}$). A typical system consists of multiple state variables, and so the value of a signal is represented as a tuple of k real numbers ($D \subseteq \mathbb{R}^k$); i.e., $\mathbf{s}(t) = (v_1, \ldots, v_k)$. For convenience, we use the subscript notation $\mathbf{s}_i(t)$ to denote the i-th component of the signal at time t (for $1 \leq i \leq k$).

Example. Suppose that the state of a vehicle at time t is modeled as tuple $\mathbf{s}(t) = (v, a)$, where v and a correspond to the velocity and acceleration of the vehicle, respectively. The signal $\mathbf{s} = \{(t_0, (30.0, 2.5)), (t_1, (32.5, 2.5)), (t_2, (35.0, 2.5))\}$ depicts a behavior of the vehicle as it speeds up from 30 to 35 km/h at a constant acceleration over a finite time sequence $\langle t_0, t_1, t_2 \rangle$.

Signal Temporal Logic (STL). STL is a logic designed for specifying and reasoning about the continuous behavior of a system over time [15]. STL is an extension of linear temporal logic (LTL) [20] with an ability to specify properties over real values and real time. An STL formula takes the following form:

$$\varphi := u \mid \neg\varphi \mid \varphi_1 \wedge \varphi_2 \mid \varphi_1 \mathbf{U}_{[a,b]}\varphi_2$$

where $a < b$ for $a, b \in \mathbb{Q}_{\geq 0}$, and u is a predicate of the form $f_u(\mathbf{s}_1(t), \ldots, \mathbf{s}_k(t)) > 0$ for a k-tuple signal $\mathbf{s} = (\mathbf{s}_1, \ldots, \mathbf{s}_k)$ at time t. Informally, the meaning of the until operator at time t is that φ_1 must hold until φ_2 becomes true sometime within the interval $[t + a, t + b]$. The until operator $\mathbf{U}$ alone is sufficient to express two other types of temporal operators that are often useful in system specification—eventually ($\mathbf{F}$) and always ($\mathbf{G}$): $\mathbf{F}_{[a,b]}\varphi = \text{True}\mathbf{U}_{[a,b]}\varphi$ and $\mathbf{G}_{[a,b]}\varphi = \neg\mathbf{F}_{[a,b]}\neg\varphi$.

Robustness of Satisfaction. In a system whose behavior is captured using continuous variables, it is often useful to be able to talk about how *close* the system is from (dis-)satisfying a property. For instance, if a property says "the distance between the ego and preceding vehicles must be at least 3.0 m", it may be useful to know not only whether the vehicles satisfy this property, but also how far above 3 m they are apart (e.g., 3.1 m vs 5 m).

In prior works, STL has been extended to define this notion of closeness as the *robustness* of satisfaction [10,11]. Formally, the robustness of $\mathbf{s}$ with respect to STL formula φ at time t, denoted $\rho(\varphi, \mathbf{s}, t)$, is defined as follows:

$$\rho(u, \mathbf{s}, t) = f_u(\mathbf{s}_1(t), \ldots, \mathbf{s}_k(t))$$
$$\rho(\neg\varphi, \mathbf{s}, t) = -\rho(\varphi, \mathbf{s}, t)$$
$$\rho(\varphi_1 \wedge \varphi_2, \mathbf{s}, t) = \min(\rho(\varphi_1, \mathbf{s}, t), \rho(\varphi_2, \mathbf{s}, t))$$
$$\rho(\varphi_1 \mathbf{U}_{[a,b]}\varphi_2, \mathbf{s}, t) = \sup_{t' \in [t+a,t+b]} \min(\rho(\varphi_2, \mathbf{s}, t'), \inf_{t'' \in [t,t']} \rho(\varphi_1, \mathbf{s}, t''))$$

where $\inf_{x \in X} f(x)$ returns the greatest lower bound of some function f over domain X (and similarly for $\sup$, the least upper bound). Given that each predicate in STL is of the form $u \equiv f_u(\mathbf{s}_1(t), \ldots, \mathbf{s}_k(t)) > 0$, robustness intuitively captures how far the signal deviates above (or below) 0.

Robustness for $\mathbf{G}$ and $\mathbf{F}$ properties can also be defined as:

$$\rho(\mathbf{G}_{[a,b]}\varphi, \mathbf{s}, t) = \inf_{t' \in [t+a,t+b]} \rho(\varphi, \mathbf{s}, t')$$
$$\rho(\mathbf{F}_{[a,b]}\varphi, \mathbf{s}, t) = \sup_{t' \in [t+a,t+b]} \rho(\varphi, \mathbf{s}, t')$$

Informally, how well $\mathbf{s}$ satisfies $\mathbf{G}\varphi$ is defined to be the point at which the system is the furthest from satisfying φ (similarly, for $\mathbf{F}\varphi$, the point at which φ is satisfied "most well" by the system).

Example. Consider the property **P1** from Sect. 2, which says that the TTC between the ego vehicle and a nearby vehicle must always be above some predefined threshold (TTC_{min}). This property can be formulated as the following STL formula: $\mathbf{G}_{[0,3]}(ttc - TTC_{min} > 0)$ (for simplicity, let us assume that $\mathbf{s}$ is a single-tuple signal that only keeps track of TTCs over time; i.e., $ttc = \mathbf{s}_1(t)$). Suppose that we are given the following pair of signals, representing two different behaviors of the system:

$$\mathbf{s}_X = \{(0, (4.0)), (1, (3.5)), (2, (4.0)), (3, (4.5))\}$$
$$\mathbf{s}_Y = \{(0, (4.0)), (1, (3.5)), (2, (3.0)), (3, (2.5))\}$$

Suppose $TTC_{min} = 4.0$ s. Then, $\rho(\mathbf{P1}, \mathbf{s}_X, 0) = -0.5$ and $\rho(\mathbf{P1}, \mathbf{s}_Y, 0) = -1.5$. Intuitively, under the scenario depicted by $\mathbf{s}_Y$, the ego vehicle comes closer to colliding with the neighboring vehicle than it does under $\mathbf{s}_X$. Thus, while the property is violated in both scenarios, $\mathbf{s}_X$ is arguably the more desirable outcome of the system.

4   Property-Driven Resolution

Given a set of conflicting feature actions, the goal of our resolution method is to determine which action is most satisfactory with respect to a desired property and allow that action to take place over the other competing actions. At high-level, for each action, our resolver generates a *predictive signal* that estimates how the system is likely to evolve over time given that particular action, and then computes its robustness with respect to the property. The resolver then selects the action with the highest robustness.

Scope. We are specifically interested in studying continuously running systems that must always stay within a safe state. Our goal is to ensure that interactions between features do not lead to a violation of *safety invariants*; i.e., properties that must be maintained by the system throughout its execution. Thus, our resolver takes an input property of form $\mathbf{G}_{[0,\infty]}\varphi$, where φ is any *bounded* STL formula. This restriction on the boundedness of φ is to ensure that prediction terminates after a finite number of steps; i.e., when the resolver performs prediction at each execution step, it only needs to look ahead a finite number of times in order to fully evaluate the robustness of the conflicting actions.

4.1   Prediction

Predictive Model. For each competing action, the resolver generates a signal that predicts how the system evolves given this action, and then evaluates this signal for robustness. Let $\mathcal{V}$ be the set of variables that hold different kinds of system quantities (e.g., speed, distance). In our approach, the model used for prediction is encoded as a transition system $M = (Q, \mathcal{A}, \delta, q_o)$, where:

- $Q \subseteq \mathbb{R}^k$ is the set of states, represented as the configurations of a k-tuple signal (i.e., $q = (v_1, \ldots, v_k)$). In particular, the state consists of n *controlled* variables (v_i for $1 \leq i \leq n \leq k$); the remaining are called *monitored* variables (i.e., $\mathcal{V} = \mathcal{V}_{controlled} \cup \mathcal{V}_{monitored}$).
- $\mathcal{A}$ is the set of actions on controlled variables.
- $\delta : Q \times \mathcal{A} \rightarrow Q$ is the transition function that takes the system from one state to another on an action.
- $q_0 \in Q$ is the initial state of the system.

The notion of controlled and monitored variables is based on the *four variable* model by Parnas et al. [18]. A controlled variable represents the part of the environment that the system can manipulate (e.g., acceleration). A monitored variable, on the other hand, represents an observation about the environment that cannot be directly manipulated but may depend on one or more controlled variables (e.g., velocity of a vehicle, which depends on its acceleration).

Each action in $\mathcal{A}$ involves the assignment of a new value to a controlled variable. In every transition, the system performs one of the available actions to modify a particular controlled variable (for example, increasing the acceleration); the change to the controlled variable, in turn, determines the values of the monitor variables in the new state. We assume that a special action called $nop \in \mathcal{A}$ is defined for all controlled variables to represent the absence of change.

Intuitively, M is a machine that can be used to generate different signals of the system (each corresponding to one possible execution), depending on the choice of the action at every transition step: Given a particular sequence of states $q_0, q_1, \ldots, q_{i-1}$, $\mathbf{s}(t) = q_t$ for $0 \leq t \leq i - 1$.

Example. Let us show how system dynamics (δ) can be specified using a set of actions and relationships among variables at consecutive time steps, t and t'. Consider a simplified version of the example from Sect. 2, with two vehicles, A and B (with B being the ego vehicle that we wish to control). The state of a predictive model for this system can be defined as (a_B, v_B, d_{AB}), where a_B is the sole controlled variable representing the acceleration of B, and the rest are monitored variables for the velocity of B and its distance to A, respectively.

The type of action for setting the acceleration of B is defined as follows:

$$set Accel(acc) \equiv a_B(t') := acc$$

where input parameter acc represents the new acceleration of the vehicle, and := denotes the assignment of a value to a controlled variable.

The dynamics of monitored variables are defined in terms of controlled variables (for simplicity, we assume that vehicle A maintains a constant speed):

$$v_B(t') = v_B(t) + a_B(t') * T_{step}$$
$$d_{AB}(t') = d_{AB}(t) + v_A * T_{step} - (v_B(t) * T_{step} + 0.5 * a_B(t') * (T_{step}^2))$$

where t and t' are used to index into the value of a variable in the current and next state, respectively; T_{step} is a constant that represents the time elapsed between each system transition (e.g., 0.1 s). The concept of TTC, which appears in property **P1**, can be derived in terms of v_B and d_{AB}, and needs not be defined as its own monitored variable: $ttc(t') = d_{AB}(t')/(v_B(t') - v_A)$

Assumption. We assume that the model of the system used for prediction is *deterministic*; i.e., executing the model from a particular state with a given action and some number of steps always returns a unique signal. This simplification results in a desirable property that feature conflicts can be resolved in a deterministic manner.

```
 1  fun resolveAll(φ, M, s)
 2  |   resolved := {}
 3  |   for v ∈ V_controlled do
 4  |   |   A_c := detectConflicts(v, M)
 5  |   |   resolved[v] := resolve(A_c, φ, M, s)
 6  |   end
 7  |   return resolved
 8  end
 9  fun resolve(A_c, φ, M, s)
10  |   rob := {}, a_max := none
11  |   for a ∈ A_c do
12  |   |   s^a := execute(M, a, s(t), window(φ))
13  |   |   rob[a] := ρ(φ, s^a, t + 1)
14  |   |   if a_max = none ∨ rob[a] > rob[a_max] then
15  |   |   |   a_max := a
16  |   |   end
17  |   end
18  |   return a_max
19  end
```

Algorithm 1. Resolution Algorithm.

4.2 Resolution Algorithm

As shown earlier in Fig. 1, our resolver is placed between the set of available features and actuators that act on the system environment as requested by the feature actions. During each system execution cycle, the resolver performs the algorithm in Algorithm 1 to resolve potential conflicts and select system actions that are most likely to maintain a given invariant φ.

The resolver attempts to resolve conflicts associated with each controlled variable one-by-one (lines 3–6). For each of the conflicting actions $a \in \mathcal{A}_c$, the resolver predicts the effect of action a by executing the system model M for a time period that is sufficiently lengthy for evaluating how well a satisfies φ (lines 12–13). After all conflicting actions have been evaluated, the resolver selects the one with the highest robustness value to be performed by the system (line 18).

Conflict Detection. The first task in resolution is to determine the *conflict set* ($\mathcal{A}_c$, line 4)—the set of feature actions that may be in a potential conflict with each other. Since the focus of this work is on resolution, not detection, we omit the details of this step. At high-level, we adopt a *variable-specific* approach proposed by [27], where two features that attempt to modify the same controlled variable are deemed to be in a possible conflict. For instance, CC attempts to speed the vehicle up by increasing its acceleration while SLC attempts to do the opposite, and so the actions from these features are placed in the conflict set. In addition, based on the system dynamics ($M.\delta$), controlled variables that affect a common monitored variable are considered to be *coupled*; any pair of actions that modify two coupled controlled variables are also included in the conflict set.

Prediction Window. The resolver must simulate the effect of actions long enough to determine their robustness with respect to the given property. This duration depends on the structure and length of intervals in the property itself. For instance, consider the following formula:

$$\varphi_{recover} \equiv (ttc \leq TTC_{min} \Rightarrow \mathbf{F}_{[0,3]}(ttc > TTC_{min}))$$

which says that if TTC falls below TTC_{min}, it must be brought back above this safe minimum threshold within the next 3 time steps[1]. In order to determine the robustness of an action with respect to this property, the resolver must generate a predictive signal of at least length 4 by executing M. More generally, the *prediction window* for a bounded STL formula, φ, is defined as follows:

$$\omega(u) = 1 \qquad \omega(\neg\varphi) = \omega(\varphi)$$
$$\omega(\varphi_1 \wedge \varphi_2) = \mathbf{max}(\omega(\varphi_1), \omega(\varphi_2))$$
$$\omega(\varphi_1 \mathbf{U}_{[a,b]}\varphi_2) = \mathbf{max}(\omega(\varphi_1) + b - 1, \omega(\varphi_2) + b)$$

The intuition behind the prediction window for the until operator is as follows: Since φ_2 must become true in at most b future steps, and φ_1 needs to hold only until φ_2 turns true, the prediction task needs to estimate future states for only $b - 1$ steps (plus the number of steps needed to predict φ_1 itself) to determine the robustness of an action for φ_1 part of the $\mathbf{U}$ formula.

Model Execution. The *execution* function (line 12) simulates M to generate a sequence of future states by iteratively applying its transition function δ to the current state and action a. We assume that throughout the prediction window, the applied action remains fixed as a. An alternative approach would involve using models of the features to predict their future actions. Although this could result in more accurate predictions, it would also introduce an additional requirement that every feature comes with its own predictive model—which, based on our interactions with automotive engineers, is rather unrealistic (particularly since many features are developed and updated by third-party suppliers beyond the control of a car manufacturer). Thus, we believe that our design decision is crucial for making the proposed resolution method applicable in practice.

In our experience, we found that our approach is still effective at predicting the system evolution. Most automotive features perform actions that change the system state in a *gradual* manner (e.g., slowly adjust the acceleration); we observed that such actions do not deviate significantly during the prediction windows that we experimented with. In addition, the accumulative effect of inaccuracies is mitigated by repeatedly performing resolution with updated feature actions at each iteration. The frequency of resolution is a parameter that can be adjusted in our framework (further discussed in Sect. 5.3. **Performance**).

Example. Consider actions, $a_1 = setAccel(0.1 \text{ m/s}^2)$ and $a_2 = setAccel(-0.45 \text{ m/s}^2)$, generated by CC and SLC, respectively. Since both manipulate the acceleration of vehicle B, they are considered to be in conflict (i.e.,

---

[1] To match the syntax of STL, the inequalities can be rewritten to the form $f(\mathbf{s}(t)) > 0$.

$\mathcal{A}_c=\{a_1, a_2\}$). The current system state is given as $(a_B(t), v_B(t), d_{AB}(t)) = (1.0 \text{ m/s}^2, 60 \text{ km/h}, 12 \text{ m})$, with $v_A = 50 \text{ km/h}$ and $TTC_{min} = 5s$. Thus, $ttc = 12/((60 - 50) * 0.2778) \approx 4.32 \leq TTC_{min}$, meaning vehicle B faces the risk of an impending collision with A. Recall the STL formula $\varphi_{recover}$ introduced earlier:

$$\varphi_{recover} \equiv (ttc \leq TTC_{min} \Rightarrow \mathbf{F}_{[0,3]}(ttc > TTC_{min}))$$

To evaluate the robustness of the two actions against this formula, the resolver generates the following predictive signals (for simplicity, we show ttc as the sole component of the signal instead of a_B, v_B, d_{AB}):

$$\mathbf{s}^{a_1} = \{(t_0, (3.19)), (t_1, (2.10)), (t_2, (1.05)), (t_3, (0.028))\}$$
$$\mathbf{s}^{a_2} = \{(t_0, (4.06)), (t_1, (3.91)), (t_2, (3.99)), (t_3, (4.59))\}$$

where t_0 is the first step in the future ($t_0 = t+1$, $t_1 = t_0+1 \ldots$). According to the robustness semantics of STL, $\rho(\varphi, \mathbf{s}^{a_1}, t_0) = 3.19 - 5 = -1.81$ and $\rho(\varphi, \mathbf{s}^{a_2}, t_0) = 4.59 - 5 = -0.41$. Even though both actions do not satisfy the invariant, a_2 is arguably a safer choice, since it pulls the vehicle closer back to the TTC_{min} threshold. Thus, the resolver selects a_2 as the next action to be performed.

5   Case Study

We present a case study applying our resolution method to a set of conflicting safety features in an automotive system. In particular, our goal was to demonstrate that given a set of conflicting feature actions, our method is effective in selecting the action that is most satisfactory with respect to a desired property.

5.1   Implementation

We built a prototype implementation of the feature resolution framework as a part of an in-house simulation environment that we had been developing for vehicle design and testing. The environment consists of two main parts: (1) The driving simulator, built on top of the Unity engine, and (2) the vehicle control system, built as a suite of models in Simulink/MATLAB, each describing the behavior of a controller (e.g., brake controller) or an ADAS feature (e.g., SLC).

The simulator is responsible for animating a model of the traffic environment, while the control system describes the internal behavior of a vehicle. Each simulation run takes place on a traffic map (e.g., a highway road) with a set of vehicles configured with an initial location (2D coordinates), orientation, and velocity. At each simulation step, the simulator sends a message to the control system with the information about the current state of the environment (i.e., surrounding vehicle locations and speeds). Given this information, the control system determines the next control action to perform (e.g., reduce acceleration) and relays this decision back to the simulator, which then accordingly updates the state of the environment by using a built-in physics engine. For our study, we implemented the following features as Simulink models:

- Cruise control (CC): Gradually increases and maintains the vehicle speed to a set value by generating a sequence of acceleration requests.
- Speed limit control (SLC): Gradually reduces the vehicle speed to a context-dependent threshold by sending a sequence of partial braking requests and decreasing its acceleration.
- Automatic emergency braking (AEB): Brings the vehicle to a stop by sending a sequence of full braking requests, drastically reducing its acceleration.
- Partial braking assistance (PB): Gradually slows down the vehicle to maintain a minimum distance to the leading vehicle by generating a sequence of partial braking requests.

5.2 Experimental Setup

We tested our resolution framework on a number of scenarios involving three vehicles (A, B, C) traveling on a single lane, as shown in Fig. 2.

Predictive Model. The model used in our simulation is more complex than the one introduced throughout Sect. 4. The state of the system is represented as the following tuple: $(a_B, v_B, d_{AB}, d_{BC}, a_A, v_A, a_C, v_C)$. In addition to observing the distance between vehicles A and B, we also keep track of information about vehicle C (which trails B). Furthermore, we assume that the speeds of both A and C may also change over time, and this information is made available to B via vehicle-to-vehicle communication.

Properties. We tested our resolution approach on the following two properties:

$$\mathbf{P1} \equiv \mathbf{G}_{[0,\infty]}(ttc > TTC_{min})$$
$$\mathbf{P2} \equiv \mathbf{G}_{[0,\infty]}(ttc \leq TTC_{min} \Rightarrow \mathbf{F}_{[0,3]}(ttc > TTC_{min}))$$

Conceptually, **P2** can be considered a weaker form of **P1** that the system attempts to satisfy if **P1** is violated: When the TTC falls below a minimum threshold, the vehicle must recover back to a safer state within the next three seconds.

The definition of TTC is also more complex than the one introduced in Sect. 4, as we now take into account the distances between B and C as well as A and B. In particular, *ttc* between A, B, C is now defined to be the minimum of the TTCs between pairs of vehicles:

$$ttc = \mathbf{min}(ttc_{AB}, ttc_{BC}) \quad ttc_{AB} = d_{AB}/(v_B - v_A) \quad ttc_{BC} = d_{BC}/(v_C - v_B)$$

Intuitively, *ttc* represents the time to the *first* potential collision. Thus, by maximizing the TTC, our resolver can be regarded as attempting to delay the first impending collision as much as possible (giving the driver more time to react).

Simulation Scenarios. For each pairwise feature combination (e.g., CC vs SLC), we simulated the four distinct scenarios and observed the changes in vehicle speeds as well as the robustness of the features. Each scenario was executed twice, with and without our property-driven resolver activated. In the run without the resolver, the action that would result in a lower acceleration was selected over the other conflicting action—the rationale being that the slower the vehicle speed, the safer it is likely to be (the resolution strategy used by [27]).

5.3   Simulation Results

Figure 3 shows the results from two scenarios involving the following feature combinations: SLC vs CC and PB vs CC, with **P1** as the property. In addition to the plotted scenarios, we tested every other pairwise combinations of features; due to limited space, we discuss only these two in detail.

SLC vs CC. Figure 3(a) and (b) shows the speed changes in the vehicles when SLC and CC are enabled, without and with the resolver active, respectively. In

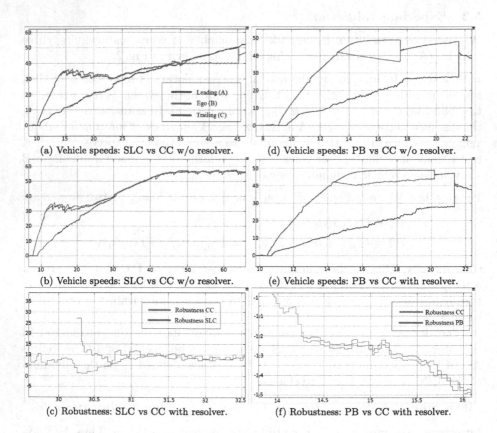

(a) Vehicle speeds: SLC vs CC w/o resolver.   (d) Vehicle speeds: PB vs CC w/o resolver.

(b) Vehicle speeds: SLC vs CC w/o resolver.   (e) Vehicle speeds: PB vs CC with resolver.

(c) Robustness: SLC vs CC with resolver.   (f) Robustness: PB vs CC with resolver.

Fig. 3. Simulation results. The x-axis in every plot represents simulation time elapsed (seconds). In plots (a), (b), (d), (e), the unit of the y-axis is in km/h; in (c) and (f), the y-axis represents the robustness value (which is, in general, unitless). In both (c) and (f), CC is enabled from the initial state, while the other feature does not become activated until certain environmental conditions are met (e.g., vehicle exceeds a SLC limit)—at which its robustness value (in blue) begins to register. (Color figure online)

Fig. 3(a), without our resolver, the system always selects the feature that results in a lower acceleration (SLC). When the trailing vehicle C (in red) speeds up, the ego vehicle B (blue) is unable to maintain ttc_{BC} above the safe threshold and eventually ends up in a collision, around 45 s. Note that when a pair of vehicles collide, their velocities simultaneously become equal (as shown by the sudden drop and increase in the plot).

In Fig. 3(b), when the resolver is active, it selects the feature that is likely to result in a higher TTC. As vehicle C approaches B from behind, ttc_{BC} begins to decrease, and the resolver selects CC to allow B to speed away from C to a state with a higher TTC. Subsequently, as vehicle B accelerates towards the leading vehicle A (in green), ttc_{AB} begins to approach the threshold, and the resolver selects SLC as the more desirable action. The resolver keeps alternating between the two features in order to maintain both ttc_{AB} and ttc_{BC} above the threshold until all three vehicles stabilize to a similar speed.

The robustness values for the two features are shown in Fig. 3(c). It starts out as CC being the only enabled feature until vehicle B reaches a certain SLC-specific speed limit, at which the SLC feature is enabled (and its robustness, in blue, begins to appear on the plot). The oscillation between the robustness of SLC and CC shows the resolver attempting to maximize ttc by alternating between the two features, until a stable speed is established by the vehicles.

PB vs CC. Figure 3(d) and (e) shows the speed changes in the vehicles when PB and CC are enabled, without and with the resolver active, respectively. In Fig. 3(d), as vehicle B catches up to vehicle A within a set distance, PB is activated and begins generating requests for decelerating vehicle B, introducing a conflict with CC. Given the two competing features, the system without our resolver selects the one that would result in a lower acceleration—in this case, PB. Around 17.5 s, the trailing vehicle C approaches and ends up colliding with B. As the leading vehicle A is traveling at a sufficiently low speed, all of the vehicles eventually end up in a three-way collision.

In Fig. 3(e), as vehicle C approaches B, the resolver continuously alternates between CC and PB in order to maximize the current ttc. However, as vehicle A is traveling at a significantly lower speed than C is, the resolver is still unable to keep the minimum TTC between the vehicles. Subsequently, vehicle B collides with C (shortly after 20 s) and eventually with vehicle A (around 21 s).

This scenario shows an example where none of the actions is sufficient to prevent the system from violating the property. In Fig. 3(f), the robustness values for both PBS and CC drop below zero and continue to fall, despite the resolver's attempt to maximize TTC, eventually resulting in a three-way collision. However, the behavior resulting from our resolver (Fig. 3(e)) is still arguably more desirable than the outcome without the resolver (3(d)). In always selecting the action that maximizes TTC, the resolver effectively delays the time of the first collision as much as possible (17.5 s vs 21 s), giving the driver more time to react.

Effect on Properties. When we initially designed our experiments, we expected to see different simulation outcomes depending on the input property (**P1** vs **P2**). Surprisingly, however, we found that the results for both sets of simulation runs were very similar, regardless of the enabled features. Note that for the invariant in **P1**, the robustness of an action is defined as $\rho(ttc > TTC_{min}, \mathbf{s}, t) = ttc(t) - TTC_{min}$. Now, consider the robustness for the invariant in **P2**:

$$\rho(ttc \leq TTC_{min} \Rightarrow \mathbf{F}_{[0,3]}(ttc > TTC_{min}), \mathbf{s}, t)$$
$$= \rho(ttc > TTC_{min} \vee \mathbf{F}_{[0,3]}(ttc > TTC_{min}), \mathbf{s}, t)$$
$$= \mathbf{max}(\rho(ttc > TTC_{min}, \mathbf{s}, t), \rho(\mathbf{F}_{[0,3]}(ttc > TTC_{min}), \mathbf{s}, t))$$
$$= \mathbf{max}(\rho(ttc > TTC_{min}, \mathbf{s}, t), \sup_{t' \in [t,t+3]} \rho(ttc > TTC_{min}, \mathbf{s}, t'))$$
$$= \mathbf{max}(ttc(t) - TTC_{min}, \sup_{t' \in [t,t+3]}(ttc(t') - TTC_{min}))$$

In other words, for **P2**, the resolver selects the action that tries to maximize TTC as much as possible during the period of the prediction window. Due to the robustness semantics, the resolver attempts to preemptively prevent TTC from falling below TTC_{min}, effectively establishing the same overall system behavior as it does under **P1** as the property. In comparison, under the conventional Boolean semantics of satisfaction, the resolver would treat competing actions equally until TTC falls below TTC_{min}. In effect, the robustness semantics of STL enables a more robust resolution of conflicts.

Performance. To assess the overhead incurred by resolution, we computed the ratio of the average simulation time with the resolver over that without the resolver. The overhead depends on the frequency of resolution, the number of features being evaluated, and the input property (which affects the prediction window). We selected the frequency of resolution to be 0.1 s, based on our estimates of how frequently messages are generated by typical electronic control units (ECUs). On average, with all of the four features enabled, the overhead was around 15.1% for **P1** and 17.8% for **P2**. The additional overhead from **P2** was due to the latter property having a larger prediction window, as expected.

It is difficult to accurately estimate how well our proposed resolver would perform in an actual vehicle. For our simulations, we are executing *models* of the features, controllers, and the environment in Simulink, which does not reflect realistic operating conditions. In a typical vehicle, these models would be realized as low-level embedded code running on ECUs or a dedicated hardware device (e.g., FPGA). In addition, in safety-critical systems like vehicles, *lookup tables* [1, 23,29] are widely used to pre-compute and reuse the results of time-consuming operations (e.g., simulation of physics dynamics), which could be used to reduce the overhead introduced by the prediction step.

6   Related Work

Our work is most closely related to the *variable-specific* resolution approach introduced in [2,27], which associates each system variable (e.g., speed) with a specific strategy for resolving conflicts between multiple actions (e.g., select the action that results in the smallest acceleration). Like ours, their approach decouples resolution decisions from the presence of particular features and is capable of handling feature addition or modification without having to modify the resolution strategies. However, since their approach still relies on fixed strategies, it may fail to produce a desirable outcome when the system runs into scenarios that are unanticipated by those strategies (as discussed in Sect. 2).

Griffeth and Velthuijsen proposed a runtime resolution method based on the notion of *negotiation*, where a central *mediator* is used to resolve conflicting actions among system agents [12]. Rather than attempting to satisfy a global system property, the goal of their resolution is different from ours, in that it attempts to come up with actions that all agents consider to be *acceptable*. Other resolution methods [4,5,13,17,24,28] rely on a priority or precedence ordering, and may not be suitable for systems where the set of features evolve over time.

STL has been leveraged for online monitoring of system properties [6,7,9]. The key difference is that monitoring attempts to detect a violation of a property *after* it has already occurred, whereas our resolution attempts to select an action that is least likely to lead to a violation *before* it occurs.

Runtime techniques for enforcing a desirable property by observing and possibly modifying system actions have been studied [19,25]. However, these approaches typically evaluate a single trace for property satisfaction, and do not involve a comparison of conflicting actions for their satisfaction or robustness.

Our approach of using a predictive model to dynamically determine the safest of the conflicting actions is similar to *online planning* [21,22], which tackles the problem of periodically computing a desirable *policy* (i.e. which actions the system should take at a given state) during the execution.

7   Conclusions and Future Directions

This paper proposes an approach that leverages a desired property of the system to resolve conflicts between competing features at runtime. Based on our experience using this framework in-house, we believe that the property-oriented method is a promising approach, especially in emerging domains such as connected vehicles where the set of installed features may change frequently.

As discussed in Sect. 4.1, our predictive model assumes that the environment evolves in a deterministic manner given a system action. Probabilistic models (e.g., Markov decision processes) may be more suitable for accurately capturing the behavior of environmental agents (e.g., how other vehicles adjust their speeds). To this end, we plan to extend our resolution framework by adopting a stochastic notion of STL satisfaction [14]. We are also exploring the possibility of incorporating enforcement techniques into our framework to *synthesize* a new action to maintain a safety invariant if none of the given feature actions is satisfactory.

References

1. Arechiga, N., Dathathri, S., Vernekar, S., Kathare, N., Gao, S., Shiraishi, S.: Osiris: a tool for abstraction and verification of control software with lookup tables. In: Proceedings of the 1st International Workshop on Safe Control of Connected and Autonomous Vehicles, SCAV@CPSWeek 2017, Pittsburgh, PA, USA, 21 April 2017, pp. 11–18 (2017)
2. Bocovich, C., Atlee, J.M.: Variable-specific resolutions for feature interactions. In: Proceedings of the 22nd ACM SIGSOFT International Symposium on Foundations of Software Engineering, (FSE-22), Hong Kong, China, 16–22 November 2014, pp. 553–563 (2014)
3. Calder, M., Kolberg, M., Magill, E.H., Reiff-Marganiec, S.: Feature interaction: a critical review and considered forecast. Comput. Netw. **41**(1), 115–141 (2003)
4. Chavan, A., Yang, L., Ramachandran, K., Leung, W.H.: Resolving feature interaction with precedence lists in the feature language extensions. In: Feature Interactions in Software and Communication Systems IX, International Conference on Feature Interactions in Software and Communication Systems, ICFI 2007, Grenoble, France, 3–5 September 2007, pp. 114–128 (2007)
5. Chen, Y., Lafortune, S., Lin, F.: Resolving feature interactions using modular supervisory control with priorities. In: Feature Interactions in Telecommunications Networks IV, Montréal, Canada, 17–19 June 1997, pp. 108–122 (1997)
6. Deshmukh, J.V., Donzé, A., Ghosh, S., Jin, X., Juniwal, G., Seshia, S.A.: Robust online monitoring of signal temporal logic. Formal Methods Syst. Des. **51**(1), 5–30 (2017)
7. Dokhanchi, A., Hoxha, B., Fainekos, G.: On-line monitoring for temporal logic robustness. In: Bonakdarpour, B., Smolka, S.A. (eds.) RV 2014. LNCS, vol. 8734, pp. 231–246. Springer, Cham (2014). https://doi.org/10.1007/978-3-319-11164-3_19
8. Dominguez, A.L.J., Day, N.A., Joyce, J.J.: Modelling feature interactions in the automotive domain. In: International Workshop on Modeling in Software Engineering (MiSE), pp. 45–50 (2008)
9. Donzé, A., Ferrère, T., Maler, O.: Efficient robust monitoring for STL. In: Sharygina, N., Veith, H. (eds.) CAV 2013. LNCS, vol. 8044, pp. 264–279. Springer, Heidelberg (2013). https://doi.org/10.1007/978-3-642-39799-8_19
10. Donzé, A., Maler, O.: Robust satisfaction of temporal logic over real-valued signals. In: Chatterjee, K., Henzinger, T.A. (eds.) FORMATS 2010. LNCS, vol. 6246, pp. 92–106. Springer, Heidelberg (2010). https://doi.org/10.1007/978-3-642-15297-9_9
11. Fainekos, G.E., Pappas, G.J.: Robustness of temporal logic specifications. In: Havelund, K., Núñez, M., Roşu, G., Wolff, B. (eds.) FATES/RV -2006. LNCS, vol. 4262, pp. 178–192. Springer, Heidelberg (2006). https://doi.org/10.1007/11940197_12
12. Griffeth, N.D., Velthuijsen, H.: The negotiating agents approach to runtime feature interaction resolution. In: Feature Interactions in Telecommunications Systems, Amsterdam, The Netherlands, 8–10 May 1994, pp. 217–235 (1994)
13. Hay, J.D., Atlee, J.M.: Composing features and resolving interactions. In: ACM SIGSOFT Symposium on Foundations of Software Engineering, Proceedings, San Diego, California, USA, 6–10 November 2000, pp. 110–119 (2000)

14. Li, J., Nuzzo, P., Sangiovanni-Vincentelli, A.L., Xi, Y., Li, D.: Stochastic contracts for cyber-physical system design under probabilistic requirements. In: Proceedings of the 15th ACM-IEEE International Conference on Formal Methods and Models for System Design, MEMOCODE 2017, Vienna, Austria, 29 September–02 October 2017, pp. 5–14 (2017)
15. Maler, O., Nickovic, D.: Monitoring temporal properties of continuous signals. Formal Techniques. Modelling and Analysis of Timed and Fault-Tolerant Systems, pp. 152–166. Springer, Heidelberg (2004). https://doi.org/10.1007/978-3-540-30206-3_12
16. Metzger, A.: Feature interactions in embedded control systems. Comput. Netw. **45**(5), 625–644 (2004)
17. Nakamura, M., Igaki, H., Yoshimura, Y., Ikegami, K.: Considering online feature interaction detection and resolution for integrated services in home network system. In: ICFI, pp. 191–206. IOS Press (2009)
18. Parnas, D.L., Madey, J.: Functional documents for computer systems. Sci. Comput. Program. **25**(1), 41–61 (1995)
19. Pinisetty, S., Roop, P.S., Smyth, S., Tripakis, S., von Hanxleden, R.: Runtime enforcement of reactive systems using synchronous enforcers. In: Proceedings of the 24th ACM SIGSOFT International SPIN Symposium on Model Checking of Software, Santa Barbara, CA, USA, 10–14 July 2017, pp. 80–89 (2017)
20. Pnueli, A.: The temporal logic of programs. In: Symposium on Foundations of Computer Science, SFCS 1977, pp. 46–57 (1977)
21. Ross, S., Pineau, J., Paquet, S., Chaib-draa, B.: Online planning algorithms for POMDPs. J. Artif. Intell. Res. **32**, 663–704 (2008)
22. Seuken, S., Zilberstein, S.: Formal models and algorithms for decentralized decision making under uncertainty. Auton. Agent. Multi-Agent Syst. **17**(2), 190–250 (2008)
23. Sundström, C., Frisk, E., Nielsen, L.: Diagnostic method combining the lookup tables and fault models applied on a hybrid electric vehicle. IEEE Trans. Control Syst. Technol. **24**(3), 1109–1117 (2016)
24. Tsang, S., Magill, E.H.: The network operator's perspective: detecting and resolving feature interaction problems. Comput. Netw. **30**(15), 1421–1441 (1998)
25. Wu, M., Zeng, H., Wang, C., Yu, H.: Safety guard: runtime enforcement for safety-critical cyber-physical systems: invited. In: Proceedings of the 54th Annual Design Automation Conference, DAC 2017, Austin, TX, USA, June 18–22 2017, pp. 84:1–84:6 (2017)
26. Yarosh, L., Zave, P.: Locked or not?: Mental models of IoT feature interaction. In: Proceedings of the 2017 CHI Conference on Human Factors in Computing Systems, Denver, CO, USA, 06–11 May 2017, pp. 2993–2997 (2017)
27. Zibaeenejad, M.H., Zhang, C., Atlee, J.M.: Continuous variable-specific resolutions of feature interactions. In: Proceedings of the 2017 11th Joint Meeting on Foundations of Software Engineering, ESEC/FSE 2017, Paderborn, Germany, 4–8 September 2017, pp. 408–418 (2017)
28. Zimmer, P.A., Atlee, J.M.: Ordering features by category. J. Syst. Softw. **85**(8), 1782–1800 (2012). https://doi.org/10.1016/j.jss.2012.03.025
29. Zurbriggen, F., Ott, T., Onder, C.H.: Fast and robust adaptation of lookup tables in internal combustion engines: feedback and feedforward controllers designed independently. Proc. Inst. Mech. Eng. Part D: J. Automob. Eng. **230**(6), 723–735 (2016)

From Parametric Trace Slicing
to Rule Systems

Giles Reger[(✉)] and David Rydeheard

University of Manchester, Manchester, UK
giles.reger@manchester.ac.uk

Abstract. Parametric runtime verification is the process of verifying
properties of execution traces of (data carrying) events produced by a
running system. This paper continues our work exploring the relationship between specification techniques for parametric runtime verification.
Here we consider the correspondence between trace-slicing automata-
based approaches and rule-systems. The main contribution is a translation from quantified automata to rule-systems, which has been implemented in SCALA. This then allows us to highlight the key differences
in how the two formalisms handle data, an important step in our wider
effort to understand the correspondence between different specification
languages for parametric runtime verification.

1 Introduction

Runtime verification [7,14,15,21] is the process of checking properties of execution traces produced by running a computational system. An execution trace is
a finite sequence of *events* generated by the computation. In many applications,
events carry *data values* – the so-called parametric, or first-order, case of runtime
verification. To apply runtime verification, we need to provide (a) a specification
language for describing properties of execution traces, and (b) a mechanism for
checking these formally-defined properties during execution, i.e. a procedure for
generating monitors from specifications. Many different specification languages
for runtime verification have been proposed and almost every new development
introduces its own specification language.

This work furthers our broader goal of organising and understanding the
space of specification languages for runtime verification. As explained later, we
see little reuse of specification languages in runtime verification and little is
understood about the relationship between the different languages that have
been introduced. We believe that the field can be considerably improved by a
better understanding of this space.

This paper specifically explores the relationship between two particular
approaches to specification for parametric runtime verification: *parametric trace*

G. Reger—The work of this author is supported by COST Action ARVI IC1402, supported by COST (European Cooperation in Science and Technology).

© Springer Nature Switzerland AG 2018
C. Colombo and M. Leucker (Eds.): RV 2018, LNCS 11237, pp. 334–352, 2018.
https://doi.org/10.1007/978-3-030-03769-7_19

slicing and *rule systems*. We begin by describing the general setting we are working in (Sect. 2) before introducing these two languages (Sect. 3). The main contribution of the paper is a translation from specifications using parametric trace slicing to those using rules (Sect. 4). We define the translation, provide some examples, and prove its correctness. The translation has been implemented and validated in SCALA, available online at https://github.com/selig/qea_to_rules. A further contribution is then a discussion of the things we have learnt about the relationship between these two languages via the development of the translation (Sect. 5). We conclude in Sect. 6.

2 Setting

In this paper we focus on the runtime verification problem at a level of abstraction where we assume that a run of a system has been abstracted in terms of a finite sequence of events via some instrumentation method. Such techniques are described elsewhere [7].

Defining the Runtime Verification Problem. We begin by defining events, traces, and properties. We assume disjoint sets of event names Σ, variables *Var*, and values *Val*. We do not directly consider sorts (e.g. variable x being an integer) as this is not essential to this work, but assume events are well-sorted where it matters.

Definition 1 (Events, Traces, and Properties). *An* event *is a pair of an event name e and a list of parameters (variables or values) $v_1, \ldots, v_n$, usually written $e(v_1, \ldots, v_n)$. An event is* ground *if it does not contain variables. A* trace *is a finite sequence of ground events. A* property *is a (possibly infinite) set of traces.*

We use x, y, z for variables and a, b, c or numbers for values (unless context requires otherwise), τ for traces and $\mathcal{P}$ for properties. For example, $\text{login}(x, 42)$ is an event where x is a variable and 42 a value; the finite sequence $\text{login}(a, 42).\text{logout}(a)$ is a trace; and the set $\{\text{login}(a, 42).\text{logout}(a), \text{login}(b, 42).\text{logout}(b)\}$ is a property. We write $\mathbf{a}, \mathbf{b}$ for events where their structure is unimportant.

We say that a property is *propositional* if all events in all traces have empty lists of parameters, otherwise it is *parametric* (or first-order). A *specification language* provides a language for writing specifications φ and provides a semantics that defines the property $\mathcal{P}(\varphi)$ that φ denotes. A specification language is propositional if it can only describe specifications denoting propositional properties, and parametric otherwise.

Definition 2 (The Runtime Verification Problem). *Given a trace τ and a specification φ decide whether $\tau \in \mathcal{P}(\varphi)$.*

Again, we can talk of the *propositional* and *parametric* versions of this problem. The propositional version should be highly familiar - typical specification languages include automata, regular expressions, and linear temporal logic, for which procedures for efficiently deciding the above problem are well known.

There are four main runtime verification approaches that handle the parametric case (see [20] for an overview). Parametric trace slicing [3,11,23] separates the issue of quantification from trace-checking using a notion of *projection*. First-order extensions to temporal logic [8,9,13,22,29] rely on the standard logical treatment of quantification, introducing (somewhat complex) monitor construction techniques to handle this. Rule systems [2,5,17] and stream processing [10,12,16] do not have inherent notions of quantification. In rule systems values are stored as rule instances (facts) and rules dictate which instances should be added or removed. Stream processing defines sets of stream operators that operate over streams to produce new streams.

We note that there are variations of the above problem e.g. deciding whether $\tau.\tau' \in \mathcal{P}(\varphi)$ for all possible extensions τ' (which acknowledges that finite traces may be prefixes of some infinite trace), or considering a property as a function from traces to some non-boolean verdict domain. In general, the specification languages for such formulations remain the same and much of our work can translate to these variations.

Our Research Question. Given this large space of specification languages our fundamental research question is as follows:

What are the fundamental differences between specification languages for describing parametric properties for runtime verification and how do these differences impact the expressiveness *and* efficiency *of the runtime verification process.*

Below we discuss (i) why we care about this question, and (ii) what our general approach to answering it is.

Why Do We Care? We outline the main motivations behind this research question:

- *Reusable research.* The four main approaches to parametric runtime verification described above have been explored in relative isolation. Developments in one area cannot be easily transferred to another. For example, notions of monitorability and complexity results remain tied to their particular language.
- *Reusable tools, benchmarks, and case studies.* Similarly, tools for one language cannot be directly used for another and related experimental data is tied to that tool. This leads to separate ecosystems where runtime verification solutions are developed in isolation.
- *Balancing Expressiveness and Efficiency.* Some approaches focus on the *expressiveness* of the language before the *efficiency* of the monitoring algorithm, and other approaches have the inverse focus. A key motivation of this work is to see where we can combine the best parts of different approaches.

For example, by identifying fragments of an expressive language that can be translated into a language with a more efficient monitoring algorithm.

- *Evaluation.* In general, it is hard to compare approaches without a good understanding of how they are related. The Runtime Verification competition [6,26] has relied on a manual translation of specifications between languages, which has been problematic in various ways. Ideally, a common language would be used. However, the close links between language and the efficiency of the monitoring algorithm mean that translations would be required from this common language.

Our Approach. We are exploring this broad research question in two complementary directions. Firstly, we are taking an *example-led* approach where we explore concrete examples of specifications in different languages and attempt to infer commonalities, differences, and general relationships. This is ongoing and has begun to highlight conceptual differences between approaches [18–20]. Secondly, we are working towards a general framework for formally exploring the relationship between specification languages. We have chosen to build this via a series of *translations* between approaches. Our previous work [27] introduced a translation from a first-order temporal logic to a language using parametric trace slicing; this current work introduces a translation from parametric trace slicing to rule systems; and we are currently exploring a translation from rule systems to a first-order temporal logic. We believe that these translations can provide a pragmatic way to move between specification languages and highlight the main differences between languages.

3   Two Languages

In this section we introduce two specification languages for parametric runtime verification – one based on parametric trace slicing and the other on rule systems. Examples in both languages are given at the end of the section.

Preliminaries. Let an *event alphabet* $\mathcal{A}(Z)$ be a set of events using variables in Z e.g. $\mathcal{A}(\{x\})$ might be $\{e(x)\}$ or $\{e(x), f(x,x)\}$ but not $\{e(x), f(x,y)\}$. A map is a partial function with finite domain. We write $\perp$ for the empty map and $\mathsf{dom}(\theta)$ for the domain of map θ. Given two maps θ_1 and θ_2 we define the following operations:

$$
\begin{aligned}
\mathsf{consistent}(\theta_1, \theta_2) \quad &\textit{iff} \quad (\forall x)\ x \in (\mathsf{dom}(\theta_1) \cap \mathsf{dom}(\theta_2)) \to \theta_1(x) = \theta_2(x) \\
\theta_1 \sqsubseteq \theta_2 \quad &\textit{iff} \quad \mathsf{dom}(\theta_1) \subseteq \mathsf{dom}(\theta_2)\ \textit{and}\ \mathsf{consistent}(\theta_1, \theta_2) \\
(\theta_1 \dagger \theta_2)(x) = v \quad &\textit{iff} \quad \theta_2(x) = v\ \textit{if}\ x \in \mathsf{dom}(\theta_2)\ \textit{otherwise}\ \theta_1(x) = v
\end{aligned}
$$

A valuation is a map from variables to values. We use θ and σ for valuations. Valuations can be applied to structures containing variables to replace those variables.

The sets *Guard(Z)* and *Assign(Z)* contain (implicitly well-sorted) guards (boolean expressions) and assignments over the set of variables Z. Such guards denote predicates on valuations with domains in Z, for example $Guard(\{x, y\})$ contains expressions such as $x = y$ and $x \leq 2$. Assignments are finite sequences of the form $x := t$ where $x \in Z$ is a variable and t is an expression over values and variables in Z that can be evaluated with respect to a valuation. We assume a true guard true and an identity assignment id.

Finally, we introduce matching. Given finite parameter sequences $\overline{v}$ and $\overline{w}$, let the predicate matches$(\overline{v}, \overline{w})$ hold if there is a valuation θ such that $\theta(\overline{v}) = \theta(\overline{w})$. Let match$(\overline{v}, \overline{w})$ be the minimal such valuation with respect to the sub-map relation $\sqsubseteq$ (if such a valuation exists, undefined otherwise). Let match$(\overline{v}, \overline{w}, Z)$ be the largest valuation θ such that $\theta \sqsubseteq$ match$(\overline{v}, \overline{w})$ and dom$(\theta) \subseteq Z$ i.e. the matching valuation is restricted to Z. We lift all definitions to events by checking equality of event names.

3.1   Parametric Trace Slicing with Quantified Event Automata

Parametric trace slicing [11] was introduced as a technique that transforms a monitoring problem involving quantification *over finite domains* into a propositional one. The idea is to take each valuation of the quantified variables and consider the specification *grounded* with that valuation for the trace *projected* with respect to the valuation. The benefit of this approach is that projection can lead to efficient indexing techniques.

Quantified event automata (QEA) [3] is a slicing-based formalism that generalises previous work on parametric trace slicing. In this work, we consider a restricted form of QEA that does not allow existential quantification (see the discussion in Sect. 5).

Definition 3 (Quantified Event Automata). *A quantified event automaton is a tuple* $\langle X, Q, \mathcal{A}(X \cup Y), \delta, \mathcal{F}, q_0, \sigma_0 \rangle$ *where X is a finite set of universally quantified variables, Q is a finite set of states, $\mathcal{A}(X \cup Y)$ is an event alphabet, $\delta \subseteq (Q \times \mathcal{A}(X \cup Y) \times Guard(Y) \times Assign(Y) \times Q)$ is a transition relation, $\mathcal{F} \subseteq Q$ is a set of final states, $q_0 \in Q$ is an initial state, and σ_0 is an initial valuation with* dom$(\sigma_0) = Y$.

The variables Y are implicitly unquantified and are to be used in guards and assignments. An advantage of the parametric trace slicing approach is that the quantified and unquantified parts of the specification can be treated separately. The quantified part is dealt with by trace slicing and the unquantified part is dealt with by the automaton.

Semantics. We now introduce a *small-step* semantics for QEA. We would normally introduce a big-step semantics in terms of the trace slicing operator and use this to motivate the (more operational) small-step presentation. But space does not allow this here and we refer the reader to other texts for this [3,24]. In the following we assume a fixed QEA of interest and refer to its components e.g. the set of quantified variables X.

Let a *monitoring state* be a map from valuations θ with dom$(\theta) \subseteq X$ to sets of *configurations*, which are pairs consisting of states $\in Q$ and valuations σ with

$\mathsf{dom}(\sigma) = Y$. The small-step semantics defines a construction that extends a monitoring state given a ground event. This construction is then lifted to traces.

Next Configurations. Given a set of configurations P, an event $\mathbf{a}$, and a valuation θ (with $\mathsf{dom}(\theta) = X$), the set $\mathsf{next}(P, \mathbf{a}, \theta)$ of next configurations is defined as the smallest set of configurations such that

$$\left\{ (q', \alpha(\sigma \dagger \mathsf{match}(\mathbf{a}, \mathbf{b}, Y))) \;\middle|\; \begin{array}{l} \exists (q, \mathbf{b}, \gamma, \alpha, q') \in \delta : \langle q, \sigma \rangle \in P \wedge \mathsf{matches}(\mathbf{a}, \mathbf{b}) \wedge \\ \gamma(\sigma \dagger \mathsf{match}(\mathbf{a}, \mathbf{b}, Y)) \wedge \mathsf{match}(\mathbf{a}, \mathbf{b}, X) \sqsubseteq \theta \end{array} \right\}$$

or P if this set is empty i.e. if no transitions can be taken then P is not updated. This says that we take a transition if we match the event, satisfy the guard, and don't capture any new variables in X not already present in θ.

Relevance. We will update the configurations related to a valuation in the monitoring state if the given event is *relevant* to that valuation. An event $\mathbf{a}$ is *relevant* to some valuation θ if there is an event in the alphabet that matches it consistently with θ i.e.

$$\mathsf{relevant}(\theta, \mathbf{a}) \leftrightarrow \exists \mathbf{b} \in \mathcal{A}(X \cup Y) : \mathsf{matches}(\mathbf{a}, \mathbf{b}) \wedge \mathsf{match}(\mathbf{a}, \mathbf{b}, X) \sqsubseteq \theta$$

Extensions. We will create a new valuation if matching the given event with an event in the alphabet binds new quantified variables. The set of valuations $\mathsf{extensions}(\theta, \mathbf{a})$ that could extend an existing valuation θ given a new ground event $\mathbf{a}$ can be defined by:

$$\mathsf{from}(\mathbf{a}) \qquad = \{\theta \mid \exists \mathbf{b} \in \mathcal{A}(X \cup Y) : \mathsf{matches}(\mathbf{a}, \mathbf{b}) \wedge \theta \sqsubseteq \mathsf{match}(\mathbf{a}, \mathbf{b}, X)\}$$
$$\mathsf{extensions}(\theta, \mathbf{a}) = \{\theta \dagger \theta' \mid \theta' \in \mathsf{from}(\mathbf{a}) \wedge \mathsf{consistent}(\theta, \theta') \wedge \theta' \neq \bot\}$$

This constructs all valuations that can be built directly and then uses the consistent ones.

Construction. We put these together into the monitoring construction.

Definition 4 (Monitoring Construction). *Given ground event $\mathbf{a}$ and monitoring state M, let $\theta_1, \ldots, \theta_m$ be a linearisation of the domain of M from largest to smallest wrt $\sqsubseteq$ i.e. if $\theta_j \sqsubset \theta_k$ then $j > k$ and every element in the domain of M is present once in the sequence, hence $m = |M|$. We define the monitoring state $(\mathbf{a} * M) = N_m$ where N_m is iteratively defined as follows for $i \in [1, m]$.*

$$N_0 = \bot \qquad N_i = N_{i-1} \dagger \mathsf{Add}_i \dagger \begin{cases} [\theta_i \mapsto \mathsf{next}(M(\theta_i), \mathbf{a}, \theta_i)] & \text{if } \mathsf{relevant}(\theta_i, \mathbf{a}) \\ [\theta_i \mapsto M(\theta_i)] & \text{otherwise} \end{cases}$$

where the additions are defined in terms of extensions not already present:

$$\mathsf{Add}_i = [(\theta' \mapsto \mathsf{next}(M(\theta_i), \mathbf{a}, \theta')) \mid \theta' \in \mathsf{extensions}(\theta_i, \mathbf{a}) \wedge \theta' \notin \underline{dom}(N_{i-1})]$$

and next is a function computing the next configurations given a valuation.

This construction iterates over valuations (of quantified variables) from *largest* to *smallest* (wrt $\sqsubseteq$). For each valuation it will add any extensions that do not already exist and then update the configuration(s) mapped to by the existing valuation. Let us now consider the aspects that have not yet been defined.

Maximality. The order of traversal in Definition 4 is important as it preserves the principle of maximality. This is the requirement that when we add a new valuation we want to extend the *most informative* or *maximal* valuation as this will be associated with all configurations relevant to the new valuation. Given a set of valuations Θ and a valuation θ let maximal$(\Theta, \theta) = \theta_M$ be the maximal valuation defined as:

$$\theta_M \in \Theta \wedge \theta_M \sqsubseteq \theta \wedge \forall \theta' \in \Theta : \theta' \sqsubseteq \theta \Rightarrow \theta_M \not\sqsubseteq \theta'$$

This relies on the fact that $\mathsf{dom}(M)$ is closed under least-upper bounds. In Definition 4, when a valuation θ is introduced its initial set of configurations is taken as those belonging to maximal$(\mathsf{dom}(M), \theta)$ as otherwise it will already have been added. This principle is important as it makes the later translation complicated.

Quantification Domain. It may not be obvious from the small-step semantics but this semantics ensures that the domain of the monitoring state captures the full cross-product of the quantification domains of X. The domain of variable $x \in X$ is given as

$$\{\mathsf{match}(\mathbf{a}, \mathbf{b})(x) \mid \mathbf{a} \in \tau \wedge \mathbf{b} \in \mathcal{A}(X \cup Y) \wedge \mathsf{matches}(\mathbf{a}, \mathbf{b}) \wedge \mathbf{b} = \mathsf{e}(\ldots, x, \ldots)\}$$

i.e. the set of values in events in the trace that match with events in the alphabet.

The Property Defined by a QEA. Let $M_\tau = \tau * [\perp \mapsto \{(q_0, \sigma_0(Y))\}]$ be the above construction transitively applied to the initial monitoring state. The property defined by the QEA is the set of traces τ such that $\forall \theta \in \mathsf{dom}(M_\tau) :$ $\mathsf{dom}(\theta) = X \Rightarrow \forall (q, \sigma) \in M_\tau(\theta) : q \in F$ i.e. *all* total valuations are only mapped to final states.

3.2   A Rule-Based Approach

We now introduce an approach first introduced in RULER [2] that uses a system of rules to compute a verdict. Our notion of a rule system here could be considered the core of the system introduced in [2] i.e. the extensions in [2] are either trivial or can be defined in terms of this core. Hence, this formulation is representative of RULER.

Let $\mathcal{R}$ be a set of rule names. A *term* is a variable, value, or a function over terms (e.g. $x + 1$). A *rule expression* is a rule name r applied to a list of terms and is *pure* if these terms are function-free. A *premise* is an event, pure rule expression or guard, or a negation of any of these (we use ! for negation). A *rule term* is of the form *lhs* $\rightarrow$ *rhs* where *lhs* is a list of premises and *rhs* is a list of rule expressions. A *rule definition* is of the form $r(\overline{x})\{body\}$ where r is a rule name, $\overline{x}$ is a list of variables and *body* is a set of rule terms. We call $r(\overline{x})\{body\}$ a rule definition for $r(\overline{x})$. Finally, A *fact* is a finite set of rule instances. A *rule instance* is a pair $\langle r, \theta \rangle$ where r is a rule name and θ is a valuation. We now define a rule system.

Definition 5 (Rule System). *A rule system is a tuple* $\langle \mathcal{D}, \mathcal{B}, \mathcal{I} \rangle$ *where* $\mathcal{D}$ *is a finite set of rule definitions,* $\mathcal{B}$ *is a finite set of* bad rule expressions *and* $\mathcal{I}$ *is an* initial *fact.*

A rule term *lhs* → *rhs* is *well-formed* if when the first occurrence of a variable in *lhs* is under a negation then this is its only occurrence in the rule term. A rule definition $r(\overline{x})\{body\}$ is *well-formed* if every *rhs* in *body* only contains variables in $\overline{x}$ or the corresponding *lhs*. A rule system is *well-formed* if (i) all rule terms are well formed, (ii) there is at most one rule definition for each $r(\overline{x})$, and (iii) every rule expression used in rule terms has a corresponding definition. A rule instance $\langle r, \theta \rangle$ is well-formed for a rule system if there is a rule definition for $r(\overline{x})$ such that $\mathrm{dom}(\theta) = \overline{x}$. Below we assume a well-formed rule system of interest and will refer to its components directly.

The semantics of rule systems can be given in terms of a rewrite relationship on *facts*. Given a fact and an event we (i) find the set of rule instances in the fact that *fire*, and then (ii) update the fact with respect to these rule instances.

An *extended fact* is a finite set of rule instances and (ground) events. We define a *firing function* for extended fact Γ, valuation θ and premise as follows:

$$
\begin{aligned}
\mathsf{fire}(\Gamma, \theta, \mathbf{b}) &= \theta \dagger \mathsf{match}(\mathbf{a}, \theta(\mathbf{b})) &&\text{if} \quad \mathbf{a} \in \Gamma \wedge \mathsf{matches}(\mathbf{a}, \theta(\mathbf{b})) \\
\mathsf{fire}(\Gamma, \theta, r(\overline{x})) &= \theta \dagger \mathsf{match}(\overline{v}, \theta(\overline{x})) &&\text{if} \quad r(\overline{v}) \in \Gamma \wedge \mathsf{matches}(\overline{v}, \theta(\overline{x})) \\
\mathsf{fire}(\Gamma, \theta, \gamma) &= \theta &&\text{if} \quad \gamma(\theta) \\
\mathsf{fire}(\Gamma, \theta, !t) &= \theta &&\text{if} \quad \mathsf{fire}(\Gamma, \theta, t) = \bot \\
\mathsf{fire}(\Gamma, \theta, t) &= \bot &&\text{otherwise}
\end{aligned}
$$

This computes the extension of θ that satisfies the premise using the given extended fact. The first two lines match against events and rule expressions, the third line checks guards, the fourth line deals with negation, and the last line handles the case where the constraints of previous lines do not hold. This is lifted to lists of premises as follows:

$$\mathsf{fire}(\Gamma, \theta, \epsilon) = \theta \qquad \mathsf{fire}(\Gamma, \theta, prems) = \mathsf{fire}(\Gamma, \mathsf{fire}(\Gamma, \theta, \mathsf{head}(prems)), \mathsf{tail}(prems))$$

We say that a rule instance $\langle r, \theta \rangle$ *fires* in an extended fact Γ if $\mathsf{fire}(\Gamma, \theta, lhs) \neq \bot$ where *lhs* → *rhs* is in the body of the rule definition for $r(\mathrm{dom}(\theta))$.

Given a rule system and extended fact Γ, we define the set of ground rule expressions that result from a rule instance $\langle r, \theta \rangle$ firing as follows:

$$\mathsf{fired}(\langle r, \theta \rangle, \Gamma) = \{\theta'(rhs) \mid lhs \to rhs \in r(\mathrm{dom}(\theta)) \wedge \theta' = \mathsf{fire}(\Gamma, \theta, lhs)\}$$

where we write *lhs* → *rhs* $\in r(\mathrm{dom}(\theta))$ to mean that *lhs* → *rhs* is in the body of the rule definition of $r(\mathrm{dom}(\theta))$. As $\theta'(rhs)$ is now ground we evaluate all functions to ensure that it is also pure e.g. $[x \mapsto 1](s(x+1)) = s(1+1) = s(2)$.

We define a rewrite relation $\Delta \xrightarrow{\mathbf{a}} \Delta'$ for facts Δ and Δ' and ground event $\mathbf{a}$. Let $\Delta' = (\Delta_{NF} \backslash \Delta_R) \cup \Delta_F$ where Δ_{NF} is the set of rule instances in Δ that do not fire in $\Delta \cup \{\mathbf{a}\}$ and Δ_F and Δ_R are the smallest facts such that:

$$
\begin{aligned}
\langle r', [\overline{x} \mapsto \overline{v}] \rangle \in \Delta_F &\quad \text{if } \langle r, \theta \rangle \text{ fires in } \Delta \cup \{\mathbf{a}\} \text{ and } r'(\overline{v}) \in \mathsf{fired}(\langle r, \theta \rangle, \Delta \cup \{\mathbf{a}\}) \\
\langle r', [\overline{x} \mapsto \overline{v}] \rangle \in \Delta_R &\quad \text{if } \langle r, \theta \rangle \text{ fires in } \Delta \cup \{\mathbf{a}\} \text{ and } !r'(\overline{v}) \in \mathsf{fired}(\langle r, \theta \rangle, \Delta \cup \{\mathbf{a}\})
\end{aligned}
$$

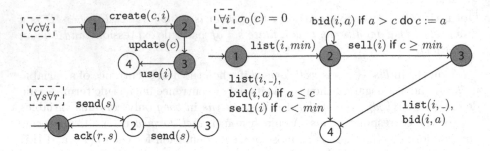

Fig. 1. QEA for (i) the *UnsafeIterator* property (top left), (ii) the *AuctionBidding* property (right), and (iii) the *Broadcast* property (bottom left).

where $r(\overline{x})$ is defined in $\mathcal{D}$. This defines Δ_F as the new rule instances after rules are fired and Δ_R as the rule instances that need to be removed after rules are fired.

This rewrite relation is transitively extended to traces to produce a final fact $\mathcal{I} \xrightarrow{\tau} \Delta$, where $\mathcal{I}$ is the initial fact. This final fact is accepting if it does not contain a rule instance $\langle r, \theta \rangle$ such that $r(\mathrm{dom}(\theta)) \in \mathcal{B}$, the set of bad rule expressions.

3.3 Examples

We now introduce three example properties and specify them in the two languages. We will later use these to motivate, demonstrate, and discuss the translation. The three properties are:

- The *UnsafeIterator* property that an iterator i created from a collection c cannot be used after c is updated.
- The *AuctionBidding* property that after an item i is listed on an auction site with a reserve price min it cannot be relisted, all bids must be strictly increasing, and it can only be sold once this min price has been reached.
- The *Broadcast* property that for every sender s and receiver r, after s sends a message it should wait for an acknowledgement from r before sending again. Receivers are identified exactly as objects that acknowledge messages.

These are formalised as QEA in Fig. 1 and as rule systems in Fig. 2. One case that may require some explanation is the rule system for the *Broadcast* property. This needs to build up knowledge about the set of sender and receiver objects explicitly (whilst in trace slicing this is done implicitly), relying on the knowledge that the set of receivers must be fixed once a sender sends for the second time.

4 Translating Quantified Event Automata to Rule Systems

We now show how to produce a rule system from a QEA. This will consist of three translations on the QEA until it is in a form where we can apply a local translation of each state to a rule definition. The translation has been implemented in SCALA (see https://github.com/selig/qea_to_rules).

4.1 An Equivalent Representation with Labelled States

We introduce an annotation of QEA that replaces states with *labelled states*. The idea is that a state will be labelled with the set of variables that are seen on all paths to that state. Let $\langle q, S \rangle$ be a *labelled state* where q is a state and S a (possibly empty) set of variables. Given a set of states Q and a set of variables X let $LS = Q \times 2^X$ be the (finite) set of labelled states.

$$\text{Start}\{ \; \texttt{create}(c, i), !\textsf{Unsafe}(c, i) \rightarrow \textsf{Created}(c, i), \textsf{Start} \; \}$$
$$\textsf{Created}(c, i)\{ \; \texttt{update}(c) \rightarrow \textsf{Unsafe}(c, i) \; \} \qquad\qquad , \{\textsf{Fail}\}, \textsf{init}$$
$$\textsf{Unsafe}(c, i)\{ \; \texttt{use}(i) \rightarrow \textsf{Fail} \; \}$$

$$\textsf{Start} \; \{ \; \texttt{list}(i, min), !\textsf{Live}(i, m), !\textsf{Sold}(i) \rightarrow \textsf{Live}(i, min, 0), \textsf{Start} \; \}$$

$$\textsf{Live}(i, m, c) \left\{ \begin{array}{l} \texttt{bid}(i, a), a > c \rightarrow \textsf{Live}(i, a) \\ \texttt{sell}(i), c \geq m \rightarrow \textsf{Sold}(i) \\ \texttt{list}(i, \_) \rightarrow \textsf{Fail} \\ \texttt{bid}(i, a), a \leq c \rightarrow \textsf{Fail} \\ \texttt{sell}(i), c < m \rightarrow \textsf{Fail} \end{array} \right\} \qquad , \{\textsf{Fail}\}, \textsf{init}$$

$$\textsf{Sold}(i) \left\{ \begin{array}{l} \texttt{list}(i, \_) \rightarrow \textsf{Fail} \\ \texttt{bid}(i, a) \rightarrow \textsf{Fail} \end{array} \right\}$$

$$\textsf{Start} \left\{ \begin{array}{l} \texttt{send}(s), !\textsf{S}(s) \rightarrow \textsf{S}(s), \textsf{Start} \\ \texttt{send}(s), !\textsf{S}(s), R(r) \rightarrow \textsf{Unsafe}(r, s), \textsf{Start} \\ \texttt{send}(s), \textsf{S}(s) \rightarrow \textsf{Fixed} \\ \texttt{ack}(r, s), !R(r) \rightarrow R(r), \textsf{Start} \end{array} \right\}$$

$$\textsf{Fixed} \left\{ \begin{array}{l} \texttt{ack}(r, s), !R(r) \rightarrow \textsf{Fail} \\ \texttt{send}(s), !\textsf{S}(s), R(r) \rightarrow \textsf{S}(s), \textsf{Unsafe}(r, s), \textsf{Fixed} \end{array} \right\} , \left\{ \begin{array}{l} \textsf{Unsafe}(r, s), \\ \textsf{Fail} \end{array} \right\} , \textsf{init}$$

$$\textsf{S}(s) \left\{ \begin{array}{l} \texttt{send}(s), R(r) \rightarrow \textsf{Unsafe}(r, s), \textsf{S}(s) \\ \texttt{ack}(r, s'), !R(r), s \neq s' \rightarrow \textsf{Unsafe}(r, s), \textsf{S}(s) \end{array} \right\}$$

$$\textsf{Unsafe}(r, s) \left\{ \begin{array}{l} \texttt{send}(s) \rightarrow \textsf{Fail} \\ \texttt{ack}(r, s) \rightarrow empty \end{array} \right\}$$

$$R(r) \; \{\}$$

Fig. 2. Rule systems for (i) the *UnsafeIterator* property (top), (ii) the *AuctionBidding* property (middle), and (iii) the *Broadcast* property (bottom). Assuming general rule definition Fail{} and init $\equiv \langle \textsf{Start}, [] \rangle$.

A QEA over labelled states is *well-labelled* if when $\langle q_2, S_2 \rangle$ is reachable from $\langle q_1, S_1 \rangle$ we have $S_1 \subseteq S_2$. The previous *Broadcast* QEA is not well-labelled as the initial state would have an empty set of labels but there is an incoming transition using r and s. The equivalent well-labelled version of this (corresponding to the result of the construction introduced next) is given in Fig. 3 (top). We show how to construct a well-labelled QEA defined over labelled states from a standard

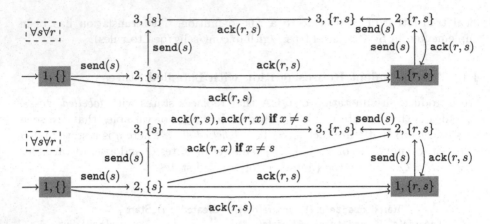

Fig. 3. *Well-labelled* and *domain-explicit* versions of the *Broadcast* QEA.

QEA. Given QEA $\langle X, Q, \mathcal{A}(X \cup Y), \delta, \mathcal{F}, q_0, \sigma_0 \rangle$ we construct $\langle X, LS, \mathcal{A}(X \cup Y), \delta', \mathcal{F}', \langle q_0, \{\} \rangle, \sigma_0 \rangle$ where δ' and $\mathcal{F}'$ are defined as the smallest sets satisfying the following:

$(\langle q, S \rangle, e(\overline{x}), \gamma, \alpha, \langle q', S \cup (\overline{x} \backslash Y) \rangle) \in \delta'$ if $(q, e(\overline{x}), \gamma, \alpha, q') \in \delta$

$(\langle q, S \rangle, e(\overline{x}), \neg(\gamma_1 \vee \ldots \vee \gamma_n), \mathsf{id}, \langle q, S \cup \overline{x} \backslash Y \rangle) \in \delta'$ for $e(\overline{x}) \in \mathcal{A}(X \cup Y)$

and all $(q, e(\overline{x}), \gamma_i, \alpha, q') \in \delta$

$\langle q, S \rangle \in \mathcal{F}'$ if $q \in \mathcal{F}$ and $S = X$

where $S \subseteq X$. The second item requires explanation; this captures the case where no transition can be taken and thus an implicit self-loop is performed as these transitions may be between states with different captured variables. Note that if no transitions for $e(\overline{x})$ exist then $\neg(\gamma_1 \vee \ldots \gamma_n)$ will be *true*. This may lead to unreachable states which can be safely removed. A special case of this would be where a guard becomes *false* by negating a *true* guard. Note that final states must have the set of quantified variables X as their label. This fits with the observation that slicing only considers total valuations.

This resultant automaton over labelled states is equivalent to the original one as no new paths to final states are introduced and none are removed. From now on we will refer to QEA over labelled states as QEA if the labelling is clear from the context or unimportant. Additionally, we will assume all QEA are well-labelled.

4.2   A Domain-Explicit Form

We make the following observation about the *Broadcast* property. Consider the trace $\mathsf{send}(1).\mathsf{ack}(2,3)$. After the first event the only (partial) valuation we can be aware of is $[s \mapsto 1]$. The second event extends the domain of r and requires us to consider $[s \mapsto 1, r \mapsto 2]$. However, $\mathsf{ack}(2,3)$ is not relevant to $[s \mapsto 1]$. This will be problematic for our translation as in the rule system the decision about whether to extend a valuation must be made locally i.e. by making a transition. Here this can be resolved by adding a transition $(\langle 2, \{s\}\rangle, \mathsf{ack}(r, x), x \neq s, \langle 2, \{r, s\}\rangle)$, which is one of two transitions added by the following construction as illustrated in Fig. 3 (bottom). However, in general, we may need to add many similar transitions to capture all possible valuation extensions. We will now introduce an intermediate form that achieves this.

We introduce a conversion to *domain-explicit* QEA that will (i) ensure that ground events that extend an evaluation will always correspond to a transition in the automaton, but (ii) will also preserve the language of the QEA. To convert to domain-explicit form, for each labelled state $\langle q, S\rangle$ and event $e(\overline{x}) \in \mathcal{A}(X \cup Y)$ where $\overline{x} \cap (X/S) \neq \emptyset$ (it contains at least one new quantified variable) we add a set of transitions

$$(\langle q, S\rangle, e(\overline{x}[x_i \mapsto \mathsf{fresh}(x_i)]), \bigwedge_{x \in R} x \neq \mathsf{fresh}(x), \mathsf{id}, \langle q, S \cup R\rangle)$$

where R is a non-empty subset of $S \cap (\overline{x}/Y)$ and $\mathsf{fresh}(x)$ produces a consistent fresh variable if $x \in R$ and x otherwise. These events are exactly those that will bind new quantified variables without needing to match the values of existing quantified variables. If $\overline{x}$ and S are disjoint then $e(\overline{z}) = e(\overline{x})$. Otherwise, a new event is created replacing one or more known quantified variables (in S) by a fresh unquantified variable along with a guard saying that the two are not equal.

The QEA resulting from this translation is well-labelled and equivalent (in terms of language accepted) to the original QEA. Equivalence is due to the fact that transitions are only created between copies of the same state, therefore no paths to final states are added or removed. Additionally, due to the skipping completion of QEA, adding events to the alphabet has no other side-effects.

4.3   A Fresh-Variable Form

Our final translation on the QEA is to ensure that we can transform transitions in a QEA directly into a rule definition. Consider the transition $\langle\langle 2, \{i\}\rangle, \mathsf{bid}(i, a), \mathbf{if}\ a > c, c := a, \langle 2, \{i\}\rangle\rangle$ from the labelled QEA for the *AuctionBidding* property (see preprint [28]). We might try and write the following rule definition for this transition where we must include the set of unquantified variables Y in the parameters of the rule definition:

$$r_2(i, min, c, a)\{\mathsf{bid}(i, a), a > c \to r_2(i, min, a, a)\}$$

This is problematic as $\mathsf{bid}(i, a)$ will try and match this a with the a in the parameter list. To avoid this, we must replace instances of unquantified variables in transitions with fresh local versions. For example, this transition would become $\langle\langle 2, \{i\}\rangle, \mathsf{bid}(i, b), \mathbf{if}\ b > c, a := b; c := a, \langle 2, \{i\}\rangle\rangle$ i.e. we replace a by b and then set $a := b$ in the assignment.

To perform this translation we replace each transition $\langle\langle q, S\rangle, e(\overline{x}), \gamma, \alpha, \langle q', S'\rangle\rangle \in \delta$ with the new transition for $y_i \in \overline{x} \cap Y$ and fresh z_i:

$$\langle\langle q, S\rangle, [y_i \mapsto z_i](e(\overline{x})), [y_i \mapsto z_i](\gamma), (z_i = y_i); \alpha, \langle q', S'\rangle\rangle$$

The resultant QEA is clearly equivalent as all paths remain the same.

4.4   The Translation

Given a domain-explicit labelled QEA $\langle X, LS, \mathcal{A}(X \cup Y), \delta, \mathsf{F}, \langle q_0, \{\} \rangle, \sigma_0 \rangle$ we construct a set of rule definitions $RD = \{r_q(S, Y) \mid \langle q, S \rangle \in LS\}$. The body for each rule definition is constructed by translating each transition starting at that state. The important step is knowing how to translate each transition based on whether the transition extends the label of quantified variables or not.

(i) Transitions with the Same Label. We first consider simple transitions that do not bind any new quantified variables. Let $(\langle q, S \rangle, e(\overline{x}), \gamma, \alpha, \langle q', S \rangle) \in \delta$ be such a transition. We introduce the following rule term for this transition

$$\mathsf{e}(\overline{x}), \gamma \rightarrow r_{q'}(S, \alpha(Y))$$

where we write $\alpha(Y)$ for the expansion of assignment α to Y e.g. $(x = y + 1)\{x, y\} = y + 1, y$. We shall call rule terms of this form kind (i).

(ii) Transitions Extending the Label. Recall that the small-step semantics for QEA depended on the principle of maximality. We need to reproduce this in the constructed rule system. The notion of maximality applies when a valuation is *extended* with information about new quantified variables and the extension is required only if there is no larger consistent valuation. For transition $(\langle q, S \rangle, e(\overline{x}), \gamma, \alpha, \langle q', S' \rangle) \in \delta$ where $S \subset S'$ we introduce the following rule term

$$\mathsf{e}(\overline{x}), \gamma, !r_1(S_1, Y_1), \dots, !r_n(S_n, Y_n) \rightarrow r_{q'}(S', \alpha(Y)), r_q(S, Y)$$

for $r_i(S_i, Y) \in RD$, $S \subset S_i$, and fresh copies Y_i of Y. We treat assignment α as the valuation given by applying it to the identity valuation. We shall call rule terms of this form kind (ii). Two features of this rule term should be explained. Firstly, $!r_1(S_1), \dots, !r_n(S_n)$ captures maximality as it states that there is no rule instance with a valuation larger than and consistent with the current one. Secondly, the two rule expressions on the right serve two separate purposes: $r_{q'}(S')$ is the new valuation in its new state and $r_q(S)$ is re-added as the initial valuation should stay in the current state.

As an example, the domain-explicit labelled QEA for the Broadcast property is translated to the following set of rule definitions (generated by our tool).

$$r_1 \begin{cases} \mathsf{ack}(r, s), !r_1(r, s), !r_2(r, s), !r_2(s), !r_3(r, s), !r_3(s) \rightarrow r_1, r_1(r, s) \\ \mathsf{send}(s), !r_1(r, s), !r_2(r, s), !r_2(s), !r_3(r, s), !r_3(s) \rightarrow r_1, r_2(s) \end{cases}$$

$$r_1(r, s) \{ \mathsf{send}(s) \rightarrow r_2(r, s) \}$$

$$r_2(s) \begin{cases} \mathsf{send}(s) \rightarrow r_3(s) \\ \mathsf{ack}(r, s_p), s \neq s_p, !r_1(r, s), !r_2(r, s), !r_3(r, s) \rightarrow r_2(s), r_2(r, s) \\ \mathsf{ack}(r, s), !r_1(r, s), !r_2(r, s), !r_3(r, s) \rightarrow r_2(s), r_1(r, s) \end{cases}$$

$$r_2(r, s) \begin{cases} \mathsf{send}(s) \rightarrow r_3(r, s) \\ \mathsf{ack}(r, s) \rightarrow r_1(r, s) \end{cases}$$

$$r_3(s) \begin{cases} \mathsf{ack}(r, s_p), s \neq s_p, !r_1(r, s), !r_2(r, s), !r_3(r, s) \rightarrow r_3(s), r_3(r, s) \\ \mathsf{ack}(r, s), !r_1(r, s), !r_2(r, s), !r_3(r, s) \rightarrow r_3(s), r_3(r, s) \end{cases}$$

$$r_3(r, s) \{\}$$

We have now described how to produce a rule body for each rule definition by translating the transitions as described above. A rule system is the set $\mathcal{D}$ of rule definitions for each state in LS, the bad rule expressions $\mathcal{B} = \{r(S) \mid \langle q, S \rangle \notin \mathcal{F}\}$ and the initial state $= \{\langle r_{q_0}, \sigma_0 \rangle\}$.

We can now state our theorem that the translation is correct i.e. it preserves the property defined by the QEA.

Theorem 1. *Given a domain-explicit Q, let RS be the rule system given by the above translation. For monitoring state M_τ and rule state Δ_τ if*

$$M_\tau = \tau * [[] \mapsto \{\langle q_0, \sigma_0(Y) \rangle\}] \qquad and \qquad \{\langle r_{q_0}, \sigma_0 \rangle\} \xrightarrow{\tau} \Delta_\tau$$

then for any valuation θ

$$M_\tau(\theta) = \{\langle q, \sigma \rangle \mid \langle r_q, \theta \cup \sigma \cup \sigma' \rangle \in \Delta_\tau \wedge \mathsf{dom}(\sigma') \cap Y = \emptyset\}$$

The proof can be found in the preprint [28]. The translation is *decidable*; any QEA of the form given in Sect. 3.1 can be translated to a rule system (which is neither unique nor minimal; no good notion of minimality exists). The size of the resulting rule system is potentially $O(|Q| \times 2^{|X|})$ due to the well-labelled translation introducing new states.

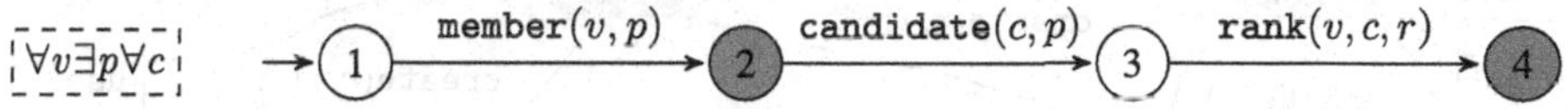

Fig. 4. A QEA for the *CandidateSelection* property taken from [3].

5   Discussion and Related Work

In this section we explore what we have learned about the relationship between the two languages introduced in Sect. 3 by the development of the previous translation. We consider the *expressiveness* of the languages, the *efficiency* of monitoring, how data is treated differently in each language, and the generality of our results.

Expressiveness. Our translation shows that rule systems are at least as expressive as the form of QEA presented here (i.e. without existential quantification, see below). The remaining questions are whether they are strictly more expressive and what effect the choice of presentation for QEA has had on this translation. The first question can be answered positively. Our previous work [18] has given an example of a property that cannot be captured via trace slicing. This was a lock-ordering inspired property but the general form relied on second-order quantification to define a notion of reachability. For the second question we consider the differences in the presentation of QEA with [3].

- *Existential Quantification.* Existential quantification can be useful in certain cases but we do not yet know how to extend the translation to include it generally. For example, it is very difficult to write a rule system for the QEA given in Fig. 4. It seems that it will be necessary to extend rule systems with additional support either via explicit quantification or a specialised notion of non-determinism that splits the state into multiple states where only one needs to be accepting. This property is formalised as a rule system in [18] but this relies on explicitly recording all facts and performing a computation on a special end of trace event.
- *Non-Determinism.* In [3], QEA were given some-path non-determinism but in [18] we observed that the most common use of non-determinism was to capture *negative* properties (the bad behaviour) and in this case all-path non-determinism is preferable. Hence, MARQ [25] supports both. To also support some-path non-determinism here (which is not commonly used) we would need to add branching and a notion of *good* facts to our rule systems (as is done in RULER).

Both existential quantification and non-determinism are rarely used features of QEA.

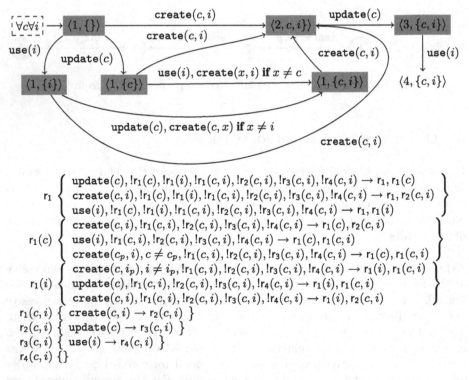

Fig. 5. Fully transformed QEA and corresponding rule system for the *UnsafeIterator* property.

Efficiency. In this translation we are able to go from QEA, which have a highly efficient monitoring algorithm [6], to rule systems, which do not [17]. This appears to be the wrong direction to make gains in efficiency. However, we can make two observations that may lead to improvements in efficiency in both systems.

Firstly, let us consider the translation of the *UnsafeIter* property given in Fig. 5 where we also give the explicit-domain labelled QEA. On inspection we can see that the rule definitions $r_1(i)$, $r_1(c)$, and $r_1(c,i)$ are redundant as every trace that leads to a rule instance $\langle r_2, \theta \rangle$ via these rules will also be produced if they are absent. This should not be surprising as if we remove these rule definitions the rule system becomes very similar to the one given in Sect. 3.3, only with the addition of maximality guards. By making some operations carried out by the slicing structure explicit, we can identify an inherent redundancy in this computation, which should lead to an optimisation of the monitoring algorithm for QEA. Formalising this redundancy both for rule systems and QEA remains further work.

Secondly, one hope for this translation was to identify a fragment of rule systems that are amenable to the efficient indexing-based monitoring algorithms used for QEA. After removing the redundancy identified above the first rule definition becomes

$$r_1 \left\{ \texttt{create}(c,i), !r_2(c,i), !r_3(c,i), !r_4(c,i) \rightarrow r_2(c,i), r_1 \right\}$$

which, when compared to the rule system in Fig. 2, includes additional negated rule expressions in the premises (which add to monitoring complexity). So taken 'as is' the resulting rule system is likely to be less efficient. However, these negated rule expressions give an explicit order in which to check rule definitions when matching incoming events (in a similar way to how indexing works for QEA) and it is plausible that this can be used to improve RULER's monitoring algorithm by either detecting rule systems of this form or automatically checking if the given rule system is equivalent to a rule system of this form (as it is in this case). Therefore, the translation suggests a future direction for developing efficient indexing for rule-based runtime verification tools.

Treatment of Data. There are two main differences in the treatment of data that this work has highlighted. Firstly, QEA makes quantification domains implicit whereas rule systems make them explicit e.g. in QEA new bindings are produced by the monitoring algorithm whereas a rule needs to fire for a new binding in a rule system. This can have implications for readability – in rule systems it is somewhat easier to see what the domains are but in some circumstances having to encode these domains can make the actual behaviour difficult to understand. For example, the resulting rule system for the *Broadcast* property is much bigger than the original QEA. An advantage of making the domain explicit in rule systems is that domain knowledge can be used to ignore some part of the domain (as seen in the *UnsafeIterator* example above). This translation provides a mechanism for understanding exactly what the domain of quantification defined by a QEA is. Secondly, the use of maximality in trace-slicing hides a lot of operational details in the semantics – making this explicit in rule systems demonstrates the implicit work required to ensure that maximality is preserved. In some cases maximality is not necessary and this work can be removed in a rule system.

Generality. We now consider how general this translation is i.e. does it apply to all trace-slicing and rule-based approaches. The first system to use the trace-slicing idea was tracematches [1]. The use of suffix-based matching meant that the authors avoided the main technical difficulty in slicing i.e. dealing with partial valuations, which required maximality. Our translation does not work with suffix-matching but this could be encoded as another transformation on the QEA. The JAVAMOP system [23] has made the slicing approach popular with its efficient implementation. The QEA formalism [3, 24] was inspired by JAVA-MOP. The notion of slicing presented here is compatible with that used in JAVAMOP as this also relies on *maximality*. Rule systems for runtime monitoring were introduced by the RULER tool [2, 4] and are used in TraceContract [5] and LOGFIRE [17] where a similar approach is taken i.e. a global set of instances or facts are rewritten by an associated set of rules. The rule systems described here can be considered a core subset of RULER and could be embedded into these other systems.

6 Conclusion

We have described the formal construction of a translation from the parametric trace slicing based QEA formalism to a rule system in the style of RULER. The translation has been shown to be equivalent to the small-step semantics for QEA. This translation gives insights into how parametric trace slicing and rule systems handle data differently. We observed that, to ensure the same property is described, it is necessary to (i) enforce complex maximality constraints on rule definitions, making them heavily interdependent, and (ii) add additional events and intermediate states to record the possible valuations as they are created. We have implemented the translation as a SCALA program. This will allow us to explore further optimisations of the translation, for example, by identifying redundant intermediate states and performing a backwards-analysis to introduce unquantified variables when they are first needed (the *AuctionBidding* translation would benefit from this). We are also looking at formalising this work in a proof assistant to give more rigorous guarantees of its correctness. In our general work on exploring the relationships between specification languages for runtime verification our next step will be to translate rule systems into a first-order temporal logic.

References

1. Allan, C.: Adding trace matching with free variables to AspectJ. SIGPLAN Not **40**, 345–364 (2005)
2. Barringer, H., Rydeheard, D., Havelund, K.: Rule systems for run-time monitoring: from EAGLE to RuleR. J Log. Comput. **20**(3), 675–706 (2010)
3. Barringer, H., Falcone, Y., Havelund, K., Reger, G., Rydeheard, D.: Quantified event automata: towards expressive and efficient runtime monitors. In: Giannakopoulou, D., Méry, D. (eds.) FM 2012. LNCS, vol. 7436, pp. 68–84. Springer, Heidelberg (2012). https://doi.org/10.1007/978-3-642-32759-9_9
4. Barringer, H., Goldberg, A., Havelund, K., Sen, K.: Rule-based runtime verification. In: Steffen, B., Levi, G. (eds.) VMCAI 2004. LNCS, vol. 2937, pp. 44–57. Springer, Heidelberg (2004). https://doi.org/10.1007/978-3-540-24622-0_5
5. Barringer, H., Havelund, K.: TRACECONTRACT: a scala DSL for trace analysis. In: Butler, M., Schulte, W. (eds.) FM 2011. LNCS, vol. 6664, pp. 57–72. Springer, Heidelberg (2011). https://doi.org/10.1007/978-3-642-21437-0_7
6. Bartocci, E., et al.: First international competition on runtime verification. Int. J. Softw. Tools Technol. Transf. (STTT) (2017)
7. Bartocci, E., Falcone, Y., Francalanza, A., Reger, G.: Introduction to runtime verification. In: Bartocci, E., Falcone, Y. (eds.) Lectures on Runtime Verification. LNCS, vol. 10457, pp. 1–23. Springer, Cham (2018). https://doi.org/10.1007/978-3-319-75632-5_1
8. Basin, D., Harvan, M., Klaedtke, F., Zălinescu, E.: MONPOLY: monitoring usage-control policies. In: Khurshid, S., Sen, K. (eds.) RV 2011. LNCS, vol. 7186, pp. 360–364. Springer, Heidelberg (2012). https://doi.org/10.1007/978-3-642-29860-8_27
9. Bauer, A., Kster, J.-C., Vegliach, G.: The ins and outs of first-order runtime verification. In: Formal Methods in System Design, pp. 1–31 (2015)
10. Bozzelli, L., Sánchez, C.: Foundations of Boolean stream runtime verification. Theor. Comput. Sci. **631**, 118–138 (2016)
11. Chen, F., Roşu, G.: Parametric trace slicing and monitoring. In: Kowalewski, S., Philippou, A. (eds.) TACAS 2009. LNCS, vol. 5505, pp. 246–261. Springer, Heidelberg (2009). https://doi.org/10.1007/978-3-642-00768-2_23
12. D'Angelo, B., et al.: LOLA: runtime monitoring of synchronous systems. In: Proceedings of the 12th International Symposium on Temporal Representation and Reasoning, pp. 166–174 (2005)
13. Decker, N., Leucker, M., Thoma, D.: Monitoring modulo theories. In: Ábrahám, E., Havelund, K. (eds.) TACAS 2014. LNCS, vol. 8413, pp. 341–356. Springer, Heidelberg (2014). https://doi.org/10.1007/978-3-642-54862-8_23
14. Falcone, Y., Havelund, K., Reger, G.: A tutorial on runtime verification. In: Broy, M., Peled, D. (eds.) Summer School Marktoberdorf 2012 - Engineering Dependable Software Systems. IOS Press (2013)
15. Falcone, Y., Krstic, S., Reger, G., Traytel, D.: A taxonomy for classifying runtime verification tools. In: Colombo, C., Leucker, M. (eds.) RV 2018. LNCS, vol. 11237, pp. 241–262 (2018)
16. Hallé, S., Khoury, R.: Runtime monitoring of stream logic formulae. In: Garcia-Alfaro, J., Kranakis, E., Bonfante, G. (eds.) FPS 2015. LNCS, vol. 9482, pp. 251–258. Springer, Cham (2016). https://doi.org/10.1007/978-3-319-30303-1_15
17. Havelund, K.: Rule-based runtime verification revisited. Int. J. Softw. Tools Technol. Transf. **17**(2), 143–170 (2015)

18. Havelund, K., Reger, G.: Specification of parametric monitors. In: Formal Modeling and Verification of Cyber-Physical Systems, 1st International Summer School on Methods and Tools for the Design of Digital Systems, Bremen, pp. 151–189 (2015)

19. Havelund, K., Reger, G.: Runtime verification logics - a language design perspective. In: Aceto, L., Bacci, G., Bacci, G., Ingólfsdóttir, A., Legay, A., Mardare, R. (eds.) Models, Algorithms, Logics and Tools. LNCS, vol. 10460, pp. 310–338. Springer, Cham (2017). https://doi.org/10.1007/978-3-319-63121-9_16

20. Havelund, K., Reger, G., Thoma, D., Zălinescu, E.: Monitoring events that carry data. In: Bartocci, E., Falcone, Y. (eds.) Lectures on Runtime Verification - Introductory and Advanced Topics. LNCS, vol. 10457, pp. 61–102. Springer, Cham (2018). https://doi.org/10.1007/978-3-319-75632-5_3

21. Leucker, M., Schallhart, C.: A brief account of runtime verification. J. Log. Algebr. Program. **78**(5), 293–303 (2008)

22. Medhat, R., Joshi, Y., Bonakdarpour, B., Fischmeister, S.: Parallelized runtime verification of first-order LTL specifications. Technical report, University of Waterloo (2014)

23. Meredith, P., Jin, D., Griffith, D., Chen, F., Roşu, G.: An overview of the MOP runtime verification framework. J Softw. Tools Technol. Transf. 1–41 (2011)

24. Reger, G.: Automata based monitoring and mining of execution traces. Ph.D. thesis, University of Manchester (2014)

25. Reger, G., Cruz, H.C., Rydeheard, D.: MARQ: monitoring at runtime with QEA. In: Baier, C., Tinelli, C. (eds.) TACAS 2015. LNCS, vol. 9035, pp. 596–610. Springer, Heidelberg (2015). https://doi.org/10.1007/978-3-662-46681-0_55

26. Reger, G., Hallé, S., Falcone, Y.: Third international competition on runtime verification. In: Falcone, Y., Sánchez, C. (eds.) RV 2016. LNCS, vol. 10012, pp. 21–37. Springer, Cham (2016). https://doi.org/10.1007/978-3-319-46982-9_3

27. Reger, G., Rydeheard, D.: From first-order temporal logic to parametric trace slicing. In: Bartocci, E., Majumdar, R. (eds.) RV 2015. LNCS, vol. 9333, pp. 216–232. Springer, Cham (2015). https://doi.org/10.1007/978-3-319-23820-3_14

28. Reger, G., Rydeheard, D.: From parametric trace slicing to rule systems. EasyChair Preprint no. 521, EasyChair (2018)

29. Stolz, V., Bodden, E.: Temporal assertions using AspectJ. In: Proceedings of the 5th International Workshop on Runtime Verification (RV 2005). ENTCS, vol. 144, no. 4, pp. 109–124. Elsevier (2006)

Scalable Online First-Order Monitoring

Joshua Schneider[(✉)], David Basin, Frederik Brix, Srđan Krstić[(✉)],
and Dmitriy Traytel[(✉)]

Institute of Information Security, Department of Computer Science, ETH Zürich,
Zurich, Switzerland
{joshua.schneider,srdan.krstic,traytel}@inf.ethz.ch

Abstract. Online monitoring is the task of identifying complex temporal patterns while incrementally processing streams of events. Existing state-of-the-art monitors can process streams of modest velocity in real-time: a few thousands events per second. We scale up monitoring to higher velocities by slicing the stream, based on the events' data values, into substreams that can be independently monitored. Because monitoring is not data parallel in general, slicing can lead to data duplication. To reduce this overhead, we adapt hash-based partitioning techniques from databases to the monitoring setting. We implement the resulting automatic data slicer in Apache Flink and use the MonPoly tool to monitor the substreams. We empirically evaluate this setup, demonstrating a substantial scalability improvement.

1 Introduction

Large-scale software systems produce millions of log events per second. Identifying interesting patterns in these high-volume, high-velocity data streams is a central challenge in the area of runtime verification and monitoring.

An *online monitor* takes a pattern, consumes a stream of data event-wise, and detects and outputs matches with the pattern. The specification language for patterns significantly influences the monitor's time and space complexity. For propositional languages, such as metric temporal logic or metric dynamic logic, current monitors are capable of handling hundreds of thousands of events per second in real time on commodity hardware [8, 13]. Propositional languages, however, are severely limited in their expressiveness. Since they regard events as atomic, they cannot formulate dependencies between data values stored in the events. First-order specification languages, such as metric first-order temporal logic (MFOTL) [11], do not have this limitation. Various online monitors [5,7,11,14,26,32,34] can handle first-order specification languages for event streams with modest velocities.

We improve the scalability of online first-order monitors using parallelization. There are two basic approaches regarding what to parallelize. *Task parallelism* adapts the monitoring algorithm to evaluate different subpatterns in parallel. The amount of parallelization offered is limited by the number of subpatterns for a given pattern. The alternative is *data parallelism*: multiple copies of the monitoring algorithm are run unchanged as a black box, in parallel, on different portions of the input data stream.

© Springer Nature Switzerland AG 2018
C. Colombo and M. Leucker (Eds.): RV 2018, LNCS 11237, pp. 353–371, 2018.
https://doi.org/10.1007/978-3-030-03769-7_20

In this paper we focus on data parallelism, which is attractive for several reasons. By being a black-box approach, data parallelism allows us to reuse existing monitors, which implement heavily optimized sequential algorithms. It also offers a virtually unbounded amount of parallelization, especially on high-volume and high-velocity data streams. Finally, it caters for the use of general-purpose libraries for data parallel stream-processing. These libraries deal with common challenges in high-performance computing, such as deployment on computing clusters, fault-tolerance, and back-pressure (i.e., velocity spikes).

Data parallelism has previously been utilized to scale up offline monitoring [9] (Sect. 2). Yet neither offline nor online monitoring is a data-parallel task in general. This means that, in some cases, parallel monitors must synchronize during their execution. Alternatively, careful data duplication across the parallel monitors allows for a non-blocking parallel architecture. An important contribution of this prior work on scalable offline monitoring is the development of a (*data*) *slicing framework* [9]. The framework takes as inputs an MFOTL formula (Sect. 3) and a splitting strategy that determines which parallel monitors the data should be sent to. It outputs an event dispatcher that forwards events to appropriate monitors and ensures that the overall parallel architecture collectively produces exactly the same results that a single-threaded monitor would do.

The previous slicing framework has three severe limitations. First, data can be sliced on only one free variable at a time. Although the single-variable slices can be composed into multi-variable slices, the composition does not offer the flexibility of simultaneously slicing on multiple variables. As a result, composition is ineffective for some formulas and adds unnecessary data duplication for others. Second, the user of the slicing framework must supply a slicing strategy, even when it is obvious what the best strategy is for the given formula. Third, the framework's implementation uses Google's MapReduce library for parallel processing, which restricts it to the offline setting.

This paper addresses all of the above limitations with the following contributions:

- We generalize the offline slicing framework [9] to support simultaneous slicing on multiple variables and adapt the framework to the online setting (Sect. 4).
- We instantiate the slicing framework with an automatic splitting strategy (Sect. 5) inspired by the hypercube algorithm [2, 27] used previously to parallelize via hashing implementations of relational join operators in databases.
- We implement our new slicing framework using the Apache Flink [3] stream processing engine (Sect. 6). We use MonPoly [11, 12] as a black-box monitor for the slices. A particular challenge in our publicly available implementation [35] was to efficiently checkpoint MonPoly's state within Flink to achieve fault-tolerance.
- We evaluate the slicing framework and automatic strategy selection on both synthetic data and real-world data based on Nokia's data collection campaign [10] (Sect. 7). We show that the overall parallel architecture has substantially improved throughput. While the optimality of the hypercube approach in terms of a balanced data distribution is out of reach for general MFOTL formulas, we demonstrate that our automatic splitting results in balanced slices on the formulas used in the Nokia case study.

2   Related Work

Our work builds on the slicing framework introduced by Basin et al. [9]. This framework ensures the sound and complete slicing of the event stream with respect to MFOTL formulas. It prescribes the use of composable operators, called slicers, that slice data associated with a single free variable, or slice based on time. We have generalized their data slicers to operate simultaneously on all free variables in a formula. Moreover, the usage of MapReduce in the implementation of the original framework limited it to the offline setting. In contrast, our implementation in Apache Flink supports online monitoring. Finally, our implementation extends the framework with an automatic strategy selection that exhibits a balanced load distribution on the slices in our empirical evaluation.

Barre et al. [4], Bianculli et al. [18], and Bersani et al. [17] use task parallelism on different subformulas to parallelize propositional offline monitors. The degree of parallelization in these approaches is limited by the specification's syntactic complexity.

Parametric trace slicing [34] lifts propositional monitoring to parametric specifications. This algorithm takes a trace with parametric events and creates propositional slices with events grouped by their parameter instances, which can be independently monitored. Parametric trace slicing considers only non-metric policies with top-level universal quantification. Barringer et al. [5] generalize this approach to more complex properties expressed using quantified event automata (QEA). Reger and Rydeheard [32], delimit the *sliceable* fragment of first-order linear temporal logic (FO-LTL) that admits a sound application of parametric trace slicing. The fragment prohibits deeply nested quantification and using the "next" operator. These restrictions originate from the time model used, in which time-points consist of exactly one event. Hence, when an event is removed from a slice, information about that time-point is lost. Our time model, based on sequences of time-stamped sets of events, avoids such pitfalls. Parametric trace slicing produces an exponential number of slices (in the domain's size) with grounded predicates, whereas we use as many slices as there are parallel monitors available.

Kuhtz and Finkbeiner [28] show that the LTL monitoring problem belongs to $AC^1(\log DCFL)$ and as such can be efficiently parallelized. However, the Boolean circuits used to establish the lower bound must be built for each trace in advance, which limits these results to the offline monitoring setting. A similar limitation applies to the work by Bundala and Ouaknine [19] and Feng et al. [22] who study variants of MTL and TPTL.

Complex event processing (CEP) systems analyze streams by recognizing composite events as (temporal) patterns of simple events. Their publish-subscribe architecture allows for ample parallelism. The languages used by CEP systems are often based on SQL extensions without a clear semantics. An exception is BeepBeep [24]: a multithreaded [25] stream processor that supports LTL-FO$^+$, another first-order variant of LTL. The parallel computation in BeepBeep must, however, be scheduled manually by the user.

Event stream processing systems have been extensively studied in the database community. We focus on the most closely related works. The hypercube partitioning scheme (also known as the *shares algorithm*) was first proposed by Afrati and Ullman [2] in the context of MapReduce. The idea underlying the algorithm can be traced back to the parallel evaluation of datalog queries [23]. The hypercube algorithm was shown to be optimal for conjunctive queries with one communication round on skew-free databases [16].

The hypercube and other hash-based partitioning schemes are sensitive to skew. Rivetti et al. [33] suggest a greedy balancing strategy after separating the heavy hitters, i.e., frequently occurring input values. This approach is restricted to multi-way joins in which all relations share a common join key. Nasir et al. [29,30] balance skew for associative stream operators without identifying heavy hitters explicitly. Vitorovic et al. [37] combines the hash-based hypercube, prone to heavy hitters, with random partitioning [31], resilient to heavy hitters. The combination only applies to multi-way joins and limits the impact of skew without improving the worst-case performance. All these approaches are unsuitable for handling general MFOTL formulas. Instead we follow a hypercube variant, which is optimal for the considered setting with skew [27]. The heavy hitters must be known in advance in this approach.

3 Preliminaries

We briefly recall the syntax and semantics of our specification language of choice, metric first-order temporal logic (MFOTL) [11], and describe the monitoring setting considered.

We fix a set of *names* $\mathbb{E}$ and for simplicity assume a single infinite *domain* $\mathbb{D}$ of values. The names $r \in \mathbb{E}$ have associated arities $\iota(r) \in \mathbb{N}$. An *event* $r(d_1, \ldots, d_{\iota(r)})$ is an element of $\mathbb{E} \times \mathbb{D}^*$. We call $1, \ldots, \iota(r)$ the *attributes* of the name r. We further fix an infinite set $\mathbb{V}$ of variables, such that $\mathbb{V}$, $\mathbb{D}$, and $\mathbb{E}$ are pairwise disjoint. Let $\mathbb{I}$ be the set of nonempty intervals $[a, b) := \{x \in \mathbb{N} \mid a \leq x < b\}$, where $a \in \mathbb{N}$, $b \in \mathbb{N} \cup \{\infty\}$ and $a < b$. Formulas φ are constructed inductively, where t_i, r, x, and I range over $\mathbb{V} \cup \mathbb{D}$, $\mathbb{E}$, $\mathbb{V}$, and $\mathbb{I}$, respectively:

$$\varphi ::= r(t_1, \ldots, t_{\iota(r)}) \mid t_1 \approx t_2 \mid \neg \varphi \mid \varphi \vee \varphi \mid \exists x. \varphi \mid \bullet_I \varphi \mid \bigcirc_I \varphi \mid \varphi \, \mathsf{S}_I \, \varphi \mid \varphi \, \mathsf{U}_I \, \varphi.$$

Along with the Boolean operators, MFOTL includes the metric past and future temporal operators $\bullet$ (*previous*), S (*since*), $\bigcirc$ (*next*), and U (*until*), which may be nested freely. We define other standard Boolean and temporal operators in terms of this minimal syntax: truth $\top := \exists x. \, x \approx x$, falsehood $\bot := \neg \top$, inequality $t_1 \not\approx t_2 := \neg(t_1 \approx t_2)$, conjunction $\varphi \wedge \psi := \neg(\neg \varphi \vee \neg \psi)$, universal quantification $\forall x. \, \varphi := \neg(\exists x. \, \neg \varphi)$, eventually $\Diamond_I \varphi := \top \, \mathsf{U}_I \, \varphi$, always $\Box_I \varphi := \neg \Diamond_I \neg \varphi$, once $\blacklozenge_I \varphi := \top \, \mathsf{S}_I \, \varphi$, and historically (always in the past) $\blacksquare_I \varphi := \neg \blacklozenge_I \neg \varphi$. Abusing notation, $\mathbb{V}_\varphi$ denotes the set of free variables of the formula φ.

MFOTL formulas are interpreted over streams of time-stamped events. We group finite sets of events that happen concurrently (from the event source's point of view) into *databases*. An *(event) stream* ρ is thus an infinite sequence $\langle \tau_i, D_i \rangle_{i \in \mathbb{N}}$ of databases D_i with associated time-stamps τ_i. We assume discrete time-stamps, modeled as natural numbers $\tau \in \mathbb{N}$. We allow the event source to use a finer notion of time than the one used as time-stamps. In particular, databases at different indices $i \neq j$ may have the same time-stamp $\tau_i = \tau_j$. The sequence of time-stamps must be non-strictly increasing ($\forall i. \, \tau_i \leq \tau_{i+1}$) and always eventually strictly increasing ($\forall \tau. \, \exists i. \, \tau < \tau_i$).

$v, i \models r(t_1, \ldots, t_n)$ if $r(v(t_1), \ldots v(t_n)) \in D_i$ | $v, i \models \exists x.\ \varphi$ if $v[x \mapsto z], i \models \varphi$ for some $z \in \mathbb{D}$

$v, i \models t_1 \approx t_2$ if $v(t_1) = v(t_2)$ | $v, i \models \bullet_I \varphi$ if $i > 0$, $\tau_i - \tau_{i-1} \in I$, and $v, i-1 \models \varphi$

$v, i \models \neg \varphi$ if $v, i \not\models \varphi$ | $v, i \models \bigcirc_I \varphi$ if $\tau_{i+1} - \tau_i \in I$ and $v, i+1 \models \varphi$

$v, i \models \varphi \vee \psi$ if $v, i \models \varphi$ or $v, i \models \psi$

$v, i \models \varphi \mathsf{S}_I \psi$ if $v, j \models \psi$ for some $j \leq i$, $\tau_i - \tau_j \in I$, and $v, k \models \varphi$ for all k with $j < k \leq i$

$v, i \models \varphi \mathsf{U}_I \psi$ if $v, j \models \psi$ for some $j \geq i$, $\tau_j - \tau_i \in I$, and $v, k \models \varphi$ for all k with $i \leq k < j$

Fig. 1. Semantics of MFOTL

The relation $v, i \models_\rho \varphi$ (Fig. 1) defines the satisfaction of the formula φ for a valuation v at an index i with respect to the stream $\rho = \langle \tau_i, D_i \rangle_{i \in \mathbb{N}}$. Whenever ρ is fixed and clear from the context, we omit the subscript on $\models$. The valuation v is a mapping $\mathbb{V} \to \mathbb{D}$, assigning domain elements to the free variables of φ. Overloading notation, v is also the extension of v to the domain $\mathbb{V} \cup \mathbb{D}$, setting $v(t) = t$ whenever $t \in \mathbb{D}$. We write $v[x \mapsto y]$ for the function equal to v, except that the argument x is mapped to y.

Let $\mathbb{S}$ be the set of streams. Although satisfaction is defined over infinite streams, a monitor will always receive only a finite stream prefix. We write $\mathbb{P}$ for the set of finite stream prefixes and $\preceq$ for the usual prefix order on streams and stream prefixes. For the prefix π and $i \in \{1, \ldots, |\pi|\}$, $\pi[i]$ denotes π's i-th element.

Abstractly, a *monitor function* maps stream prefixes to verdict outputs from a set $\mathbb{O}$. A monitor is an algorithm that implements a monitor function. An online monitor receives incremental updates of a stream prefix and computes the corresponding verdicts. We consider time-stamped databases to be the atomic units of the input. The monitor may produce the verdicts incrementally, too. To represent this behavior on the level of monitor functions, we assume that verdicts are equipped with a partial order $\sqsubseteq$ indicating refinement and that a monitor function is a monotone map $\langle \mathbb{P}, \preceq \rangle \to \langle \mathbb{O}, \sqsubseteq \rangle$. This captures the intuition that as the monitor function receives more input, it produces more output, and (depending on the refinement ordering), does not retract previous verdicts.

Concretely, the MonPoly monitor [12] implements a monitor function $\mathscr{M}_\varphi$ for φ from a practically relevant fragment of MFOTL [11]. Whenever φ is violated for a particular index, MonPoly outputs the valuations of the free variables that cause φ to become false. Because some violations may be found only after a time delay, we ignore the order of MonPoly's output and model it as a set, with $\sqsubseteq$ being the subset relation:

$$\mathscr{M}_\varphi(\pi) = \{(v, i) \mid i \leq |\pi| \text{ and for all } \rho \in \mathbb{S} \text{ with } \pi \preceq \rho, (v, i) \not\models_\rho \varphi\}.$$

4 Slicing Framework

We introduce a general framework for parallel online monitoring based on slicing. Basin et al. [9] provide operators that split finite logs offline into independently monitorable slices, based on the events' data values and time-stamps. Each slice contains only a subset of the events from the original trace, which reduces the computational effort to monitor the slice. We adapt this idea to online monitoring. Since slicing with respect to time is not particularly useful in the online setting, we focus on the data in the events.

4.1   Abstract Slicing

Parallelizing a monitor should not affect its input-output behavior. We formulate this correctness requirement abstractly using the notion of a slicer for a monitor function. The slicer indicates how to split the stream prefix into independently monitorable substreams and how to combine the verdict outputs of the parallel submonitors into a single verdict.

Definition 1. *A* slicer *for a monitor function* $\mathcal{M}$ *is a tuple* (K, M, S, J), *where K is a set of slice identifiers, the* submonitor *family* $M \in K \to (\mathbb{P} \to \mathbb{O})$ *is a K-indexed family of monitor functions, the* splitter $S \in \mathbb{P} \to (K \to \mathbb{P})$ *splits prefixes into K-indexed slices, and the* joiner $J \in (K \to \mathbb{O}) \to \mathbb{O}$ *indicates how to combine K-indexed verdicts into one, satisfying the following properties:*

Monotonicity *For all* $\pi_1, \pi_2 \in \mathbb{P}$, $\pi_1 \preceq \pi_2$ *implies* $S(\pi_1)_k \preceq S(\pi_2)_k$, *for all* $k \in K$.
Soundness *For all* $\pi \in \mathbb{P}$, $J\big(\lambda k.\, M_k(S(\pi)_k)\big) \sqsubseteq \mathcal{M}(\pi)$.
Completeness *For all* $\pi \in \mathbb{P}$, $\mathcal{M}(\pi) \sqsubseteq J\big(\lambda k.\, M_k(S(\pi)_k)\big)$.

For an input prefix π, $S(\pi)$ denotes the collection of its slices. Each slice is identified by an element of K, which we write as a subscript. We require the splitter S to be monotone so that the submonitors M_k, which may differ from the monitor function $\mathcal{M}$, can process the sliced prefixes incrementally. Composing the splitter, the corresponding submonitor for each slice, and the joiner yields the parallelized monitor function $J\big(\lambda k.\, M_k(S(\pi)_k)\big)$. It is sound and complete if and only if it computes the same verdicts as $\mathcal{M}$.

For example, parametric trace slicing [32, 34] can be seen as a particular slicer for monitor functions that arise from sliceable FO-LTL formulas [32, Sect. 4]. Thereby, K is the cross-product of finite domains for the formulas' variables. Thus elements of K are valuations and the splitter is defined as the restriction of the trace to the values occurring in the valuation. The submonitor M_k is a propositional LTL monitor and the joiner simply takes the union of the results (which may be marked with the valuation).

The splitter S as defined above is overly general. In practice, we would like a highly efficient implementation of S since it is a centralized operation in front of the parallel inner monitors M, which must inspect every input event. Parametric trace slicing determines the target slice for an event by inspecting events individually (and not as part of the whole prefix). We call splitter with this property event-separable. Event-separable splitters are desirable because they cater to a parallel implementation of the splitter S.

Definition 2. *A splitter S is called* event-separable *if there is a function* $\hat{S} \in (\mathbb{E} \times \mathbb{D}^*) \to \mathscr{P}(K)$ *such that* $S(\pi)_k[i] = \langle \tau_i, \{e \in D_i \mid k \in \hat{S}(e)\} \rangle$ *for all* $\pi \in \mathbb{P}$, $k \in K$, $i \leq |\pi|$.

Lemma 1. *If S is event-separable, then* $\pi_1 \preceq \pi_2$ *implies* $S(\pi_1)_k \preceq S(\pi_2)_k$ *for all* $k \in K$.

We also call slicers with event-separable splitters *event-separable*. We identify event-separable slicers (K, M, S, J) with $(K, M, \hat{S}, J)$.

4.2 Joint Data Slicer

We describe an event-separable slicer for the monitor function $\mathcal{M}_\varphi$ that arises from the MFOTL formula φ. Our *joint data slicer* distributes events according to the valuations they induce in the formula. Recall that the output of $\mathcal{M}_\varphi$ consists of all valuations that do not satisfy the formula at some timepoint. We would like to evaluate φ for each valuation to determine whether the valuation is a violation. However, there are infinitely many valuations in the presence of infinite domains. The joint data slicer uses finitely many (possibly overlapping) slices, which taken together cover all possible valuations. For a given valuation, only a subset of the events is relevant to evaluate the formula.

We assume that the bound variables in φ are disjoint from the free variables. Given an event $e = r(d_1, \ldots, d_n)$, the set $matches(\varphi, e)$ contains all valuations $v \in \mathbb{V}_\varphi \to \mathbb{D}$ for which there is a subformula $r(t_1, \ldots, t_n)$ in φ where $v(t_i) = d_i$ for all $i \in \{1, \ldots, n\}$. We implicitly extend v to $\mathbb{V} \cup \mathbb{D}$, such that it is the identity on $(\mathbb{V} \setminus \mathbb{V}_\varphi) \cup \mathbb{D}$.

Definition 3. *Let φ be an MFOTL formula and $f \in (\mathbb{V}_\varphi \to \mathbb{D}) \to \mathscr{P}(K)$ be a mapping from valuations to nonempty sets of slice identifiers. The* joint data slicer *for φ with splitting strategy f is the tuple $(K, \lambda k. \, \mathcal{M}_\varphi, \hat{S}_f, J_f)$, where*

$$\hat{S}_f(e) = \bigcup\nolimits_{v \in matches(\varphi, e)} f(v), \qquad J_f(s) = \bigcup\nolimits_{k \in K} (s_k \cap (\{v \mid k \in f(v)\} \times \mathbb{N})).$$

The intersection with $\{v \mid k \in f(v)\} \times \mathbb{N}$ in the definition of J_f is needed only for some formulas, notably those that involve equality. Consider, e.g., the formula $x \approx a \to Q(x)$, where a is a constant. Even if a prefix contains $Q(a)$, so that no violation occurs, the event will be omitted from all slices that do not have an associated valuation with $x = a$. If we do not filter the erroneous verdict from those slices, the result will be unsound.

Proposition 1. *The joint data slicer $(K, \lambda k. \, \mathcal{M}_\varphi, \hat{S}_f, J_f)$ is a slicer for $\mathcal{M}_\varphi$.*

Proof. Monotonicity follows from Lemma 1. For soundness and completeness, we must show that $(v, i) \in J_f(\mathcal{M}_\varphi \circ S_f(\pi))$ if and only if $(v, i) \in \mathcal{M}_\varphi(\pi)$ for an arbitrary v and i. By the definitions of J_f and $\mathcal{M}_\varphi$, this is equivalent to

$$(\forall k \in f(v). \forall \rho. \, \rho \succeq S_f(\pi)_k \implies v, i \models_\rho \neg\varphi) \iff (\forall \sigma. \, \sigma \succeq \pi \implies v, i \models_\sigma \neg\varphi).$$

For an arbitrary $k \in f(v)$, it suffices to consider streams ρ and σ such that $\rho[i] = S_f(\pi)_k[i]$ and $\sigma[i] = \pi[i]$ for all $i \leq |S_f(\pi)_k| = |\pi|$, and $\rho[i] = \sigma[i]$ otherwise. Then $v, i \models_\rho \varphi \iff v, i \models_\sigma \varphi$ follows by induction on the structure of φ generalizing over v and i. $\square$

Example 1. Consider the formula $P(x, y) \to \Diamond_{[0,5]}(P(y, x) \wedge Q(x))$. We apply the joint data slicer for two slices ($K = \{1, 2\}$). Its splitting strategy f maps all valuations to the first slice, except for $\langle x = 5, y = 7 \rangle$. (Note that the intersection with $\{v \mid k \in f(v)\} \times \mathbb{N}$ is redundant in the definition of J_f for this formula. For any violating valuation, there must be a matching P event in the slice, which determines the values of all free variables.)

Let π be the prefix $\langle 11, \{P(5, 1), Q(2)\} \rangle, \langle 12, \{P(5, 7), Q(3), Q(5)\} \rangle, \langle 21, \{P(7, 5)\} \rangle$. We obtain the slices

$$S_f(\pi)_1 = \langle 11, \{P(5,1), Q(2)\} \rangle, \, \langle 12, \{P(5,7), Q(3)\} \rangle, \, \langle 21, \{P(7,5)\} \rangle$$
$$S_f(\pi)_2 = \langle 11, \{\} \rangle, \, \langle 12, \{P(5,7), Q(5)\} \rangle, \, \langle 21, \{P(7,5)\} \rangle.$$

The events $P(5,7)$ and $P(7,5)$ are duplicated across the slices because both $\langle x = 5, y = 7 \rangle$ and $\langle x = 7, y = 5 \rangle$ are matching valuations for either event.

The data slicer used in the offline slicing framework [9] is defined for a single free variable x and a collection $(S_k)_{k \in K}$ of slicing sets. Each slicing set is a subset of the domain, and $\bigcup_{k \in K} S_k = \mathbb{D}$. This single variable slicer is a special case of our joint data slicer. To see this, define $f(v)$ to be the set of all k satisfying $v(x) \in S_k$. At least one such k must exist because the S_k cover the domain. In contrast, some instances of the joint data slicer cannot be simulated by a composition of single variable slicers. Consider a formula with the atoms $P(x,y)$, $P(y,z)$, and $P(z,x)$. Any single variable slicer will send all P events to all slices because each atom misses one free variable. We show in Sect. 5 that our joint data slicer is more precise for such formulas.

5   Automatic Slicing

The joint data slicer (Sect. 4.2) is parameterized by a splitting strategy. Ideally, the chosen strategy optimally utilizes the available computing resources. In particular, computation and communication costs should be evenly distributed, while keeping the overhead low. As an approximation of the overall computational cost, we consider the event rate, i.e., the number of events in a period of time, of each slice. We chose this as minimizing the event rate should reduce the submonitors' execution time and memory consumption. We do not optimize the amount of communication in this paper. However, the number of slices is a parameter that affects the communication cost due to data duplication.

We base our splitting strategy on the hypercube algorithm [2,16,23,27,36]. Below, we describe this algorithm within our framework and address challenges that arise in the online setting. We decided on the hypercube algorithm as our starting point because its skew-aware variant by Koutris et al. [27] has been shown to yield strategies that are optimal with respect to the worst-case load for conjunctive queries. Query evaluation and monitoring are closely related: reporting violations of some formula φ with free variables is equivalent to evaluating the query $\neg \varphi$. Therefore, conjunctive queries constitute a specific subset of all monitoring tasks. While this does not imply optimality for arbitrary formulas, we are still able to effectively slice formulas containing operators other than conjunctions.

Let $[n] = \{1, \ldots, n\}$ for $n \in \mathbb{N}$. We assume a linear ordering $x_1, \ldots, x_k$ on the free variables of the formula φ. The basic idea of the hypercube algorithm is to organize N submonitors into a hypercube (or more precisely, an orthotope) $K = [n_1] \times \ldots \times [n_k]$ such that $\prod_{i \in [k]} n_i = N$. The parameters $n_1, \ldots, n_k$ are called *shares*. At the beginning of the monitoring, hash functions $h_i \in \mathbb{D} \to [n_i]$ are chosen randomly and independently. To decide which submonitors should receive an event, the hypercube algorithm applies the hash function h_i to the values of the free variable x_i, for all $x_i \in \mathbb{V}_\varphi$. This is done for each valuation that is inferred from the event by the data slicer. Each tuple of hash values represents a coordinate in K, which is the target slice for that valuation. Therefore, the splitting strategy f maps valuations v to (sets of) slice identifiers $\{\langle h_1(v(x_1)), \ldots, h_k(v(x_k)) \rangle\}$.

The shares are chosen to optimize the maximum event rate over all submonitors. For now, we assume that all values have low *degree*. The degree of a data value denotes the number of events that contain this value in a specific attribute. Then, the maximum event rate of the monitors given the shares n is estimated by the following cost function [2, 15]:

$$cost(n, \varphi, Z) = \sum_{r(d_1,\ldots,d_n) \in \varphi} \frac{Z(r)}{\prod_{x_i \in \{d_1,\ldots,d_n\} \cap \mathbb{V}_\varphi} n_i}.$$

The term $r(d_1,\ldots,d_n)$ ranges over all atoms in the formula φ. The function Z is a parameter of the optimization, where $Z(r)$ is the rate of events with name r. We use a simplified version of the algorithm by Chu et al. [21] to optimize the cost function. The algorithm enumerates all possible integer shares with product N. This is feasible because the number of share combinations is small for realistic N, even when N has many small prime divisors. In fact, we assume that N is a power of two in our implementation.

It is not obvious how the statistics Z can be meaningfully obtained in the context of online monitoring. We cannot collect them from the entire stream for two reasons. First, it is impossible to observe future events at the time when the splitting strategy must be fixed. Second, if the rates increase due to a temporary change in the stream characteristics, some monitor instance might become overwhelmed, events must be buffered, and latency increases. The optimization cannot account for such local changes if we use statistics collected over a long period of time, as one would do in offline processing. However, some buffering to handle transient rate spikes is acceptable. Therefore, we estimate the statistics using a recorded prefix of the stream and aggregate them over short time windows.

Example 2. Consider the formula $\varphi = P(x,y) \wedge Q(y,z) \rightarrow \neg R(z,x)$ and a stream consisting of $3m$ events in a given period of time. We assume that the events with names P, Q, and R occur equally often, such that $Z(P) = Z(Q) = Z(R) = m$. The optimal shares for the hypercube composed of N monitors are $n_x = n_y = n_z = N^{1/3}$. Each slice contains approximately $cost(n, \varphi, Z) = 3m/N^{2/3}$ events. We obtain the same results for the formula $\varphi' = P(x,y) \wedge P(y,z) \rightarrow \neg P(z,x)$ and $Z(P) = m$ because each event is replicated three times. Yet, the event rate per slice is lower than the rate of the input stream if $N \geq 8$. This is an improvement over the single variable slicer (Sect. 4.2).

Next, we show how the joint data slicer with the optimal hypercube strategy for φ distributes some events. We assume $N = 64$ and simplify the hash functions to $h(x) = x \bmod 4$. The slices are thus identified by strings of three numbers between 0 and 3, with one number for each variable x, y, and z.

event	containing slices	event	containing slices
$P(0,1)$	010, 011, 012, 013	$Q(1,7)$	013, 113, 213, 313
$P(1,1)$	110, 111, 112, 113	$R(7,0)$	003, 013, 023, 033

The events $P(0,1)$, $Q(1,7)$, and $R(7,0)$ are sent to slice 013, which ensures completeness.

Data distributions without skew, in which all values have low degree, are too limited in practice. Hash-based partitioning schemes such as the hypercube fail to distribute events evenly if the input is skewed. A standard solution it to use a different splitting strategy for the highly skewed portions of the data [27]. Following the terminology of [27], a *heavy hitter* is a value with degree at least $Z(r)/N$ in events with name r. We collect heavy hitter information along with the Z statistics. A value is considered a heavy hitter if it is a heavy hitter in at least one of the time windows over which we collect the Z statistics.

To compute the slice for a valuation, our skew-aware strategy first determines the set H of variables that are heavy hitters. A value d is a heavy hitter for a variable x if there is an atom $r(\ldots, t_{j-1}, x, t_{j+1}, \ldots)$ in the formula such that d is a heavy hitter in the j-th attribute of r. For each set H, a separate collection of shares n_x^H and independent hash functions h_x^H is used, where $x \in \mathbb{V}_\varphi$. Note that there are 2^k different sets H, where $k = |\mathbb{V}_\varphi|$. For $x \in H$, we fix $n_x^H = 1$ in the share optimization. The remaining shares are computed as before, as is $f(v)$, but using the hash functions h_x^H.

Example 3. Consider the same formula φ and stream as before, but suppose now that the stream has some heavy hitters. We analyze the optimal shares for the heavy-hitter sets $A = \{x\}$, $B = \{x, y\}$, and $C = \{x, y, z\}$. The remaining cases have symmetrical solutions. In the case A, the shares are $n_x^A = 1$ and $n_y^A = n_z^A = N^{1/2}$. Each slice then contains at most $1/N^{1/2}$ of the events for which only x is assigned a heavy hitter. In the case B, the optimal shares are $n_x^B = n_y^B = 1$ and $n_z^B = N$, so there are at most $1/N$ of the corresponding events in each slice. Finally, in the case C, one must broadcast the events. Note that there can be at most N different heavy hitters per attribute. Therefore, there are at most $3wN^2$ events to which the set C applies, where w is the number of databases in the time period that we consider. If w is bounded by a constant, the overall fraction of events in each slice is asymptotically equal to the maximum of the three cases, which is $O(1/N^{1/2})$.

Now assume that 0 is a heavy hitter in the first attribute of P, and $N = 64$. Therefore, we need to consider the heavy-hitter sets $\{\}$ and $\{x\}$. Let the hash functions be the modulus as in the previous example (e.g., $h_y^{\{x\}}(y) = y \bmod 8$). We overlay the slices for the different heavy-hitter sets and assign identifiers from $[N]$ according to their lexicographic ordering: both valuations $\langle x = 1, y = 1, z = 3 \rangle$ and $\langle y = 2, z = 7 \rangle$ map to 23.

event	containing slices	event	containing slices
$P(0,1)$	$8, 9, 10, 11, 12, 13, 14, 15$	$Q(1,7)$	$7, 23, 39, 55; 15$
$P(1,1)$	$20, 21, 22, 23$	$R(7,0)$	$7, 15, 23, 31, 39, 47, 55, 63$

Both $\{\}$ and $\{x\}$ are possible for $Q(1,7)$ because $Q(y,z)$ does not induce a valuation for x.

In general, the possible rate reduction depends on the pattern of free variables in the formula's atoms. A detailed discussion is provided by Koutris et al. [27]. The ideal case is a formula in which all atoms with a significant event count share a variable, together with a stream that never assigns a heavy hitter to that variable. Then the load per slice is proportional to $1/N$. Atoms with missing variables, and equivalently variables with heavy hitters, increase the fraction to $1/N^q$ for some $q > 1$. Our approach affects only

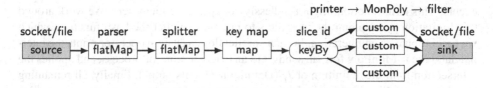

Fig. 2. Stream operators in the online monitor

the event rate, but not the index rate, which is the number of databases per unit of time. The index rate impacts the performance of monitors such as MonPoly because each database triggers an update step in the monitoring algorithm. For a syntactic fragment of MFOTL, MonPoly reduces the number of update steps skipping empty databases [9].

6   Implementation

We implemented a parallel online monitor based on the joint data slicer in Scala on top of the Apache Flink stream processing framework. Given a formula, the slicer reads events from a TCP socket or a text file, monitors them in parallel, and writes the collected verdicts to a second socket or file. The monitoring of the slices is delegated to MonPoly [12].

The Flink API provides the means to construct a logical dataflow graph. The graph consists of operators that retrieve data streams from external sources, apply processing functions to stream elements, and output the elements to sinks. Operators and the flows between them can execute in parallel; elements are partitioned according to user-specified keys. At runtime, Flink maps the graph to a distributed cluster of computing nodes. We chose Flink for its low latency stream processing and its support for fault tolerant computation. Fault tolerance is ensured using a distributed checkpointing mechanism [20]: The system recovers from failures by restarting from regularly created checkpoints. Operators must expose their state to the framework to participate in the checkpoints.

Figure 2 shows the dataflow graph of our slicer. Its main parameters are the number N of parallel monitors and the inputs for the shares optimization, which is performed during initialization. Events are read line by line as strings. We support both MonPoly's input format and the CSV format used in the first RV competition [6]. The parser converts the input lines into an internal datatype that stores the event name and the list of data values. We flatten the parser's results into a stream of single events because a single line in MonPoly's format may describe several events, i.e., an entire database, at once.

After parsing, the splitter computes the set of target slices for each event. To do so, it first determines the matching valuations as described in Sect. 4.2. As this set may be infinite, the splitter encodes it as a partial mappings from variables to data values. For each target slice, a copy of the event is sent to the next operator along with the slice identifier.

At this point, we would like to distribute the events to N parallel submonitors. However, the keyBy operation in the Flink API applies its own hash function to shuffle the events. This hash function might needlessly collapse slice identifiers. We work around this limitation by mapping the identifiers to preimages under the hash function, which we precompute by enumeration. In each parallel flow, a custom operator prints the internal datatype in MonPoly format, sends it to an external monitor process, and applies the intersection from the definition of J_f (Definition 3) to its output. Finally, all remaining verdicts are combined into a single stream, which is written to an output socket or file.

The custom operator is responsible for starting and interacting with the MonPoly process. The operator writes one database at a time to standard input and simultaneously reads violations from standard output of the process. Reading and writing is asynchronous to the Flink pipeline in order to prevent blocking other operators. Flink's AsyncWaitOperator supports asynchronous requests to external processes without managing their state. We must, however, include the submonitors' states in the checkpointing because they summarize the events seen so far. Thus, our custom operator tracks MonPoly's state. To this end, we extend MonPoly with control commands for saving and loading its state. Whenever Flink instructs the custom operator to create a checkpoint, it first waits until all prior events have been processed. Then, the command for saving state is issued and MonPoly writes its state to a temporary file. Violations reported after the checkpoint instruction's arrival at the custom operator are included in the checkpoint. This ensures that no violation is lost because other operators might create their own checkpoint concurrently. We evaluate the overhead of checkpointing in Sect. 7.

The part of the dataflow before the submonitors is not parallel. This is a bottleneck that limits scalability: all events in the input must be processed sequentially by the splitter. Despite this limitation of our implementation, the splitter and the surrounding operators could be parallelized too: As its splitter operates on individual events, the joint data slicer is event-separable (Sect. 4.1). A parallel splitter would be particularly effective if the event source itself is distributed. However, we would have to ensure that events arrive at the submonitors in chronological order after reshuffling. This order is no longer guaranteed if the splitter is partitioned into concurrent tasks. A possible solution is to buffer and reorder events. We leave the analysis of such an extension to future work.

7 Evaluation

With our evaluation, we aim to answer the following research questions:

RQ1: How does our monitor scale with respect to the index and event rate?
RQ2: How does our monitor scale with respect to different variable occurrence patterns?
RQ3: How much overhead is incurred by supporting fault tolerance (FT)?
RQ4: Can knowledge about the frequency of event names improve performance?
RQ5: Can knowledge about heavy hitter values improve performance?
RQ6: Can our monitor handle data in a real-world online setting?
RQ7: How does it compare to MonPoly running on a single core?

$star$ $= \Box \forall a.\forall b.\forall c.\forall d.\ (\blacklozenge_{[0,10s)} P(a,b)) \rightarrow Q(a,c) \rightarrow \Box_{[0,10s)} \neg R(a,d)$

$linear$ $= \Box \forall a.\forall b.\forall c.\forall d.\ (\blacklozenge_{[0,10s)} P(a,b)) \rightarrow Q(b,c) \rightarrow \Box_{[0,10s)} \neg R(c,d)$

$triangle$ $= \Box \forall a.\forall b.\forall c.\quad (\blacklozenge_{[0,10s)} P(a,b)) \rightarrow Q(b,c) \rightarrow \Box_{[0,10s)} \neg R(c,a)$

$script$ $= \Box \forall db.\forall dt.\ select(\text{script1},db,dt) \vee insert(\text{script1},db,dt) \vee$
$\qquad\qquad delete(\text{script1},db,dt) \vee update(\text{script1},db,dt) \rightarrow$
$\quad ((\neg \blacklozenge_{[0,1s)} \Diamond_{[0,1s)}\ end(\text{script1}))\ \mathsf{S}\ (\blacklozenge_{[0,1s)} \Diamond_{[0,1s)}\ start(\text{script1}))) \vee \blacklozenge_{[0,1s)} \Diamond_{[0,1s)}\ end(\text{script1})$

$insert$ $= \Box \forall u.\forall dt.\ insert(u,\text{db1},dt) \wedge dt \not\approx \text{unknown} \rightarrow$
$\qquad \blacklozenge_{[0,1s)} \Diamond_{[0,30h]} \exists u'.\ insert(u',\text{db2},dt) \vee delete(u',\text{db1},dt)$

$delete$ $= \Box \forall u.\forall dt.\ delete(u,\text{db1},dt) \wedge dt \not\approx \text{unknown} \rightarrow$
$\qquad \big(\blacklozenge_{[0,1s)} \Diamond_{[0,30h]} \exists u'.\ delete(u',\text{db2},dt) \big) \vee$
$\qquad \big((\Diamond_{[0,1s)} \blacklozenge_{[0,30h]} \exists u'.\ insert(u',\text{db1},dt)) \wedge (\blacksquare_{[0,30h]} \Box_{[0,30h]} \neg \exists u'.\ insert(u',\text{db2},dt)) \big)$

Fig. 3. MFOTL formulas used in the evaluation

To answer the research questions, we organize our evaluation into two families of experiments, each monitoring a different type of input stream (synthetic or real-world). The synthetic streams are used to analyze the effects of individual parameters, e.g., event rate, while real-world streams attest to our tool's ability to scalably solve realistic problems.

We implemented a generator that takes a random seed and synthesizes streams with specific characteristics. It produces streams containing binary events labeled with P, Q, or R with configurable event rate, index rate, and rate of violations for the three fixed formulas $star$, $linear$, and $triangle$ (Fig. 3). This setup allows us to test RQ1. Furthermore, to test RQ4 and RQ5, the generator synthesizes event labels with configurable rates $(Z(P), Z(Q),$ and $Z(R))$ and forces some event attribute values to be heavy hitters.

We use logs collected during the Nokia's Data Collection Campaign [10] as real-world streams. The campaign collected data from mobile phones of 180 participants and propagated it through three databases db1, db2, and db3. The phones uploaded their data directly to db1, while a synchronization script script1 periodically copied the data from db1 to db2. Then, database triggers on db2 anonymized and copied the data to db3. The participants could query and delete their own data in db1 and such deletions were propagated to all databases. To obtain streams suitable for online monitoring, we have developed a tool that replays log events and simulates the event rate at the log creation time, which is captured by the events' time-stamps. The tool can also replay the log proportionally faster than its event rate which is useful to evaluate the monitor's performance while retaining log's other characteristics. Since the log from the campaign spans a year, to evaluate our tool in a reasonable amount of time, we pick a one day fragment from the log with the highest average event rate and we use our replayer tool to speed it up between up to 5,000 times. The fragment contains roughly 9.5 million events and has an average event rate of 110 events per second. Combined with the speedup, we have subjected our tool to streams of over half a million events per second. The used logs [1] and the scripts that synthesize and replay streams [35] are publicly available.

Figure 3 shows the formulas we monitored in our evaluation. The formulas *star*, *linear*, and *triangle* are tailored for the synthetic streams. Different occurrence patterns of free variables in the formulas allows us to test RQ2. We aimed to cover common data patterns in database queries [16] and extend them with temporal aspects. The formulas *script*, *insert*, and *delete* stem from the Nokia's Data Collection Campaign and have been shown there to be challenging to monitor [10]. Since we monitor only a one day fragment of the log from Nokia, we must initialize our monitor with the appropriate state in order for it to produce the correct output. Therefore, we monitor each formula once on the part of the log preceding the chosen fragment, store the monitor's state, and start the monitor with the stored state as its initial state in the experiments.

We ran all our experiments on a server with two sockets, each containing twelve Intel Xeon 2.20GHz CPU cores with hyperthreading that effectively gives us 48 independent computation threads. We use the UNIX time command to measure total execution time, i.e., the time between the moment when the replayer tool starts emitting events to the monitor until the moment the monitor processes the last emitted event. We also measure the maximal memory usage of each submonitor. To measure latency during execution, the replayer tool injects a special event (called a latency marker) into the stream tagged with the current time. The marker is propagated by the monitor and the latency is measured at the output by comparing the current time with the time in the marker's tag. Besides the current latency measurement, we also calculate the rolling average and maximum latency up to the current point in the experiment. Flink supports latency markers and provides us with separate latency measurements for each operator in our monitor's implementation. Our replayer tool generates latency markers every second. When the latency is higher than one second, the latency marker gets delayed, too, and a timely value cannot be produced. Flink reports zeros for the current latency in this case, while we consider the latest non-zero value. This significantly reduces the noise in our measurements. Flink also measures the number of events each submonitor receives. Since we focus on performance measurements, we discard the tool's output during the experiments. Each run of a monitor with a specific configuration is repeated three times and the collected metrics are averaged to minimize the noise in the measurements.

Figure 4 shows the results for synthetic streams. Figure 4a (top) shows the maximum latency when monitoring the formula *star* with different numbers of cores. With the event rate of 2,200 events per second, the single core variant of our tool already exhibits 5 s latency. Similar latency is exhibited with 4 cores when monitoring events rates above 8,000. In contrast, using 16 cores achieves sub-second latency for all event rates in our experiments. We also show the maximal memory consumption across all submonitors in Fig. 4a (bottom). With an increasing number of submonitors, each submonitor receives fewer events and hence uses less memory. This experiment answers RQ1: our tool handles significantly higher event rates by using more parallel submonitors.

Figure 4b shows maximum latency (top) and memory consumption (bottom) of our tool when monitoring *star*, *triangle*, and *linear* formulas using 4 cores. The plots show six graphs, where a graph shows results of monitoring one of the three formulas over a stream with an index rate of 1 or 1,000. Since the index rate affects the performance of MonPoly [11], our tool is also affected. The event rate gain enabled by

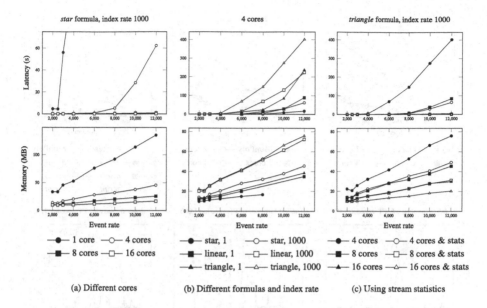

star formula, index rate 1000   4 cores   triangle formula, index rate 1000

(a) Different cores   (b) Different formulas and index rate   (c) Using stream statistics

Fig. 4. Monitoring synthetic streams with fault tolerance

more submonitors depends on the variable occurrence patterns in the monitored formula (RQ2). Figure 4b also demonstrates that the *star* pattern is the one that exhibits the best scalability.

In the above experiments, we did not supply our monitor with the information on the rates of event labels in the stream. Figure 4c positively answers RQ4 by showing that both our tool's latency (top) and memory consumption (bottom) decrease independently of the number of cores when such statistics about the stream are known in advance.

Figure 5 summarizes the results of monitoring the real-world log from the Nokia case study. The event and index rates are defined by the log, while we only control the replay speed. The experiments answer RQ7 and show that we achieve better performance then MonPoly on its own, on all three formulas. We improve latency even when using a single core, due the optimized implementation of the slicer that filters the unnecessary events more efficiently than MonPoly. In this experiment, our tool's performance does not improve beyond 4 cores, since for event rates higher than 500,000 the centralized parsing and slicing becomes a bottleneck. The top left and middle plots contrast the performance overhead of fault tolerance (RQ3). The maximal latency is not affected; however the bottom three plots show that the current and average latency are. These plots correspond to three individual runs and depict how the current latency changes over time. The leftmost plot shows the monitoring of the *delete* formula with respect to the stream sped up 1,000 times, not accounting for fault tolerance. The middle and rightmost plots show runs with enabled fault tolerance support for the speedups of 1,000 and 1,500. The regular spikes in the current latency stem from Flink's state snapshot algorithm.

Figure 6a shows the number of events sent per submonitor when no skew is present in the stream. In the presence of skew, the event distribution is much less uniform

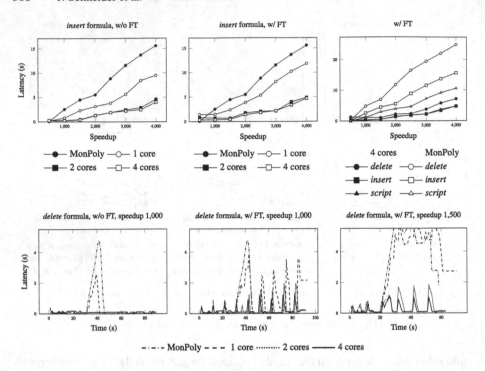

Fig. 5. Monitoring the real-world stream

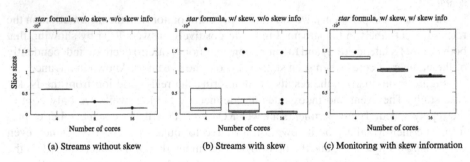

Fig. 6. Impact of the skew and skew information on parallel monitoring

(Fig. 6b). However, when our monitor is aware of the variables in the formula whose instantiations in the stream are skewed, it can balance the events evenly (Fig. 6c), effectively reducing the maximum load of the submonitors.

8 Conclusion and Future Work

We generalized the offline slicing framework [9] to support online monitoring and the simultaneous slicing with respect to all free variables in the formula. We adapted hash-based partitioning techniques from databases to obtain an automatic slicing strategy.

We implemented the automatic slicing combining MonPoly with Flink and experimentally demonstrated a significant performance improvement: while retaining sub-second latency, 16-way parallelization allows us to increase the event rate by one order of magnitude.

We plan to extend our framework to include slicing on bound variables and to optimize slicing of rigid predicates. Checkpointing MonPoly's state coupled with the online collection of the stream's varying statistics can be used to dynamically reconfigure the automatic slicing strategy. We intend to implement this natural extension and analyze the tradeoff between the reconfiguration costs and the cost of using imperfect statistics. We also plan to refine our automatic splitting strategy to take communication costs explicitly into account and evaluate our approach on a distributed computing cluster.

Acknowledgment. Joshua Schneider is supported by the US Air Force grant "Monitoring at Any Cost" (FA9550-17-1-0306). Srđan Krstić is supported by the Swiss National Science Foundation grant "Big Data Monitoring" (167162).

References

1. The Nokia case study log file (2014). https://sourceforge.net/projects/monpoly/files/ldcc.tar/download
2. Afrati, F.N., Ullman, J.D.: Optimizing multiway joins in a map-reduce environment. IEEE Trans. Knowl. Data Eng. **23**(9), 1282–1298 (2011)
3. Alexandrov, A., et al.: The stratosphere platform for big data analytics. VLDB J. **23**(6), 939–964 (2014)
4. Barre, B., Klein, M., Soucy-Boivin, M., Ollivier, P.-A., Hallé, S.: MapReduce for parallel trace validation of LTL properties. In: Qadeer, S., Tasiran, S. (eds.) RV 2012. LNCS, vol. 7687, pp. 184–198. Springer, Heidelberg (2013). https://doi.org/10.1007/978-3-642-35632-2_20
5. Barringer, H., Falcone, Y., Havelund, K., Reger, G., Rydeheard, D.: Quantified event automata: towards expressive and efficient runtime monitors. In: Giannakopoulou, D., Méry, D. (eds.) FM 2012. LNCS, vol. 7436, pp. 68–84. Springer, Heidelberg (2012). https://doi.org/10.1007/978-3-642-32759-9_9
6. Bartocci, E., Bonakdarpour, B., Falcone, Y.: First international competition on software for runtime verification. In: Bonakdarpour, B., Smolka, S.A. (eds.) RV 2014. LNCS, vol. 8734, pp. 1–9. Springer, Cham (2014). https://doi.org/10.1007/978-3-319-11164-3_1
7. Bartocci, E., Falcone, Y., Francalanza, A., Reger, G.: Introduction to runtime verification. In: Bartocci, E., Falcone, Y. (eds.) Lectures on Runtime Verification. LNCS, vol. 10457, pp. 1–33. Springer, Cham (2018). https://doi.org/10.1007/978-3-319-75632-5_1
8. Basin, D., Bhatt, B.N., Traytel, D.: Almost event-rate independent monitoring of metric temporal logic. In: Legay, A., Margaria, T. (eds.) TACAS 2017. LNCS, vol. 10206, pp. 94–112. Springer, Heidelberg (2017). https://doi.org/10.1007/978-3-662-54580-5_6
9. Basin, D., Caronni, G., Ereth, S., Harvan, M., Klaedtke, F., Mantel, H.: Scalable offline monitoring of temporal specifications. Form. Methods Syst. Des. **49**(1–2), 75–108 (2016)
10. Basin, D., Harvan, M., Klaedtke, F., Zălinescu, E.: Monitoring data usage in distributed systems. IEEE Trans. Softw. Eng. **39**(10), 1403–1426 (2013)
11. Basin, D., Klaedtke, F., Müller, S., Zălinescu, E.: Monitoring metric first-order temporal properties. J. ACM **62**(2), 15:1–15:45 (2015)

12. Basin, D., Klaedtke, F., Zălinescu, E.: The MonPoly monitoring tool. In: Reger, G., Havelund, K., (eds.) RV-CuBES 2017, Kalpa Publications in Computing, vol. 3, pp. 19–28. EasyChair (2017)
13. Basin, D., Krstić, S., Traytel, D.: Almost event-rate independent monitoring of metric dynamic logic. In: Lahiri, S., Reger, G. (eds.) RV 2017. LNCS, vol. 10548, pp. 85–102. Springer, Cham (2017). https://doi.org/10.1007/978-3-319-67531-2_6
14. Bauer, A., Küster, J.-C., Vegliach, G.: From propositional to first-order monitoring. In: Legay, A., Bensalem, S. (eds.) RV 2013. LNCS, vol. 8174, pp. 59–75. Springer, Heidelberg (2013). https://doi.org/10.1007/978-3-642-40787-1_4
15. Beame, P., Koutris, P., Suciu, D.: Skew in parallel query processing. In: Hull, R., Grohe, M. (eds.) PODS 2014, pp. 212–223. ACM (2014)
16. Beame, P., Koutris, P., Suciu, D.: Communication steps for parallel query processing. J. ACM 64(6), 40:1–40:58 (2017)
17. Bersani, M.M., Bianculli, D., Ghezzi, C., Krstić, S., Pietro, P.S.: Efficient large-scale trace checking using MapReduce. In: Dillon, L.K., Visser, W., Williams, L. (eds.) ICSE 2016, pp. 888–898. ACM (2016)
18. Bianculli, D., Ghezzi, C., Krstić, S.: Trace checking of metric temporal logic with aggregating modalities using MapReduce. In: Giannakopoulou, D., Salaün, G. (eds.) SEFM 2014. LNCS, vol. 8702, pp. 144–158. Springer, Cham (2014). https://doi.org/10.1007/978-3-319-10431-7_11
19. Bundala, D., Ouaknine, J.: On the complexity of temporal-logic path checking. In: Esparza, J., Fraigniaud, P., Husfeldt, T., Koutsoupias, E. (eds.) ICALP 2014. LNCS, vol. 8573, pp. 86–97. Springer, Heidelberg (2014). https://doi.org/10.1007/978-3-662-43951-7_8
20. Carbone, P., Ewen, S., Fóra, G., Haridi, S., Richter, S., Tzoumas, K.: State management in Apache Flink®: consistent stateful distributed stream processing. PVLDB 10(12), 1718–1729 (2017)
21. Chu, S., Balazinska, M., Suciu, D.: From theory to practice: efficient join query evaluation in a parallel database system. In: Sellis, T.K., Davidson, S.B., Ives, Z.G. (eds.) SIGMOD 2015, pp. 63–78. ACM (2015)
22. Feng, S., Lohrey, M., Quaas, K.: Path checking for MTL and TPTL over data words. Log. Methods Comput. Sci. 13(3), (2017)
23. Ganguly, S., Silberschatz, A., Tsur, S.: Parallel bottom-up processing of datalog queries. J. Log. Program. 14(1&2), 101–126 (1992)
24. Hallé, S., Khoury, R.: Event stream processing with BeepBeep 3. In: Reger, G., Havelund, K. (eds.) RV-CuBES 2017, Kalpa Publications in Computing, pp. 81–88. EasyChair (2017)
25. Hallé, S., Khoury, R., Gaboury, S.: Event stream processing with multiple threads. In: Lahiri, S., Reger, G. (eds.) RV 2017. LNCS, vol. 10548, pp. 359–369. Springer, Cham (2017). https://doi.org/10.1007/978-3-319-67531-2_22
26. Havelund, K., Peled, D., Ulus, D.: First order temporal logic monitoring with BDDs. In: Stewart, D., Weissenbacher, G. (eds.) FMCAD 2017, pp. 116–123. IEEE (2017)
27. Koutris, P., Beame, P., Suciu, D.: Worst-case optimal algorithms for parallel query processing. In: Martens, W., Zeume, T. (eds.) ICDT 2016, LIPIcs, vol. 48, pp. 8:1–8:18. Schloss Dagstuhl – Leibniz-Zentrum für Informatik (2016)
28. Kuhtz, L., Finkbeiner, B.: LTL path checking is efficiently parallelizable. In: Albers, S., Marchetti-Spaccamela, A., Matias, Y., Nikoletseas, S., Thomas, W. (eds.) ICALP 2009. LNCS, vol. 5556, pp. 235–246. Springer, Heidelberg (2009). https://doi.org/10.1007/978-3-642-02930-1_20
29. Nasir, M.A.U., Morales, G.D.F., García-Soriano, D., Kourtellis, N., Serafini, M.: The power of both choices: practical load balancing for distributed stream processing engines. In: Gehrke, J., Lehner, W., Shim, K., Cha, S.K., Lohman, G.M. (eds.) ICDE 2015, pp. 137–148. IEEE Computer Society (2015)

30. Nasir, M.A.U., Morales, G.D.F., Kourtellis, N., Serafini, M.: When two choices are not enough: balancing at scale in distributed stream processing. In: ICDE 2016, pp. 589–600. IEEE Computer Society (2016)
31. Okcan, A., Riedewald, M.: Processing theta-joins using MapReduce. In: Sellis, T.K., Miller, R.J., Kementsietsidis, A., Velegrakis, Y. (eds.) SIGMOD 2011, pp. 949–960. ACM (2011)
32. Reger, G., Rydeheard, D.: From first-order temporal logic to parametric trace slicing. In: Bartocci, E., Majumdar, R. (eds.) RV 2015. LNCS, vol. 9333, pp. 216–232. Springer, Cham (2015). https://doi.org/10.1007/978-3-319-23820-3_14
33. Rivetti, N., Querzoni, L., Anceaume, E., Busnel, Y., Sericola, B.: Efficient key grouping for near-optimal load balancing in stream processing systems. In: Eliassen, F., Vitenberg, R. (eds.) DEBS 2015, pp. 80–91. ACM (2015)
34. Roşu, G., Chen, F.: Semantics and algorithms for parametric monitoring. Log. Methods Comput. Sci. 8(1), (2012)
35. Schneider, J., Basin, D., Brix, F., Krstić, S., Traytel, D.: Implementation associated with this paper (2018). https://bitbucket.org/krle/scalable-online-monitor
36. Suri, S., Vassilvitskii, S.: Counting triangles and the curse of the last reducer. In: Srinivasan, S., Ramamritham, K., Kumar, A., Ravindra, M.P., Bertino, E., Kumar, R. (eds.) WWW 2011, pp. 607–614. ACM (2011)
37. Vitorovic, A., et al.: Squall: scalable real-time analytics. PVLDB 9(13), 1553–1556 (2016)

Practical Information Flow Control
for Web Applications

Angel Luis Scull Pupo$^{(\boxtimes)}$, Laurent Christophe, Jens Nicolay, Coen de Roover,
and Elisa Gonzalez Boix

Vrije Universiteit Brussel, Pleinlaan 2, 1050 Brussels, Belgium
{ascullpu,lachrist,jnicolay,cderoove,egonzale}@vub.be

Abstract. Current browser-level security solutions do not provide a
mechanism for information flow control (IFC) policies. As such, they
need to be combined with language-based security approaches. Practical implementations for ICF enforcement remains a challenge when the
full spectrum of web applications features is taken into account (i.e.
JavaScript features, web APIs, DOM, portability, performance, etc.). In
this work we develop GIFC, a permissive-upgrade-based inlined monitoring mechanism to detect unwanted information flow in web applications.
GIFC covers a wide range of JavaScript features that give rise to implicit
flows. In contrast to related work, GIFC also handles dynamic code evaluation online, and it features an API function model mechanism that
enables information tracking through APIs calls. As a result, GIFC can
handle information flows that use DOM nodes as channels of information.
We validate GIFC by means of a benchmark suite from literature specifically designed for information flow verification, which we also extend.
We compare GIFC qualitatively with respect to closest related work and
show that GIFC performs better at detecting unwanted implicit flows.

Keywords: Information flow control · JavaScript
Runtime monitoring · Browser security · Programming language

1 Introduction

Large parts of many contemporary client-side web applications are implemented
in or compiled to HTML and JavaScript. In these web applications, developers
reuse content, code, and services provided by third parties to avoid reimplementing everything from scratch. The default code inclusion mechanism in web
applications are `script` elements that point to a resource providing JavaScript
source code. The code a browser downloads in this manner is, however, executed in the same environment and with the same privileges as the code provided by the hosted page itself. This implies that, without additional measures,
third-party JavaScript code may have access to sensitive data provided by users.
For example, consider a web application including a *password strength checker*
component to provide users with visual feedback about the quality of their password. In order for the component to perform this task, it must be provided with

© Springer Nature Switzerland AG 2018
C. Colombo and M. Leucker (Eds.): RV 2018, LNCS 11237, pp. 372–388, 2018.
https://doi.org/10.1007/978-3-030-03769-7_21

the password value. However, nothing prevents the component from leaking the password to other third party code.

To help mitigate exploits of such security vulnerabilities, modern browsers provide mechanisms such as *Same-Origin Policy* (SOP) and *Content Security Policy* (CSP). SOP allows to isolate content from different web origins coexisting within the same web page [1], but it does not apply to the src content of script tags. On the other hand, CSP enables developers to specify from which domains the browser can load resources [33,34], but it does not prevent white-listed third-party components that access users data from leaking this data [25,34]. As a result, SOP and CSP must be complemented with application-level security mechanisms to ensure data privacy and confidentiality.

The goal of *Information Flow Control* (IFC) is precisely to enforce data confidentiality and integrity guarantees in software systems. In this paper we focus on dynamic IFC analysis through runtime monitoring for web applications. Dynamic analysis is said to be more suitable for JavaScript than static verification since statically approximating the behaviour of programs is particularly difficult given the dynamic nature of JavaScript [3,8]. However, several JavaScript language features still make dynamic IFC analysis a particularly challenging task [3], being the most relevant ones, how to reason about DOM and other web APIs, eval, prototype inheritance and finally, how to handle *implicit flows*, i.e. flows caused by non-executed branches. In this paper we explore a practical dynamic IFC mechanism that tackles all these relevant features without requiring VM modifications.

1.1 Problem Statement

We surveyed recent and relevant dynamic IFC approaches for JavaScript that have a publicly accessible implementation and are described in related work: IF-TRANSPILER [32], JSFLOW [19], ZAPHODFACETS [6], FLOWFOX [14,16], and JEST [13]. In general, existing work aims at tackling some of the aforementioned language feature challenges while keeping the performance penalties at a reasonable level.

Table 1. Overview of recent and relevant dynamic IFC approaches for JavaScript.

	eval/DOM	Libraries	Permissive	Portable	Performant
IF-TRANSPILER			✓	✓	✓
JSFLOW	✓	✓			
ZAPHODFACETS			✓		
FLOWFOX	✓	✓	✓		
JEST	✓	✓		✓	✓
GIFC	✓	✓	✓	✓	✓

Table 1 summarizes our survey of dynamic IFC approaches. Only JSFLOW, FLOWFOX, and JEST offer support for the DOM and eval, with JEST requiring a server-side component to handle eval. Yet, support for the DOM and eval is crucial when analyzing web applications, because the DOM models an important part of the application state and eval is widely used in web applications [22, 30]. Moreover, only those three approaches support modeling the behavior of (external) libraries in terms of information flow.

Permissiveness is considered to be an important factor in making IFC practical [18,32]. In this regard, JSFLOW and JEST are not as permissive as IF-TRANSPILER, meaning that these approaches will prematurely end a secure program execution. On the other hand, FLOWFOX is permissive.

In terms of performance, applying JSFLOW, ZAPHODFACETS, or FLOWFOX incurs a high performance penalty because JSFLOW and ZAPHODFACETS add a complete layer of interpretation between the application code and the underlying JavaScript runtime, while FLOWFOX relies on multiple executions of an application. Overall, approaches that modify the VM (FLOWFOX) or develop a new interpreter (ZAPHODFACETS and JSFLOW) are expensive.

Finally, JSFLOW, ZAPHODFACETS, and FLOWFOX are not portable, as they are tied to a particular implementation of a JavaScript or browser environment, greatly diminishing their applicability in a landscape of JavaScript and web standards which is constantly evolving.

In this paper we present GIFC, a permissive and portable dynamic IFC mechanism with support for dynamic code evaluation, external libraries and DOM. GIFC exhibits the following properties:

Support for eval. GIFC handles dynamic code evaluation online. This is possible because we employ an instrumentation platform running alongside the instrumented program.

Support for libraries. GIFC features an API function model mechanism that enables information tracking through APIs calls. To handle external function calls we took inspiration from the specification of function models described in [21].

Permissive. The monitor of GIFC is based on the *permissive upgrade* (PU) technique of Austin and Flanagan [5].

Portable. GIFC does not require modifications to the underlying JavaScript interpreter or rely on a specific JavaScript runtime environment, but instead works with any ECMAScript 5 compliant JavaScript interpreter.

Performant. The monitor of GIFC is inlined in the source code, so that the instrumented program (including the monitor) can still benefit from the optimizations offered by the underlying JavaScript runtime.

To the best of our knowledge, the combination of these properties are novel and ensures that GIFC is well-suited to perform practical information flow control for contemporary web applications.

The remainder of this paper is structured as follows. Section 2, informally introduces the key IFC concepts. Next, Sect. 3 introduces the principal aspects of our approach that drove the implementation of GIFC described in Sect. 4.

In Sect. 5, we evaluate qualitatively GIFC based on a benchmark suite from literature. We also did a quantitative study to evaluate the performance of GIFC with respect to the state of the art. Finally, Sect. 6 compares the features introduced in Sect. 3 with the state of the art on dynamic IFC.

2 Background Information on IFC

IFC can be used to enforce data privacy and integrity guarantees in software systems [20]. The semantic foundation for IFC is based on the concept of *noninterference* [17,20]. This property holds for an application when, given the same public inputs, the variation of its secret inputs does not affect its public outputs. Dynamic IFC mechanisms track the dissemination of program values as they are produced and combined during program execution to prevent the flow of a sensitive value to a *public sink* [20].

An IFC policy defines *labels* that express the security level of program values, and identifies the sources that produce values with a particular label. For example, a *low* label L can be associated with non-sensitive program values that are allowed to be publicly observable. In contrast, *high* labels H can be associated with sensitive values that should remain private to the application. Additionally, an IFC policy identifies *information sinks* in a program and associates them with a label as well. IFC then only allows values flowing into a sink that are less sensitive than that sink's label. An IFC policy therefore establishes how the different security levels are related, for example through the use of a total or partial order (lattice) between labels. In our example, we would have L ⊏ H, expressing that H is more sensitive than L, so that H values are not allowed to flow to L sinks.

Explicit and Implicit Flows. Information flows can be categorized into two types [15,20]. *Explicit flows* arise from the direct copy of information. For example, the assignment expression y = x causes an explicit flow from variable x to y, and after the assignment y will have the same value with the same label as x. *Implicit flows* arise from control flow structures such as if, **return** in a nonfinal position, **break**, **continue**, and **throw**. For example, after executing the statement if (z) y=0 else y=1 the value of variable y depends on the value of z. This results in an implicit flow from z to y, and after the if statement the value of y will have the same label as z.

Permissiveness. Permissiveness can be understood as the ability of a monitoring mechanism to allow the execution of semantically secure programs [13,18]. Implicit flows from private variables holding secret values to public variables holding non-secret values enables attackers to infer information about these secret values. Austin and Flanagan [4] proposed the *No-Sensitive Upgrade* (NSU) technique, in which any side effect that depends on secret information will terminate the execution. NSU monitors, however, make a coarse approximation of the all paths of executions of the program in order to ensure soundness. For example, consider the program in Listing 1.1. NSU terminates the execution when it reaches the assignment to y because the occurrence this side-effect depends on the secret value of variable x. Although this behavior is sound, the termination of the program execution is premature since the value of y is never used afterwards.

Listing 1.1.	Listing 1.2.	Listing 1.3.

```
let x = true; //H    let x = true; //H    let x = false;//H
let y = false;//L    let y = false;//L    let y = false;//L
let z = true; //L    let z = true; //L    let z = true; //L
if (x) {y=false};//P if (x) {y=false};//P if (x) {y=false};
print(z)             print(y)             print(y)
```

Permissive Upgrade (PU) [5] is an alternative to NSU that provides a more permissive approach to handle implicit flows. A PU monitor keeps track of secret-dependent values by means of a special label P that indicates that the information is *partially leaked*, i.e., it is currently secret but in other executions may remain public. The execution is terminated only when a partially leaked value is used in a conditional statement or flows to a public sink. Therefore, at the assignment to y in Listing 1.1, instead of stopping the execution as a NSU monitor would, a PU monitor tags the value of variable y with P and execution continues until the end. However, a PU monitor would halt the execution of the program in Listing 1.2 when reaching the `print` statement. For completeness, we mention that both NSU and PU deem the execution of the program in Listing 1.3 to be safe, although there is an implicit flow from variable x to y. Therefore, these monitors are able to enforce *termination-insensitive* noninterference (TINI) which is weaker than *noninterference* [4,5,10].

3   GIFC

This work introduces GIFC, a permissive and portable inlined monitoring mechanism that supports the DOM and dynamic code evaluation and offers support for modeling external libraries. To the best of our knowledge, this combination of properties for a dynamic IFC approach is unique. Before delving into how GIFC offers all the properties from Table 1, we first lay out the attacker assumptions.

3.1   Attacker Model

We adhere to the *gadget attacker model* [7]. We assume the user visits a trusted web application in a legitimate browser. The attacker is somehow able to run his malicious JavaScript code on the trusted site, for example because the application includes a script from the attacker's server or by using an improper sanitized input. The attacker does not have any network privileges that allows them to mount a *man-in-the-middle* attack [2]. The only outputs the attacker can observe are those sent to his own server. For that, he can use APIs in the browser environment (e.g `XMLHTTPRequest`). Those APIs are considered sinks of information.

Therefore, the duty of the IFC monitor is to prevent the flow of any high or sensitive value to those sinks.

3.2 Permissiveness

GIFC's monitor is a flow-sensitive variation on the PU strategy introduced in Austin et al. [5]. GIFC proposes to use AST information of the program to extend the *pc* label context of language constructs such as

Listing 1.4.

```
1  if (!h) {throw new Error()};
2  y = z;
3  f();
4  g();
```

return, break, throw, etc., when their execution depends on secret values. This information is crucial and must be handled carefully by approaches like NSU or PU to ensure soundness and permissiveness guarantees. If the aforementioned language features are not handled, the monitor will potentially leak information and hence, will become unsound. On the other hand, if they are used with an approach like NSU, the monitor could become excessively restrictive. For example, consider the code snippet in Listing 1.4 in which h is secret. The execution of lines from 2 to 4 depends on the value of h, given the throw statement will execute based on the value h. Therefore, a NSU-based monitor will stop the execution at the assignment statement (line 2). In this example this problem is extended until the program encounters the first error handler.

3.3 Portability

GIFC does not rely on a modified VM like [9,16], nor provides an IFC-aware interpreter like [6,19] since those solutions are inherently not portable. Instead, GIFC relies on code instrumentation. Similarly to [12,13,27,31,32], GIFC inlines the monitor within the program.

Inlining the monitor in the program source code has, however, security implications given that the program runs alongside the monitor and an attacker may attempt to tamper with the monitor state to compromise security. To increase the monitor's security, GIFC and JEST obfuscates all variables names introduced by the monitor. This is a naive approach because an attacker can use the reflective capabilities of JavaScript to inspect and modify the monitor state. A possible way to ensure the security of the monitor could be by means of *freeze/seal* of ECMAScript 5. These functions can be used to protect the monitor which will prevent an attacker from altering the monitor functionality. This will imply freezing Object, Array, String and other objects from the standard library. Also, all the object in the prototype chain of the monitor should be secured to prevent an attacker from tampering with its prototype chain. Nevertheless, the security of our monitor is ongoing work.

3.4 Eval

Function eval allows the execution of arbitrary code represented by a string value. Existing dynamic and hybrid approaches that rely on source code instrumentation do not support `eval()`. For a source code instrumentation approach to support `eval()` with minimum performance implications, the instrumentation mechanism must run alongside the instrumented program. In GIFC, we specialized `eval()` to track information flow on the string value that this function receive as argument. Since our code instrumenter is part of the execution environment, when `eval()` is called, its argument is instrumented before its evaluation.

3.5   External Library Calls

JavaScript web applications do not live in isolation in the browser, but they instead interact with the rest of the system in order to do something useful like processing user input/output, sending data over the network, displaying a web form, etc. All these interactions performed by the application are done by means of calls to web APIs, implemented by the browser in other languages (e.g., C++).

Listing 1.5 shows an example of an external function call, `Math.pow`. When executing that code with GIFC to track the flow of information, the application is actually running with augmented semantics, e.g. values are labeled and monitored. Since external libraries do not understand the values used in the augmented semantics, the monitoring mechanism should not pass label information to `Math.pow`. However, after the external library call, the monitor cannot know which label assign to x's value.

Listing 1.5.

```
let y = 13; //H
let x = Math.pow(y,2);
```

A conservative approach to solve this problem is to label the result value with the most sensitive label of the values involved in the call. However, this is considered to be restrictive [19]. To solve this problem in GIFC, we defined an API function model with two functions φ and γ, inspired by the ones presented by Hedin et al. in [21]. The φ knows how to marshal the values from the monitored program to the external function. Also, it has to store the label all values involved in the call. Those stored labels are then used by γ to decide which label should be attached to the return value of the API function call.

3.6   Document Object Model

The Document Object Model (DOM) is the main web API offering page rendering and input/output facilities [24]. DOM elements are exposed to JavaScript as objects. However, their semantics is different from regular ordinary JavaScript objects. Properties of DOM elements are actually pairs of getter/setter functions provided by the browser that cannot handle labeled values.

Monitoring flows from the DOM is crucial as attackers could store secret information as DOM element or as part of their properties or attributes to then later retrieve them and leak that information.

To be able to reason about the DOM without VM modifications, JavaScript proxies [28] seem a good approach to enhance DOM elements operations with information flow control semantics. However, the DOM is unable to handle proxified nodes because type checks that inspect actual DOM elements will fail for proxies. Also, our function model from Sect. 3.5 is stateless, while many DOM elements model state.

In order to monitor the DOM API, GIFC associates a meta-object with each DOM element. This meta-object keeps track the element properties' labels and is stored in its target DOM object as an "anonymous" property, using a symbol property key. Note, however, that this approach is transparent but not tamper-proof. This is because the attacker can gain access to the meta-object by mean the language reflective features (i.e. `Object.getOwnPropertySymbols()`).

3.7 Performance

As explained in the introduction dynamic IFC incurs on non-neglegible performance penalties. In particular, the performance of FLOWFOX depends on the number of security level and the number of cores of the CPU given that the program needs to execute once per each security level. On the other hand, providing an IFC aware interpreter like JSFLOW and ZAPHODFACETS incurs in a big performance penalty (as we also later show in Sect. 5.2).

Similar to IF-TRANSPILER, GIFC employs code instrumentation to inline its monitor within the target program. Inlining the source code is potentially better performant than the aforementioned solutions since the resulting code can benefit from JIT compilation as pointed out in [13]. Section 5 evaluates this research statement and measures the impact of GIFC on the original application.

4 Implementation

We implemented GIFC[1] as a JavaScript framework that takes a JavaScript or an HTML page as input program. GIFC then inlines the IFC monitor by instrumenting the source code of the application. More precisely, the JavaScript code is instrumented to trap relevant operations and call the monitor through a well-defined interface, decoupling the monitor from the instrumentation platform used. Our current prototype assumes that developers tag the sources and sinks in the input program and provide the specification of function models to handle external libraries. In what follows, we will first briefly introduce the used code instrumentation platform, and then provide details on the monitor, how it deals with implicit flows and non-JavaScript APIs.

4.1 Code Instrumentation Platform

GIFC uses *Linvail* [11] as code instrumentation platform for implementing its monitor. More precisely, it employs Linvail's source-to-source transpiler for

---

[1] https://gitlab.soft.vub.ac.be/ascullpu/guardia-ifc.

JavaScript called *Aran*[2]. Aran takes as input a target program and an analysis and produces an instrumented JavaScript program that can be executed on any ES5-compliant interpreter. The analysis is a JavaScript file that describes how JavaScript operations should be embellished. In the case of GIFC, the analysis file provides the traps for language operations (function calls, variable assignment, object property access, etc.) that require calling the IFC monitor.

4.2   Monitor

The instrumented code interacts with the monitor using a well-defined interface shown in Fig. 1, distilled from the semantics of the PU monitor presented by Austin et al. [5].

	Monitor function	Description
callbacks	pushContext(x, t)	Push a context label given a type
	popContext(t)	Pop a context label given its type
	join(x,y)	Returns the least upper bound of the labels
	permissiveCheck()	Determine if there is no PU violation in a branching point
	enforce(y,...xs)	Enforce IFC if y is a sink and some of xs is a source
	leave(fn)	Remember all values' labels of an external function call before its execution
	enter(fn, val)	Attach a computed label to the return value of an external function
impl	tagAsSource(x)	Tags x as source (i.e. sensitive data)
	tagAsSink(x)	Tags x as sink (i.e. produce a public observable data)
	addFnModel(φ, γ))	Registers a model γ for an external function φ

Fig. 1. Monitor interface

The monitor interface decouples its implementation from the instrumentation platform, which enables changing parts of the monitoring mechanism independently. We would also like to exploit this decoupling in future work to experiment with other code instrumentation platforms.

Figure 1 distinguishes two categories of monitor functions. Calls to the functions marked as "callbacks" are automatically inserted into the target program during code instrumentation (see Sect. 4.4). Calls to the functions marked as "impl" have to be manually called by the IFC implementor, i.e. developer performing IFC analysis. Those calls refer to the tagging functions for tagging sources and sinks, and to add a function model (see Sect. 4.3).

4.3   Implementer Monitor Functions

GIFC provides functions `tagAsSource` and `tagAsSink` that developers have to insert into a program to identify sensitive sources and sinks. For example, the

---

[2] https://github.com/lachrist/aran.

program in Listing 1.6 shows the required tagging for enabling the IFC monitor to prevent the flow of the user password to the browser console output. Function console.log is tagged as a sink, and the value property of the HTML element with id #pass as a source.

Listing 1.6. Prevent password leakage

```
tagAsSink(console.log);
const onClickHandler = () => {
    const $ = document.querySelector;
    let pass = tagAsSource($('#pass').value);
    ...
    console.log(pass);
}
```

Although developers currently have to manually tag sources and sinks in the code, it would be possible to devise a more declarative (external) manner for specifying sources and sinks, which the code instrumenter can then use to introduce the tag functions in the target program where appropriate. We are currently building plugin support enhanced with AI machinery to automate the marking sources and sinks in the future.

Besides identifying sources and sinks, GIFC also expects that external functions are registered using addFnModel(fun, γ). Function γ has to approximate the flow of information of function fun in terms of the labels of the arguments. For example, for Math.pow(x,y) shown in Listing 1.5, we would register $\gamma(x,y) = x \sqcup y$, correctly capturing the notion that if Math.pow is called with one or two sensitive argument values, then the resulting value is also sensitive. We implemented models for some objects of the standard libraries including Math, Array, and String. However, the monitor fallback to default conservative model for functions calls that do not have precise model implementation.

4.4   Callback Monitor Functions

GIFC uses a shadow stack to maintain the *pc* label. The pushContext() function pushes a security label into the stack every time the program encounters a control flow statement. The label value is the join of all values that influences control flow in a control flow statement.

popContext() removes the top element of the stack when the execution reaches the end of a control flow structure body.

Our monitor actually maintains an *exception* stack that keeps track of implicit flows that arise from throwing exceptions in sensitive contexts. We push into the *exception* stack when the execution of a throw statement depends on sensitive information. This is because there is no syntactic way to know when an exception will be handled. Then, when a catch handler is reached, we pop all values from the *exception* stack.

The join(a,b) operation is used whenever the label of a value depends on multiple values (i.e. the *least upper bound* of the elements). As a concrete example, consider let z = x + y;. The label of z depends on the more sensitive label involved in the values of the binary operation (also, in the label of the pc context, etc.).

The `permissiveCheck()` enforces the PU invariant at the branching point of control flow structures to avoid total leak of information. `enforce()` is then used at code locations (e.g. function application, setters) where information can leak the system to prevent information flow violations. It checks if there is any sensitive value flowing to a setter or function annotated as sink.

Functions `addFnModel(fun, γ)`, `leave`, and `enter` enable the IFC monitor to interact with non-instrumented functions, i.e. external function calls. As mentioned, external functions need to be registered using `addFnModel(fun, γ)`. During program execution, upon the call to an external function, function `leave` looks up the corresponding γ function, splits the labels from the argument values and applies γ, and stores the resulting label ℓ. Next, the actual external function is called with the unlabeled argument values. Finally, function `enter` attaches the stored label ℓ to the value returned from the non-instrumented function call.

Recall that to reason about the DOM, GIFC associates a meta-object with each DOM element. When a getter or setter is executed on a DOM element, the instrumentation ensures that each element property write operation updates its corresponding label in the meta-object, while every value resulting from a property read operation will be labeled with its corresponding label. For handling DOM elements methods, the function model associated to the method is used.

5   Evaluation

In order to evaluate our approach, we performed a qualitative and quantitative evaluation of our GIFC implementation. The qualitative evaluation provides an indication of how effective our approach is in detecting illicit information flows. The quantitative evaluation shows the performance implications of our approach to an uninstrumented baseline and compares it to related approaches.

5.1   Qualitative Evaluation

To evaluate the effectiveness of GIFC in a practical way, we compare it with IF-TRANSPILER, JSFLOW, and ZAPHODFACETS by determining whether or not illicit flows are detected in a suite of benchmark programs[3]. The benchmark suite was designed by Sayed et al. [32] and consists of 33 programs specifically designed for testing information flow control. It contains a wide variety of (combinations of) language features that challenge any IFC approach. We extended the benchmark with 5 new programs to test features such as `eval`, API function calls, and property getters/setters not present in the original one. In the GIFC repository we describe the 28 programs included in the original benchmark suite[4]. The

---

[3] Unfortunately we were unable to set up a functional test environment for FLOWFOX and JEST. In the case of JEST certain models are required that are undocumented and not trivial to develop.

[4] https://gitlab.soft.vub.ac.be/ascullpu/guardia-ifc.

last entries in the table describe the new 5 additions. Each benchmark program takes as input a secret string value, which the program attempts to leak explicitly or implicitly in various ways. We ran all tools on all benchmark programs in NodeJS, except for ZAPHODFACETS, of which the experiments were performed in *Mozilla Firefox 8.0* as required by the tool.

Table 2 shows how GIFC compares to the other three IFC approaches. The ✓ means that a tool was able to detect the illicit information flow, while ✗ indicates that a tool was unable to detect the illicit flow. *R.Err* indicates that a tool threw a runtime exception and was unable to execute the program properly. *In.Err* indicates that the tool was unable to inline the monitor into the original program source code. *Exp* indicates that the tool threw an exception at a point where an illicit information flow could be. However, in these cases it was premature because at that point there was no invalid information flow. This observation was also made in [32].

The results in Table 2 show that GIFC is able to detect and prevent illicit information flows in all test programs. For the 28 programs from the original suite we were able to reproduce the findings reported by Sayed et al. [32] for IF-TRANSPILER, JSFLOW, and ZAPHODFACETS. For the 5 test programs that we extended the suite, GIFC and JSFLOW successfully detected all illicit flows. Both IF-TRANSPILER and ZAPHODFACETS were able to successfully detect an illicit flow in only one out of 5 new test programs.

Adding online support for `eval()` in IF-TRANSPILER needs the static analysis component and the transpiler in the same process of the application. Supporting APIs will require the refactoring of the transformation rules to include function models. Also, it will require implementing the mechanism that allows assigning models to APIs functions which need to be configured at runtime.

From this we conclude that GIFC is on par with the existing tools in terms of detecting illicit information flows in the presence of different JavaScript features.

5.2   Quantitative Evaluation

We conducted performance benchmarks to measure the impact of GIFC on the performance of the original application (the baseline), and to gauge how our approach compares with IF-TRANSPILER, JSFLOW, and ZAPHODFACETS in this regard. The set of benchmark programs consists of 9 different algorithms used in Sayed et al. [32]. Table 3 shows the time in milliseconds to run the algorithms. More concretely, it reports the average time of 10 executions of each algorithm. Both JSFLOW and ZAPHODFACETS failed to execute the AES algorithm. This was also reported in [32].

The results in Table 3 show that the approaches that rely on code instrumentation (GIFC and IF-TRANSPILER) have a performance impact which is one or more orders of magnitude smaller than the performance impact of approaches that rely on an additional interpreter (JSFLOW and ZAPHODFACETS). IF-TRANSPILER performs better than GIFC, although performance is still comparable. Important sources of performance overhead in GIFC's dynamic monitor are

Table 2. Effectiveness comparison

Program	JSFLOW	ZAPHODFACETS	IF-TRANSPILER	GIFC
Test 1	✓	✓	✓	✓
Test 2	✓	✓	✓	✓
Test 3	✓	✓	✓	✓
Test 4	✓	✓	✓	✓
Test 5	✓	R.Err	✓	✓
Test 6	Exp	R.Err	✓	✓
Test 7	Exp	R.Err	✓	✓
Test 8	Exp	R.Err	✓	✓
Test 9	Exp	R.Err	✓	✓
Test 11	Exp	R.Err	✓	✓
Test 11	Exp	R.Err	✓	✓
Test 12	Exp	R.Err	✓	✓
Test 13	✗	R.Err	✓	✓
Test 14	✓	R.Err	✓	✓
Test 15	✓	R.Err	✓	✓
Test 16	✓	R.Err	✓	✓
Test 17	✓	R.Err	✓	✓
Test 18	✓	R.Err	✓	✓
Test 19	✓	R.Err	✓	✓
Test 20	✗	R.Err	✓	✓
Test 21	Exp	R.Err	✓	✓
Test 22	✓	R.Err	✓	✓
Test 23	✓	R.Err	✓	✓
Test 24	✓	R.Err	✓	✓
Test 25	✗	R.Err	✓	✓
Test 26	✗	R.Err	✓	✓
Test 27	✗	R.Err	✓	✓
Test 28	✗	R.Err	✓	✓
Test 29	✓	✗	✗	✓
Test 30	✓	R.Err	In.Err	✓
Test 31	✓	R.Err	✗	✓
Test 32	✓	✗	✓	✓
Test 33	✓	✓	✗	✓

Table 3. Performance benchmarks

Approach	FFT	LZW	KS	FT	HN	24	MD5	SHA	AES
Baseline	4 ms	4 ms	22 ms	3 ms	16 ms	13 ms	2 ms	2 ms	9 ms
IF-TRANSPILER	14 ms	11 ms	363 ms	10 ms	327 ms	126 ms	33 ms	29 ms	284 ms
GIFC	23 ms	34 ms	747 ms	35 ms	1238 ms	1233 ms	31 ms	35 ms	780 ms
JSFLOW	404 ms	421 ms	5206 ms	661 ms	5165 ms	4371 ms	491 ms	566 ms	fails
ZAPHODFACETS	100 ms	188 ms	15563 ms	145 ms	12657 ms	6403 ms	124 ms	197 ms	fails

the wrapping and unwrapping of values before and after API calls, and the emulation of implicit calls to functions `toString()` and `valueOf()` due to implicit value coercion in the target program.

6 Related Work

In this section, we discuss the most recent and relevant dynamic IFC approaches for JavaScript previously mentioned (IF-TRANSPILER, JSFLOW, ZAPHOD-FACETS, FLOWFOX) and some additional related work. All but IF-TRANSPILER and JEST are also part of the most recent survey on IFC by Bielova et al. [10].

Sayed et al. [32] introduce IF-TRANSPILER, an hybrid flow-sensitive monitor inlining framework for JavaScript applications. The static component is used to improve the permissiveness of the monitor by collecting at branching points, the side effects and function calls of branches not taken. At a branching point, the static analysis collects all variables that could have been assigned or functions that could have been called in the untaken branch. In contrast to GIFC, IF-TRANSPILER does not offer support for external libraries neither `eval()` nor DOM, which prevent it from being used in a practical scenario. Also, its static analysis do not handle side effects inside the body of function calls in the untaken branches. Therefore, the soundness of the static analysis is compromised.

JSFLOW [19] is an IFC-aware interpreter for JavaScript that uses NSU to handle implicit flows. To relax NSU, JSFLOW uses upgrade instructions for public labels before entering to a more sensitive context. However, this requires programmer intervention to specify where and what the interpreter should upgrade, which can lead to misconfigurations. JSFLOW is not portable, because it needs to be adapted for each JavaScript engine. Also, it has a considerable performance impact due to the addition of a complete layer of interpretation.

ZAPHODFACETS [6] is an IFC-aware interpreter featuring *faceted values* which capture the multidimensional view of a value with respect to confidentiality levels. They provide formal proofs with respect to TINI and also evaluated their as a plugin implementation for the Firefox browser. However, they lack support for DOM and external libraries. They do not support eval and the application performance is heavily affected due to the added interpretation layer. Also, the ZAPHODFACETS portability is limited to the Firefox browser.

Secure Multi-Execution (SME) [16,29] takes a different approach that traditional monitoring approaches for IFC. Programs under SME are executed multiple times, once for each security level, using special rules for input and output operations. The FLOWFOX implementation require large browser modifications in order to synchronize all the executions. Executions that are not allowed to access sensitive information are provided with dummy values representing more sensitive values. Therefore, any leak of information will not release the secrets of the application. However, it is unclear how dummy values can ensure the transparency of the system.

JEST [13] is an IFC monitor inliner for JavaScript implementing NSU like JSFLOW. It uses the concept of *boxes* to associate label information with program values. To allow the program work on boxes, they rewrite the program using special functions for all JavaScript operations (e.g. function calls, assignments, etc.). Like GIFC, JEST has a shadow stack to handle unstructured implicit flows. However, JEST implements the NSU technique which requires the intervention of the programmer to indicate the upgrading points. They also rely on an external process to handle dynamic code evaluation, which degrades the application performance on calls to `eval()`.

Santos and Rezk [31] were the first that developed an IFC inlining compiler for a core of JavaScript. They proved that the compiler is able to enforce TINI and developed a practical implementation of it. However, their implementation does not cover external libraries neither DOM.

Bichhawat et al. [9] implemented a dynamic IFC mechanism for the JavaScript bytecode produced by Safari's WebKit Engine. They formalize the Webkit's bytecode syntax and semantics, their instrumentation mechanism and prove non-interference. To improve permissiveness, they implement a variant of PU but their work does not support the DOM or other Web APIs.

Le Guernic et al. [23] developed a sound hybrid monitor that enforces non-interference for a sequential language with loops and outputs. The monitoring mechanism is composed by a variation of the *edit automata* [26] and the semantics of monitored executions. It enforces non-interference by authorizing, editing or forbidding the an specific action during the execution.

Magazinius et al. [27] formalized a framework to inline a monitor on the fly for an small language with dynamic code evaluation.

7   Conclusion

We introduced GIFC, a practical portable dynamic IFC monitoring mechanism. GIFC implements the PU strategy to improve the permissiveness of the monitoring. It offers support for DOM and external libraries enabling a practical use of IFC. Having static information at runtime makes it possible to develop a more precise model of implicit flows. GIFC is the first inlining mechanism that supports dynamic code evaluation online.

Benchmarks results show that the performance impact is better than approaches which rely on a IFC-aware interpreter but it is non-neglegible. Nevertheless, we believe that the approach can be used in settings where security plays a key role. Also, GIFC can aid developers if it is used as IFC testing tool at development time.

In spite of the achievements presented here, there are still some challenges that this kind of approaches need to overcome. First, the performance impact needs to be addressed. Second, the monitor state must be secured given the fact that its state is visible to the application.

References

1. Same Origin Policy - Web Security. https://www.w3.org/Security/wiki/SameOriginPolicy
2. Man-in-the-middle attack - OWASP, August 2015. https://www.owasp.org/index.php/Man-in-the-middle_attack
3. Andreasen, E., et al.: A survey of dynamic analysis and test generation for JavaScript. ACM Comput. Surv. **50**(5), 1–36 (2017)
4. Austin, T.H., Flanagan, C.: Efficient purely-dynamic information flow analysis. In: PLAS, p. 113 (2009)
5. Austin, T.H., Flanagan, C.: Permissive dynamic information flow analysis. In: PLAS, pp. 1–12 (2010)
6. Austin, T.H., Flanagan, C.: Multiple facets for dynamic information flow. In: POPL, p. 165 (2012)
7. Barth, A., Jackson, C., Mitchell, J.C.: Securing frame communication in browsers. Commun. ACM **52**(6), 83–91 (2009)
8. Bichhawat, A., Rajani, V., Garg, D., Hammer, C.: Generalizing permissive-upgrade in dynamic information flow analysis. CoRR cs.CR, pp. 15–24 (2015)
9. Bichhawat, A., Rajani, V., Garg, D., Hammer, C.: Information flow control in WebKit's JavaScript bytecode. In: Abadi, M., Kremer, S. (eds.) POST 2014. LNCS, vol. 8414, pp. 159–178. Springer, Heidelberg (2014). https://doi.org/10.1007/978-3-642-54792-8_9
10. Bielova, N., Rezk, T.: A taxonomy of information flow monitors. In: POST vol. 9635, no. 1, pp. 46–67 (2016)
11. Christophe, L., Boix, E.G., De Meuter, W., De Roover, C.: Linvail - a general-purpose platform for shadow execution of JavaScript. In: SANER, pp. 260–270 (2016)
12. Chudnov, A., Naumann, D.A.: Information flow monitor Inlining. In: 2010 IEEE 23rd Computer Security Foundations Symposium (CSF), pp. 200–214. IEEE (2010)
13. Chudnov, A., Naumann, D.A.: Inlined information flow monitoring for JavaScript. In: the 22nd ACM SIGSAC Conference, pp. 629–643. ACM Press, New York (2015)
14. De Groef, W., Devriese, D., Nikiforakis, N., Piessens, F.: Flowfox: a web browser with flexible and precise information flow control. In: Proceedings of the 2012 ACM Conference on Computer and Communications Security (CCS 2012), pp. 748–759. ACM (2012). DOIurl10.1145/2382196.2382275, https://lirias.kuleuven.be/handle/123456789/354589
15. Denning, D.E., Denning, P.J.: Certification of programs for secure information flow. Commun. ACM **20**(7), 504–513 (1977)
16. Devriese, D., Piessens, F.: Noninterference through secure multi-execution. In: 2010 IEEE Symposium on Security and Privacy (SP), pp. 109–124. IEEE (2010)
17. Goguen, J.A., Meseguer, J.: Security policies and security models. In: IEEE Symposium on Security and Privacy, p. 11 (1982)
18. Hedin, D., Bello, L., Sabelfeld, A.: Value-sensitive hybrid information flow control for a JavaScript-like language. In: 2015 IEEE 28th Computer Security Foundations Symposium (CSF), pp. 351–365. IEEE (2015)

19. Hedin, D., Birgisson, A., Bello, L., Sabelfeld, A.: JSFlow: tracking information flow in JavaScript and its APIs. In: Proceedings of the 29th Annual ACM Symposium on Applied Computing, pp. 1663–1671. ACM, New York (2014)
20. Hedin, D., Sabelfeld, A.: A Perspective on Information-Flow Control. In: Software Safety and Security (2012)
21. Hedin, D., Sjösten, A., Piessens, F., Sabelfeld, A.: A principled approach to tracking information flow in the presence of libraries. In: Maffei, M., Ryan, M. (eds.) POST 2017. LNCS, vol. 10204, pp. 49–70. Springer, Heidelberg (2017). https://doi.org/10.1007/978-3-662-54455-6_3
22. Jensen, S.H., Jonsson, P.A., Møller, A.: Remedying the Eval that men Do. In: the 2012 International Symposium, pp. 34–44. ACM Press, New York (2012)
23. Le Guernic, G., Banerjee, A., Jensen, T., Schmidt, D.A.: Automata-based confidentiality monitoring. In: Okada, M., Satoh, I. (eds.) ASIAN 2006. LNCS, vol. 4435, pp. 75–89. Springer, Heidelberg (2007). https://doi.org/10.1007/978-3-540-77505-8_7
24. Le Hégaret, P.: W3c Document Object Model, January 2005. https://www.w3.org/DOM/
25. Lekies, S., Kotowicz, K., Groß, S., Nava, E.A.V., Johns, M.: Code-reuse attacks for the web - breaking cross-site scripting mitigations via script gadgets. In: CCS, pp. 1709–1723 (2017)
26. Ligatti, J., Bauer, L., Walker, D.: Edit automata - enforcement mechanisms for run-time security policies. Int. J. Inf, Sec. (2005)
27. Magazinius, J., Russo, A., Sabelfeld, A.: On-the-fly inlining of dynamic security monitors. Comput. Secur. **31**(7), 827–843 (2012)
28. MDN: Proxy (Mar 2018). https://developer.mozilla.org/en-US/docs/Web/JavaScript/Reference/Global_Objects/Proxy
29. Rafnsson, W., Sabelfeld, A.: Secure multi-execution - fine-grained, declassification-aware, and transparent. J. Comput. Secur. **24**(1), 39–90 (2016)
30. Richards, G., Hammer, C., Burg, B., Vitek, J.: The eval that men do - a large-scale study of the use of eval in JavaScript applications. In: Mezini, M. (ed.) ECOOP 2011. LNCS, vol. 6813, pp. 52–78. Springer, Heidelberg (2011). https://doi.org/10.1007/978-3-642-22655-7_4
31. Santos, J.F., Rezk, T.: An information flow monitor-inlining compiler for securing a core of JavaScript. In: Cuppens-Boulahia, N., Cuppens, F., Jajodia, S., Abou El Kalam, A., Sans, T. (eds.) SEC 2014. IAICT, vol. 428, pp. 278–292. Springer, Heidelberg (2014). https://doi.org/10.1007/978-3-642-55415-5_23
32. Sayed, B., Traoré, I., Abdelhalim, A.: If-transpiler: Inlining of hybrid flow-sensitive security monitor for JavaScript. Comput. Secur. **75**, 92–117 (2018)
33. Stamm, S., Sterne, B., Markham, G.: Reining in the web with content security policy. In: the 19th International Conference, pp. 921–930. ACM Press, New York (2010)
34. Weichselbaum, L., Spagnuolo, M., Lekies, S., Janc, A.: CSP is dead, long live CSP! on the insecurity of whitelists and the future of content security policy. In: ACM Conference on Computer and Communications Security, pp. 1376–1387. ACM Press, New York (2016)

Time-Series Learning Using Monotonic Logical Properties

Marcell Vazquez-Chanlatte[1]([✉]), Shromona Ghosh[1], Jyotirmoy V. Deshmukh[2],
Alberto Sangiovanni-Vincentelli[1], and Sanjit A. Seshia[1]

[1] University of California, Berkeley, USA
{marcell.vc,shromona.ghosh,alberto,sseshia}@eecs.berkeley.edu
[2] University of Southern California, Berkeley, USA
jdeshmuk@usc.edu

Abstract. Cyber-physical systems of today are generating large volumes of time-series data. As manual inspection of such data is not tractable, the need for learning methods to help discover logical structure in the data has increased. We propose a logic-based framework that allows domain-specific knowledge to be embedded into formulas in a parametric logical specification over time-series data. The key idea is to then map a time series to a surface in the parameter space of the formula. Given this mapping, we identify the Hausdorff distance between surfaces as a natural distance metric between two time-series data under the lens of the parametric specification. This enables embedding non-trivial domain-specific knowledge into the distance metric and then using off-the-shelf machine learning tools to label the data. After labeling the data, we demonstrate how to extract a logical specification for each label. Finally, we showcase our technique on real world traffic data to learn classifiers/monitors for slow-downs and traffic jams.

Keywords: Specification mining · Time-series learning
Dimensionality reduction

1 Introduction

Recently, there has been a proliferation of sensors that monitor diverse kinds of real-time data representing *time-series behaviors* or *signals* generated by systems and devices that are monitored through such sensors. However, this deluge can place a heavy burden on engineers and designers who are not interested in the details of these signals, but instead seek to discover higher-level insights.

More concisely, one can frame the key challenge as: "How does one automatically identify logical structure or relations within the data?" To this end, modern machine learning (ML) techniques for signal analysis have been invaluable in domains ranging from healthcare analytics [7] to smart transportation [5]; and from autonomous driving [14] to social media [12]. However, despite the success of ML based techniques, we believe that easily leveraging the domain-specific knowledge of non-ML experts remains an open problem.

© Springer Nature Switzerland AG 2018
C. Colombo and M. Leucker (Eds.): RV 2018, LNCS 11237, pp. 389–405, 2018.
https://doi.org/10.1007/978-3-030-03769-7_22

At present, a common way to encode domain-specific knowledge into an ML task is to first transform the data into an *a priori* known *feature space*, e.g., the statistical properties of a time series. While powerful, translating the knowledge of domain-specific experts into features remains a non-trivial endeavor. More recently, it has been shown that a *parametric signal temporal logic* formula along with a total ordering on the parameter space can be used to extract feature vectors for learning temporal logical predicates characterizing driving patterns, overshoot of diesel engine re-flow rates, and grading for simulated robot controllers in a massive open online coursei (MOOC) [16]. Crucially, the technique of learning through the lens of a logical formula means that learned artifacts can be readily leveraged by existing formal methods infrastructure for verification, synthesis, falsification, and monitoring. Unfortunately, the usefulness of the results depend intimately on the total ordering used. The following example illustrates this point.

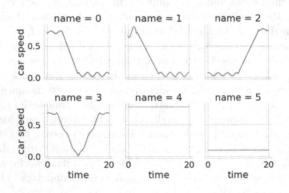

Fig. 1. Example signals of car speeds on a freeway.

Example: Most freeways have bottlenecks that lead to traffic congestion, and if there is a stalled or a crashed vehicle at this site, then upstream traffic congestion can severely worsen.[1] For example, Fig. 1 shows a series of potential time-series signals to which we would like to assign pairwise distances indicating the similarity (small values) or differences (large values) between any two time series. To ease exposition, we have limited our focus to the car's speed. In signals 0 and 1, both cars transition from high speed freeway driving to stop and go traffic. Conversely, in signal 2, the car transitions from stop and go traffic to high speed freeway driving. Signal 3 corresponds to a car slowing to a stop and then accelerating, perhaps due to difficulty merging lanes. Finally, signal 4 signifies a car encountering no traffic and signal 5 corresponds to a car in heavy traffic, or a possibly stalled vehicle.

Suppose a user wished to find a feature space equipped with a measure to distinguish cars being stuck in traffic. Some properties might be:

---

[1] We note that such data can be obtained from fixed mounted cameras on a freeway, which is then converted into time-series data for individual vehicles, such as in [4].

1. Signals 0 and 1 should be *very* close together since both show a car entering stop and go traffic in nearly the same manner.
2. Signals 2, 3, and 4 should be close together since the car ultimately escapes stop and go traffic.
3. Signal 5 should be far from all other examples since it does not represent entering or leaving stop and go traffic.

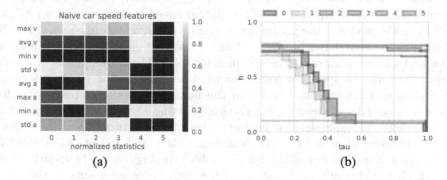

Fig. 2. (a) Statistical feature space (b) Trade-off boundaries in specification.

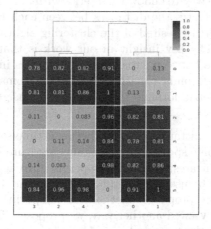

Fig. 3. Adjacency matrix and clustering of Fig. 1. Smaller numbers mean that the time series are more similar with respect to the logical distance metric.

For a strawman comparison, we consider two ways the user might assign a distance measure to the above signal space. Further, we omit generic time series distance measures such as Dynamic Time Warping [8] which do not offer the ability to embed domain specific knowledge into the metric. At first, the user might treat the signals as a series of independent measurements and attempt to characterize the signals via standard statistical measures on the speed and acceleration (mean, standard deviation, etc.). Figure 2a illustrates how the example signals look in this feature space with each component normalized between 0 and 1. The user might then use the Euclidean distance of each feature to assign a distance between signals. Unfortunately, in this measure, signal 4 is not close to signal 2 or 3, violating the second desired property. Further, signals 0 and 1 are not "very" close together violating the first property. Next, the user attempts to capture traffic slow downs by the following (informal) parametric temporal specification: "Between time τ and 20, the car speed is always less than h." As will be made precise in the preliminaries (for each individual time-series) Fig. 2b illustrates the boundaries between values of τ and h that make the specification true and values which make the specification false. The techniques in [16] then require the user to specify a particular total ordering on the parameter space. One then uses the maximal point on the boundary as the representative for the entire boundary. However, in practice, selecting a good ordering a-priori is non-obvious. For example, [16] suggests a lexicographic ordering of the parameters. However, since most of the boundaries start and end at essentially the same point, applying any of the lexicographic orderings to the boundaries seen in Fig. 2b would result in almost all of the boundaries collapsing to the same points. Thus, such an ordering would make characterizing a slow down impossible.

In the sequel, we propose using the Hausdorff distance between boundaries as a general ordering-free way to endow time series with a "logic respecting distance metric". Figure 3 illustrates the distances between each boundary. As is easily confirmed, all 3 properties desired of the clustering algorithm hold.

Contributions. The key insight in our work is that in many interesting examples, the distance between satisfaction boundaries in the parameter space of parametric logical formula can characterize the domain-specific knowledge implicit in the parametric formula. Leveraging this insight we provide the following contributions:

1. We propose a new distance measure between time-series through the lens of a chosen monotonic specification. Distance measure in hand, standard ML algorithms such as nearest neighbors (supervised) or agglomerative clustering (unsupervised) can be used to glean insights into the data.
2. Given a labeling, we propose a method for computing representative points on each boundary. Viewed another way, we propose a form of dimensionality reduction based on the temporal logic formula.
3. Finally, given the representative points and their labels, we can use the machinery developed in [16] to extract a simple logical formula as a classifier for each label.

2   Preliminaries

The main object of analysis in this paper are time-series.[2]

---

[2] Nevertheless, the material presented in the sequel easily generalizes to other objects.

Definition 1 (Time Series, Signals, Traces). *Let T be a subset of $\mathbb{R}^{\geq 0}$ and $\mathcal{D}$ be a nonempty set. A time series (signal or trace), $\mathbf{x}$ is a map:*

$$\mathbf{x} : T \rightarrow \mathcal{D} \tag{1}$$

Where T and $\mathcal{D}$ are called the time domain and value domain respectively. The set of all time series is denoted by $\mathcal{D}^T$.

Between any two time series one can define a metric which measures their similarity.

Definition 2 (Metric). *Given a set X, a metric is a map,*

$$d : X \times X \rightarrow \mathbb{R}^{\geq 0} \tag{2}$$

such that $d(x,y) = d(y,x)$, $d(x,y) = 0 \iff x = y$, $d(x,z) \leq d(x,y) + d(y,z)$.

Example 1 (Infinity Norm Metric). Let X be $\mathbb{R}^n$. The infinity norm induced distance $d_\infty(\boldsymbol{x}, \boldsymbol{y}) \overset{\text{def}}{=} \max_i (|x_i - y_i|)$ is a metric.

Example 2 (Hausdorff Distance). Given a set X with a distance metric d, the Hausdorff distance is a distance metric between closed subsets of X. Namely, given closed subsets $A, B \subseteq X$:

$$d_H(A, B) \overset{\text{def}}{=} \max \left(\sup_{x \in A} \inf_{y \in B} (d(x, y)), \sup_{y \in B} \inf_{x \in A} (d(y, x)) \right) \tag{3}$$

We use the following property of the Hausdorff distance throughout the paper: Given two sets A and B, there necessarily exists points $a \in A$ and $b \in B$ such that:

$$d_H(A, B) = d(a, b) \tag{4}$$

Within a context, the platonic ideal of a metric between traces respects any domain-specific properties that make two elements "similar".[3] A logical trace property, also called a specification, assigns to each timed trace a truth value.

Definition 3 (Specification). *A specification is a map, ϕ, from time series to true or false.*

$$\phi : \mathcal{D}^T \rightarrow \{1, 0\} \tag{5}$$

A time series, $\mathbf{x}$, is said to satisfy a specification iff $\phi(\mathbf{x}) = 1$.

Example 3. Consider the following specification related to the specification from the running example:

$$\phi_{ex}(\mathbf{x}) \overset{\text{def}}{=} \mathbb{1}\left[\forall t \in T \;.\; (t > 0.2 \implies \mathbf{x}(t) < 1) \right](\mathbf{x}) \tag{6}$$

where $\mathbb{1}[\cdot]$ denotes an indicator function. Informally, this specification says that after $t = 0.2$, the value of the time series, $x(t)$, is always less than 1.

---

[3] Colloquially, if it looks like a duck and quacks like a duck, it should have a small distance to a duck.

Given a finite number of properties, one can then "fingerprint" a time series as a Boolean feature vector. That is, given n properties, $\phi_1 \ldots \phi_n$ and the corresponding indicator functions, $\phi_1 \ldots \phi_n$, we map each time series to an n-tuple as follows.

$$\mathbf{x} \mapsto (\phi_1(\mathbf{x}), \ldots, \phi_n(\mathbf{x})) \tag{7}$$

Notice however that many properties are not naturally captured by a *finite* sequence of binary features. For example, imagine a single quantitative feature $f : \mathcal{D}^T \to [0,1]$ encoding the percentage of fuel left in a tank. This feature implicitly encodes an uncountably infinite family of Boolean features $\phi_k(\mathbf{x}) = \mathbb{1}[f(\mathbf{x}) = k](\mathbf{x})$ indexed by the percentages $k \in [0,1]$. We refer to such families as parametric specifications. For simplicity, we assume that the parameters are a subset of the unit hyper-box.

Definition 4 (Parametric Specifications). *A parametric specification is a map:*

$$\varphi : \mathcal{D}^T \to \left([0,1]^n \to \{0,1\} \right) \tag{8}$$

where $n \in \mathbb{N}$ is the number of parameters and $\left([0,1]^n \to \{0,1\} \right)$ denotes the set of functions from the hyper-square, $[0,1]^n$ to $\{0,1\}$.

Remark 1. The signature, $\varphi : [0,1]^n \to (\mathcal{D}^T \to \{0,1\})$ would have been an alternative and arguably simpler definition of parametric specifications; however, as we shall see, (8) highlights that a trace induces a structure, called the validity domain, embedded in the parameter space.

Parametric specifications arise naturally from syntactically substituting constants with parameters in the description of a specification.

Example 4. The parametric specification given in Example 3 can be generalized by substituting τ for 0.2 and h for 1 in Example 3.

$$\varphi_{ex}(\mathbf{x})(\tau, h) \stackrel{\text{def}}{=} \mathbb{1}\left[\forall t \in T \, . \, (t > \tau \implies \mathbf{x}(t) < h) \right](\mathbf{x}) \tag{9}$$

At this point, one could naively extend the notion of the "fingerprint" of a parametric specification in a similar manner as the finite case. However, if $[0,1]^n$ is equipped with a distance metric, it is fruitful to instead study the geometry induced by the time series in the parameter space. To begin, observe that the value of a Boolean feature vector is exactly determined by which entries map to 1. Analogously, the set of parameter values for which a parameterized specification maps to true on a given time series acts as the "fingerprint". We refer to this characterizing set as the validity domain.

Definition 5 (Validity domain). *Given an n parameter specification, φ, and a trace, $\mathbf{x}$, the validity domain is the pre-image of 1 under $\varphi(\mathbf{x})$,*

$$\mathcal{V}_\varphi(\mathbf{x}) \stackrel{\text{def}}{=} PreImg_{\varphi(\mathbf{x})}[1] = \left\{ \theta \in [0,1]^n \mid \varphi(\mathbf{x})(\theta) = 1 \right\} \tag{10}$$

Thus, $\mathcal{V}_\varphi$, can be viewed as the map that returns the structure in the parameter space indexed by a particular trace.

Note that in general, the validity domain can be arbitrarily complex making reasoning about its geometry intractable. We circumvent such hurdles by specializing to monotonic specifications.

Definition 6 (Monotonic Specifications). *A parametric specification is said to be monotonic if for all traces,* $\mathbf{x}$:

$$\theta \trianglelefteq \theta' \implies \varphi(\mathbf{x})(\theta) \leq \varphi(\mathbf{x})(\theta') \tag{11}$$

where $\trianglelefteq$ *is the standard product ordering on* $[0,1]^n$, *e.g.* $(x,y) \leq (x',y')$ *iff* $(x < x' \wedge y < y')$.

Remark 2. The parametric specification in Example 4 is monotonic.

Proposition 1. *Given a monotonic specification,* φ, *and a time series,* $\mathbf{x}$, *the boundary of the validity domain,* $\partial\mathcal{V}_\varphi(x)$, *of a monotonic specification is a hyper-surface that segments* $[0,1]^n$ *into two components.*

Next, we develop a distance metric between validity domains which characterizes the similarity between two time series under the lens of a monotonic specification.

3   Logic-Respecting Distance Metric

In this section, we define a class of metrics on the signal space that is derived from corresponding parametric specifications. First, observe that the validity domains of monotonic specifications are uniquely defined by the hyper-surface that separates them from the rest of the parameter space. Similar to Pareto fronts in a multi-objective optimization, these boundaries encode the trade-offs required in each parameter to make the specification satisfied for a given time series. This suggests a simple procedure to define a distance metric between time series that respects their logical properties: Given a monotonic specification, a set of time series, and a distance metric between validity domain boundaries:

1. Compute the validity domain boundaries for each time series.
2. Compute the distance between the validity domain boundaries.

Of course, the benefits of using this metric would rely entirely on whether (i) The monotonic specification captures the relevant domain-specific details (ii) The distance between validity domain boundaries is sensitive to outliers. While the choice of specification is highly domain-specific, we argue that for many monotonic specifications, the distance metric should be sensitive to outliers as this represents a large deviation from the specification. This sensitivity requirement seems particularly apt if the number of satisfying traces of the specification grows linearly or super-linearly as the parameters increase. Observing that Hausdorff distance (3) between two validity boundaries satisfy these properties, we define our new distance metric between time series as:

Definition 7. *Given a monotonic specification, φ, and a distance metric on the parameter space $([0,1]^n, d)$, the logical distance between two time series, $\mathbf{x}(t), \mathbf{y}(t) \in \mathcal{D}^T$ is:*

$$d_\varphi(\mathbf{x}(t), \mathbf{y}(t)) \stackrel{\text{def}}{=} d_H\left(\partial \mathcal{V}_\varphi(\mathbf{x}), \partial \mathcal{V}_\varphi(\mathbf{y})\right) \tag{12}$$

3.1 Approximating the Logical Distance

Next, we discuss how to approximate the logical distance metric within arbitrary precision. First, observe that the validity domain boundary of a monotonic specification can be recursively approximated to arbitrary precision via binary search on the diagonal of the parameter space [13]. This approximation yields a series of overlapping axis aligned rectangles that are guaranteed to contain the boundary (see Fig. 4).

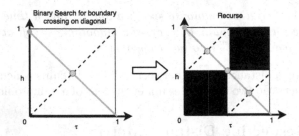

Fig. 4. Illustration of procedure introduced in [13] to recursively approximate a validity domain boundary to arbitrary precision.

To formalize this approximation, let $I(\mathbb{R})$ denote the set of closed intervals on the real line. We then define an axis aligned rectangle as the product of closed intervals.

Definition 8. *The set of axis aligned rectangles is defined as:*

$$I(\mathbb{R}^n) \stackrel{\text{def}}{=} \prod_{i=1}^{n} I(\mathbb{R}) \tag{13}$$

The approximation given in [13] is then a family of maps,

$$\text{approx}^i : \mathcal{D}^T \to \mathcal{P}\left(I(\mathbb{R}^n)\right) \tag{14}$$

where i denotes the recursive depth and $\mathcal{P}(\cdot)$ denotes the powerset.[4] For example, approx^0 yields the bounding box given in the leftmost subfigure in Fig. 4 and approx^1 yields the subdivision of the bounding box seen on the right.[5]

---

[4] The co-domain of (14) could be tightened to $\left(2^n - 2\right)^i$, but to avoid also parameterizing the discretization function, we do not strengthen the type signature.

[5] If the rectangle being subdivided is degenerate, i.e., lies entirely within the boundary of the validity domain and thus all point intersect the boundary, then the halfway point of the diagonal is taken to be the subdivision point.

Next, we ask the question: Given a discretization of the rectangle set approximating a boundary, how does the Hausdorff distance between the discretization relate to the true Hausdorff distance between two boundaries? In particular, consider the map that takes a set of rectangles to the set of the corner points of the rectangles. Formally, we denote this map as:

$$\text{discretize} : \mathcal{P}\left(I(\mathbb{R}^n)\right) \to \mathcal{P}\left(\mathbb{R}^n\right) \tag{15}$$

As the rectangles are axis aligned, at this point, it is fruitful to specialize to parameter spaces equipped with the infinity norm. The resulting Hausdorff distance is denoted d_H^∞. This specialization leads to the following lemma:

Lemma 1. *Let* $\mathbf{x}$, $\mathbf{x}'$ *be two time series and* $\mathcal{R}, \mathcal{R}'$ *the approximation of their respective boundaries. Further, let* p, p' *be points in* $\mathcal{R}, \mathcal{R}'$ *such that:*

$$\hat{d} \stackrel{\text{def}}{=} d_H^\infty(\text{ discretize}(\mathcal{R}),\ \text{discretize}(\mathcal{R}')) = d_\infty(p, p') \tag{16}$$

and let r, r' *be the rectangles in* $\mathcal{R}$ *and* $\mathcal{R}'$ *containing the points* p *and* p' *respectively. Finally, let* $\frac{\epsilon}{2}$ *be the maximum edge length in* $\mathcal{R}$ *and* $\mathcal{R}'$, *then:*

$$\max(0, \hat{d} - \epsilon) \le d_\varphi(\mathbf{x}, \mathbf{x}') \le \hat{d} + \epsilon \tag{17}$$

Proof. First, observe that (i) each rectangle intersects its boundary (ii) each rectangle set over-approximates its boundary. Thus, by assumption, each point within a rectangle is at most $\epsilon/2$ distance from the boundary w.r.t. the infinity norm. Thus, since there exist two points p, p' such that $\hat{d} = d_\infty(p, p')$, the maximum deviation from the logical distance is at most $2\frac{\epsilon}{2} = \epsilon$ and $\hat{d} - \epsilon \le d_\varphi(\mathbf{x}, \mathbf{x}') \le \hat{d} + \epsilon$. Further, since d_φ must be in $\mathbb{R}^{\geq 0}$, the lower bound can be tightened to $\max(0, \hat{d} - \epsilon)$. ∎

We denote the map given by (17) from the points to the error interval as:

$$d_H^\infty \pm \epsilon : \mathcal{P}(\mathbb{R}) \times \mathcal{P}(\mathbb{R}) \to I(\mathbb{R}^+) \tag{18}$$

Next, observe that this approximation can be made arbitrarily close to the logical distance.

Theorem 1. *Let* $d^\star = d_\varphi(\mathbf{x}, \mathbf{y})$ *denote the logical distance between two traces* $\mathbf{x}, \mathbf{y}$. *For any* $\epsilon \in \mathbb{R}^{\geq 0}$, *there exists* $i \in \mathbb{N}$ *such that:*

$$d_H^\infty(\text{ discretize}(\text{ approx}^i(\mathcal{R})),\ \text{discretize}(\text{ approx}^i(\mathcal{R}'))) \in [d^\star - \epsilon, d^\star + \epsilon] \tag{19}$$

Proof. By Lemma 1, given a fixed approximate depth, the above approximation differs from the true logical distance by at most two times the maximum edge length of the approximating rectangles. Note that by construction, incrementing the approximation depth results in each rectangle having at least one edge being halved. Thus the maximum edge length across the set of rectangles must at least halve. Thus, for any ϵ there exists an approximation depth $i \in \mathbb{N}$ such that:

$$d_H^\infty(\text{ discretize}(\text{ approx}^i(\mathcal{R})),\ \text{discretize}(\text{ approx}^i(\mathcal{R}'))) \in [d^\star - \epsilon, d^\star + \epsilon] .$$

∎

Finally, Algorithm 1 summarizes the above procedure.

Algorithm 1. Approximate Logical Distance

1: **procedure** APPROX_DIST$(\mathbf{x}, \mathbf{x}', \delta)$
2:     $lo, hi \leftarrow 0, \infty$
3:     **while** $hi - lo > \delta$ **do**
4:         $\mathcal{R}, \mathcal{R}' \leftarrow \text{approx}^i(\mathbf{x}), \text{approx}^i(\mathbf{x}')$
5:         $points, points' \leftarrow \text{discretize}(\mathcal{R}), \text{discretize}(\mathcal{R}')$
6:         $lo, hi \leftarrow (d_H^\infty \pm \epsilon)(\mathcal{R}, \mathcal{R}')$
7:     **return** lo, hi

Remark 3. An efficient implementation should of course memoize previous calls to approx^i and use approx^i to compute approx^{i+1}. Further, since certain rectangles can be quickly determined to not contribute to the Hausdorff distance, they need not be subdivided further.

3.2 Learning Labels

The distance interval (lo, hi) returned by Algorithm 1 can be used by learning techniques, such as *hierarchical or agglomerative clustering*, to estimate clusters (and hence the labels). While the technical details of these learning algorithms are beyond the scope of this work, we formalize the result of the learning algorithms as a labeling map:

Definition 9 (Labeling). *A k-labeling is a map:*

$$L : \mathcal{D}^T \rightarrow \{0, \ldots, k\} \tag{20}$$

for some $k \in \mathbb{N}$. If k is obvious from context or not important, then the map is simply referred to as a labeling.

4 Artifact Extraction

In practice, many learning algorithms produce labeling maps that provide little to no insight into why a particular trajectory is given a particular label. In the next section, we seek a way to systematically summarize a labeling in terms of the parametric specification used to induce the logical distance.

4.1 Post-Facto Projections

To begin, observe that due to the nature of the Hausdorff distance, when explaining why two boundaries differ, one can remove large segments of the boundaries without changing their Hausdorff distance. This motivates us to find a small summarizing set of parameters for each label. Further, since the Hausdorff distance often reduces to the distance between two points, we aim to summarize each boundary using a particular projection map. Concretely,

Definition 10. *Letting* $\partial \mathcal{V}_\varphi(\mathcal{D}^T)$ *denote the set of all possible validity domain boundaries, a projection is a map:*

$$\text{proj} : \partial \mathcal{V}_\varphi(\mathcal{D}^T) \to \mathbb{R}^n \qquad (21)$$

where n *is the number of parameters in* φ.

Remark 4. In principle, one could extend this to projecting to a finite tuple of points. For simplicity, we do not consider such cases.

Systematic techniques for picking the projection include *lexicographic projections* and solutions to *multi-objective optimizations*; however, as seen in the introduction, a-priori choosing the projection scheme is subtle. Instead, we propose performing a post-facto optimization of a collection of projections in order to be maximally representative of the labels. That is, we seek a projection, proj^*, that maximally disambiguates between the labels, i.e., maximizes the minimum distance between the clusters. Formally, given a set of traces associated with each label $L_1, \ldots L_k$ we seek:

$$\text{proj}^* \in \arg \max_{\text{proj}} \min_{i,j \in \binom{k}{2}} d_\infty(\text{proj}(L_i), \text{proj}(L_j)) \qquad (22)$$

For simplicity, we restrict our focus to projections induced by the intersection of each boundary with a line intersecting the base of the unit box $[0,1]^n$. Just as in the recursive boundary approximations, due to monotonicity, this intersection point is guaranteed to be unique. Further, this class of projections is in one-one correspondence with the boundary. In particular, for any point p on boundary, there exists exactly one projection that produces p. As such, each projection can be indexed by a point in $[0,1]^{n-1}$.

Example 5. Let $n = 2$, φ denote a parametric specification, and let $\theta \in [0, \pi/2]$ denote an angle from one of the axes. The projection induced by a line with angle θ is implicitly defined as:

$$\text{proj}_\theta(\mathbf{x}) \cdot [\cos(\theta), -\sin(\theta)] \in \partial \mathcal{V}_\varphi(\mathbf{x}) \qquad (23)$$

Remark 5. Since we expect clusters of boundaries to be near each other, we also expect their intersection points to be near each other.

Remark 6. For our experiment, we search for the optimal projection (22) in the space of projections defined by $\{\text{proj}_\theta \mid \theta = \frac{i}{100}\frac{\pi}{2}, i \in \{0, 1, \ldots, 100\}\}$.

4.2 Label Specifications

Next, observe that given a projection, when studying the infinity norm distance between labels, it suffices to consider only the bounding box of each label in parameter space. Namely, letting $B : \mathcal{P}(\mathbb{R}^n) \to I[\mathbb{R}^n]$ denote the map that computes the bounding box of a set of points in $\mathbb{R}^n$, for any two labels i and j:

$$d_\infty(\text{proj}(L_i), \text{proj}(L_j)) = d_\infty(B \circ \text{proj}(L_i), B \circ \text{proj}(L_j)). \qquad (24)$$

This motivates using the projection's bounding box as a surrogate for the cluster. Next, we observe that one can encode the set of trajectories whose boundaries intersect (and thus can project to) a given bounding box as a simple Boolean combination of the specifications corresponding to instantiating φ with the parameters of at most $n+1$ corners of the box [16, Lemma 2]. While a detailed exposition is outside the scope of this article, we illustrate with an example.

Example 6. Consider examples 0 and 1 from the introductory example viewed as validity domain boundaries under (9). Suppose that the post-facto projection mapped example 0 to $(1/4, 1/2)$ and mapped example 1 to $(0.3, 0.51)$. Such a projection is plausibly near the optimal for many classes of projections since none of the other example boundaries (who are in different clusters) are near the boundaries for 0 and 1 at these points. The resulting specification is:

$$\phi(\mathbf{x}) = \varphi_{ex}(\mathbf{x})(1/4, 1/2) \wedge \neg\varphi_{ex}(\mathbf{x})(1/4, 0.51) \wedge \neg\varphi_{ex}(\mathbf{x})(0.3, 1/2)$$
$$= \mathbb{1}\left[t \in [1/4, 0.3] \implies \mathbf{x}(t) \in [1/2, 0.51] \wedge t > 0.3 \implies \mathbf{x}(t) \ge 0.51\right] \tag{25}$$

4.3   Dimensionality Reduction

Finally, observe that the line that induces the projection can serve as a mechanism for dimensionality reduction. Namely, if one parameterizes the line $\gamma(t)$ from $[0,1]$, where $\gamma(0)$ is the origin and $\gamma(1)$ intersects the unit box, then the points where the various boundaries intersect can be assigned a number between 0 and 1. For high-dimensional parameter spaces, this enables visualizing the projection histogram and could even be used for future classification/learning. We again illustrate using our running example.

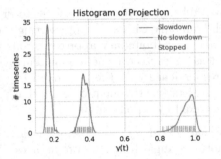

Fig. 5. Figure of histogram resulting from projecting noisy variations of the traffic slow down example time series onto the diagonal of the unit box.

Example 7. For all six time series in the traffic slow down example, we generate 100 new time series by modulating the time series with noise drawn from $\mathcal{N}(1, 0.3)$. Using our previously labeled time series, the projection using the line with angle 45° (i.e., the diagonal of the unit box) from the x-axis yields the distribution seen in Fig. 5. Observe that all three clusters are clearly visible.

Remark 7. If one dimension is insufficient, this procedure can be extended to an arbitrary number of dimensions using more lines. An interesting extension may be to consider how generic dimensionality techniques such as principle component analysis would act in the limit where one approximates the entire boundary.

5   Case Study

To improve driver models and traffic on highways, the Federal Highway Administration collected detailed traffic data on southbound US-101 freeway, in Los Angeles [4]. Traffic through the segment was monitored and recorded through eight synchronized cameras, next to the freeway. A total of 45 minutes of traffic data was recorded including vehicle trajectory data providing lane positions of each vehicle within the study area. The data-set is split into 5979 time series. For simplicity, we constrain our focus to the car's speed. In the sequel, we outline a technique for first using the parametric specification (in conjunction with off-the-shelf machine learning techniques) to filter the data, and then using the logical distance from an idealized slow down to find the slow downs in the data. This final step offers a key benefit over the closest prior work [16]. Namely given an over approximation of the desired cluster, one can use the logical distance to further refine the cluster.

Rescale Data. As in our running example, we seek to use (9) to search for traffic slow downs; however, in order to do so, we must re-scale the time series. To begin, observe that the mean velocity is 62 mph with 80% of the vehicles remaining under 70 mph. Thus, we linearly scale the velocity so that 70mph $\mapsto$ 1 arbitrary unit (a.u.). Similarly, we re-scale the time axis so that each tick is 2 s. Figure 6a shows a subset of the time series.

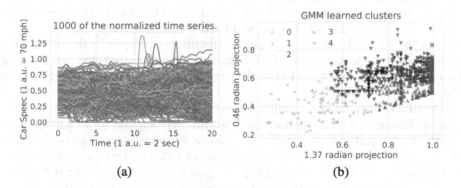

(a)   (b)

Fig. 6. (a) 1000/5000 of the rescaled highway 101 time series. (b) Projection of Time-Series to two lines in the parameter space of (9) and resulting GMM labels.

Filtering. Recall that if two boundaries have small Hausdorff distances, then the points where the boundaries intersect a line (that intersects the origin of the parameter space) must be close. Since computing the Hausdorff distance is a fairly expensive operation, we use this one way implication to group time series which may be near each other w.r.t. the Hausdorff distance.

In particular, we (arbitrarily) selected two lines intersecting the parameter space origin at 0.46 and 1.36 rad from the τ axis to project to. We filtered out time-series that did not intersect the line within $[0,1]^2$. We then fit a 5 cluster Gaussian Mixture Model (GMM) to label the data. Figure 6b shows the result.

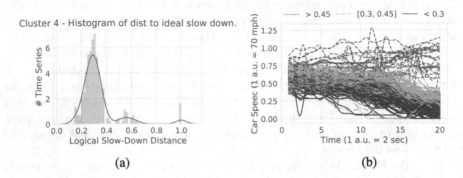

Fig. 7. (a) Cluster 4 Logical distance histogram. (b) Time-series in Cluster 4 colored by distance to ideal slow down.

Matching Idealized Slow Down. Next, we labeled the idealized slow down, (trace 0 from Fig. 2b) using the fitted GMM. This identified cluster 4 (with 765 data points) as containing potential slow downs. To filter for the true slow downs, we used the logical distance[6] from the idealized slow down to further subdivide the cluster. Figure 7b shows the resulting distribution. Figure 7a shows the time series in cluster 4 annotated by their distance for the idealized slow down. Using this visualization, one can clearly identify 390 slow downs (distance less than 0.3)

Artifact Extraction. Finally, we first searched for a single projection that gave a satisfactory separation of clusters, but were unable to do so. We then searched over pairs of projections to create a specification as the conjunction of two box specifications. Namely, in terms of (9), our first projection yields the specification: $\phi_1 = \varphi_{ex}(0.27, 0.55) \wedge \neg\varphi_{ex}(0.38, 0.55) \wedge \neg\varphi_{ex}(0.27, 0.76)$. Similarly, our second projection yields the specification: $\phi_2 = \varphi_{ex}(0.35, 0.17) \wedge \neg\varphi_{ex}(0.35, 0.31) \wedge \neg\varphi_{ex}(0.62, 0.17)$. The learned slow down specification is the conjunction of these two specifications.

6   Related Work and Conclusion

Time-series clustering and classification is a well-studied area in the domain of machine learning and data mining [10]. Time series clustering that work with raw time-series data combine clustering schemes such as agglomerative clustering, hierarchical clustering, k-means clustering among others, with similarity

---

[6] again associated with (9).

measures between time-series data such as the dynamic time-warping (DTW) distance, statistical measures and information-theoretic measures. Feature-extraction based methods typically use generic sets of features, but algorithmic selection of the right set of meaningful features is a challenge. Finally, there are model-based approaches that seek an underlying generative model for the time-series data, and typically require extra assumptions on the data such as linearity or the Markovian property. Please see [10] for detailed references to each approach. It should be noted that historically time-series learning focused on univariate time-series, and extensions to multivariate time-series data have been relatively recent developments.

More recent work has focused on automatically identifying features from the data itself, such as the work on *shapelets* [11,15,17], where instead of comparing entire time-series data using similarity measures, algorithms to automatically identify distinguishing motifs in the data have been developed. These motifs or shapelets serve not only as features for ML tasks, but also provide visual feedback to the user explaining why a classification or clustering task, labels given data, in a certain way. While we draw inspiration from this general idea, we seek to expand it to consider logical shapes in the data, which would allow leveraging user's domain expertise.

Automatic identification of motifs or basis functions from the data while useful in several documented case studies, comes with some limitations. For example, in [1], the authors define a subspace clustering algorithm, where given a set of time-series curves, the algorithm identifies a subspace among the curves such that every curve in the given set can be expressed as a linear combination of a deformations of the curves in the subspace. We note that the authors observe that it may be difficult to associate the natural clustering structure with specific predicates over the data (such as patient outcome in a hospital setting).

The use of logical formulas for learning properties of time-series has slowly been gaining momentum in communities outside of traditional machine learning and data mining [2,3,6,9]. Here, fragments of Signal Temporal Logic have been used to perform tasks such as supervised and unsupervised learning. A key distinction from these approaches is our use of libraries of signal predicates that encode domain expertise that allow human-interpretable clusters and classifiers.

Finally, preliminary exploration of this idea appeared in prior work by some of the co-authors in [16]. The key difference is the previous work required users to provide a ranking of parameters appearing in a signal predicate, in order to project time-series data to unique points in the parameter space. We remove this additional burden on the user in this paper by proposing a generalization that projects time-series signals to trade-off curves in the parameter space, and then using these curves as features.

Conclusion. We proposed a family of distance metrics for time-series learning centered *monotonic specifications* that respect the logical characteristic of the specification. The key insight was to first map each time-series to characterizing surfaces in the parameter space and then compute the Hausdorff Distance between the surfaces. This enabled embedding non-trivial domain specific knowledge into the distance metric usable by standard machine learning. After labeling the data, we demonstrate how this technique produces artifacts that can be used for dimensionality reduction or as a logical specification for each label. We concluded with a simple automotive case study show casing the technique on real world data. Future work includes investigating how to the leverage massively parallel natural in the boundary and Hausdorff computation using graphical processing units and characterizing alternative boundary distances (see Remark 7).

Acknowledgments. Some of the key ideas in this paper were influenced by discussions with Oded Maler, especially those pertaining to computing the boundaries of monotonic specifications. The work of the authors on this paper was funded in part by the NSF VeHICaL project (#1545126), NSF project #1739816, the DARPA BRASS program under agreement number FA8750–16–C0043, the DARPA Assured Autonomy program, Berkeley Deep Drive, the Army Research Laboratory under Cooperative Agreement Number W911NF–17–2–0196, and by Toyota under the iCyPhy center.

References

1. Bahadori, M.T., Kale, D., Fan, Y., Liu, Y.: Functional subspace clustering with application to time series. In: Proceedings of ICML, pp. 228–237 (2015)
2. Bartocci, E., Bortolussi, L., Sanguinetti, G.: Data-driven statistical learning of temporal logic properties. In: Legay, A., Bozga, M. (eds.) FORMATS 2014. LNCS, vol. 8711, pp. 23–37. Springer, Cham (2014). https://doi.org/10.1007/978-3-319-10512-3_3
3. Bombara, G., Vasile, C.I., Penedo, F., Yasuoka, H., Belta, C.: A decision tree approach to data classification using signal temporal logic. In: Proceedings of HSCC, pp. 1–10 (2016)
4. Colyar, J., Halkias, J.: US highway 101 dataset. Federal Highway Administration (FHWA), Tech. Rep. FHWA-HRT-07-030 (2007)
5. Deng, D., Shahabi, C., Demiryurek, U., Zhu, L., Yu, R., Liu, Y.: Latent space model for road networks to predict time-varying traffic. In: Proceedings of the 22nd ACM SIGKDD International Conference on Knowledge Discovery and Data Mining, pp. 1525–1534. ACM (2016)
6. Jones, A., Kong, Z., Belta, C.: Anomaly detection in cyber-physical systems: a formal methods approach. In: Proceedings of CDC, pp. 848–853 (2014)
7. Kale, D.C., et al.: An examination of multivariate time series hashing with applications to health care. In: 2014 IEEE International Conference on Data Mining (ICDM), pp. 260–269. IEEE (2014)
8. Keogh, E.J., Pazzani, M.J.: Scaling up dynamic time warping for data mining applications. In: Proceedings of KDD, pp. 285–289 (2000)
9. Kong, Z., Jones, A., Medina Ayala, A., Aydin Gol, E., Belta, C.: Temporal logic inference for classification and prediction from data. In: Proceedings of HSCC, pp. 273–282 (2014)
10. Liao, T.W.: Clustering of time series data survey. Pattern Recognit. **38**(11), 1857–1874 (2005)
11. Lines, J., Davis, L.M., Hills, J., Bagnall, A.: A shapelet transform for time series classification. In: Proceedings of the 18th ACM SIGKDD International Conference on Knowledge Discovery and Data Mining, pp. 289–297. ACM (2012)

12. Liu, Y., Bahadori, T., Li, H.: Sparse-GEV: sparse latent space model for multivariate extreme value time series modeling. In: Proceedings of ICML (2012)
13. Maler, O.: Learning Monotone Partitions of Partially-Ordered Domains (Work in Progress), Jul 2017. https://hal.archives-ouvertes.fr/hal-01556243, working paper or preprint
14. McCall, J.C., Trivedi, M.M.: Driver behavior and situation aware brake assistance for intelligent vehicles. Proc. IEEE **95**(2), 374–387 (2007)
15. Mueen, A., Keogh, E., Young, N.: Logical-shapelets: an expressive primitive for time series classification. In: Proceedings of the 17th ACM SIGKDD International Conference on Knowledge Discovery and Data Mining, pp. 1154–1162. ACM (2011)
16. Vazquez-Chanlatte, M., Deshmukh, J.V., Jin, X., Seshia, S.A.: Logic-based clustering and learning for time-series data. In: Proceedings of International Conference on Computer-Aided Verification (CAV) (2017)
17. Ye, L., Keogh, E.: Time series shapelets: a new primitive for data mining. In: Proceedings of the 15th ACM SIGKDD International Conference on Knowledge Discovery and Data Mining, pp. 947–956. ACM (2009)

Short Papers

Short Papers

Evaluating Perception Systems for Autonomous Vehicles Using Quality Temporal Logic

Adel Dokhanchi[1][(✉)], Heni Ben Amor[1], Jyotirmoy V. Deshmukh[2], and Georgios Fainekos[1]

[1] Arizona State University, Tempe, AZ 85281, USA
{adokhanc,hbenamor,fainekos}@asu.edu
[2] University of Southern California, Los Angeles, CA 90089, USA
jyotirmoy.deshmukh@usc.edu

Abstract. For reliable situation awareness in autonomous vehicle applications, we need to develop robust and reliable image processing and machine learning algorithms. Currently, there is no general framework for reasoning about the performance of perception systems. This paper introduces Timed Quality Temporal Logic (TQTL) as a formal language for monitoring and testing the performance of object detection and situation awareness algorithms for autonomous vehicle applications. We demonstrate that it is possible to describe interesting properties as TQTL formulas and detect cases where the properties are violated.

Keywords: Temporal logic · Monitoring · Autonomous vehicles
Perception · Image processing · Machine Learning

1 Introduction

The wide availability of high-performance GPU-based hardware has led to an explosion in the applications of Machine Learning (ML) techniques to real-time image recognition problems, especially using deep learning [12]. Such techniques are being used in *safety-critical* applications such as self-driving vehicles [17]. Testing of these systems is largely based on either (a) measuring the recognition error on a pre-recorded data-set, or (b) running actual driving tests on the road with a backup human driver and focusing on the *disengagements*. A *disengagement* is an event when the autonomous car returns control back to the human driver [1,2]. There is, thus, an urgent need for techniques to formally reason about the correctness and performance of such driving applications that use perception systems based on Deep Neural Networks (DNN) and ML algorithms.

The key challenge in formal verification is that it is infeasible to specify functional correctness of components using learning-based models in an abstract fashion. However, we can vastly improve the confidence in the vision-based system by extensive, *safety-driven* virtual testing of the vision algorithms [9,15].

© Springer Nature Switzerland AG 2018
C. Colombo and M. Leucker (Eds.): RV 2018, LNCS 11237, pp. 409–416, 2018.
https://doi.org/10.1007/978-3-030-03769-7_23

In this work in progress, we focus on deep learning algorithms that analyze images or sequences of images in order to detect and classify objects for intention recognition and scenario classification. In order to evaluate the performance of the perception algorithms over time, we need to provide quality requirements that capture temporal dependencies between detected objects. Most importantly, going beyond ad-hoc validation and testing, we need a formal framework that facilitates temporal reasoning over the quality of the perception systems. Such a formal framework would enable the community to create a precise and real-life set of requirements that need to be met by any learning-based model.

In this paper, we consider temporal logic based quality requirements for scoring or grading the results of perception algorithms. Then, a quality monitor considers the quality requirements to score the learning-based perception results. We consider evaluating timed object data with respect to quality requirements presented in Timed Quality Temporal Logic (TQTL), which is based on Timed Propositional Temporal Logic (TPTL) [4,8].

2   Problem Formulation

We assume a *data stream* $\mathcal{D}$ is provided by a perception algorithm, LIDAR, RADAR, or other devices. An atomic block in a data stream is a frame which is a set $\{data_1, ..., data_m\}$, where each $data_j$ is an element of a data domain or data object. A stream $\mathcal{D}$ is a sequence of frames $\mathcal{D}(i)$ where i is the *timestamp* over a linearly ordered set. Each frame i contains data object $data_j \in \mathcal{D}(i)$ in a datastructure (a tuple) format, for example $data_j$ = (ID, Class, Probability, BBOX (Bounding Box),...). This data structure depends on the ML algorithm. Our method assumes that for each ML algorithm there exists a customized retrieve function $\mathcal{R}$ which can extract and access the information of the corresponding data object ($data_j$). In addition, there exists a customized attribute with quality metric which can be evaluated by a *quality function* to provide us the quality of the data objects in the stream.

In the case study, we assume that each data object of the ML algorithm has the following format $data_j$ =(ID, Class, Probability, BBOX), where ID $\in \mathbb{N}$ is a number uniquely identifying an object, Probability $\in \mathbb{R} \cap [0,1]$, Class $\in \{Car, Cyclist, Pedestrian\}$, and BBOX is a tuple of four integers [top, left, bottom, right] $\in \mathbb{N}^4$ representing the coordinates of the bounding box in pixels. For example, a data stream for 3 different detected objects would look like:

Data Frame 0: $\mathcal{D}(0) = \{(1, \text{``Car''}, 0.9, [283, 181, 413, 231])\}$
Data Frame 1: $\mathcal{D}(1) = \{(2, \text{``Car''}, 0.8, [...]), (1, \text{``Car''}, 0.9, [...])\}$
Data Frame 2: $\mathcal{D}(2) = \{(3, \text{``Car''}, 0.95, [...]), (2, \text{``Pedestrian''}, 0.9, [...])\}$

$\vdots$

We also assume that there exists a function $\mathcal{SO}$ (short for Set of Objects) which can retrieve the object IDs from a data frame $\mathcal{D}(i)$. For the above streaming data $\mathcal{D}$, the function $\mathcal{SO}$ returns the following values of object IDs: $\mathcal{SO}(\mathcal{D}(0)) =$

$\{1\}$, $\mathcal{SO}(\mathcal{D}(1)) = \{1,2\}$, $\mathcal{SO}(\mathcal{D}(2)) = \{2,3\}$. In order to retrieve the other fields (non-ID) from the data objects, we assume that these fields are available through the function $\mathcal{R}$. We use object-oriented notation "." to retrieve the "XYZ" fields (attributes) from $\mathcal{D}(i)$ for object ID. So, $\mathcal{R}(\mathcal{D}(i), id)$. XYZ retrieves the "XYZ" attribute of object id from frame i. For the above vision stream example, $\mathcal{R}(\mathcal{D}(1), 2)$. Class $= Car$, and $\mathcal{R}(\mathcal{D}(1), 2)$. Probability $= 0.8$.

Without loss of generality, we assume that each data object in the stream $\mathcal{D}$ is provided by the ML algorithm with a unique object ID, where the specific object ID is unique over different frames of the video. In other words, we assume that the ML algorithm can match the objects of different frames and provide a unique ID of the object within the whole data stream. This is a necessary assumption to help us track these objects through frames and to apply temporal reasoning over the specific objects.

Given a finite stream $\mathcal{D}$ and Quality Temporal Logic formula φ, our goal is to compute the quality value of formula φ with respect to stream $\mathcal{D}$. Throughout this paper, we use the notation $[\![\phi]\!]$ to represent the quality value of formula ϕ. Finally, we assume that the quality can be quantified by a real-valued number similar to the robust semantics of temporal logics [6,10].

3   Timed Quality Temporal Logic

In this section, we consider the important aspects of stream reasoning for object detection algorithms. Also, the corresponding syntax and semantics will be provided to address the problem of quality reasoning. One important differentiating factor of quality monitoring to Signal Temporal Logic (STL) [6,13] monitoring is that the number of objects in the video is dynamically changing. Therefore, we need to introduce Existential and Universal quantifiers to reason about the dynamically changing number of data objects (e.g. as in [14]). In addition, we need to be able to record the time in order to extract the data objects using function $\mathcal{R}$ at different timestamps [7,8].

Timed Quality Temporal Logic (TQTL) is defined to reason about a stream $\mathcal{D}$. Assume that $\mathcal{P} = \{\pi_1, \pi_2, ..., \pi_n\}$ is a set of predicates which define assertions about data objects. Each π_j corresponds to $\pi_j \equiv f(j_1, ..., j_n, id_1, ..., id_n) \sim c$, where $f(j_1, ..., j_n, id_1, ..., id_n)$ is a scoring function which extracts/processes information about data objects $id_1, ..., id_n$ from frames $j_1, ..., j_n$, and compares it with a constant c to resolve the quality of the data objects. It should be noted that c can be a string, integer, real, enumerator, or any constant data type that the ML algorithm uses to represent data. The symbols $\sim \in \{=, \geq, >, <, \leq\}$ are relational operators.

Definition 1 (TQTL Syntax). *The set of TQTL formulas ϕ over a finite set of predicates $\mathcal{P}$, a finite set of time variables (V_t), and a finite set of object indexes (V_o) is inductively defined according to the following grammar:*

$$\phi ::= \top \mid \pi \mid x.\phi \mid \exists id@x, \phi \mid x \leq y + n \mid \neg\phi \mid \phi_1 \vee \phi_2 \mid \phi_1 U \phi_2$$

where $\pi \in \mathcal{P}$, $\top$ is *true*, $x, y \in V_t$, $n \in \mathbb{N}$, $id \in V_o$, U is the Until operator. The time constraints of TQTL are represented in the form of $x \leq y + n$. The freeze time quantifier $x.\phi$ assigns the current time i to time variable x before processing the subformula ϕ. The Existential quantifier is denoted as $\exists$. The Universal quantifier is defined as $\forall id@x, \phi \equiv \neg(\exists id@x, \neg\phi)$. For TQTL formulas ψ, ϕ, we define $\psi \wedge \phi \equiv \neg(\neg\psi \vee \neg\phi)$, $\perp \equiv \neg\top$ (False), $\psi \rightarrow \phi \equiv \neg\psi \vee \phi$ (ψ Implies ϕ), $\Diamond\psi \equiv \top U\psi$ (Eventually ψ), $\Box\psi \equiv \neg\Diamond\neg\psi$ (Always ψ) using syntactic manipulation. The semantics of TQTL is defined over an evaluation function $\epsilon : V_t \cup V_o \rightarrow \mathbb{N}$ which is an environment for the time variables and object IDs.

Definition 2 (TQTL Semantics). *Consider the data stream $\mathcal{D}$, $i \in \mathbb{N}$ is the index of current frame, $\pi \in \mathcal{P}$, $\phi, \phi_1, \phi_2 \in TQTL$ and evaluation function $\epsilon : V_t \cup V_o \rightarrow \mathbb{N}$. The quality value of formula ϕ with respect to $\mathcal{D}$ at frame i with evaluation ϵ is recursively assigned as follows:*

$$[\![\top]\!](\mathcal{D}, i, \epsilon) := +\infty$$
$$[\![\pi]\!](\mathcal{D}, i, \epsilon) := [\![f_\pi(j_1, ..., j_n, id_1, ..., id_n) \sim c]\!](\mathcal{D}, i, \epsilon)$$
$$[\![x.\phi]\!](\mathcal{D}, i, \epsilon) := [\![\phi]\!](\mathcal{D}, i, \epsilon[x \Leftarrow i])$$
$$[\![\exists id@x, \phi]\!](\mathcal{D}, i, \epsilon) := \max_{k \in \mathcal{SO}(\mathcal{D}(\epsilon(x)))}([\![\phi]\!](\mathcal{D}, i, \epsilon[id \Leftarrow k]))$$
$$[\![x \leq y + n]\!](\mathcal{D}, i, \epsilon) := \begin{cases} +\infty \ if \epsilon(x) \leq \epsilon(y) + n \\ -\infty \ otherwise \end{cases}$$
$$[\![\neg\phi]\!](\mathcal{D}, i, \epsilon) := -[\![\phi]\!](\mathcal{D}, i, \epsilon)$$
$$[\![\phi_1 \vee \phi_2]\!](\mathcal{D}, i, \epsilon) := \max([\![\phi_1]\!](\mathcal{D}, i, \epsilon), [\![\phi_2]\!](\mathcal{D}, i, \epsilon))$$
$$[\![\phi_1 U \phi_2]\!](\mathcal{D}, i, \epsilon) := \max_{i \leq j} \left(\min \left([\![\phi_2]\!](\mathcal{D}, j, \epsilon), \min_{i \leq k < j} [\![\phi_1]\!](\mathcal{D}, k, \epsilon) \right) \right)$$

Here, $\epsilon[x \Leftarrow a]$ assigns the value a into the variable $x \in V$ in the environment ϵ. Given a variable $x \in V$ and a value $q \in \mathbb{N}$, we define the environment $\epsilon' = \epsilon[x \Leftarrow q]$ to be equivalent to the environment ϵ on all variables in V except variable x which now has value q. We say that $\mathcal{D}$ satisfies φ ($\mathcal{D} \models \varphi$) iff $[\![\phi]\!](\mathcal{D}, 0, \epsilon_0) > 0$, where ϵ_0 is the initial environment. On the other hand, a data stream $\mathcal{D}'$ does not satisfy a TQTL formula ϕ (denoted by $\mathcal{D}' \not\models \phi$), iff $[\![\phi]\!](\mathcal{D}, 0, \epsilon_0) \leq 0$. The quantifier $\exists id@x$ is the maximum operation on the quality values of formula $[\![\phi]\!]$ corresponding to the objects IDs $= \epsilon(id)$ that are detected at frame $\epsilon(x)$.

We assume that for each the ML algorithm there exists a corresponding retrieve function $\mathcal{R}$ to extract the values corresponding to data objects. The set of predicates $\mathcal{P} = \{\pi_1, \pi_2, ..., \pi_n\}$ evaluate object data values and return a quality value in $\mathbb{R} \cup \{\pm\infty\}$. Each quality predicate π has an associated scoring function f_π. The scoring function $f_\pi(j_1, ..., j_n, id_1, ..., id_n)$ extracts specific information about object id_k at frame j_k for each $k \in \{1, ..., n\}$ and compares it with c to compute the quality value of the predicate π represented as $[\![f_\pi(j_1, ..., j_n, id_1, ..., id_n) \sim c]\!] \in \mathbb{R} \cup \{\pm\infty\}$ similar to robustness semantics [10]. The scoring functions of the quality predicates depend on the ML algorithm,

Fig. 1. SqueezeDet [16] object classification of KITTI [11] images from a cyclist. Bounding boxes are classified as Cyclist (yellow), Pedestrian (purple), and Car (blue). (Color figure online)

$\mathcal{R}$, data fields of $\mathcal{D}$, operator $\sim$, and type of c. Each scoring function f_π uses the application dependent customized function h_π to compute the quality of the corresponding objects. The function h_π then returns a value about the quality of the data objects which will be used by f_π to compute the quality value of the predicate π which is denoted as $[\![\pi]\!]$.

In general, $[\![f_\pi(j_1, ..., j_n, id_1, ..., id_n) \sim c]\!]$ may be of two types. The first returns a Boolean result of comparing values from sets without scalar metrics, i.e., comparing the object class of *pedestrian* with respect to $\{car, cyclist\}$. For example, in this case, for equality $=$, we can define:

$$[\![f_e(j_1, ..., j_n, id_1, ..., id_n) = c]\!](\mathcal{D}, i, \epsilon) :=$$
$$\begin{cases} +\infty & \text{if } h_e([\mathcal{R}(\mathcal{D}(\epsilon(j_k)), \epsilon(id_k))]_{k=1}^n) = c \wedge \forall k \in \{1, ..., n\}, \epsilon(id_k) \in \mathcal{SO}(\mathcal{D}(\epsilon(j_k))) \\ -\infty & \text{otherwise} \end{cases}$$

The second type is for predicates comparing values from sets with well-defined metrics similar to the various temporal logic robust semantics [6]. For example, for "greater than", we could define:

$$[\![f_n(j_1, ..., j_n, id_1, ..., id_n) > c]\!](\mathcal{D}, i, \epsilon) :=$$
$$\begin{cases} h_n([\mathcal{R}(\mathcal{D}(\epsilon(j_k)), \epsilon(id_k))]_{k=1}^n) - c & \text{if } \forall k \in \{1, ..., n\}, \epsilon(id_k) \in \mathcal{SO}(\mathcal{D}(\epsilon(j_k))) \\ -\infty & \text{otherwise} \end{cases}$$

where k is index of the kth object variable (id_k) and j_k is the kth time variable of the formula. Here, h_e and h_n are application dependent functions on the data fields of $\mathcal{D}$ which process the retrieved values of data objects $\epsilon(id_k)$ at $\epsilon(j_k)$ if $\epsilon(id_k) \in \mathcal{SO}(\mathcal{D}(\epsilon(j_k)))$. The second predicate type can return finite real values.

TQTL Example: Now consider Fig. 1. When a car is following a cyclist, it is important that the cyclist is correctly classified in order to utilize the appropriate predictive motion model. We consider the following vision quality requirement: *"At every time step, for all the objects* (id_1) *in the frame, if the object class is cyclist with probability more than 0.7, then in the next 5 frames the object* id_1 *should still be classified as a cyclist with probability more than 0.6"*. The requirement can be formalized in TQTL as follows:

$$\phi_1 = \Box\Big(x.\forall id_1 @x, (C(x, id_1) = Cyclist \land P(x, id_1) > 0.7)$$

$$\rightarrow \Box\big(y.((x \le y \land y \le x + 5) \rightarrow C(y, id_1) = Cyclist \land P(y, id_1) > 0.6)\big)\Big)$$

where $[\![C(x, id_1) = Cyclist]\!](\mathcal{D}, i, \epsilon) :=$

$$\begin{cases} +\infty & \epsilon(id_1) \in \mathcal{SO}(\mathcal{D}(\epsilon(x))) \text{ and } \mathcal{R}(\mathcal{D}(\epsilon(x)), \epsilon(id_1)).\text{Class} = Cyclist \\ -\infty & \epsilon(id_1) \notin \mathcal{SO}(\mathcal{D}(\epsilon(x))) \text{ or} \\ & \epsilon(id_1) \in \mathcal{SO}(\mathcal{D}(\epsilon(x))) \text{ and } \mathcal{R}(\mathcal{D}(\epsilon(x)), \epsilon(id_1)).\text{Class} \ne Cyclist \end{cases}$$

and $[\![P(y, id_1) > 0.6]\!](\mathcal{D}, i, \epsilon) :=$

$$\begin{cases} -\infty & \epsilon(id_1) \notin \mathcal{SO}(\mathcal{D}(\epsilon(y))) \\ \mathcal{R}(\mathcal{D}(\epsilon(y)), \epsilon(id_1)).\text{Probability} - 0.6 & \epsilon(id_1) \in \mathcal{SO}(\mathcal{D}(\epsilon(y))) \end{cases}$$

4   Experimental Results

The implementation of our TQTL monitor is based on the publicly available S-TaLiRo toolbox [3,5,8]. We evaluated our TQTL monitor using the KITTI benchmark dataset [11]. The KITTI dataset is a well-known benchmark for autonomous driving which contains real traffic situations from Karlsruhe, Germany. We ran the SqueezeDet object detection algorithm [16] on some KITTI data streams. It should be noted that the object matching is manually annotated in these data streams since we assume that the objects are matched correctly. However, automated reliability reasoning about object matching throughout video streams is a challenging problem and it is the focus of our on-going research.

In Fig. 1, we provide the results of SqueezeDet on a KITTI data stream (following a cyclist). We evaluate the TQTL formula ϕ_1 from the previous section with respect to $\mathcal{D}$. The monitor tool obtained a negative result when evaluating $[\![\phi_1]\!]$, i.e., $\mathcal{D} \not\models \phi_1$. This is because the data stream $\mathcal{D}$ does not contain an object classified as cyclist in Frames 84 and 85 in Fig. 1. A closer investigation of Frames 84 and 85 shows that although a cyclist is not detected (yellow box), a pedestrian is detected at the position of the cyclist with purple color. If our motion prediction algorithm had the capability to tolerate an object classification change, e.g., from *cyclist* to *pedestrian* and back, then the formal specification should be able to reflect that. To specify such a behavior, the second $\Box$ of ϕ_1 should be changed to:

$$\Box(y.((x \le y \land y \le x + 5) \rightarrow C(y, id_1) = Cyclist \land P(y, id_1) > 0.6$$

$$\lor \exists id_2 @y, (C(y, id_2) = Pedestrian \land dist(x, y, id_1, id_2) < 40 \land P(y, id_2) > 0.6)))$$

where the scoring function of *dist* extracts the coordinates of the bounding boxes of object id_1 at frame x and object id_2 at frame y for computing the center to center distance between these boxes. The requirement is now satisfied by $\mathcal{D}$.

5   Conclusion and Future Works

In this paper, we provided a temporal logic monitoring framework for evaluating the quality of perception algorithms for autonomous vehicle applications. We highlighted that we can represent complex quality requirements over object detection data streams using Timed Quality Temporal Logic (TQTL). Our prototype monitoring tool is built upon our off-line monitor for TPTL requirements [8]. Our on-going work extends the presented framework to automated reasoning over object classification data streams without object tracking.

Acknowledgements. This work was partially supported by the NSF I/UCRC Center for Embedded Systems and by NSF grants 1350420, 1361926 and 1446730.

References

1. Autonomous vehicle disengagement reports 2016. https://www.dmv.ca.gov/portal/dmv/detail/vr/autonomous/disengagement_report_2016
2. IEEE Connected Vehicles: Google reports self-driving car disengagements. http://sites.ieee.org/connected-vehicles/2015/12/15/google-reports-self-driving-car-disengagements
3. S-TaLiRo Toolbox. https://sites.google.com/a/asu.edu/s-taliro/s-taliro
4. Alur, R., Henzinger, T.A.: A really temporal logic. J. ACM **41**(1), 181–204 (1994)
5. Annpureddy, Y., Liu, C., Fainekos, G., Sankaranarayanan, S.: S-TaLiRo: a tool for temporal logic falsification for hybrid systems. In: Abdulla, P.A., Leino, K.R.M. (eds.) TACAS 2011. LNCS, vol. 6605, pp. 254–257. Springer, Heidelberg (2011). https://doi.org/10.1007/978-3-642-19835-9_21
6. Bartocci, E., Deshmukh, J., Donzé, A., Fainekos, G., Maler, O., Ničković, D., Sankaranarayanan, S.: Specification-based monitoring of cyber-physical systems: a survey on theory, tools and applications. In: Bartocci, E., Falcone, Y. (eds.) Lectures on Runtime Verification - Introductory and Advanced Topics. LNCS, vol. 10457, pp. 135–175. Springer, Cham (2018). https://doi.org/10.1007/978-3-319-75632-5_5
7. Deshmukh, J.V., Majumdar, R., Prabhu, V.S.: Quantifying conformance using the skorokhod metric. In: 27th International Conference on Computer Aided Verification (CAV), pp. 234–250 (2015)
8. Dokhanchi, A., Hoxha, B., Tuncali, C.E., Fainekos, G.: An efficient algorithm for monitoring practical TPTL specifications. In: The ACM/IEEE International Conference on Formal Methods and Models for System Design (MEMOCODE), pp. 184–193 (2016)
9. Dreossi, T., Ghosh, S., Sangiovanni-Vincentelli, A.L., Seshia, S.A.: Systematic testing of convolutional neural networks for autonomous driving. In: ICML Workshop on Reliable Machine Learning in the Wild (RMLW) (2017)
10. Fainekos, G., Pappas, G.J.: Robustness of temporal logic specifications for continuous-time signals. Theor. Comput. Sci. **410**(42), 4262–4291 (2009)
11. Geiger, A., Lenz, P., Stiller, C., Urtasun, R.: Vision meets robotics: the KITTI dataset. Int. J. Robot. Res. (IJRR) **32**, 1229–1235 (2013)
12. Goodfellow, I., Bengio, Y., Courville, A.: Deep Learning. MIT Press (2016). http://www.deeplearningbook.org

13. Maler, O., Nickovic, D.: Monitoring temporal properties of continuous signals. In: Lakhnech, Y., Yovine, S. (eds.) FORMATS/FTRTFT -2004. LNCS, vol. 3253, pp. 152–166. Springer, Heidelberg (2004). https://doi.org/10.1007/978-3-540-30206-3_12

14. Nguyen, L.V., Kapinski, J., Jin, X., Deshmukh, J.V., Johnson, T.T.: Hyperproperties of real-valued signals. In: The ACM-IEEE International Conference on Formal Methods and Models for System Design (MEMOCODE), pp. 104–113 (2017)

15. Tuncali, C.E., Fainekos, G., Ito, H., Kapinski, J.: Simulation-based adversarial test generation for autonomous vehicles with machine learning components. In: IEEE Intelligent Vehicles Symposium (IV) (2018)

16. Wu, B., Iandola, F., Jin, P.H., Keutzer, K.: Squeezedet: Unified, small, low power fully convolutional neural networks for real-time object detection for autonomous driving. arXiv:1612.01051 (2016)

17. Xu, H., Gao, Y., Yu, F., Darrell, T.: End-to-end learning of driving models from large-scale video datasets. In: IEEE Conference on Computer Vision and Pattern Recognition (CVPR) (2017). https://doi.org/10.1109/CVPR.2017.376

Tracing Distributed Component-Based Systems, a Brief Overview

Yliès Falcone[1]([⊠]), Hosein Nazarpour[2], Mohamad Jaber[3], Marius Bozga[2], and Saddek Bensalem[2]

[1] Univ. Grenoble Alpes, CNRS, Inria, Grenoble INP, LIG,
38000 Grenoble, France
ylies.falcone@univ-grenoble-alpes.fr

[2] Univ. Grenoble Alpes, CNRS, Inria, Grenoble INP, Verimag, 38000 Grenoble,
France
{hosein.nazarpour,marius.bozga,saddek.bensalem}@univ-grenoble-alpes.fr

[3] American University of Beirut, Beirut, Lebanon
mj54@aub.edu.lb

Abstract. We overview a framework for tracing asynchronous distributed component-based systems with multiparty interactions managed by distributed schedulers. Neither the global state nor the total ordering of the system events is available at runtime. We instrument the system to retrieve local events from the local traces of the schedulers. Local events are sent to a global observer which reconstructs on-the-fly the global traces that are compatible with the local traces, in a concurrency-preserving and communication-delay insensitive fashion. The global traces are represented as an original lattice over partial states, such that any path of the lattice projected on a scheduler represents the corresponding local partial trace according to that scheduler (soundness), and all possible global traces of the system are recorded (completeness).

1 Introduction

Component-based design consists in constructing complex systems using predefined components which are atomic entities with some actions and interfaces. The behavior of a component-based system with multiparty interactions (CBS) depends on the behavior of each component as well as the interactions between the components. A multiparty interaction is a set of simultaneously executed actions of components [9]. To allow for the concurrent execution of non-conflicting interactions (with no shared component), interactions are distributed on several schedulers. Schedulers and components interact (by exchanging messages) to ensure the correct execution of multiparty interactions [10].

Problem Statement. Our goal is to conduct runtime verification [4,5,17] of a distributed CBS against properties referring to the global states of the system. This implies, in particular, that properties cannot be projected and checked on individual components. We use neither a global clock nor a shared memory. On

C. Colombo and M. Leucker (Eds.): RV 2018, LNCS 11237, pp. 417–425, 2018.
https://doi.org/10.1007/978-3-030-03769-7_24

the one hand, this makes the execution of the system more dynamic and parallel by avoiding synchronization to take global snapshots [11], which would go against the distribution of the system. On the other hand, it complicates the monitoring problem because no component can be aware of the global trace. Since the execution of interactions is based on sending/receiving messages, communication is asynchronous, and delays in the reception of messages are inevitable. Moreover, the absence of ordering between the execution of the interactions in different schedulers makes the actual execution trace unobservable. To allow for the RV of distributed CBSs, we instrument them so as to *trace* and *reconstruct* their global behavior in a concurrency-preserving and communication-delay insensitive fashion. We shall leverage the component-based nature of the system under scrutiny and account for the existing causalities in the execution of distributed CBSs.

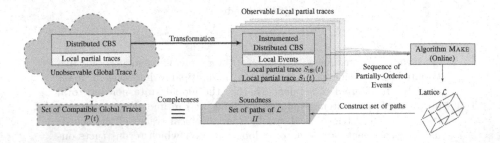

Fig. 1. Overview of the computation lattice construction

Approach Overview (Fig. 1). We define a *monitoring hypothesis* by defining an abstract semantic model that encompasses a variety of distributed CBSs. Our model relies only on partial-state semantics of CBSs, in terms of (1) Labeled Transition Systems with unobservable internal actions and observable actions and (2) a set of schedulers defining multiparty interactions (i.e, barriers) on sets of observable actions from different components. Our model is, however, not bound to any CBS framework. Due to the parallel executions in schedulers (i) events (i.e., actions changing the state of the system) are not totally ordered, and (ii) the actual global trace is unobservable. Although each scheduler is aware of its local behavior (local partial trace) and its local events, to evaluate the global behavior, we need the set of possible orderings of the events of all schedulers, that is, the set of compatible global traces. In our setting, schedulers do not communicate together and only communicate with their associated components. Indeed, only the shared components involved in several multiparty interactions managed by different schedulers make the actions of different schedulers causally related. In other words, the executions of two actions managed by two schedulers and involving a shared component are causally related, because each execution requires the termination of the other execution to release the shared component. To account for existing causality, we (i) employ vector clocks to define the ordering of events (ii) instrument the system to compose each scheduler with a controller to compute the correct vector clock of each generated event (iii) compose each shared component with a controller to resolve the causality, and (iv) introduce a procedure to reconstruct a set of compatible global traces that could possibly have happened with the received events. We represent the set of compatible global traces using a computation lattice tailored for CBSs. Such a computation lattice consists of a set of partially connected nodes. Created nodes are partial states and become global states during monitoring. Any path of the lattice projected on a scheduler represents the corresponding local partial trace according to that scheduler (soundness). All possible global traces are exactly recorded (completeness).

An extended version of this paper with more details and proofs is available in [28].

2   Semantics of Distributed CBSs with Multiparty Interactions

We describe a general semantics of CBSs, where neither the exact model nor the behavior of the system are known. How the behaviors of the components and the schedulers are obtained is irrelevant for monitoring. Inspiring from conformance-testing theory [30], we refer to this as the *monitoring hypothesis*. *Components* are in the set $\mathbf{B} = \{B_1, \ldots, B_{|\mathbf{B}|}\}$ and *schedulers* in $\mathbf{S} = \{S_1, \ldots, S_{|\mathbf{S}|}\}$. Each component B_i is endowed with a set of actions Act_i. Joint actions of components, aka multiparty interactions, involve several components. An interaction is a non-empty subset of $\cup_{i=1}^{|\mathbf{B}|} Act_i$; Int denotes the set of interactions. At most one action of each component is involved in an interaction: $\forall a \in Int . |a \cap Act_i| \leq 1$. Moreover, each component B_i has internal actions modeled as a unique action β_i. Schedulers coordinate the execution of interactions and ensure that each multiparty interaction is jointly executed. We describe the behavior of components, schedulers, and their composition. Component B (i) has actions in set Act_B which are possibly shared with some of the other components, (ii) has an internal action $\beta_B \notin Act_B$ which models internal computations of component B, (iii) the state of B is busy (unknown) while it is performing its internal action, and (iv) alternates moving from a ready state to a busy state (after executing an action), and vice-versa (after executing an internal action). Intuitively, when a scheduler executes an interaction, it triggers the execution of the associated actions on the involved components, and updates its internal vector clock. Moreover, when a component executes an internal action, it triggers the execution of the corresponding action on the associated schedulers and also sends the updated state of the component to the associated schedulers, the component sends a message including its current state to the schedulers. Note, by construction, schedulers are always ready to receive such a state update.

Global Behavior. The global execution of the system can be described as the parallel execution of interactions managed by the schedulers. Components execute independently according to the decisions of schedulers. Any executed global action contains at most one interaction involving each component. Whenever an interaction managed by a scheduler is executed, this scheduler and all components involved in this interaction must be ready to execute it. Internal actions are executed whenever the corresponding components are ready to execute them. Moreover, schedulers are aware of internal actions of components in their scope. The awareness of internal actions of a component results in transferring the updated state of the component to the schedulers. The components and schedulers not involved in an interaction remain in the same state.

Traces of Distributed CBSs with Multiparty Interactions. A trace is a sequence of states traversed by the system at runtime, from some initial state and following the transition relation of the LTS. For clarity and our monitoring purposes, the states of schedulers are irrelevant in the trace, and thus we restrict the system states to those of the components. A *partial trace* has partial states where at least one component is busy (with internal computation). Although the partial trace of the system exists, it is not observable because it would require a perfect observer having simultaneous access to the states of components. Introducing such an observer requires to synchronize all components and defeat the purpose of building a distributed system. Instead, we shall instrument the system to observe the sequence of states through schedulers.

3   Computation Lattice of Distributed Component-Based Systems

We briefly overview the on-the-fly construction of a computation lattice representing the possible global traces compatible with the local partial traces (Algorithm MAKE). Since schedulers do not interact directly, the execution of an interaction by one scheduler is concurrent with the execution of all interactions by other schedulers.

System Instrumentation. To retrieve the actual ordering and obtain the local partial traces, one needs to instrument the system by adding controllers to the schedulers and to the shared components. Each time a scheduler executes an interaction, the involved components are notified by the scheduler to execute their corresponding actions. Moreover, the controller of the scheduler updates its local clock and notifies the controller of the shared components involved in the interaction by sending its vector clock (be stored in the controller). Whenever a shared component executes its internal action β, schedulers that have the shared component in their scope are notified by receiving the updated state. Moreover, the vector clock stored in the controller of the shared component is sent to the controller of the associated schedulers. Consequently, schedulers having a shared component in their scope exchange their vector clocks through the shared component. Intuitively, for scheduler S_j, the execution of an interaction (labeled by a vector clock), or notification by the internal action of a component which the execution of its latest action has been managed by scheduler S_j, is defined as an *event* of scheduler S_j.

Extended Computation Lattice (Overview). Intuitively, an extended computation lattice (lattice for short) consists of a set of partially connected nodes, where each node is a pair, made of a state of the system and a vector clock. A system state consists in the states of all components. The computation lattice is represented implicitly using vector clocks. The construction mainly performs the two following operations: (i) *creations of new nodes* and (ii) *updates* of existing nodes in the lattice. The observer, which is charge of building the lattice, receives two sorts of events: (1) events related to the execution of an interaction in *Int*, referred to as *action events*, and (2) events related to internal actions referred to as *update events*. (Recall that internal actions carry the state of the component which has performed the action – the state is sent to the observer by the controller that is notified of this action). Action events lead to the creation of new nodes, while update events complete the information in the nodes of the lattice related to the state of the component related to the event. Since the received events are not totally ordered (because of communication delay), we construct the computation lattice based on the vector clocks attached to the received events. Note, we assume that the events received from a scheduler are totally ordered.

Intermediate Operations. We consider a lattice $\mathcal{L}$. A newly received event either modifies $\mathcal{L}$ or is kept in a queue for later. Action events extend $\mathcal{L}$ and update events update the existing nodes of $\mathcal{L}$ by adding the missing state information into them. By extending the lattice with new nodes, one needs to further complete the lattice by computing joints of created nodes with existing ones so as to complete the set of possible global traces.

Receiving an action or update event might not always lead to extending or updating the current computation lattice. Due to communication delay, an event that happened before another event might be received later by the observer. It is necessary for the construction of the lattice to use events in a specific order. Such events must be kept in a waiting queue to be used later.

Properties Guaranteed by Lattice Construction. The first property states that the ordering of the events does not affect the lattice. The second property is *correctness* (soundness), meaning that the resulting computation lattice encodes a set of the sequences of global states, s.t. each sequence represents a global trace of the system. The third property is *completeness*, meaning that for any sequence of events, we construct a lattice whose set of paths consists of all the compatible global traces.

Remark 1 (Garbage Collection). For performance reasons, a garbage collector regularly removes non-frontier nodes from the lattice and checks for the existence of events that can be treated. This ensures that the lattice size remains almost constant at runtime, while maintaining soundness and completeness.

4 Evaluation

We implemented the RVDIST tool [1] to evaluate our approach on a robot navigation system and the two-phase commit protocol. We consider metrics related to lattice construction. Our experiment show that the size of the constructed lattice remain constant at runtime when executed on two systems generating a few thousands of events. Moreover, the size of the constructed lattice and the number of paths of the lattices is *inversely proportional* to the number of shared components.

5 Related Work

This paper extends our runtime verification frameworks for component-based systems, in the sequential [19] and multi-threaded [27] settings. Regarding distributed systems, a lot of tracing and debugging frameworks have been defined for instance in the system community, however, generally with an offline, less general and less formal approach (e.g., no correctness guarantees). Henceforth, we rather focus in this section on the formal approaches to monitoring distributed systems (see [21] for an overview). The approach in [8] presents an algorithm for decentralized monitoring LTL formulas for synchronous distributed systems. We rather target asynchronous distributed CBSs with a partial-state semantics, where the global state of the system is unavailable at runtime. Hence, instead of having a global trace at runtime, we deal with the compatible partial traces which could have happened at runtime. The approach in [7] presents a framework for detecting and analyzing synchronous distributed systems faults in a centralized manner using local LTL properties that require only the local traces. In our setting, the global trace allows monitoring global properties that cannot be projected and checked on individual components/schedulers. Thus, local traces cannot be directly used for verifying properties. In [29], the authors design a method for monitoring safety properties in distributed systems relying on existing process communication. Compared to [29], our algorithm is sound as we reconstruct the behavior of the distributed system based on all possible partial traces. In our work, each trace could have happened as the actual trace of the system, and could have generated the same events. The approach in [23] shows that the trace monitoring problem with automata is NP-complete in the number of concurrent processes. The approaches in [2,12,22], generalized in [26], monitor temporal requirements over distributed processes where local monitors are attached to processes and circulate tokens. Interestingly, the approach [26] is decentralized (as is [8]). Compared to [23,26] which use simpler computational models, our approach is tailored to and leverages CBS where traces are defined over partial states. Also close to our work is [24] for the monitoring of violations of invariants using knowledge. Model-checking the system allows to pre-calculate the states where a violation can be reported by a process alone. When communication (i.e., more knowledge) is needed between processes, synchronizations are added. The focus of [24] is to minimize communication induced by synchronization while our approach does not impose synchronization to the system. The approach in [3] introduces a component-based model of Apache ZooKeeper for testing using a model-checker. It describes code that maintains an event graph similar to our lattice construction. However, [3] is specific to Zookeeper, whereas our method can be applied to any distributed system.

6 Conclusions and Perspectives

We efficiently trace distributed CBSs where interactions are partitioned over distributed schedulers. Our technique (i) transforms the system to generate events associated with the partial traces of schedulers, (ii) synthesizes a centralized observer which collects the local events of all schedulers (iii) reconstructs on-the-fly the possible orderings of the received events which form a computation lattice. We showed that the constructed lattice encodes exactly the set of compatible global traces: each could have occurred as the actual execution trace of the system. The experimental results show that, even for long execution traces, the size of the constructed lattice is constant.

Tracing distributed CBSs in a sound and complete allows us to tackle the problem of the runtime verification of distributed CBSs. We plan to address this problem in the future as well as the following ones:

- (i) define specification formalisms tailored to our model of CBSs and study their monitorability [16];
- (ii) decentralize observers/monitors according to the system architecture by using decentralized runtime verification frameworks [6,13,15];
- (iii) adapt techniques for runtime enforcement [20] of sequential CBSs [18] to the distributed setting;
- (iv) use heteregoneous communication primitives (synchronous and asynchronous) [25] for facilitating the implementation of optimized monitors;
- (v) leverage aspect-oriented programming on CBSs [14] to define source-to-source transformations to inject runtime verification monitors.

Acknowledgement. This article is based upon work from COST Action ARVI IC1402, supported by COST (European Cooperation in Science and Technology). The authors acknowledge the support of the Brain-IoT project (www.brain-iot.eu). This work was supported by the French national program "Programme Investissements d'Avenir IRT Nanoelec" (ANR-10-AIRT-05).

References

1. RVDist: Runtime Verification for Distributed Component-Based Systems. https://gitlab.inria.fr/monitoring/rv-dist-pub
2. Agarwal, A., Garg, V.K., Ogale, V.: Modeling and analyzing periodic distributed computations. In: Dolev, S., Cobb, J., Fischer, M., Yung, M. (eds.) SSS 2010. LNCS, vol. 6366, pp. 191–205. Springer, Heidelberg (2010). https://doi.org/10.1007/978-3-642-16023-3_17

3. Artho, C., et al.: Model-based API testing of apache zookeeper. In: 2017 IEEE International Conference on Software Testing, Verification and Validation, pp. 288–298 (2017)
4. Bartocci, E., et al.: First international competition on runtime verification: rules, benchmarks, tools, and final results of CRV 2014. Int. J. Softw. Tools Technol. Transf., 1–40 (2017)
5. Bartocci, E., Falcone, Y., Francalanza, A., Reger, G.: Introduction to runtime verification. In: Bartocci, E., Falcone, Y. (eds.) Lectures on Runtime Verification. LNCS, vol. 10457, pp. 1–33. Springer, Cham (2018). https://doi.org/10.1007/978-3-319-75632-5_1
6. Bauer, A., Falcone, Y.: Decentralised LTL monitoring. Formal Methods Syst. Des. **48**(1–2), 46–93 (2016)
7. Bauer, A., Leucker, M., Schallhart, C.: Model-based runtime analysis of distributed reactive systems. In: ASWEC 2006, Australian Software Engineering Conference, pp. 243–252. IEEE (2006)
8. Bauer, A., Falcone, Y.: Decentralised LTL monitoring. In: Giannakopoulou, D., Méry, D. (eds.) FM 2012. LNCS, vol. 7436, pp. 85–100. Springer, Heidelberg (2012). https://doi.org/10.1007/978-3-642-32759-9_10
9. Bliudze, S., Sifakis, J.: A notion of glue expressiveness for component-based systems. In: van Breugel, F., Chechik, M. (eds.) CONCUR 2008. LNCS, vol. 5201, pp. 508–522. Springer, Heidelberg (2008). https://doi.org/10.1007/978-3-540-85361-9_39
10. Bonakdarpour, B., Bozga, M., Jaber, M., Quilbeuf, J., Sifakis, J.: A framework for automated distributed implementation of component-based models. Distrib. Comput. **25**(5), 383–409 (2012)
11. Chandy, K.M., Lamport, L.: Distributed snapshots: determining global states of distributed systems. ACM Trans. Comput. Syst. (TOCS) **3**(1), 63–75 (1985)
12. Cooper, R., Marzullo, K.: Consistent detection of global predicates. In: Workshop on Parallel and Distributed Debugging, Santa Cruz, California, pp. 167–174 (1991)
13. El-Hokayem, A., Falcone, Y.: Monitoring decentralized specifications. In: Bultan, T., Sen, K. (eds.) Proceedings of the 26th ACM SIGSOFT International Symposium on Software Testing and Analysis, Santa Barbara, CA, USA, 10–14 July 2017, pp. 125–135. ACM (2017)
14. El-Hokayem, A., Falcone, Y., Jaber, M.: Modularizing behavioral and architectural crosscutting concerns in formal component-based systems - application to the behavior interaction priority framework. J. Log. Algebr. Meth. Program. **99**, 143–177 (2018)
15. Falcone, Y., Cornebize, T., Fernandez, J.-C.: Efficient and generalized decentralized monitoring of regular languages. In: Ábrahám, E., Palamidessi, C. (eds.) FORTE 2014. LNCS, vol. 8461, pp. 66–83. Springer, Heidelberg (2014). https://doi.org/10.1007/978-3-662-43613-4_5
16. Falcone, Y., Fernandez, J., Mounier, L.: What can you verify and enforce at runtime? STTT **14**(3), 349–382 (2012). https://doi.org/10.1007/s10009-011-0196-8
17. Falcone, Y., Havelund, K., Reger, G.: A tutorial on runtime verification. In: Broy, M., Peled, D.A., Kalus, G. (eds.) Engineering Dependable Software Systems, NATO Science for Peace and Security Series, D: Information and Communication Security, vol. 34, pp. 141–175. IOS Press (2013)
18. Falcone, Y., Jaber, M.: Fully automated runtime enforcement of component-based systems with formal and sound recovery. STTT **19**(3), 341–365 (2017)

19. Falcone, Y., Jaber, M., Nguyen, T., Bozga, M., Bensalem, S.: Runtime verification of component-based systems in the BIP framework with formally-proved sound and complete instrumentation. Softw. Syst. Model. **14**(1), 173–199 (2015)
20. Falcone, Y., Mounier, L., Fernandez, J., Richier, J.: Runtime enforcement monitors: composition, synthesis, and enforcement abilities. Formal Methods Syst. Des. **38**(3), 223–262 (2011)
21. Francalanza, A., Pérez, J.A., Sánchez, C.: Runtime verification for decentralised and distributed systems. In: Bartocci, E., Falcone, Y. (eds.) Lectures on Runtime Verification. LNCS, vol. 10457, pp. 176–210. Springer, Cham (2018). https://doi.org/10.1007/978-3-319-75632-5_6
22. Fromentin, E., Jard, C., Jourdan, G., Raynal, M.: On-the-fly analysis of distributed computations. Inf. Process. Lett. **54**(5), 267–274 (1995)
23. Genon, A., Massart, T., Meuter, C.: Monitoring distributed controllers: when an efficient LTL algorithm on sequences is needed to model-check traces. In: Misra, J., Nipkow, T., Sekerinski, E. (eds.) FM 2006. LNCS, vol. 4085, pp. 557–572. Springer, Heidelberg (2006). https://doi.org/10.1007/11813040_37
24. Graf, S., Peled, D., Quinton, S.: Monitoring distributed systems using knowledge. In: Bruni, R., Dingel, J. (eds.) FMOODS/FORTE -2011. LNCS, vol. 6722, pp. 183–197. Springer, Heidelberg (2011). https://doi.org/10.1007/978-3-642-21461-5_12
25. Kobeissi, S., Utayim, A., Jaber, M., Falcone, Y.: Facilitating the implementation of distributed systems with heterogeneous interactions. In: Furia, C.A., Winter, K. (eds.) IFM 2018. LNCS, vol. 11023, pp. 255–274. Springer, Cham (2018). https://doi.org/10.1007/978-3-319-98938-9_15
26. Mostafa, M., Bonakdarpour, B.: Decentralized runtime verification of LTL specifications in distributed systems. In: International Parallel and Distributed Processing Symposium, pp. 494–503 (2015)
27. Nazarpour, H., Falcone, Y., Bensalem, S., Bozga, M.: Concurrency-preserving and sound monitoring of multi-threaded component-based systems: theory, algorithms, implementation, and evaluation. Formal Aspects Comput. **29**(6), 951–986 (2017). https://doi.org/10.1007/s00165-017-0422-6
28. Nazarpour, H., Falcone, Y., Jaber, M., Bensalem, S., Bozga, M.: Monitoring distributed component-based systems. CoRR abs/1705.05242 (2017)
29. Sen, K., Vardhan, A., Agha, G., Rosu, G.: Efficient decentralized monitoring of safety in distributed systems. In: 26th International Conference on Software Engineering, pp. 418–427. IEEE (2004)
30. Tretmans, J.: A formal approach to conformance testing. In: Sixth International Workshop on Protocol Test Systems, IFIP TC6/WG6.1, pp. 257–276 (1993)

MLTL Benchmark Generation
via Formula Progression

Jianwen Li$^{(\boxtimes)}$ and Kristin Y. Rozier

Iowa State University, Ames, IA, USA
{jianwen,kyrozier}@iastate.edu

Abstract. Safe cyber-physical system operation requires runtime verification (RV), yet the burgeoning collection of RV technologies remain
comparatively untested due to a dearth of benchmarks with oracles
enabling objectively evaluating their performance. Mission-time LTL
(MLTL) adds integer temporal bounds to LTL to intuitively describe missions of such systems. An MLTL benchmark for runtime verification is a
3-tuple consisting of (1) an MLTL specification φ; (2) a set of finite input
streams representing propositional system variables (call this computa-
tion π) over the alphabet of φ; (3) an oracle stream of $\langle v, t \rangle$ pairs where
verdict v is the result (true or false) for time t of evaluating whether
$\pi_t \models \varphi$ (computation π at time t satisfies formula φ). We introduce
an algorithm for reliably generating MLTL benchmarks via formula pro-
gression. We prove its correctness, demonstrate it executes efficiently,
and show how to use it to generate a variety of useful patterns for the
evaluation and comparative analysis of RV tools.

1 Introduction

Runtime Verification (RV) provides the essential check that a system upholds its
requirements during execution. Tools performing *online* or *stream-based* verification run on-board safety-critical systems, checking the current execution against
the system's requirements in real time. RV is often expected, or even required,
on-board modern human-interactive systems as it provides the essential capability to detect, and possibly mitigate, failures that could cause harm to people,
property, or the environment. RV on-board an aircraft can provide the crucial
trigger to abandon a mission or switch to safe mode in the face of the failure of a
critical sensor. However it is essential that the RV tool be *correct*; a false-positive
could trigger an abort unnecessarily and a false-negative would be equivalent to
not running RV at all.

RV requirements are frequently expressed in Mission-time LTL (MLTL) [11],
one of the many variations on Metric Temporal Logic [9], which has the syntax
of Linear Temporal Logic with the option of integer bounds on the temporal
operators. It provides the readability of LTL while assuming, when a different

Work supported by NASA ECF NNX16AR57G and NSF CAREER Award CNS-
1552934.

© Springer Nature Switzerland AG 2018
C. Colombo and M. Leucker (Eds.): RV 2018, LNCS 11237, pp. 426–433, 2018.
https://doi.org/10.1007/978-3-030-03769-7_25

duration is not specified, that all requirements must be upheld during the (a priori known) length of a given mission, such as during the half-hour battery life of an Unmanned Aerial System (UAS). Using integer bounds instead of real-number or real-time bounds leads to more generic specifications that are adaptable to monitoring on different platforms (e.g., in software vs in hardware) with different granularities of time (e.g., because monitoring on-board an embedded system with more limited resources for storing the monitors may necessitate a wider granularity of time to fit the monitor encodings). We choose MLTL because it has been used for the Runtime Verification Benchmark Challenge [10] and in many industrial case studies [5,8,11,13–16]. Many specifications from other case studies, in logics such as MTL [1] and STL [7], can be represented in MLTL.

Arguably the biggest challenge facing the RV community today is the dearth of benchmarks for checking the correctness of RV tools and comparatively analyzing them [12]. An RV benchmark has three parts: (a) an input stream or *computation* π representing the values of the system variables over time; (b) an MLTL requirement φ; (c) an oracle $\mathcal{O}$, or output stream of tuples $\langle v, t \rangle$ where v is the valuation of φ (true or false) at time t for all $0 \leq t \leq M$ where M is the mission bound, or the number of time steps in the benchmark instance. The oracle is crucially required to evaluate correctness of RV algorithms but checking whether computation π satisfies requirement φ at each timestep in M is hard. Therefore, we create RV benchmarks by generating an MLTL requirement φ and deciding what pattern we'd like to see in our oracle (e.g., to achieve goals of code coverage for the RV tool under test). We utilize a new algorithm based on *formula progression* [3] over MLTL formulas to generate a π that satisfies φ at each timestep accordingly.

The contributions of this paper include a definition of formula progression for MLTL along with proofs of decomposibility and correctness. We design an RV benchmark generation algorithm based on MLTL formula progression, argue for its correctness, and show how to use it to generate different interesting benchmark patterns. Section 2 provides base definitions of MLTL semantics and benchmarks. We define MLTL formula progression in Sect. 3 and use it for benchmark generation algorithms in Sect. 4. Section 5 concludes.

2   Mission-Time Linear Temporal Logic (MLTL)

MLTL was first introduced in [11] as a variation on LTL with closed, finite integer intervals on the temporal operators that translate to practical concepts, such as mission bounds. A closed interval over naturals $I = [a, b]$ ($0 \leq a \leq b$ are natural numbers) is a set of naturals $\{i \mid a \leq i \leq b\}$. We focus on *bounded* intervals such that $b < +\infty$. All MLTL intervals I are closed because every open or half-open interval, e.g., in Metric Temporal Logic (MTL) [2], is reducible to an equivalent closed bounded interval. For example, $(1,2) = \emptyset$, $(1,3) = [2,2]$, $(1,3] = [2,3]$, etc. Let $\mathcal{P}$ be a set of atomic propositions, then the syntax of a formula in Mission-Time LTL (abbreviated as MLTL) is:

$$\varphi ::= \text{true} \mid \text{false} \mid p \mid \neg\varphi \mid \varphi \vee \varphi \mid \varphi \wedge \varphi \mid \varphi U_I \varphi \mid \varphi R_I \varphi,$$

where I is a bounded interval, and $p \in \mathcal{P}$ is an *atom*. We use the abbreviations $F_I \varphi$ for $\mathsf{true} U_I \varphi$, $G_I \varphi$ for $\mathsf{false} R_I \varphi$, and $F_{[1,1]} \varphi$ for the equivalent of the LTL formula $X \varphi$.

The semantics of MLTL formulas are interpreted over finite traces. Let π be a finite trace in which every timestamp $\pi[i : i \geq 0]$ is over $2^{\mathcal{P}}$, and $|\pi|$ denotes the length of π; $|\pi| < +\infty$ because π is a finite trace. We use π^i (where $i \geq 1$) to represent the prefix of π ending at timestamp i (excluding i), and π_i (where $i \geq 0$) to represent the suffix of π starting from timestamp i (including i). Note that $\pi_i = \epsilon$ (empty trace) if $i \geq |\pi|$. Let $a, b : a \leq b$ be two natural numbers; we define that π models (satisfies) an MLTL formula φ, denoted as $\pi \models \varphi$, as follows:

- $\pi \models p$ iff $p \in \pi[0]$; $\quad$ - $\pi \models \neg \varphi$ iff $\pi \not\models \varphi$;
- $\pi \models \varphi_1 \vee \varphi_2$ iff $\pi \models \varphi_1$ or $\pi \models \varphi_2$; $\quad$ - $\pi \models \varphi_1 \wedge \varphi_2$ iff $\pi \models \varphi_1$ and $\pi \models \varphi_2$;
- $\pi \models \varphi_1 U_{[a,b]} \varphi_2$ iff $|\pi| > a$ and, there exists $i \in [a, b]$ such that $\pi_i \models \varphi_2$ and for every $j \in [a, b] : j < i$, it holds that $\pi_j \models \varphi_1$;
- $\pi \models \varphi_1 R_{[a,b]} \varphi_2$ iff $|\pi| \leq a$ or for every $i \in [a, b]$, either $\pi_i \models \varphi_2$ holds or there exists $j \in [a, b]$ s.t. $\pi_j \models \varphi_1$ and $\forall i, a \leq i \leq j, \pi_j \models \varphi_2$.

The Until and Release operators are interpreted slightly differently in MLTL than in the traditional MTL-over-naturals[1] [4]. In MTL-over-naturals, the satisfaction of $\varphi_1 U_I \varphi_2$ requires φ_1 to hold from position 0 to the position where φ_2 holds (in I), while in MLTL φ_1 is only required to hold within the interval I, before the time φ_2 holds. The same applies to the Release operator. From our experience in writing specifications, cf. [5,11,13–15], this adjustment is more user-friendly. Meanwhile, it is not hard to see that MLTL is as expressive as MTL-over-naturals: the formula $\varphi_1 U_{[a,b]} \varphi_2$ in MTL-over-naturals can be represented as $(G_{[0,a-1]} \varphi_1) \wedge (\varphi_1 U_{[a,b]} \varphi_2)$ in MLTL; $\varphi_1 U_{[a,b]} \varphi_2$ in MLTL can be represented as $F_{[a,a]}(\varphi_1 U_{[0,b-a]} \varphi_2)$ in MTL-over-naturals.

MLTL*Benchmarks*. One *benchmark instance* is a triple $\langle \pi, \varphi, \mathcal{O} \rangle$, where π is a finite trace of length $|\pi|$ over $(2^{\Sigma})^{|\pi|}$ representing the propositional variable input streams, φ is the MLTL requirement being monitored, and $\mathcal{O}$ is an oracle, itself a stream of pairs $\langle v, t \rangle$ such that verdict $v = true$ if $\pi_t \models \varphi$ and $v = false$ if not. An RV tool takes as input the formula φ and the finite trace set π and uses φ to generate a monitor; $\mathcal{O}$ is required to verify that the monitor operates correctly.

3   Formula Progression on MLTL

We introduce the concept of *formula progression* [3] over MLTL formulas.

Definition 1. *Given an MLTL formula φ and a finite trace π, let φ' be one formula progression of φ. We define the* progression function $prog(\varphi, \pi) = \varphi'$ *recursively:*

---

[1] In this paper, MTL-over-naturals is interpreted over finite traces.

- *if $|\pi| = 1$, then*
  - $prog(\text{true}, \pi) = \text{true}$ *and* $prog(\text{false}, \pi) = \text{false}$;
  - *if* $\varphi = p$ *is an atom,* $prog(\varphi, \pi) = \text{true}$ *iff* $p \in \pi[0]$;
  - *if* $\varphi = \neg\psi$, $prog(\varphi, \pi) = \neg prog(\psi, \pi)$;
  - *if* $\varphi = \psi_1 \vee \psi_2$, $prog(\varphi, \pi) = prog(\psi_1, \pi) \vee prog(\psi_2, \pi)$;
  - *if* $\varphi = \psi_1 \wedge \psi_2$, $prog(\varphi, \pi) = prog(\psi_1, \pi) \wedge prog(\psi_2, \pi)$;
  - *if* $\varphi = \psi_1 U_{[a,b]} \psi_2$,

$$prog(\varphi, \pi) = \begin{cases} \psi_1 U_{[a-1,b-1]} \psi_2 & \text{if } 0 < a \leq b; \\ prog(\psi_2, \pi) \vee (prog(\psi_1, \pi) \wedge \psi_1 U_{[0,b-1]} \psi_2) & \text{if } 0 = a < b; \\ prog(\psi_2, \pi) & \text{if } 0 = a = b; \end{cases}$$

  - *if* $\varphi = F_{[a,b]} \psi_2$,

$$prog(\varphi, \pi) = \begin{cases} F_{[a-1,b-1]} \psi_2 & \text{if } 0 < a \leq b; \\ prog(\psi_2, \pi) \vee F_{[0,b-1]} \psi_2 & \text{if } 0 = a < b; \\ prog(\psi_2, \pi) & \text{if } 0 = a = b; \end{cases}$$

  - *if* $\varphi = \psi_1 R_{[a,b]} \psi_2$, $prog(\varphi, \pi) = \neg prog((\neg\psi_1) U_{[a,b]} (\neg\psi_2), \pi)$;
  - *if* $\varphi = G_{[a,b]} \psi_2$, $prog(\varphi, \pi) = \neg prog(F_{[a,b]}(\neg\psi_2), \pi)$;
- *else* $prog(\varphi, \pi) = prog(prog(\varphi, \pi[0]), \pi_1)$.

The procedure $prog$ takes an MLTL formula φ and finite trace π as the input, and returns another MLTL formula by progressing π over φ. Figure 1 exemplifies formula progression over $\varphi = F_{[2,3]}a$ with respect to the trace $\pi = \{\neg a\}\{\neg a\}\{a\}$. From the figure, we have $prog(\varphi, \pi^1(= \{\neg a\})) = F_{[1,2]}a$, $prog(\varphi, \pi^2(= \{\neg a\}\{\neg a\})) = F_{[0,1]}a$, and $prog(\varphi, \pi^3(= \{\neg a\}\{\neg a\}\{a\})) = \text{true}$. Based on Definition 1, we have the following theorems.

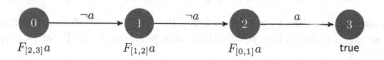

Fig. 1. The schema of $prog(F_{[2,3]}a, \pi = \{\neg a\}\{\neg a\}\{\neg a\}\{a\})$.

Theorem 1. Formula Progression Decomposition. *Let φ be an MLTL formula and π be a finite trace. Then formula progression on π can be decomposed into two progressions on the sub-traces (i.e. π^k, π_k) of π for an arbitrary k in the range $1 \leq k \leq |\pi|$. Formally, $prog(\varphi, \pi) = prog(prog(\varphi, \pi^k), \pi_k)$ for every $1 \leq k \leq |\pi|$.*

Proof. When $k = 1$, $prog(\varphi, \pi) = prog(prog(\varphi, \pi^1), \pi_1)$ is true based on Definition 1. Assume $prog(\varphi, \pi) = prog(prog(\varphi, \pi^k), \pi_k)$ is true for $1 \leq k < |\pi|$. Since $prog(prog(\varphi, \pi^k), \pi_k) = prog(prog(prog(\varphi, \pi^k), \pi[k]), \pi_{k+1})$ and $prog(prog(\varphi, \pi^k), \pi[k]) = prog(\varphi, \pi^{k+1})$ are true by Definition 1, we have the following is also true: $prog(\varphi, \pi) = prog(prog(\varphi, \pi^{k+1}), \pi_{k+1}) = prog(prog(\varphi, \pi^{k+1}), \pi_{k+1})$. $\square$

Theorem 1 generalizes the recursive part of Definition 1. To perform formula progression over φ with respect to the finite trace π, it is equivalent first perform formula progression over φ with respect to the prefix of π up to k, i.e. π^k, and then perform formula progression over $prog(\varphi, \pi^k)$ with respect to the subfix of π from k, i.e., π_k.

Theorem 2. Satisfiability Preservation. *Let φ be an* MLTL *formula and π be a finite trace. Then π satisfies φ iff the suffix of π, i.e., π_k for some k, satisfies the formula obtained from formula progression over φ with respect to the prefix of π, i.e., π^k. Formally, $\pi \models \varphi$ iff $\pi_k \models prog(\varphi, \pi^k)$ for every $1 \le k \le |\pi|$.*

Proof. (Sketch.) When $k = 1$, the proof can be done by an induction over the construction of $prog(\varphi, \pi^1)$ (the base case in Definition 1). Inductively, assume $\pi \models \varphi$ iff $\pi_k \models prog(\varphi, \pi^k)$ is true for $1 \le k < |\pi|$. From the hypothesis assumption, $\pi_k \models prog(\varphi, \pi^k)$ iff $\pi_{k+1} \models prog(prog(\varphi, \pi^k), \pi[k]) = prog(\varphi, \pi^{k+1})$ holds. As a result, we have that $\pi \models \varphi$ iff $\pi_{k+1} \models prog(\varphi, \pi^{k+1})$ holds.   □

Theorem 2 states that the formula progression is able to preserve the satisfaction of π in terms of the MLTL formula φ.

Theorem 3. Correctness. *Let φ be an* MLTL *formula and π be a finite trace. Then $\pi \models \varphi$ holds iff $prog(\varphi, \pi) = \text{true}$ holds.*

Proof. (Sketch.) For the base case when $|\pi| = 1$, the inductive proof can be done over the construction of $prog(\varphi, \pi)$ (the base case in Definition 1). When $|\pi| > 1$, we have $\pi \models \varphi$ iff $\pi_{|\pi|-1} \models prog(\varphi, \pi^{|\pi|-1})$ according to Theorem 2. Moreover, since $|\pi_{|\pi|-1}| = 1$ and we have proved that $\pi_{|\pi|-1} \models prog(\varphi, \pi^{|\pi|-1})$ iff $prog(prog(\varphi, \pi^{|\pi|-1}), \pi[|\pi| - 1]) = prog(\varphi, \pi) = \text{true}$ holds (from Theorem 1), it is true that $\pi \models \varphi$ holds iff $prog(\varphi, \pi) = \text{true}$ holds when $|\pi| > 1$.   □

Theorem 3 is a direct conclusion from Theorem 2, considering the particular situation when formula progression has been performed on all timestamps of π.

Corollary 1. *For the* MLTL *formula φ and finite trace π, $\pi \models \varphi$ implies $\pi \cdot \pi' \models \varphi$ for any arbitrary finite trace π'.*

Proof. From Theorem 3, $\pi \models \varphi$ implies that $prog(\varphi, \pi) = \text{true}$ holds. Since $\pi' \models \text{true}$ and $prog(\varphi, \pi) = \text{true}$ hold, it is true that $\pi \cdot \pi' \models \varphi$ based on Theorem 2.   □

We use the theorems and corollary introduced above as the theoretic correctness guarantee of our benchmark construction algorithms in the following section.

4   Benchmark Generation

4.1   Random Pattern

We use the MLTL generation tool released in [6] to construct random MLTL formulas. Once the formula φ is generated, we create a finite trace over the alphabet of the formula, i.e., Σ, with a random length (≥ 1) and assign a random assignment $P \in 2^{|\Sigma|}$ to each timestamp of the trace. We use the algorithm *prog* and Theorem 3 to generate π such that $\pi_k \models \varphi$ holds iff $prog(\varphi, \pi_k) =$ true for $0 \leq k < |\pi|$. In this way, we can efficiently generate large sets of always-satisfiable benchmark instances, representing the case where the system always upholds its requirements.

4.2 Almost-Satisfiable Pattern

For an instance $\langle \varphi, \pi, \mathcal{O} \rangle$ under the *Almost-Satisfiable Pattern*, $\pi_k \models \varphi$ must be true for as many k as possible ($1 \leq k < |\pi|$). To generate such instances, we leverage both the MLTL-SAT [6] and formula progression techniques in the following procedure:

- Use the MLTL-SAT solver to generate a model (satisfying finite trace) π for the given formula φ. If no such model exists, φ is unsatisfiable and we discard it. Otherwise, $\pi(= \pi_0) \models \varphi$ and we push the pair $\langle 0, \text{true} \rangle$ into $\mathcal{O}$;
- To pursue $\pi_k \models \varphi$ ($1 \leq k < |\pi|$) also being true, we extend π as follows:
  - First apply the formula progression technique to obtain the formula $prog(\varphi, \pi_k)$;
  - Use the MLTL-SAT solver to generate a model π' for $prog(\varphi, \pi_k)$. It may be possible that such model π' does not exist, in which case we push $\langle k, \text{false} \rangle$ into $\mathcal{O}$ and terminate our attempt to make $\pi_k \models \varphi$;
  - If π' exists, update π with $\pi \cdot \pi'$. Theorem 2 guarantees that $\pi_k \models \varphi$ holds for the updated π. Push $\langle k, \text{true} \rangle$ into $\mathcal{O}$;
  - The updated π also preserves the fact that $\pi_{k-1} \models \varphi$, i.e., the extension of π does not affect the previous truth evaluations, according to Corollary 1.
- To ensure termination, we set a mission length bound for the finite trace π.

The procedure SAT(φ) calls the MLTL-SAT solver to check the satisfiability of φ. Taking the MLTL formula φ and fixed length bound K for the generated trace in the instance, the procedure returns an instance of an Almost-Satisfiable Pattern.

Theorem 4 (Correctness). *Let $\langle \varphi, \pi, \mathcal{O} \rangle$ be the instance generated from Algorithm 1. Then we have $\pi_k \models \varphi$ iff $\langle k, \text{true} \rangle \in \mathcal{O}$ for $1 \leq k \leq |\varphi|$.*

4.3 Almost-Unsatisfiable and Median-Satisfiable Patterns

We also consider the dual of Almost-Satisfiable Pattern, namely Almost-Unsatisfiable Pattern, each instance under which requires that $\pi_k \not\models \varphi$ be true for as many k as possible ($1 \leq k < |\pi|$). First we create an Almost-Satisfiable Pattern instance $\langle \varphi, \pi, \mathcal{O} \rangle$ as shown in the previous section. Then we negate the formula in the instance and set $\mathcal{O}' = \{\langle k, \text{true} \rangle | \langle k, \text{false} \rangle \in \mathcal{O}\} \cup \{\langle k, \text{false} \rangle | \langle k, \text{true} \rangle \in \mathcal{O}\}$. As a result, the instance $\langle \neg\varphi, \pi, \mathcal{O}' \rangle$ is under the Almost-Unsatisfiable Pattern.

Algorithm 1. The Pseudo-code to generate the Almost-Satisfiable Pattern instances

---

Require: An MLTL formula φ, and the length bound K for the generated finite trace.
Ensure: An instance $\langle \varphi, \pi, \mathcal{O} \rangle$ that is under Almost-Satisfiable Pattern.
  1: **if** SAT(φ) return UNSAT **then**
  2:    **return** $\langle \varphi, \epsilon, \mathcal{O} \rangle$ (ϵ is the empty trace);
  3: **end if**
  4: Let π be the model returned from SAT(φ);
  5: **while** $1 \le k < |\pi|$ **do**
  6:    **if** $|\pi| > K$ **then**
  7:       **return** $\langle \varphi, \pi, \mathcal{O} \rangle$;
  8:    **end if**
  9:    Let $\varphi' = prog(\varphi, \pi_k)$;
 10:    **if** SAT(φ') return UNSAT **then**
 11:       Push the pair $\langle k, \mathsf{false} \rangle$ into $\mathcal{O}$;
 12:    **else**
 13:       Let π' be the model returned from SAT(φ');
 14:       Update $\pi = \pi \cdot \pi'$;
 15:       Push the pair $\langle k, \mathsf{true} \rangle$ into $\mathcal{O}$;
 16:    **end if**
 17: **end while**
 18: **return** π;

The Median-Satisfiable Pattern is a combination of the Almost-Satisfiable and Almost-Unsatisfiable Patterns; in each instance the number of timestamps on which the formula are satisfied is almost the same as that of timestamps on which the formula are falsified. To generate such an instance, we simply create an Almost-Satisfiable and Almost-Unsatisfiable Pattern instance respectively, i.e. $\langle \varphi, \pi_1, \mathcal{O}_1 \rangle$ and $\langle \varphi, \pi_2, \mathcal{O}_2 \rangle$, which have the same MLTL formula. Then the instance $\langle \varphi_1, \pi_1 \cdot \pi_2, \mathcal{O} \rangle$, where $\mathcal{O} = \mathcal{O}_1 \cup \mathcal{O}_2$, is under the Median-Satisfiable Pattern.

5 Conclusions and Future Work

By introducing algorithms for generating several crafted patterns of RV benchmarks, we have paved the way for the creation of a benchmark generation tool and the ability to create a large set of publicly-available benchmarks. Next, we plan to implement and experimentally evaluate the performance of our benchmark generation algorithms. After we optimize the performance to enable efficient generation of large sets of each type of benchmark, we plan to release our code and a database of generated instances.

References

1. Alur, R., Henzinger, T.: Real-time logics: complexity and expressiveness. In: Proceedings 5th IEEE Symposium on Logic in Computer Science, pp. 390–401 (1990)
2. Alur, R., Henzinger, T.A.: A really temporal logic. J. ACM **41**(1), 181–204 (1994)
3. Bacchus, F., Kabanza, F.: Planning for temporally extended goals. Ann. Math. Artif. Intell. **22**, 5–27 (1998)
4. Furia, C.A., Spoletini, P.: Tomorrow and all our yesterdays: MTL satisfiability over the integers. In: Fitzgerald, J.S., Haxthausen, A.E., Yenigun, H. (eds.) ICTAC 2008. LNCS, vol. 5160, pp. 126–140. Springer, Heidelberg (2008). https://doi.org/10.1007/978-3-540-85762-4_9
5. Geist, J., Rozier, K.Y., Schumann, J.: Runtime observer pairs and bayesian network reasoners on-board FPGAs: flight-certifiable system health management for embedded systems. In: Bonakdarpour, B., Smolka, S.A. (eds.) RV 2014. LNCS, vol. 8734, pp. 215–230. Springer, Cham (2014). https://doi.org/10.1007/978-3-319-11164-3_18
6. Li, J., Rozier, K.Y., Vardi, M.Y.: Evaluating the satisfiability of mission-time LTL: a bounded MTL over naturals. Under submission (2018)
7. Maler, O., Nickovic, D.: Monitoring temporal properties of continuous signals. In: Lakhnech, Y., Yovine, S. (eds.) FORMATS/FTRTFT -2004. LNCS, vol. 3253, pp. 152–166. Springer, Heidelberg (2004). https://doi.org/10.1007/978-3-540-30206-3_12
8. Moosbrugger, P., Rozier, K.Y., Schumann, J.: R2U2: monitoring and diagnosis of security threats for unmanned aerial systems. FMSD **51**, 1–31 (2017)
9. Ouaknine, J., Worrell, J.: Some recent results in metric temporal logic. In: Cassez, F., Jard, C. (eds.) FORMATS 2008. LNCS, vol. 5215, pp. 1–13. Springer, Heidelberg (2008). https://doi.org/10.1007/978-3-540-85778-5_1
10. Reger, G., Rozier, K.Y., Stolz, V.: Runtime verification benchmark challenge, November 2018. https://www.rv-competition.org/2018-2/
11. Reinbacher, T., Rozier, K.Y., Schumann, J.: Temporal-logic based runtime observer pairs for system health management of real-time systems. In: Ábrahám, E., Havelund, K. (eds.) TACAS 2014. LNCS, vol. 8413, pp. 357–372. Springer, Heidelberg (2014). https://doi.org/10.1007/978-3-642-54862-8_24
12. Rozier, K.Y.: On the evaluation and comparison of runtime verification tools for hardware and cyber-physical systems. In: RV-CUBES, vol. 3, pp. 123–137. Kalpa Publications (2017)
13. Rozier, K.Y., Schumann, J., Ippolito, C.: Intelligent hardware-enabled sensor and software safety and health management for autonomous UAS. In: Technical Memorandum NASA/TM-2015-218817, NASA Ames Research Center, Moffett Field, CA 94035, May 2015
14. Schumann, J., Moosbrugger, P., Rozier, K.Y.: R2U2: Monitoring and diagnosis of security threats for unmanned aerial systems. In: RV. Springer-Verlag (2015)
15. Schumann, J., Moosbrugger, P., Rozier, K.Y.: Runtime Analysis with R2U2: A Tool Exhibition Report. In: RV. Springer-Verlag (2016)
16. Schumann, J., Rozier, K.Y., Reinbacher, T., Mengshoel, O.J., Mbaya, T., Ippolito, C.: Towards real-time, on-board, hardware-supported sensor and software health management for unmanned aerial systems. IJPHM **6**(1), 1–27 (2015)

Tool Papers

An Environment for the PARTRAP Trace Property Language (Tool Demonstration)

Ansem Ben Cheikh, Yoann Blein, Salim Chehida, German Vega,
Yves Ledru$^{(\boxtimes)}$, and Lydie du Bousquet

Univ. Grenoble Alpes, CNRS, Grenoble INP, LIG, 38000 Grenoble, France
{Yoann.Blein,Yves.Ledru}@univ-grenoble-alpes.fr

Abstract. We present PARTRAP and its associated toolset, supporting a lightweight approach to formal methods. In critical systems, such as medical systems, it is often easy to enhance the code with tracing information. PARTRAP is an expressive language that allows to express properties over traces of parametric events. It is designed to ease the understanding and writing of properties by software engineers without background in formal methods. In this tool demonstration, we will present the language and its toolset: compiler, syntax directed editor, and a prototype generator of examples and counter-examples.

1 Introduction

Many applications, such as software intensive medical devices, require high quality software but their criticality does not mandate the use of formal proofs. Therefore, the formal methods community has promoted a lightweight approach to formal methods [17]. The PARTRAP language [8] goes into that direction. Most computer systems can easily be augmented to produce traces of their activity. PARTRAP allows to express properties of these traces which are evaluated by monitoring. PARTRAP and its associated toolset are designed to support software engineers not trained in formal methods. The language supports a unique combination of features: it is parametric and provides temporal operators to increase expressiveness; it is declarative and uses descriptive keywords to favour user-friendliness. It reuses Dwyer's specification patterns [14] to express intuitive properties. Properties of parameters can be expressed in Python, a language familiar to our target users. Its toolset includes a syntax-directed editor. It generates detailed explanations to help understand why a property evaluates to true or false on a given trace. We also prototyped a generator of examples and counter-examples, to help users understand the meaning of their properties.

Section 2 gives an overview of the PARTRAP language. Section 3 presents its associated toolset, and Sect. 4 draws the conclusions and perspectives of this study. On the PARTRAP web site[1], you will find a companion video demonstrating the tool, links to reference documents describing the syntax and semantics of PARTRAP, and instructions on how to download the PARTRAP eclipse plugin.

This work is funded by the ANR MODMED project (ANR-15-CE25-0010).
[1] http://vasco.imag.fr/tools/partrap/.

C. Colombo and M. Leucker (Eds.): RV 2018, LNCS 11237, pp. 437–446, 2018.
https://doi.org/10.1007/978-3-030-03769-7_26

2   The PARTRAP Language

Context. The design of PARTRAP was performed in cooperation with Blue
Ortho, a medical devices manufacturer, and MinMaxMedical, a software com-
pany. Together, we considered a medical system (TKA) that guides Total Knee
Arthroplasty surgeries, i.e. the replacement of both tibial and femoral cartilages
with implants. TKA produces traces of the sensors acquisitions and interactions
with the surgeon. Over time, more than 10 000 traces of actual surgeries have
been collected by Blue Ortho. Each trace counts about 500 significant events.
Figure 1 gives a simplified excerpt of such a trace, in JSON format.

```
00. [{"state": "Connect", "id": "EnterState", "time": 4042.7},
01.  {"state": "Connect", "id": "ExitState", "time": 4042.7},
...
04.  {"id": "CameraConnected", "time": 4747.34},
...
13.  {"ty": "P", "id": "TrackerDetected", "time": 4783.8},
14.  {"ty": "T", "id": "TrackerDetected", "time": 4798.0},
15.  {"v1": 41.44, "id": "Temp", "time": 4816.6},
16.  {"state": "Save", "id": "EnterState", "time": 4816.611},
...
20.  {"v1": 55.62, "id": "Temp", "time": 4847.6}]
```

Fig. 1. A trace excerpt in JSON Format

We identified 15 properties, listed in [19], representative of such medical
devices for assisted surgery. These properties specify the TKA traces. A careful
analysis of the properties revealed that they express temporal relations between
events, involve event parameters, and may apply to a restricted scope of the trace.
A few properties also refer to physical time or involve 3D calculations. Based on
these properties, we designed PARTRAP (Parametric Trace Property language)
[8,9]. The language is aimed at being used for *offline* trace checking. In [19],
we discussed how the language can be used during development to express and
check properties of traces produced by system tests, but also during exploitation
in order to identify how the system is used or mis-used.

2.1   Structure of PARTRAP Properties

A PARTRAP temporal property is described by its scope in the trace, and a temporal pattern over events satisfying some predicate. For example, the following
property expresses that *"once the camera is connected, the device temperature
does not go below 45 °C"*.

```
VAlidTemp1 : after first CameraConnected,
                absence_of Temp t where t.v1 < 45.0
```

The first line defines the scope of the property, here it is the suffix of the trace starting after the first event of type `CameraConnected`. The second line expresses a temporal pattern. Here, it is an absence pattern, stating that no event should be a `Temp` whose v1 parameter is less than 45.0. `t` is a local variable designating an event of type `Temp`. The `where` clause refers to this event and its parameter. The evaluation of this property on the trace of Fig. 1 yields false and returns the following message[2]:

```
[WARNING] False on trace unit-tests_Trace.json:
-In the scope from 5 to 20 with the environment:{}
found 1 event that should not occur:
{trace_occ_index=15, time=4816.6, id=Temp, v1=41.44}
```

Actually, event `CameraConnected` appears on line 4 of Fig. 1. So the scope of the property ranges from lines 5 to 20 which corresponds to the last event of the trace. The error message tells that line 15 features a `Temp` event which violates the property because its v1 has value `41.44` which is actually below 45 °C.

PARTRAP allows to express more complex properties. For example, property `ValidTrackers` in Fig. 3 features nested scopes and universal quantification to express that all types of trackers have been detected before entering a state whose name includes '*TrackersVisibCheck*'.

PARTRAP offers a variety of operators to express scopes and patterns. Scopes refer to events located before or after an event or between two events. The scope may consider the first or the last occurrence of the event, but also be repeated for each occurrence of the event. Patterns may refer to the absence or occurrence of an event, but may also refer to pairs of events where one event enables or disables the occurrence of the other. Moreover, it is possible to express physical time constraints stating that a property holds within a time interval. Finally, expressions occurring in the `where` clause may be written either in a basic language with support for numeric and string expressions, or in Python as in [3]. Python allows to take advantage of software libraries to express complex or domain dependent properties, e.g. properties based on 3D calculations.

Basic PARTRAP temporal properties can be combined using propositional logic connectors (`and`, `or`, `implies`, `equiv`) or quantifiers (`exists` and `forall`). PARTRAP properties are defined on finite traces and evaluated after completion of the trace. A detailed description of the language is given in [8] or [9].

2.2 Related Work

Several languages based on temporal logic have been proposed to express trace properties. In [8], we compared PARTRAP to several temporal specification languages using multiple criteria. Table 1 summarizes this study and groups languages with similar features combination. Please refer to [8] for detailed explanations about this table. The "Parametric" column indicates whether a language

---

[2] The message has been slightly simplified to fit in the size of the paper. See the console in Fig. 3 for the actual message.

supports parametric events, i.e. events carrying data. If so, "Comp. values" specify if *compound values* in parameters (e.g. records or lists) may be exploited. If quantification is supported, it may be *global*, i.e. the domain value of a quantified variable is defined as the values taken by this variable in a whole trace, or *local*, where the quantification domain may only depend on the current state. The "Ref. past data" column indicates whether it is possible to use parameters values of past events. We also consider if physical time ("wall-clock time") is supported at the language level, in which case specifications involving timing constraints are easier to express. Finally, the specification style of a language can be *declarative, operational*, or *mixed* between the two and offers the choice to the user. As shown in Table 1, PARTRAP supports a unique combination of these features, appropriate for our industrial context and motivated by the need for expressiveness. Other approaches, like [12], have similar goals as ours, and use a controlled natural language. However, the resulting language is domain specific and can not be applied to our industrial application.

Table 1. Comparison of PARTRAP with several temporal specification languages

Language	Parametric	Comp. values	Quantification	Ref. past data	Wall-clock time	Style
Dwyer's patterns [14], Propel [23], LTL$_f$ [6], CFLTL [21]	✗	n/a	n/a	n/a	✗	decl.
RSL [22], SALT [7], TLTL$_f$ [6]	✗	n/a	n/a	n/a	✓	decl.
EAGLE [2]	✓	✗	global	✓	✗	decl.
Stolz's Param. Prop. [24]	✓	✗	local	✗	✗	decl.
FO-LTL$^+$ [15]	✓	✓	local	✗	✗	decl.
MFOTL/MONPOLY [5,11]	✓	✗	global	✓	✓	decl.
JavaMOP [18]	✓	✗	global	✓	✗	mixed
QEA/MarQ [1,20], Mufin [13]	✓	✗	global	✓	✗	oper.
RULER [4], Logfire [16]	✓	✗	n/a	✓	✗	oper.
LOGSCOPE [3]	✓	✗	global	✗	✗	mixed
PARTRAP	✓	✓	local	✓	✓	decl.

3   Associated Toolset

ParTraP-IDE is a toolset designed to edit and execute the PARTRAP language directly on a set of trace files. Given a set of properties, the tool provides the set of traces violating them and an explanation of the error causes.

ParTraP-IDE relies on the Eclipse IDE and the XText framework[3]. Xtext provides a complete infrastructure including: parser, lexer, typechecker and a compiler generator. Figure 2 shows the ParTraP-IDE architecture. Part A presents how XText generates the toolset. Part B presents the usage of the tool.

---

[3] https://www.eclipse.org/Xtext/

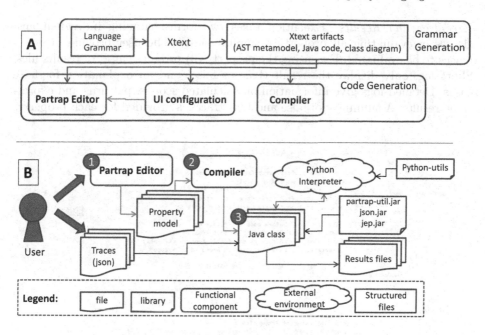

Fig. 2. Architecture of the PARTRAP toolset

3.1 Tool Generation (Part A of Fig. 2)

This section deals with the tool generation architecture (Part A). The PAR-TRAP Language grammar is defined in EBNF (XText's default grammar language). After being parsed, a set of language models is generated (AST metamodel, Java code and class diagram). These Xtext artifacts are used to configure the language editor and to generate a compiler that transforms each PAR-TRAP property to a Java monitor. When a large set of properties is considered, ParTraP-IDE allows to compute the whole set of properties at the same time. It is less time consuming than executing separate Java classes for each property.

3.2 ParTraP-IDE by Example (Part B of Fig. 2)

The PARTRAP *Editor.* (1) helps the user to write syntactically correct properties. The configured editor provides syntax coloring according to concepts (name, keyword, python script,..) as shown in Fig. 3 under the editor window. Python expressions are delimited by dollars signs ('$') as featured by property VAlidTemp2 in Fig. 3. Moreover, some validation constraints are enforced by the editor in order to forbid undesired language expressions like double use of property names or recursivity when referencing properties. Saving the file automatically calls the PARTRAP compiler (2) and produces the set of Java classes under package 'src-gen' (see project explorer in Fig. 3).

Execution and Results. Execution takes two forms: running individual java classes or evaluating all properties simultaneously. The user provides a set of traces to be evaluated. Executing the property (3) produces a set of results files. Short logs only display the result (true or false) and an explanation for false cases. Detailed logs give information on calculated scopes, patterns and expressions results. A summary of false and true traces is provided for each property.

Fig. 3. Screen capture of the environment

The example property presented in Sect. 2.1 is typed in the editor of Fig. 3 and named `VAlidTemp1`. When applied on the trace of Fig. 1, the console reports that one event having the temperature value '41.44' violates this property.

Python Expressions. Property `VAlidTemp2` is an alternate expression of the same property whose **where** clause is expressed in Python and uses the Python **math** module. As it is important for our envisioned users to define complex calculations in properties expressions, PARTRAP properties support the integration of Python expressions using declared Python libraries. As a consequence, the designed IDE allows the import of Python modules and the execution of Python scripts. This is made possible by the use of JEP (Java Embedded Python)[4] which is a Python package generating a jar file 'jep.jar' added in the Java build path to exchange data and scripts between the JVM and the Python Interpreter.

Performance. Although we traded performance off against expressiveness of the language, we carried out several experiments to check that the generated monitors featured sufficient performance in the context of our industrial partner,

---

[4] https://github.com/ninia/jep.

Table 2. Performance evaluation (times in seconds)

Property	100 traces	with Python	1 trace with 521 events	with Python
1	0.307	2.988	0.064	0.105
2	0.326	2.378	0.064	0.088
3	n/a	1.736	n/a	0.070
4	17.605	51.639	0.255	0.728
5	0.674	2.170	0.065	0.116
6	1.517	4.969	0.074	0.118

who typically collects and analyzes several dozens of traces every day. Therefore, we collected 100 traces from our partner[5]. The traces range from 304 to 1163 events, with an average of 530 events. We evaluated the 6 PARTRAP properties presented in Chapter 5 of [10]. These properties typically combine a scope with a temporal pattern. For each property, we constructed a variant whose **where** clause is expressed in Python (except property 3 which already has its assertion in Python). We led the experiments on a Windows 10 machine with an Intel(R) Core(TM) i7-6600U CPU @ 2.60 GHz, and 16 Go of RAM. Each experiment was performed 50 times and the average execution times are reported in Table 2.

Column 2 reports the time in milliseconds to evaluate the property on 100 traces. The 100 traces are covered in a few seconds for each property. Property 4 takes longer because it features a complex scope involving pairs of events. Column 3 reports on the same properties but with their **where** clause expressed in Python. Their evaluations are slower because of the extra cost of interactions between the java monitor and the Python interpreter.

Columns 4 and 5 report on the time needed to evaluate a property on a single trace. Actually, the initialisation of the monitor involves some overhead independently of the number of traces. Hence, we arbitrarily selected one of the traces whose length, 521 events, was close to the average length of our set. As expected, the average time to evaluate each property is significantly longer than one hundredth of the time of columns 2 or 3.

In summary, these experiments show that PARTRAP monitors perform well on traces provided by our partner. Most results are computed in less than one second, even if they involve Python assertions. These performances match the needs of our industrial partner. But further experiments should be led to evaluate how these performances scale up for much longer traces.

3.3 Example and Counter-Example Generator

To help software engineers understand or write PARTRAP formulae, we are working on a prototype that generates examples and counter-examples and lets

---

[5] These traces are not publicly available for confidentiality reasons.

engineers check that they match their intuition of the meaning of the formula. We use the Z3 SMT solver[6]. Its input is a script composed of declarations (constants or functions) and assertions. Z3 computes whether the current assertions are satisfiable or not, and gives a valuation of the variables, for satisfiable formulae.

We have defined the semantics of PARTRAP operators as Z3 functions. PAR-TRAP properties are translated as Z3 assertions which use these functions. Z3 then checks these assertions for satisfiability and, if possible, produces a trace satisfying the property. For example, the following Z3 assertion expresses property VAlidTemp1 (absence of temperature below 45 °C after the camera is connected).

```
(assert (afterFirst "CameraConnected"
            (absence_of_where "Temp" t (< (v1 t) 45.0))))
```

This property is satisfiable and the solver generates the following example, which trivially satisfies the property by avoiding `Temp` events.

```
[{"id": "CameraConnected", "time": 5263, "v1": 2.0},
 {"id": "C",               "time": 5264, "v1": 0.0},
 {"id": "CameraConnected", "time": 5853, "v1": 4.0},]
```

Counter-examples are generated by evaluating satisfiability of the negation of the property. In our example, it produces the following trace where a `Temp` event with low temperature (0.0) is generated after the `CameraConnected` event.

```
[{"id": "C",               "time": 8,    "v1": 5.0},
 {"id": "a",               "time": 9,    "v1": 7.0},
 {"id": "CameraConnected", "time": 2436, "v1": 2.0},
 {"id": "Temp",            "time": 2437, "v1": 0.0},]
```

This part of the tool is currently at a prototyping stage. It will be included in the PARTRAP distribution in the coming months. A major limitation of this tool is that it does not support Python expressions.

4   Conclusion

This paper has briefly presented PARTRAP and its associated toolset. PAR-TRAP is aimed at software engineers with poor knowledge of formal methods. Hence, we designed a keyword oriented language based on intuitive constructs such as Dwyer's patterns. We also integrated Python expressions in PAR-TRAP properties to give access to domain specific libraries. Moreover, the evaluation of PARTRAP expressions produces detailed logs to explain why a property was verified or failed. An examples and counter-examples generator is currently prototyped to help engineers understand the meaning of their formulae.

The companion video of this paper illustrates the main constructs of the language and shows how the toolset helps to edit them, generates Java monitors,

[6] https://github.com/Z3Prover/z3

evaluates properties and explains the result of their evaluation. The tool was successfully experimented on 6 properties evaluated on 100 traces of surgical operations, provided by our partner. Work in progress applies the tool to home automation traces. Future work will apply the tool to other medical devices.

References

1. Barringer, H., Falcone, Y., Havelund, K., Reger, G., Rydeheard, D.: Quantified event automata: towards expressive and efficient runtime monitors. In: Giannakopoulou, D., Méry, D. (eds.) FM 2012. LNCS, vol. 7436, pp. 68–84. Springer, Heidelberg (2012). https://doi.org/10.1007/978-3-642-32759-9_9
2. Barringer, H., Goldberg, A., Havelund, K., Sen, K.: Rule-based runtime verification. In: Steffen, B., Levi, G. (eds.) VMCAI 2004. LNCS, vol. 2937, pp. 44–57. Springer, Heidelberg (2004). https://doi.org/10.1007/978-3-540-24622-0_5
3. Barringer, H., Groce, A., Havelund, K., Smith, M.H.: Formal analysis of log files. JACIC 7(11), 365–390 (2010). https://doi.org/10.2514/1.49356
4. Barringer, H., Rydeheard, D.E., Havelund, K.: Rule systems for run-time monitoring: from Eagle to RuleR. J. Log. Comput. 20(3), 675–706 (2010). https://doi.org/10.1093/logcom/exn076
5. Basin, D.A., Klaedtke, F., Müller, S., Zalinescu, E.: Monitoring metric first-order temporal properties. J. ACM 62(2), 15 (2015). https://doi.org/10.1145/2699444
6. Bauer, A., Leucker, M., Schallhart, C.: Runtime verification for LTL and TLTL. ACM Trans. Softw. Eng. Methodol. 20(4), 14 (2011). https://doi.org/10.1145/2000799.2000800
7. Bauer, A., Leucker, M., Streit, J.: SALT—structured assertion language for temporal logic. In: Liu, Z., He, J. (eds.) ICFEM 2006. LNCS, vol. 4260, pp. 757–775. Springer, Heidelberg (2006). https://doi.org/10.1007/11901433_41
8. Blein, Y., Ledru, Y., du Bousquet, L., Groz, R.: Extending specification patterns for verification of parametric traces. In: Proceedings of the 6th Conference on Formal Methods in Software Engineering, FormaliSE 2018, collocated with ICSE 2018, Gothenburg, Sweden, 2 June 2018, pp. 10–19. ACM (2018). https://doi.org/10.1145/3193992.3193998
9. Blein, Y., Ledru, Y., du Bousquet, L., Groz, R., Clère, A., Bertrand, F.: MODMED WP1/D1: preliminary definition of a domain specific specification language. Technical report, LIG, MinMaxMedical, BlueOrtho (2017)
10. Blein, Y., Tabikh, M.A., Ledru, Y.: MODMED WP4/D1: test assessment - preliminary study and tool prototype. Technical report, LIG, MinMaxMedical, BlueOrtho (2017)
11. Basin, D., Harvan, M., Klaedtke, F., Zălinescu, E.: MONPOLY: monitoring usage-control policies. In: Khurshid, S., Sen, K. (eds.) RV 2011. LNCS, vol. 7186, pp. 360–364. Springer, Heidelberg (2012). https://doi.org/10.1007/978-3-642-29860-8_27
12. Calafato, A., Colombo, C., Pace, G.J.: A controlled natural language for tax fraud detection. In: Davis, B., Pace, G.J.J., Wyner, A. (eds.) CNL 2016. LNCS (LNAI), vol. 9767, pp. 1–12. Springer, Cham (2016). https://doi.org/10.1007/978-3-319-41498-0_1
13. Decker, N., Harder, J., Scheffel, T., Schmitz, M., Thoma, D.: Runtime monitoring with union-find structures. In: Chechik, M., Raskin, J.-F. (eds.) TACAS 2016. LNCS, vol. 9636, pp. 868–884. Springer, Heidelberg (2016). https://doi.org/10.1007/978-3-662-49674-9_54

14. Dwyer, M.B., Avrunin, G.S., Corbett, J.C.: Patterns in property specifications for finite-state verification. In: Boehm, B.W., Garlan, D., Kramer, J. (eds.) Proceedings of the 1999 International Conference on Software Engineering, ICSE 1999, Los Angeles, CA, USA, 16–22 May 1999, pp. 411–420. ACM (1999). https://doi.org/10.1145/302405.302672

15. Hallé, S., Villemaire, R.: Runtime monitoring of message-based workflows with data. In: 12th International IEEE Enterprise Distributed Object Computing Conference, ECOC 2008, Munich, Germany, 15–19 September 2008, pp. 63–72. IEEE Computer Society (2008). https://doi.org/10.1109/EDOC.2008.32

16. Havelund, K.: Rule-based runtime verification revisited. STTT **17**(2), 143–170 (2015). https://doi.org/10.1007/s10009-014-0309-2

17. Jackson, D., Wing, J.: Lightweight formal methods. ACM Comput. Surv. **28**(4), 121 (1996). https://doi.org/10.1145/242224.242380

18. Jin, D., Meredith, P.O., Lee, C., Rosu, G.: JavaMOP: efficient parametric runtime monitoring framework. In: Glinz, M., Murphy, G.C., Pezzè, M. (eds.) 34th International Conference on Software Engineering, ICSE 2012, Zurich, Switzerland, 2–9 June 2012, pp. 1427–1430. IEEE Computer Society (2012). https://doi.org/10.1109/ICSE.2012.6227231

19. Ledru, Y., Blein, Y., du Bousquet, L., Groz, R., Clère, A., Bertrand, F.: Requirements for a trace property language for medical devices. In: 2018 IEEE/ACM International Workshop on Software Engineering in Healthcare Systems, SEHS@ICSE 2018, Gothenburg, Sweden, 28 May 2018, pp. 30–33. ACM (2018). http://ieeexplore.ieee.org/document/8452638

20. Reger, G., Cruz, H.C., Rydeheard, D.: MARQ: monitoring at runtime with QEA. In: Baier, C., Tinelli, C. (eds.) TACAS 2015. LNCS, vol. 9035, pp. 596–610. Springer, Heidelberg (2015). https://doi.org/10.1007/978-3-662-46681-0_55

21. Regis, G., Degiovanni, R., D'Ippolito, N., Aguirre, N.: Specifying event-based systems with a counting fluent temporal logic. In: ICSE (1), pp. 733–743. IEEE Computer Society (2015). https://doi.org/10.1109/ICSE.2015.86

22. Reinkemeier, P., Stierand, I., Rehkop, P., Henkler, S.: A pattern-based requirement specification language: mapping automotive specific timing requirements. In: Reussner, R.H., Pretschner, A., Jähnichen, S. (eds.) Software Engineering 2011 - Workshopband (inkl. Doktorandensymposium), Fachtagung des GI-Fachbereichs Softwaretechnik, 21.-25.02.2011, Karlsruhe. LNI, vol. 184, pp. 99–108. GI (2011). http://subs.emis.de/LNI/Proceedings/Proceedings184/article6316.html

23. Smith, R.L., Avrunin, G.S., Clarke, L.A., Osterweil, L.J.: PROPEL: an approach supporting property elucidation. In: Proceedings of the 24th International Conference on Software Engineering, ICSE 2002, Orlando, Florida, USA, 19–25 May 2002, pp. 11–21 (2002). https://doi.org/10.1145/581339.581345

24. Stolz, V.: Temporal assertions with parametrised propositions. In: Sokolsky, O., Taşiran, S. (eds.) RV 2007. LNCS, vol. 4839, pp. 176–187. Springer, Heidelberg (2007). https://doi.org/10.1007/978-3-540-77395-5_15

Writing Domain-Specific Languages for BeepBeep

Sylvain Hallé[✉] and Raphaël Khoury

Laboratoire d'informatique formelle, Université du Québec à Chicoutimi,
Saguenay, Canada
shalle@acm.org

Abstract. This paper describes a plug-in extension of the BeepBeep 3 event stream processing engine. The extension allows one to write a custom grammar defining a particular specification language on event traces. A built-in interpreter can then convert expressions of the language into chains of BeepBeep processors through just a few lines of code, making it easy for users to create their own domain-specific languages.

1 Introduction

The field of Runtime Verification (RV) has seen a proliferation of specification languages over the years. Among the various formal notations that have been put forward, we can mention logic-based specifications such as LTL-FO$^+$ [16] and MFOTL [3]; automata-based specifications like DATE [6] and QEA [2]; stream-based languages like ArtiMon [20], Lola [7], Lustre [11] and TeSSLa [8]. Each specification language seems to have a "niche" of problem domains whose properties can be expressed more easily and more clearly than others. The recent trend towards the development of *domain-specific languages* (DSL) can be seen as a natural consequence of this observation. As its name implies, a DSL is a custom language, often with limited scope, whose syntax is designed to express properties of a particular nature in a succinct way.

Unfortunately, current RV tools are often implemented to evaluate expressions of a single language following a single grammar. They offer very few in the way of easily customizing their syntax to design arbitrary DSLs. In this respect, the BeepBeep event stream processor is designed differently, as it does not provide any imposed, built-in query language. However, a special extension to the system's core makes it possible for a user to define the grammar for a language of their choice, and to set up an interpreter that can build chains of processor objects for expressions of that language. In this paper, we describe the BeepBeep DSL plug-in, and illustrate its purpose by showing how to build interpreters allowing BeepBeep to read and evaluate specifications of multiple existing specification languages.

© Springer Nature Switzerland AG 2018
C. Colombo and M. Leucker (Eds.): RV 2018, LNCS 11237, pp. 447–457, 2018.
https://doi.org/10.1007/978-3-030-03769-7_27

2   An Overview of BeepBeep 3

BeepBeep 3 is an event stream processing engine implemented as an open source Java library.[1] It is organized around the concept of *processors*. In a nutshell, a processor is a basic unit of computation that receives one or more event traces as its input, and produces one or more event traces as its output. BeepBeep's core library provides a handful of generic processor objects performing basic tasks over traces; they can be represented graphically as boxes with input/output "pipes", as is summarized in Fig. 1.

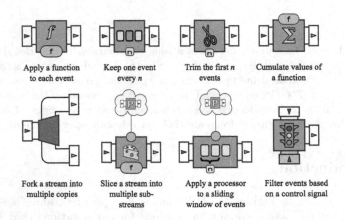

Fig. 1. BeepBeep's basic processors.

In order to create custom computations over event traces, BeepBeep allows processors to be *composed*; this means that the output of a processor can be redirected to the input of another, creating complex processor chains. Events can either be *pushed* through the inputs of a chain, or *pulled* from the outputs, and BeepBeep takes care of managing implicit input and output event queues for each processor. In addition, users also have the freedom of creating their own custom processors and functions, by extending the `Processor` and `Function` objects, respectively. Extensions of BeepBeep with predefined custom objects are called *palettes*; there exist palettes for various purposes, such as signal processing, XML manipulation, plotting, and finite-state machines.

Over the past few years, BeepBeep has been involved in a variety of case studies [4,13–15,19,21], and provides built-in support for multi-threading [17]. For a complete description of BeepBeep, the reader is referred to a recent tutorial [12] or to BeepBeep's detailed user manual [1].

3   The DSL Palette

Like many other extensions, BeepBeep's DSL capabilities come in the form of an auxiliary JAR library (a *palette*) for creating languages and parsing expressions.

---

[1] https://liflab.github.io/beepbeep-3.

It can be freely downloaded from the palette repository[2]. This palette provides a special object for creating domain-specific languages called the `Grammar-ObjectBuilder`. The operation of the `GrammarObjectBuilder` can be summarized as follows: (1) The object builder is given the syntactical rules of the language in the form of a Backus-Naur grammar; this grammar must be LL(k), a limitation imposed by the underlying parsing library. (2) Given an expression of the language as a character string, the object builder parses the expression according to the grammar and produces a parsing tree. (3) The builder then performs a postfix traversal of the tree and progressively builds the object represented by the expression.

We shall illustrate the operation of the `GrammarObjectBuilder` using a very simple example, and then show how it has been used to implement interpreters for various existing languages. The first step consists of defining the grammar for the targeted language and expressing it in Backus-Naur Form (BNF). In our simple example, suppose the language only supports a few constructs: filtering, comparing numbers with the greater-than operator, summing numbers, and referring to an input stream by a number. A possible way to organize these functionalities into a language would be the small grammar shown in Fig. 2a. Given such a grammar, an expression like "FILTER (INPUT 0) ON ((INPUT 1) GT (INPUT 0))" is syntactically correct; parsing it results in the tree shown in Fig. 2b.

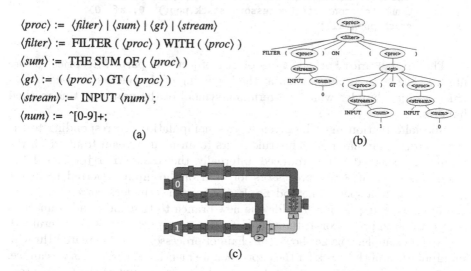

⟨*proc*⟩ := ⟨*filter*⟩ | ⟨*sum*⟩ | ⟨*gt*⟩ | ⟨*stream*⟩

⟨*filter*⟩ := FILTER (⟨*proc*⟩) WITH (⟨*proc*⟩)

⟨*sum*⟩ := THE SUM OF (⟨*proc*⟩)

⟨*gt*⟩ := (⟨*proc*⟩) GT (⟨*proc*⟩)

⟨*stream*⟩ := INPUT ⟨*num*⟩ ;

⟨*num*⟩ := ^[0-9]+;

(a)

(b)

(c)

Fig. 2. (a) A simple grammar; (b) the parsing tree for the expression "FILTER (INPUT 0) ON ((INPUT 1) GT (INPUT 0))"; (c) the chain of processors created by the `GrammarObjectBuilder` from this expression.

---

[2] https://github.com/liflab/beepbeep-3-palettes/.

The next step is to create a new interpreter, which extends Grammar-ObjectBuilder and implements handler methods for the various symbols of the grammar. The parsing tree is traversed in postfix fashion using the Visitor design pattern; Java objects are pushed and pulled from a persistent stack. By default, the GrammarObjectBuilder treats any terminal symbol of the tree as a character string. Therefore, when visiting a leaf of the parsing tree, the builder puts on its stack a String object whose value is the contents of that specific literal. When visiting a parse node that corresponds to a non-terminal token, such as <gt>, the builder looks for a method that handles this symbol. "Handling" a symbol generally means popping objects from the stack, creating one or more new objects, and pushing some of them back onto the stack.

Let us start with a simple case, that of the <gt> symbol. When a <gt> node is visited in the parsing tree, as per the postfix traversal we described earlier, we know that the top of the stack contains two strings with the constants that were parsed earlier. The task of the handler method is to create a new processor evaluating the "greater than" function, pipe into the inputs of this processor the two objects popped from the stack, and push this new processor back onto the stack. Therefore, we can create a method called handleGt that reads as follows:

```
@Builds(rule="<gt>")
public void handleGt(ArrayDeque<Object> stack) {
  ApplyFunction af = new ApplyFunction(Numbers.greaterThan);
  Connector.connect((Processor) stack.pop(), 0, af, 1);
  Connector.connect((Processor) stack.pop(), 0, af, 0);
  stack.push(af);
}
```

The ApplyFunction and Connector objects are part of BeepBeep's core library. The Builds annotation at the beginning of the method is used to signal the object builder what non-terminal symbol of the grammar this method handles.

Special attention must be given to the manipulations corresponding to the <stream> grammar rule. This rule refers to an input stream from which the events are expected to be produced. Internally, the GrammarObjectBuilder maintains a set of Fork processors for each of the inputs referred to in the query. A call to a special method forkInput fetches the fork corresponding to the input pipe at position n, adds one new branch to that fork, and connects a Passthrough processor at the end of it. This Passthrough is then returned.

As an example, Fig. 2c shows the chain of processor objects created through manipulations of the stack for the expression we mentioned earlier. As we can see, the GrammarObjectBuilder takes care of a good amount of the tedious task of parsing a string and performing specific actions for each non-terminal symbol of a grammar. In the example shown here, a complete running interpreter for expressions of the language can be obtained for 6 lines of BNF grammar and 30 lines of Java code[3]. With some experience, such an interpreter can be written in a few minutes.

4   Extending Existing Specification Languages

The example shown in the previous section is only meant to illustrate the operation of the `GrammarObjectBuilder` through a very simple case. Several features available in the DSL palette have been left out due to lack of space. For instance, the `GrammarObjectBuilder` can also be used to build Beep-Beep's `Function` objects instead of processors, and additional annotations can be appended to handler methods in order to further simplify the manipulations of the object stack.[4]

Obviously, the syntax of the language does not need to look like the example we have shown earlier, and it is not necessary to impose a one-to-one correspondence between grammar rules and BeepBeep's `Processor` objects. A single rule can spawn and push on the stack as many objects as one wishes, making it possible for a short grammatical construct to represent a potentially complex chain of processors. In the following, we briefly describe interpreters for three existing languages that have been implemented using BeepBeep's DSL palette. In all three cases, additional functionalities have been included into the original language "for free", by taking advantage of BeepBeep's available palettes and generic event model. All the interpreters described in this section are freely available online.[5]

4.1   Linear Temporal Logic

The four basic operators of Linear Temporal Logic ($\mathbf{F}$, $\mathbf{G}$, $\mathbf{X}$ and $\mathbf{U}$) can easily be accommodated by a simple LTL palette that was already discussed in Beep-Beep's original tutorial [12, Sect. 5.1]. The grammar and stack manipulations for handling these operators, as well as Boolean connectives, are straightforward and result in an interpreter with around 50 lines of Java code. We shall rather focus on the extensions to that have been added to the original LTL by leveraging BeepBeep's architecture.

Arbitrary Ground Terms. Special syntactical rules for ground terms can be added to LTL's syntax, depending on the underlying trace's type. For example, if events in a trace are made of numeric values, the ground terms of the language can be defined as arithmetic operations over numbers (many of which are already included in BeepBeep's core); if events are XML or JSON documents, ground terms can be XPath or JPath expressions fetching fragments of these events, using BeepBeep's XML and JSON palettes, respectively.

---

[3] The code for the interpreter can be found in the BeepBeep example repository: https://liflab.github.io/beepbeep-3-examples/classdsl_1_1_simple_processor _builder.html.

[4] More details can be found in Chap. 8 of BeepBeep's user manual [1].

[5] https://github.com/liflab/beepbeep-3-polyglot.

First-order Quantification. BeepBeep's Slice processor performs exactly the equivalent of LTL-FO$^+$'s first-order quantifiers. This places the expressiveness of BeepBeep 3's LTL interpreter to the level of its ancestor, BeepBeep 1 [16].

New Operators. Additional temporal operators can easily be defined as new Processor objects and added to LTL's syntax. As an example, our LTL interpreter adds an operator **C**, which counts the number of times a formula is true on a given stream. For example, the expression **G** $(\neg c\, \mathbf{U}\, (\mathbf{C}\, (a \wedge \mathbf{X} b) = 3)$ expresses the fact that c cannot hold until a has been immediately followed by b three times.

4.2   Quantified Event Automata

Quantified Event Automata (QEAs) is the formalism used by the MarQ runtime monitor [2]. BeepBeep has a palette called FSM that allows users to define generalized Moore Machines, whose expressiveness is similar to QEAs. In its current version, MarQ does not provide an input language, and QEAs need to be built programmatically using Java objects. Our interpreter proposes a tentative syntax, shown in Fig. 3, reminiscent of the Graphviz library for drawing graphs [10].

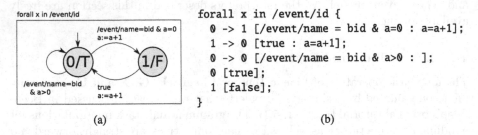

```
forall x in /event/id {
    0 -> 1 [/event/name = bid & a=0 : a=a+1];
    1 -> 0 [true : a=a+1];
    0 -> 0 [/event/name = bid & a>0 : ];
    0 [true];
    1 [false];
}
```

(a)   (b)

Fig. 3. A simple QEA with two states (a); a textual notation that defines the same automaton (b).

The quantifier part of the QEA is taken care of by BeepBeep's Slice processor. The interpreter for this language is interesting in that the postfix traversal of the parsing tree does not create a chain of processors, but rather updates a single MooreMachine object (itself a descendant of Processor) with new transitions; the Moore machine is repeatedly popped and pushed on the stack at each new transition. The interpreter also generalizes the original QEAs in a few ways.

Event Types. As with the LTL interpreter, the syntax for fetching event content is type-dependent. The code example above shows that quantifiers and guards on transitions are written as XPath conditions, suitable for events in the XML format.

State Symbols. Since the automaton is a Moore machine, each state can be set to output a symbol when visited. Moreover, this symbol does not need to be a Boolean value. The quantifier part of the automaton is actually an aggregation function over the set of the last symbols output by each instance of the automaton; the `forall` statement is the special case of conjunction over Boolean values. For instance, one can associate a number to each state, and compute the sum of these numbers as the output of the quantified automaton.

4.3 LOLA

Our last example is an interpreter for version 1.0 of LOLA, which is the specification language for the tool of the same name [7]. A LOLA specification is a set of equations over typed stream variables. Figure 4 shows an example of such a specification, taken from the original paper, and summarizing most of the language's features. It defines ten streams, based on three independent variables t_1, t_2 and t_3. A stream expression may involve the value of a previously defined stream. The values of the streams corresponding to s_1 to s_6 are obtained by evaluating their defining expressions place-wise at each position.

$$s_1 = t_1 \vee (t_3 \leq 1)$$
$$s_2 = ((t_3)^2 + 7) \mod 15$$
$$s_3 = \text{ite}(s_3; s_4; s_4 + 1)$$
$$s_4 = \text{ite}(t_1; t_3 \leq s_4; \neg s_3)$$
$$s_5 = t_1[+1; \text{false}]$$
$$s_6 = s_9[-1; 0] + (t_3 \mod 2)$$

Fig. 4. An example of a LOLA specification showing various features of the language.

Using the DSL palette, the complete BeepBeep interpreter for LOLA 1.0 has less than 100 lines of Java code. Since the original LOLA language corresponds to a subset of BeepBeep's existing processors and features, we proceeded as in the previous examples and added a few new features to it.

Generalized Offset. The original LOLA construct $s[n, c]$ denotes the value of stream s, offset by n events from the current position, with n a fixed integer. In contrast, the construction of $s[x, c]$ in BeepBeep accepts constructs of the form $s[ax + n, c]$, where x is the index of the current position in the stream and $a, n \in \mathbb{N}$.

Filtering and Non-Uniform Processors. In LOLA, every stream is expected to be *uniform*: exactly one output is produced for each input. In BeepBeep however, processors do not need to be uniform. One example is the `Filter` processor, which may discard events from its input trace based on a condition. We can hence create the LOLA construct "filter φ on ψ", where φ and ψ are two arbitrary stream expressions (with ψ of Boolean type). For example, to let out only events that are positive, one can write filter t on $t > 0$.

Scoping and Sub-streams. LOLA lacks a scoping mechanism for defining streams. If the same kind of processing (requiring intermediate streams) must be done on multiple input streams, this processing must be repeated for each input stream. Moreover, since stream specifications all live in the same global scope, intermediate streams must be given different names to avoid clashes. Our extended version of LOLA provides a new construct, called define, that allows a user to create a processing chain and encapsulate it as a named object with parameters. Consider the following specification:

$$\text{define } \$p(x_1, x_2)$$
$$y_1 = \text{ite}(x_1 < x_2, x_2[1,0], x_2)$$
$$y_2 = \text{ite}(x_2 < x_1, x_2[-1,0], x_1)$$
$$\text{out} = x_1 + x_2$$
$$\text{end define}$$
$$s_1 = \$p(t_1, t_2)$$
$$s_2 = \$p(t_2, t_3)$$

It starts with a define block, which creates a new template stream called p, which takes two input streams called x_1 and x_2. The next two lines define two intermediate streams, and the last specifies the output of p, using the reserved stream name *out*. From then on, p can be used in an expression wherever a stream name is accepted. The next two lines show how streams s_1 and s_2 are defined by applying p to the input stream pairs (t_1, t_2) and (t_2, t_3), respectively. Streams y_1 and y_2 exist only in the local scope of p.

Generalized Windows. User-defined blocks open the way to generic sliding window processors. Version 2.0 of LOLA already supports classical aggregation functions over a sliding window, such as sum or average. In contrast, BeepBeep provides a generic Window processor, which can make a window out of any event trace and apply any processor to the contents of the window. Moreover, this window can be set as the input of an arbitrary chain of other processors, and receive input from an arbitrary chain of other processors. We can therefore create the generalized construct "window($p(s)$,n)". Here, p can be any sub-stream name, defined according to the syntax described above.

4.4   Additional Features

In addition to BeepBeep's core processors and functions, functionalities of external palettes can also be added to an interpreter. For example, new grammatical constructs can be defined to use the Signal palette, which provides a peak-finding processor on an incoming stream of numerical values. Should these extensions prove insufficient, we remind the reader that any other extension can also be designed by creating new processors and functions, and adding them to an interpreter through the means described in this paper. Therefore, BeepBeep is a convenient testbed for trying out new monitoring features, while leveraging the existing syntax of another language.

One last feature of BeepBeep's DSL palette is the possibility to mix multiple languages in the same specification. Case in point, we compiled a "multi-interpreter", called *Polyglot*, which is able to read specifications from input files, and to dispatch them to the proper interpreter instance based on the file extension. If multiple files are specified, the output of processor chain built from file n is piped into the input of processor chain built from file $n+1$. It is therefore possible to call the multi-interpreter from the command line as follows:

```
$ java -jar polyglot.jar spec1.qea spec2.lola spec3.ltl
```

This would in effect evaluate a specification that is a mix of a QEA, piped into a set of LOLA equations, whose output is sent to an LTL formula. To the best of our knowledge, BeepBeep's Polyglot extension is one of few tools that provides such a flexible way of accepting specifications.[6]

5   Conclusion

In this paper, we have seen how an extension of the BeepBeep event stream processing engine allows a user to easily define the syntax and construction rules for arbitrary domain-specific languages. The DSL palette provides facilities for parsing expressions according to a grammar, and takes care of many tedious tasks related to the processing of the parsing tree. Combined with BeepBeep's generic streaming model and large inventory of available processors and functions, we have seen how the DSL palette also makes it possible to write interpreters for a variety of *existing* specification languages, and even add new features to them. In the future, the performance of these interpreters should be compared with the original tools.

References

1. Event stream processing with BeepBeep 3. https://liflab.gitbooks.io/event-stream-processing-with-beepbeep-3
2. Barringer, H., Falcone, Y., Havelund, K., Reger, G., Rydeheard, D.: Quantified event automata: towards expressive and efficient runtime monitors. In: Giannakopoulou, D., Méry, D. (eds.) FM 2012. LNCS, vol. 7436, pp. 68–84. Springer, Heidelberg (2012). https://doi.org/10.1007/978-3-642-32759-9_9
3. Basin, D.A., Klaedtke, F., Müller, S., Zalinescu, E.: Monitoring metric first-order temporal properties. J. ACM 62(2), 15:1–15:45 (2015). https://doi.org/10.1145/2699444
4. Boussaha, M.R., Khoury, R., Hallé, S.: Monitoring of security properties using BeepBeep. In: Imine, A., Fernandez, J.M., Marion, J.-Y., Logrippo, L., Garcia-Alfaro, J. (eds.) FPS 2017. LNCS, vol. 10723, pp. 160–169. Springer, Cham (2018). https://doi.org/10.1007/978-3-319-75650-9_11

[6] The other being MOP [5], which also handles specifications in multiple languages.

5. Chen, F., Rosu, G.: Mop: an efficient and generic runtime verification framework. In: Gabriel, R.P., Bacon, D.F., Lopes, C.V., Jr., G.L.S. (eds.) Proceedings of the 22nd Annual ACM SIGPLAN Conference on Object-Oriented Programming, Systems, Languages, and Applications, OOPSLA 2007, 21–25 October 2007, Montreal, Quebec, Canada, pp. 569–588. ACM (2007). https://doi.org/10.1145/1297027.1297069

6. Colombo, C., Pace, G.J.: Runtime verification using LARVA. In: Reger, G., Havelund, K. (eds.) An International Workshop on Competitions, Usability, Benchmarks, Evaluation, and Standardisation for Runtime Verification Tools, RV-CuBES 2017, vol. 3, 15 September 2017, Seattle, WA, USA, pp. 55–63. Kalpa Publications in Computing. EasyChair (2017). http://www.easychair.org/publications/paper/Jwmr

7. D'Angelo, B., et al.: LOLA: runtime monitoring of synchronous systems. In: 12th International Symposium on Temporal Representation and Reasoning (TIME 2005), 23–25 June 2005, Burlington, Vermont, USA, pp. 166–174. IEEE Computer Society (2005). https://doi.org/10.1109/TIME.2005.26

8. Decker, N., et al.: Rapidly adjustable non-intrusive online monitoring for multi-core systems. In: Cavalheiro, S., Fiadeiro, J. (eds.) SBMF 2017. LNCS, vol. 10623, pp. 179–196. Springer, Cham (2017). https://doi.org/10.1007/978-3-319-70848-5_12

9. Falcone, Y., Sánchez, C. (eds.): RV 2016. LNCS, vol. 10012. Springer, Cham (2016). https://doi.org/10.1007/978-3-319-46982-9

10. Gansner, E.R., Koutsofios, E., North, S.: Drawing graphs with dot (2015). http://www.graphviz.org/pdf/dotguide.pdf

11. Halbwachs, N., Lagnier, F., Ratel, C.: Programming and verifying real-time systems by means of the synchronous data-flow language LUSTRE. IEEE Trans. Software Eng. 18(9), 785–793 (1992)

12. Hallé, S.: When RV meets CEP. In: Falcone, Y., Sánchez, C. (eds.) RV 2016. LNCS, vol. 10012, pp. 68–91. Springer, Cham (2016). https://doi.org/10.1007/978-3-319-46982-9_6

13. Hallé, S., Gaboury, S., Bouchard, B.: Activity recognition through complex event processing: First findings. In: Bouchard, B., Giroux, S., Bouzouane, A., Gaboury, S. (eds.) Artificial Intelligence Applied to Assistive Technologies and Smart Environments, Papers from the 2016 AAAI Workshop, Phoenix, Arizona, USA, 12 February 2016, AAAI Workshops, vol. WS-16-01. AAAI Press (2016). http://www.aaai.org/ocs/index.php/WS/AAAIW16/paper/view/12561

14. Hallé, S., Gaboury, S., Bouchard, B.: Towards user activity recognition through energy usage analysis and complex event processing. In: Proceedings of the 9th ACM International Conference on PErvasive Technologies Related to Assistive Environments, PETRA 2016, Corfu Island, Greece, 29 June–1 July 2016, p. 3. ACM (2016). http://dl.acm.org/citation.cfm?id=2910707

15. Hallé, S., Gaboury, S., Khoury, R.: A glue language for event stream processing. In: Joshi, J., et al. (eds.) 2016 IEEE International Conference on Big Data, BigData 2016, Washington DC, USA, 5–8 December 2016, pp. 2384–2391. IEEE (2016). https://doi.org/10.1109/BigData.2016.7840873

16. Hallé, S., Villemaire, R.: Runtime enforcement of web service message contracts with data. IEEE Trans. Services Comput. 5(2), 192–206 (2012). https://doi.org/10.1109/TSC.2011.10

17. Hallé, S., Khoury, R., Gaboury, S.: Event stream processing with multiple threads. In: Lahiri, S., Reger, G. (eds.) RV 2017. LNCS, vol. 10548, pp. 359–369. Springer, Cham (2017). https://doi.org/10.1007/978-3-319-67531-2_22

18. Lahiri, S., Reger, G. (eds.): RV 2017. LNCS, vol. 10548. Springer, Cham (2017). https://doi.org/10.1007/978-3-319-67531-2
19. Khoury, R., Hallé, S., Waldmann, O.: Execution trace analysis using LTL-FO$^+$. In: Margaria, T., Steffen, B. (eds.) ISoLA 2016. LNCS, vol. 9953, pp. 356–362. Springer, Cham (2016). https://doi.org/10.1007/978-3-319-47169-3_26
20. Rapin, N.: Reactive property monitoring of hybrid systems with aggregation. In: Falcone, Y., Sánchez, C. (eds.) RV 2016. LNCS, vol. 10012, pp. 447–453. Springer, Cham (2016). https://doi.org/10.1007/978-3-319-46982-9_28
21. Varvaressos, S., Lavoie, K., Gaboury, S., Hallé, S.: Automated bug finding in video games: A case study for runtime monitoring. Comput. Entertain. **15**(1), 1:1–1:28 (2017). https://doi.org/10.1145/2700529

A Framework for Non-intrusive Trace-driven Simulation of Manycore Architectures with Dynamic Tracing Configuration

Jasmin Jahic[1]([✉]), Matthias Jung[1], Thomas Kuhn[1], Claus Kestel[2], and Norbert Wehn[2]

[1] Fraunhofer IESE, Fraunhofer-Platz 1, Kaiserslautern, Germany
{jasmin.jahic,matthias.jung,thomas.kuhn}@iese.fraunhofer.de
[2] Microelectronic Systems Design Research Group, University of Kaiserslautern, Erwin-Schroedinger-Strasse 1, Kaiserslautern, Germany
{kestel,wehn}@eit.uni-kl.de

Abstract. Traditional software testing methods are inefficient for multithreaded software. In order to verify such software, testing is often complemented by analysis of the execution trace. To monitor the execution trace, most approaches today use binary instrumentation or rigid frameworks based on system simulators. Most existing approaches are intrusive, as they tend to change the monitored software. Furthermore, their monitoring configuration is static, resulting in huge, often non-relevant, traces. In this paper, we present a light, non-intrusive execution monitoring and control approach, implemented using the *gem5* system simulator. We complement existing approaches with dynamic configuration of the monitoring, making it possible to dynamically change the monitoring focus to the parts of the software that are of interest. This configuration results in reduced execution trace size. Our approach does not change the software under test, but rather the virtual platform that executes the software.

Keywords: Runtime verification · Execution monitoring · Data race gem5 · Lockset

1 Introduction

Runtime verification is the process of checking whether an execution trace satisfies a specification. For multithreaded software, runtime verification (*RV*) executes software and performs analysis on the execution trace (e.g., *Happens-before* [17] and *Lockset* [27] algorithms) to find concurrency bugs.

Existing execution monitoring approaches can be roughly classified into three groups: (1) approaches that use specialized hardware [1] and those that are implemented near hardware [32], (2) approaches that use virtual platforms, and

© Springer Nature Switzerland AG 2018
C. Colombo and M. Leucker (Eds.): RV 2018, LNCS 11237, pp. 458–468, 2018.
https://doi.org/10.1007/978-3-030-03769-7_28

(3) simple intrusive techniques that instrument the target program (i.e., at the source, intermediate representation, or binary level) and produce an execution trace as the program executes (e.g., *PIN* [20], *Valgrind* [24]). Hardware-based techniques are often non-intrusive, but require specialized hardware and a complex setup. Virtual-platform-based approaches enable fast prototyping and execution of a program on a virtual target platform, but often instrument software at the source code level [8,14,25]. Software instrumentation introduces probe effects, as explained by Song and Lee [29]. These instrumentation operations can perturb program execution in two ways. First, the execution of the additional instrumentation instructions can delay the occurrence of an execution event. As a consequence, the interacting time with other threads and with the external environment can change. Second, due to the changes in the timing of invoking guarded resources and critical sections, scheduling decisions can be different. The second effect is critical for embedded systems because they often try to predict the execution time of threads to ensure a strict scheduling order between them, and use scheduling as an implicit synchronization mechanism [13]. In order to resolve these challenges, in this paper we present our framework for *non-intrusive* monitoring of multithreaded and other complex software, to avoid probe effects. Instead of changing the monitored software, we change the virtual platform on which the software executes. Our framework provides additional features that enable dynamic monitoring configuration, and it relates the monitored instructions to the source code information in cases where debug information exists. Dynamic, online configuration of monitoring enables us to choose which instructions to trace during the execution and reduces the execution trace size. The price to pay for non-intrusiveness is obviously the overhead due to the simulation of virtual hardware. The framework is based on the *gem5* system simulator [5], using the syscall execution (*SE*) mode. However, the presented approach is not limited on the gem5 simulator and can be employed on similar processor simulators. We evaluated our approach using the *SPLASH-2* [31] and *TACLeBench* [9] benchmarks. The results show that the dynamic monitoring configuration can significantly reduce the size of the execution trace as well as the tracing overhead.

The paper is organized as follows. Section 2 describes related work in the areas of execution monitoring and provides more details about the *gem5* system simulator. Section 3 describes the abstract concept of our approach. Section 4 describes the design and the implementation of our approach with the *gem5* system simulator. In Sect. 5, we present our evaluation results. We explain the advantages of our approach and conclude in Sect. 6.

2 Related Work

2.1 Monitoring an Execution Trace

In time-triggered runtime verification (*TTRV*), the monitor runs in parallel with the system under inspection and reads the system state at a fixed frequency for property evaluation [7]. Such a monitor ensures bounded overhead and time-predictable intervention in the system execution, but risks missing some events in cases of low polling frequency [22]. The conventional monitoring approach in *RV* is event-triggered, which can lead to unpredictable monitoring overhead and potentially to bursts of monitoring invocations at run time, but has the advantage of capturing all configured events.

Some approaches instrument a program at the source code level [2,23] and at the intermediate level [3,4,10,18,30]. On binary level, *PIN* [20] tool, for example, re-compiles the target binary using a just-in-time (*JIT*) compiler, adds new instructions, and runs the modified binary. *Valgrind* [24], another well-known tool, also uses a *JIT* compiler, but re-compiles the binary's machine code, one small code block at a time. The instrumentation is a straightforward, but error-prone approach for monitoring execution traces, with probe effects [29] being the main challenge, as mentioned in the introduction.

RACEZ [28] is a classical example of a non-intrusive monitoring that requires hardware performance monitoring unit to sample memory accesses. *HARD* [32] is an implementation of a monitoring approach in hardware. It uses a bloom filter [6] and augments cache lines with additional bits to record the memory states. *R2U2* [21] implements monitoring on dedicated FPGA hardware and traces the values of the variables passed over the system bus. In vehicles, traces are often obtained through passive observation of the data within the CAN messages being broadcast between system components [15]. There already exist approaches for monitoring execution traces based on the *gem5* system simulator ([8,12,14,25]). However, their focus is either on fast performance exploration of hardware, or requires software instrumentation. Besides, these approaches do not relate machine instructions to source code symbols. Our approach is not intrusive, it does not disturb the relative execution order between threads, and therefore avoids probe effects. We relate raw machine instructions with the source code to provide enough information for finding the origin of a bug.

2.2   The gem5 System Simulator

The most mature cycle-accurate open source system simulator is the *gem5* framework, which is a modular platform for computer-system architecture research [5]. Each CPU model supports multiple instruction set architectures, including Alpha, x86, ARM, and RISCV. The provided CPU models can simulate the execution of software in either one of two modes:

- The *Systemcall Emulation* (SE) mode executes simple Linux applications without the need for modeling peripheral devices and an operating system. Whenever an application performs a system call, gem5 emulates an operating system by handling this system call internally. In most cases, gem5 will forward the system call to the host operating system. In comparison to abstract simulators like QEMU the core model still represents the real hardware architecture.

– The *Full-System* (FS) mode executes both kernel-level and user-level code. In this mode, gem5 models all the peripheral devices. This is similar to a bare-metal execution on real hardware.

The semantics of the gem5 simulator is a discrete event model, similar to the ones provided in SystemC [11] or FERAL [16]. A discrete event model uses the concept of an event queue in combination with a two-dimensional time in order to deterministically simulate concurrent processes in a sequential executing simulation engine. The event queue sorts the events in time denoted in ticks (1 tick = 1 ps). After the initialization of the simulator has been performed, the discrete event model picks the first event in the queue and updates the current simulation time to match the time of this event. During the execution of an event, new events are created (either in the future or maybe for the current simulation time). New events are insertion-sorted into the event queue based on their tick. Events generated with the same tick as the current simulation time will thus happen after any existing events at this simulation time, which is therefore called two-dimensional time or delta-cycling. If there are no pending events in the event queue for the current simulation time, the current simulation time is advanced to the next event in the queue.

3 Non-intrusive Trace-driven Simulation of Manycore Architectures

In order to monitor the execution, instead of modifying the target software, we modify the system simulator. We introduce two components, an *interceptor* and a *controller*, along the system simulator's work-flow to monitor the execution and to perform online changes of the *interceptor* monitoring configuration. Our approach enables online configuration of the *interceptor* so that it intercepts only specified instructions, without inspecting all instructions. In order to achieve this, we incorporate the execution control of the system simulator and the *controller* into the *FERAL* framework [16]. *FERAL* stands for Framework for Efficient simulator coupling on Requirements and Architecture Level. It enables the integration of specialized and focused simulators with heterogeneous models of computation and communication into one holistic simulation scenario. *FERAL* manages the system simulator and the *controller* as simulation components (Fig. 1).

The *interceptor* module consists of changes introduced to the system simulator and is fully located within the system simulator. Its configuration contains identifiers of instructions that should be intercepted and is responsible for interrupting the system simulator's regular execution flow. The *interceptor* exists in the form of probes located within virtual hardware components. After an instruction is fully executed, the interceptor probes contain enough information to relate the respective instruction to the source code. The *controller* is responsible for handling the instruction reported from the *interceptor* (i.e., control procedures). *Controller* procedures are responsible for recording execution traces, performing analysis (e.g., *Lockset algorithm*), and making online changes to the monitoring configuration of the *interceptor*.

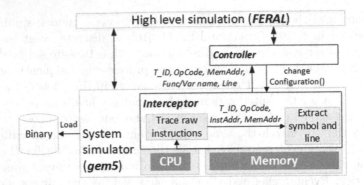

Fig. 1. Simulation framework concept overview. The *Interceptor* intercepts raw instruction data from *gem5*: thread id(*T_ID*), operation code (*OpCode*), instruction address (*InstAddr*), and memory address (*MemAddr*).

3.1   Non-intrusive Monitoring of Raw Data

A system simulator consists of software components that match the logical functionality of the simulated hardware (Fig. 1). These components execute distinct software procedures, for different instruction *operation types*. During software procedures for reading from memory (i.e., *LOAD* instructions) and writing to memory (*STORE* instructions), the probes directly extract the target memory addresses. Depending on a probe's location, it also has information about a memory *operation type*. Besides this information, probes also record an *instruction's memory address* located in the program counter (*instAddr*). The raw data record collected by the probes consists of *thread ID*, *instAddr*, instruction *operation type*, and accessed *memory location*.

The configuration of the *interceptor* consists of activating probes at software procedures of simulated hardware components and setting instruction identifiers defining the instructions to be intercepted. An instruction identifier can be generic, such as an instruction type (e.g., *LOAD*), in which case the *interceptor* would intercept all instructions of the same type. In the default case, the *interceptor* reacts to memory manipulation instructions (e.g., *LOAD*, *STORE*), function calls, and branching instructions. When the *interceptor* detects that an instruction matches an identifier, it calls a *controller procedure*, which, for example, records the instruction in the execution trace and continues with the execution.

3.2   Relating Raw Trace Data to the Source Code

A compiler can generate debug information together with the machine code, which represents the relation between the machine code and the source code.

For binaries in Executable and Linkable Format (*ELF*), the common debugging data format is *DWARF*. The debugging format defines the debugging sections and their attributes. For example, a section contains *DW_AT_low_pc*, a program-counter value for the beginning of the function. Relating raw instruction data records to debug data is enabled via instruction memory addresses. However, it is a computationally demanding task. The configuration of the *interceptor* supports focused monitoring by dynamically activating probes at software procedures of simulated hardware components.

4 Design and Implementation

Applications in *gem5* SE mode are running directly on the virtual hardware, so *gem5* has to take over the thread management. Every thread is directly mapped to one virtual core [26]. The tracing of raw data is an existing feature in *gem5*, but forces us to react to every processed instruction and only when all raw data is recorded. Therefore, we have changed *gem5* to improve control of the monitoring. During execution, *gem5* handles instructions based on their type (i.e., operation code). *gem5* handles each type in a separate function. Inside each handling function, we implemented monitoring probes (Figure 2). Before reaching *postExecute*, we can, based on the information from our probes, decide what to do with the executing instruction.

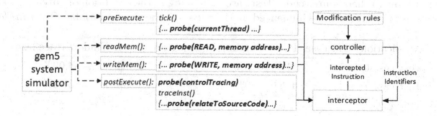

Fig. 2. Implementation of the concept in the gem5 system simulator.

In order to retrieve the function name of the current function call, we relate the current instruction address from the program counter to the debug infor-mation. Once *main* is reached, for memory *LOAD* and *STORE* operations, we retrieve the debug symbol name by relating the memory address of the executing instruction and the current executing instruction to the debug information. In the same manner, we retrieve the source code line number (as explained in the previous section). In *gem5 SE* mode, there exist only threads of the executing application. A function for creating a new thread (e.g., *pthread_create*) will exe-cute like any other function. As an argument, it takes a function name that a new thread will execute. By tracing a function name that creates threads and its arguments, the *interceptor* is able to conclude which function a new thread will execute. In the *preExecute()* phase of the CPU, the *interceptor* retrieves

Table 1. Execution times and execution trace size when applications were executed with *gem5* without tracing, with tracing (*gem5 TD*), with tracing of raw data and our probes (*gem5 TD**), with tracing and online calculation of debug symbols (*gem5 DBG*), with tracing and online calculation of debug symbols while ignoring external functions (*gem5 DBG**).

Application	barnes	fmm	ocean-con	radiosity	PowerWindow	PowerWindow*
gem5 [s]	156	53	1053	23	1.04	20
gem5 TD [s]	171	57	1161	26	1.1	21.7
gem5 TD* [s]	262	83	1690	40	1.51	36
gem5 DBG [s]	1495	646	14 475	440	6.77	124
gem5 DBG* [s]	1623	678	14 873	446	7.81	63
gem5 DBG [MB]	1 404	172	19 796	221	5.88	207
gem5 DBG* [MB]	1 305	163	19 732	218	5.84	6.6

the identifier of the currently executing thread (i.e., *thread ID*). Therefore, well before reaching the *postExecute* phase of the CPU, the *interceptor* has the *thread ID* executing the current instruction.

Table 2. Test case 6: Decrease (−) of execution overhead and execution trace size when tracing only two tasks from the parallelized *PowerWindow*, compared with the case when gem5 traced all instructions of the parallelized *PowerWindow* and related them online to their source code. Test case 7: Tracing of the execution of only two tasks from the moment it can be influenced by the access to the shared variable *OverrunFlag*.

Application/Test case	PowerWindow[s]; overhead	PowerWindow trace size
Test case 6	41[s]; −49%	1.05[MB]; −84.09%
Test case 7	41[s]; −49%	0.89[MB]; −86.52%

5 Evaluation

In order to evaluate the overhead of our approach, we used four applications (i.e., *barnes*, *fmm*, *ocean-con*, and *radiosity*) from the famous *SPLASH-2* benchmark [31], and a parallelized *PowerWindow* application [19] from the *TACLeBench* [9] benchmark. As the default setup, we executed the applications with *gem5* but without the tracing option. We designed seven test cases: (1) execution of the applications with *gem5* tracing (but without printing the trace) (*gem5 TD*). (2) *gem5* execution when tracing raw data with our probes (*gem5 TD**). (3) tracing all instructions with online computation of their debug symbols (*gem5 DBG*). (4) computation of the debug symbols online, while ignoring the external functions (e.g., *printf*). (6) testing the parallelized *PowerWindow* to demonstrate how the *interceptor's* monitoring configuration changes dynamically, and influences the overhead and the execution trace size. We traced the execution of only two tasks (*powerwindow_DRV* and *powerwindow_PSG_BackR*) while relating their instructions to the source code online and compare the overhead and the size of the execution trace with the case when we traced the instructions of all tasks of the parallelized *PowerWindow*. (7) kept the setup from the sixth test case, but only started to record memory operations once one of the two traced tasks accessed the global variable *OverrunFlag*. When these tasks completed, the *controller* restarted the monitoring configuration of the *interceptor* to trace only function calls (in order to detect when the same tasks start again). (7) trace the execution of two tasks from the moment it can be influenced by the access to the shared variable *OverrunFlag*.

The results (Table 1) show that our probes introduced an average overhead of 50.23% compared to the unmodified execution of *gem5* with tracing (*gem5 TD*/gem5 TD*[%]). Calculating debug symbols is a demanding task, and on average introduced 6.83x overhead compared to the execution of *gem5* with tracing and our probes (*gem5 DBG/gem5 TD**[%]). When external functions were ignored, the execution time was slightly higher in all but the parallelized *PowerWindow* application. The reason for this is that the filter for reasoning *"if an instruction belongs to an external function"* is executed for every instruction. The parallelized *PowerWindow* however, creates four new threads in every execution cycle, calling functions of the *pthread* library. Therefore, the number of executed external function instructions is significantly higher than in other cases. Test cases 6 and 7 (Table 2) show that the tracing of particular tasks or events of interest using dynamic monitoring configuration led to a significant decrease in the overhead and size of the execution trace.

6   Conclusion and Future Work

In this paper, we presented a framework for non-intrusive monitoring of software execution, which takes the binary as input and provides as output an execution trace with a source code symbols. Our approach mitigates the probe effects, as it does not change the binary, nor does it change the relative execution path by introducing new instructions. However, due to the combination of hardware emulation, handling some system calls internally, and forwarding some system calls to the host operating system, there still is a certain change of the original software behavior, which we aim at addressing in the future. The online monitoring configuration enables the creation of adaptive rules for tracing particular software instructions and software parts, producing execution traces with desired granularity. The result is a reasonable overhead of 58.53% on average when executing applications from the *SPLASH-2* and *TACLe* benchmarks, while enabling some unique features. In the future, we are planning to implement the same approach using commercial simulators.

Acknowledgments. This work was funded by the German Federal Ministry of Education and Research (BMBF) under grant no. 01IS16025 (ARAMiS II) and supported by the the Fraunhofer *High Performance Center for Simulation- and Software-based Innovation*. We thank Sonnhild Namingha from Fraunhofer IESE for reviewing this article.

References

1. Adrien, V., Naser, E.J., Dagenais, M.R.: Hardware-assisted software event tracing. Concurr. Comput.: Pract. Exp. **29**(10), e4069 (2017). https://doi.org/10.1002/cpe. 4069. https://onlinelibrary.wiley.com/doi/abs/10.1002/cpe.4069
2. Agarwal, R., Sasturkar, A., Wang, L., Stoller, S.D.: Optimized run-time race detection and atomicity checking using partial discovered types. In: Proceedings of the 20th IEEE/ACM International Conference on Automated Software Engineering, ASE 2005, pp. 233–242. ACM, New York (2005). https://doi.org/10.1145/1101908. 1101944, http://doi.acm.org/10.1145/1101908.1101944
3. Alpern, B., et al.: The jalapeno virtual machine. IBM Syst. J. **39**(1), 211–238 (2000). https://doi.org/10.1147/sj.391.0211
4. Apache-commons: the byte code engineering library (apache commons bcel) (2017). http://jakarta.apache.org/bcel/
5. Binkert, N., et al.: The gem5 simulator. SIGARCH Comput. Archit. News **39**(2), 1–7 (2011). https://doi.org/10.1145/2024716.2024718, https://doi.acm.org/10.1145/2024716.2024718
6. Bloom, B.H.: Space/time trade-offs in hash coding with allowable errors. Commun. ACM **13**(7), 422–426 (1970). https://doi.org/10.1145/362686.362692, https://doi.acm.org/10.1145/362686.362692
7. Bonakdarpour, B., Navabpour, S., Fischmeister, S.: Time-triggered runtime verification. Form. Methods Syst. Des. **43**(1), 29–60 (2013). https://doi.org/10.1007/s10703-012-0182-0
8. Butko, A., et al.: A trace-driven approach for fast and accurate simulation of many-core architectures. In: The 20th Asia and South Pacific Design Automation Conference, pp. 707–712 (Jan 2015). https://doi.org/10.1109/ASPDAC.2015.7059093
9. Falk, H., et al.: TACLeBench: a benchmark collection to support worst-case execution time research. In: Schoeberl, M. (ed.) 16th International Workshop on Worst-Case Execution Time Analysis (WCET 2016). OpenAccess Series in Informatics (OASIcs), vol. 55, pp. 2:1–2:10. Schloss Dagstuhl-Leibniz-Zentrum fuer Informatik, Dagstuhl, Germany (2016). https://doi.org/10.4230/OASIcs.WCET.2016. 2, http://drops.dagstuhl.de/opus/volltexte/2016/6895
10. Goldberg, A., Havelund, K.: Instrumentation of java bytecode for runtime analysis. Technical Reports from ETH Zurich 408, ETH Zurich, Zurich, Switzerland (2003)
11. IEEE: IEEE standard for standard systemc language reference manual. Std 1666–2011 (Revision of IEEE Std 1666–2005), pp. 1–638, January 2012. https://doi.org/10.1109/IEEESTD.2012.6134619
12. Jagtap, R., Diestelhorst, S., Hansson, A., Jung, M., Wehn, N.: Exploring system performance using elastic traces: fast, accurate and portable. In: IEEE International Conference on Embedded Computer Systems Architectures Modeling and Simulation (SAMOS), July 2016, Samos Island, Greece (2016)
13. Jahic, J., Kuhn, T., Jung, M., Wehn, N.: Supervised testing of concurrent software in embedded systems. In: 2017 International Conference on Embedded Computer Systems: Architectures, Modeling, and Simulation (SAMOS), pp. 233–238, July 2017. https://doi.org/10.1109/SAMOS.2017.8344633
14. Ji, W., Liu, Y., Huo, Y., Wang, Y., Shi, F.: Extracting threaded traces in simulation environments. In: Hsu, C.-H., Li, X., Shi, X., Zheng, R. (eds.) NPC 2013. LNCS, vol. 8147, pp. 27–38. Springer, Heidelberg (2013). https://doi.org/10.1007/978-3-642-40820-5_3

15. Kane, A., Chowdhury, O., Datta, A., Koopman, P.: A case study on runtime monitoring of an autonomous research vehicle (ARV) system. In: Bartocci, E., Majumdar, R. (eds.) RV 2015. LNCS, vol. 9333, pp. 102–117. Springer, Cham (2015). https://doi.org/10.1007/978-3-319-23820-3_7

16. Kuhn, T., Forster, T., Braun, T., Gotzhein, R.: Feral - framework for simulator coupling on requirements and architecture level. In: 2013 Eleventh ACM/IEEE International Conference on Formal Methods and Models for Codesign (MEMOCODE 2013), pp. 11–22, October 2013

17. Lamport, L.: Time, clocks, and the ordering of events in a distributed system. Commun. ACM **21**(7), 558–565 (1978)

18. Lattner, C., Adve, V.: Llvm: a compilation framework for lifelong program analysis & transformation. In: International symposium on Code Generation and Optimization: Feedback-Directed and Runtime Optimization. CGO 2004, p. 75. IEEE, San Jose (2004)

19. Li, H., De Meulenaere, P., Hellinckx, P.: Powerwindow: a multi-component taclebench benchmark for timing analysis. Advances on P2P, Parallel, Grid, Cloud and Internet Computing. LNDECT, vol. 1, pp. 779–788. Springer, Cham (2017). https://doi.org/10.1007/978-3-319-49109-7_75

20. Luk, C.K., et al.: Pin: Building customized program analysis tools with dynamic instrumentation. SIGPLAN Not. **40**(6), 190–200, June 2005. https://doi.org/10.1145/1064978.1065034, https://doi.acm.org/10.1145/1064978.1065034

21. Moosbrugger, P., Rozier, K.Y., Schumann, J.: R2u2: monitoring and diagnosis of security threats for unmanned aerial systems. Formal Methods in System Design **51**(1), 31–61 (2017). https://doi.org/10.1007/s10703-017-0275-x

22. Navabpour, S., Bonakdarpour, B., Fischmeister, S.: Time-triggered runtime verification of component-based multi-core systems. In: Bartocci, E., Majumdar, R. (eds.) RV 2015. LNCS, vol. 9333, pp. 153–168. Springer, Cham (2015). https://doi.org/10.1007/978-3-319-23820-3_10

23. Necula, G.C., McPeak, S., Rahul, S.P., Weimer, W.: CIL: intermediate language and tools for analysis and transformation of C programs. In: Horspool, R.N. (ed.) CC 2002. LNCS, vol. 2304, pp. 213–228. Springer, Heidelberg (2002). https://doi.org/10.1007/3-540-45937-5_16

24. Nethercote, N., Seward, J.: Valgrind: A framework for heavyweight dynamic binary instrumentation. SIGPLAN Not. **42**(6), 89–100 (2007). https://doi.org/10.1145/1273442.1250746, https://doi.acm.org/10.1145/1273442.1250746

25. Nocua, A., Bruguier, F., Sassatelli, G., Gamatie, A.: Elasticsimmate: a fast and accurate gem5 trace-driven simulator for multicore systems. In: 2017 12th International Symposium on Reconfigurable Communication-centric Systems-on-Chip (ReCoSoC). pp. 1–8, July 2017. https://doi.org/10.1109/ReCoSoC.2017.8016146

26. Potter, B.: Supporting native pthreads in syscall emulation mode, June 2015. http://gem5.org/wiki/images/8/80/2015_ws_07_pthread.pdf

27. Savage, S., Burrows, M., Nelson, G., Sobalvarro, P., Anderson, T.: Eraser: a dynamic data race detector for multithreaded programs. ACM Trans. Comput. Syst. **15**(4), 391–411 (1997). https://doi.org/10.1145/265924.265927, https://doi.acm.org/10.1145/265924.265927

28. Sheng, T., Vachharajani, N., Eranian, S., Hundt, R., Chen, W., Zheng, W.: Racez: a lightweight and non-invasive race detection tool for production applications. In: 2011 33rd International Conference on Software Engineering (ICSE), pp. 401–410, May 2011. https://doi.org/10.1145/1985793.1985848

29. Song, Y.W., Lee, Y.H.: On the existence of probe effect in multi-threaded embedded programs. In: International Conference on Embedded Software. EMSOFT. IEEE, Jaypee Greens, India (2014)
30. Vallée-Rai, R., Co, P., Gagnon, E., Hendren, L., Lam, P., Sundaresan, V.: Soot - a java bytecode optimization framework. In: Proceedings of the 1999 Conference of the Centre for Advanced Studies on Collaborative Research. pp. 13-. CASCON 1999. IBM Press (1999). http://dl.acm.org/citation.cfm?id=781995.782008
31. Woo, S.C., Ohara, M., Torrie, E., Singh, J.P., Gupta, A.: The splash-2 programs: characterization and methodological considerations. In: Proceedings 22nd Annual International Symposium on Computer Architecture. pp. 24–36, June 1995. https://doi.org/10.1109/ISCA.1995.524546
32. Zhou, P., Teodorescu, R., Zhou, Y.: Hard: Hardware-assisted lockset-based race detection. In: Proceedings of the 2007 IEEE 13th International Symposium on High Performance Computer Architecture. pp. 121–132. HPCA '07, IEEE Computer Society, Washington, DC, USA (2007). https://doi.org/10.1109/HPCA.2007.346191, https://doi.org/10.1109/HPCA.2007.346191

Author Index

Printed in the United States
By Bookmasters